SCHOLARSHIP ALMANAC

6th Edition

THOMSON

PETERSON'S

Australia • Canada • Mexico • Singapore • Spain • United Kingdom • United States

About The Thomson Corporation and Peterson's

With revenues of US$7.2 billion, The Thomson Corporation (www.thomson.com) is a leading global provider of integrated information solutions for business, education, and professional customers. Its Learning businesses and brands (www.thomsonlearning.com) serve the needs of individuals, learning institutions, and corporations with products and services for both traditional and distributed learning.

Peterson's, part of The Thomson Corporation, is one of the nation's most respected providers of lifelong learning online resources, software, reference guides, and books. The Education Supersite[SM] at www.petersons.com—the Internet's most heavily traveled education resource—has searchable databases and interactive tools for contacting U.S.-accredited institutions and programs. In addition, Peterson's serves more than 105 million education consumers annually.

For more information, contact Peterson's, 2000 Lenox Drive, Lawrenceville, NJ 08648; 800-338-3282; or find us on the World Wide Web at www.petersons.com/about.

ISSN 0894-9336
ISBN 0-7689-0943-0

Printed in Canada

10 9 8 7 6 5 4 3 2   04 03 02

CONTENTS

PART III Appendix and Indexes

INTRODUCTION

The news media seem to constantly remind us that a college education is expensive. It certainly appears to be beyond the means of many Americans. The sticker price for four years at state-supported colleges can be more than $40,000, and private colleges and universities could cost more than $100,000. And these costs continue to spiral upward!

But there is good news. The system operates to provide the needed money so that most families and students are able to afford a college education while making only a reasonable financial sacrifice. Although most families will have to plan on bearing the primary burden of college costs, almost all colleges truly want to admit students regardless of a family's ability to pay. Colleges will try to find various forms of student financial aid to make up enough of the difference between what a family can afford and what an education will cost so all admitted students will be able to enroll in the college that best fits their requirements.

First in any family's consideration is the large amount of federal government money available to students and parents in the form of scholarships, work-study salaries, and low-interest loans. Second, colleges themselves have increased their own student aid efforts, and many colleges also have ways to assist families who are not eligible for need-based assistance. These include an increasing number of merit scholarships as well as direct student loans and jobs and various forms of parental loans. Third, private sources of aid, including civic organizations, labor and trade groups, religious and ethnic groups, and associations provide billions of dollars in scholarship aid each year.

The college financial aid system is complex. It demands study, planning, calculation, flexibility, filling out forms, and meeting deadlines. However, for most people it can produce positive results. Because this may be the first guide to student financial aid that you buy, we have provided a quick review of the elements of this system in our three introductory chapters.

Most of the rest of this book is about the third stream of student financial aid—the $2–$3 billion made available annually by sources outside the colleges and college-channeled federal aid. Parents and students planning for college need to keep in mind that despite the immense size of this third stream and the tremendous help it can provide, it is a fraction of the $61 billion that comes from colleges and college-administered federal sources. If you find that you want a more complete explanation of the system, including details about the student financial aid programs offered by individual colleges, we recommend that you look at *Peterson's College Money Handbook,* which is available in bookstores, libraries, and guidance offices everywhere.

CHAPTER

1

How Can You Pay for College?

There are four basic sources of funds you can use to pay for college:

1. Family resources, including income, savings, and borrowing
2. A student's contribution from savings, loans, and jobs
3. Need-based scholarships or grants
4. Aid that is based on factors other than financial need

Loans are borrowed money that must be repaid (either after graduation or while attending college); the amount you have to pay back is the total you have borrowed plus an interest charge.

Scholarships and grants are outright gifts and do not have to be repaid.

A student's contribution (other than a loan) usually takes the form of student employment, or work-study, which is a job arranged for a student during the academic year.

Colleges are the primary contact point for most student financial aid. The college's financial aid office, using information submitted by you on the Free Application for Federal Student Aid (FAFSA), constructs an aid "package" that will be awarded after the family contribution has been determined. In most cases, this package consists of a combination of grants, scholarships, loans, and campus work.

ESTIMATING COLLEGE COSTS*

The starting point for organizing a plan to pay for your college education is to make a good estimate of the yearly cost. You can use the
College Cost Worksheet on the next page to do this. Most colleges
publish annual tuition and room and board charges in their catalogs
and often include an estimate of how much a student can expect to
spend for books and incidentals. Any college should be able to provide
you with figures for the current year's tuition and mandatory fee
charges, as well as estimates for room and board and other expenses.
Peterson's publishes a number of comprehensive guides, including
*Peterson's Guide to Four-Year Colleges, Peterson's Guide to Two-
Year Colleges,* and *Peterson's College Money Handbook,* that are
one-stop resources for college cost information. You can find these in
bookstores, libraries, and high school guidance offices.

To estimate your college costs for 2003–04, use 2002–03 tuition
and fees and room and board figures, and inflate the numbers by 5
percent (or, if it is available, use the college's estimate for 2003–04
expenses). Add $750 for books and $1300 for personal expenses. If
you will commute from your home, use $2000 instead of the college's
given room and board charges and $900 for transportation. Finally,
estimate the cost of two round trips if your home is more than a few
hundred miles from the college. Add the items to calculate the total
budget. You should now have a reasonably good estimate of college
costs for 2003–04. (To determine the costs for later years, add 5
percent per year for a fairly accurate estimate.)

The next step is to evaluate whether or not you are likely to
qualify for financial aid based on need. This step is critical, since more
than 90 percent of the yearly total of $74.4 billion in student aid is
awarded only after a determination is made that the family lacks
sufficient financial resources to pay the full cost of college on its own.
To judge your chance of receiving need-based aid, it is necessary to
estimate an Expected Family Contribution (EFC) according to a government formula known as the Federal Methodology (FM). You can do so
by referring to the Family Contribution Table in this chapter.

---

*Excerpted from "A Guide to Financing Your Child's College Education" in *Peterson's
College Money Handbook 2003.* © 2002 by Peterson's.

College Cost Worksheet

	College 1	College 2	College 3	Commuter College
Tuition and Fees	___	___	___	___
Room and Board	___	___	___	$2000
Books	$ 750	$ 750	$ 750	$ 750
Personal Expenses	$1300	$1300	$1300	$1300
Travel	___	___	___	$ 900
Total Budget	===	===	===	===

How Aid Matches Need

	COLLEGE X	COLLEGE Y
Cost of Attendance	$10,000	$24,000
− Expected Family Contribution	− 5500	− 5500
= Financial Need	$ 4500	$18,500
Financial Need	$ 4500	$18,500
− Grant Aid Awarded	− 675	−14,575
− Campus Job (Work-Study) Awarded	− 1400	− 1300
− Student Loan Awarded	− 2425	− 2625
= Unmet Need	0	0

Expected Family Contribution Table

Consult the following expected family contribution table using estimated 2002 income and likely asset holdings as of December 31, 2002. First, locate the approximate parental contribution in the table. If more than one family member will be in college at least half-time during 2003-04, divide the parental contribution by the number in college. If your child has savings, add 35 percent of that amount. If your child earned in excess of $2200 in 2002, include 50 percent of the amount over $2200 in the income figure. To see whether or not you might qualify for need-based aid, subtract the family contribution from each college's budget. If the family contribution is only a few thousand dollars over the budget, it is still worthwhile to apply for aid since this procedure is only intended to give you a preliminary estimate of college costs and your family contribution.

Table Used to Approximate Expected Family Contribution for 2003–04

	ASSETS	INCOME BEFORE TAXES								
		$ 20,000	30,000	40,000	50,000	60,000	70,000	80,000	90,000	100,000
	$ 20,000									
FAMILY SIZE	3	$ 220	2,100	3,200	5,400	8,700	11,800	14,800	17,600	20,400
	4	0	1,400	2,000	4,000	7,400	10,500	13,400	15,900	19,300
	5	0	300	1,300	3,000	6,200	9,300	12,200	15,100	18,100
	6	0	0	600	2,100	5,000	7,800	10,800	13,700	16,600
	$ 30,000									
FAMILY SIZE	3	$ 220	2,100	3,200	5,400	8,700	11,800	14,800	17,600	20,400
	4	0	1,400	2,000	4,000	7,400	10,500	13,400	15,900	19,300
	5	0	300	1,300	3,000	6,200	9,300	12,200	15,100	18,100
	6	0	0	600	2,100	5,000	7,800	10,800	13,700	16,600
	$ 40,000									
FAMILY SIZE	3	$ 220	2,200	3,300	5,600	8,900	11,900	14,900	14,700	21,700
	4	0	1,500	2,100	4,100	7,500	10,700	13,600	16,000	20,400
	5	0	400	1,400	3,100	6,300	9,400	12,300	15,200	18,100
	6	0	0	600	2,200	5,100	8,000	11,000	13,900	16,700
	$ 50,000									
FAMILY SIZE	3	$ 600	2,500	3,800	6,200	9,500	12,500	15,500	18,300	21,200
	4	0	1,800	2,400	4,600	8,200	11,300	14,200	16,700	20,000
	5	0	600	1,600	3,500	6,900	10,000	12,900	15,700	18,700
	6	0	0	900	2,500	5,700	8,600	11,600	14,500	17,300
	$ 60,000									
FAMILY SIZE	3	$ 800	2,900	4,200	6,700	10,100	13,100	16,000	18,900	21,800
	4	140	2,000	2,700	5,100	8,700	11,900	14,800	17,600	20,600
	5	0	900	1,900	3,900	7,500	10,600	13,500	16,300	19,300
	6	0	0	1,200	2,900	6,300	9,200	12,200	15,100	17,900
	$ 80,000									
FAMILY SIE	3	$ 1,400	3,500	5,100	7,800	11,000	14,200	17,100	20,000	22,900
	4	600	2,600	3,400	6,100	9,800	12,900	15,700	18,300	21,600
	5	0	1,400	2,500	4,800	8,600	11,700	14,600	17,400	20,400
	6	0	300	1,700	3,600	7,300	10,200	13,200	16,000	19,100

	ASSETS	$ 20,000	30,000	40,000	50,000	60,000	70,000	80,000	90,000	100,000
								INCOME BEFORE TAXES		
	$100,000									
FAMILY SIZE	3	$ 1,800	4,400	6,100	8,900	12,300	15,300	18,200	21,100	24,000
	4	1,200	3,300	4,200	7,200	10,900	14,000	16,800	15,400	22,700
	5	100	1,900	3,200	5,800	9,700	12,800	15,600	18,500	21,500
	6	0	900	2,300	4,400	8,400	11,400	14,400	17,200	20,100
	$120,000									
FAMILY SIZE	3	$ 2,500	5,300	7,300	10,100	13,400	16,300	19,300	22,300	25,100
	4	1,700	4,100	5,100	8,400	12,100	15,200	18,000	20,600	23,900
	5	600	2,500	4,000	6,900	10,800	13,900	16,600	19,600	22,600
	6	250	1,400	2,900	5,400	9,600	12,500	15,500	18,300	21,200
	$140,000									
FAMILY SIZE	3	$ 3,200	6,500	8,400	11,200	14,500	17,400	20,400	23,300	26,200
	4	2,300	5,100	6,200	9,500	13,200	16,200	19,100	21,700	25,000
	5	1,200	3,200	4,900	8,100	11,900	15,100	17,900	20,800	23,800
	6	800	1,900	3,700	6,500	10,700	13,600	16,500	19,400	22,400

SCHOLARSHIPS

What Are Scholarships? What Importance Should You Give Them?

The word "scholarship" can cause confusion. Precise usage limits the use of scholarship to "free money" given to cover educational costs for undergraduate students. However, many people, including college financial aid officials and program sponsors, use the word generically to refer to all forms of student gift aid, including fellowships and grants, especially if a program covers both undergraduate and graduate levels of study. In the profiles of scholarship programs in this book, we use whatever term the sponsor uses.

However, so that you will be aware of the differences in meaning when you encounter the terms, here are further definitions:

- *Scholarships:* Undergraduate gift aid that is used to pay educational costs.

- *Need-Based Scholarships:* Gift aid based on demonstrated need. Need, as defined by colleges and the federal government, is the difference between the cost of attending a college and the EFC, which is determined by a federal and/or institutional formula.

- *Merit-Based Scholarships:* Financial aid based on criteria other than financial need, including academic major, career goals, grades, test scores, athletic ability, hobbies, talents, place of residence or birth, ethnic identity, religious affiliation, your own or your parents' military or public safety service, disability, union membership, employment history, community service, or club affiliations. The preponderance of scholarship programs described in this book are merit based, although many also use need to set the size of the award.

- *Grants:* Graduate or postdoctoral awards to support specific research or other projects. Grants cover expenses directly related to carrying out the proposed research (e.g., materials, interview costs, or computer time). Sometimes a grant includes allowances for travel and living expenses incurred while conducting research away from the home institution. Usually, living expenses at the home university are not covered. (NOTE: The word grant is also used to refer to undergraduate gift aid, for example, the Federal Pell Grant.)

- *Fellowships:* Graduate- and postgraduate-level awards to individuals to cover their living expenses while they take advanced courses, carry out research, or work on a project. Some fellowships include a tuition waiver.

- *Prizes:* Money given in recognition of an outstanding achievement. Prizes often are awarded to winners of competitions.

- *Internships:* A defined period of time working in the intern's field of interest with and under the supervision of the professional staff of a host organization. Often the intern works part-time or during the summer. Some internships offer stipends in the form of an hourly wage or fixed allowance.

- *Assistantships:* Graduate-level awards, usually waiving all or some tuition, plus an allowance for living expenses. In return, the recipient works at teaching or research facilities. Teaching assistants teach in their field of study. Research assistants often work on projects related to their dissertation or thesis.

- *Work-Study:* When capitalized, Work-Study refers to a federally supported program that provides students with part-time employment during the school year. The federal government pays part of the student's salary. Employers are usually college departments. Local agencies also can participate in the program. Eligibility for Federal Work-Study is based on demonstrated need. Work-study (not capitalized) is used to describe any student job in an aid package.

Sources of financial aid include private agencies, foundations, corporations, clubs, fraternal and service organizations, civic associations, unions, and religious groups. These sponsors provide grants, scholarships, and low-interest loans. Some employers also provide tuition reimbursement benefits for employees and their dependents.

It is always worthwhile to look into scholarships that can be found beyond the college financial aid office's network. For a family that does not qualify for need-based aid, these "outside" scholarships and merit scholarships available from colleges are the only form of gift aid available. No matter what your situation regarding need-based aid, scholarships from noninstitutional sources (those not administered by colleges or the U.S. Department of Education) are almost always useful. Be aware that the amounts received from "outside" scholarships to pay tuition and expenses may be deducted from the amount of aid offered in your college financial aid package. An "outside" scholarship may prove most useful in reducing the loan and work-study components of the college-offered package.

Use the following checklist when investigating merit scholarships:

- Take advantage of any scholarships for which you are automatically eligible based on employer benefits, military service, association or church membership, other affiliations, or student or parent attributes (ethnic background, nationality, etc.). Company or union tuition remissions are the most common examples of these awards.

- Look for other awards for which you might be eligible based on the characteristics and affiliations indicated above, but where there is a selection process and an application required. *Peterson's Scholarship Almanac* provides information about the largest scholarship programs, but there are thousands of smaller programs that may be right for you. Scholarship directories, such as *Peterson's Scholarships, Grants & Prizes*, which details more than 2,000 scholarship programs, are useful resources.

- See if your state has a merit scholarship program. Also, check to see if the state scholarships are "portable," meaning they can be used in other states or must be used at in-state institutions.

- Look into national scholarship competitions. High school guidance counselors usually know about these scholarships. Examples of these awards are the National Merit Scholarship, Coca-Cola Scholarship, Aid Association for Lutherans, Intel Science Talent Search, and the U.S. Senate Youth Program.

- ROTC (Reserve Officers' Training Corps) scholarships are offered by the Army, Navy, Marines, and Air Force. A full ROTC scholarship covers all tuition, fees, and textbook costs. Acceptance of an ROTC scholarship entails a commitment to take military science courses and to serve as an officer in the sponsoring branch of the service. Competition is heavy, and preference may be given to students in certain fields of study, such as engineering science. Application procedures vary by service. Contact an armed services recruiter or your high school guidance counselor for further information.

- Investigate community scholarships. High school guidance counselors usually have a list of these awards, and announcements are published in the town newspaper. Most common are awards given by service organizations such as the American Legion, Rotary International, and the local women's club.

- If you are strong academically (for example, a National Merit Commended Scholar or better), or very talented in fields such as athletics or performing/creative arts, you may want to consider colleges that offer their own merit awards to gifted students they wish to enroll.

Federal Scholarship Programs*

The federal government is the single largest source of financial aid for students, accounting for about $61 billion available annually. At the present time there are two federal grant programs—the Federal Pell Grant and the Federal Supplemental Educational Opportunity Grant (FSEOG); three loan programs—the Federal Perkins Loan, the Direct Loan, and the Stafford Loan; and a job program that helps colleges provide jobs for students—Federal Work-Study (FWS).

The application and need evaluation process is controlled by Congress and the U.S. Department of Education. The application is the Free Application for Federal Student Aid (FAFSA). In addition, nearly every state that offers student assistance uses the federal government's system to award its own aid. By completing the FAFSA, you automatically apply for state aid. However, you should check with your state Higher Education agency or high school guidance counselor for any other forms that may be required in addition to the FAFSA. (NOTE: In addition to the FAFSA, some colleges also ask the family to complete the PROFILE application.)

The FAFSA is your "passport" to receiving your share of the billions of dollars awarded annually in need-based aid. If the college cost worksheet shows that you might qualify for aid, pick up a FAFSA

---

*Excerpted from "Federal Financial Aid Programs" in *Peterson's College Money Handbook 2003.* © 2002 by Peterson's.

from your high school guidance office after mid-November. The form will ask for your current year's financial data, and it should be filed after January 1, in time to meet the earliest college or state scholarship deadline. Online application can be made through accessing the FAFSA Web site at www.fafsa.ed.gov/. Both the student and at least one parent should apply for a federal PIN number at http://www.pin.ed. gov. The PIN serves as your electronic signature when applying for aid on the Web. Within two to four weeks after you submit the form, you will receive a summary of the FAFSA information, which is called the Student Aid Report (SAR). The SAR will give you your EFC and also allow you to make corrections to the data you submitted.

Federal Pell Grant

The Federal Pell Grant is the largest grant program: almost 4 million students receive awards annually. This grant is intended to be the starting point of assistance for lower-income families. Eligibility for a Federal Pell Grant depends on the EFC. The amount you receive will depend on your EFC and the cost of education at the college you will attend. The highest award depends on how much the program is funded. The maximum for 2001–02 school year ranged from $400 to $3750. The maximum for 2002–03 will be $4000.

To give you some idea of your possible eligibility for a Federal Pell Grant, the following table may be helpful. The amounts shown are based on a family size of 4, with 1 in college, no emergency expenses, no contribution from student income or assets, and college costs of at least $4000 per year.

Table Used to Estimate Federal Pell Grants for 2002–03

Adjusted Gross Income	Family Assets							
	$50,000	$55,000	$60,000	$65,000	$70,000	$75,000	$80,000	$85,000
$ 5000	$4000	$4000	$4000	$4000	$4000	$4000	$4000	$4000
$10,000	4000	4000	4000	4000	4000	4000	4000	4000
$15,000	4000	4000	4000	4000	4000	3950	3750	3650
$20,000	3650	3450	3250	3150	3050	2950	2850	2750
$25,000	2750	2550	2450	2350	2150	2050	1950	1750
$30,000	1750	1650	1550	1450	1350	1250	950	650
$35,000	1250	1150	950	750	450	400	—	—

Federal Supplemental Educational Opportunity Grant (FSEOG)

As its name implies, the Federal Supplemental Educational Opportunity Grant provides additional need-based federal grant money to supplement the Federal Pell Grant. Each participating college is given funds to award to especially needy students. The maximum award is $4000 per year, but the amount you receive depends on the college's policy, the availability of FSEOG funds, the total cost of education, and the amount of other aid awarded.

Federal Financial Aid Programs

Name of Program	Type of Program	Maximum Award Per Year
Federal Pell Grant	Need-based grant	$4000
Federal Supplemental Educational Opportunity Grant	Need-based grant	$4000
Federal Work-Study	Need-based part-time job	no maximum
Federal Perkins Loan	Need-based loan	$4000
Subsidized Stafford Direct Loan	Need-based student loan	$2625 (first year)
Unsubsidized Stafford Direct Loan	Non-need-based student loan	$2625 (first year, dependent student)
PLUS Loan	Non-need-based parent loan	Up to the cost of education

Note: Both Direct and Stafford Loans have higher maximums after the freshman year. Students who meet the federal qualifications for independent status are eligible for increased loan limits in these programs.

College-Based Gift Aid

Next to the federal government, colleges provide the largest amount of financial aid to students. In addition, they control most of the money channeled to students from the federal government.

College need-based scholarships frequently are figured into students' financial aid packages. Most colleges award both need- and merit-based scholarships, although a small number of colleges (most notably the Ivy League) offer only need-based scholarships. Colleges may offer merit-based scholarships to freshmen with specific academic strengths, talents in the creative or performing arts, special achievements or activities, and a wide variety of particular circumstances. Some of these circumstances are parents in specific professions; residents of particular geographic areas; spouses, children, and siblings of other students; and students with disabilities.

A college's financial aid office can inform you about the need-based scholarships available from that college. Usually, the admissions office is the primary source to get information about any merit-based scholarships the college offers. Some colleges have information about their scholarships on their Web sites. *Peterson's College Money Handbook* is a one-stop reference guide to the financial aid programs at more than 1,600 four-year colleges and universities. You may notice that private colleges usually have larger financial aid programs, but public colleges are usually less expensive, especially for in-state students.

Colleges have different requirements regarding necessary financial aid application forms. Be prepared to check early with the colleges you are interested in about which forms they need. All colleges require the FAFSA for students applying for federal aid. The other most commonly required form is PROFILE, the College Scholarship Service's financial aid form. To see if the college you are applying to requires PROFILE, read the financial aid section of the admission material.

Athletic Scholarships*

Some scholarships for athletic ability or participation are available from various noninstitutional sources, but the great preponderance comes directly from the colleges themselves. Athletic scholarships may be the most widely used single category of merit scholarship, and certainly they are the most widely known and sought by students. Athletic scholarships are controlled by the coaches in the athletic department of a college.

Most financial aid provided on the basis of athletic ability or achievement is in the form of scholarship aid. Loans for athletic participation are uncommon. Some coaches may describe the aid that they are offering to athletes as scholarships, when the aid really is in the form of a loan. If you believe that you are being offered a scholarship (that is money *given* to you based on need or athletic ability), insist that it be confirmed in writing and that it is not a loan or

---

*Excerpted from *Athlete's Game Plan for College & Career.* © 1984 by Stephen Figler and Howard Figler.

"indebtedness." Remember, scholarship money is *given* to you, while loans must be repaid. Be sure you are clear about which type of aid a coach may be offering.

Athletes who are good enough even to consider competing at the collegiate level frequently dream of being awarded an athletic scholarship, whether or not their family can afford to pay for their education. Potential college athletes want to be "on scholarship" because it is a reward, an honor, a status symbol. An athletic scholarship is a reward for your hard work and success in high school or junior college. It is a status symbol because it tells other students that the college wants and needs you at least as much as you want to attend the college.

Many students struggle to pay for their years in college, while the athlete with a full scholarship (tuition, room, board, a book allowance) cashes in just for being an athlete. This may give you high status in the minds of many students, but it has a downside in two ways. First, athletic scholarships sometimes generate resentment and jealousy among other students. Where money is available to "buy" athletes, there is a temptation to bring in star athletes who might not meet the same academic standards that others must meet. Nonathlete students may resent the "free ride" that athletes get, while they have to work, save their money, deplete their savings and other assets, go begging to their parents, fill out numerous forms, wait in long financial lines, and hunt for money to make ends meet in college.

A second problem for scholarship athletes is that coaches often demand a tight reign over the athletes to whom they have given money. Many coaches believe they have a right to control their investment. As a scholarship athlete, you run the risk of being treated as an employee with much of your life being governed by your boss/coach. Athletes who have scholarships might lose their place on the team if they displease the coach or if they do not perform up to the coach's expectations. If you need that money to continue in college, having it taken away could be devastating. You might not have even chosen that school if not for the scholarship. But even if you do not absolutely need the money to pay for your education, losing the scholarship could mean a struggle to find new sources of money, often after the financial aid application season has passed and the available funds have been awarded to other students.

According to current national athletic association guidelines and practices, athletic scholarships are given on a one-year, renewable basis. While your coach may have "sold" you on his or her college with the promise of having your entire education paid by an athletic scholarship, the money and free tuition could disappear at the end of any year, leaving you to search for some other way to pay for the rest of your education. Worse, if you then want to transfer to another college, you lose a season of eligibility for athletics. The chances of getting another athletic scholarship elsewhere are much less if the coach at your new school will not be able to use your talents until the following year.

So, if you are eligible to be a scholarship athlete, the primary question you must decide is whether you want *and* need an athletic scholarship or whether you just want one. The status and honor that may come with an athletic scholarship can be enjoyable, but is it worth the cost? While some coaches feel more of a commitment to athletes who are their "employees," other coaches will appreciate your getting funds for college some other way, freeing up a scholarship for them to offer to another athlete.

In any case, the availability of an athletic scholarship should not be your primary reason for selecting one college over others. There are too many nonathletic sources of financial aid available for you to let the offer of an athletic scholarship determine which school you attend.

Who Gets Scholarship Offers?

Most athletic scholarships at schools with top-level teams are reserved for the best high school and junior college athletes, the ones who have established a reputation in their sport. Especially in football and men's basketball, college coaches do much of their hunting for talent with the help of computer-based scouting services, which keep records of the statistics of the nation's best prospects. Athletes at that level—"blue-chip" prospects—do not have to search for athletic scholarships; recruiters come knocking at *their* door (sometimes knocking *down* the door). Occasionally an unrecruited athlete in those sports (a "walk-on") may be given a partial or full scholarship after proving him- or herself under fire.

Virtually all NCAA Division I schools (except for the Ivy League and Patriot League colleges) offer athletic scholarships, and in most sports the coach does his or her own scouting rather than using computerized scouting services. The same is true at Division II schools, a lower level of athletic competition. These schools are allowed fewer scholarships, and many of these cover only part of the educational costs. Division III NCAA schools—the lowest level—are not allowed to offer scholarships directly for athletic talent, yet most of them still scout high school and junior college prospects.

NCAA colleges may compete at a particular level in one sport and at another level in other sports. For example, a school with a Division II basketball team (athletic scholarships allowed) may field a Division III soccer team (no athletic scholarships). While this may be confusing, you only need to be concerned about the level at which they field a team in *your* sport.

Many colleges affiliated with the NAIA (National Association for Intercollegiate Athletics) also offer scholarships. These schools are among the smaller and less well-known for their sports teams, so they generally do not have as much money to put into athletic scholarships. A number of junior colleges, or community colleges, also offer athletic scholarships. As at NCAA Division II schools, NAIA and junior college scholarships are more likely to be partial (i.e., quarter, half, or tuition-only) rather than "full rides."

Athletic scholarships for women have increased tremendously in recent years. In large part this is a result of Title IX (part of a federal law called the Education Amendments of 1972). Within this law, colleges must provide athletic scholarship aid to female and male athletes in proportion to their enrollment. Also, all resources, support, and opportunities to compete in athletics must be shared equitably by men and women. Title IX was reinforced in 1997 by a Supreme Court ruling in a case filed by women student-athletes against Brown University.

Despite these advances, the opportunities women have for obtaining athletic scholarships at some schools still may lag behind the financial aid offered to men. Once you are in college and can see what types and amounts of aid are available to female athletes as compared to male athletes, you will be in a better position to determine whether female athletes are being discriminated against at that school. Contact the campus affirmative action office and ask its staff to look into the situation if you think that female athletes are not getting their fair share. You may be considered a troublemaker by some people in the athletic department, but you deserve what the law allows and should be allowed to stand up for your rights.

How to Generate an Offer

While colleges at all levels of athletic competition scout and recruit athletes, those at levels *below* Division I of the NCAA are more likely to consider information submitted by an individual student seeking an athletic scholarship. The amount of scholarship money available each year in any given sport varies greatly, and even if recruiters have not been knocking down your door, you still may have the chance to get a scholarship offer if you follow the approach described below:

1. Draw up a preliminary list of colleges that meet the criteria that are important to you, such as location, size, overall cost, type of academic environment, availability of particular academic programs or majors, and sports opportunities. (You should check on whether the school has a junior varsity team in case you do not make the varsity your first year.)

2. Find out the name of the head coach in your sport at the colleges on your list. Starting with the top contenders on your preliminary list (three to six colleges), write a letter to the head coach at each school. In the letter describe several important reasons why you want to attend his or her college. Explain that you are interested in competing on the team and that you would like to know what sources of financial aid are available for athletes. Don't be shy about telling the coach of your athletic strengths, including statistics (true ones!), that might generate the coach's interest in you. Include copies of newspaper write-ups and action photos, if you have them. A videotape of you in competition can also help in selling yourself to the coach. That is what you are really doing, *selling yourself.* There is absolutely no shame in that. In fact, it is good practice for when you graduate and have to sell an employer on your qualifications and accomplishments.

3. If you do not receive encouragement from the first group of head coaches you write to, work down your list of college choices. There are no guarantees, but using this process certainly is more likely to result in finding athletic-related financial aid than doing nothing.

4. Ask your current or former coach to write a letter on your behalf to specific coaches on your list. A letter to a specific, named coach carries more weight than a generic letter to any coach (i.e., "Dear Coach"). The letter of recommendation should stress how much of an asset you have been to your team and would be on that coach's team. Letters from two coaches are better than one, three are better than two, etc.

Seldom will a coach offer financial aid to an athlete sight unseen. Since most coaches operate with a tight recruiting budget, you may have to pay your own travel expenses to see a coach who shows some interest. If you are then offered financial aid—full or partial scholarship, loan, work-study, or some combination—your efforts have paid off *and* that coach knows you as more than just another "wanna-be." He or she knows that you are hungry to compete on that team and that you are an aggressive seeker of success, a trait all coaches want in their athletes. But beware when a coach promises financial aid in the future, if things work out. The coach may come through for you, but do not bank on such promises because they are "written on air."

Even if, after all that effort, you receive no athletics-related financial aid, you are likely to be in a better position to be accepted by the school and to be considered for other types of aid not directly tied to athletics. Students who have special talents—i.e., those who are "well-rounded" and take the initiative to make these talents known—are often more desired by schools than those who present only academic credentials. If you get only a partial athletic scholarship or none at all—like the majority of college athletes—you may be eligible for financial aid based on need.

Great athletes and good ones are sometimes tempted to accept—or even to ask for—money or other financial benefits beyond the amount the rules allow them. It is not worth whatever "extra" you might get, since there are penalties and other liabilities. For example, in 1997, the University of Massachusetts men's basketball team forfeited its "Final Four" standing (achieved a few years before) and had to return $151,000 because one of its players took money that he should not have. Why compromise friendships, your teammates' goals, your own ethics, possibly your athletic career, and even your chance at the aid you deserve by trying to take more than you should?

State and Local Scholarships

Each state government has established one or more financial aid programs for qualified students. Usually, only legal residents of the state are eligible to benefit from such programs. However, some are available to out-of-state students attending colleges within the state. In addition to residential status, other qualifications frequently exist. States may also offer internship or work-study programs, graduate fellowships and grants, or low-interest loans in addition to grant and forgivable loan programs.

If you are interested in learning more about state-sponsored programs, the state higher education office should be able to provide information. Information brochures and application forms for state scholarship programs are usually available in your high school guidance office or from a college financial aid office in your state.

Increasingly, state government agencies are putting state scholarship information on their Web sites. The financial aid page of state-administered college or university sites frequently has a list of state-sponsored scholarships and financial aid programs. You can access college and university Web sites easily through Peterson's Education Center (www.petersons.com).

Businesses, community service clubs, and local organizations often sponsor scholarship programs for residents of a specific town or county. These can be attractive to a scholarship seeker because the odds of winning can be higher than they would be for scholarships drawing from a wider pool of applicants. However, because the information network at the local level is spotty, it is often difficult to find information about their existence. Some of the best sources of information about these local programs are high school guidance offices, community college financial aid offices, high school district administrative offices, and public libraries. In addition, you may want to check with the local offices of organizations that traditionally sponsor scholarships, such as the International Kiwanis Club, the Benevolent and Protective Order of Elks, the Lions Club International, or the National Association of American Business Clubs (AMBUCS).

Private Aid

Billions of dollars every year are given by private donors to students and their families to help with the expenses of a college education. Last year, noninstitutional and nongovernment sponsors gave more than $3 billion in financial aid to help undergraduate students pay for college costs.

Foundations, fraternal and ethnic organizations, community service clubs, churches and religious groups, philanthropies, companies and industry groups, labor unions and public employees' associations, veterans' groups, and trusts and bequests all make up a large network of possible sources.

It is always worthwhile for any prospective student to look into these scholarships, but they are especially important to students who do not qualify for need-based financial aid, to students and families who wish to supplement the aid being given by governmental or university sources, and to students who possess special abilities, achievements, or personal qualifications (e.g., memberships in church or civic organizations, specific ethnic backgrounds, parents who served in the armed forces, etc.) that fit the criteria of one or more of the various private scholarship sponsors.

Some factors that can affect eligibility for these awards, such as ethnic heritage and parental status, are beyond a student's control. Other criteria, such as academic, scientific, technological, athletic, artistic, or creative merit, are not easily or quickly met unless one has previously committed himself or herself to a particular endeavor. However, eligibility for many programs is within your control, especially if you plan ahead. For example, you can start or keep up current membership in a church or civic organization, participate in volunteer service efforts, or pursue an interest, from amateur radio to golf to raising animals to writing and more. Any of these actions might give you an edge for a particular scholarship or grant opportunity.

The eligibility criteria for private scholarships, grants, and prizes are a real mosaic; they vary widely and include financial need as well as personal characteristics and merit. The number and amounts of the awards available from individual sponsors can vary each year depending upon the number of grantees, fund contributions, and other factors. However, practically anyone can find awards to fit his or her individual circumstances.

Peterson's Scholarship Almanac was created to provide students and their families access to the biggest and most lucrative private financial aid programs. In this publication you will find detailed information about the top 500 scholarship/grant programs and prize sources. *Peterson's Scholarships, Grants & Prizes* is a comprehensive guide to the more than 2,800 scholarship/grant programs and prize sources that will provide nearly 1.6 million financial awards to undergraduates in the 2003–04 school year.

SOURCES OF COLLEGE FINANCING OTHER THAN SCHOLARSHIPS

Financing strategies are important because the high cost of a college education today often requires families, whether or not they receive aid, to think about stretching the payment for college beyond the four-year period of enrollment. For high-cost colleges it is not unreasonable to think about a 10-4-10 plan: ten years of saving; four years of paying college bills out of current income, savings, and borrowing; and ten years to repay a parental loan.

Family Savings*

Although saving for college is always a good idea, many families are unclear about its advantages. Families do not save for two reasons. First, after expenses have been covered, many families do not have much money to set aside. An affordable but regular savings plan through a payroll deduction is usually the answer to the problem of spending your entire paycheck every month.

The second reason that saving for college is not a high priority is the belief that the financial aid system penalizes a family by lowering aid eligibility. The Federal Methodology determination is very kind to savers. In fact, savings are ignored completely for families that earn less than $50,000 and who are eligible to file a short form federal tax return (1040A or EZ). Savings in the form of home equity and retirement plans are excluded from the calculation. And even when savings are counted, a maximum of 5.6 percent of the total is expected each year. In other words, if a family has $40,000 in savings after an asset protection allowance is considered, the contribution is no greater than $2240, an amount very close to the yearly interest that is accumulated. Therefore, it is possible for a family to meet its savings contribution without depleting the face value of its investments.

A sensible savings plan is important because of the financial advantage of saving compared to borrowing. The amount of money students borrow for college is now greater than the amount they receive in grants and scholarships. With loans becoming so widespread, savings should be carefully considered as an alternative to borrowing. Your incentive for saving is that a dollar saved is a dollar not borrowed.

State governments in increasing number are enacting new programs to help families save for college education. There are two basic categories of these programs. Under a prepaid or guaranteed tuition program, in exchange for early tuition purchase (usually in installments), a tuition rate is locked in at the plan's participating colleges or universities, almost always public institutions. In a college savings plan trust program, participants save money in a special college savings account on behalf of a prospective student. These accounts usually have a guaranteed minimum return and offer favorable treatment for state and federal taxes. In many cases, the interest earned in these programs will result in no tax liability. You should check with your state's higher education agency for more details.

---

*Excerpted from "Federal Financial Aid Programs" in *Peterson's College Money Handbook 2003.* © *2002 by Peterson's.*

Work-Study and Jobs

Federal Work-Study (FWS)

The Federal Work-Study program provides jobs for students who need financial aid to pay for their educational expenses. Funds from the federal government and the college (or the employer) pay the salary. The student works on an hourly basis on or off campus and must be paid at least the federal minimum wage. Students may earn only up to the amount awarded, which depends on the calculated financial need and the total amount of money available to the college.

Many colleges, after assigning jobs to students who qualify for Federal Work-Study (FWS), offer other part-time positions to nonqualifying students from regular college funds. In fact, at many colleges, the ratio is about 50-50, meaning half are employed under the FWS program while the other half are paid directly by the college. Students who qualify for FWS are usually assigned jobs through the student employment office. Other students should contact the Career Planning Office, or check with individual offices and departments for possible openings. In addition, there are usually off-campus employment opportunities available to everyone.

AmeriCorps

AmeriCorps is a national umbrella group of service programs for a limited number of students. Participants work in a public or private nonprofit agency providing service to the community in one of four priority areas: education, human services, the environment, and public safety. In exchange, they earn a stipend of $7400 to $14,800 a year for living expenses and up to $4725 for two years to apply toward college expenses. Students can work either before, during, or after they go to college and can use the funds to either pay current educational expenses or repay federal student loans. Speak to a college financial aid officer for more details about this program and any other new initiatives available to students.

Cooperative Education Programs

Co-op programs, also known as cooperative education, are special programs usually administered at the departmental level. A formal arrangement with off-campus employers allows students to combine work and study, either at the same time or in alternating terms. Generally, these programs begin at the end of the sophomore year and add a year or a semester to the length of the degree program. Co-op programs enable students to earn regular marketplace wages while gaining experience, often specifically related to the field they are studying. The National Commission for Cooperative Education, 360 Huntington Avenue, Boston, Massachusetts 02115-5096, 617-373-3770, is a central source of information about these programs.

Loans

In addition to scholarships and work-study, there are loan opportunities available for all students. The federal loan programs are called the Stafford and Direct. Student and parent loans are provided by both programs. Some of the organizations that sponsor scholarships, such as the Air Force Aid Society, also provide loans.

For those students who demonstrate need, the interest on the loans is paid by the federal government during the time the student is in school. If you do not demonstrate financial need, or your need has been met with other forms of aid, you can apply for the unsubsidized Stafford or Direct Loan. Unsubsidized loans begin to accrue interest as soon as the money is received.

Federal Perkins Loan

This loan is a low-interest (5 percent) loan for students with exceptional financial need. Federal Perkins Loans are made through the college's financial aid office with the college as the lender. Students may borrow a maximum of $4000 per year for up to five years of undergraduate study. They may take up to ten years to repay the loan, beginning nine months after they graduate, leave school, or drop below half-time status. No interest accrues while they are in school and, under certain conditions (e.g., they teach in low-income areas, work in law enforcement, are full-time nurses or medical technicians, serve as Peace Corps or VISTA volunteers, etc.), some or all of the loan can be canceled or payments deferred.

Stafford and Direct Loans

Stafford and Direct Loans have the same interest rates, loan maximums, deferments, and cancellation benefits. A Stafford Loan may be borrowed from a commercial lender such as a bank or credit union. A Direct Loan is borrowed directly from the U.S. Department of Education. Once you have decided on the college you plan to attend, the financial aid office will inform you of the program it participates in and advise you on all application procedures.

The interest rate varies annually up to a maximum of 8.25 percent. If you qualify for a need-based subsidized Stafford Loan, the interest is paid by the federal government while you are enrolled in college. There is also an unsubsidized Stafford Loan that is not based on need, for which you are eligible regardless of your family income.

The maximum amount dependent students may borrow in any one year is $2625 for freshmen, $3500 for sophomores, and $5500 for juniors and seniors, with a maximum of $23,000 for the total undergraduate program. The maximum amount independent students can borrow is $6625 for freshmen (of which no more than $2625 can be subsidized), $7500 for sophomores (of which no more than $3500 can be subsidized), and $10,500 for juniors and seniors (of which no more than $5500 can be subsidized). Borrowers must pay a fee of up to 4 percent of the loan, which is deducted from the loan proceeds.

To apply for a Stafford Loan, you must first complete a FAFSA to determine eligibility for a subsidized loan then a separate loan application that is submitted to a lender. The financial aid office can help in selecting a lender, or you can contact your state department of higher education to find a participating lender. The lender will send a promissory note where you agree to repay the loan. The proceeds of the loan, less the origination fee, will be sent to your college to be either credited to your account or released to you. Longer term repayment plans may be available depending on your overall debt level, income, and other factors.

If you qualify for a subsidized Stafford Loan, you do not have to pay interest while in school. For an unsubsidized Stafford Loan, you will be responsible for paying the interest from the time the loan is established. However, some lenders will permit borrowers to delay making payments and will add the interest to the loan. Once the repayment period starts, borrowers of both subsidized and unsubsidized Stafford Loans will have to pay a combination of interest and principal monthly for up to ten years.

PLUS Loans

PLUS is for parents of dependent students to help families who may not have the cash available to pay their share of the charges. There is no needs test to qualify. The loan has a variable interest rate that cannot exceed 9 percent. There is no yearly limit; you can borrow up to the cost of your education less other financial aid received. Repayment begins sixty days after the money is advanced. A fee of up to 4 percent of the loan is subtracted from the proceeds. Parent borrowers must generally have a good credit record to qualify. Parents are urged to contact the financial aid office to determine if the PLUS program is the best source of alternative loan funds. Many schools have arranged other private loan programs that may offer better loan terms. Some programs administered by the state higher education agency may have parental loan programs with better terms and conditions.

Famous Scholarship Programs

The two most famous and prestigious scholarship programs are the Fulbright and Rhodes scholarships. Here is a quick overview of the programs.

The Fulbright Scholarship Program

The Fulbright Scholarship Program is the U.S. government's premier scholarship program available for international study. The Fulbright Program sponsors study, research, or teaching by American graduate scholars and artists in more than 100 host countries and by graduate-level students, teachers, or researchers from more than 125 countries at U.S. universities. In its fifty-five years of operation, the Fulbright program has sponsored nearly 200,000 scholars. The program was established in 1946 to foster mutual understanding through educational and cultural exchanges of persons, knowledge, and skills between the United States and other countries. It is named for Senator J. William Fulbright, who sponsored the legislation in the United States Senate as a step toward constructing alternatives to armed conflict. The program's primary source of funding is the United States Information Agency (USIA).

The U.S. Student Program is designed to give recent baccalaureate-level graduates, master's and doctoral candidates, and beginning professionals and artists an opportunity for personal development and international experience. Recipients plan their own programs. Projects may include course-related work, library or field research, classes in music or art, research projects in the sciences or social sciences, or various hybrid projects. The Fulbright Scholar Program is designed to provide senior teachers and professionals the opportunity to conduct research, teach, or study abroad and to make a major contribution to global understanding.

There are five basic types of Fulbright grants open to U.S. citizens:

- *Fulbright Full Grants:* Provide round-trip transportation; language or orientation courses; tuition, in some cases; book and research allowances; maintenance for the academic year, based on living costs in the host country; and supplemental health and accident insurance. Fulbright Full Grants are payable in local currency or U.S. dollars, depending on the country of assignment.

- *Fulbright Travel Grants:* Available only to Germany, Hungary, Italy, or Korea. They are available to supplement a student's own funds or an award from a non-Fulbright source that does not provide funds for travel or to supplement study. Travel grants provide round-trip transportation to the country where the student will pursue studies for an academic year, supplemental health and accident insurance, and the cost of an orientation course abroad, if applicable.
- *Foreign and Private Grants:* Offered by international governments, universities, and private donors in specific host countries. The benefits and special requirements of the grants are determined by the sponsoring agency. If the awards do not cover the entire expense of international study, candidates are expected to cover the additional costs from their own funds, although some international grants may be supplemented by Fulbright travel grants.
- *Teaching Opportunities:* Belgium/Luxembourg, France, Germany, Hungary, Korea, Taiwan, and Turkey offer assistantships for teaching English in secondary schools, middle schools, or higher educational institutions.
- *Fulbright Scholar Program:* Offers grants for college and university faculty and administrators, professionals (lawyers, government officials, journalists, research scientists, and others), artists, and independent scholars to conduct research, teach, or study abroad.

Fulbright recipients are selected on the basis of their academic or professional record, language preparation, the feasibility of the proposed project, and personal qualifications. The decision-making procedure involves review of the application by three groups: a National Screening Committee (NSC) of the Institute for International Education that consists of specialists in various fields and area studies, the supervising agency (the USIS post at the American Embassy or a special binational Fulbright Commission in the host country), and the J. William Fulbright Foreign Scholarship Board.

An application form is available from the Fulbright Program Advisor at the graduate's campus or from the Institute of International Education, 809 United Nations Plaza, New York, NY 10017-3580. Applications should be submitted between May 1 and mid-October. Check with the Fulbright Program Advisor or the Institute of International Education for the specific year's deadline.

The Rhodes Scholarship
Cecil Rhodes, a remarkable public figure of late Victorian Britain, made a fortune in diamond mining in South Africa and forcefully

advocated a single world international government. On his death in 1902 at the age of 49, he left his fortune to Oxford University to establish the Rhodes scholarship program. The aim of the Rhodes scholarship is to bring from throughout the world young men and women of proven intellectual and academic achievement, integrity of character, interest in and respect for their fellow beings, the ability to lead, and the energy to use their talents to make an effective contribution to the world around them.

Because of a long history of prominent individuals who have been Rhodes scholars and the extreme selectivity of the award, the Rhodes scholarship is regarded in academe as an extremely high honor. Colleges and universities take great pride in their students who go on to win Rhodes scholarships and view the cultivation of a Rhodes scholar to be a great status symbol.

The Rhodes scholarship provides payment of all tuition and related fees in any field of study at Oxford plus a stipend for living expenses. The Rhodes trustees assist successful applicants with their travel expenses to and from Oxford.

Appointment to a Rhodes scholarship is made for two years with a possible third year if the scholar's plan of study and record at Oxford warrant extension of the award. An American Rhodes scholar with a degree from an approved American university or college is entitled to Senior Status. Subject to the consent of their college, Senior Status entitles students to read for the Oxford B.A. in any of the Final Honour Schools. If qualified by previous training and with the consent of their colleges and relevant faculty, Rhodes scholars may be admitted to read for a higher degree.

Candidates must be citizens, between the ages of 18 and 23 as of October 1 of the year of their application, and have sufficient credits to ensure completion of a bachelor's degree before the October 1 following application. Selection is made on four criteria: scholarship, character, leadership, and physical vigor. Participation in varsity sports is a usual way to demonstrate physical vigor, but it is not essential if applicants are able to demonstrate physical vigor in other ways.

Each of the world's nations is assigned a number of Rhodes scholarship slots that they may fill each year. The United States of America selects 32 Rhodes scholars annually. Applications are made through the Office of the Institutional Representative for the Rhodes scholarships at the candidate's college or university. A campus committee evaluates applicants and sends the evaluations to a state Committee of Selection. In each state a Committee of Selection may nominate 2 or 3 applicants to appear before the District Committee (the U.S. is organized into eight districts of six or seven states each). The Rhodes trustees will pay round-trip transportation of applicants nominated by State Committees to the place of the District Committee meeting. Applicants must pay their own lodging, food, and other expenses when appearing before State Committees. The names of scholarship winners are announced at the close of the District Committee meetings in December.

After selection of the scholars, the Rhodes scholarship authorities in Oxford seek places for them in Oxford Colleges, following the electees' preferences, if possible. Because the Colleges make their own admissions, there is no guarantee of a place. Two samples of written work, approximately 2,000 words each, are required for college placement. The award of the scholarship is not confirmed by the Rhodes Trustees until the scholar-elect has been accepted for admission by a college. Rhodes scholars are expected to be full-time students at Oxford for the duration of their degree programs. Scholars-elect enter Oxford University in October following their election. Deferment of the scholarship is not allowed except for medical internships.

Prospective applicants should study the academic system of Oxford University to determine if their plan of study is one that is feasible at Oxford. The best sources of information are the current issues of the *University of Oxford Undergraduate Prospectus* and *Graduate Studies Prospectus*, published by the Oxford University Press and available in the offices of Institutional Representatives for the Rhodes scholarships in colleges and universities. In addition, the *Oxford University Examination Decrees* is available for a charge from the Oxford University Press Bookshop, 116 High Street, Oxford OX1 4BZ, England. Copies of a brochure, *Oxford and the Rhodes Scholarships*, giving information about the scholarships and life and study at Oxford, may be obtained from Institutional Representatives at each campus as well as from the Office of the American Secretary. Students who wish further information or have difficulty in obtaining application forms should write to: Office of the American Secretary, The Rhodes Scholarship Trust, PO Box 7490, McLean, Virginia 22106-7490.

CHAPTER

2

Where Can You Find Help?

THE COLLEGE FINANCIAL AID OFFICE

The cost of education at a private college likely will fall in the range of $12,000 to $35,000 annually for tuition, room, and board. Public college education is about half this amount. Your actual cost, though, depends upon your financial aid award. No matter what your family's income level or your academic record, you are likely to be eligible for some form of financial aid. Whether through scholarships, awards, grants, loans, or student employment, most colleges endeavor to provide financial assistance to admitted freshmen that will enable these students to enroll at their institution. That's why it is important to look beyond the "sticker price" of attending the college of your choice and apply for financial aid before ruling out a college based on cost.

Most financial aid is based on financial need. However, whether you demonstrate 100 percent financial need or hardly any, you can look to the financial aid office of the college that has accepted you to work with you to create a financial aid package that addresses your unique situation and makes your college education an investment that you can afford. The primary purpose of the college student financial aid office is to remove financial barriers to student enrollment and ensure that any qualified student can obtain sufficient resources to attend their college. The essential job of the financial aid administrator is to help students who would otherwise be unable to attend their college seek, obtain, and make the best use of all financial resources available.

The financial aid office in any college will guide you to the financial aid options available from a variety of sources—state and federal government programs, friends of the college, alumni, and the college itself. The actual amount of a financial aid package is determined not only from the evaluation of your personal financial situation but also by the unique financial resources, policies, and practices of each institution.

Financial aid packages vary significantly from school to school. Moreover, the amount of aid available from each college can fluctuate widely from year to year, depending on the number of applicants, the amount of need to be met, and the financial resources and policies of the college.

After you have narrowed down the colleges in which you are interested based on academic and personal criteria, we recommend that you contact the college's financial aid office. Here are just a few questions you might want to ask the financial aid officers at the colleges you are seriously considering attending:

- What are the types and sources of the aid provided to freshmen at this school?
- What factors do the college consider in determining whether a financial aid applicant is qualified for its need-based aid programs?
- How does the college determine the combination of types of aid that make up an individual's package?
- How are non-need awards treated—as a part of the aid package or as a part of the parental/family contribution?
- Does this school "guarantee" financial aid and, if so, how is its policy implemented? Guaranteed aid means that, by policy, 100 percent of need is met for all students judged to have need. Implementation determines how need is met and varies widely from school to school. For example, grade point average may determine the proportioning of scholarship, loan, and work-study aid. Rules for freshmen may be different from those for upperclass students.
- To what degree is the admission process "need-blind"? Need-blind means that admission decisions are made without regard to the student's need for financial aid.
- What are the norms and practices for upperclass student aid? A college might offer a wonderful package for the freshman year, then leave you relatively on your own to fund the remaining three years. Or the school may provide a higher proportion of scholarship money for freshmen, then rebalance its aid packages to contain more self-help aid (loans and work-study) in upperclass years. There is an assumption that, all other factors being equal, students who have settled into the pattern of college time management can handle more work-study hours than freshmen. Grade point average,

tuition increases, changes in parental financial circumstances, and other factors may also affect the redistribution. If you feel your financial situation warrants additional review, the financial aid office is always willing to work with you to help you find solutions to financing your education.

THE HIGH SCHOOL GUIDANCE OFFICE

The high school guidance office is often the first source of information that students and parents have to learn about their college options, including financing. High school guidance counselors, among other responsibilities, work to educate students and their parents about college options and the college admission and financial assistance process. They counsel individual students about their postsecondary career and educational choices.

Many guidance offices are well equipped for this task, with libraries of college catalogs, college guides, interactive career or college selection software (such as *Peterson's Career & College Quest* multimedia CD-ROM). Many high school students have access to a first-rate college and career information center and a counselor who has great knowledge about specific colleges, college selection, admissions processes, and student financial aid options and can work with students as they make the transition from high school to postsecondary education. Thousands of high schools are fortunate to have this type of resource.

Resources devoted to college advisement vary tremendously from district to district. Guidance counselors sometimes have an overwhelming number of students to counsel and urgent responsibilities in other areas that can demand a greater share of their time, energy, and expertise. They often cannot find the time to provide personalized consultation to individual students about their college options. It is always necessary for parents to assess the situation at their children's particular high school. If college counseling resources at your high school are limited, it may be necessary to fill in, either by yourself or, if you can afford it, with an independent college advisement counselor.

With respect to financial aid, any high school guidance office should be able to provide you with the current FAFSA, forms for state-sponsored financial aid programs, and information about locally sponsored scholarship programs.

College fairs are a worthwhile resource available to many parents and students. There are college fairs sponsored by school districts as well as a program of National College Fairs sponsored by the National

Association for College Admission Counseling (NACAC). These usually offer exhibits and presentations by individual colleges and universities. Students and parents are able to meet with admissions representatives of different colleges; view their information presentations; take home a range of informative brochures, periodicals, and other products; and attend information sessions on college admissions and financing. Many high schools allow time off during the school day for students to attend a college fair.

NACAC's National College Fair program probably draws the greatest number of college representatives. NACAC sponsors thirty-six fairs in different parts of the country, which attract more than 300,000 students each year. Contact them at National Association for College Admission Counseling, 1631 Prince Street, Alexandria, Virginia 22314-2818; telephone: 703-836-2222; fax: 703-836-8015; or look at their Web site (www.nacac.com/) to receive an up-to-date list of college fairs.

CHAPTER

3

What Do You Need to Know About Application Forms?

BASIC AID APPLICATION FORMS

FAFSA

Because the federal government provides about 75 percent of all aid awarded, the Free Application for Federal Student Aid (FAFSA) and the Federal Methodology (FM) are the most important application forms and need analysis process with which you will have to deal. The information on the FAFSA—parental and student income and assets, the number of family members, and the number attending college as well as other variables—is analyzed to derive the Expected Family Contribution. This one form is required by every college. It is also the basis for almost all student financial aid provided by state governments and colleges themselves.

The FAFSA is available from any college financial aid office as well as most high school guidance offices. Students and families can apply for federal student aid over the Internet using the interactive FAFSA on the Web. Most applicants will find the Web version of the FAFSA relatively easy and fast. FAFSA on the Web can be accessed at www.fafsa.ed.gov/ and does not require users to download programs or install software.

Submit the FAFSA after January 1 to meet the earliest deadline of your state, college, or private aid program. The aid decision process favors those who apply on time. Once you have passed the deadline, your application may not be considered. Because of early program deadlines, you may have to use an estimated tax return to complete the FAFSA. This is permitted, and even advisable. Far too many parents and students wait to submit the FAFSA and lose their chance at thousands of financial aid dollars. Many colleges provide the option to apply for early decision admission. If you apply for this before January 1, follow the college's aid application instructions.

You should be prepared when you start to complete the FAFSA. Here are the records that you will need (all income records are for the year immediately prior to college start):

- Federal tax returns (if available)
- If no tax return is available, a complete record of all taxable income
- Untaxed income (including Earned Income Credit; Social Security benefits; child support)
- Bank statements for checking, savings, money market, and CD accounts
- Investment statements concerning interest, dividends, and capital gains
- Second home or rental property value and debt records
- Business value and debt records
- Farm investment value and debt records

PROFILE

Some colleges require an aid application in addition to the FAFSA. Among the approximately 2,000 four-year colleges, about 600 are private institutions with more than $2 billion of their own scholarships. Many of these colleges feel that the federal aid system (FAFSA and FM) does not collect or evaluate information thoroughly enough to be used to award their own funds. These colleges have made an arrangement with the College Scholarship Service, a branch of the College Board, to establish a separate application system called PROFILE.

The need formula connected to PROFILE is the Institutional Methodology (IM). If you apply for financial aid at one of the colleges that uses PROFILE, the admission material will state that PROFILE is required in addition to the FAFSA. You should read this information carefully and file PROFILE to meet the earliest deadline among the colleges involved. Before you can receive the PROFILE form, however, you must register, providing enough basic information so the PROFILE package can be designed specifically for you. Also, while the FAFSA is free, there is a charge for PROFILE.

In addition to the requirement by certain colleges that you submit both the FAFSA and PROFILE (PROFILE is always in addition to the FAFSA; it does not replace it), you should also realize that each system has its own method for analyzing family ability to pay for college. The main differences between PROFILE's Institutional Methodology and FAFSA's Federal Methodology are as follows:

- PROFILE includes equity in the family home as an asset; the FAFSA doesn't.
- PROFILE expects a minimum student contribution, usually in the form of summer earnings. The FAFSA has no such minimum.
- PROFILE allows for more professional judgment than the FAFSA. Medical expenses, private secondary school costs, and a variety of special circumstances are considered under PROFILE subject to the discretion of the aid counselor on campus.
- PROFILE collects information on the noncustodial parent; the FAFSA doesn't.
- PROFILE collects information on assets not reported on the FAFSA, including life insurance, annuities, retirement plans, etc.

PROFILE's Institutional Methodology tends to be both more complete in its data collection and more rigorous in its analysis than the FAFSA's Federal Methodology. When IM results are compared to FM results for thousands of applicants, IM will usually come up with a somewhat higher Expected Family Contribution than FM.

To prepare to complete the PROFILE application form, you will need to gather all of the information that you would need to complete the FAFSA. In addition, you will need to show the market value of your home less the outstanding mortgage.

After the applications are submitted, you will receive the aid award letter. Your aid package will show you how much to subtract from the college's cost of attendance to arrive at your actual contribution. If you are an aid recipient, it is not until you have calculated your "bottom line" that you will learn the actual cost of an individual college.

PRIVATE AID SCHOLARSHIP APPLICATIONS

The types of applications that you will need to apply for scholarships from the noninstitutional sector can be as varied as the sponsors themselves. Be prepared to spend some time and effort gathering the material that each application requires. The amount of time you have to do this should be a factor in considering how many scholarships you wish to pursue. Weigh this against the fact that the chances for most students of receiving a privately sponsored scholarship will likely be less than of getting help from the federal government or the college.

Need-based scholarships, especially many state scholarships, use the FAFSA as the primary application. Application for state aid is automatically done when you complete the FAFSA. However, check the aid information for your specific state, because the sources and programs vary considerably. It is advisable to keep a record of your FAFSA and PROFILE data in the event that you may wish to reproduce them for a noninstitutional sponsor or if questions arise.

Merit-based scholarship sponsors frequently require a secondary school transcript and one or more letters of recommendation. The source of the letter of recommendation may be specified in the sponsor's materials. If not, you will want to find one or more individuals of appropriate professional authority or credence in the area directly related to that which forms the basis for the award. If, for example, the award is given for academic quality, typically a teacher or school administrator should be sought; if community service, a leader or organizer of relevant community service projects is the best choice. A document written and signed by this individual will attest to the quality of an applicant's qualifications, work, character, abilities, or accomplishments. Usually it is preferable that the letter be specifically addressed, but if a number of similar awards are being sought, you may have to settle for a generically addressed letter to any recipient who may be interested. Sponsors may request that the signer send the letter directly to them. If so, follow the sponsor's directions.

The best advice in applying for private scholarships is to request descriptive information from the sponsor about the scholarship program that you may be interested in and review it carefully in respect to the scholarship's eligibility criteria, application requirements, and deadlines. If you do not precisely match the scholarship's eligibility criteria, you almost certainly will not receive the award. Be careful to supply *all* of the application forms and supporting documentation that the sponsor requests. Pay attention to deadlines; begin the process of gathering information and preparing letters and forms well in advance of the deadline, and try to beat the deadline by as much as you can. Many sponsors' procedures give some advantage to earlier applicants.

In addition to the application, your case usually can be enhanced by a concise cover letter. Provide basic information about your grade in school or year of college, graduation date, major, and goals. If the basis for the award is academic, information about your GPA and class rank is relevant. Test scores appropriate to your level and field of study will be needed. High school students may wish to provide their PSAT, SAT, ACT, and/or Advanced Placement scores.

Summary

There are reasons to be optimistic about your prospects of finding the help you need to pay for college. Although the "sticker price" of a college education may be high, there is an extensive network available to help students and families in paying their college expenses. If typical financial aid packages are taken into consideration, the actual cost of four years of college is likely to be less than what most families spend on a car, and, unlike a car, the value a college education will increase as time goes on. The majority of students should *expect* to receive aid to make their college costs manageable, whether this comes from the government, the college, or the many noninstitutional sponsors that offer scholarships. There are many ways to manage college costs and many channels through which you can receive help. This process requires preparation, organization, and resourcefulness.

We wish you success in your quest and hope that *Peterson's Scholarship Almanac* proves to be helpful.

HOW TO USE THE PROFILES

WHAT ARE THE CRITERIA FOR SELECTING THE TOP 500 SCHOLARSHIPS?

Between January and April of each year, Peterson's conducts a survey of more than 4,000 organizations and agencies in the U.S. and Canada that sponsor scholarships, prizes, fellowships, grants, and forgivable loans for undergraduate- and graduate-level students.

Scholarship sponsors provide Peterson's with data about the number and dollar amounts of the awards they give in a year. These are frequently described as ranges. To determine the 500 largest scholarships available in the U.S. out of a list of thousands, we multiplied the highest number in the range representing the number of awards given in a year (never less than 1) by the highest number in the range representing the dollar amounts given.

The information is constructed from Peterson's questionnaires that went to the sponsoring bodies in December 2001. The information was verified and correct as of April 2002. The number of awards, funding amounts, and procedures can change at any time. There is no way to guarantee that the number of awards or dollar amounts reported by a sponsor will be duplicated in a new year. You should request written descriptive materials for the program in which you are interested directly from the sponsor.

HOW TO UNDERSTAND THE PROFILES

The 500 scholarships described in this book are organized into categories that represent the major factors used to determine eligibility for scholarship awards and prizes. To find a basic list of scholarships available to you, look under the specific category or categories that fit your particular academic goals, skills, personal characteristics, or background.

The categories are divided into two broad classes: **Academic Fields/Career Goals** and **Nonacademic/Noncareer Criteria**.

Because your major academic field of study and/or career goal has central importance in college planning, the *Academic Fields/ Career Goals* section appears first. The *Academic Fields/Career Goals* category is subdivided into individual subject areas that are organized alphabetically.

These are:

Agribusiness
Agriculture
Animal/Veterinary Sciences
Applied Sciences
Architecture
Area/Ethnic Studies
Arts
Aviation/Aerospace
Biology
Business/Consumer Services
Chemical Engineering
Civil Engineering
Communications
Computer Science/Data Processing
Dental Health/Services
Drafting
Earth Science
Economics
Education
Electrical Engineering/Electronics
Engineering-Related Technologies
Engineering/Technology
Fashion Design
Filmmaking
Fire Sciences
Food Science/Nutrition
Food Service/Hospitality
Foreign Language
Funeral Services/Mortuary Science
Graphics/Graphic Arts/Printing
Health Administration
Health and Medical Sciences
Health Information Management/
    Technology
History
Home Economics

Horticulture/Floriculture
Hospitality Management
Humanities
Interior Design
International Migration
Journalism
Landscape Architecture
Law/Legal Services
Literature/English/Writing
Materials Science, Engineering, and
    Metallurgy
Mechanical Engineering
Meteorology/Atmospheric Science
Natural Resources
Natural Sciences
Nuclear Science
Nursing
Peace and Conflict Studies
Performing Arts
Photojournalism
Physical Sciences and Math
Political Science
Real Estate
Religion/Theology
Science, Technology, and Society
Social Sciences
Social Services
Special Education
Sports-Related
Surveying, Surveying Technology,
    Cartography, or Geographic
    Information Science
Therapy/Rehabilitation
Trade/Technical Specialties
Transportation
TV/Radio Broadcasting

The second class of awards, *Nonacademic/Noncareer Criteria*, are those that are primarily based on a personal characteristic of the award recipient. We have organized these criteria into ten categories:

Civic, Professional, Social, or Union Affiliation
Corporate Affiliation
Employment Experience

Impairment
Military Service
Nationality or Ethnic Heritage
Religious Affiliation
State of Residence
Talent
Miscellaneous Criteria

Full descriptive profiles of scholarship awards are sequentially numbered from 1 through 500. This number appears in the upper right-hand corner of the profile with a bullet in front of it (it is this profile number, not the page number the award appears on, that is referenced in all indexes). A full profile of an award appears in only one location in the book. Most awards have more than one criterion that needs to be met before a student can be eligible. Cross-references by name and sequential number are made to the full program description from the other relevant criteria categories under which the award might also have been listed if one of its multiple criteria had not come earlier in the alphabet. The full description appears in the first relevant location, the cross-references in the later ones.

Cross-references are not provided from the *Nonacademic/ Noncareer Criteria* section to programs in the *Academic Fields/ Career Goals* section. You will be able to locate relevant awards in this section by any personal qualifying criteria through the indexes in the back of the book, which repeat the organizing scheme of the profiles.

For example, the numbered full profile of a scholarship for any kind of engineering student who resides in Ohio, Pennsylvania, or West Virginia may appear under *Aviation/Aerospace*, the alphabetically first relevant engineering category heading in the *Academic/ Career Areas* section of the book. Cross-references to this first listing, by name and number, may occur from any other relevant engineering or technological academic field subject areas, such as *Chemical Engineering, Civil Engineering, Engineering-Related Technologies, Engineering/Technology, Mechanical Engineering,* or *Nuclear Science.* There would not be a cross-reference from the *State of Residence* category. However, the name of the scholarship will appear in the Index under the State section. You will always want to check the relevant indexes to get the most out of the guide's listings.

Within the appropriate categories, the descriptive profiles are organized alphabetically by the name of the sponsoring organization. If more than one scholarship from the same organization appears in a particular section, the awards are then listed alphabetically by the name of the award under the name of the sponsor.

WHAT IS IN THE DESCRIPTIVE PROFILES?

Here are the elements of a full descriptive profile:

1. Name of sponsoring organization (In most instances acronyms are given as full names. However, occasionally a sponsor will refer to itself throughout by acronym, and in deference to this seeming preference, we present their name as an acronym.)
2. Award name and sequence number
3. Brief description of the award
4. Academic/Career Areas (this is only in the *Academic/Career Areas* section)
5. Award descriptors (Is it a scholarship? A prize for winning a competition? A forgivable loan? An internship? For what years of college can it be used? Is it renewable or is it for only one year? How many awards are given? For what amounts?)
6. Eligibility Requirements
7. Application Requirements, which also lists the application deadline
8. Sponsoring organization's Web site address
9. Contact name, address, phone and fax numbers, and e-mail address

A STRATEGY FOR FINDING RELEVANT AWARDS

Private scholarships and awards are frequently characterized by unpredictable, sometimes seemingly bizarre, criteria. Before you begin your search for a relevant award, draw up a personal profile of yourself that will help establish as many as possible criteria that might form the basis for your award grant. Here is a basic checklist of what you should give consideration to:

What is your career goal? Be both narrow and broad in your designation. If, for example, you have a career goal to be a TV news reporter, you will find many awards specific to this field in the *TV/Radio Broadcasting* section. However, collegiate broadcasting courses can be offered in departments or schools of communication. So, be sure to consider *Communications* as a relevant section for your search. Also, consider *Journalism* for the same reasons. Then, look under some more broadly inclusive, but possibly relevant areas, such as *Trade/Technical Specialties.* Or, possibly, check a related, but different field, such as *Performing Arts.* Finally, look under marginally related, basic academic fields, such as *Humanities, Social Sciences,* or *Political Science.* We make every attempt to provide superior cross-reference aids, but the nuances of specific awards can be difficult to capture with even the most flexible cross-referencing systems. You will need to be broadly associative in your thinking in order to get the most out of this wealth of information.

If you have no clear career goal at this stage of your life, browsing through the huge variety of academic/career awards may well spark new interest in a career path. Be open to imagining yourself filling different career roles that you may not have previously considered.

In what academic subject fields are you interested in majoring? Your educational experiences to this point or your sense about your personal talents or interests may have given you a good idea of what academic discipline you wish to pursue. Again, use both broad and narrow focuses in designing your search and look to related subject fields. For example, if you want to major in history, there is a *History* section. But be sure to also check out *Social Sciences* and *Humanities* and, maybe *Area/Ethnic Studies.* In addition, *Education* could also have the perfect scholarship for a future historian.

In what jobs, industries, or occupations have your parents or other members of your immediate family been engaged? What employment experiences do you have? Individual companies, employee organizations, trade unions, government agencies, and industry associations frequently set up scholarships for workers or children or other relatives of workers from specific companies or industries. These awards may sometimes require that you study to stay in the same career field, but most are offered regardless of the field of study you wish to undertake. Also, if one of your parents worked as a public service employee, especially as a firefighter or police officer, and most especially if he or she was killed or disabled in the line of duty, there are many relevant awards available.

Do you have any hobbies or special interests? Have you ever been an officer of an organization? Do you have special skills or talents? Have you won any competitions? Are you a good writer? From bowling to clarinet playing, from caddying to ham radio, from winning a beauty contest to simply "being interested in leadership," there are a host of special interests that can win for you awards from groups that wish to promote and/or reward these pursuits.

Where do you live? Where have you lived? Where are you going to college? Residence criteria are among the most common qualifications for scholarship aid. Local clubs and companies provide millions of dollars in scholarship aid to students who live in a particular state, province, region, or section of a state. This means that your residential identity puts you at the head of the line for these grants. State of residence can—depending on the sponsor's criteria—include the place of your official residence, the place you attend college, the place you were born, or any place you lived for more than a year.

What is your family's ethnic heritage? Hundreds of scholarships have been endowed for students who can claim a particular nationality or racial or ethnic descent. Partial ethnic descent frequently qualifies, so don't be put off if you do not think of yourself as having a specific "ethnic" background. There are awards for Colonial American, English, Welsh, Scottish, descendants of signers of the Declaration of Independence, European, and other backgrounds that students may be inclined to consider as not especially "ethnic."

Do you have any physical impairment? There are many awards given to individuals with physical impairments. In addition to commonly recognized impairments of mobility, sight, communication, and hearing, learning disabilities and chronic diseases, such as asthma and epilepsy, are criteria for some awards.

Are you now in, or have you served in, a branch of the armed services? Did one of your parents serve? In a war? Was one of your parents lost or disabled in the armed services? There are hundreds of awards that use one or more of these qualifications.

Do you belong to a civic association, union, or religious organization? Do your parents belong? Hundreds of clubs and religious groups provide scholarship assistance to members or children of members.

Are you male or female?

What is your age?

Do you qualify for need-based aid?

Did you graduate in the upper half, upper third, or upper quarter of your class?

Do you plan to attend a two-year college, a four-year college, or a vocational/technical school?

What year (freshman, sophomore, etc.) of school are you entering?

Be expansive in considering your possible qualifications. Although some awards may be small, you may qualify for more than one award, and these can add up significantly in the end.

PROFILES

ACADEMIC FIELDS/
CAREER GOALS

AGRIBUSINESS_____

CALIFORNIA FARM BUREAU SCHOLARSHIP FOUNDATION

CALIFORNIA FARM BUREAU SCHOLARSHIP   • 1

Renewable award given to students attending a four-year college or university in California. Applicants must be California residents preparing for a career in the agricultural industry.

Academic/Career Areas Agribusiness; Agriculture.
Award Scholarship for use in any year; renewable. *Number:* 23. *Amount:* $2000–$2750.
Eligibility Requirements: Applicant must be enrolled full or part-time at a four-year institution; resident of California and studying in California.
Application Requirements Application, essay, interview, references, transcript. *Deadline:* March 1.
World Wide Web: http://www.cfbf.com/cfbfapp.htm
Contact: Darlene Licciardo, Scholarship Coordinator
        California Farm Bureau Scholarship Foundation
        2300 River Plaza Drive
        Sacramento, CA 95833
        Phone: 800-698-3276

CENEX HARVEST STATES FOUNDATION

CENEX HARVEST STATES FOUNDATION COOPERATIVE STUDIES SCHOLARSHIPS   • 2

Renewable awards for college juniors and seniors attending agricultural colleges of participating universities. Must be enrolled in courses on cooperative principles and business practices. Each university selects a recipient in the spring. If the award is given in the junior year, the student is eligible for an additional $750 in their senior year without reapplying provided that eligibility requirements are met. A maximum of $1500 will be awarded to any one student in the cooperative studies program.

Academic/Career Areas Agribusiness; Agriculture.
Award Scholarship for use in junior or senior years; renewable. *Number:* up to 79. *Amount:* $750–$1500.
Eligibility Requirements: Applicant must be enrolled full-time at a four-year institution; resident of Colorado, Idaho, Iowa, Kansas, Minnesota, Montana,

Nebraska, North Dakota, Oklahoma, Oregon, South Dakota, Utah, Washington, Wisconsin, or Wyoming and studying in Colorado, Idaho, Iowa, Kansas, Minnesota, Montana, Nebraska, North Dakota, Oregon, South Dakota, Utah, or Washington.

Application Requirements Application, transcript.

Contact: Scholarship Director
Cenex Harvest States Foundation
5500 Cenex Drive
Inver Grove Heights, MN 55077
Phone: 651-451-5129
Fax: 651-451-5073
E-mail: wnels@chsco-ops.com

HISPANIC COLLEGE FUND, INC.

HISPANIC COLLEGE FUND SCHOLARSHIP PROGRAM • 3

This program awards scholarships to full-time students of Hispanic origin who have demonstrated academic excellence, leadership skills and financial need to pursue an undergraduate degree in a business or technology-related field.

Academic/Career Areas Agribusiness; Business/Consumer Services; Chemical Engineering; Communications; Computer Science/Data Processing; Drafting; Economics; Electrical Engineering/Electronics; Engineering/Technology; Engineering-Related Technologies; Graphics/Graphic Arts/Printing; Mechanical Engineering.

Award Scholarship for use in freshman, sophomore, junior, or senior years; not renewable. *Number:* 200–250. *Amount:* $1000–$5000.

Eligibility Requirements: Applicant must be Hispanic, Latin American/Caribbean, Mexican, Nicaraguan, or Spanish and enrolled full-time at a two-year or four-year institution or university. Applicant must have 3.0 GPA or higher. Available to U.S. citizens.

Application Requirements Application, essay, financial need analysis, resume, references, test scores, transcript, college acceptance letter. *Deadline:* April 15.

World Wide Web: http://www.hispanicfund.org

Contact: Tatiana Pham, Program Manager
Hispanic College Fund, Inc.
1717 Pennsylvania Avenue, NW, Suite 460
Washington, DC 20006
Phone: 202-296-5400
Fax: 202-296-3774
E-mail: hispaniccollegefund@earthlink.net

THE HISPANIC COLLEGE FUND/INROADS/SPRINT SCHOLARSHIP PROGRAM • 4

One-time award open to undergraduates of Hispanic descent pursuing a degree in a business- or technology-related major. Must be a U.S. citizen and have a

The Hispanic College Fund/INROADS/Sprint Scholarship Program (continued)
minimum 3.0 GPA. Recipients will participate in INROADS Leadership Development Training while interning at Sprint during the summer. Deadline: April 15.

Academic/Career Areas Agribusiness; Business/Consumer Services; Chemical Engineering; Communications; Computer Science/Data Processing; Drafting; Economics; Electrical Engineering/Electronics; Engineering/Technology; Engineering-Related Technologies; Graphics/Graphic Arts/Printing; Mechanical Engineering.

Award Scholarship for use in freshman, sophomore, junior, or senior years; not renewable. *Number:* 20–25. *Amount:* $1000–$2500.

Eligibility Requirements: Applicant must be Hispanic, Latin American/ Caribbean, Mexican, Nicaraguan, or Spanish and enrolled full-time at a two-year or four-year institution or university. Applicant must have 3.0 GPA or higher. Available to U.S. citizens.

Application Requirements Application, essay, financial need analysis, resume, references, test scores, transcript, college acceptance letter, copy of taxes, copy of SAR. *Deadline:* April 15.

World Wide Web: http://www.hispanicfund.org

Contact: Tatiana Pham, Program Manager
Hispanic College Fund, Inc.
1717 Pennsylvania Avenue, NW, Suite 460
Washington, DC 20006
Phone: 202-296-5400
Fax: 202-296-3774
E-mail: hispaniccollegefund@earthlink.net

UNITED AGRIBUSINESS LEAGUE

UNITED AGRIBUSINESS LEAGUE SCHOLARSHIP PROGRAM • 5

Award of $1000-$5000 available to students enrolled or planning to enroll in a full-time degree program in agribusiness at a two-or four-year institution. Minimum 2.5 GPA required. Application deadline is March 29.

Academic/Career Areas Agribusiness; Agriculture; Animal/Veterinary Sciences; Economics; Food Science/Nutrition; Horticulture/Floriculture; Landscape Architecture.

Award Scholarship for use in any year; renewable. *Number:* 10–15. *Amount:* $1000–$5000.

Eligibility Requirements: Applicant must be enrolled full-time at a two-year or four-year institution or university. Applicant must have 2.5 GPA or higher. Available to U.S. and non-U.S. citizens.

Application Requirements Application, essay, financial need analysis, resume, references, test scores, transcript. *Deadline:* March 29.

World Wide Web: http://www.ual.org

Contact: Christiane Steele, Scholarship Coordinator
United Agribusiness League
54 Corporate Park
Irvine, CA 92606-5105
Phone: 949-975-1424
Fax: 949-975-1671
E-mail: csteele@ual.org

AGRICULTURE

CALIFORNIA FARM BUREAU SCHOLARSHIP FOUNDATION

CALIFORNIA FARM BUREAU SCHOLARSHIP
see number 1

CENEX HARVEST STATES FOUNDATION

CENEX HARVEST STATES FOUNDATION COOPERATIVE STUDIES SCHOLARSHIPS
see number 2

MARYLAND STATE HIGHER EDUCATION COMMISSION

HOPE SCHOLARSHIP
• 6

Student must be a high school senior at the time of application and must enroll in an eligible major. Family income may not exceed $95,000 annually. Recipients must agree to work in the state of Maryland for one year for each year they accept the award.

Academic/Career Areas Agriculture; Arts; Business/Consumer Services; Communications; Foreign Language; Health and Medical Sciences; Home Economics; Humanities; Literature/English/Writing; Natural Resources; Political Science; Social Sciences.

Award Forgivable loan for use in freshman, sophomore, junior, or senior years; renewable. *Number:* up to 300. *Amount:* $1000–$3000.

Eligibility Requirements: Applicant must be high school student; planning to enroll full-time at a two-year or four-year institution; resident of Maryland and studying in Maryland. Applicant must have 3.0 GPA or higher. Available to U.S. citizens.

Application Requirements Application, financial need analysis, transcript. *Deadline:* March 1.

World Wide Web: http://www.mhec.state.md.us

Hope Scholarship (continued)
Contact: Debbie Smith, Scholarship Administration
Maryland State Higher Education Commission
16 Francis Street
Annapolis, MD 21401-1781
Phone: 410-260-4594
Fax: 410-974-5994
E-mail: ssamail@mhec.state.md.us

UNITED AGRIBUSINESS LEAGUE

UNITED AGRIBUSINESS LEAGUE SCHOLARSHIP PROGRAM

see number 5

ANIMAL/VETERINARY SCIENCES_____

AMERICAN ORNITHOLOGISTS' UNION

AMERICAN ORNITHOLOGISTS' UNION RESEARCH AWARDS • 7

One-time award for students without recourse to regular funding for research on any aspect of avian biology. Must be members of the American Ornithologists' Union. Write for further information.

Academic/Career Areas Animal/Veterinary Sciences; Biology; Natural Sciences.
Award Grant for use in any year; not renewable. *Number:* 28–30. *Amount:* up to $1800.
Eligibility Requirements: Applicant must be enrolled full or part-time at a four-year institution or university and member of American Ornithologist's Union. Available to U.S. and non-U.S. citizens.
Application Requirements Application, references, self-addressed stamped envelope. *Deadline:* February 1.
World Wide Web: http://www.aou.org
Contact: Dr. Gary Ritchison, AOU Awards Committee Chair
American Ornithologists' Union
Department of Biology, Eastern Kentucky University
Richmond, KY 40475
E-mail: gritchis@acs.eku.edu

LOUISIANA OFFICE OF STUDENT FINANCIAL ASSISTANCE

ROCKEFELLER STATE WILDLIFE SCHOLARSHIP • 8

For Louisiana residents attending a public college within the state studying wildlife, forestry, or marine sciences full-time. Renewable up to five years as an undergraduate and two years as a graduate. Must have at least a 2.5 GPA and have taken the ACT or SAT.

Academic/Career Areas Animal/Veterinary Sciences; Applied Sciences; Natural Resources.
Award Scholarship for use in any year; renewable. *Number:* 60. *Amount:* $1000.
Eligibility Requirements: Applicant must be enrolled full-time at a two-year or four-year institution or university; resident of Louisiana and studying in Louisiana. Applicant must have 2.5 GPA or higher. Available to U.S. citizens.
Application Requirements Application, test scores, transcript. *Deadline:* July 1.
World Wide Web: http://www.osfa.state.la.us
Contact: Public Information
Louisiana Office of Student Financial Assistance
PO Box 91202
Baton Rouge, LA 70821-9202
Phone: 800-259-5626 Ext. 1012
E-mail: custserv@osfa.state.la.us

UNITED AGRIBUSINESS LEAGUE

UNITED AGRIBUSINESS LEAGUE SCHOLARSHIP PROGRAM
see number 5

APPLIED SCIENCES

AMERICAN INSTITUTE OF AERONAUTICS AND ASTRONAUTICS

AIAA UNDERGRADUATE SCHOLARSHIP • 9
Renewable award available to college sophomores, juniors and seniors enrolled full-time in an accredited college/university. Must be AIAA student member or become one prior to receiving award. Course of study must provide entry into some field of science or engineering encompassed by AIAA. Minimum 3.0 GPA required.

Academic/Career Areas Applied Sciences; Aviation/Aerospace; Electrical Engineering/Electronics; Engineering/Technology; Materials Science, Engineering and Metallurgy; Mechanical Engineering; Physical Sciences and Math; Science, Technology and Society.
Award Scholarship for use in sophomore, junior, or senior years; renewable. *Number:* 30. *Amount:* $2000.
Eligibility Requirements: Applicant must be enrolled full-time at a two-year or four-year or technical institution or university. Applicant must have 3.0 GPA or higher. Available to U.S. and non-U.S. citizens.

AIAA Undergraduate Scholarship (continued)
Application Requirements Application, essay, references, transcript.
Deadline: January 31.
World Wide Web: http://www.aiaa.org
Contact: Stephen Brock, Student Programs Director
American Institute of Aeronautics and Astronautics
1801 Alexander Bell Drive, Suite 500
Reston, VA 20191
Phone: 703-264-7536
Fax: 703-264-7551
E-mail: stephenb@aiaa.org

AMERICAN SOCIETY OF NAVAL ENGINEERS

AMERICAN SOCIETY OF NAVAL ENGINEERS SCHOLARSHIP • 10

Award for naval engineering students in the final year of an undergraduate program or after one year of graduate study at an accredited institution. Must be full-time student and a U.S. citizen. Must study in specified fields. Minimum 2.5 GPA required. One-time award of $2500 for undergraduates and $3500 for graduate students. No doctoral candidates or candidates who already have an advanced degree.

Academic/Career Areas Applied Sciences; Aviation/Aerospace; Civil Engineering; Electrical Engineering/Electronics; Engineering/Technology; Materials Science, Engineering and Metallurgy; Mechanical Engineering; Nuclear Science; Physical Sciences and Math.
Award Scholarship for use in senior, or graduate years; not renewable. *Number:* 18–22. *Amount:* $2500–$3500.
Eligibility Requirements: Applicant must be enrolled full-time at a four-year institution or university. Applicant must have 2.5 GPA or higher. Available to U.S. citizens.
Application Requirements Application, references, test scores, transcript.
Deadline: February 15.
World Wide Web: http://www.navalengineers.org
Contact: Dennis Pignotti, Operations Manager
American Society of Naval Engineers
1452 Duke Street
Alexandria, VA 22314
Phone: 703-836-6727
Fax: 703-836-7491
E-mail: scholarships@navalengineers.org

ASTRONAUT SCHOLARSHIP FOUNDATION

ASTRONAUT SCHOLARSHIP FOUNDATION • 11

Provides scholarships for deserving college science and engineering students.

Academic/Career Areas Applied Sciences; Aviation/Aerospace; Biology; Chemical Engineering; Computer Science/Data Processing; Earth Science; Electrical Engineering/Electronics; Engineering/Technology; Engineering-Related Technologies; Materials Science, Engineering and Metallurgy; Mechanical Engineering; Meteorology/Atmospheric Science.

Award Scholarship for use in junior, senior, graduate, or post graduate years; renewable. *Number:* 17. *Amount:* $8500.

Eligibility Requirements: Applicant must be enrolled full-time at an institution or university. Available to U.S. citizens.

Application Requirements Financial need analysis, references, transcript. *Deadline:* April 15.

World Wide Web: http://www.astronautscholarship.org

Contact: Mr. Howard Benedict, Executive Director
Astronaut Scholarship Foundation
6225 Vectorspace Boulevard
Titusville, FL 32780
Phone: 321-269-6119
Fax: 321-267-3970
E-mail: mercurysvn@aol.com

BARRY M. GOLDWATER SCHOLARSHIP AND EXCELLENCE IN EDUCATION FOUNDATION

BARRY M. GOLDWATER SCHOLARSHIP AND EXCELLENCE IN EDUCATION PROGRAM • 12

One-time award to college juniors and seniors who will pursue advanced degrees in mathematics, natural sciences, or engineering. Students planning to study medicine are eligible if they plan a career in research. Candidates must be nominated by their college or university. Must be U.S. citizen or resident alien. Minimum 3.0 GPA required. Nomination deadline: February 1. Please visit website for further updates. (http://www.act.org/goldwater)

Academic/Career Areas Applied Sciences; Biology; Chemical Engineering; Civil Engineering; Computer Science/Data Processing; Earth Science; Engineering/Technology; Materials Science, Engineering and Metallurgy; Mechanical Engineering; Natural Sciences; Nuclear Science; Physical Sciences and Math.

Award Scholarship for use in junior or senior years; renewable. *Number:* up to 300. *Amount:* up to $7500.

Eligibility Requirements: Applicant must be enrolled at a four-year institution or university. Applicant must have 3.0 GPA or higher. Available to U.S. citizens.

Application Requirements Application, autobiography, essay, references, transcript, school nomination. *Deadline:* February 1.

World Wide Web: http://www.act.org/goldwater

Barry M. Goldwater Scholarship and Excellence in Education Program (continued)
Contact: Col. Gerald Smith, President
Barry M. Goldwater Scholarship and Excellence in Education
Foundation
6225 Brandon Avenue, Suite 315
Springfield, VA 22150-2519
Phone: 703-756-6012
Fax: 703-756-6015
E-mail: goldh2o@erols.com

INTERNATIONAL SOCIETY FOR OPTICAL ENGINEERING-SPIE

SPIE EDUCATIONAL SCHOLARSHIPS IN OPTICAL SCIENCE AND ENGINEERING • 13

Application forms must show demonstrated personal commitment to and involvement of the applicant in the fields of optics, optical science and engineering, and indicate how the granting of the award will contribute to these fields. Applications will be judged by the SPIE Scholarship Committee on the basis of the long range contribution which the granting of the award will make to these fields.

Academic/Career Areas Applied Sciences; Aviation/Aerospace; Chemical Engineering; Electrical Engineering/Electronics; Engineering/Technology; Engineering-Related Technologies; Materials Science, Engineering and Metallurgy; Mechanical Engineering.
Award Scholarship for use in any year; not renewable. *Number:* 30–80. *Amount:* $1000–$10,000.
Eligibility Requirements: Applicant must be enrolled full or part-time at a two-year or four-year or technical institution or university. Available to U.S. and non-U.S. citizens.
Application Requirements Application, references, self-addressed stamped envelope. *Deadline:* February 2.
World Wide Web: http://www.spie.org/info/scholarships
Contact: Scholarship Committee
International Society for Optical Engineering-SPIE
PO Box 10
Bellingham, WA 98227
Phone: 360-676-3290
Fax: 360-647-1445
E-mail: scholarships@spie.org

LOUISIANA OFFICE OF STUDENT FINANCIAL ASSISTANCE

ROCKEFELLER STATE WILDLIFE SCHOLARSHIP   see number 8

ARCHAEOLOGY_____

FOUNDATION FOR THE ADVANCEMENT OF MESOAMERICAN STUDIES, INC.

FAMSI 2002 ANNUAL GRANT COMPETITION ● 14

Provides funds to support research projects that suggest significant contributions to the understanding of ancient Mesoamerican cultures. Grant recipients are determined through an annual grant competition.

Academic/Career Areas Archaeology; Architecture; Area/Ethnic Studies; Art History; Arts; History; Humanities; Museum Studies; Political Science; Religion/ Theology; Social Sciences.

Award Grant for use in any year; not renewable. *Number:* 1–35. *Amount:* $500–$10,000.

Eligibility Requirements: Applicant must be enrolled full or part-time at a two-year or four-year or technical institution or university. Available to U.S. and non-U.S. citizens.

Application Requirements Application, references, curriculum vitae. *Deadline:* September 30.

World Wide Web: http://www.famsi.org

Contact: Jessica Crank, Assistant to the Director
Foundation for the Advancement of MesoAmerican Studies, Inc.
268 S. Suncoast Boulevard
Crystal River, FL 34429-5498
Phone: 352-795-5990
Fax: 352-795-7970
E-mail: jessica@famsi.org

ARCHITECTURE_____

AACE INTERNATIONAL

AACE INTERNATIONAL COMPETITIVE SCHOLARSHIP ● 15

One-time awards to full-time students pursuing a degree in engineering, construction management, quantity surveying and related fields. Application deadline is November 8.

Academic/Career Areas Architecture; Aviation/Aerospace; Chemical Engineering; Civil Engineering; Computer Science/Data Processing; Electrical Engineering/ Electronics; Engineering/Technology; Engineering-Related Technologies; Mechanical Engineering.

Award Scholarship for use in sophomore, junior, senior, or graduate years; not renewable. *Number:* 15–25. *Amount:* $750–$3000.

AACE International Competitive Scholarship (continued)

Eligibility Requirements: Applicant must be enrolled full-time at a two-year or four-year or technical institution or university. Available to U.S. and non-U.S. citizens.

Application Requirements Application, essay, transcript. *Deadline:* November 8.

World Wide Web: http://www.aacei.org

Contact: Charla Miller, Staff Director, Education and Administration
AACE International
209 Prairie Avenue, Suite 100
Morgantown, WV 26501
E-mail: cmiller@aacei.org

AMERICAN ARCHITECTURAL FOUNDATION

AMERICAN INSTITUTE OF ARCHITECTS MINORITY/ DISADVANTAGED SCHOLARSHIP • 16

Renewable award for high school seniors and college freshmen who are entering an architecture degree program. Must be nominated by architect, firm, teacher, dean, civic organization director by December. Must include drawing. Deadline for nominations: December 6. Deadline for applications: January 15. Co-sponsored by AIA and AAF.

Academic/Career Areas Architecture.

Award Scholarship for use in freshman year; renewable. *Number:* 20. *Amount:* $500–$2500.

Eligibility Requirements: Applicant must be Native American or Eskimo, Asian, African American, or Hispanic and enrolled full-time at a four-year institution or university. Available to U.S. citizens.

Application Requirements Application, financial need analysis, references, test scores, transcript, drawing.

World Wide Web: http://www.archfoundation.org

Contact: Mary Felber, Director of Scholarship Programs
American Architectural Foundation
1735 New York Avenue, NW
Washington, DC 20006-5292
Phone: 202-626-7511
Fax: 202-626-7420
E-mail: mfelber@archfoundation.org

AMERICAN INSTITUTE OF ARCHITECTS/AMERICAN ARCHITECTURAL FOUNDATION SCHOLARSHIP FOR PROFESSIONAL DEGREE CANDIDATES • 17

One-time award available to students in the final two years of a professional degree, NAAB-accredited program leading to a bachelor of arts or master's. Applications available from head of department. One-time award. Cosponsored by AIA and AAF.

Academic/Career Areas Architecture.

Award Scholarship for use in junior, senior, or graduate years; not renewable. *Number:* 250. *Amount:* $500–$2500.

Eligibility Requirements: Applicant must be enrolled full-time at a four-year institution or university. Available to U.S. and non-U.S. citizens.

Application Requirements Application, essay, financial need analysis, references, transcript. *Deadline:* February 1.

World Wide Web: http://www.archfoundation.org

Contact: Mary Felber, Director of Scholarship Programs
American Architectural Foundation
1735 New York Avenue, NW
Washington, DC 20006-5292
Phone: 202-626-7511
Fax: 202-626-7420
E-mail: mfelber@archfoundation.org

FOUNDATION FOR THE ADVANCEMENT OF MESOAMERICAN STUDIES, INC.

FAMSI 2002 ANNUAL GRANT COMPETITION   see number 14

INTERNATIONAL FACILITY MANAGEMENT ASSOCIATION FOUNDATION

IFMA FOUNDATION SCHOLARSHIPS   • 18

One-time scholarship of up to $5,000 awarded to students enrolled in full-time facility management programs. Minimum 2.5 GPA required.

Academic/Career Areas Architecture; Engineering-Related Technologies.

Award Scholarship for use in junior, senior, graduate, or post graduate years; not renewable. *Number:* 10. *Amount:* $1000–$5000.

Eligibility Requirements: Applicant must be enrolled full-time at a four-year institution or university. Applicant must have 2.5 GPA or higher. Available to U.S. and non-U.S. citizens.

Application Requirements Application, autobiography, references, transcript. *Deadline:* June 1.

World Wide Web: http://www.ifma.org

Contact: Heidi Suprun, Foundation Manager
International Facility Management Association Foundation
One East Greenway Plaza, Suite 1100
Houston, TX 77046-0194
Phone: 713-623-4362
Fax: 713-623-6124
E-mail: foundation@ifma.org

JOHN F. KENNEDY LIBRARY FOUNDATION

KENNEDY RESEARCH GRANTS • 19

One-time grants for students and scholars doing research on any topic relating to the Kennedy period. Must include ten-page writing sample, project budget and a vita. See application for further details. Preference given to Ph.D. dissertation research, research in recently opened or unused collections, and recent dissertations being prepared for publication. Deadlines for spring grants, March 15; for fall grants, August 15.

Academic/Career Areas Architecture; Criminal Justice/Criminology; Economics; Education; History; Humanities; Library Sciences; Literature/English/Writing; Political Science; Social Sciences.

Award Grant for use in any year; not renewable. *Number:* 15–20. *Amount:* $500–$2500.

Eligibility Requirements: Applicant must be studying in Massachusetts. Available to U.S. citizens.

Application Requirements Application, driver's license, essay, financial need analysis, references, transcript.

World Wide Web: http://www.jfklibrary.org

Contact: Grant and Fellowship Coordinator
John F. Kennedy Library Foundation
Columbia Point
Boston, MA 02125
Phone: 617-929-1200

NATIONAL ASSOCIATION OF WOMEN IN CONSTRUCTION

NAWIC UNDERGRADUATE SCHOLARSHIPS • 20

One-time award for any student having at least one year of study remaining in a construction-related program leading to an associate or higher degree. Awards range from $500-$2000. Submit academic advisor evaluation, application, and transcript of grades.

Academic/Career Areas Architecture; Civil Engineering; Drafting; Electrical Engineering/Electronics; Engineering/Technology; Engineering-Related Technologies; Interior Design; Landscape Architecture; Mechanical Engineering; Trade/Technical Specialties.

Award Scholarship for use in sophomore, junior, or senior years; not renewable. *Number:* 40–50. *Amount:* $500–$2000.

Eligibility Requirements: Applicant must be enrolled full-time at a two-year or four-year or technical institution or university. Applicant must have 3.0 GPA or higher. Available to U.S. and non-U.S. citizens.

Application Requirements Application, essay, financial need analysis, interview, references, transcript. *Deadline:* February 1.

World Wide Web: http://nawic.org

Contact: Scholarship Administrator
National Association of Women in Construction
327 South Adams Street
Fort Worth, TX 76104

NEW YORK STATE EDUCATION DEPARTMENT

REGENTS PROFESSIONAL OPPORTUNITY SCHOLARSHIP PROGRAM—NEW YORK • 21

Renewable award for New York residents in programs leading to a degree in a profession licensed by the Board of Regents. Priority given to minority or disadvantaged students. Must practice full time, professionally in New York for one year for each award received.

Academic/Career Areas Architecture; Business/Consumer Services; Civil Engineering; Dental Health/Services; Electrical Engineering/Electronics; Food Science/Nutrition; Interior Design; Landscape Architecture; Law/Legal Services; Nursing; Social Sciences; Therapy/Rehabilitation.

Award Forgivable loan for use in freshman, sophomore, junior, senior, or graduate years; renewable. *Number:* 220. *Amount:* $1000–$5000.

Eligibility Requirements: Applicant must be Native American or Eskimo, African American, or Hispanic; enrolled full-time at a two-year or four-year institution or university; resident of New York and studying in New York. Available to U.S. citizens.

Application Requirements Application. *Deadline:* May 1.

Contact: Lewis J. Hall, Coordinator
New York State Education Department
Room 1078 EBA
Albany, NY 12234
Phone: 518-486-1319
Fax: 518-486-5346

REAL ESTATE AND LAND USE INSTITUTE

CALIFORNIA STATE UNIVERSITY REAL ESTATE SCHOLARSHIP AND INTERNSHIP GRANT PROGRAM • 22

Targeted at low income and educationally disadvantaged undergraduate and graduate students at one of twenty-three California State University campuses. Must be enrolled at least half-time in a program related to land use or real estate. Minimum GPA is 2.5 for undergraduate students and 3.0 for graduate students.

Academic/Career Areas Architecture; Business/Consumer Services; Civil Engineering; Landscape Architecture; Real Estate.

Award Scholarship for use in any year; not renewable. *Number:* 22–31. *Amount:* $500–$2350.

California State University Real Estate Scholarship and Internship Grant Program (continued)

Eligibility Requirements: Applicant must be enrolled full or part-time at a four-year institution or university and studying in California. Applicant must have 2.5 GPA or higher. Available to U.S. citizens.

Application Requirements Application, essay, financial need analysis, transcript. *Deadline:* Continuous.

Contact: Pam Amundsen, Project Manager
Real Estate and Land Use Institute
7700 College Town Drive, Suite 200
Sacramento, CA 95826-2304
Phone: 916-278-6633
Fax: 916-278-4500
E-mail: amundsenpl@csus.edu

WORLDSTUDIO FOUNDATION

WORLDSTUDIO FOUNDATION SCHOLARSHIP PROGRAM • 23

Worldstudio Foundation provides scholarships to minority and economically disadvantaged students who are studying the design/architecture/arts disciplines in American colleges and universities. Among the foundation's primary aims are to increase diversity in the creative professions and to foster social and environmental responsibility in the artists, designers, and studios of tomorrow. To this end, scholarship recipients are selected not only for their ability and their need, but also for their demonstrated commitment to giving back to the larger community through their work.

Academic/Career Areas Architecture; Arts; Fashion Design; Interior Design.

Award Scholarship for use in any year; not renewable. *Number:* 30–50. *Amount:* $1000–$5000.

Eligibility Requirements: Applicant must be enrolled full-time at a two-year or four-year or technical institution or university. Available to U.S. and non-U.S. citizens.

Application Requirements Application, essay, financial need analysis, photo, portfolio, references, self-addressed stamped envelope, transcript. *Deadline:* April 19.

World Wide Web: http://www.worldstudio.org

Contact: Scholarship Coordinator
Worldstudio Foundation
225 Varick Street, 9th Floor
New York, NY 10014
Phone: 212-366-1317
Fax: 212-807-0024
E-mail: scholarships@worldstudio.org

AREA/ETHNIC STUDIES_____

FOUNDATION FOR THE ADVANCEMENT OF MESOAMERICAN STUDIES, INC.

FAMSI 2002 ANNUAL GRANT COMPETITION   see number 14

IRISH-AMERICAN CULTURAL INSTITUTE

IRISH RESEARCH FUNDS   • 24

One-time award for research which has an Irish-American theme in any discipline of humanities and social science. Primary research preferred, but will fund such projects as museum exhibits, curriculum development, and the compilation of bibliographies. Submit proposal.

Academic/Career Areas Area/Ethnic Studies; Humanities; Social Sciences.
Award Grant for use in any year; not renewable. *Number:* 1–10. *Amount:* $1000–$5000.
Eligibility Requirements: Available to U.S. and non-U.S. citizens.
Application Requirements Application, resume, references. *Deadline:* October 1.
World Wide Web: http://www.iaci-usa.org
Contact: Irish Research Funds Coordinator
Irish-American Cultural Institute
1 Lackawanna Place
Morristown, NJ 07960
Phone: 973-605-1991
Fax: 973-605-8875
E-mail: irishwaynj@aol.com

ART HISTORY_____

FOUNDATION FOR THE ADVANCEMENT OF MESOAMERICAN STUDIES, INC.

FAMSI 2002 ANNUAL GRANT COMPETITION   see number 14

ARTS_____

ALLIANCE FOR YOUNG ARTISTS AND WRITERS, INC.

SCHOLASTIC ART AND WRITING AWARDS-ART SECTION   • 25

Award for students in grades 7-12. Winners of preliminary judging advance to national level. Contact regarding application fee and deadlines, which vary.

Scholastic Art and Writing Awards-Art Section (continued)

Academic/Career Areas Arts; Literature/English/Writing.

Award Scholarship for use in freshman, sophomore, junior, or senior years; not renewable. *Number:* 800. *Amount:* $100–$20,000.

Eligibility Requirements: Applicant must be high school student and must have an interest in art. Available to U.S. and Canadian citizens.

Application Requirements Application, applicant must enter a contest, essay, portfolio, references.

Contact: Alliance for Young Artists and Writers, Inc.
555 Broadway
New York, NY 10012-1396

SCHOLASTIC ART AND WRITING AWARDS-WRITING SECTION SCHOLARSHIP • 26

Award for students in grades 7-12. Winners of preliminary judging advance to national level. Contact regarding application fee and deadlines, which vary.

Academic/Career Areas Arts; Literature/English/Writing.

Award Scholarship for use in freshman, sophomore, junior, or senior years; not renewable. *Number:* 400. *Amount:* $100–$10,000.

Eligibility Requirements: Applicant must be high school student and must have an interest in writing. Available to U.S. and Canadian citizens.

Application Requirements Application, applicant must enter a contest, essay, manuscript.

Contact: Alliance for Young Artists and Writers, Inc.
555 Broadway
New York, NY 10012-1396

ELIZABETH GREENSHIELDS FOUNDATION

ELIZABETH GREENSHIELDS AWARD/GRANT • 27

Award of Can$10,000 grant available to candidates working in painting, drawing, printmaking, or sculpture. Work must be representational or figurative. Must submit at least one color slide of each of six works. Must reapply to renew. Applications from self-taught individuals are also accepted.

Academic/Career Areas Arts.

Award Grant for use in any year; not renewable. *Number:* 40–60. *Amount:* $10,000.

Eligibility Requirements: Applicant must be enrolled full or part-time at a two-year or four-year or technical institution or university and must have an interest in art. Available to U.S. and non-U.S. citizens.

Application Requirements Application, slides. *Deadline:* Continuous.

Contact: Diane Pitcher, Applications Coordinator
Elizabeth Greenshields Foundation
1814 Sherbrooke Street West, Suite 1
Montreal, QC H3H IE4
Canada
Phone: 514-937-9225
Fax: 514-937-0141
E-mail: egreen@total.net

FOUNDATION FOR THE ADVANCEMENT OF MESOAMERICAN STUDIES, INC.

FAMSI 2002 ANNUAL GRANT COMPETITION

see number 14

MARYLAND STATE HIGHER EDUCATION COMMISSION

HOPE SCHOLARSHIP

see number 6

WORLDSTUDIO FOUNDATION

WORLDSTUDIO FOUNDATION SCHOLARSHIP PROGRAM

see number 23

AVIATION/AEROSPACE_____

AACE INTERNATIONAL

AACE INTERNATIONAL COMPETITIVE SCHOLARSHIP

see number 15

AMERICAN INSTITUTE OF AERONAUTICS AND ASTRONAUTICS

AIAA UNDERGRADUATE SCHOLARSHIP

see number 9

AMERICAN SOCIETY OF NAVAL ENGINEERS

AMERICAN SOCIETY OF NAVAL ENGINEERS SCHOLARSHIP

see number 10

ASTRONAUT SCHOLARSHIP FOUNDATION

ASTRONAUT SCHOLARSHIP FOUNDATION

see number 11

INSTRUMENTATION, SYSTEMS, AND AUTOMATION SOCIETY (ISA)

INSTRUMENTATION, SYSTEMS, AND AUTOMATION SOCIETY (ISA) SCHOLARSHIP PROGRAM
• 28

The ISA grants scholarships worldwide to full-time students studying in technical fields related to instrumentation systems and automation. Minimum 3.0 GPA required. Applications available at http://www.isa.org

Academic/Career Areas Aviation/Aerospace; Chemical Engineering; Electrical Engineering/Electronics; Engineering/Technology; Engineering-Related Technologies; Heating, Air-Conditioning, and Refrigeration Mechanics.

Award Scholarship for use in any year; not renewable. *Number:* 10–25. *Amount:* $500–$5000.

Eligibility Requirements: Applicant must be enrolled full-time at a two-year or four-year or technical institution or university. Applicant must have 3.0 GPA or higher. Available to U.S. and non-U.S. citizens.

Application Requirements Application, references, self-addressed stamped envelope, transcript. *Deadline:* February 1.

World Wide Web: http://www.isa.org

Contact: Dale Lee, Director of Education Services
Instrumentation, Systems, and Automation Society (ISA)
67 Alexander Drive
Research Triangle Park, NC 27709
Phone: 919-990-9442
Fax: 919-549-8288
E-mail: dlee@isa.org

INTERNATIONAL SOCIETY FOR OPTICAL ENGINEERING-SPIE

SPIE EDUCATIONAL SCHOLARSHIPS IN OPTICAL SCIENCE AND ENGINEERING
see number 13

NAMEPA NATIONAL SCHOLARSHIP FOUNDATION

NATIONAL ASSOCIATION OF MINORITY ENGINEERING PROGRAM ADMINISTRATORS NATIONAL SCHOLARSHIP FUND
• 29

NAMEPA offers one-time scholarships for African-American, Hispanic, and American Indian students who have demonstrated potential and interest in pursuing an undergraduate degree in engineering. Must have a minimum 3.0 GPA. Must have a score above 25 on ACT, or above 1000 on SAT. Deadline may vary. Visit website for application materials and further details.

Academic/Career Areas Aviation/Aerospace; Chemical Engineering; Civil Engineering; Computer Science/Data Processing; Electrical Engineering/ Electronics; Engineering/Technology; Engineering-Related Technologies; Materials Science, Engineering and Metallurgy; Mechanical Engineering.

Award Scholarship for use in freshman or junior years; not renewable. *Number:* 10–50. *Amount:* $10,000–$50,000.

Eligibility Requirements: Applicant must be Native American or Eskimo, African American, or Hispanic and enrolled full-time at a two-year or four-year institution or university. Applicant must have 3.0 GPA or higher. Available to U.S. and non-U.S. citizens.

Application Requirements Application, essay, resume, references, test scores, transcript. *Deadline:* March 30.

World Wide Web: http://www.namepa.org

Contact: Latisha Moore, Administrative Assistant
Namepa National Scholarship Foundation
1133 West Morse Boulevard, Suite 201
Winter Park, FL 32789
Phone: 407-647-8839
Fax: 407-629-2502
E-mail: namepa@namepa.org

NASA MINNESOTA SPACE GRANT CONSORTIUM

MINNESOTA SPACE GRANT CONSORTIUM MINNESOTA SPACE GRANT CONSORTIUM • 30

Between twenty-five and fifty scholarships ranging from $500 to $2000 are awarded to students registered with affiliate schools and currently interested in pursuing studies in fields related to aerospace sciences and engineering. Preference is given to students currently involved in aerospace science or engineering. The deadline is March 1. Minimum 3.0 GPA required.

Academic/Career Areas Aviation/Aerospace; Computer Science/Data Processing; Engineering/Technology; Physical Sciences and Math.

Award Scholarship for use in freshman, sophomore, junior, senior, or graduate years; not renewable. *Number:* 25–50. *Amount:* $500–$2000.

Eligibility Requirements: Applicant must be enrolled full-time at a four-year or technical institution or university and studying in Minnesota. Applicant must have 3.0 GPA or higher. Available to U.S. citizens.

Application Requirements Application, essay, references, transcript. *Deadline:* March 1.

World Wide Web: http://www.aem.umn.edu/other/msgc

Minnesota Space Grant Consortium Minnesota Space Grant Consortium (continued)
Contact: Randi Quanbeck-Lundell, Program Coordinator
NASA Minnesota Space Grant Consortium
University of Minnesota, Department of Aerospace Engineering &
Mechanics
107 Akerman Hall, 110 Union Street SE
Minneapolis, MN 55455
Phone: 612-626-9295
Fax: 612-626-1558
E-mail: quanbeck@aem.umn.edu

NASA NEVADA SPACE GRANT CONSORTIUM

UNIVERSITY AND COMMUNITY COLLEGE SYSTEM OF NEVADA NASA SPACE GRANT AND FELLOWSHIP PROGRAM • 31

Nevada Space Grant provides graduate fellowships and undergraduate scholarship to qualified student majoring in aerospace science, technology and related fields. Must be Nevada resident studying at a Nevada college/university.

Academic/Career Areas Aviation/Aerospace; Chemical Engineering; Computer Science/Data Processing; Electrical Engineering/Electronics; Engineering/Technology; Meteorology/Atmospheric Science; Physical Sciences and Math.
Award Scholarship for use in freshman, sophomore, junior, senior, or graduate years; renewable. *Number:* 15–25. *Amount:* $500–$10,000.
Eligibility Requirements: Applicant must be enrolled full-time at a two-year or four-year institution or university; resident of Nevada and studying in Nevada. Available to U.S. citizens.
Application Requirements Application, autobiography, essay, resume, references, transcript. *Deadline:* April 1.
World Wide Web: http://www.unr.edu/spacegrant
Contact: Lori Rountree, Program Coordinator
NASA Nevada Space Grant Consortium
University of Nevada, Reno
MS 172
Reno, NV 89557-0138
Phone: 775-784-6261
Fax: 775-327-2235
E-mail: lori@mines.unr.edu

SOCIETY OF AUTOMOTIVE ENGINEERS

SAE ENGINEERING SCHOLARSHIPS • 32

Scholarships available to graduating high school seniors to pursue a four-year degree in engineering or a related science. Must have a minimum 3.0 GPA and must be a U.S. citizen. Renewable awards. Application fee: $5. Application should be retrieved from the SAE website at http://www.sae.org/students/stuschol.htm.

Academic/Career Areas Aviation/Aerospace; Chemical Engineering; Electrical Engineering/Electronics; Engineering/Technology; Engineering-Related Technologies; Materials Science, Engineering and Metallurgy; Mechanical Engineering.

Award Scholarship for use in freshman year; renewable. *Number:* 30–50. *Amount:* $400–$16,000.

Eligibility Requirements: Applicant must be high school student and planning to enroll full-time at a four-year institution or university. Applicant must have 3.0 GPA or higher. Available to U.S. citizens.

Application Requirements Application, essay, test scores, transcript. *Fee:* $5. *Deadline:* December 1.

World Wide Web: http://www.sae.org/students/stuschol.htm

Contact: Connie Harnish, Scholarship and Loan Coordinator
Society of Automotive Engineers
400 Commonwealth Drive
Warrendale, PA 15096-0001
Phone: 724-772-4047
Fax: 724-776-0890
E-mail: connie@sae.org

BIOLOGY

ALBERTA HERITAGE SCHOLARSHIP FUND

ALBERTA HERITAGE SCHOLARSHIP FUND ABORIGINAL HEALTH CAREERS BURSARY • 33

Award for aboriginal students in Alberta entering their second or subsequent year of postsecondary education in a health field. Must be Indian, Inuit, or Metis and a resident of Alberta for a minimum of three years prior to applying. Awards are valued up to Can$13,000. Deadline: May 15. Must be ranked in upper half of class or have a minimum 2.5 GPA.

Academic/Career Areas Biology; Dental Health/Services; Health Administration; Health and Medical Sciences; Nursing; Therapy/Rehabilitation.

Award Scholarship for use in sophomore, junior, senior, or graduate years; not renewable. *Number:* 20–40. *Amount:* $1000–$13,000.

Eligibility Requirements: Applicant must be Canadian; Native American or Eskimo; enrolled full-time at a two-year or four-year or technical institution or university and resident of Alberta. Applicant must have 2.5 GPA or higher.

Application Requirements Application, essay, financial need analysis, references, transcript. *Deadline:* May 15.

World Wide Web: http://www.alis.gov.ab.ca/scholarships

Alberta Heritage Scholarship Fund Aboriginal Health Careers Bursary (continued)
Contact: Alberta Heritage Scholarship Fund
9940 106th Street, 9th Floor, Box 28000 Station Main
Edmonton, AB T5J 4R4
Canada
Phone: 780-427-8640
Fax: 780-422-4516
E-mail: heritage@gov.ab.ca

AMERICAN LIVER FOUNDATION

STUDENT RESEARCH FELLOWSHIPS-AMERICAN LIVER FOUNDATION • 34

Nonrenewable research awards available to full-time undergraduate college students who are currently involved with laboratory research. Must submit detailed research proposal in field of liver disease.

Academic/Career Areas Biology; Health and Medical Sciences; Physical Sciences and Math.

Award Scholarship for use in freshman, sophomore, junior, or senior years; not renewable. *Number:* 10–20. *Amount:* $2500.

Eligibility Requirements: Applicant must be enrolled full-time at a four-year institution. Available to U.S. and non-U.S. citizens.

Application Requirements Application, references, description of project, curriculum vitae, and bibliography. *Deadline:* January 5.

World Wide Web: http://www.liverfoundation.org
Contact: Arlene Fraraccio, Research Grants Coordinator
American Liver Foundation
1425 Pompton
Cedar Grove, NJ 07009
Phone: 973-256-2550 Ext. 225
Fax: 973-256-3214
E-mail: afraraccio@liverfoundation.org

AMERICAN ORNITHOLOGISTS' UNION

AMERICAN ORNITHOLOGISTS' UNION RESEARCH AWARDS
see number 7

ARKANSAS DEPARTMENT OF HIGHER EDUCATION

EMERGENCY SECONDARY EDUCATION LOAN PROGRAM • 35

Must be Arkansas resident enrolled full-time in approved Arkansas institution. Renewable award for students majoring in secondary math, chemistry, physics, biology, physical science, general science, special education, or foreign language. Must teach in Arkansas at least five years. Must rank in upper half of class or have a minimum 2.5 GPA.

Academic/Career Areas Biology; Education; Foreign Language; Physical Sciences and Math; Special Education.

Award Forgivable loan for use in sophomore, junior, senior, or graduate years; renewable. *Number:* up to 50. *Amount:* up to $2500.

Eligibility Requirements: Applicant must be enrolled full-time at a two-year or four-year institution or university; resident of Arkansas and studying in Arkansas. Applicant must have 2.5 GPA or higher. Available to U.S. citizens.

Application Requirements Application, transcript. *Deadline:* April 1.

World Wide Web: http://www.arscholarships.com

Contact: Assistant Coordinator
Arkansas Department of Higher Education
114 East Capitol
Little Rock, AR 72201
Phone: 501-371-2050
Fax: 501-371-2001

ASTRONAUT SCHOLARSHIP FOUNDATION

ASTRONAUT SCHOLARSHIP FOUNDATION   see number 11

BARRY M. GOLDWATER SCHOLARSHIP AND EXCELLENCE IN EDUCATION FOUNDATION

BARRY M. GOLDWATER SCHOLARSHIP AND EXCELLENCE IN EDUCATION PROGRAM   see number 12

BAT CONSERVATION INTERNATIONAL

BAT CONSERVATION INTERNATIONAL STUDENT SCHOLARSHIP PROGRAM   • 36

The goal of this program is to support student research that will answer ecological or behavioral questions essential to bat conservation or management; document key ecological or economic roles of bats; or educate people who are directly relevant to conservation success. Submission of research proposal and budget required. Only senior level biology students and graduate students in biological disciplines are eligible.

Academic/Career Areas Biology; Natural Resources; Natural Sciences.

Award Grant for use in senior, or graduate years; not renewable. *Number:* 12–20. *Amount:* $500–$2500.

Eligibility Requirements: Applicant must be enrolled full-time at a four-year institution or university. Available to U.S. and non-U.S. citizens.

Bat Conservation International Student Scholarship Program (continued)
Application Requirements Application, references, research proposal, budget.
Deadline: December 15.
World Wide Web: http://www.batcon.org
Contact: Ms. Angela England, Scholarship Awards Coordinator
Bat Conservation International
PO Box 162603
Austin, TX 78716-2603
Phone: 512-327-9721 Ext. 35
Fax: 512-327-9724
E-mail: aengland@batcon.org

BUSINESS AND PROFESSIONAL WOMEN'S FOUNDATION

BPW CAREER ADVANCEMENT SCHOLARSHIP PROGRAM FOR WOMEN
• 37

Scholarships ranging from $500-$1000 each are awarded for full-or part-time study. Applicant must be studying in one of the following fields: biological sciences, teacher education certification, engineering, social science, paralegal studies, humanities, business studies, mathematics, computer science, physical sciences, or for a professional degree (JD, MD, DDS). The Career Advancement Scholarship Program was established to assist women seeking the education necessary for entry or re-entry into the work force, or advancement within a career field. Must be 25 or over. Send self-addressed double-stamped envelope between January 1 and April 1 for application.

Academic/Career Areas Biology; Computer Science/Data Processing; Dental Health/Services; Education; Engineering/Technology; Engineering-Related Technologies; Health and Medical Sciences; Humanities; Law/Legal Services; Physical Sciences and Math; Social Sciences.

Award Scholarship for use in junior, senior, or graduate years; not renewable. *Number:* 100–200. *Amount:* $500–$1000.

Eligibility Requirements: Applicant must be age 25; enrolled full or part-time at a two-year or four-year or technical institution or university and female. Applicant must have 2.5 GPA or higher. Available to U.S. citizens.

Application Requirements Application, essay, financial need analysis, references, self-addressed stamped envelope, transcript. *Deadline:* April 15.
World Wide Web: http://www.bpwusa.org
Contact: Jennifer Miller, Education Director
Business and Professional Women's Foundation
2012 Massachusetts Avenue, NW
Washington, DC 20036
Phone: 202-293-1100 Ext. 182
Fax: 202-293-0298

MARYLAND STATE HIGHER EDUCATION COMMISSION

SCIENCE AND TECHNOLOGY SCHOLARSHIP • 38

Provides assistance to full-time students in an academic program that will address career shortage areas in the state (computer science, engineering, biological sciences, mathematics, and physical sciences). Must be Maryland resident. Must have cumulative unweighted 3.0 GPA in math, natural or physical science, social science, social studies, English, foreign language, and computer science.

Academic/Career Areas Biology; Chemical Engineering; Civil Engineering; Computer Science/Data Processing; Earth Science; Electrical Engineering/Electronics; Engineering/Technology; Engineering-Related Technologies; Fire Sciences; Physical Sciences and Math.

Award Forgivable loan for use in freshman, sophomore, junior, or senior years; renewable. *Number:* up to 2500. *Amount:* $1000–$3000.

Eligibility Requirements: Applicant must be enrolled full-time at a two-year or four-year institution or university; resident of Maryland and studying in Maryland. Applicant must have 3.0 GPA or higher. Available to U.S. citizens.

Application Requirements Application, transcript. *Deadline:* March 1.

World Wide Web: http://www.mhec.state.md.us

Contact: Julie Perrotta, Scholarship Administration
Maryland State Higher Education Commission
16 Francis Street
Annapolis, MD 21401-1781
Phone: 410-260-4564
Fax: 410-974-5994
E-mail: ssamail@mhec.state.md.us

SOCIETY OF TOXICOLOGY

MINORITY UNDERGRADUATE STUDENT AWARDS • 39

Travel funds are provided for members of groups under-represented in the Sciences to attend a special program at the Society of Toxicology Annual Meeting. Must have a 3.0 GPA. The deadline is October 9.

Academic/Career Areas Biology; Health and Medical Sciences.

Award Grant for use in freshman, sophomore, junior, or senior years; not renewable. *Number:* 20–50. *Amount:* $1000–$1200.

Eligibility Requirements: Applicant must be Native American or Eskimo, African American, or Hispanic and enrolled full-time at a two-year or four-year institution or university. Applicant must have 3.0 GPA or higher. Available to U.S. citizens.

Application Requirements Application, essay, references, transcript. *Deadline:* October 9.

World Wide Web: http://www.toxicology.org

Minority Undergraduate Student Awards (continued)
Contact: Society of Toxicology
1767 Business Center Drive, Suite 302
Reston, VA 20190

UNITED STATES DEPARTMENT OF HEALTH AND HUMAN SERVICES

NIH UNDERGRADUATE SCHOLARSHIP FOR INDIVIDUALS FROM DISADVANTAGED BACKGROUNDS • 40

Renewable awards of up to $20,000 per year for individuals from disadvantaged backgrounds to pursue degrees in physical and life sciences (including chemistry). Must complete one year of National Institutes of Health employment for each year of scholarship plus ten weeks during each year of scholarship. Minimum 3.5 GPA required.

Academic/Career Areas Biology; Health and Medical Sciences; Physical Sciences and Math.
Award Scholarship for use in freshman, sophomore, junior, or senior years; renewable. *Number:* 15–20. *Amount:* up to $20,000.
Eligibility Requirements: Applicant must be enrolled full-time at a four-year institution or university. Applicant must have 3.5 GPA or higher.
Application Requirements Application, essay, financial need analysis, references, transcript. *Deadline:* March 31.
World Wide Web: http://helix.nih.gov:8001/oe/student/ugsp.html
Contact: Marc Horowitz, Office of Loan Repayment and Scholarship
United States Department of Health and Human Services
2 Center Drive, Room 2E30
Bethesda, MD 20892-0230
Phone: 800-528-7689
Fax: 301-402-8098
E-mail: mhorowitz@nih.gov

BUSINESS/CONSUMER SERVICES_____

AMERICAN FLORAL ENDOWMENT

VICTOR AND MARGARET BALL PROGRAM • 41

Award for undergraduate students majoring in business, floriculture, and ornamental horticulture. A paid training experience for students who are interested in a "production related" career (growing), and up to a $6000 grant upon satisfactory completion of six months of training. Deadlines: March 1 for fall/winter training; November 1 for spring/summer training.

Academic/Career Areas Business/Consumer Services; Horticulture/ Floriculture.

Award Scholarship for use in freshman, sophomore, junior, or senior years; not renewable. *Number:* 20. *Amount:* $3000–$6000.

Eligibility Requirements: Applicant must be enrolled full-time at a two-year or four-year institution or university. Applicant must have 2.5 GPA or higher. Available to U.S. and non-U.S. citizens.

Application Requirements Application, photo, references, transcript.

World Wide Web: http://www.endowment.org

Contact: Steve F. Martinez, Executive Vice President
American Floral Endowment
11 Glen-Ed Professional Park
Glen Carbon, IL 62034
Phone: 618-692-0045
Fax: 618-692-4045
E-mail: afe@endowment.org

APICS-EDUCATIONAL AND RESEARCH FOUNDATION, INC.

DONALD W. FOGARTY INTERNATIONAL STUDENT PAPER COMPETITION
• 42

Annual competition on topics pertaining to resource management only. Must be original work of one or more authors. May submit one paper only. Must be in English. Open to full- and part-time undergraduate and graduate students. High school students ineligible. All queries are directed to website. Other queries must submit e-mail address and SASE.

Academic/Career Areas Business/Consumer Services; Natural Resources.

Award Prize for use in freshman, sophomore, junior, senior, or graduate years; not renewable. *Number:* 90. *Amount:* $100–$1750.

Eligibility Requirements: Applicant must be enrolled full or part-time at a four-year institution or university. Available to U.S. and non-U.S. citizens.

Application Requirements Application, applicant must enter a contest, essay, self-addressed stamped envelope. *Deadline:* May 15.

World Wide Web: http://www.apics.org/E&R

Contact: Communications/Educational Research Associate
APICS- Educational and Research Foundation, Inc.
5301 Shawnee Road
Alexandria, VA 22312-2317
Phone: 703-354-8851 Ext. 2283
Fax: 703-354-8794
E-mail: foundation@apicshq.org

CASUALTY ACTUARIAL SOCIETY/SOCIETY OF ACTUARIES JOINT COMMITTEE ON MINORITY RECRUITING

ACTUARIAL SCHOLARSHIPS FOR MINORITY STUDENTS • 43

Award for underrepresented minority students planning careers in actuarial science or mathematics. Applicants should have taken the ACT Assessment or the SAT. Number and amount of awards vary with merit and financial need. Must be a U.S. citizen or permanent resident. All scholarship information including application is available online. Do not send award inquiries to address.

Academic/Career Areas Business/Consumer Services.

Award Scholarship for use in freshman, sophomore, junior, senior, or graduate years; not renewable. *Number:* 20–35. *Amount:* $500–$3000.

Eligibility Requirements: Applicant must be Native American or Eskimo, African American, or Hispanic and enrolled full or part-time at a two-year or four-year institution or university. Available to U.S. and Canadian citizens.

Application Requirements Application, financial need analysis, references, test scores, transcript. *Deadline:* May 1.

World Wide Web: http://www.BeAnActuary.org

Contact: Minority Scholarship Coordinator
  Phone: 847-706-3509
  Fax: 847-706-3599
  E-mail: snelson@soa.org

CUBAN AMERICAN NATIONAL FOUNDATION

MAS FAMILY SCHOLARSHIPS • 44

Graduate and undergraduate scholarships in the fields of engineering, business, international relations, economics, communications, and journalism. Applicants must be Cuban-American and have graduated in the top 10% of high school class or have minimum 3.5 college GPA. Selection based on need, academic performance, leadership. Those who have already received awards and maintained high level of performance are given preference over new applicants.

Academic/Career Areas Business/Consumer Services; Chemical Engineering; Communications; Economics; Electrical Engineering/Electronics; Engineering/Technology; Engineering-Related Technologies; Journalism; Mechanical Engineering; Political Science.

Award Scholarship for use in any year; renewable. *Number:* 10–15. *Amount:* $1000–$10,000.

Eligibility Requirements: Applicant must be Latin American/Caribbean; enrolled full-time at a two-year or four-year institution or university and must have an interest in leadership. Applicant must have 3.5 GPA or higher. Available to U.S. citizens.

Application Requirements Application, autobiography, essay, financial need analysis, references, test scores, transcript. *Deadline:* March 31.
Contact: Director
Cuban American National Foundation
Mas Family Scholarships
1312 SW 27th Avenue, 3rd Floor
Miami, FL 33145
Phone: 305-592-7768
Fax: 305-592-7889

DECA (DISTRIBUTION EDUCATION CLUB OF AMERICA)

HARRY A. APPLEGATE SCHOLARSHIP • 45

Available to DECA members for undergraduate or graduate study. Must major in marketing education, merchandising, and/or management. Nonrenewable award for high school students based on DECA activities, grades, and need. Submit application to state office by state application deadline. National office must receive applications by the second Monday in March.

Academic/Career Areas Business/Consumer Services; Education; Food Service/Hospitality.
Award Scholarship for use in any year; not renewable. *Number:* 30–100. *Amount:* $1000–$1500.
Eligibility Requirements: Applicant must be high school student; planning to enroll full or part-time at a two-year or four-year institution or university; member of Distribution Ed Club or Future Business Leaders of America and must have an interest in leadership. Applicant must have 2.5 GPA or higher. Available to U.S. and Canadian citizens.
Application Requirements Application, references, test scores, transcript.
World Wide Web: http://www.deca.org
Contact: Kathy Onion, Marketing Specialist
DECA (Distribution Education Club of America)
1908 Association Drive
Reston, VA 20191-4013
Phone: 703-860-5000
Fax: 703-860-4013
E-mail: kathy_onion@deca.org

FLORIDA INSTITUTE OF CPAS EDUCATIONAL FOUNDATION

EDUCATIONAL FOUNDATION SCHOLARSHIPS • 46

Scholarships are for accounting majors who are Florida residents attending Florida college/universities. Applicants must be planning to sit for CPA exam and indicate desire to practice accounting in Florida. Scholarships are granted

Educational Foundation Scholarships (continued)
based on educational achievement, financial need and demonstrated professional, social, and charitable activities. Citizens of other countries may apply, if planning to work in Florida. Minimum 3.0 GPA required.

Academic/Career Areas Business/Consumer Services.

Award Scholarship for use in senior, or graduate years; not renewable. *Number:* 50. *Amount:* $1250.

Eligibility Requirements: Applicant must be enrolled full-time at a four-year institution or university; resident of Florida and studying in Florida. Applicant must have 3.0 GPA or higher. Available to U.S. and non-U.S. citizens.

Application Requirements Application, financial need analysis, photo, references, transcript. *Deadline:* April 1.

World Wide Web: http://www.ficpa.org

Contact: Betsy Wilson, Educational Foundation Assistant
Florida Institute of CPAs Educational Foundation
325 West College Avenue
PO Box 5437
Tallahassee, FL 32314
Phone: 850-224-2724 Ext. 200
Fax: 850-222-8190
E-mail: wilsonb@ficpa.org

FICPA CHAPTER SCHOLARSHIP PROGRAM • 47

Scholarships are for accounting majors who are Florida residents attending Florida college/universities. Applicants must be planning to sit for CPA exam and indicate desire to practice accounting in Florida. Scholarships are granted based on educational achievement, financial need and demonstrated professional, social, and charitable activities. Citizens of other countries may apply, if planning to work in Florida. Minimum 3.0 GPA required. Deadlines: 4/1 and 10/1.

Academic/Career Areas Business/Consumer Services.

Award Scholarship for use in senior, or graduate years; not renewable. *Number:* 30–60. *Amount:* $1000–$1250.

Eligibility Requirements: Applicant must be enrolled full or part-time at a four-year institution or university; resident of Florida and studying in Florida. Applicant must have 3.0 GPA or higher. Available to U.S. and non-U.S. citizens.

Application Requirements Application, financial need analysis, photo, references, transcript.

World Wide Web: http://www.ficpa.org

Contact: Betsy Wilson, Educational Foundation Assistant
Florida Institute of CPAs Educational Foundation
325 West College Avenue
PO Box 5437
Tallahassee, FL 32314
Phone: 850-224-2724 Ext. 200
Fax: 850-222-8190
E-mail: wilsonb@ficpa.org

HISPANIC COLLEGE FUND, INC.

HISPANIC COLLEGE FUND SCHOLARSHIP PROGRAM   see number 3

THE HISPANIC COLLEGE FUND/INROADS/SPRINT SCHOLARSHIP PROGRAM   see number 4

KNIGHT RIDDER

KNIGHT RIDDER MINORITY SCHOLARSHIP PROGRAM   • 48

Five $40,000 scholarships are given to graduating high school seniors who have plans of pursuing journalism as a study and eventually as a career. Funds are given out over a four year period: $5,000 is given the first and second years, $15,000 is given out the third and fourth years. Recipients must work as an intern for a Knight-Ridder Company and maintain a "B" average. Must be sponsored by local Knight Ridder newspaper.

Academic/Career Areas Business/Consumer Services; Graphics/Graphic Arts/Printing; Journalism.

Award Scholarship for use in freshman, sophomore, junior, or senior years; renewable. *Number:* 5. *Amount:* $500–$15,000.

Eligibility Requirements: Applicant must be Native American or Eskimo, Asian, African American, or Hispanic; high school student; planning to enroll full-time at a two-year or four-year institution or university and must have an interest in designated field specified by sponsor. Available to U.S. citizens.

Application Requirements Autobiography, essay, interview, references, test scores, transcript. *Deadline:* January 3.

World Wide Web: http://www.kri.com

Contact: Jacqui Love Marshall, Vice President, HR/Diversity and
　　　　　　　Development
　　　　　　　Knight Ridder
　　　　　　　50 West San Fernando Street, Suite 1200
　　　　　　　San Jose, CA 95113-2413
　　　　　　　Phone: 408-938-7734
　　　　　　　Fax: 408-938-0205
　　　　　　　E-mail: jlovemar@knightridder.com

MARYLAND ASSOCIATION OF PRIVATE CAREER SCHOOLS

MARYLAND ASSOCIATION OF PRIVATE CAREER SCHOOLS SCHOLARSHIP   • 49

Awards for study at trade schools only. Must enter school same year high school is completed. For use only in Maryland and by Maryland residents. Write for further information. One-time award of $1000 to $16,458.

Academic/Career Areas Business/Consumer Services; Computer Science/Data Processing; Dental Health/Services; Engineering/Technology; Food Science/Nutrition; Home Economics; Trade/Technical Specialties; TV/Radio Broadcasting.

Maryland Association of Private Career Schools Scholarship (continued)

Award Scholarship for use in freshman year; not renewable. *Number:* 38. *Amount:* $1000–$16,458.

Eligibility Requirements: Applicant must be high school student; planning to enroll full-time at a technical institution; resident of Maryland and studying in Maryland. Available to U.S. citizens.

Application Requirements Application, references, transcript. *Deadline:* April 7.

Contact: Administrative Assistant
Maryland Association of Private Career Schools
1205 Stonewood Court
Annapolis, MD 21401
Phone: 410-974-4472
Fax: 410-757-3809

MARYLAND STATE HIGHER EDUCATION COMMISSION

HOPE SCHOLARSHIP
see number 6

NATIONAL ASSOCIATION OF BLACK ACCOUNTANTS, INC.

NATIONAL ASSOCIATION OF BLACK ACCOUNTANTS NATIONAL SCHOLARSHIP
• 50

One-time award for minority college students to study full-time, any business-related discipline at an accredited institution. Candidate must be a member of the National Association of Black Accountants with a minimum GPA of 2.5. Must submit a copy of visa, if a non-U.S. citizen.

Academic/Career Areas Business/Consumer Services; Economics.

Award Scholarship for use in freshman, sophomore, junior, or senior years; not renewable. *Number:* 40. *Amount:* $500–$6000.

Eligibility Requirements: Applicant must be Native American or Eskimo, Asian, African American, or Hispanic; enrolled full-time at a four-year institution or university and member of National Association of Black Accountants. Applicant must have 2.5 GPA or higher. Available to U.S. and non-U.S. citizens.

Application Requirements Application, autobiography, essay, financial need analysis, resume, transcript, visa, if non-U.S. citizen. *Deadline:* December 31.

World Wide Web: http://www.nabainc.org

Contact: Charles Quinn, Director, CAMA
National Association of Black Accountants, Inc.
7249-A Hanover Parkway
Greenbelt, MD 20770
Phone: 301-474-6222 Ext. 114
Fax: 301-474-3114
E-mail: cquinn@nabainc.org

NEW JERSEY SOCIETY OF CERTIFIED PUBLIC ACCOUNTANTS

NEW JERSEY SOCIETY OF CERTIFIED PUBLIC ACCOUNTANTS HIGH SCHOOL SCHOLARSHIP PROGRAM • 51

This program is open to all NJ high school seniors. Selection is based on a one-hour aptitude exam and the highest scorers on this exam are invited for an interview. The winners receive accounting scholarships to the college of their choice. Five-year awards range in value from $6500-$8500.

Academic/Career Areas Business/Consumer Services.
Award Scholarship for use in freshman year; renewable. *Number:* 15–20. *Amount:* $6500–$8500.
Eligibility Requirements: Applicant must be high school student; planning to enroll full-time at an institution or university and resident of New Jersey. Available to U.S. citizens.
Application Requirements Interview, test scores. *Deadline:* October 31.
World Wide Web: http://www.njscpa.org
Contact: Janice Amatucci, Student Programs Coordinator
New Jersey Society of Certified Public Accountants
425 Eagle Rock Avenue
Roseland, NJ 07068
Phone: 973-226-4494
Fax: 973-226-7425
E-mail: jamatucci@njscpa.org

NEW JERSEY SOCIETY OF CERTIFIED PUBLIC ACCOUNTANTS COLLEGE SCHOLARSHIP PROGRAM • 52

Award for college juniors based upon academic merit. Must be a New Jersey resident attending a four-year New Jersey institution. Must be nominated by Accounting Department Chair. Minimum 3.5 GPA required. Interview required. One-time award of up to $4000.

Academic/Career Areas Business/Consumer Services.
Award Scholarship for use in junior year; not renewable. *Number:* 10–20. *Amount:* $3000–$4000.
Eligibility Requirements: Applicant must be enrolled full or part-time at a four-year institution or university; resident of New Jersey and studying in New Jersey. Applicant must have 3.5 GPA or higher. Available to U.S. citizens.
Application Requirements Interview, transcript. *Deadline:* January 18.
World Wide Web: http://www.njscpa.org
Contact: Ms. Janice Amatucci, Student Programs Coordinator
New Jersey Society of Certified Public Accountants
425 Eagle Rock Avenue
Roseland, NJ 07068
Phone: 973-226-4494
Fax: 973-226-7425
E-mail: jamatucci@njscpa.org

NEW YORK STATE EDUCATION DEPARTMENT

REGENTS PROFESSIONAL OPPORTUNITY SCHOLARSHIP PROGRAM—NEW YORK
see number 21

NORTH CAROLINA CPA FOUNDATION, INC.

NORTH CAROLINA CPA FOUNDATION ACCOUNTING SCHOLARSHIP PROGRAM • 53

Awards are made to juniors, seniors and fifth-year students pursuing undergraduate and graduate degrees in accounting. The essay requests the students describe the "CPA of the Future" and why they want to become one. The amount of the award will be determined by the best essay. Applicants must be a North Carolina resident attending a North Carolina four-year college or university.

Academic/Career Areas Business/Consumer Services.

Award Scholarship for use in junior, senior, or graduate years; not renewable. *Number:* 20–30. *Amount:* $1000–$3000.

Eligibility Requirements: Applicant must be enrolled full-time at a four-year institution or university; resident of North Carolina and studying in North Carolina. Applicant must have 2.5 GPA or higher. Available to U.S. citizens.

Application Requirements Application, applicant must enter a contest, essay, transcript. *Deadline:* December 31.

World Wide Web: http://www.ncacpa.org

Contact: Jim Ahler, CAE, Executive Director
North Carolina CPA Foundation, Inc.
PO Box 80188
Raleigh, NC 27623-0188
Phone: 919-469-1040
Fax: 919-469-3959
E-mail: jtahler@ncacpa.org

OSCPA EDUCATIONAL FOUNDATION

OSCPA EDUCATIONAL FOUNDATION SCHOLARSHIP PROGRAM • 54

One-time award for students majoring in accounting. Must attend an accredited Oregon college/university or community college on full-time basis. High school seniors must have a minimum 3.5 GPA. Must be a U.S. citizen and Oregon resident. Deadline is February 6.

Academic/Career Areas Business/Consumer Services.

Award Scholarship for use in any year; not renewable. *Number:* 50–100. *Amount:* $500–$3000.

Eligibility Requirements: Applicant must be enrolled full-time at a two-year or four-year institution or university; resident of Oregon and studying in Oregon. Applicant must have 3.5 GPA or higher. Available to U.S. citizens.
Application Requirements Application, resume, references, test scores, transcript. *Deadline:* February 6.
World Wide Web: http://www.orcpa.org
Contact: Jessica Martin, Member Services/Communications Assistant
OSCPA Educational Foundation
PO Box 4555
Beaverton, OR 97076-4555
Phone: 503-641-7200 Ext. 11
Fax: 503-626-2942
E-mail: jessica@orcpa.org

PENNSYLVANIA INSTITUTE OF CERTIFIED PUBLIC ACCOUNTANTS

PENNSYLVANIA INSTITUTE OF CERTIFIED PUBLIC ACCOUNTANTS SOPHOMORE SCHOLARSHIP • 55
To promote the accounting profession and CPA credential as an exciting and rewarding career path, the PICPA awards $34,000 annually in new scholarships to full-time sophomore undergraduate students enrolled at Pennsylvania colleges and universities. Minimum 3.0 GPA required.

Academic/Career Areas Business/Consumer Services.
Award Scholarship for use in sophomore year; renewable. *Number:* 18. *Amount:* $1000–$9000.
Eligibility Requirements: Applicant must be enrolled full-time at a two-year or four-year institution or university and studying in Pennsylvania. Applicant must have 3.0 GPA or higher. Available to U.S. and non-U.S. citizens.
Application Requirements Application, essay, resume, references, test scores. *Deadline:* March 2.
World Wide Web: http://www.picpa.org
Contact: Craig Brodbeck, Marketing Administrator
Pennsylvania Institute of Certified Public Accountants
1650 Arch Street
17th Floor
Philadelphia, PA 19103-2099
Phone: 215-496-9272

REAL ESTATE AND LAND USE INSTITUTE

CALIFORNIA STATE UNIVERSITY REAL ESTATE SCHOLARSHIP AND INTERNSHIP GRANT PROGRAM   see number 22

SOCIETY OF PLASTICS ENGINEERS (SPE) FOUNDATION

SOCIETY OF PLASTICS ENGINEERS SCHOLARSHIP PROGRAM • 56

The SPE Foundation offers scholarships to full-time students who have demonstrated or expressed an interest in the plastics industry. They must be majoring in or taking courses that would be beneficial to a career in the plastics industry.

Academic/Career Areas Business/Consumer Services; Chemical Engineering; Civil Engineering; Engineering/Technology; Materials Science, Engineering and Metallurgy; Mechanical Engineering; Trade/Technical Specialties.

Award Scholarship for use in any year; not renewable. *Number:* 20. *Amount:* $1000–$5000.

Eligibility Requirements: Applicant must be enrolled full-time at a two-year or four-year or technical institution or university. Available to U.S. and non-U.S. citizens.

Application Requirements Application, essay, financial need analysis, references, transcript. *Deadline:* December 15.

World Wide Web: http://www.4spe.org

Contact: Gail Bristol, Managing Director
Society of Plastics Engineers (SPE) Foundation
14 Fairfield Drive
Brookfield, CT 06804
Phone: 203-740-5447
Fax: 203-775-8490
E-mail: grbristol@4spe.org

UNITED NEGRO COLLEGE FUND

CITIGROUP FELLOWS PROGRAM • 57

In addition to the $6400 scholarship, recipients receive a Citigroup mentor and attend the annual leadership conference for fellows and mentors. Ten freshmen with a business-related major attending a UNCF member college or university or an historically black college or university are selected each year. Minimum 3.0 GPA required.

Academic/Career Areas Business/Consumer Services.

Award Scholarship for use in freshman year; not renewable. *Number:* 10. *Amount:* $6400.

Eligibility Requirements: Applicant must be African American and enrolled at a four-year institution or university. Applicant must have 3.0 GPA or higher.

Application Requirements Application. *Deadline:* March 8.

World Wide Web: http://www.uncf.org

Contact: Program Services Department
United Negro College Fund
8260 Willow Oaks Corporate Drive
Fairfax, VA 22031

COCA-COLA CORPORATE SCHOLARSHIP/INTERN PROGRAM • 58

Provides educational opportunities for minority students. Must be undergraduate sophomore with a minimum GPA of 3.0. Scholarship based on successful internship performance. Open to majors in engineering, business, finance, computer science/MIS, chemistry, communications, journalism, retail and human resources.

Academic/Career Areas Business/Consumer Services; Communications; Computer Science/Data Processing; Engineering/Technology; Journalism.
Award Scholarship for use in sophomore year; not renewable. *Number:* up to 50. *Amount:* $10,000.
Eligibility Requirements: Applicant must be Native American or Eskimo, Asian, African American, or Hispanic. Applicant must have 3.0 GPA or higher.
Application Requirements Application, references, transcript. *Deadline:* December 14.
World Wide Web: http://www.uncf.org
Contact: Program Services Department
United Negro College Fund
8260 Willow Oaks Corporate Drive
Fairfax, VA 22031

CHEMICAL ENGINEERING_____

AACE INTERNATIONAL

AACE INTERNATIONAL COMPETITIVE SCHOLARSHIP   see number 15

AMERICAN CHEMICAL SOCIETY

AMERICAN CHEMICAL SOCIETY SCHOLARS PROGRAM   • 59

Renewable award for minority students pursuing studies in chemistry, biochemistry, chemical technology, chemical engineering or any chemical sciences. Must be U.S. citizen or permanent resident and have minimum 3.0 GPA. May be Native American, African-American, or Hispanic. Scholarship amount for freshmen is up to $2500, and up to $3000 for sophomores, juniors and seniors.

Academic/Career Areas Chemical Engineering; Materials Science, Engineering and Metallurgy; Natural Sciences.

American Chemical Society Scholars Program (continued)
Award Scholarship for use in freshman, sophomore, or junior years; renewable. *Number:* 100–200. *Amount:* $600–$3000.
Eligibility Requirements: Applicant must be Native American or Eskimo, African American, or Hispanic and enrolled full-time at a two-year or four-year or technical institution or university. Applicant must have 3.0 GPA or higher. Available to U.S. citizens.
Application Requirements Application, financial need analysis, references, test scores, transcript. *Deadline:* March 1.
World Wide Web: http://www.acs.org
Contact: Robert Hughes, Manager
American Chemical Society
1155 16th Street, NW
Washington, DC 20036
E-mail: scholars@acs.org

ASTRONAUT SCHOLARSHIP FOUNDATION

ASTRONAUT SCHOLARSHIP FOUNDATION   see number 11

BARRY M. GOLDWATER SCHOLARSHIP AND EXCELLENCE IN EDUCATION FOUNDATION

BARRY M. GOLDWATER SCHOLARSHIP AND EXCELLENCE IN EDUCATION PROGRAM   see number 12

CONSULTING ENGINEERS AND LAND SURVEYORS OF CALIFORNIA SCHOLARSHIP PROGRAM

CONSULTING ENGINEERS AND LAND SURVEYORS OF CALIFORNIA SCHOLARSHIP AWARD   • **60**
Five to seven awards to engineering and land surveying students in their third, fourth, or fifth year of study. Must have a minimum GPA of 3.2. For California residents and for study in California only.

Academic/Career Areas Chemical Engineering; Civil Engineering; Electrical Engineering/Electronics; Engineering/Technology; Engineering-Related Technologies; Mechanical Engineering; Surveying; Surveying Technology, Cartography, or Geographic Information Science.
Award Scholarship for use in junior, senior, or graduate years; not renewable. *Number:* 5–7. *Amount:* up to $7500.
Eligibility Requirements: Applicant must be enrolled full-time at a four-year institution or university; resident of California and studying in California. Available to U.S. citizens.

Application Requirements Application, essay, references, transcript.
Deadline: January 8.
World Wide Web: http://www.celsoc.org
Contact: Christine Hoek, Communications Associate
   Consulting Engineers and Land Surveyors of California Scholarship
      Program
   1303 J Street, Suite 450
   Sacramento, CA 95814
   Phone: 916-441-7991
   Fax: 916-441-6312
   E-mail: choek@celsoc.org

CUBAN AMERICAN NATIONAL FOUNDATION

MAS FAMILY SCHOLARSHIPS see number 44

HISPANIC COLLEGE FUND, INC.

HISPANIC COLLEGE FUND SCHOLARSHIP PROGRAM see number 3

THE HISPANIC COLLEGE FUND/INROADS/SPRINT SCHOLARSHIP PROGRAM see number 4

INSTRUMENTATION, SYSTEMS, AND AUTOMATION SOCIETY (ISA)

INSTRUMENTATION, SYSTEMS, AND AUTOMATION SOCIETY (ISA) SCHOLARSHIP PROGRAM see number 28

INTERNATIONAL SOCIETY FOR OPTICAL ENGINEERING-SPIE

SPIE EDUCATIONAL SCHOLARSHIPS IN OPTICAL SCIENCE AND ENGINEERING see number 13

MARYLAND STATE HIGHER EDUCATION COMMISSION

SCIENCE AND TECHNOLOGY SCHOLARSHIP see number 38

NAMEPA NATIONAL SCHOLARSHIP FOUNDATION

NATIONAL ASSOCIATION OF MINORITY ENGINEERING PROGRAM ADMINISTRATORS NATIONAL SCHOLARSHIP FUND see number 29

NASA NEVADA SPACE GRANT CONSORTIUM

UNIVERSITY AND COMMUNITY COLLEGE SYSTEM OF NEVADA
NASA SPACE GRANT AND FELLOWSHIP PROGRAM   see number 31

SOCIETY OF AUTOMOTIVE ENGINEERS

SAE ENGINEERING SCHOLARSHIPS   see number 32

SOCIETY OF PLASTICS ENGINEERS (SPE) FOUNDATION

SOCIETY OF PLASTICS ENGINEERS SCHOLARSHIP PROGRAM
see number 56

USENIX ASSOCIATION

USENIX STUDENT PROGRAMS   • 61

Funding for students and student research projects. Proposals accepted until September 1. See web site for deadlines and more information (http://www. usenix.org).

Academic/Career Areas Chemical Engineering; Civil Engineering; Computer Science/Data Processing; Electrical Engineering/Electronics; Engineering/ Technology; Engineering-Related Technologies; Materials Science, Engineering and Metallurgy; Mechanical Engineering.

Award Grant for use in any year; not renewable. *Number:* 1–50. *Amount:* $500–$50,000.

Eligibility Requirements: Applicant must be enrolled full or part-time at a two-year or four-year or technical institution or university. Available to U.S. and non-U.S. citizens.

Application Requirements Application. *Deadline:* September 1.

World Wide Web: http://www.usenix.org

Contact: Gale Berkowitz, Deputy Executive Director
USENIX Association
2560 Ninth Street, Suite 215
Berkeley, CA 94710
Phone: 510-528-8649
Fax: 510-548-5738
E-mail: gale@usenix.org

CIVIL ENGINEERING_____

AACE INTERNATIONAL

AACE INTERNATIONAL COMPETITIVE SCHOLARSHIP   see number 15

AMERICAN SOCIETY OF NAVAL ENGINEERS

AMERICAN SOCIETY OF NAVAL ENGINEERS SCHOLARSHIP
see number 10

ASSOCIATED GENERAL CONTRACTORS EDUCATION AND RESEARCH FOUNDATION

AGC EDUCATION AND RESEARCH FOUNDATION UNDERGRADUATE SCHOLARSHIPS • 62

Fifty-five or more named scholarships are available to college freshmen, first- or second-year students at a two-year school who plan to transfer to a four-year program for the fall term, or college sophomores, juniors, or beginning seniors in a five-year program. Junior- and senior-level applicants must have one full academic year of coursework remaining at the beginning of the fall term. Applicant must pursue a B.S. degree in construction or construction/civil engineering. Must be a U.S. citizen or permanent resident. Maximum award of $2,000 per year is renewable for up to four years. Application and complete guidelines are available on the web.

Academic/Career Areas Civil Engineering; Engineering/Technology; Trade/Technical Specialties.
Award Scholarship for use in freshman, sophomore, junior, or senior years; renewable. *Number:* 55. *Amount:* up to $2000.
Eligibility Requirements: Applicant must be enrolled full-time at a four-year institution. Available to U.S. citizens.
Application Requirements Application, essay, references, transcript. *Deadline:* November 1.
World Wide Web: http://www.agcfoundation.org
Contact: Floretta Slade, Director of Programs
　　　　　Associated General Contractors Education and Research
　　　　　　Foundation
　　　　　333 John Carlyle Street, Suite 200
　　　　　Alexandria, VA 22314
　　　　　Phone: 703-837-5342
　　　　　Fax: 703-837-5402
　　　　　E-mail: sladef@agc.org

BARRY M. GOLDWATER SCHOLARSHIP AND EXCELLENCE IN EDUCATION FOUNDATION

BARRY M. GOLDWATER SCHOLARSHIP AND EXCELLENCE IN EDUCATION PROGRAM
see number 12

CONSULTING ENGINEERS AND LAND SURVEYORS OF CALIFORNIA SCHOLARSHIP PROGRAM

CONSULTING ENGINEERS AND LAND SURVEYORS OF CALIFORNIA SCHOLARSHIP AWARD
see number 60

KENTUCKY TRANSPORTATION CABINET

KENTUCKY TRANSPORTATION CABINET CIVIL ENGINEERING SCHOLARSHIP PROGRAM
• 63

Established in 1948, the Kentucky Transportation Cabinet has awarded over 1,400 scholarships to civil engineers, amounting to over $10 million in the 53 years. There are currently 77 scholarships available to eligible applicants at 3 ABET-accredited universities in Kentucky. Our mission is to continually pursue statewide recruitment and retention of bright, motivated civil engineers in the Kentucky Transportation Cabinet.

Academic/Career Areas Civil Engineering.

Award Scholarship for use in freshman, sophomore, junior, or senior years; renewable. *Number:* 70. *Amount:* $3200–$3600.

Eligibility Requirements: Applicant must be enrolled full-time at an institution or university; resident of Kentucky and studying in Kentucky. Available to U.S. citizens.

Application Requirements Application, essay, interview, references, test scores, transcript. *Deadline:* March 1.

World Wide Web: http://www.kytc.state.ky.us/person/ScholarshipProgram.htm

Contact: Jo Anne Tingle, P.E., Scholarship Program Manager
Kentucky Transportation Cabinet
Attn: Scholarship Coordinator, State Office Building
501 High Street, Room 913
Frankfort, KY 40622
Phone: 877-273-5222
Fax: 502-564-6683
E-mail: jo.tingle@mail.state.ky.us

MARYLAND STATE HIGHER EDUCATION COMMISSION

SCIENCE AND TECHNOLOGY SCHOLARSHIP
see number 38

NAMEPA NATIONAL SCHOLARSHIP FOUNDATION

NATIONAL ASSOCIATION OF MINORITY ENGINEERING PROGRAM ADMINISTRATORS NATIONAL SCHOLARSHIP FUND
see number 29

NATIONAL ASSOCIATION OF WOMEN IN CONSTRUCTION

NAWIC UNDERGRADUATE SCHOLARSHIPS see number 20

NEW YORK STATE EDUCATION DEPARTMENT

REGENTS PROFESSIONAL OPPORTUNITY SCHOLARSHIP PROGRAM—NEW YORK see number 21

REAL ESTATE AND LAND USE INSTITUTE

CALIFORNIA STATE UNIVERSITY REAL ESTATE SCHOLARSHIP AND INTERNSHIP GRANT PROGRAM see number 22

SOCIETY OF PLASTICS ENGINEERS (SPE) FOUNDATION

SOCIETY OF PLASTICS ENGINEERS SCHOLARSHIP PROGRAM see number 56

TEXAS DEPARTMENT OF TRANSPORTATION

CONDITIONAL GRANT PROGRAM • 64

A grant that provides female minorities financial education assistance up to $3,000 per semester for approved degree plans. At present, it is for civil engineering degrees. Must be a Texas resident and study in Texas.

Academic/Career Areas Civil Engineering.

Award Grant for use in freshman, sophomore, junior, or senior years; renewable. *Number:* 50. *Amount:* up to $3000.

Eligibility Requirements: Applicant must be Native American or Eskimo, Asian, African American, or Hispanic; enrolled full-time at a four-year institution; female; resident of Texas and studying in Texas. Applicant must have 2.5 GPA or higher. Available to U.S. citizens.

Application Requirements Application, essay, interview, references, test scores, transcript. *Deadline:* March 1.

World Wide Web: http://www.dot.state.tx.us

Contact: Minnie Brown, Program Coordinator
Texas Department of Transportation
125 East 11th Street
Austin, TX 78701-2483
Phone: 512-416-4979
Fax: 512-416-4980
E-mail: www.mbrown2@dot.state.tx.us

USENIX ASSOCIATION

USENIX STUDENT PROGRAMS
see number 61

COMMUNICATIONS_____

CALIFORNIA CHICANO NEWS MEDIA ASSOCIATION (CCNMA)

JOEL GARCIA MEMORIAL SCHOLARSHIP • 65

Scholarships for Latinos interested in pursuing a career in journalism and related fields. Awards based on scholastic achievement, financial need, and community awareness. Submit sample of work. Award for California residents or those attending school in California. Deadline is first Friday of April.

Academic/Career Areas Communications; Journalism; Photojournalism; TV/Radio Broadcasting.
Award Scholarship for use in any year; not renewable. *Number:* 20–30. *Amount:* $500–$2000.
Eligibility Requirements: Applicant must be Latin American/Caribbean; Hispanic; enrolled full-time at a two-year or four-year institution or university; resident of California and studying in California. Available to U.S. and non-U.S. citizens.
Application Requirements Application, autobiography, essay, financial need analysis, interview, references, transcript, work samples.
World Wide Web: http://www.ccnma.org
Contact: Julio Moran, Executive Director
California Chicano News Media Association (CCNMA)
3502 Watt Way, ASC
Los Angeles, CA 90089-0281
Phone: 213-740-5263
Fax: 213-740-8524
E-mail: info@ccnma.org

CHARLES AND LUCILLE KING FAMILY FOUNDATION, INC.

CHARLES AND LUCILLE KING FAMILY FOUNDATION SCHOLARSHIPS • 66

Renewable award for college undergraduates at junior or senior level pursuing television or film or communication studies to further their education. Must attend a four-year undergraduate institution. Minimum 3.0 GPA required to renew scholarship. Must have completed at least two years of study and be currently enrolled in a U.S. college or university. Must submit personal statement with application materials by April 15.

Academic/Career Areas Communications; Filmmaking; TV/Radio Broadcasting.
Award Scholarship for use in junior or senior years; renewable. *Number:* 10–20. *Amount:* $1250–$2500.
Eligibility Requirements: Applicant must be enrolled full-time at a four-year institution or university. Applicant must have 3.0 GPA or higher. Available to U.S. and non-U.S. citizens.
Application Requirements Application, essay, financial need analysis, references, transcript. *Deadline:* April 15.
World Wide Web: http://www.kingfoundation.org
Contact: Michael Donovan, Educational Director
Charles and Lucille King Family Foundation, Inc.
366 Madison Avenue, 10th Floor
New York, NY 10017
Phone: 212-682-2913
Fax: 212-949-0728
E-mail: info@kingfoundation.org

CUBAN AMERICAN NATIONAL FOUNDATION

MAS FAMILY SCHOLARSHIPS   see number 44

HISPANIC COLLEGE FUND, INC.

HISPANIC COLLEGE FUND SCHOLARSHIP PROGRAM   see number 3

THE HISPANIC COLLEGE FUND/INROADS/SPRINT SCHOLARSHIP PROGRAM   see number 4

LOS ANGELES TIMES

LOS ANGELES TIMES SCHOLARSHIP PROGRAM   • 67

Award for students attending community colleges and campuses of California State University and the University of California in the Los Angeles Times market area. Must be pursuing career in newspapers or related field. Deadline: March 1.

Academic/Career Areas Communications; Journalism; Photojournalism; TV/Radio Broadcasting.
Award Scholarship for use in sophomore or junior years; not renewable. *Number:* up to 60. *Amount:* $750–$5000.
Eligibility Requirements: Applicant must be enrolled full-time at a two-year or four-year institution or university; resident of California and studying in California. Applicant must have 2.5 GPA or higher. Available to U.S. citizens.
Application Requirements Application, essay, financial need analysis, references, transcript. *Deadline:* March 1.

Los Angeles Times Scholarship Program (continued)
World Wide Web: http://www.latimes.com
Contact: Scholarship Fund Administrator
  Los Angeles Times
  202 West 1st Street
  Los Angeles, CA 90012
  Phone: 213-237-5771
  Fax: 213-237-4609

MARYLAND STATE HIGHER EDUCATION COMMISSION

HOPE SCHOLARSHIP   see number 6

UNITED NEGRO COLLEGE FUND

COCA COLA CORPORATE SCHOLARSHIP/INTERN PROGRAM
                                              see number 58

COMPUTER SCIENCE/DATA PROCESSING

AACE INTERNATIONAL

AACE INTERNATIONAL COMPETITIVE SCHOLARSHIP   see number 15

ASTRONAUT SCHOLARSHIP FOUNDATION

ASTRONAUT SCHOLARSHIP FOUNDATION   see number 11

BARRY M. GOLDWATER SCHOLARSHIP AND EXCELLENCE IN EDUCATION FOUNDATION

BARRY M. GOLDWATER SCHOLARSHIP AND EXCELLENCE IN
EDUCATION PROGRAM   see number 12

BUSINESS AND PROFESSIONAL WOMEN'S FOUNDATION

BPW CAREER ADVANCEMENT SCHOLARSHIP PROGRAM FOR
WOMEN   see number 37

HISPANIC COLLEGE FUND, INC.

HISPANIC COLLEGE FUND SCHOLARSHIP PROGRAM   see number 3

THE HISPANIC COLLEGE FUND/INROADS/SPRINT SCHOLARSHIP PROGRAM   see number 4

MARYLAND ASSOCIATION OF PRIVATE CAREER SCHOOLS

MARYLAND ASSOCIATION OF PRIVATE CAREER SCHOOLS SCHOLARSHIP   see number 49

MARYLAND STATE HIGHER EDUCATION COMMISSION

SCIENCE AND TECHNOLOGY SCHOLARSHIP   see number 38

NAMEPA NATIONAL SCHOLARSHIP FOUNDATION

NATIONAL ASSOCIATION OF MINORITY ENGINEERING PROGRAM ADMINISTRATORS NATIONAL SCHOLARSHIP FUND   see number 29

NASA MINNESOTA SPACE GRANT CONSORTIUM

MINNESOTA SPACE GRANT CONSORTIUM MINNESOTA SPACE GRANT CONSORTIUM   see number 30

NASA NEVADA SPACE GRANT CONSORTIUM

UNIVERSITY AND COMMUNITY COLLEGE SYSTEM OF NEVADA NASA SPACE GRANT AND FELLOWSHIP PROGRAM   see number 31

UNITED NEGRO COLLEGE FUND

COCA COLA CORPORATE SCHOLARSHIP/INTERN PROGRAM   see number 58

EDS CORPORATE SCHOLARS PROGRAM • 68

Ten scholarships for juniors majoring in computer science or information systems attending a UNCF member college or university. Minimum 3.0 GPA required.

Academic/Career Areas Computer Science/Data Processing.
Award Scholarship for use in junior year; not renewable. *Number:* 10. *Amount:* $7750.
Eligibility Requirements: Applicant must be African American and enrolled at a four-year institution or university. Applicant must have 3.0 GPA or higher.
Application Requirements Application. *Deadline:* March 1.
World Wide Web: http://www.uncf.org
Contact: Program Services Department
United Negro College Fund
8260 Willow Oaks Corporate Drive
Fairfax, VA 22031

USENIX ASSOCIATION

USENIX STUDENT PROGRAMS see number 61

CRIMINAL JUSTICE/CRIMINOLOGY___

JOHN F. KENNEDY LIBRARY FOUNDATION

KENNEDY RESEARCH GRANTS see number 19

DENTAL HEALTH/SERVICES___

ALBERTA HERITAGE SCHOLARSHIP FUND

ALBERTA HERITAGE SCHOLARSHIP FUND ABORIGINAL HEALTH CAREERS BURSARY see number 33

BUSINESS AND PROFESSIONAL WOMEN'S FOUNDATION

BPW CAREER ADVANCEMENT SCHOLARSHIP PROGRAM FOR WOMEN see number 37

HEALTH PROFESSIONS EDUCATION FOUNDATION

HEALTH PROFESSIONS EDUCATION SCHOLARSHIP PROGRAM
• 69

The scholarship is awarded to students pursuing a career as a dentist, dental hygienist, nurse practitioner, certified nurse midwives and physician assistant. Eligible scholarship applicants may receive $10,000 per year in financial assistance. Applicants must agree to practice in a medically under-served area of California for a minimum of two years. Deadline: March 27. Must be a resident of CA and U.S. citizen.

Academic/Career Areas Dental Health/Services; Health and Medical Sciences; Nursing.

Award Scholarship for use in senior, graduate, or post graduate years; not renewable. *Number:* 10–15. *Amount:* $5000–$10,000.

Eligibility Requirements: Applicant must be enrolled full or part-time at an institution or university; resident of California and studying in California. Available to U.S. citizens.

Application Requirements Application, driver's license, financial need analysis, references, transcript, 2 copies of application. *Deadline:* March 27.

World Wide Web: http://www.healthprofessions.ca.gov

Contact: Lisa Montgomery, Program Director
Health Professions Education Foundation
1600 Ninth Street, Suite 436
Sacramento, CA 95814
Phone: 800-773-1669
Fax: 916-653-1438
E-mail: lmontgom@oshpd.state.ca.us

MARYLAND ASSOCIATION OF PRIVATE CAREER SCHOOLS

MARYLAND ASSOCIATION OF PRIVATE CAREER SCHOOLS SCHOLARSHIP
see number 49

MARYLAND STATE HIGHER EDUCATION COMMISSION

PROFESSIONAL SCHOLARSHIP PROGRAM-MARYLAND **• 70**

Professional scholarships provide need-based financial assistance to full-time students attending a Maryland school of medicine, dentistry, law, pharmacy, social work, or nursing. Must be a Maryland resident.

Academic/Career Areas Dental Health/Services; Health and Medical Sciences; Law/Legal Services; Nursing; Social Services.

Professional Scholarship Program-Maryland (continued)

Award Scholarship for use in freshman, sophomore, junior, senior, or graduate years; renewable. *Number:* 200–500. *Amount:* $200–$1000.

Eligibility Requirements: Applicant must be enrolled full-time at a two-year or four-year institution or university; resident of Maryland and studying in Maryland. Available to U.S. citizens.

Application Requirements Application, financial need analysis. *Deadline:* March 1.

World Wide Web: http://www.mhec.state.md.us

Contact: Cis Whittington, Scholarship Administration
Maryland State Higher Education Commission
16 Francis Street
Annapolis, MD 21401-1781
Phone: 410-260-4546
Fax: 410-974-5994
E-mail: ssamail@mhec.state.md.us

NATIONAL DENTAL ASSOCIATION FOUNDATION

NDAF/COLGATE PALMOLIVE SCHOLARSHIP PROGRAM • 71

The National Dental Association Foundation, through a grant from the Colgate-Palmolive Company, awards grants to African-American post doctoral dental undergraduate dental, dental hygiene and dental assistant students annually. $10,000 in one-time postdoctoral grants are awarded to candidates who are pursuing clinical research careers in dentistry. $2,000 special scholar awards to dental school freshmen. Balance of scholarships are between $300-$1,000.

Academic/Career Areas Dental Health/Services.

Award Grant for use in any year; renewable. *Number:* 100-125. *Amount:* $500-$10,000.

Eligibility Requirements: Applicant must be African American and enrolled full-time at a two-year or four-year or technical institution or university. Available to U.S. citizens.

Application Requirements Application, financial need analysis, photo, references, test scores, transcript. *Deadline:* May 15.

World Wide Web: http://ndaonline.org

Contact: National Dental Association Foundation
3517 16th Street NW
Washington, DC 20010

NEW MEXICO COMMISSION ON HIGHER EDUCATION

ALLIED HEALTH STUDENT LOAN PROGRAM-NEW MEXICO • 72

Renewable loans for New Mexico residents enrolled in an undergraduate allied health program. Loans can be forgiven through service in a medically underserved area or can be repaid. Penalties apply for failure to provide service. May borrow up to $12,000 per year for four years. Apply by calling the Commission at the CHE Student Helpline: 1-800-279-9777.

Academic/Career Areas Dental Health/Services; Health and Medical Sciences; Nursing; Social Sciences; Therapy/Rehabilitation.

Award Forgivable loan for use in freshman, sophomore, junior, or senior years; renewable. *Number:* 1–40. *Amount:* up to $12,000.

Eligibility Requirements: Applicant must be enrolled full or part-time at a two-year or four-year institution or university; resident of New Mexico and studying in New Mexico. Available to U.S. citizens.

Application Requirements Application, financial need analysis, transcript. *Deadline:* July 1.

World Wide Web: http://www.nmche.org

Contact: Barbara Serna, Clerk Specialist
New Mexico Commission on Higher Education
PO Box 15910
Santa Fe, NM 87506-5910
Phone: 505-827-4026
Fax: 505-827-7392

NEW YORK STATE EDUCATION DEPARTMENT

REGENTS PROFESSIONAL OPPORTUNITY SCHOLARSHIP PROGRAM—NEW YORK
see number 21

STATE OF GEORGIA

SERVICE-CANCELLABLE STAFFORD LOAN-GEORGIA • 73

To assist Georgia students enrolled in critical fields of study in allied health (e.g., nursing, physical therapy). For use at GSFA-approved schools. $3500 forgivable loan for dentistry students only. Contact school financial aid officer for more details.

Academic/Career Areas Dental Health/Services; Health and Medical Sciences; Nursing.

Award Forgivable loan for use in freshman, sophomore, junior, senior, or graduate years; not renewable. *Number:* 500–1200. *Amount:* $2000–$4500.

Eligibility Requirements: Applicant must be enrolled full or part-time at a two-year or four-year or technical institution or university; resident of Georgia and studying in Georgia. Available to U.S. citizens.

Application Requirements Application, financial need analysis. *Deadline:* Continuous.

World Wide Web: http://www.gsfc.org

Service-Cancellable Stafford Loan-Georgia (continued)
Contact: Peggy Matthews, Manager/GSFA Originations
State of Georgia
2082 East Exchange Place, Suite 230
Tucker, GA 30084-5305
Phone: 770-724-9230
Fax: 770-724-9263
E-mail: peggy@mail.gsfc.state.ga.us

DRAFTING

HISPANIC COLLEGE FUND, INC.

HISPANIC COLLEGE FUND SCHOLARSHIP PROGRAM see number 3

THE HISPANIC COLLEGE FUND/INROADS/SPRINT SCHOLARSHIP PROGRAM see number 4

NATIONAL ASSOCIATION OF WOMEN IN CONSTRUCTION

NAWIC UNDERGRADUATE SCHOLARSHIPS see number 20

EARTH SCIENCE

ASTRONAUT SCHOLARSHIP FOUNDATION

ASTRONAUT SCHOLARSHIP FOUNDATION see number 11

BARRY M. GOLDWATER SCHOLARSHIP AND EXCELLENCE IN EDUCATION FOUNDATION

BARRY M. GOLDWATER SCHOLARSHIP AND EXCELLENCE IN EDUCATION PROGRAM see number 12

MARYLAND STATE HIGHER EDUCATION COMMISSION

SCIENCE AND TECHNOLOGY SCHOLARSHIP see number 38

SOCIETY OF EXPLORATION GEOPHYSICISTS FOUNDATION (SEG)

SOCIETY OF EXPLORATION GEOPHYSICISTS FOUNDATION SCHOLARSHIP • 74

Renewable award available to undergraduate and graduate students. Applicants must be preparing for a career in geophysics or a related earth science at a four-year college or university. High school seniors may apply. Minimum 3.0 GPA required. Average award is $1500 per year.

Academic/Career Areas Earth Science; Physical Sciences and Math.
Award Scholarship for use in freshman, sophomore, junior, senior, or graduate years; renewable. *Number:* 70–110. *Amount:* $500–$3000.
Eligibility Requirements: Applicant must be enrolled full-time at a four-year institution or university. Applicant must have 3.0 GPA or higher. Available to U.S. and non-U.S. citizens.
Application Requirements Application, financial need analysis, references, test scores, transcript. *Deadline:* March 1.
World Wide Web: http://www.seg.org
Contact: Sue LoBianco, Scholarship Coordinator
Society of Exploration Geophysicists Foundation (SEG)
PO Box 702740
Tulsa, OK 74170-2740
Phone: 918-497-5500
Fax: 918-497-5557
E-mail: slobianco@seg.org

ECONOMICS

CUBAN AMERICAN NATIONAL FOUNDATION

MAS FAMILY SCHOLARSHIPS see number 44

HISPANIC COLLEGE FUND, INC.

HISPANIC COLLEGE FUND SCHOLARSHIP PROGRAM see number 3

THE HISPANIC COLLEGE FUND/INROADS/SPRINT SCHOLARSHIP PROGRAM see number 4

JOHN F. KENNEDY LIBRARY FOUNDATION

KENNEDY RESEARCH GRANTS see number 19

NATIONAL ASSOCIATION OF BLACK ACCOUNTANTS, INC.

NATIONAL ASSOCIATION OF BLACK ACCOUNTANTS NATIONAL SCHOLARSHIP
see number 50

UNITED AGRIBUSINESS LEAGUE

UNITED AGRIBUSINESS LEAGUE SCHOLARSHIP PROGRAM
see number 5

EDUCATION

ALASKA COMMISSION ON POSTSECONDARY EDUCATION

ALASKA COMMISSION ON POST-SECONDARY EDUCATION TEACHER EDUCATION SCHOLARSHIP LOAN • 75

Renewable loans for Alaska residents who are graduates of an Alaskan high school and pursuing teaching careers in rural elementary and secondary schools in Alaska. Must be nominated by rural school district. Eligible for 100% forgiveness if loan recipient teaches in Alaska upon graduation. Several awards of up to $7500 each. Must maintain good standing at institution. Contact for deadline.

Academic/Career Areas Education.
Award Forgivable loan for use in freshman, sophomore, junior, or senior years; renewable. *Number:* 100. *Amount:* up to $7500.
Eligibility Requirements: Applicant must be enrolled full-time at a four-year institution or university; resident of Alaska and studying in Alaska.
Application Requirements Application, transcript.
World Wide Web: http://www.state.ak.us/acpe/
Contact: Lori Stedman, Administrative Assistant, Special Programs
Alaska Commission on Postsecondary Education
3030 Vintage Boulevard
Juneau, AK 99801-7100
Phone: 907-465-6741
Fax: 907-465-5316

ALPHA DELTA KAPPA FOUNDATION

INTERNATIONAL TEACHER EDUCATION SCHOLARSHIP • 76

Enables women from foreign countries to study in the United States. Applicants must be single with no dependents, age 20-35, non-U.S. citizens residing outside the U.S., have at least one year of college completed, and plan to enter the teaching profession.

Academic/Career Areas Education.

Award Scholarship for use in sophomore, junior, senior, or graduate years; renewable. *Number:* up to 7. *Amount:* up to $10,000.

Eligibility Requirements: Applicant must be age 20-35; enrolled full-time at a four-year institution or university and single female. Applicant must have 3.5 GPA or higher. Available to Canadian and non-U.S. citizens.

Application Requirements Application, autobiography, financial need analysis, photo, references, test scores, transcript, certificates of health from physician and dentist, TOEFL scores, college acceptance. *Deadline:* January 1.

World Wide Web: http://www.alphadeltakappa.org

Contact: Dee Frost, Scholarships and Grants Coordinator
Alpha Delta Kappa Foundation
1615 West 92nd Street
Kansas City, MO 64114-3296
Phone: 816-363-5525
Fax: 816-363-4010
E-mail: dfrost@www.alphadeltakappa.org

ARKANSAS DEPARTMENT OF HIGHER EDUCATION

ARKANSAS MINORITY TEACHER SCHOLARS PROGRAM • 77

Renewable award for Native American, African-American, Hispanic and Asian-American students who have completed at least 60 semester hours and are enrolled full-time in a teacher education program in Arkansas. Award may be renewed for one year. Must be Arkansas resident with minimum 2.5 GPA. Must teach for three to five years in Arkansas to repay scholarship funds received. Must pass PPST exam.

Academic/Career Areas Education.

Award Forgivable loan for use in junior or senior years; renewable. *Number:* up to 100. *Amount:* up to $5000.

Eligibility Requirements: Applicant must be Native American or Eskimo, Asian, African American, or Hispanic; enrolled full-time at a four-year institution or university; resident of Arkansas and studying in Arkansas. Applicant must have 2.5 GPA or higher. Available to U.S. citizens.

Application Requirements Application, transcript. *Deadline:* June 1.

World Wide Web: http://www.arscholarships.com

Contact: Lillian Williams, Assistant Coordinator
Arkansas Department of Higher Education
114 East Capitol
Little Rock, AR 72201
Phone: 501-371-2050
Fax: 501-371-2001

EMERGENCY SECONDARY EDUCATION LOAN PROGRAM

see number 35

BUSINESS AND PROFESSIONAL WOMEN'S FOUNDATION

BPW CAREER ADVANCEMENT SCHOLARSHIP PROGRAM FOR WOMEN
see number 37

DECA (DISTRIBUTION EDUCATION CLUB OF AMERICA)

HARRY A. APPLEGATE SCHOLARSHIP
see number 45

DELAWARE HIGHER EDUCATION COMMISSION

CHRISTA MCAULIFFE TEACHER SCHOLARSHIP LOAN—DELAWARE
• 78

Award for Delaware residents who are pursuing teaching careers. Must agree to teach in Delaware public schools as repayment of loan. Minimum award is $1000 and is renewable for up to four years. Available only at Delaware colleges. Based on academic merit. Must be ranked in upper half of class, and have a score of 1050 on SAT or 25 on the ACT.

Academic/Career Areas Education.
Award Forgivable loan for use in freshman, sophomore, junior, or senior years; renewable. *Number:* 1–50. *Amount:* $1000–$5000.
Eligibility Requirements: Applicant must be enrolled full-time at a four-year institution or university; resident of Delaware and studying in Delaware. Applicant must have 2.5 GPA or higher. Available to U.S. citizens.
Application Requirements Application, essay, test scores, transcript. *Deadline:* March 31.
World Wide Web: http://www.doe.state.de.us/high-ed
Contact: Maureen Laffey, Associate Director
Delaware Higher Education Commission
820 North French Street
Wilmington, DE 19801
Phone: 302-577-3240
Fax: 302-577-6765
E-mail: dhec@state.de.us

FLORIDA STATE DEPARTMENT OF EDUCATION

CRITICAL TEACHER SHORTAGE TUITION REIMBURSEMENT-FLORIDA
• 79

One-time awards for full-time Florida public school employees who are certified to teach in Florida and are teaching or preparing to teach in critical teacher shortage subject areas. Must earn minimum grade of 3.0 in approved courses. May receive tuition reimbursement up to 9 semester hours or equivalent per academic year, not to exceed $78 per semester hour, for maximum 36 hours. Contact for application and deadline. Must be resident of Florida.

Academic/Career Areas Education.
Award Scholarship for use in any year; not renewable. *Number:* 1000–1200. *Amount:* up to $700.
Eligibility Requirements: Applicant must be enrolled part-time at a two-year or four-year institution or university; resident of Florida; studying in Florida and have employment experience in teaching. Applicant must have 3.0 GPA or higher. Available to U.S. citizens.
Application Requirements Application, financial need analysis. *Deadline:* September 15.
World Wide Web: http://www.firn.edu/doe/osfa
Contact: Bureau of Student Financial Assistance
Florida State Department of Education
1940 North Monroe
Suite 70
Tallahassee, FL 32303-4759
Phone: 888-827-2004
E-mail: osfa@mail.doe.state.fl.us

GEORGIA ASSOCIATION OF EDUCATORS

GAE GFIE SCHOLARSHIP FOR EDUCATION SUPPORT PROFESSIONALS FOR PROFESSIONAL DEVELOPMENT ● 80

At least seven scholarships for up to $10,000 will be awarded to Education Support Professional members who enroll in classes or college programs, which improve their work skills. Scholarships are intended to subsidize applicant's tuition expenses. Must be a member of GAE.

Academic/Career Areas Education.
Award Scholarship for use in any year; not renewable. *Number:* 7. *Amount:* up to $10,000.
Eligibility Requirements: Applicant must be resident of Georgia and studying in Georgia. Available to U.S. citizens.
Application Requirements Application, essay, transcript. *Deadline:* January 18.
World Wide Web: http://www.gae.org
Contact: Sally Bennett, Professional Development Specialist
Georgia Association of Educators
100 Crescent Centre Parkway
Suite 500
Tucker, GA 30084-7049
Phone: 678-837-1103
E-mail: sally.bennett@gae.org

GEORGIA STUDENT FINANCE COMMISSION

GEORGIA PROMISE TEACHER SCHOLARSHIP PROGRAM • 81

Renewable, forgivable loans for junior undergraduates at Georgia colleges who have been accepted for enrollment into a teacher education program leading to initial certification. Minimum cumulative 3.0 GPA required. Recipient must teach at a Georgia public school for one year for each $1500 awarded. Available to seniors for renewal only. Write for deadlines.

Academic/Career Areas Education.

Award Forgivable loan for use in junior or senior years; renewable. *Number:* 700–1400. *Amount:* $3000–$6000.

Eligibility Requirements: Applicant must be enrolled full or part-time at a four-year institution or university and studying in Georgia. Applicant must have 3.0 GPA or higher. Available to U.S. citizens.

Application Requirements Application, transcript. *Deadline:* Continuous.

World Wide Web: http://www.gsfc.org

Contact: William Flook, Director of Scholarships and Grants Division
Georgia Student Finance Commission
2082 East Exchange Place, Suite 100
Tucker, GA 30084

GOLDEN APPLE FOUNDATION

GOLDEN APPLE SCHOLARS OF ILLINOIS • 82

Between 75 and 100 forgivable loans are given to undergraduate students. Loans are $7,000 a year for 4 years. Applicants must be between 17 and 21 and carry a minimum GPA of 2.5. Eligible applicants will be residents of Illinois who are studying in Illinois. The deadline is December 1. Recipients must agree to teach in high-need Illinois schools.

Academic/Career Areas Education.

Award Forgivable loan for use in freshman, sophomore, junior, or senior years; renewable. *Number:* 75–100. *Amount:* $7000.

Eligibility Requirements: Applicant must be age 17-21; enrolled full-time at a four-year institution or university; resident of Illinois and studying in Illinois. Applicant must have 2.5 GPA or higher. Available to U.S. citizens.

Application Requirements Application, autobiography, essay, interview, photo, references, test scores, transcript. *Deadline:* December 1.

World Wide Web: http://www.goldenapple.org

Contact: Pat Kilduff, Director of Recruitment and Placement
Golden Apple Foundation
8 South Michigan Avenue, Suite 700
Chicago, IL 60603-3318
Phone: 312-407-0006 Ext. 105
Fax: 312-407-0344
E-mail: patnk@goldenapple.org

ILLINOIS STUDENT ASSISTANCE COMMISSION (ISAC)

DAVID A. DEBOLT TEACHER SHORTAGE SCHOLARSHIP PROGRAM • 83

Award to assist Illinois students planning to teach at an Illinois pre-school, elementary school, or high school in a teacher shortage discipline. Must agree to teach one year in teacher shortage area for each year of award assistance received. Deadline: May 1.

Academic/Career Areas Education; Special Education.
Award Forgivable loan for use in sophomore, junior, senior, or graduate years; not renewable. *Number:* 300–350. *Amount:* $4000–$5000.
Eligibility Requirements: Applicant must be enrolled full or part-time at a two-year or four-year institution or university; resident of Illinois and studying in Illinois. Applicant must have 2.5 GPA or higher. Available to U.S. and non-U.S. citizens.
Application Requirements Application, transcript. *Deadline:* May 1.
World Wide Web: http://www.isac-online.org
Contact: Dave Barinholtz, Client Information
    Illinois Student Assistance Commission (ISAC)
    1755 Lake Cook Road
    Deerfield, IL 60015-5209
    Phone: 847-948-8500 Ext. 2385

MINORITY TEACHERS OF ILLINOIS SCHOLARSHIP PROGRAM • 84

Award for minority students planning to teach at an approved Illinois preschool, elementary, or secondary school. Deadline: May 1. Must be Illinois resident.

Academic/Career Areas Education; Special Education.
Award Forgivable loan for use in sophomore, junior, or senior years; renewable. *Number:* 400–500. *Amount:* $4000–$5000.
Eligibility Requirements: Applicant must be Native American or Eskimo, Asian, African American, or Hispanic; enrolled full-time at a four-year institution or university; resident of Illinois and studying in Illinois. Applicant must have 2.5 GPA or higher. Available to U.S. and non-U.S. citizens.
Application Requirements Application. *Deadline:* May 1.
World Wide Web: http://www.isac-online.org
Contact: David Barinholtz, Client Information
    Illinois Student Assistance Commission (ISAC)
    1755 Lake Cook Road
    Deerfield, IL 60015-5209
    Phone: 847-948-8500 Ext. 2385

JOHN F. KENNEDY LIBRARY FOUNDATION

KENNEDY RESEARCH GRANTS

see number 19

KANSAS BOARD OF REGENTS

KANSAS TEACHER SERVICE SCHOLARSHIP • 85

Several scholarships for Kansas residents pursuing teaching careers. Must teach in a hard-to-fill discipline for underserved area of the state of Kansas for one year for each award received. Renewable award of $5000. Application fee is $10. Deadline: April 1. Must be U.S. citizen.

Academic/Career Areas Education.

Award Forgivable loan for use in freshman, sophomore, junior, or senior years; renewable. *Number:* 60–80. *Amount:* $5000.

Eligibility Requirements: Applicant must be enrolled full-time at a two-year or four-year institution or university; resident of Kansas and studying in Kansas. Applicant must have 3.0 GPA or higher. Available to U.S. citizens.

Application Requirements Application, references, test scores, transcript. *Fee:* $10. *Deadline:* April 1.

World Wide Web: http://www.kansasregents.com

Contact: Diane Lindeman, Director of Student Financial Assistance
Kansas Board of Regents
1000 Southwest Jackson, Suite 520
Topeka, KS 66612-1368
Phone: 785-296-3517
Fax: 785-296-0983
E-mail: dlindeman@ksbor.org

KENTUCKY HIGHER EDUCATION ASSISTANCE AUTHORITY (KHEAA)

KENTUCKY TEACHER SCHOLARSHIP PROGRAM • 86

Award for Kentucky resident attending Kentucky institutions and pursuing initial teacher certification. Must teach one semester for each semester of award received. In critical shortage areas, must teach one semester for every two semesters of award received. Repayment obligation if teaching requirement not met. Submit Free Application for Federal Student Aid and Teacher Scholarship Application by May 1.

Academic/Career Areas Education; Special Education.

Award Forgivable loan for use in freshman, sophomore, junior, senior, or graduate years; not renewable. *Number:* 600–700. *Amount:* $100–$5000.

Eligibility Requirements: Applicant must be enrolled full-time at a two-year or four-year institution or university; resident of Kentucky and studying in Kentucky. Available to U.S. citizens.

Application Requirements Application, financial need analysis. *Deadline:* May 1.

World Wide Web: http://www.kheaa.com

Distinguished Scholar-Teacher Education Awards (continued)

Application Requirements Application, test scores, transcript, must be recipient of the Distinguished Scholar Award. *Deadline:* Continuous.

World Wide Web: http://www.mhec.state.md.us

Contact: Margaret Riley, Scholarship Administration
Maryland State Higher Education Commission
16 Francis Street
Annapolis, MD 21401-1781
Phone: 410-260-4568
Fax: 410-974-5994
E-mail: ssamail@mhec.state.md.us

JANET L. HOFFMANN LOAN ASSISTANCE REPAYMENT PROGRAM • 89

Provides assistance for repayment of loan debt to Maryland residents working full-time in non-profit organizations and state or local governments. Must submit Employment Verification Form and Lender verification form.

Academic/Career Areas Education; Law/Legal Services; Nursing; Social Services; Therapy/Rehabilitation.

Award Forgivable loan for use in any year; not renewable. *Number:* up to 400. *Amount:* up to $7500.

Eligibility Requirements: Applicant must be resident of Maryland and studying in Maryland. Available to U.S. citizens.

Application Requirements Application, transcript, 1040 Tax Form. *Deadline:* September 30.

World Wide Web: http://www.mhec.state.md.us

Contact: Cis Whittington, Scholarship Administration
Maryland State Higher Education Commission
16 Francis Street
Annapolis, MD 21401-1781
Phone: 410-260-4546
Fax: 410-974-5994
E-mail: ssamail@mhec.state.md.us

MARYLAND TEACHER SCHOLARSHIP • 90

Available to Maryland residents attending a college in Maryland with a major in teacher education. Must work as public school teachers within the state of Maryland.

Academic/Career Areas Education; Special Education.

Award Forgivable loan for use in any year; renewable. *Number:* up to 2300. *Amount:* $2000–$5000.

Eligibility Requirements: Applicant must be enrolled full-time at a two-year or four-year institution or university; resident of Maryland and studying in Maryland. Applicant must have 3.0 GPA or higher. Available to U.S. citizens.

Application Requirements Application, transcript. *Deadline:* March 1.

World Wide Web: http://www.mhec.state.md.us

Contact: Pam Polly, Program Coordinator
Kentucky Higher Education Assistance Authority (KHEA/
1050 U.S. 127 South
Frankfort, KY 40601-4323
Phone: 502-696-7392
Fax: 502-696-7345
E-mail: ppolly@kheaa.com

MARYLAND STATE HIGHER EDUCATION COMMISSION

CHILD CARE PROVIDER PROGRAM-MARYLAND

Scholarship provides assistance for Maryland undergraduates atte
Maryland institution and pursuing studies in a child development pr
an early childhood education program. Must serve as a professional
provider in Maryland for one year for each year award received. Must
minimum 2.0 GPA. Contact for further information.

Academic/Career Areas Education.

Award Scholarship for use in freshman, sophomore, junior, or senic
renewable. *Number:* up to 90. *Amount:* $500–$2000.

Eligibility Requirements: Applicant must be enrolled full or part-ti
two-year or four-year institution or university; resident of Maryland an
ing in Maryland. Available to U.S. citizens.

Application Requirements Application, transcript. *Deadline:* June 1

World Wide Web: http://www.mhec.state.md.us

Contact: Margaret Crutchley, Scholarship Administration
Maryland State Higher Education Commission
16 Francis Street
Annapolis, MD 21401-1781
Phone: 410-260-4545
Fax: 410-974-5994
E-mail: ssamail@mhec.state.md.us

DISTINGUISHED SCHOLAR-TEACHER EDUCATION AWARDS

Up to $3,000 scholarship for Maryland high school seniors who have rec
the Distinguished Scholar Award. Recipient must enroll as a full-time underg
ate in a Maryland institution and pursue a program of study leading
Maryland teaching certificate. Must maintain 3.0 GPA for renewal. Must
in a Maryland public school one year for each year scholarship is receiv

Academic/Career Areas Education.

Award Scholarship for use in freshman, sophomore, junior, or senior y
renewable. *Number:* 20–80. *Amount:* up to $3000.

Eligibility Requirements: Applicant must be high school student; plan
to enroll full-time at a two-year or four-year institution or university; resid
of Maryland and studying in Maryland. Applicant must have 3.0 GPA or hig
Available to U.S. citizens.

Contact: Julie Perrotta, Scholarship Administration
Maryland State Higher Education Commission
16 Francis Street
Annapolis, MD 21401-1781
Phone: 410-260-4564
Fax: 410-974-5994
E-mail: ssamail@mhec.state.md.us

SHARON CHRISTA MCAULIFFE TEACHER EDUCATION-CRITICAL SHORTAGE GRANT PROGRAM ● 91

Renewable awards for Maryland residents who are college juniors, seniors, or graduate students enrolled in a Maryland teacher education program. Must agree to enter profession in a subject designated as a critical shortage area. Must teach in Maryland for one year for each award year.

Academic/Career Areas Education.
Award Scholarship for use in junior, senior, or graduate years; renewable. *Number:* up to 100. *Amount:* $200–$12,981.
Eligibility Requirements: Applicant must be enrolled full or part-time at a four-year institution or university; resident of Maryland and studying in Maryland. Applicant must have 3.0 GPA or higher. Available to U.S. citizens.
Application Requirements Application, essay, resume, transcript. *Deadline:* December 31.
World Wide Web: http://www.mhec.state.md.us
Contact: Margaret Crutchley, Scholarship Administration
Maryland State Higher Education Commission
16 Francis Street
Annapolis, MD 21401-1781
Phone: 410-260-4545
Fax: 410-974-5994
E-mail: ssamail@mhec.state.md.us

MISSOURI DEPARTMENT OF ELEMENTARY AND SECONDARY EDUCATION

MISSOURI MINORITY TEACHING SCHOLARSHIP ● 92

Award may be used any year up to four years at an approved, participating Missouri institution. Scholarship is for minority Missouri residents with a minimum 3.5 GPA in teaching programs. Recipients must commit to teach for five years in a Missouri public elementary or secondary school. Graduate students must teach math or science. Otherwise, award must be repaid.

Academic/Career Areas Education.
Award Scholarship for use in any year; renewable. *Number:* 100. *Amount:* $3000.
Eligibility Requirements: Applicant must be Native American or Eskimo, Asian, African American, or Hispanic; enrolled full-time at a two-year or four-

Missouri Minority Teaching Scholarship (continued)
year institution or university; resident of Missouri and studying in Missouri. Applicant must have 3.5 GPA or higher. Available to U.S. citizens.

Application Requirements Application, essay, financial need analysis, references, test scores, transcript. *Deadline:* February 15.

World Wide Web: http://www.dese.state.mo.us

Contact: Laura Harrison, Administrative Assistant II
Missouri Department of Elementary and Secondary Education
PO Box 480
Jefferson City, MO 65102-0480
Phone: 573-751-1668
Fax: 573-526-3580
E-mail: lharriso@mail.dese.state.mo.us

MISSOURI TEACHER EDUCATION SCHOLARSHIP (GENERAL) • 93

Nonrenewable award for Missouri high school seniors or Missouri resident college freshmen or sophomores. Must attend approved teacher training program at Missouri four-year institution. Nonrenewable. Must rank in top fifteen percent of high school class or ACT/SAT. Merit-based award.

Academic/Career Areas Education.

Award Scholarship for use in freshman or sophomore years; not renewable. *Number:* 200–240. *Amount:* $2000.

Eligibility Requirements: Applicant must be enrolled full-time at a four-year institution or university; resident of Missouri and studying in Missouri. Applicant must have 3.5 GPA or higher. Available to U.S. citizens.

Application Requirements Application, essay, references, test scores, transcript. *Deadline:* February 15.

World Wide Web: http://www.dese.state.mo.us

Contact: Laura Harrison, Administrative Assistant II
Missouri Department of Elementary and Secondary Education
PO Box 480
Jefferson City, MO 65102-0480
Phone: 573-751-1668
Fax: 573-526-3580
E-mail: lharriso@mail.dese.state.mo.us

NORTH CAROLINA TEACHING FELLOWS COMMISSION

NORTH CAROLINA TEACHING FELLOWS SCHOLARSHIP PROGRAM
• 94

Renewable award for North Carolina high school seniors pursuing teaching careers. Must agree to teach in a North Carolina public or government school for four years or repay award. Must attend one of the fourteen approved schools in North Carolina. Merit-based. Must interview at the local level and at the regional level as a finalist.

Academic/Career Areas Education.

Award Forgivable loan for use in freshman, sophomore, junior, or senior years; renewable. *Number:* up to 400. *Amount:* $6500.

Eligibility Requirements: Applicant must be high school student; planning to enroll full-time at a four-year institution; resident of North Carolina and studying in North Carolina. Applicant must have 3.5 GPA or higher. Available to U.S. citizens.

Application Requirements Application, essay, interview, references, test scores, transcript. *Deadline:* October 31.

World Wide Web: http://www.teachingfellows.org

Contact: Ms. Sherry Woodruff, Program Officer
North Carolina Teaching Fellows Commission
3739 National Drive, Suite 210
Raleigh, NC 27612
Phone: 919-781-6833
Fax: 919-781-6527
E-mail: tfellows@ncforum.org

ORDEAN FOUNDATION

ORDEAN LOAN PROGRAM • 95

Renewable award for low-income students who are from Hermantown, Proctor, or Duluth. Students must be fully admitted into social work, management, education, accounting or nursing. Students must work in their designated field in the Duluth area for up to 3 years after graduation. Open to full-time junior or senior undergraduates. Must be U.S. citizens. Minimum 2.5 GPA required.

Academic/Career Areas Education; Health Administration; Health Information Management/Technology; Nursing; Social Services.

Award Forgivable loan for use in junior or senior years; renewable. *Number:* 30–45. *Amount:* $1000–$2000.

Eligibility Requirements: Applicant must be enrolled full-time at a four-year institution; resident of Minnesota and studying in Minnesota. Applicant must have 2.5 GPA or higher. Available to U.S. citizens.

Application Requirements Application, financial need analysis, transcript. *Deadline:* Continuous.

Contact: Trish Johnson, Financial Aid Counselor
Ordean Foundation
College of Saint Scholastica
1200 Kenwood Avenue
Duluth, MN 55811
Phone: 218-723-7027
Fax: 218-733-2229
E-mail: tjohnson@css.edu

PHI DELTA KAPPA INTERNATIONAL

SCHOLARSHIP GRANTS FOR PROSPECTIVE EDUCATORS • 96

One-time award available to high school seniors in the top fifty percent of their graduating class. Applicants must plan to major in education and pursue a teaching career. Contact local Phi Delta Kappa chapter for more information. Do not send application to headquarters. Must have minimum 2.5 GPA.

Academic/Career Areas Education.
Award Grant for use in freshman year; not renewable. *Number:* 30. *Amount:* $1000–$5000.
Eligibility Requirements: Applicant must be high school student and planning to enroll full-time at a two-year or four-year institution or university. Applicant must have 2.5 GPA or higher. Available to U.S. and non-U.S. citizens.
Application Requirements Application, essay, references, self-addressed stamped envelope, transcript. *Deadline:* January 31.
World Wide Web: http://www.pdkintl.org
Contact: Dr. James Fogarty, Associate Executive Director
Phi Delta Kappa International
408 North Union Avenue, PO Box 789
Bloomington, IN 47402-0789
Fax: 812-339-0018
E-mail: headquarters@pdkintl.org

SOUTH CAROLINA STUDENT LOAN CORPORATION

SOUTH CAROLINA TEACHER LOAN PROGRAM • 97

One-time awards for South Carolina residents attending four-year postsecondary institutions in South Carolina. Recipients must teach in the South Carolina public school system in a critical-need area after graduation. 20% of loan forgiven for each year of service. Write for additional requirements.

Academic/Career Areas Education; Special Education.
Award Forgivable loan for use in any year; not renewable. *Number:* up to 1121. *Amount:* $2500–$5000.
Eligibility Requirements: Applicant must be enrolled full or part-time at a four-year institution or university; resident of South Carolina and studying in South Carolina. Applicant must have 3.0 GPA or higher.
Application Requirements Application, test scores. *Deadline:* June 1.
World Wide Web: http://www.slc.sc.edu
Contact: Jennifer Jones-Gaddy, Vice President
South Carolina Student Loan Corporation
PO Box 21487
Columbia, SC 29221
Phone: 803-798-0916
Fax: 803-772-9410
E-mail: jgaddy@slc.sc.edu

STATE OF UTAH

TERREL H. BELL TEACHING INCENTIVE LOAN • 98

Designed to provide financial assistance to outstanding Utah students pursuing a degree in education. The incentive loan funds full-time tuition and general fees for eight semesters. After graduation/certification the loan may be forgiven if the recipient teaches in a Utah public school or accredited private school (K-12). Loan forgiveness is done on a year for year basis. Application deadline depends on institution.

Academic/Career Areas Education.

Award Forgivable loan for use in freshman, sophomore, junior, or senior years; renewable. *Number:* 365. *Amount:* $600–$1500.

Eligibility Requirements: Applicant must be enrolled full-time at a two-year or four-year institution or university; resident of Utah and studying in Utah. Available to U.S. citizens.

Application Requirements Application, essay, test scores, transcript.

World Wide Web: http://www.utahsbr.edu

Contact: Angie Loving, Manager for Programs and Administration
State of Utah
3 Triad Center, Suite 550
Salt Lake City, UT 84180
Phone: 801-321-7124
Fax: 801-321-7199
E-mail: aloving@utahsbr.edu

STATE STUDENT ASSISTANCE COMMISSION OF INDIANA (SSACI)

INDIANA MINORITY TEACHER AND SPECIAL EDUCATION SERVICES SCHOLARSHIP PROGRAM • 99

For Black or Hispanic students seeking teaching certification or for students seeking special education teaching certification or occupational or physical therapy certification. Must be a U.S. citizen and Indiana resident enrolled full-time at an eligible Indiana institution. Must teach in an Indiana-accredited elementary or secondary school after graduation. Contact institution for application and deadline. Minimum 2.0 GPA required.

Academic/Career Areas Education; Special Education; Therapy/Rehabilitation.

Award Scholarship for use in any year; not renewable. *Number:* 340–370. *Amount:* $1000–$4000.

Eligibility Requirements: Applicant must be African American or Hispanic; enrolled full-time at a four-year institution or university; resident of Indiana and studying in Indiana. Available to U.S. citizens.

Application Requirements Application, financial need analysis. *Deadline:* Continuous.

World Wide Web: http://www.ssaci.in.gov

Indiana Minority Teacher and Special Education Services Scholarship Program (continued)

Contact: Ms. Yvonne Heflin, Director, Special Programs
State Student Assistance Commission of Indiana (SSACI)
150 West Market Street, Suite 500
Indianapolis, IN 46204-2805
Phone: 317-232-2350
Fax: 317-232-3260
E-mail: grants@ssaci.state.un.is

TENNESSEE STUDENT ASSISTANCE CORPORATION

MINORITY TEACHING FELLOWS PROGRAM/TENNESSEE • 100

Forgivable loan for minority Tennessee residents pursuing teaching careers. High school applicant minimum 2.75 GPA. Must be in the top quarter of the class or score an 18 on ACT. College applicant minimum 2.50 GPA. Submit statement of intent, test scores, and transcripts with application and two letters of recommendation. Must teach one year per year of award or repay as a loan.

Academic/Career Areas Education; Special Education.
Award Forgivable loan for use in freshman, sophomore, junior, or senior years; renewable. *Number:* 19–29. *Amount:* $5000.
Eligibility Requirements: Applicant must be Native American or Eskimo, Asian, African American, or Hispanic; enrolled full-time at a two-year or four-year institution or university; resident of Tennessee and studying in Tennessee. Available to U.S. citizens.
Application Requirements Application, essay, references, test scores, transcript. *Deadline:* April 15.
World Wide Web: http://www.state.tn.us/tsac
Contact: Michael Roberts, Compliance Administrator
Tennessee Student Assistance Corporation
404 James Robertson Parkway, Suite 1950, Parkway Towers
Nashville, TN 37243-0820
Phone: 615-741-1346
Fax: 615-741-6101
E-mail: michael.roberts@state.tn.us

TENNESSEE TEACHING SCHOLARS PROGRAM • 101

Forgivable loan for college juniors, seniors, and college graduates admitted to an education program in Tennessee with a minimum GPA of 2.5. Students must commit to teach in a Tennessee public school one year for each year of the award.

Academic/Career Areas Education.
Award Forgivable loan for use in junior, senior, or graduate years; not renewable. *Number:* 30–250. *Amount:* $1000–$3900.

Eligibility Requirements: Applicant must be enrolled full-time at a four-year institution or university; resident of Tennessee and studying in Tennessee. Applicant must have 2.5 GPA or higher. Available to U.S. citizens.

Application Requirements Application, references, test scores, transcript, letter of intent. *Deadline:* April 15.

World Wide Web: http://www.state.tn.us/tsac

Contact: Mike McCormack, Scholarship Administrator
Tennessee Student Assistance Corporation
Suite 1950, Parkway Towers
Nashville, TN 37243-0820
Phone: 615-741-1346
Fax: 615-741-6101

WEST VIRGINIA HIGHER EDUCATION POLICY COMMISSION-STUDENT SERVICES

UNDERWOOD-SMITH TEACHER SCHOLARSHIP PROGRAM • 102

For West Virginia residents at West Virginia institutions pursuing teaching careers. Must have a 3.25 GPA after completion of two years of course work. Must teach two years in West Virginia public schools for each year the award is received. Recipients will be required to sign an agreement acknowledging an understanding of the program's requirements and their willingness to repay the award if appropriate teaching service is not rendered.

Academic/Career Areas Education.

Award Scholarship for use in junior, senior, or graduate years; renewable. *Number:* 53. *Amount:* up to $5000.

Eligibility Requirements: Applicant must be enrolled full-time at a four-year institution or university; resident of West Virginia and studying in West Virginia. Available to U.S. citizens.

Application Requirements Application, essay, references. *Deadline:* April 15.

World Wide Web: http://www.hepc.wvnet.edu

Contact: Michelle Wicks, Scholarship Coordinator
West Virginia Higher Education Policy Commission-Student
Services
1018 Kanawha Boulevard East, Suite 700
Charleston, WV 25301
Phone: 304-558-4618
Fax: 304-558-4622
E-mail: wicks@hepc.wvnet.edu

ELECTRICAL ENGINEERING/ ELECTRONICS_____

AACE INTERNATIONAL

AACE INTERNATIONAL COMPETITIVE SCHOLARSHIP see number 15

AMERICAN INSTITUTE OF AERONAUTICS AND ASTRONAUTICS

AIAA UNDERGRADUATE SCHOLARSHIP see number 9

AMERICAN SOCIETY OF NAVAL ENGINEERS

AMERICAN SOCIETY OF NAVAL ENGINEERS SCHOLARSHIP
see number 10

ASTRONAUT SCHOLARSHIP FOUNDATION

ASTRONAUT SCHOLARSHIP FOUNDATION see number 11

CONSULTING ENGINEERS AND LAND SURVEYORS OF CALIFORNIA SCHOLARSHIP PROGRAM

CONSULTING ENGINEERS AND LAND SURVEYORS OF
CALIFORNIA SCHOLARSHIP AWARD see number 60

CUBAN AMERICAN NATIONAL FOUNDATION

MAS FAMILY SCHOLARSHIPS see number 44

HISPANIC COLLEGE FUND, INC.

HISPANIC COLLEGE FUND SCHOLARSHIP PROGRAM see number 3

THE HISPANIC COLLEGE FUND/INROADS/SPRINT SCHOLARSHIP
PROGRAM see number 4

INSTRUMENTATION, SYSTEMS, AND AUTOMATION SOCIETY (ISA)

INSTRUMENTATION, SYSTEMS, AND AUTOMATION SOCIETY (ISA) SCHOLARSHIP PROGRAM
see number 28

INTERNATIONAL SOCIETY FOR OPTICAL ENGINEERING-SPIE

SPIE EDUCATIONAL SCHOLARSHIPS IN OPTICAL SCIENCE AND ENGINEERING
see number 13

MARYLAND STATE HIGHER EDUCATION COMMISSION

SCIENCE AND TECHNOLOGY SCHOLARSHIP
see number 38

NAMEPA NATIONAL SCHOLARSHIP FOUNDATION

NATIONAL ASSOCIATION OF MINORITY ENGINEERING PROGRAM ADMINISTRATORS NATIONAL SCHOLARSHIP FUND
see number 29

NASA NEVADA SPACE GRANT CONSORTIUM

UNIVERSITY AND COMMUNITY COLLEGE SYSTEM OF NEVADA NASA SPACE GRANT AND FELLOWSHIP PROGRAM
see number 31

NATIONAL ASSOCIATION OF WOMEN IN CONSTRUCTION

NAWIC UNDERGRADUATE SCHOLARSHIPS
see number 20

NEW YORK STATE EDUCATION DEPARTMENT

REGENTS PROFESSIONAL OPPORTUNITY SCHOLARSHIP PROGRAM—NEW YORK
see number 21

SOCIETY OF AUTOMOTIVE ENGINEERS

SAE ENGINEERING SCHOLARSHIPS
see number 32

USENIX ASSOCIATION

USENIX STUDENT PROGRAMS
see number 61

WEST VIRGINIA HIGHER EDUCATION POLICY COMMISSION-STUDENT SERVICES

WEST VIRGINIA ENGINEERING, SCIENCE & TECHNOLOGY SCHOLARSHIP PROGRAM
• 103

For students attending WV institutions full-time pursuing a career in engineering, science or technology. Must have a 3.0 GPA on a 4.0 scale. Must work in the fields of engineering, science or technology in West Virginia one year for each year the award is received.

Academic/Career Areas Electrical Engineering/Electronics; Engineering/Technology; Engineering-Related Technologies; Science, Technology and Society.

Award Scholarship for use in freshman, sophomore, junior, or senior years; renewable. *Number:* 300. *Amount:* up to $3000.

Eligibility Requirements: Applicant must be enrolled full-time at a two-year or four-year or technical institution or university and studying in West Virginia. Applicant must have 3.0 GPA or higher. Available to U.S. citizens.

Application Requirements Application, essay, test scores, transcript. *Deadline:* April 1.

World Wide Web: http://www.hepc.wvnet.edu

Contact: Michelle Wicks, Scholarship Coordinator
West Virginia Higher Education Policy Commission-Student Services
1018 Kanawha Boulevard East, Suite 700
Charleston, WV 25301
Phone: 304-558-4618
Fax: 304-558-4622
E-mail: wicks@hepc.wvnet.edu

ENGINEERING-RELATED TECHNOLOGIES

AACE INTERNATIONAL

AACE INTERNATIONAL COMPETITIVE SCHOLARSHIP
see number 15

AMERICAN WELDING SOCIETY

AMERICAN WELDING SOCIETY DISTRICT SCHOLARSHIP PROGRAM • 104

Award for students in vocational training, community college, or a degree program in welding or a related field of study. Applicants must be high school graduates or equivalent. Must reside in the U.S. and attend a U.S. institution. Recipients may reapply. Must include personal statement of career goals. Also must rank in upper half of class or have a minimum GPA of 2.5.

Academic/Career Areas Engineering-Related Technologies; Trade/Technical Specialties.
Award Scholarship for use in any year; not renewable. *Number:* 88–150. *Amount:* $500–$1000.
Eligibility Requirements: Applicant must be age 18 and enrolled full or part-time at a two-year or four-year or technical institution or university. Applicant must have 2.5 GPA or higher. Available to U.S. and non-U.S. citizens.
Application Requirements Application, autobiography, financial need analysis, photo, transcript. *Deadline:* March 1.
World Wide Web: http://www.aws.org
Contact: Ms. Jo Ann Castrillo, Development Coordinator
American Welding Society
550 Northwest 42nd Avenue
Miami, FL 33126
Phone: 800-443-9353 Ext. 461
Fax: 305-443-7559
E-mail: joann@aws.org

ASTRONAUT SCHOLARSHIP FOUNDATION

ASTRONAUT SCHOLARSHIP FOUNDATION see number 11

BUSINESS AND PROFESSIONAL WOMEN'S FOUNDATION

BPW CAREER ADVANCEMENT SCHOLARSHIP PROGRAM FOR WOMEN see number 37

CONSULTING ENGINEERS AND LAND SURVEYORS OF CALIFORNIA SCHOLARSHIP PROGRAM

CONSULTING ENGINEERS AND LAND SURVEYORS OF CALIFORNIA SCHOLARSHIP AWARD see number 60

CUBAN AMERICAN NATIONAL FOUNDATION

MAS FAMILY SCHOLARSHIPS see number 44

HISPANIC COLLEGE FUND, INC.

HISPANIC COLLEGE FUND SCHOLARSHIP PROGRAM see number 3

THE HISPANIC COLLEGE FUND/INROADS/SPRINT SCHOLARSHIP PROGRAM see number 4

INSTRUMENTATION, SYSTEMS, AND AUTOMATION SOCIETY (ISA)

INSTRUMENTATION, SYSTEMS, AND AUTOMATION SOCIETY (ISA) SCHOLARSHIP PROGRAM see number 28

INTERNATIONAL FACILITY MANAGEMENT ASSOCIATION FOUNDATION

IFMA FOUNDATION SCHOLARSHIPS see number 18

INTERNATIONAL SOCIETY FOR OPTICAL ENGINEERING-SPIE

SPIE EDUCATIONAL SCHOLARSHIPS IN OPTICAL SCIENCE AND ENGINEERING see number 13

MARYLAND STATE HIGHER EDUCATION COMMISSION

SCIENCE AND TECHNOLOGY SCHOLARSHIP see number 38

NAMEPA NATIONAL SCHOLARSHIP FOUNDATION

NATIONAL ASSOCIATION OF MINORITY ENGINEERING PROGRAM ADMINISTRATORS NATIONAL SCHOLARSHIP FUND see number 29

NATIONAL ASSOCIATION OF WOMEN IN CONSTRUCTION

NAWIC UNDERGRADUATE SCHOLARSHIPS see number 20

PLASTICS INSTITUTE OF AMERICA

PLASTICS PIONEERS SCHOLARSHIPS • 105

Financial grants awarded to undergraduate students needing help in their education expenses to enter into a full time career in any and all segments of the plastics industry, with emphasis on "hands on" participation in the many fields where members of the Plastics Pioneers Association have spent their professional years. Applicants must be U.S. citizens.

Academic/Career Areas Engineering/Technology; Engineering-Related Technologies; Materials Science, Engineering and Metallurgy; Trade/Technical Specialties.
Award Scholarship for use in freshman, sophomore, junior, or senior years; renewable. *Number:* 30–40. *Amount:* $1500.
Eligibility Requirements: Applicant must be enrolled full or part-time at a two-year or four-year or technical institution. Available to U.S. citizens.
Application Requirements Application, essay, references, transcript. *Deadline:* April 1.
World Wide Web: http://www.plasticsinstitute.org
Contact: Plastics Institute of America
University of Massachusetts-Lowell
333 Aiken Street
Lowell, MA 01854

SOCIETY OF AUTOMOTIVE ENGINEERS

SAE ENGINEERING SCHOLARSHIPS see number 32

USENIX ASSOCIATION

USENIX STUDENT PROGRAMS see number 61

WEST VIRGINIA HIGHER EDUCATION POLICY COMMISSION-STUDENT SERVICES

WEST VIRGINIA ENGINEERING, SCIENCE & TECHNOLOGY SCHOLARSHIP PROGRAM see number 103

ENGINEERING/TECHNOLOGY_____

AACE INTERNATIONAL

AACE INTERNATIONAL COMPETITIVE SCHOLARSHIP see number 15

AMERICAN INSTITUTE OF AERONAUTICS AND ASTRONAUTICS

AIAA UNDERGRADUATE SCHOLARSHIP see number 9

AMERICAN SOCIETY OF NAVAL ENGINEERS

AMERICAN SOCIETY OF NAVAL ENGINEERS SCHOLARSHIP
see number 10

ASSOCIATED GENERAL CONTRACTORS EDUCATION AND RESEARCH FOUNDATION

AGC EDUCATION AND RESEARCH FOUNDATION UNDERGRADUATE SCHOLARSHIPS see number 62

ASTRONAUT SCHOLARSHIP FOUNDATION

ASTRONAUT SCHOLARSHIP FOUNDATION see number 11

BARRY M. GOLDWATER SCHOLARSHIP AND EXCELLENCE IN EDUCATION FOUNDATION

BARRY M. GOLDWATER SCHOLARSHIP AND EXCELLENCE IN EDUCATION PROGRAM see number 12

BUSINESS AND PROFESSIONAL WOMEN'S FOUNDATION

BPW CAREER ADVANCEMENT SCHOLARSHIP PROGRAM FOR WOMEN see number 37

CONSULTING ENGINEERS AND LAND SURVEYORS OF CALIFORNIA SCHOLARSHIP PROGRAM

CONSULTING ENGINEERS AND LAND SURVEYORS OF CALIFORNIA SCHOLARSHIP AWARD see number 60

CUBAN AMERICAN NATIONAL FOUNDATION

MAS FAMILY SCHOLARSHIPS see number 44

HISPANIC COLLEGE FUND, INC.

HISPANIC COLLEGE FUND SCHOLARSHIP PROGRAM see number 3

THE HISPANIC COLLEGE FUND/INROADS/SPRINT SCHOLARSHIP PROGRAM see number 4

INSTRUMENTATION, SYSTEMS, AND AUTOMATION SOCIETY (ISA)

INSTRUMENTATION, SYSTEMS, AND AUTOMATION SOCIETY (ISA) SCHOLARSHIP PROGRAM see number 28

INTERNATIONAL SOCIETY FOR OPTICAL ENGINEERING-SPIE

SPIE EDUCATIONAL SCHOLARSHIPS IN OPTICAL SCIENCE AND ENGINEERING see number 13

MARYLAND ASSOCIATION OF PRIVATE CAREER SCHOOLS

MARYLAND ASSOCIATION OF PRIVATE CAREER SCHOOLS SCHOLARSHIP see number 49

MARYLAND STATE HIGHER EDUCATION COMMISSION

SCIENCE AND TECHNOLOGY SCHOLARSHIP see number 38

NAMEPA NATIONAL SCHOLARSHIP FOUNDATION

NATIONAL ASSOCIATION OF MINORITY ENGINEERING PROGRAM ADMINISTRATORS NATIONAL SCHOLARSHIP FUND see number 29

NASA MINNESOTA SPACE GRANT CONSORTIUM

MINNESOTA SPACE GRANT CONSORTIUM MINNESOTA SPACE GRANT CONSORTIUM
see number 30

NASA NEVADA SPACE GRANT CONSORTIUM

UNIVERSITY AND COMMUNITY COLLEGE SYSTEM OF NEVADA NASA SPACE GRANT AND FELLOWSHIP PROGRAM
see number 31

NATIONAL ASSOCIATION OF WOMEN IN CONSTRUCTION

NAWIC UNDERGRADUATE SCHOLARSHIPS
see number 20

PLASTICS INSTITUTE OF AMERICA

PLASTICS PIONEERS SCHOLARSHIPS
see number 105

SOCIETY OF AUTOMOTIVE ENGINEERS

SAE ENGINEERING SCHOLARSHIPS
see number 32

SOCIETY OF MANUFACTURING ENGINEERS EDUCATION FOUNDATION

SME FAMILY SCHOLARSHIP
• 106

Three scholarships awarded to children or grandchildren of Society of Manufacturing Engineers members. Must be graduating high school senior planning to pursue full-time studies for an undergraduate degree in manufacturing engineering, manufacturing engineering technology, or a closely related engineering study at an accredited college or university. Undergraduate students must have completed 30 credit hours. Minimum GPA of 3.0 and SAT score of 1000 required, or ACT score of 21.

Academic/Career Areas Engineering/Technology.
Award Scholarship for use in freshman, sophomore, junior, or senior years; renewable. *Number:* 3. *Amount:* $5000–$20,000.
Eligibility Requirements: Applicant must be enrolled full-time at a four-year institution or university. Applicant must have 3.0 GPA or higher. Available to U.S. and non-U.S. citizens.
Application Requirements Application, essay, resume, references, test scores, transcript. *Deadline:* February 1.
World Wide Web: http://www.sme.org/foundation

Contact: Cindy Monzon, Program Coordinator
Society of Manufacturing Engineers Education Foundation
One SME Drive
PO Box 930
Dearborn, MI 48121-0930
Phone: 313-271-1500 Ext. 1707
Fax: 313-240-6095
E-mail: monzcyn@sme.org

SOCIETY OF PLASTICS ENGINEERS (SPE) FOUNDATION

SOCIETY OF PLASTICS ENGINEERS SCHOLARSHIP PROGRAM
see number 56

TAU BETA PI ASSOCIATION

TAU BETA PI SCHOLARSHIP PROGRAM • 107

One-time award for initiated members of Tau Beta Pi in their senior year of full-time undergraduate engineering study. Submit typewritten application and two letters of recommendation. Contact for complete details.

Academic/Career Areas Engineering/Technology.
Award Scholarship for use in senior year; not renewable. *Number:* 95–100. *Amount:* $2000.
Eligibility Requirements: Applicant must be enrolled full-time at a four-year institution or university. Applicant must have 3.5 GPA or higher. Available to U.S. and non-U.S. citizens.
Application Requirements Application, references. *Deadline:* March 1.
World Wide Web: http://www.tbp.org/
Contact: D. Stephen Pierre Jr., Director of Fellowships
Tau Beta Pi Association
PO Box 2697
Knoxville, TN 37901-2697
Fax: 334-694-2310
E-mail: dspierre@southernco.com

UNITED NEGRO COLLEGE FUND

COCA COLA CORPORATE SCHOLARSHIP/INTERN PROGRAM
see number 58

USENIX ASSOCIATION

USENIX STUDENT PROGRAMS
see number 61

WEST VIRGINIA HIGHER EDUCATION POLICY COMMISSION-STUDENT SERVICES

WEST VIRGINIA ENGINEERING, SCIENCE & TECHNOLOGY SCHOLARSHIP PROGRAM
see number 103

FASHION DESIGN_____

WORLDSTUDIO FOUNDATION

WORLDSTUDIO FOUNDATION SCHOLARSHIP PROGRAM
see number 23

FILMMAKING_____

CHARLES AND LUCILLE KING FAMILY FOUNDATION, INC.

CHARLES AND LUCILLE KING FAMILY FOUNDATION SCHOLARSHIPS
see number 66

PRINCESS GRACE FOUNDATION—USA

PRINCESS GRACE SCHOLARSHIPS IN DANCE, THEATER, AND FILM
• 108

Scholarships are offered as follows: Dance for any year of training after the first year; Theater for last year of study in acting, directing, designing; Film for senior/master's thesis projects. Must be a U.S. citizen or permanent resident. Must include a video and nominator's statements. Deadlines: Theater: March 31, Dance: April 30, and Film: June 1.

Academic/Career Areas Filmmaking; Performing Arts.
Award Scholarship for use in senior, or graduate years; not renewable. *Number:* 15-20. *Amount:* $5000-$25,000.
Eligibility Requirements: Applicant must be enrolled full-time at a four-year institution or university. Available to U.S. citizens.
Application Requirements Application, essay, photo, portfolio, resume, references, self-addressed stamped envelope, nomination.
World Wide Web: http://www.pgfusa.com

Contact: Ms. Toby Boshak, Executive Director
Princess Grace Foundation—USA
150 East 58th Street, 21st Floor
New York, NY 10155
Phone: 212-317-1470
Fax: 212-317-1473
E-mail: tboshak@pgfusa.com

FIRE SCIENCES_____

MARYLAND STATE HIGHER EDUCATION COMMISSION

FIREFIGHTER, AMBULANCE, AND RESCUE SQUAD MEMBER TUITION REIMBURSEMENT PROGRAM-MARYLAND • 109

Award intended to reimburse members of rescue organizations serving Maryland communities for tuition costs of course work towards a degree or certificate in fire service or medical technology. Must attend a two- or four-year school in Maryland.

Academic/Career Areas Fire Sciences; Health and Medical Sciences; Trade/Technical Specialties.

Award Scholarship for use in any year; not renewable. *Number:* 100–300. *Amount:* $200–$4000.

Eligibility Requirements: Applicant must be enrolled full or part-time at a two-year or four-year institution or university; resident of Maryland; studying in Maryland and have employment experience in police/firefighting. Available to U.S. citizens.

Application Requirements Application, transcript. *Deadline:* July 1.

World Wide Web: http://www.mhec.state.md.us

Contact: Margaret Riley, Scholarship Administration
Maryland State Higher Education Commission
16 Francis Street
Annapolis, MD 21401-1781
Phone: 410-264-4568
Fax: 410-974-5994
E-mail: ssamail@mhec.state.md.us

SCIENCE AND TECHNOLOGY SCHOLARSHIP

see number 38

FOOD SCIENCE/NUTRITION_____

AMERICAN SCHOOL FOOD SERVICE ASSOCIATION

SCHWAN'S FOOD SERVICE SCHOLARSHIP • 110

Program is designed to assist members of the American School Food Service Association and their dependents as they pursue educational advancement in the field of child nutrition. Must rank in upper half of class or have a minimum 2.5 GPA.

Academic/Career Areas Food Science/Nutrition; Food Service/Hospitality.
Award Scholarship for use in any year; not renewable. *Number:* 50–60. *Amount:* $100–$1000.
Eligibility Requirements: Applicant must be enrolled full or part-time at a two-year or four-year or technical institution or university; member of American School Food Service Association and have employment experience in food service. Applicant must have 2.5 GPA or higher. Available to U.S. citizens.
Application Requirements Application, essay, resume, references, transcript, proof of enrollment. *Deadline:* April 15.
World Wide Web: http://www.asfsa.org
Contact: Ruth O'Brien, Scholarship Coordinator
American School Food Service Association
700 South Washington Street, Suite 300
Alexandria, VA 22314
Phone: 703-739-3900 Ext. 150
E-mail: robrien@asfsa.org

INSTITUTE OF FOOD TECHNOLOGISTS

INSTITUTE OF FOOD TECHNOLOGISTS FOOD ENGINEERING DIVISION JUNIOR/SENIOR SCHOLARSHIP • 111

One-time award for junior or senior-level students in an Institute of Food Technologists-approved program, with demonstrated intent to pursue profes-sional activities in food science or food technology. Submit recommendation. Applications must be sent to department head of educational institution, not IFT.

Academic/Career Areas Food Science/Nutrition.
Award Scholarship for use in sophomore, junior, or senior years; not renewable. *Number:* 50. *Amount:* $1000–$2250.
Eligibility Requirements: Applicant must be enrolled at a four-year institu-tion or university. Available to U.S. citizens.
Application Requirements Application, references, transcript. *Deadline:* February 1.
World Wide Web: http://www.ift.org

Contact: Administrator
Institute of Food Technologists
221 North LaSalle Street, Suite 300
Chicago, IL 60601
Phone: 312-782-8424
Fax: 312-782-8348

INTERNATIONAL ASSOCIATION OF CULINARY PROFESSIONALS FOUNDATION (IACP)

IACP FOUNDATION CULINARY SCHOLARSHIPS • 112

Beginning, continuing and specialty education scholarships for students and/or professionals currently involved in the culinary industry or studying culinary arts. Minimum 3.0 GPA required. $25 application fee.

Academic/Career Areas Food Science/Nutrition; Food Service/Hospitality.
Award Scholarship for use in any year; not renewable. *Number:* 8–10. *Amount:* $500–$10,000.
Eligibility Requirements: Applicant must be enrolled full or part-time at a two-year or four-year or technical institution or university and have employment experience in food service. Applicant must have 3.0 GPA or higher. Available to U.S. and non-U.S. citizens.
Application Requirements Application, essay, references, transcript. *Fee:* $25. *Deadline:* December 1.
World Wide Web: http://www.iacp.com
Contact: Kristi Kelty, Program Coordinator
International Association of Culinary Professionals Foundation (IACP)
304 West Liberty Street, Suite 201
Louisville, KY 40202-3068
Phone: 502-581-9786
Fax: 502-589-3602
E-mail: kkelty@hqtrs.com

JAMES BEARD FOUNDATION, INC.

JAMES BEARD FOUNDATION SCHOLARSHIP PROGRAM • 113

Scholarships are offered for study in the U.S. and abroad. All candidates must demonstrate a strong commitment to the culinary arts, an exceptional academic or work record, and financial need. Restrictions vary according to each program.

Academic/Career Areas Food Science/Nutrition; Home Economics.
Award Scholarship for use in senior, or graduate years; not renewable. *Number:* 125–150. *Amount:* $500–$20,000.
Eligibility Requirements: Applicant must be enrolled full or part-time at a two-year or four-year or technical institution or university. Available to U.S. and non-U.S. citizens.

James Beard Foundation Scholarship Program (continued)

Application Requirements Application, essay, financial need analysis, references, transcript. *Deadline:* April 15.

World Wide Web: http://www.jamesbeard.org

Contact: Caroline Stuart, Scholarship Director
James Beard Foundation, Inc.
167 West 12th. Street
New York, NY 10011
Phone: 212-675-4984
Fax: 212-645-1438
E-mail: jamesbeardfound@hotmail.com

KENTUCKY RESTAURANT ASSOCIATION EDUCATIONAL FOUNDATION

KENTUCKY RESTAURANT ASSOCIATION EDUCATIONAL FOUNDATION SCHOLARSHIP • 114

One-time award to Kentucky residents enrolled in a food service program. Submit application, transcript, and references. Application deadlines are January 1 and July 1.

Academic/Career Areas Food Science/Nutrition; Food Service/Hospitality; Hospitality Management.

Award Scholarship for use in any year; not renewable. *Number:* 30–40. *Amount:* $500–$1500.

Eligibility Requirements: Applicant must be enrolled full-time at a two-year or four-year or technical institution or university and resident of Kentucky. Available to U.S. citizens.

Application Requirements Application, references, transcript, letters from school and employer.

World Wide Web: http://www.kyra.org/

Contact: Betsy Byrd, Director of Member Relations
Kentucky Restaurant Association Educational Foundation
512 Executive Park
Louisville, KY 40207
Phone: 502-896-0464
Fax: 502-896-0465
E-mail: info@kyra.org

MARYLAND ASSOCIATION OF PRIVATE CAREER SCHOOLS

MARYLAND ASSOCIATION OF PRIVATE CAREER SCHOOLS SCHOLARSHIP

see number 49

NATIONAL RESTAURANT ASSOCIATION EDUCATIONAL FOUNDATION

NATIONAL RESTAURANT ASSOCIATION EDUCATIONAL FOUNDATION UNDERGRADUATE SCHOLARSHIPS FOR COLLEGE STUDENTS • 115

This scholarship is awarded to college students who have demonstrated a commitment to both postsecondary hospitality education and to a career in the industry with 750 hours of industry work experience. Must have a 2.75 GPA, and be enrolled for a full academic term for the school year beginning in fall.

Academic/Career Areas Food Science/Nutrition.

Award Scholarship for use in sophomore, junior, or senior years; not renewable. *Number:* 159–200. *Amount:* $2000.

Eligibility Requirements: Applicant must be enrolled full-time at an institution or university and have employment experience in food service. Available to U.S. citizens.

Application Requirements Application, essay, transcript. *Deadline:* March 1.

World Wide Web: http://www.nraef.org

Contact: Emilee N. Rogan, Director, Scholarship Program
National Restaurant Association Educational Foundation
175 West Jackson Boulevard, Suite 1500
Chicago, IL 60604-2702
Phone: 800-765-2122
Fax: 312-715-1362
E-mail: scholars@foodtrain.org

NATIONAL RESTAURANT ASSOCIATION EDUCATIONAL FOUNDATION UNDERGRADUATE SCHOLARSHIPS FOR HIGH SCHOOL SENIORS • 116

This scholarship is awarded to high school students who have demonstrated a commitment to both postsecondary hospitality education and to a career in the industry. Must have 250 hours of industry experience, age 17-19 with a 2.75 GPA.

Academic/Career Areas Food Science/Nutrition.

Award Scholarship for use in freshman year; not renewable. *Number:* 50–100. *Amount:* $2000.

Eligibility Requirements: Applicant must be high school student; age 17-19; planning to enroll full-time at an institution or university and have employment experience in food service.

Application Requirements Application, essay, references, transcript. *Deadline:* March 1.

World Wide Web: http://www.nraef.org

National Restaurant Association Educational Foundation Undergraduate Scholarships for High School Seniors (continued)

Contact: Emilee N. Rogan, Director, Scholarship Program
National Restaurant Association Educational Foundation
175 West Jackson Boulevard, Suite 1500
Chicago, IL 60604-2702
Phone: 800-765-2122
Fax: 312-715-1362
E-mail: scholars@foodtrain.org

NEW YORK STATE EDUCATION DEPARTMENT

REGENTS PROFESSIONAL OPPORTUNITY SCHOLARSHIP PROGRAM—NEW YORK
see number 21

UNITED AGRIBUSINESS LEAGUE

UNITED AGRIBUSINESS LEAGUE SCHOLARSHIP PROGRAM
see number 5

FOOD SERVICE/HOSPITALITY_____

AMERICAN SCHOOL FOOD SERVICE ASSOCIATION

SCHWAN'S FOOD SERVICE SCHOLARSHIP
see number 110

DECA (DISTRIBUTION EDUCATION CLUB OF AMERICA)

HARRY A. APPLEGATE SCHOLARSHIP
see number 45

ILLINOIS RESTAURANT ASSOCIATION EDUCATIONAL FOUNDATION

ILLINOIS RESTAURANT ASSOCIATION EDUCATIONAL FOUNDATION SCHOLARSHIPS
• 117

Scholarship available to Illinois residents enrolled with a food service management, culinary arts, or hospitality management concentration in an accredited program of a two or four-year college or university.

Academic/Career Areas Food Service/Hospitality; Hospitality Management.
Award Scholarship for use in any year; not renewable. *Number:* 40–60.
Amount: $500–$10,000.
Eligibility Requirements: Applicant must be enrolled full or part-time at a two-year or four-year institution or university and resident of Illinois.
Application Requirements Application, references, transcript. *Deadline:* June 1.
World Wide Web: http://www.illinoisrestaurants.org
Contact: Matthew Bass, Program and Office Coordinator
　　　　　Illinois Restaurant Association Educational Foundation
　　　　　200 North LaSalle, Suite 880
　　　　　Chicago, IL 60601-1014
　　　　　Phone: 312-787-4000
　　　　　Fax: 312-787-4792
　　　　　E-mail: edfound@illinoisrestaurants.org

INTERNATIONAL ASSOCIATION OF CULINARY PROFESSIONALS FOUNDATION (IACP)

IACP FOUNDATION CULINARY SCHOLARSHIPS　　　see number 112

KENTUCKY RESTAURANT ASSOCIATION EDUCATIONAL FOUNDATION

KENTUCKY RESTAURANT ASSOCIATION EDUCATIONAL FOUNDATION SCHOLARSHIP　　　see number 114

FOREIGN LANGUAGE_____

ALBERTA HERITAGE SCHOLARSHIP FUND

ALBERTA HERITAGE SCHOLARSHIP FUND FELLOWSHIPS FOR FULL-TIME STUDIES IN FRENCH—COLLEGE/TECHNICAL SCHOOLS　　　**• 118**
Award to assist francophone students in pursuing studies in French at a college or technical institute in any discipline in Canada. Must be Alberta resident, with French as a first language, and be enrolled full-time in a college or technical school. Awards valued at Can$1000 per semester, as well as Can$200 travel grant per semester for studies outside of Alberta. Deadline: November 15.

Alberta Heritage Scholarship Fund Fellowships for full-time Studies in French—College/Technical Schools (continued)

Academic/Career Areas Foreign Language.

Award Scholarship for use in freshman, sophomore, junior, or senior years; not renewable. *Number:* 50. *Amount:* $1000–$2400.

Eligibility Requirements: Applicant must be Canadian; enrolled full-time at a two-year or four-year or technical institution and resident of Alberta. Applicant must have 2.5 GPA or higher.

Application Requirements Application, transcript. *Deadline:* November 15.

World Wide Web: http://www.alis.gov.ab.ca/scholarships

Contact: Alberta Heritage Scholarship Fund
9940 106th Street, 9th Floor, Box 28000 Station Main
Edmonton, AB T5J 4R4
Canada
Phone: 780-427-8640
Fax: 780-422-4516
E-mail: heritage@gov.ab.ca

FELLOWSHIPS FOR FULL-TIME STUDIES IN FRENCH—UNIVERSITY • 119

One-time awards for Canadian citizens who are Alberta residents pursuing full-time postsecondary studies in French in any discipline at a Canadian university. Travel grant is available for studies outside of Alberta. Awards valued at Can$500-Can$1,400 per semester.

Academic/Career Areas Foreign Language.

Award Scholarship for use in freshman, sophomore, junior, or senior years; not renewable. *Number:* 250. *Amount:* $1000–$2000.

Eligibility Requirements: Applicant must be Canadian; enrolled full-time at a four-year institution or university and resident of Alberta.

Application Requirements Application, transcript. *Deadline:* November 15.

World Wide Web: http://www.alis.gov.ab.ca/scholarships

Contact: Director
Alberta Heritage Scholarship Fund
9940 106th Street, 9th Floor, Box 28000 Station Main
Edmonton, AB T5J 4R4
Canada
Phone: 780-427-8640
Fax: 780-422-4516
E-mail: heritage@gov.ab.ca

ARKANSAS DEPARTMENT OF HIGHER EDUCATION

EMERGENCY SECONDARY EDUCATION LOAN PROGRAM

see number 35

MARYLAND STATE HIGHER EDUCATION COMMISSION

HOPE SCHOLARSHIP

see number 6

NEW HAMPSHIRE POSTSECONDARY EDUCATION COMMISSION

NEW HAMPSHIRE CAREER INCENTIVE PROGRAM • 120

Grants available to New Hampshire residents attending New Hampshire institutions in programs leading to certification in special education, foreign language education or licensure as an LPN, RN or an Associate, Baccalaureate or advanced nursing degree. Must work in shortage area following graduation. Deadline: June 1 for fall or December 15 for spring. Foreign language or special education students must be juniors, seniors or graduate students with a 3.0 GPA or higher. Forgivable loan is not automatically renewable. Applicant must reapply.

Academic/Career Areas Foreign Language; Nursing; Special Education.
Award Forgivable loan for use in freshman, sophomore, junior, senior, or graduate years; not renewable. *Number:* 1–50. *Amount:* $1000–$3000.
Eligibility Requirements: Applicant must be enrolled full or part-time at a two-year or four-year or technical institution or university; resident of New Hampshire and studying in New Hampshire. Available to U.S. citizens.
Application Requirements Application, financial need analysis, references.
World Wide Web: http://www.state.nh.us/postsecondary
Contact: Judith Knapp, Student Financial Assistant Coordinator
New Hampshire Postsecondary Education Commission
Two Industrial Park Drive
Concord, NH 03301-8512
Phone: 603-271-2555
Fax: 603-271-2696
E-mail: jknapp@nhsa.state.nh.us

ROTARY FOUNDATION OF ROTARY INTERNATIONAL

ROTARY FOUNDATION ACADEMIC-YEAR AMBASSADORIAL SCHOLARSHIPS • 121

One-time award funds travel, tuition, room and board for one academic year of study in foreign country. Applicant must have completed at least two years of university course work and be proficient in language of host country. Application through local Rotary club; appearances before clubs required during award period. Deadlines vary (March-July). See website for updated information.

Academic/Career Areas Foreign Language.

Rotary Foundation Academic-Year Ambassadorial Scholarships (continued)

Award Scholarship for use in junior, senior, graduate, or post graduate years; not renewable. *Number:* 900–1000. *Amount:* $11,000–$25,000.

Eligibility Requirements: Applicant must be enrolled at a four-year or technical institution or university and must have an interest in foreign language.

Application Requirements Application, autobiography, essay, interview, references, transcript.

World Wide Web: http://www.rotary.org

Contact: Scholarship Program
Rotary Foundation of Rotary International
1560 Sherman Avenue
Evanston, IL 60203
Phone: 847-866-4459

ROTARY FOUNDATION CULTURAL AMBASSADORIAL SCHOLARSHIP   • 122

One-time award funds three or six months (depending on availability through sponsoring Rotary district) of intensive language study and cultural immersion abroad. Applicant must have completed at least two years of university course work or one year in proposed language of study. Application through local Rotary club; appearances before clubs required during award period. Applications accepted March through July. See website for updated information.

Academic/Career Areas Foreign Language.

Award Scholarship for use in junior, senior, or graduate years; not renewable. *Number:* 150–200. *Amount:* $12,000–$19,000.

Eligibility Requirements: Applicant must have an interest in leadership.

Application Requirements Application, autobiography, essay, interview, references, transcript.

World Wide Web: http://www.rotary.org

Contact: Scholarship Program
Rotary Foundation of Rotary International
1560 Sherman Avenue
Evanston, IL 60203
Phone: 847-866-4459

SOCIEDAD HONORARIA HISPÁNICA

JOSEPH S. ADAMS SCHOLARSHIP   • 123

Applicants must be members of the Sociedad Honoraria Hispánica and a high school senior. Must have major/career interest in Spanish/Portuguese. Applicants must demonstrate high academic achievement, depth of character, leadership, patriotism, seriousness of purpose. Award available to citizens of other countries as long as they are members of the Sacred Honoraria Hispánica. For information contact local sponsor of Sociedad Honoraria Hispánica. For high school students only.

Academic/Career Areas Foreign Language.

Award Scholarship for use in freshman year; not renewable. *Number:* 44. *Amount:* $1000–$2000.

Eligibility Requirements: Applicant must be high school student; planning to enroll full-time at a four-year institution or university and must have an interest in Portuguese language or Spanish language. Available to U.S. and non-U.S. citizens.

World Wide Web: http://www.sociedadhonorariahispanica.org

Contact: Local sponsor of SHH at high school
Sociedad Honoraria Hispánica
PO Box 10
Turbeville, SC 29162-0010

GRAPHICS/GRAPHIC ARTS/PRINTING__

HISPANIC COLLEGE FUND, INC.

HISPANIC COLLEGE FUND SCHOLARSHIP PROGRAM   see number 3

THE HISPANIC COLLEGE FUND/INROADS/SPRINT SCHOLARSHIP PROGRAM   see number 4

KNIGHT RIDDER

KNIGHT RIDDER MINORITY SCHOLARSHIP PROGRAM   see number 48

PRINT AND GRAPHIC SCHOLARSHIP FOUNDATION

PRINT AND GRAPHICS SCHOLARSHIPS   • 124

Applicant must be interested in a career in graphic communications. Must have and maintain a 3.0 cumulative GPA. Selection based on academic record, class rank, recommendations, biographical information and extracurricular activities. Deadline for high school students is March 1 and April 1 for enrolled college students. Award available to citizens outside U.S. as long as they are attending a U.S. institution.

Academic/Career Areas Graphics/Graphic Arts/Printing.

Award Scholarship for use in freshman, sophomore, junior, senior, or graduate years; renewable. *Number:* 320. *Amount:* $1000–$3000.

Eligibility Requirements: Applicant must be enrolled full-time at a two-year or four-year or technical institution or university and must have an interest in designated field specified by sponsor. Applicant must have 3.0 GPA or higher. Available to U.S. and non-U.S. citizens.

Print and Graphics Scholarships (continued)
Application Requirements Application, essay, references, self-addressed stamped envelope, test scores, transcript.
World Wide Web: http://www.gatf.org
Contact: Bernie Eckert, Program Coordinator
Print and Graphic Scholarship Foundation
200 Deer Run Road
Sewickley, PA 15143-2600
Phone: 412-741-6860
Fax: 412-741-2311
E-mail: pgsf@gatf.org

HEALTH ADMINISTRATION_____

ALBERTA HERITAGE SCHOLARSHIP FUND

ALBERTA HERITAGE SCHOLARSHIP FUND ABORIGINAL HEALTH CAREERS BURSARY   see number 33

ORDEAN FOUNDATION

ORDEAN LOAN PROGRAM   see number 95

HEALTH AND MEDICAL SCIENCES_____

ALBERTA HERITAGE SCHOLARSHIP FUND

ALBERTA HERITAGE SCHOLARSHIP FUND ABORIGINAL HEALTH CAREERS BURSARY   see number 33

ALICE M. YARNOLD AND SAMUEL YARNOLD SCHOLARSHIP TRUST

ALICE M. AND SAMUEL YARNOLD SCHOLARSHIP   **• 125**
For New Hampshire resident, attending school in any state; applicant must already have begun postsecondary education (graduating high school seniors not eligible); must major in medicine, nursing or health-related field but not in management within those fields.

Academic/Career Areas Health and Medical Sciences; Nursing; Therapy/ Rehabilitation.

Award Scholarship for use in sophomore, junior, senior, graduate, or post graduate years; not renewable. *Number:* 20–30. *Amount:* $1000–$3000.

Eligibility Requirements: Applicant must be enrolled full or part-time at a two-year or four-year or technical institution or university and resident of New Hampshire. Available to U.S. citizens.

Application Requirements Application, essay, financial need analysis, references, transcript. *Deadline:* May 10.

Contact: Ms. Jacqueline Lambert, Assistant to Trustees of Yarnold Trust
Alice M. Yarnold and Samuel Yarnold Scholarship Trust
One Glenwood Avenue
Dover, NH 03820-2456
Phone: 603-742-1300
Fax: 603-742-1863

AMERICAN LIVER FOUNDATION

STUDENT RESEARCH FELLOWSHIPS-AMERICAN LIVER FOUNDATION
see number 34

BUSINESS AND PROFESSIONAL WOMEN'S FOUNDATION

BPW CAREER ADVANCEMENT SCHOLARSHIP PROGRAM FOR WOMEN
see number 37

CENTER FOR RURAL HEALTH INITIATIVES-TEXAS

TEXAS PHYSICIAN ASSISTANT LOAN REIMBURSEMENT PROGRAM
• 126

Educational loan reimbursement program for physician assistants who have worked twelve consecutive months in a qualified rural Texas county. Submit a copy of diploma from accredited physician assistant school.

Academic/Career Areas Health and Medical Sciences.

Award Grant for use in any year; not renewable. *Number:* 18–36. *Amount:* $2500–$5000.

Eligibility Requirements: Applicant must be resident of Texas.

Application Requirements Application. *Deadline:* June 30.

World Wide Web: http://www.crhi.state.tx.us

Contact: Susan Kolliopoulos, Program Administrator
Center for Rural Health Initiatives- Texas
PO Drawer 1708
Austin, TX 78767-1708
Phone: 512-479-8891
Fax: 512-479-8898
E-mail: crhi@crhi.state.tx.us

HEALTH PROFESSIONS EDUCATION FOUNDATION

HEALTH PROFESSIONS EDUCATION SCHOLARSHIP PROGRAM
see number 69

KAISER PERMANENTE ALLIED HEALTHCARE SCHOLARSHIP • 127

One-time award to all students enrolled in or accepted to California accredited allied health education programs for school related expenses. Priority is given to students enrolled in the following fields: medical imaging, occupational therapy, physical therapy, respiratory care, social work, pharmacy, pharmacy technician, medical laboratory technologist, surgical technician, ultrasound technician and diagnostic medical sonography. Eligible applicants may receive up to $2,500 per year in financial assistance. Deadlines: March 27 and September 11. Must be resident of CA and U.S. citizen.

Academic/Career Areas Health and Medical Sciences; Social Services; Therapy/Rehabilitation.

Award Scholarship for use in any year; not renewable. *Number:* 20–40. *Amount:* $2000–$2500.

Eligibility Requirements: Applicant must be enrolled full or part-time at a two-year or four-year or technical institution or university; resident of California and studying in California. Applicant must have 2.5 GPA or higher. Available to U.S. citizens.

Application Requirements Application, driver's license, financial need analysis, references, transcript.

World Wide Web: http://www.healthprofessions.ca.gov

Contact: Lisa Montgomery, Program Director
Health Professions Education Foundation
1600 Ninth Street, Suite 436
Sacramento, CA 95814
Phone: 800-773-1669
Fax: 916-653-1438
E-mail: lmontgom@oshpd.state.ca.us

YOUTH FOR ADOLESCENT PREGNANCY PREVENTION LEADERSHIP RECOGNITION PROGRAM • 128

Over the next two years the Youth for Adolescent Pregnancy Prevention (YAPP) Leadership Recognition Program (LRP) will recognize 16 youths throughout California who have made an outstanding contribution to their communities by promoting healthy adolescent sexuality and teen pregnancy prevention. Youth selected to receive this scholarship award will receive up to $5,000 per year for up to 5 years to assist them in pursing careers in the health field (e.g., medicine, ancillary services, dentistry, mental health). Must be resident of CA and U.S. citizen between the ages of 16-24.

Academic/Career Areas Health and Medical Sciences; Nursing.

Award Scholarship for use in freshman, sophomore, junior, or senior years; not renewable. *Number:* 8. *Amount:* $25,000.

Eligibility Requirements: Applicant must be age 16-24; enrolled full or part-time at a two-year or four-year or technical institution or university; resident of California and studying in California. Available to U.S. citizens.

Application Requirements Application, financial need analysis, interview, photo, references, transcript, 2 copies of application. *Deadline:* January 23.

World Wide Web: http://www.healthprofessions.ca.gov

Contact: Ms. LaTanya Henley, Project Officer
Health Professions Education Foundation
1600 9th Street, Suite 436
Sacramento, CA 95814
Phone: 916-653-0860
Fax: 916-653-1438
E-mail: lhenley@oshpd.state.ca.us

J.D. ARCHBOLD MEMORIAL HOSPITAL

ARCHBOLD SCHOLARSHIP PROGRAM • 129

Service cancelable loan awarded for a clinical degree. Awarded to residents of Southwest Georgia and North Florida. Specific clinical degree may vary, depending on need in area. Must agree to full-time employment for 1-3 years upon graduation.

Academic/Career Areas Health and Medical Sciences; Nursing.

Award Forgivable loan for use in junior year; not renewable. *Number:* 50. *Amount:* $600–$6000.

Eligibility Requirements: Applicant must be enrolled full or part-time at a two-year or four-year or technical institution or university and resident of Florida or Georgia. Available to U.S. citizens.

Application Requirements Application, interview, transcript. *Deadline:* Continuous.

World Wide Web: http://www.archbold.org

Contact: Donna McMillan, Education Coordinator
J.D. Archbold Memorial Hospital
PO Box 1018
Thomasville, GA 31799
Phone: 229-228-2795
Fax: 229-228-8584

MARYLAND STATE HIGHER EDUCATION COMMISSION

DEVELOPMENTAL DISABILITIES TUITION ASSISTANCE PROGRAM • 130

Provides tuition assistance to students who are service employees that provide direct support or care to individuals with mental health disabilities. Must be a Maryland resident attending a Maryland college.

Developmental Disabilities Tuition Assistance Program (continued)

Academic/Career Areas Health and Medical Sciences; Nursing; Social Services; Special Education; Therapy/Rehabilitation.

Award Forgivable loan for use in freshman, sophomore, junior, senior, or graduate years; renewable. *Number:* up to 400. *Amount:* $500–$3000.

Eligibility Requirements: Applicant must be enrolled full or part-time at a two-year or four-year institution or university; resident of Maryland; studying in Maryland and have employment experience in designated career field. Available to U.S. citizens.

Application Requirements Application, transcript. *Deadline:* July 1.

World Wide Web: http://www.mhec.state.md.us

Contact: Deanne Alspach, Scholarship Administration
Maryland State Higher Education Commission
16 Francis Street
Annapolis, MD 21401-1781
Phone: 410-260-4553
Fax: 410-974-5994
E-mail: ssamail@mhec.state.md.us

FIREFIGHTER, AMBULANCE, AND RESCUE SQUAD MEMBER TUITION REIMBURSEMENT PROGRAM-MARYLAND
see number 109

HOPE SCHOLARSHIP
see number 6

PROFESSIONAL SCHOLARSHIP PROGRAM-MARYLAND
see number 70

NATIONAL AMBUCS, INC.

AMBUCS SCHOLARS-SCHOLARSHIPS FOR THERAPISTS • 131

Scholarships are open to students who are U.S. citizens at a junior level in college or above. These students must be enrolled in an accredited program by the appropriate health therapy profession authority in physical therapy, occupational therapy, speech-language pathology, or audiology and must demonstrate a financial need. Application available on website. Paper applications are not accepted.

Academic/Career Areas Health and Medical Sciences; Therapy/Rehabilitation.

Award Scholarship for use in junior, senior, graduate, or post graduate years; not renewable. *Number:* 300. *Amount:* $500–$6000.

Eligibility Requirements: Applicant must be enrolled full-time at a four-year institution or university. Available to U.S. citizens.

Application Requirements Application, essay, financial need analysis. *Deadline:* April 15.

World Wide Web: http://www.ambucs.com

Contact: Janice Blankenship, Scholarship Coordinator
National AMBUCS, Inc.
PO Box 5127
High Point, NC 27262
Phone: 336-869-2166
Fax: 336-887-8451
E-mail: janiceb@ambucs.com

NEW MEXICO COMMISSION ON HIGHER EDUCATION

ALLIED HEALTH STUDENT LOAN PROGRAM-NEW MEXICO

see number 72

PHYSICIAN ASSISTANT FOUNDATION

PHYSICIAN ASSISTANT FOUNDATION ANNUAL SCHOLARSHIP

• 132

One-time award for student members of the American Academy of Physician Assistants enrolled in accredited physician assistant programs. Award based on financial need, academic achievement, and goals. Must submit two passport-type photographs for promotional reasons.

Academic/Career Areas Health and Medical Sciences.
Award Scholarship for use in junior or senior years; not renewable. *Number:* 40–50. *Amount:* $2000–$3000.
Eligibility Requirements: Applicant must be enrolled full or part-time at a two-year or four-year institution or university and member of American Academy of Physicians Assistants. Available to U.S. citizens.
Application Requirements Application, essay, financial need analysis, photo, transcript. *Deadline:* February 1.
World Wide Web: http://www.aapa.org
Contact: Physician Assistant Foundation
950 North Washington Street
Alexandria, VA 22304-1552
Phone: 703-836-2272
Fax: 703-684-1924

SOCIETY OF TOXICOLOGY

MINORITY UNDERGRADUATE STUDENT AWARDS

see number 39

STATE OF GEORGIA

SERVICE-CANCELLABLE STAFFORD LOAN-GEORGIA

see number 73

UNITED STATES DEPARTMENT OF HEALTH AND HUMAN SERVICES

NIH UNDERGRADUATE SCHOLARSHIP FOR INDIVIDUALS FROM DISADVANTAGED BACKGROUNDS
see number 40

HEALTH INFORMATION MANAGEMENT/ TECHNOLOGY_____

FOUNDATION OF RESEARCH AND EDUCATION OF AMERICAN HEALTH INFORMATION MANAGEMENT ASSOCIATION

FOUNDATION OF RESEARCH AND EDUCATION UNDERGRADUATE MERIT SCHOLARSHIPS
• 133

Multiple scholarships for undergraduate Health Information Management students. One standard application for all available scholarships. Must have a 3.0 GPA. Applications can be downloaded at http://www.ahima.org. Must be a member of AHIMA.

Academic/Career Areas Health Information Management/Technology.
Award Scholarship for use in freshman, sophomore, junior, or senior years; not renewable. *Number:* 35–45. *Amount:* $1000–$5000.
Eligibility Requirements: Applicant must be enrolled full or part-time at a two-year or four-year or technical institution or university. Applicant must have 3.0 GPA or higher. Available to U.S. and non-U.S. citizens.
Application Requirements Application, references, transcript. *Deadline:* May 31.
World Wide Web: http://www.ahima.org
Contact: Ms. Alison Bergum, Research and Development Coordinator
233 North Michigan Avenue, Suite 2150
Chicago, IL 60601-5800
Phone: 312-233-1100
E-mail: fore@ahima.org

ORDEAN FOUNDATION

ORDEAN LOAN PROGRAM
see number 95

HEATING, AIR-CONDITIONING, AND REFRIGERATION MECHANICS_____

INSTRUMENTATION, SYSTEMS, AND AUTOMATION SOCIETY (ISA)

INSTRUMENTATION, SYSTEMS, AND AUTOMATION SOCIETY (ISA) SCHOLARSHIP PROGRAM see number 28

HISTORY_____

FOUNDATION FOR THE ADVANCEMENT OF MESOAMERICAN STUDIES, INC.

FAMSI 2002 ANNUAL GRANT COMPETITION see number 14

HUGH FULTON BYAS MEMORIAL FUNDS, INC.

HUGH FULTON BYAS MEMORIAL GRANT • 134

Grants for UK citizens who are full-time students intending to pursue a course of study in the United States devoted to world peace, journalism, Anglo-American relations, or the creative arts. Submit copy of UK passport.

Academic/Career Areas History; International Migration; Journalism; Peace and Conflict Studies.
Award Grant for use in sophomore, junior, senior, graduate, or post graduate years; renewable. *Number:* 3–10. *Amount:* $1000–$25,000.
Eligibility Requirements: Applicant must be Ukrainian and enrolled full-time at a four-year institution or university. Available to Canadian and non-U.S. citizens.
Application Requirements Application, essay, financial need analysis, photo, self-addressed stamped envelope, transcript, UK passport. *Deadline:* Continuous.
Contact: Linda Maffei, Administrator
Hugh Fulton Byas Memorial Funds, Inc.
261 Bradley Street
New Haven, CT 06511
Phone: 203-777-8356
Fax: 203-562-6288

JOHN F. KENNEDY LIBRARY FOUNDATION

KENNEDY RESEARCH GRANTS
see number 19

HOME ECONOMICS_____

FAMILY, CAREER AND COMMUNITY LEADERS OF AMERICA-TEXAS ASSOCIATION

FCCLA HOUSTON LIVESTOCK SHOW AND RODEO SCHOLARSHIP
• 135

Ten, four-year $10,000 scholarships to be awarded to outstanding members of the Texas FCCLA. Applicants should visit the web site or write to Texas FCCLA for complete information, submission guidelines, and restrictions. Minimum 3.5 GPA required. Must be Texas resident and attend a Texas institution.

Academic/Career Areas Home Economics.

Award Scholarship for use in freshman, sophomore, junior, or senior years; not renewable. *Number:* 10. *Amount:* $10,000.

Eligibility Requirements: Applicant must be high school student; planning to enroll full-time at a four-year institution or university; resident of Texas; studying in Texas and member of Family, Career and Community Leaders of America. Applicant must have 3.5 GPA or higher. Available to U.S. citizens.

Application Requirements Application, essay, photo, references, test scores, transcript. *Deadline:* March 1.

World Wide Web: http://www.texasfccla.org

Contact: FCCLA Staff
Family, Career and Community Leaders of America- Texas
    Association
3530 Bee Caves Road, #101
Austin, TX 78766
Phone: 512-306-0099
Fax: 512-306-0041
E-mail: fccla@texasfccla.org

JAMES BEARD FOUNDATION, INC.

JAMES BEARD FOUNDATION SCHOLARSHIP PROGRAM
see number 113

MARYLAND ASSOCIATION OF PRIVATE CAREER SCHOOLS

MARYLAND ASSOCIATION OF PRIVATE CAREER SCHOOLS SCHOLARSHIP
see number 49

MARYLAND STATE HIGHER EDUCATION COMMISSION

HOPE SCHOLARSHIP
see number 6

HORTICULTURE/FLORICULTURE_____

AMERICAN FLORAL ENDOWMENT

VICTOR AND MARGARET BALL PROGRAM
see number 41

GOLF COURSE SUPERINTENDENTS ASSOCIATION OF AMERICA

GCSAA SCHOLARS COMPETITION
• 136

For outstanding students planning careers in golf course management. Must be full-time college undergraduates currently enrolled in a two-year or more accredited program related to golf course management and have completed one year of program. Must be member of GCSAA.

Academic/Career Areas Horticulture/Floriculture.
Award Scholarship for use in sophomore, junior, or senior years; not renewable. *Number:* up to 17. *Amount:* $500–$3500.
Eligibility Requirements: Applicant must be enrolled full-time at a two-year or four-year institution or university and member of Golf Course Superintendents Association of America. Available to U.S. and non-U.S. citizens.
Application Requirements Application, essay, references, transcript. *Deadline:* June 1.
World Wide Web: http://www.gcsaa.org
Contact: Pam Smith, Scholarship Coordinator
Golf Course Superintendents Association of America
1421 Research Park Drive
Lawrence, KS 66049-3859
Phone: 800-472-7878 Ext. 678
Fax: 785-832-3673
E-mail: psmith@gcsaa.org

JOSEPH SHINODA MEMORIAL SCHOLARSHIP FOUNDATION

JOSEPH SHINODA MEMORIAL SCHOLARSHIP
• 137

One-time award for undergraduates in accredited colleges and universities. Must be furthering their education in the field of floriculture (production, distribution, research, or retail). Must be U.S. citizen. Deadline is May 30.

Joseph Shinoda Memorial Scholarship (continued)

Academic/Career Areas Horticulture/Floriculture.

Award Scholarship for use in sophomore, junior, or senior years; not renewable. *Number:* 10–20. *Amount:* $250–$3000.

Eligibility Requirements: Applicant must be enrolled full-time at a four-year institution or university. Available to U.S. citizens.

Application Requirements Application, essay, financial need analysis, references, transcript. *Deadline:* May 30.

World Wide Web: http://www.shinodascholarship.org

Contact: Virginia Walter, Professor, Horticulture and Crop Science
      Department
      Joseph Shinoda Memorial Scholarship Foundation
      234 Via La Paz
      San Luis Obispo, CA 93407
      E-mail: vwalter@calpoly.edu

UNITED AGRIBUSINESS LEAGUE

UNITED AGRIBUSINESS LEAGUE SCHOLARSHIP PROGRAM

see number 5

HOSPITALITY MANAGEMENT

ILLINOIS RESTAURANT ASSOCIATION EDUCATIONAL FOUNDATION

ILLINOIS RESTAURANT ASSOCIATION EDUCATIONAL FOUNDATION SCHOLARSHIPS

see number 117

KENTUCKY RESTAURANT ASSOCIATION EDUCATIONAL FOUNDATION

KENTUCKY RESTAURANT ASSOCIATION EDUCATIONAL FOUNDATION SCHOLARSHIP

see number 114

HUMANITIES

BUSINESS AND PROFESSIONAL WOMEN'S FOUNDATION

BPW CAREER ADVANCEMENT SCHOLARSHIP PROGRAM FOR WOMEN

see number 37

FOUNDATION FOR THE ADVANCEMENT OF MESOAMERICAN STUDIES, INC.

FAMSI 2002 ANNUAL GRANT COMPETITION　　　see number 14

IRISH-AMERICAN CULTURAL INSTITUTE

IRISH RESEARCH FUNDS　　　see number 24

JOHN F. KENNEDY LIBRARY FOUNDATION

KENNEDY RESEARCH GRANTS　　　see number 19

MARYLAND STATE HIGHER EDUCATION COMMISSION

HOPE SCHOLARSHIP　　　see number 6

INTERIOR DESIGN_____

NATIONAL ASSOCIATION OF WOMEN IN CONSTRUCTION

NAWIC UNDERGRADUATE SCHOLARSHIPS　　　see number 20

NEW YORK STATE EDUCATION DEPARTMENT

REGENTS PROFESSIONAL OPPORTUNITY SCHOLARSHIP PROGRAM—NEW YORK　　　see number 21

WORLDSTUDIO FOUNDATION

WORLDSTUDIO FOUNDATION SCHOLARSHIP PROGRAM
see number 23

INTERNATIONAL MIGRATION_____

HUGH FULTON BYAS MEMORIAL FUNDS, INC.

HUGH FULTON BYAS MEMORIAL GRANT　　　see number 134

JOURNALISM_____

CALIFORNIA CHICANO NEWS MEDIA ASSOCIATION (CCNMA)

JOEL GARCIA MEMORIAL SCHOLARSHIP   see number 65

CUBAN AMERICAN NATIONAL FOUNDATION

MAS FAMILY SCHOLARSHIPS   see number 44

HUGH FULTON BYAS MEMORIAL FUNDS, INC.

HUGH FULTON BYAS MEMORIAL GRANT   see number 134

KNIGHT RIDDER

KNIGHT RIDDER MINORITY SCHOLARSHIP PROGRAM   see number 48

LOS ANGELES TIMES

LOS ANGELES TIMES SCHOLARSHIP PROGRAM   see number 67

UNITED NEGRO COLLEGE FUND

COCA COLA CORPORATE SCHOLARSHIP/INTERN PROGRAM
                    see number 58

LANDSCAPE ARCHITECTURE_____

NATIONAL ASSOCIATION OF WOMEN IN CONSTRUCTION

NAWIC UNDERGRADUATE SCHOLARSHIPS   see number 20

NEW YORK STATE EDUCATION DEPARTMENT

REGENTS PROFESSIONAL OPPORTUNITY SCHOLARSHIP PROGRAM—NEW YORK
see number 21

REAL ESTATE AND LAND USE INSTITUTE

CALIFORNIA STATE UNIVERSITY REAL ESTATE SCHOLARSHIP AND INTERNSHIP GRANT PROGRAM
see number 22

UNITED AGRIBUSINESS LEAGUE

UNITED AGRIBUSINESS LEAGUE SCHOLARSHIP PROGRAM
see number 5

LAW ENFORCEMENT/POLICE ADMINISTRATION_____

ARKANSAS POLICE CORPS PROGRAM

ARKANSAS POLICE CORPS SCHOLARSHIP • 138
Federal funded programs which recruits and offers educational assistance to individual who wish to pursue a career in law enforcement.

Academic/Career Areas Law Enforcement/Police Administration.
Award Scholarship for use in sophomore, junior, senior, or graduate years; renewable. *Number:* 15. *Amount:* $7500.
Eligibility Requirements: Applicant must be enrolled full-time at a four-year institution or university. Available to U.S. citizens.
Application Requirements Application, autobiography, driver's license, essay, interview, photo, resume, references, test scores, transcript.
World Wide Web: http://www.ualr.edu/~cjdept/polcorps.html
Contact: Candis Wheat, Assistant Director
Arkansas Police Corps Program
Criminal Justice Department, University of Arkansas at Little Rock
2801 South University Avenue
Little Rock, AR 72204-1099
Phone: 501-569-3195
Fax: 501-569-3075
E-mail: caloveless@ualr.edu

LAW/LEGAL SERVICES_____

BUSINESS AND PROFESSIONAL WOMEN'S FOUNDATION

BPW CAREER ADVANCEMENT SCHOLARSHIP PROGRAM FOR WOMEN
see number 37

FLORIDA EDUCATION FUND

FLORIDA MINORITY PARTICIPATION IN LEGAL EDUCATION (MPLE) SCHOLARSHIP PROGRAM
• 139

Renewable award to a member of an historically disadvantaged minority group that is underrepresented in the membership of the Florida Bar. Must be a Florida resident and attend a pre-law program at an accredited four-year college or university in the state of Florida. Must be a U.S. citizen. Visit website for additional information.

Academic/Career Areas Law/Legal Services.
Award Scholarship for use in freshman, sophomore, junior, or senior years; renewable. *Number:* 34. *Amount:* up to $7500.
Eligibility Requirements: Applicant must be Native American or Eskimo, Asian, African American, or Hispanic; enrolled full-time at a four-year institution or university; resident of Florida and studying in Florida. Available to U.S. citizens.
Application Requirements Application, essay, financial need analysis, references, test scores, transcript. *Deadline:* April 30.
World Wide Web: http://www.mpleonline.org
Contact: Lyra Logan, Vice President
Florida Education Fund
15485 Eagle Nest Lane, Suite 200
Miami Lakes, FL 33014
Phone: 305-364-3111
Fax: 305-364-3128
E-mail: mplemail@aol.com

MARYLAND STATE HIGHER EDUCATION COMMISSION

JANET L. HOFFMANN LOAN ASSISTANCE REPAYMENT PROGRAM
see number 89

PROFESSIONAL SCHOLARSHIP PROGRAM-MARYLAND
see number 70

NEW YORK STATE EDUCATION DEPARTMENT

REGENTS PROFESSIONAL OPPORTUNITY SCHOLARSHIP PROGRAM—NEW YORK
see number 21

LIBRARY SCIENCES_____

ALA-ALSC ASSOCIATION FOR LIBRARY SERVICE TO CHILDREN

ECONO-CLAD LITERATURE PROGRAM AWARD • 140
One-time award to honor a member of the ALSC who has developed an outstanding reading or literature program for children. Award provides expenses to attend the ALA Annual Conference.

Academic/Career Areas Library Sciences.
Award Prize for use in any year; not renewable. *Number:* 1–1000. *Amount:* $1000.
Eligibility Requirements: Applicant must be member of American Library Association and have employment experience in designated career field. Available to U.S. and Canadian citizens.
Application Requirements Application. *Deadline:* December 31.
World Wide Web: http://www.ala.org/alsc./scholars.html
Contact: ALSC Awards Program
ALA-ALSC Association For Library Service to Children
50 East Huron Street
Chicago, IL 60611
Phone: 800-545-2433 Ext. 2163
E-mail: alsc@ala.org

JOHN F. KENNEDY LIBRARY FOUNDATION

KENNEDY RESEARCH GRANTS
see number 19

LITERATURE/ENGLISH/WRITING_____

ALLIANCE FOR YOUNG ARTISTS AND WRITERS, INC.

SCHOLASTIC ART AND WRITING AWARDS-ART SECTION
see number 25

SCHOLASTIC ART AND WRITING AWARDS-WRITING SECTION SCHOLARSHIP
see number 26

INTERNATIONAL READING ASSOCIATION

INTERNATIONAL READING ASSOCIATION ELVA KNIGHT RESEARCH GRANT
• 141

One award annually to researcher outside the United States and/or Canada, one to teacher-initiated research project, and up to five additional grants. To assist researcher in reading and literacy project. Must be member of International Reading Association. One-time award of up to $10,000. Contact to obtain application procedures. Application deadline: January 15.

Academic/Career Areas Literature/English/Writing.
Award Grant for use in any year; not renewable. *Number:* 1–7. *Amount:* up to $10,000.
Eligibility Requirements: Applicant must be member of International Reading Association.
Application Requirements Application. *Deadline:* January 15.
World Wide Web: http://www.reading.org
Contact: Marcella Moore, Senior Secretary
International Reading Association
800 Barksdale Road, PO Box 8139
Newark, DE 19714-8139
Phone: 302-731-1600 Ext. 423
Fax: 302-731-1057
E-mail: research@reading.org

JOHN F. KENNEDY LIBRARY FOUNDATION

KENNEDY RESEARCH GRANTS
see number 19

MARYLAND STATE HIGHER EDUCATION COMMISSION

HOPE SCHOLARSHIP
see number 6

MATERIALS SCIENCE, ENGINEERING AND METALLURGY_____

AMERICAN CHEMICAL SOCIETY

AMERICAN CHEMICAL SOCIETY SCHOLARS PROGRAM
see number 59

AMERICAN INSTITUTE OF AERONAUTICS AND ASTRONAUTICS

AIAA UNDERGRADUATE SCHOLARSHIP
see number 9

AMERICAN SOCIETY OF NAVAL ENGINEERS

AMERICAN SOCIETY OF NAVAL ENGINEERS SCHOLARSHIP
see number 10

ASTRONAUT SCHOLARSHIP FOUNDATION

ASTRONAUT SCHOLARSHIP FOUNDATION
see number 11

BARRY M. GOLDWATER SCHOLARSHIP AND EXCELLENCE IN EDUCATION FOUNDATION

BARRY M. GOLDWATER SCHOLARSHIP AND EXCELLENCE IN EDUCATION PROGRAM
see number 12

INTERNATIONAL SOCIETY FOR OPTICAL ENGINEERING-SPIE

SPIE EDUCATIONAL SCHOLARSHIPS IN OPTICAL SCIENCE AND ENGINEERING
see number 13

NAMEPA NATIONAL SCHOLARSHIP FOUNDATION

NATIONAL ASSOCIATION OF MINORITY ENGINEERING PROGRAM ADMINISTRATORS NATIONAL SCHOLARSHIP FUND
see number 29

PLASTICS INSTITUTE OF AMERICA

PLASTICS PIONEERS SCHOLARSHIPS
see number 105

SOCIETY OF AUTOMOTIVE ENGINEERS

SAE ENGINEERING SCHOLARSHIPS
see number 32

SOCIETY OF PLASTICS ENGINEERS (SPE) FOUNDATION

SOCIETY OF PLASTICS ENGINEERS SCHOLARSHIP PROGRAM

see number 56

USENIX ASSOCIATION

USENIX STUDENT PROGRAMS

see number 61

MECHANICAL ENGINEERING_____

AACE INTERNATIONAL

AACE INTERNATIONAL COMPETITIVE SCHOLARSHIP   see number 15

AMERICAN INSTITUTE OF AERONAUTICS AND ASTRONAUTICS

AIAA UNDERGRADUATE SCHOLARSHIP   see number 9

AMERICAN SOCIETY OF NAVAL ENGINEERS

AMERICAN SOCIETY OF NAVAL ENGINEERS SCHOLARSHIP

see number 10

ASTRONAUT SCHOLARSHIP FOUNDATION

ASTRONAUT SCHOLARSHIP FOUNDATION   see number 11

BARRY M. GOLDWATER SCHOLARSHIP AND EXCELLENCE IN EDUCATION FOUNDATION

BARRY M. GOLDWATER SCHOLARSHIP AND EXCELLENCE IN EDUCATION PROGRAM   see number 12

CONSULTING ENGINEERS AND LAND SURVEYORS OF CALIFORNIA SCHOLARSHIP PROGRAM

CONSULTING ENGINEERS AND LAND SURVEYORS OF CALIFORNIA SCHOLARSHIP AWARD   see number 60

CUBAN AMERICAN NATIONAL FOUNDATION

MAS FAMILY SCHOLARSHIPS   see number 44

HISPANIC COLLEGE FUND, INC.

HISPANIC COLLEGE FUND SCHOLARSHIP PROGRAM   see number 3

THE HISPANIC COLLEGE FUND/INROADS/SPRINT SCHOLARSHIP PROGRAM   see number 4

INTERNATIONAL SOCIETY FOR OPTICAL ENGINEERING-SPIE

SPIE EDUCATIONAL SCHOLARSHIPS IN OPTICAL SCIENCE AND ENGINEERING   see number 13

NAMEPA NATIONAL SCHOLARSHIP FOUNDATION

NATIONAL ASSOCIATION OF MINORITY ENGINEERING PROGRAM ADMINISTRATORS NATIONAL SCHOLARSHIP FUND   see number 29

NATIONAL ASSOCIATION OF WOMEN IN CONSTRUCTION

NAWIC UNDERGRADUATE SCHOLARSHIPS   see number 20

SOCIETY OF AUTOMOTIVE ENGINEERS

SAE ENGINEERING SCHOLARSHIPS   see number 32

SOCIETY OF PLASTICS ENGINEERS (SPE) FOUNDATION

SOCIETY OF PLASTICS ENGINEERS SCHOLARSHIP PROGRAM   see number 56

USENIX ASSOCIATION

USENIX STUDENT PROGRAMS   see number 61

METEOROLOGY/ATMOSPHERIC SCIENCE_____

ASTRONAUT SCHOLARSHIP FOUNDATION

ASTRONAUT SCHOLARSHIP FOUNDATION   see number 11

NASA NEVADA SPACE GRANT CONSORTIUM

UNIVERSITY AND COMMUNITY COLLEGE SYSTEM OF NEVADA
NASA SPACE GRANT AND FELLOWSHIP PROGRAM   see number 31

MUSEUM STUDIES_____

FOUNDATION FOR THE ADVANCEMENT OF MESOAMERICAN STUDIES, INC.

FAMSI 2002 ANNUAL GRANT COMPETITION   see number 14

NATURAL RESOURCES_____

APICS-EDUCATIONAL AND RESEARCH FOUNDATION, INC.

DONALD W. FOGARTY INTERNATIONAL STUDENT PAPER
COMPETITION   see number 42

BAT CONSERVATION INTERNATIONAL

BAT CONSERVATION INTERNATIONAL STUDENT SCHOLARSHIP
PROGRAM   see number 36

LOUISIANA OFFICE OF STUDENT FINANCIAL ASSISTANCE

ROCKEFELLER STATE WILDLIFE SCHOLARSHIP   see number 8

MARYLAND STATE HIGHER EDUCATION COMMISSION

HOPE SCHOLARSHIP
see number 6

NATIONAL FISH AND WILDLIFE FOUNDATION

BUDWEISER CONSERVATION SCHOLARSHIP PROGRAM • 142

The Budweiser Conservation Scholarship Program supports and promotes innovative research or study that seeks to respond to today's most pressing conservation issues. This competitive scholarship program is designed to respond to many of the most significant challenges in fish, wildlife, and plant conservation in the United States by providing scholarships to eligible graduate and undergraduate students who are poised to make a significant contribution to the field of conservation.

Academic/Career Areas Natural Resources.
Award Scholarship for use in sophomore, junior, or graduate years; not renewable. *Number:* 20. *Amount:* $10,000.
Eligibility Requirements: Applicant must be enrolled full-time at a four-year institution or university. Available to U.S. citizens.
Application Requirements Application, essay, references, transcript, title of proposed research and a short abstract. *Deadline:* January 18.
World Wide Web: http://www.nfwf.org
Contact: Tom Kelsch, Director, Conservation Education
National Fish and Wildlife Foundation
1120 Connecticut Avenue, NW
Suite 900
Washington, DC 20036
Phone: 202-857-0166
Fax: 202-857-0162
E-mail: tom.kelsch@nfwf.org

UNITED STATES ENVIRONMENTAL PROTECTION AGENCY

NATIONAL NETWORK FOR ENVIRONMENTAL MANAGEMENT STUDIES FELLOWSHIP • 143

The NNEMS Fellowship Program is designed to provide undergraduate and graduate students with research opportunities at one of EPA's facilities nationwide. EPA awards approximately 80-90 NNEMS fellowships per year. Selected students receive a stipend for performing their research project. EPA develops an annual catalog of research projects available for student application. The application deadline is generally between January-February each year. Submit a complete application package as described in the annual catalog. Minimum 3.0 GPA required.

National Network for Environmental Management Studies Fellowship (continued)
Academic/Career Areas Natural Resources.
Award Grant for use in any year; not renewable. *Number:* 80–90. *Amount:* $5564–$9600.
Eligibility Requirements: Applicant must be enrolled full or part-time at a two-year or four-year institution or university. Applicant must have 3.0 GPA or higher. Available to U.S. citizens.
Application Requirements Application, applicant must enter a contest, resume, references, transcript, application package.
World Wide Web: http://www.epa.gov/enviroed/students.html
Contact: Sheri Jojokian, Environmental Education Specialist
United States Environmental Protection Agency
Office of Environmental Education, 1200 Pennsylvania Avenue,
NW (1704A)
Washington, DC 20460
Phone: 202-564-0452
Fax: 202-564-2754
E-mail: jojokian.sheri@epa.gov

NATURAL SCIENCES_____

AMERICAN CHEMICAL SOCIETY

AMERICAN CHEMICAL SOCIETY SCHOLARS PROGRAM
see number 59

AMERICAN ORNITHOLOGISTS' UNION

AMERICAN ORNITHOLOGISTS' UNION RESEARCH AWARDS
see number 7

BARRY M. GOLDWATER SCHOLARSHIP AND EXCELLENCE IN EDUCATION FOUNDATION

BARRY M. GOLDWATER SCHOLARSHIP AND EXCELLENCE IN EDUCATION PROGRAM
see number 12

BAT CONSERVATION INTERNATIONAL

BAT CONSERVATION INTERNATIONAL STUDENT SCHOLARSHIP PROGRAM
see number 36

NUCLEAR SCIENCE_____

AMERICAN SOCIETY OF NAVAL ENGINEERS

AMERICAN SOCIETY OF NAVAL ENGINEERS SCHOLARSHIP
see number 10

BARRY M. GOLDWATER SCHOLARSHIP AND EXCELLENCE IN EDUCATION FOUNDATION

BARRY M. GOLDWATER SCHOLARSHIP AND EXCELLENCE IN EDUCATION PROGRAM
see number 12

NATIONAL ACADEMY FOR NUCLEAR TRAINING

NATIONAL ACADEMY FOR NUCLEAR TRAINING UNDERGRADUATE SCHOLARSHIP
• 144

Scholarships are available to students at U.S. colleges and universities majoring in nuclear, mechanical and electrical engineering, power-generation health physics, and chemical engineering with a nuclear or power option. Eligible applicants will be U.S. citizens, rising sophomores, juniors and seniors with a minimum GPA of 3.0. For more information visit http://www.nei.org.

Academic/Career Areas Nuclear Science.
Award Scholarship for use in sophomore, junior, or senior years; renewable. *Number:* 150. *Amount:* $2500.
Eligibility Requirements: Applicant must be enrolled full-time at a four-year institution or university. Applicant must have 3.0 GPA or higher. Available to U.S. citizens.
Application Requirements Application, transcript. *Deadline:* February 1.
World Wide Web: http://www.nei.org
Contact: National Academy for Nuclear Training
Attn: Educational Assistance Program
700 Galleria Parkway, NW, Suite 100
Atlanta, GA 30339-5957

NURSING_____

ALBERTA HERITAGE SCHOLARSHIP FUND

ALBERTA HERITAGE SCHOLARSHIP FUND ABORIGINAL HEALTH CAREERS BURSARY
see number 33

ALICE M. YARNOLD AND SAMUEL YARNOLD SCHOLARSHIP TRUST

ALICE M. AND SAMUEL YARNOLD SCHOLARSHIP   see number 125

AMERICAN ASSOCIATION OF CRITICAL-CARE NURSES (AACN)

AACN EDUCATIONAL ADVANCEMENT SCHOLARSHIPS-BSN COMPLETION • 145

One-time award for juniors and seniors currently enrolled in an NLN or CCNE accredited nursing program. Must be AACN member with active RN license who is currently or has recently worked in critical care. Must have 3.0 GPA. Supports RN members completing a baccalaureate degree in nursing.

Academic/Career Areas Nursing.
Award Scholarship for use in junior or senior years; not renewable. *Number:* 50–100. *Amount:* $1500.
Eligibility Requirements: Applicant must be enrolled full or part-time at a four-year institution or university; member of American Association of Critical Care Nurses and have employment experience in designated career field. Applicant must have 3.0 GPA or higher. Available to U.S. citizens.
Application Requirements Application, essay, references, transcript. *Deadline:* April 1.
World Wide Web: http://www.aacn.org
Contact: American Association of Critical-Care Nurses (AACN)
101 Columbia
Aliso Viejo, CA 92656
Phone: 800-899-2226

AMERICAN LEGION, EIGHT AND FORTY

EIGHT & FORTY LUNG AND RESPIRATORY DISEASE NURSING SCHOLARSHIP FUND • 146

Available to registered nurses with work experience who are taking courses leading to full-time employment in lung or respiratory disease nursing and teaching. Candidates should have proven leadership qualities in emergency situations.

Academic/Career Areas Nursing.
Award Scholarship for use in junior, senior, or graduate years; not renewable. *Number:* 20–25. *Amount:* up to $3000.
Eligibility Requirements: Applicant must be enrolled full or part-time at a four-year institution or university; have employment experience in designated career field and must have an interest in leadership. Available to U.S. citizens.
Application Requirements Application, references, transcript. *Deadline:* May 15.

World Wide Web: http://www.legion.org
Contact: Program Administrator
American Legion, Eight and Forty
PO Box 1055
Indianapolis, IN 46206-1055

DELAWARE HIGHER EDUCATION COMMISSION

DELAWARE NURSING INCENTIVE SCHOLARSHIP LOAN • 147

Award for Delaware residents pursuing a nursing career. Must be repaid with nursing practice at a Delaware state-owned hospital. Based on academic merit. Must have minimum 2.5 GPA. Renewable for up to four years.

Academic/Career Areas Nursing.
Award Forgivable loan for use in freshman, sophomore, junior, or senior years; renewable. *Number:* 1–40. *Amount:* $1000–$5000.
Eligibility Requirements: Applicant must be enrolled full-time at a two-year or four-year institution or university and resident of Delaware. Applicant must have 2.5 GPA or higher. Available to U.S. citizens.
Application Requirements Application, essay, test scores, transcript. *Deadline:* March 31.
World Wide Web: http://www.doe.state.de.us/high-ed
Contact: Maureen Laffey, Associate Director
Delaware Higher Education Commission
820 North French Street
Wilmington, DE 19801
Phone: 302-577-3240
Fax: 302-577-6765
E-mail: dhec@state.de.us

FLORIDA DEPARTMENT OF HEALTH

NURSING SCHOLARSHIP PROGRAM • 148

Provides financial assistance for full- or part-time nursing students enrolled in an approved nursing program in Florida. Must be a Florida resident in graduate school or an undergraduate in junior or senior year.

Academic/Career Areas Nursing.
Award Scholarship for use in junior, senior, or graduate years; renewable. *Number:* 15–30. *Amount:* $4000–$6000.
Eligibility Requirements: Applicant must be enrolled full or part-time at a four-year institution or university; resident of Florida and studying in Florida. Available to U.S. and non-U.S. citizens.
Application Requirements Application.

Nursing Scholarship Program (continued)
Contact: Florida Department of Health
Division of EMS and Community Health Resources
4052 Bald Cypress Way, Mail Bin C-15
Tallahassee, FL 32399-1735

FOUNDATION OF THE NATIONAL STUDENT NURSES' ASSOCIATION

FOUNDATION OF THE NATIONAL STUDENT NURSES' ASSOCIATION SCHOLARSHIPS • 149

One-time award for National Student Nurses' Association members and nonmembers enrolled in nursing programs leading to RN license. Based on need, academic ability, and health-related nursing school or community involvement. Send self-addressed stamped envelope with two stamps for application. Graduating high school seniors are not eligible.

Academic/Career Areas Nursing.
Award Scholarship for use in freshman, sophomore, junior, or senior years; not renewable. *Number:* 40–50. *Amount:* $1000–$2000.
Eligibility Requirements: Applicant must be enrolled at a two-year or four-year institution. Available to U.S. citizens.
Application Requirements Application, financial need analysis, self-addressed stamped envelope, transcript. *Deadline:* February 1.
World Wide Web: http://www.nsna.org
Contact: Scholarship Chairperson
Foundation of the National Student Nurses' Association
555 West 57th Street, Suite 1327
New York, NY 10019
Phone: 212-581-2215
Fax: 212-581-2368
E-mail: nsna@nsna.org

HAVANA NATIONAL BANK, TRUSTEE

MCFARLAND CHARITABLE NURSING SCHOLARSHIP • 150

For registered nursing students only. Must sign contract obliging student to work in Havana, Illinois for two years for each year of funding or repay award with interest and liquidated damages. Submit test scores, essay, transcripts, references, financial need analysis, and autobiography with application. Preference given to local residents. GPA is an important consideration in selection. Application fee is $5.

Academic/Career Areas Nursing.
Award Forgivable loan for use in any year; renewable. *Number:* 3–5. *Amount:* $1000–$15,000.
Eligibility Requirements: Applicant must be enrolled full-time at an institution or university. Available to U.S. and non-U.S. citizens.

Application Requirements Application, autobiography, essay, financial need analysis, interview, photo, references, test scores, transcript. *Fee:* $5. *Deadline:* May 1.

World Wide Web: http://www.havanabank.com

Contact: Larry Thomson, Vice President and Senior Trust Officer
Havana National Bank, Trustee
PO Box 200
Havana, IL 62644
Phone: 309-543-3361
Fax: 309-543-3441

HEALTH PROFESSIONS EDUCATION FOUNDATION

ASSOCIATE DEGREE NURSING PILOT SCHOLARSHIP PROGRAM
• 151

One-time award to nursing students accepted to or enrolled in associate degree nursing programs and who agree to obtain a B.S.N. at a nursing program in California within five years of obtaining an A.D.N. Eligible applicants may receive up to $4,000 per year in financial assistance. Deadlines: March 27 and September 11. Must be a resident of California.

Academic/Career Areas Nursing.

Award Scholarship for use in any year; not renewable. *Number:* 30. *Amount:* $4000.

Eligibility Requirements: Applicant must be enrolled full or part-time at a two-year or technical institution or university; resident of California and studying in California. Applicant must have 2.5 GPA or higher. Available to U.S. citizens.

Application Requirements Application, driver's license, financial need analysis, references, transcript.

World Wide Web: http://www.healthprofessions.ca.gov

Contact: Lisa Montgomery, Program Director
Health Professions Education Foundation
1600 Ninth Street, Suite 436
Sacramento, CA 95814
Phone: 800-773-1669
Fax: 916-653-1438
E-mail: lmontgom@oshpd.state.ca.us

HEALTH PROFESSIONS EDUCATION SCHOLARSHIP PROGRAM

see number 69

REGISTERED NURSE EDUCATION LOAN REPAYMENT PROGRAM
• 152

Repays governmental and commercial loans that were obtained for tuition expenses, books, equipment and reasonable living expenses associated with

Registered Nurse Education Loan Repayment Program (continued)

attending college. In return for the repayment of educational debt, loan repayment recipients are required to practice full-time in direct patient care in a medically underserved area or county health facility. Eligible applicants may receive up to $19,000 for repayment of educational debt. Deadlines: March 27 and September 11. Must be resident of CA and U.S. citizen.

Academic/Career Areas Nursing.

Award Grant for use in any year; not renewable. *Number:* 50–70. *Amount:* $4000–$8000.

Eligibility Requirements: Applicant must be enrolled full or part-time at an institution or university and resident of California. Available to U.S. citizens.

Application Requirements Application, driver's license, financial need analysis, references, transcript.

World Wide Web: http://www.healthprofessions.ca.gov

Contact: Lisa Montgomery, Program Director
Health Professions Education Foundation
1600 Ninth Street, Suite 436
Sacramento, CA 95814
Phone: 800-773-1669
Fax: 916-653-1438
E-mail: lmontgom@oshpd.state.ca.us

RN EDUCATION SCHOLARSHIP PROGRAM   • 153

One-time award to nursing students accepted to or enrolled in baccalaureate degree nursing programs in California. Eligible applicants may receive up to $8,000 per year in financial assistance. Deadlines: March 27 and September 11. Must be resident of California and a U.S. citizen.

Academic/Career Areas Nursing.

Award Scholarship for use in any year; not renewable. *Number:* 50–70. *Amount:* $6000–$8000.

Eligibility Requirements: Applicant must be enrolled full or part-time at a four-year or technical institution or university; resident of California and studying in California. Applicant must have 2.5 GPA or higher. Available to U.S. citizens.

Application Requirements Application, driver's license, financial need analysis, references, transcript.

World Wide Web: http://www.healthprofessions.ca.gov

Contact: Lisa Montgomery, Program Director
Health Professions Education Foundation
1600 Ninth Street, Suite 436
Sacramento, CA 95814
Phone: 800-773-1669
Fax: 916-653-1438
E-mail: lmontgom@oshpd.state.ca.us

YOUTH FOR ADOLESCENT PREGNANCY PREVENTION LEADERSHIP RECOGNITION PROGRAM   see number 128

J.D. ARCHBOLD MEMORIAL HOSPITAL

ARCHBOLD SCHOLARSHIP PROGRAM

see number 129

KANSAS BOARD OF REGENTS

KANSAS NURSING SERVICE SCHOLARSHIP PROGRAM • 154

This program is designed to encourage Kansans to enroll in nursing programs and commit to practicing in Kansas. Recipients sign agreements to practice nursing at specific facilities one year for each year of support. Application fee is $10. Deadline: May 15.

Academic/Career Areas Nursing.
Award Forgivable loan for use in junior or senior years; renewable. *Number:* 100–200. *Amount:* $2500–$3500.
Eligibility Requirements: Applicant must be enrolled full-time at a two-year or four-year institution or university; resident of Kansas and studying in Kansas. Available to U.S. citizens.
Application Requirements Application, financial need analysis, sponsor agreement form. *Fee:* $10. *Deadline:* May 15.
World Wide Web: http://www.kansasregents.com
Contact: Diane Lindeman, Director of Student Financial Assistance
Kansas Board of Regents
1000 Southwest Jackson, Suite 520
Topeka, KS 66612-1368
Phone: 785-296-3517
Fax: 785-296-0983
E-mail: dlindeman@ksbor.org

MARYLAND STATE HIGHER EDUCATION COMMISSION

DEVELOPMENTAL DISABILITIES TUITION ASSISTANCE PROGRAM

see number 130

JANET L. HOFFMANN LOAN ASSISTANCE REPAYMENT PROGRAM

see number 89

MARYLAND STATE NURSING SCHOLARSHIP AND LIVING EXPENSES GRANT • 155

Renewable grant for Maryland residents enrolled in a two-or four-year Maryland institution nursing degree program. Recipients must agree to serve as a full-time nurse in a Maryland shortage area and must maintain a 3.0 GPA in college. Application deadline is June 30. Submit Free Application for Federal Student Aid.

Academic/Career Areas Nursing.

Maryland State Nursing Scholarship and Living Expenses Grant (continued)

Award Forgivable loan for use in freshman, sophomore, junior, senior, or graduate years; renewable. *Number:* 186–600. *Amount:* $200–$4800.

Eligibility Requirements: Applicant must be enrolled full or part-time at a two-year or four-year institution or university; resident of Maryland and studying in Maryland. Applicant must have 3.0 GPA or higher. Available to U.S. citizens.

Application Requirements Application, financial need analysis, transcript. *Deadline:* June 30.

World Wide Web: http://www.mhec.state.md.us

Contact: Cis Whittington, Scholarship Administration
Maryland State Higher Education Commission
16 Francis Street
Annapolis, MD 21401-1781
Phone: 410-260-4546
Fax: 410-974-5994
E-mail: ssamail@mhec.state.md.us

PROFESSIONAL SCHOLARSHIP PROGRAM-MARYLAND

see number 70

MISSOURI DEPARTMENT OF HEALTH AND SENIOR SERVICES

MISSOURI PROFESSIONAL AND PRACTICAL NURSING STUDENT LOAN PROGRAM • 156

For Missouri residents attending institutions in Missouri. Forgivable loan for nursing student. Upon graduation, the student must work with a non-profit Health Service program or at a non-profit Health Service Public Agency in Missouri. Minimum 2.5 GPA required for applicants. Deadlines: 7/15 and 12/15.

Academic/Career Areas Nursing.

Award Forgivable loan for use in any year; not renewable. *Number:* up to 67. *Amount:* up to $5000.

Eligibility Requirements: Applicant must be enrolled full-time at a two-year or four-year or technical institution or university; resident of Missouri and studying in Missouri. Applicant must have 2.5 GPA or higher. Available to U.S. and non-U.S. citizens.

Application Requirements Application, driver's license.

Contact: Cindy Cox
Missouri Department of Health and Senior Services
PO Box 570
Jefferson City, MO 65102-0570
Phone: 573-751-6219
Fax: 572-522-8146
E-mail: coxc@dhss.state.mo.us

NEW HAMPSHIRE POSTSECONDARY EDUCATION COMMISSION

NEW HAMPSHIRE CAREER INCENTIVE PROGRAM   see number 120

NEW MEXICO COMMISSION ON HIGHER EDUCATION

ALLIED HEALTH STUDENT LOAN PROGRAM-NEW MEXICO
see number 72

NEW YORK STATE EDUCATION DEPARTMENT

REGENTS PROFESSIONAL OPPORTUNITY SCHOLARSHIP PROGRAM—NEW YORK   see number 21

NORTH CAROLINA STATE EDUCATION ASSISTANCE AUTHORITY

NURSE SCHOLARS PROGRAM—UNDERGRADUATE (NORTH CAROLINA)   • 157

Forgivable loans to residents of North Carolina who have gained full acceptance to a North Carolina institution of higher education that offers a nursing program. Must apply to the North Carolina State Education and Welfare division. Must serve as a registered nurse in North Carolina for one year for each year of funding. Minimum 3.0 GPA required.

Academic/Career Areas Nursing.

Award Forgivable loan for use in freshman, sophomore, junior, or senior years; renewable. *Number:* up to 450. *Amount:* $3000–$5000.

Eligibility Requirements: Applicant must be enrolled full-time at a two-year or four-year institution or university; resident of North Carolina and studying in North Carolina. Applicant must have 3.0 GPA or higher. Available to U.S. citizens.

Application Requirements Application, essay, references, test scores, transcript.

World Wide Web: http://www.cfnc.org

Contact: Christy Campbell, Manager-Health, Education and Welfare
North Carolina State Education Assistance Authority
PO Box 14223
Research Triangle, NC 27709-3663
Phone: 919-549-8614
Fax: 919-248-4687

NORTH DAKOTA BOARD OF NURSING

NORTH DAKOTA BOARD OF NURSING EDUCATION LOAN PROGRAM
• 158

One-time loan for North Dakota residents pursuing a nursing degree. Must sign repayment note agreeing to repay loan by nursing employment in North Dakota after graduation. Repayment rate is $1 per hour of employment. For juniors, seniors, and graduate students.

Academic/Career Areas Nursing.

Award Forgivable loan for use in junior, senior, or graduate years; not renewable. *Number:* 30–35. *Amount:* $2000–$5000.

Eligibility Requirements: Applicant must be enrolled full or part-time at a two-year or four-year institution or university and resident of North Dakota.

Application Requirements Application, financial need analysis, references, transcript. *Fee:* $15. *Deadline:* July 1.

World Wide Web: http://www.ndbon.org

Contact: Ms. Constance Kalanek, Executive Director
North Dakota Board of Nursing
919 South 7th Street, Suite 504
Bismarck, ND 58504-5881
Phone: 701-328-9777
Fax: 701-328-9785
E-mail: executivedir@nbdon.org

NORTHWEST COMMUNITY NURSING AND HEALTH SERVICE, INC.

ALBERT AND FLORENCE NEWTON NURSE SCHOLARSHIP NEWTON FUND
• 159

For schools in RI only. Must be a RI resident. Ascribes funds to: registered nurses seeking BS degree in nursing; senior nursing students in final year of education to become a registered nurse; registered nurses with BS degree seeking graduate degree; programs selected which are targeted to increase the availability of new registered nurses. Application deadline: April and October.

Academic/Career Areas Nursing.

Award Scholarship for use in senior, or graduate years; not renewable. *Number:* 5–20. *Amount:* $250–$2500.

Eligibility Requirements: Applicant must be enrolled full or part-time at a two-year or four-year institution or university; resident of Rhode Island and studying in Rhode Island. Available to U.S. and non-U.S. citizens.

Application Requirements Application, essay, financial need analysis.

World Wide Web: http://northwesthealthcare.org

Contact: Beverly McGuire, CEO
Northwest Community Nursing and Health Service, Inc.
PO Box 234
Harmony, RI 02829
Phone: 401-949-3801
Fax: 401-949-5115
E-mail: bmcguire@northwesthealthcare.org

ORDEAN FOUNDATION

ORDEAN LOAN PROGRAM see number 95

STATE OF GEORGIA

NORTHEAST GEORGIA PILOT NURSE SERVICE CANCELABLE LOAN • 160

Up to 100 forgivable loans between $2,500 and $4,500 will be awarded to undergraduate students who are residents of Georgia studying nursing at a four-year school in Georgia. Loans can be repaid by working as a nurse in northeast Georgia.

Academic/Career Areas Nursing.
Award Forgivable loan for use in freshman, sophomore, junior, or senior years; not renewable. *Number:* up to 100. *Amount:* $2500–$4500.
Eligibility Requirements: Applicant must be enrolled full or part-time at a four-year institution; resident of Georgia and studying in Georgia. Available to U.S. citizens.
Application Requirements Application, financial need analysis. *Deadline:* Continuous.
World Wide Web: http://www.gsfc.org
Contact: Peggy Matthews, Manager/GSFA Originations
State of Georgia
2082 East Exchange Place, Suite 230
Tucker, GA 30084-5305
Phone: 770-724-9230
Fax: 770-724-9263
E-mail: peggy@mail.gsfc.state.ga.us

SERVICE-CANCELLABLE STAFFORD LOAN-GEORGIA see number 73

STATE STUDENT ASSISTANCE COMMISSION OF INDIANA (SSACI)

INDIANA NURSING SCHOLARSHIP FUND • 161

Need-based tuition funding for nursing students enrolled full- or part-time at an eligible Indiana institution. Must be an Indiana resident and have a minimum

Indiana Nursing Scholarship Fund (continued)
2.0 GPA or meet the minimum requirements for the nursing program. Upon graduation, recipients must practice as a nurse in an Indiana health care setting for two years.

Academic/Career Areas Nursing.
Award Scholarship for use in any year; not renewable. *Number:* 510–595. *Amount:* $200–$5000.
Eligibility Requirements: Applicant must be enrolled full or part-time at a two-year or four-year institution or university; resident of Indiana and studying in Indiana. Available to U.S. citizens.
Application Requirements Application, financial need analysis. *Deadline:* Continuous.
World Wide Web: http://www.ssaci.in.gov
Contact: Ms. Yvonne Heflin, Director, Special Programs
State Student Assistance Commission of Indiana (SSACI)
150 West Market Street, Suite 500
Indianapolis, IN 46204-2805
Phone: 317-232-2350
Fax: 317-232-3260

PEACE AND CONFLICT STUDIES_____

HUGH FULTON BYAS MEMORIAL FUNDS, INC.

HUGH FULTON BYAS MEMORIAL GRANT   see number 134

PERFORMING ARTS_____

AMERICAN SOCIETY OF COMPOSERS, AUTHORS, AND PUBLISHERS FOUNDATION

AMERICAN SOCIETY OF COMPOSERS, AUTHORS, AND PUBLISHERS FOUNDATION MORTON GOULD YOUNG COMPOSER AWARDS   • 162
Cash grants for U.S. citizens or permanent residents or those with student visas, up to age 30 as of March 1. Applicants must be composers and must submit score, with or without tape or CD recording, for competition. Original music of any style will be considered. Works that have earned national prizes are ineligible, as are arrangements.

Academic/Career Areas Performing Arts.

Award Prize for use in any year; not renewable. *Number:* 20–25. *Amount:* $250–$3500.

Eligibility Requirements: Applicant must be age 30 or under and must have an interest in music/singing. Available to U.S. and Canadian citizens.

Application Requirements Application, applicant must enter a contest, autobiography, references, self-addressed stamped envelope. *Deadline:* March 1.

World Wide Web: http://www.ascap.com

Contact: Frances Richard, Vice President, Concert Music
American Society of Composers, Authors, and Publishers
  Foundation
One Lincoln Plaza
New York, NY 10023
Phone: 212-621-6327
Fax: 212-621-6504
E-mail: frichard@ascap.com

CLARICE SMITH PERFORMING ARTS CENTER

UNIVERSITY OF MARYLAND INTERNATIONAL LEONARD ROSE CELLO COMPETITION
• **163**

One-time prize earned through a competitive international music competition. Cello competition takes place every four years. Award for those ages 18 to 30. Application fee: $80. Submit audition tape. Contact center in order to find out when next competition will take place.

Academic/Career Areas Performing Arts.

Award Prize for use in any year; not renewable. *Number:* up to 12. *Amount:* $1000–$20,000.

Eligibility Requirements: Applicant must be age 18-30 and must have an interest in music/singing. Available to U.S. and non-U.S. citizens.

Application Requirements Application, applicant must enter a contest, autobiography, photo, portfolio, references. *Fee:* $80. *Deadline:* December 15.

World Wide Web: http://www.inform.umd.edu/smithcenter

Contact: George Moquin, Director, International Competitions
Clarice Smith Performing Arts Center
University of Maryland, Suite 3800, Clarice Smith Performing Arts
  Center
College Park, MO 20742-1625
Phone: 301-405-8174
Fax: 301-405-5977
E-mail: gmoquin@deans.umd.edu

UNIVERSITY OF MARYLAND INTERNATIONAL MARIAN ANDERSON VOCAL ARTS COMPETITION AND FESTIVAL • 164

One-time prize earned through a competitive international music competition. Voice competition takes place every four years. Next competition is May 22 to 31, 2003. Submit audiocassette audition tape. Award for those 21 through 39 years of age. $80 application fee.

Academic/Career Areas Performing Arts.

Award Prize for use in any year; not renewable. *Number:* up to 12. *Amount:* $1000–$20,000.

Eligibility Requirements: Applicant must be age 21-39 and must have an interest in music/singing. Available to U.S. and non-U.S. citizens.

Application Requirements Application, applicant must enter a contest, autobiography, photo, portfolio, references. *Fee:* $80. *Deadline:* December 13.

World Wide Web: http://www.inform.umd.edu/smithcenter

Contact: George Moquin, Director, International Competitions
Clarice Smith Performing Arts Center
University of Maryland, Suite 3800, Clarice Smith Performing Arts Center
College Park, MD 20742-1625
Phone: 301-405-8174
Fax: 301-405-5977
E-mail: gmoquin@deans.umd.edu

UNIVERSITY OF MARYLAND INTERNATIONAL WILLIAM KAPELL PIANO COMPETITION • 165

One-time prize earned through a competitive international music competition June 1. Submit audiocassette audition. For those ages 18-33. $80 application fee. Contact center in order to find out when next competition will take place.

Academic/Career Areas Performing Arts.

Award Prize for use in any year; not renewable. *Number:* up to 12. *Amount:* $1000–$25,000.

Eligibility Requirements: Applicant must be age 18-33 and must have an interest in music/singing. Available to U.S. and non-U.S. citizens.

Application Requirements Application, applicant must enter a contest, autobiography, photo, portfolio, references. *Fee:* $80. *Deadline:* December 14.

World Wide Web: http://www.inform.umd.edu/smithcenter

Contact: George Moquin, Director, International Competitions
Clarice Smith Performing Arts Center
University of Maryland, Suite 3800, Clarice Smith Performing Arts
Center
College Park, MD 20742-1625
Phone: 301-405-8174
Fax: 301-405-5977
E-mail: gmoquin@deans.umd.edu

DONNA REED FOUNDATION FOR THE PERFORMING ARTS

DONNA REED PERFORMING ARTS SCHOLARSHIPS • 166

Award to recognize, encourage, and support individuals who demonstrate excellence and a high level of interest in the performing arts. Must be a graduating high school senior. Applications are accepted in acting, dance, vocal, instrumental, and musical theater. To remain eligible for the four-year scholarship, you must be attending an accredited postsecondary or approved program of study. Finalists must compete at the Donna Reed Festival in Iowa during the third full-week of June.

Academic/Career Areas Performing Arts.
Award Scholarship for use in any year; not renewable. *Number:* 15. *Amount:* $500–$4000.
Eligibility Requirements: Applicant must be high school student and planning to enroll full-time at a two-year or four-year or technical institution or university. Available to U.S. citizens.
Application Requirements Application, applicant must enter a contest, video/audio tape, CD. *Fee:* $35. *Deadline:* April 1.
World Wide Web: http://www.donnareed.org
Contact: Donna Reed Foundation for the Performing Arts
1305 Broadway
Denison, IA 51442

GINA BACHAUER INTERNATIONAL PIANO FOUNDATION

GINA BACHAUER INTERNATIONAL ARTISTS PIANO COMPETITION AWARD • 167

Piano competition sponsored every four years (next in 2002). Includes solo, chamber music, and orchestral performances. Prizes of over $100,000 include cash awards, concerts, CD recording, and residency in various countries. Submit birth certificate copy, passport copy, tapes of last two year's programs, and audition tape. May also audition live.

Academic/Career Areas Performing Arts.

Gina Bachauer International Artists Piano Competition Award (continued)
Award Prize for use in any year; not renewable. *Number:* 6. *Amount:* $4000–$30,000.
Eligibility Requirements: Applicant must have an interest in music/singing. Available to U.S. and non-U.S. citizens.
Application Requirements Application, applicant must enter a contest, photo, tapes, passport and birth certificate copies. *Fee:* $50. *Deadline:* December 1.
World Wide Web: http://www.bachauer.com
Contact: Massimiliano Frani, Associate Artistic Director
　　　　　Gina Bachauer International Piano Foundation
　　　　　PO Box 11664
　　　　　Salt Lake City, UT 84147-1664
　　　　　Phone: 801-521-9200
　　　　　Fax: 801-521-9202
　　　　　E-mail: frani@bachauer.com

JOHANN SEBASTIAN BACH INTERNATIONAL COMPETITIONS

THE RAISSA TSELENTIS MEMORIAL, JOHANN SEBASTIAN BACH INTERNATIONAL COMPETITIONS • 168

Cash award with public appearances for serious musicians ages 20-40. Must perform pieces by Bach in solo recital program in international competition, requiring an extensive, mature repertoire. Requirements change for each competition. $50 registration fee. Contact for application deadline.

Academic/Career Areas Performing Arts.
Award Prize for use in any year; not renewable. *Number:* 3–12. *Amount:* $15,000.
Eligibility Requirements: Applicant must be age 20-40 and must have an interest in music/singing. Available to U.S. and non-U.S. citizens.
Application Requirements Application, applicant must enter a contest, self-addressed stamped envelope. *Fee:* $50.
Contact: James Marra, President
　　　　　Johann Sebastian Bach International Competitions
　　　　　21 Stratford Court
　　　　　Cohoes, NY 12047-2330
　　　　　Phone: 518-233-1139

PRINCESS GRACE FOUNDATION—USA

PRINCESS GRACE SCHOLARSHIPS IN DANCE, THEATER, AND FILM
see number 108

WAMSO-MINNESOTA ORCHESTRA VOLUNTEER ASSOCIATION

YOUNG ARTIST COMPETITION • 169

Created in 1956, the contest is designed to discover and encourage exceptional young talented musicians through a regional competition. Applicants submit taped performances. From that group, selected participants compete in the semi-finals with finalists advancing to the final round. Applicant must play an instrument which has a permanent chair in the Minnesota orchestra. Only residents of Michigan, Minnesota, Iowa, Illinois, Kansas, Missouri, Nebraska, North Dakota, South Dakota, Indiana, Wisconsin, Ontario and Manitoba are eligible. Application fee is $65.

Academic/Career Areas Performing Arts.

Award Prize for use in any year; not renewable. *Number:* 9–14. *Amount:* $500–$5250.

Eligibility Requirements: Applicant must be age 15-26; enrolled full or part-time at a two-year or four-year or technical institution or university; resident of Illinois, Indiana, Iowa, Kansas, Manitoba, Michigan, Minnesota, Missouri, Nebraska, North Dakota, Ontario, South Dakota, or Wisconsin and must have an interest in music. Available to U.S. and non-U.S. citizens.

Application Requirements Application, applicant must enter a contest, taped performance of specific repertoire. *Fee:* $65. *Deadline:* September 15.

World Wide Web: http://www.wamso.org

Contact: YAC Chair
WAMSO-Minnesota Orchestra Volunteer Association
Orchestra Hall
1111 Nicollet Mall
Minneapolis, MN 55403-2477
Phone: 612-371-5654
Fax: 612-371-7176
E-mail: wamso@mnorch.org

YOUNG MUSICIANS FOUNDATION

YMF SCHOLARSHIP PROGRAM • 170

Applicants must demonstrate exceptional talent and financial need, and must be residents of Southern California. Instrumentalists must be under 18 years of age and not beyond junior year in high school at audition time. Vocalists must be under 26 at audition time. Application fee: $12.

Academic/Career Areas Performing Arts.

Award Scholarship for use in any year; not renewable. *Number:* 40-60. *Amount:* $500–$2500.

Eligibility Requirements: Applicant must be age 8-25; enrolled full or part-time at a two-year or four-year or technical institution or university; resident of California; studying in California and must have an interest in music/singing. Available to U.S. citizens.

YMF Scholarship Program (continued)
Application Requirements Application, applicant must enter a contest, financial need analysis, references, audition. *Fee:* $12. *Deadline:* May 1.
World Wide Web: http://www.ymf.org
Contact: Programs Director
Young Musicians Foundation
195 South Beverly Drive, Suite 414
Beverly Hills, CA 90212
Phone: 310-859-7668
E-mail: ymfmusic@aol.com

PHOTOJOURNALISM_____

CALIFORNIA CHICANO NEWS MEDIA ASSOCIATION (CCNMA)

JOEL GARCIA MEMORIAL SCHOLARSHIP
see number 65

LOS ANGELES TIMES

LOS ANGELES TIMES SCHOLARSHIP PROGRAM
see number 67

PHYSICAL SCIENCES AND MATH_____

AMERICAN INSTITUTE OF AERONAUTICS AND ASTRONAUTICS

AIAA UNDERGRADUATE SCHOLARSHIP
see number 9

AMERICAN LIVER FOUNDATION

STUDENT RESEARCH FELLOWSHIPS-AMERICAN LIVER FOUNDATION
see number 34

AMERICAN SOCIETY OF NAVAL ENGINEERS

AMERICAN SOCIETY OF NAVAL ENGINEERS SCHOLARSHIP
see number 10

ARKANSAS DEPARTMENT OF HIGHER EDUCATION

EMERGENCY SECONDARY EDUCATION LOAN PROGRAM

see number 35

BARRY M. GOLDWATER SCHOLARSHIP AND EXCELLENCE IN EDUCATION FOUNDATION

BARRY M. GOLDWATER SCHOLARSHIP AND EXCELLENCE IN EDUCATION PROGRAM

see number 12

BUSINESS AND PROFESSIONAL WOMEN'S FOUNDATION

BPW CAREER ADVANCEMENT SCHOLARSHIP PROGRAM FOR WOMEN

see number 37

MARYLAND STATE HIGHER EDUCATION COMMISSION

SCIENCE AND TECHNOLOGY SCHOLARSHIP

see number 38

NASA MINNESOTA SPACE GRANT CONSORTIUM

MINNESOTA SPACE GRANT CONSORTIUM MINNESOTA SPACE GRANT CONSORTIUM

see number 30

NASA NEVADA SPACE GRANT CONSORTIUM

UNIVERSITY AND COMMUNITY COLLEGE SYSTEM OF NEVADA NASA SPACE GRANT AND FELLOWSHIP PROGRAM

see number 31

SOCIETY OF EXPLORATION GEOPHYSICISTS FOUNDATION (SEG)

SOCIETY OF EXPLORATION GEOPHYSICISTS FOUNDATION SCHOLARSHIP

see number 74

UNITED STATES DEPARTMENT OF HEALTH AND HUMAN SERVICES

NIH UNDERGRADUATE SCHOLARSHIP FOR INDIVIDUALS FROM DISADVANTAGED BACKGROUNDS see number 40

POLITICAL SCIENCE

CUBAN AMERICAN NATIONAL FOUNDATION

MAS FAMILY SCHOLARSHIPS see number 44

FOUNDATION FOR THE ADVANCEMENT OF MESOAMERICAN STUDIES, INC.

FAMSI 2002 ANNUAL GRANT COMPETITION see number 14

JOHN F. KENNEDY LIBRARY FOUNDATION

KENNEDY RESEARCH GRANTS see number 19

MARYLAND STATE HIGHER EDUCATION COMMISSION

HOPE SCHOLARSHIP see number 6

REAL ESTATE

REAL ESTATE AND LAND USE INSTITUTE

CALIFORNIA STATE UNIVERSITY REAL ESTATE SCHOLARSHIP AND INTERNSHIP GRANT PROGRAM see number 22

RELIGION/THEOLOGY

ED E. AND GLADYS HURLEY FOUNDATION

ED E. AND GLADYS HURLEY FOUNDATION SCHOLARSHIP • 171

The Hurley Foundation provides scholarships (maximum of $1,000/year per student) to worthy and deserving young men and women, residing in any state, who wish to study at a school within the State of Texas to become ministers, missionaries or religious workers of the Protestant faith.

Academic/Career Areas Religion/Theology.

Award Scholarship for use in any year; not renewable. *Number:* 100–150. *Amount:* up to $1000.

Eligibility Requirements: Applicant must be Protestant; enrolled full or part-time at a two-year or four-year institution or university and studying in Texas. Available to U.S. citizens.

Application Requirements Application, financial need analysis, references. *Deadline:* April 30.

Contact: Lori Campbell, Vice President
Ed E. and Gladys Hurley Foundation
Bank of America, N.A., Trustee
PO Box 831515
Dallas, TX 75283
Phone: 214-559-6329
Fax: 214-559-6364
E-mail: lori.j.campbell@bankofamerica.com

FOUNDATION FOR THE ADVANCEMENT OF MESOAMERICAN STUDIES, INC.

FAMSI 2002 ANNUAL GRANT COMPETITION   see number 14

UNITED METHODIST CHURCH

ERNEST AND EURICE MILLER BASS SCHOLARSHIP FUND ● 172

One-time award for undergraduate student enrolled at an accredited institution and entering United Methodist Church ministry as a deacon or elder. Must be an active member of United Methodist Church for at least one year. Merit-based award. Minimum 3.0 GPA required.

Academic/Career Areas Religion/Theology.

Award Scholarship for use in freshman, sophomore, junior, or senior years; not renewable. *Number:* 75–80. *Amount:* $800–$1200.

Eligibility Requirements: Applicant must be Methodist and enrolled full-time at a two-year or four-year institution or university. Applicant must have 3.0 GPA or higher. Available to U.S. citizens.

Application Requirements Application, essay, references, transcript. *Deadline:* June 1.

World Wide Web: http://www.umc.org/

Contact: Patti J. Zimmerman, Scholarships Administrator
United Methodist Church
PO Box 34007
Nashville, TN 37203-0007
Phone: 615-340-7344
E-mail: pzimmer@gbhem.org

SCIENCE, TECHNOLOGY AND SOCIETY_

AMERICAN INSTITUTE OF AERONAUTICS AND ASTRONAUTICS

AIAA UNDERGRADUATE SCHOLARSHIP　　　　see number 9

WEST VIRGINIA HIGHER EDUCATION POLICY COMMISSION-STUDENT SERVICES

WEST VIRGINIA ENGINEERING, SCIENCE & TECHNOLOGY SCHOLARSHIP PROGRAM　　　　see number 103

SOCIAL SCIENCES_____

BUSINESS AND PROFESSIONAL WOMEN'S FOUNDATION

BPW CAREER ADVANCEMENT SCHOLARSHIP PROGRAM FOR WOMEN　　　　see number 37

FOUNDATION FOR THE ADVANCEMENT OF MESOAMERICAN STUDIES, INC.

FAMSI 2002 ANNUAL GRANT COMPETITION　　　　see number 14

IRISH-AMERICAN CULTURAL INSTITUTE

IRISH RESEARCH FUNDS　　　　see number 24

JOHN F. KENNEDY LIBRARY FOUNDATION

KENNEDY RESEARCH GRANTS　　　　see number 19

MARYLAND STATE HIGHER EDUCATION COMMISSION

HOPE SCHOLARSHIP　　　　see number 6

NEW MEXICO COMMISSION ON HIGHER EDUCATION

ALLIED HEALTH STUDENT LOAN PROGRAM-NEW MEXICO
see number 72

NEW YORK STATE EDUCATION DEPARTMENT

REGENTS PROFESSIONAL OPPORTUNITY SCHOLARSHIP PROGRAM—NEW YORK
see number 21

SOCIAL SERVICES_____

HEALTH PROFESSIONS EDUCATION FOUNDATION

KAISER PERMANENTE ALLIED HEALTHCARE SCHOLARSHIP
see number 127

MARYLAND STATE HIGHER EDUCATION COMMISSION

DEVELOPMENTAL DISABILITIES TUITION ASSISTANCE PROGRAM
see number 130

JANET L. HOFFMANN LOAN ASSISTANCE REPAYMENT PROGRAM
see number 89

PROFESSIONAL SCHOLARSHIP PROGRAM-MARYLAND
see number 70

ORDEAN FOUNDATION

ORDEAN LOAN PROGRAM
see number 95

SPECIAL EDUCATION_____

ARKANSAS DEPARTMENT OF HIGHER EDUCATION

EMERGENCY SECONDARY EDUCATION LOAN PROGRAM
see number 35

ILLINOIS STUDENT ASSISTANCE COMMISSION (ISAC)

DAVID A. DEBOLT TEACHER SHORTAGE SCHOLARSHIP
PROGRAM   see number 83

MINORITY TEACHERS OF ILLINOIS SCHOLARSHIP PROGRAM
                                                       see number 84

KENTUCKY HIGHER EDUCATION ASSISTANCE AUTHORITY (KHEAA)

KENTUCKY TEACHER SCHOLARSHIP PROGRAM   see number 86

MARYLAND STATE HIGHER EDUCATION COMMISSION

DEVELOPMENTAL DISABILITIES TUITION ASSISTANCE PROGRAM
                                                       see number 130

MARYLAND TEACHER SCHOLARSHIP   see number 90

NEW HAMPSHIRE POSTSECONDARY EDUCATION COMMISSION

NEW HAMPSHIRE CAREER INCENTIVE PROGRAM   see number 120

SOUTH CAROLINA STUDENT LOAN CORPORATION

SOUTH CAROLINA TEACHER LOAN PROGRAM   see number 97

STATE STUDENT ASSISTANCE COMMISSION OF INDIANA (SSACI)

INDIANA MINORITY TEACHER AND SPECIAL EDUCATION
SERVICES SCHOLARSHIP PROGRAM   see number 99

TENNESSEE STUDENT ASSISTANCE CORPORATION

MINORITY TEACHING FELLOWS PROGRAM/TENNESSEE
                                                       see number 100

SPORTS-RELATED_____

NATIONAL ATHLETIC TRAINERS' ASSOCIATION

NATIONAL ATHLETIC TRAINER'S ASSOCIATION RESEARCH AND EDUCATION FOUNDATION SCHOLARSHIP PROGRAM • 173

One-time award available to full-time students who are members of NATA. Minimum 3.2 GPA required. Open to undergraduate upper-classmen and graduate/post-graduate students.

Academic/Career Areas Sports-related.

Award Scholarship for use in junior, senior, graduate, or post graduate years; not renewable. *Number:* 55–60. *Amount:* $2000.

Eligibility Requirements: Applicant must be enrolled full-time at a four-year institution or university. Available to U.S. and non-U.S. citizens.

Application Requirements Application, essay, references, transcript. *Deadline:* February 1.

World Wide Web: http://www.nata.org

Contact: Barbara Niland, Scholarship Coordinator
National Athletic Trainers' Association
2952 Stemmons Freeway, Suite 200
Dallas, TX 75247-6103
Phone: 214-637-6282 Ext. 121
Fax: 214-637-2206
E-mail: barbara@nata.org

SURVEYING; SURVEYING TECHNOLOGY, CARTOGRAPHY, OR GEOGRAPHIC INFORMATION SCIENCE_____

CONSULTING ENGINEERS AND LAND SURVEYORS OF CALIFORNIA SCHOLARSHIP PROGRAM

CONSULTING ENGINEERS AND LAND SURVEYORS OF CALIFORNIA SCHOLARSHIP AWARD   see number 60

THERAPY/REHABILITATION_____

ALBERTA HERITAGE SCHOLARSHIP FUND

ALBERTA HERITAGE SCHOLARSHIP FUND ABORIGINAL HEALTH CAREERS BURSARY see number 33

ALICE M. YARNOLD AND SAMUEL YARNOLD SCHOLARSHIP TRUST

ALICE M. AND SAMUEL YARNOLD SCHOLARSHIP see number 125

HEALTH PROFESSIONS EDUCATION FOUNDATION

KAISER PERMANENTE ALLIED HEALTHCARE SCHOLARSHIP see number 127

MARYLAND STATE HIGHER EDUCATION COMMISSION

DEVELOPMENTAL DISABILITIES TUITION ASSISTANCE PROGRAM see number 130

JANET L. HOFFMANN LOAN ASSISTANCE REPAYMENT PROGRAM see number 89

NATIONAL AMBUCS, INC.

AMBUCS SCHOLARS- SCHOLARSHIPS FOR THERAPISTS see number 131

NEW MEXICO COMMISSION ON HIGHER EDUCATION

ALLIED HEALTH STUDENT LOAN PROGRAM-NEW MEXICO see number 72

NEW YORK STATE EDUCATION DEPARTMENT

REGENTS PROFESSIONAL OPPORTUNITY SCHOLARSHIP PROGRAM—NEW YORK see number 21

STATE STUDENT ASSISTANCE COMMISSION OF INDIANA (SSACI)

INDIANA MINORITY TEACHER AND SPECIAL EDUCATION SERVICES SCHOLARSHIP PROGRAM

see number 99

TRADE/TECHNICAL SPECIALTIES____

AMERICAN WELDING SOCIETY

AMERICAN WELDING SOCIETY DISTRICT SCHOLARSHIP PROGRAM

see number 104

ASSOCIATED GENERAL CONTRACTORS EDUCATION AND RESEARCH FOUNDATION

AGC EDUCATION AND RESEARCH FOUNDATION UNDERGRADUATE SCHOLARSHIPS

see number 62

KANSAS BOARD OF REGENTS

VOCATIONAL EDUCATION SCHOLARSHIP PROGRAM-KANSAS

• 174

Several scholarships for Kansas residents who graduated from a Kansas accredited high school. Must be enrolled in a vocational education program at an eligible Kansas institution. Based on ability and aptitude. Deadline is July 1. Renewable award of $500. Must be U.S. citizen.

Academic/Career Areas Trade/Technical Specialties.
Award Scholarship for use in freshman or sophomore years; renewable. *Number:* 100–200. *Amount:* $500.
Eligibility Requirements: Applicant must be enrolled full-time at a two-year or technical institution; resident of Kansas and studying in Kansas. Available to U.S. citizens.
Application Requirements Application, test scores. *Deadline:* July 1.
World Wide Web: http://www.kansasregents.com
Contact: Diane Lindeman, Director of Student Financial Assistance
    Kansas Board of Regents
    1000 Southwest Jackson, Suite 520
    Topeka, KS 66612-1368
    Phone: 785-296-3517
    Fax: 785-296-0983
    E-mail: dlindeman@ksbor.org

MARYLAND ASSOCIATION OF PRIVATE CAREER SCHOOLS

MARYLAND ASSOCIATION OF PRIVATE CAREER SCHOOLS SCHOLARSHIP
see number 49

MARYLAND STATE HIGHER EDUCATION COMMISSION

FIREFIGHTER, AMBULANCE, AND RESCUE SQUAD MEMBER TUITION REIMBURSEMENT PROGRAM-MARYLAND
see number 109

NATIONAL ASSOCIATION OF WOMEN IN CONSTRUCTION

NAWIC UNDERGRADUATE SCHOLARSHIPS
see number 20

PLASTICS INSTITUTE OF AMERICA

PLASTICS PIONEERS SCHOLARSHIPS
see number 105

SOCIETY OF PLASTICS ENGINEERS (SPE) FOUNDATION

SOCIETY OF PLASTICS ENGINEERS SCHOLARSHIP PROGRAM
see number 56

STATE OF GEORGIA

INTELLECTUAL CAPITAL PARTNERSHIP PROGRAM, ICAPP • 175
Forgivable loans will be awarded to undergraduate students who are residents of Georgia studying high-tech related fields at a Georgia institution. Repayment for every $2500 that is awarded is one-year service in a high-tech field in Georgia. Can be enrolled in a certificate or degree program.

Academic/Career Areas Trade/Technical Specialties.
Award Forgivable loan for use in freshman, sophomore, junior, or senior years; not renewable. *Number:* up to 328. *Amount:* $7000–$10,000.
Eligibility Requirements: Applicant must be enrolled full or part-time at a two-year or four-year institution or university; resident of Georgia and studying in Georgia. Available to U.S. citizens.
Application Requirements Application, financial need analysis. *Deadline:* Continuous.
World Wide Web: http://www.gsfc.org

Contact: Peggy Matthews, Manager/GSFA Originations
State of Georgia
2082 East Exchange Place, Suite 230
Tucker, GA 30084-5305
Phone: 770-724-9230
Fax: 770-724-9263
E-mail: peggy@mail.gsfc.state.ga.us

WOMEN'S JEWELRY ASSOCIATION

WOMEN'S JEWELRY ASSOCIATION SCHOLARSHIP PROGRAM • 176

Program is designed to encourage talented female students and help support their studies in the jewelry field.

Academic/Career Areas Trade/Technical Specialties.
Award Scholarship for use in any year; not renewable. *Number:* 5-10. *Amount:* $500-$5000.
Eligibility Requirements: Applicant must be enrolled full or part-time at a two-year or four-year or technical institution or university; female and must have an interest in designated field specified by sponsor. Available to U.S. citizens.
Application Requirements Application, essay, portfolio, references. *Deadline:* June 1.
World Wide Web: http://www.womens.jewelry.org
Contact: Scholarship Committee
Women's Jewelry Association
333 Route 46 West, B-201
Fairfield, NJ 07004
Phone: 973-575-7190
Fax: 973-575-1445
E-mail: info@womens.jewelry.org

TV/RADIO BROADCASTING_____

CALIFORNIA CHICANO NEWS MEDIA ASSOCIATION (CCNMA)

JOEL GARCIA MEMORIAL SCHOLARSHIP   see number 65

CHARLES AND LUCILLE KING FAMILY FOUNDATION, INC.

CHARLES AND LUCILLE KING FAMILY FOUNDATION SCHOLARSHIPS   see number 66

JOHN BAYLISS BROADCAST FOUNDATION

BAYLISS RADIO SCHOLARSHIP ● 177

One-time award for college juniors, seniors, or graduate students majoring in broadcast communications with a concentration in radio broadcasting. Must have history of radio-related activities and a GPA of at least 3.0. Essay outlining future broadcasting goals required. Request information by mail, including stamped, self-addressed envelope, or by e-mail rather than by telephone. Must be attending school in U.S. Application is available at website, http://www. baylissfoundation.org.

Academic/Career Areas TV/Radio Broadcasting.
Award Scholarship for use in junior, senior, or graduate years; not renewable. *Number:* 20. *Amount:* up to $5000.
Eligibility Requirements: Applicant must be enrolled full-time at a four-year institution or university. Applicant must have 3.0 GPA or higher. Available to U.S. and Canadian citizens.
Application Requirements Application, essay, references, self-addressed stamped envelope, transcript. *Deadline:* April 30.
World Wide Web: http://www.baylissfoundation.org
Contact: Kit Hunter Franke, Executive Director
John Bayliss Broadcast Foundation
PO Box 51126
Pacific Grove, CA 93950
E-mail: info@baylissfoundation.org

LOS ANGELES TIMES

LOS ANGELES TIMES SCHOLARSHIP PROGRAM
see number 67

MARYLAND ASSOCIATION OF PRIVATE CAREER SCHOOLS

MARYLAND ASSOCIATION OF PRIVATE CAREER SCHOOLS SCHOLARSHIP
see number 49

NONACADEMIC/ NONCAREER CRITERIA

CIVIC, PROFESSIONAL, SOCIAL, OR UNION AFFILIATION

AMERICAN FOREIGN SERVICE ASSOCIATION

AMERICAN FOREIGN SERVICE ASSOCIATION (AFSA) FINANCIAL AID AWARD PROGRAM • 178

Need-based financial aid scholarship program open to children whose parents are in the U.S. Government Foreign Service. Must attend a U.S. school full-time and maintain a "C" average. Children whose parents are in the military and international students are not eligible.

Award Scholarship for use in freshman, sophomore, junior, or senior years; not renewable. *Number:* 50–60. *Amount:* $500–$3000.

Eligibility Requirements: Applicant must be enrolled full-time at a two-year or four-year or technical institution or university; single; member of American Foreign Service Association and have employment experience in U.S. Foreign Service. Applicant must have 2.5 GPA or higher. Available to U.S. citizens.

Application Requirements Application, financial need analysis, transcript, CSS Profile. *Deadline:* February 6.

World Wide Web: http://www.afsa.org

Contact: Ms. Lori Dec, Scholarship Administrator
American Foreign Service Association
2101 E Street, NW
Washington, DC 20037
Phone: 202-944-5504
Fax: 202-338-6820
E-mail: dec@afsa.org

AMERICAN LEGION, DEPARTMENT OF OHIO

AMERICAN LEGION SCHOLARSHIP—OHIO • 179

For descendants of Ohio Legionnaires only. Nonrenewable award for full-time study only. Must rank in upper third of class or have a minimum 3.0 GPA. Must include descendancy proofs. Deadline: April 15.

Award Scholarship for use in freshman, sophomore, junior, or senior years; not renewable. *Number:* 15–20. *Amount:* $2000–$3000.

Eligibility Requirements: Applicant must be enrolled full-time at a two-year or four-year or technical institution or university and member of American Legion or Auxiliary. Applicant must have 3.0 GPA or higher. Available to U.S. and non-U.S. citizens.

American Legion Scholarship—Ohio (continued)
Application Requirements Application, test scores, transcript. *Deadline:* April 15.
World Wide Web: http://www.ohioamericanlegion.org
Contact: Donald Lanthorn, Service Director
American Legion, Department of Ohio
PO Box 8007
Delaware, OH 43015-8007
Phone: 740-362-7478
Fax: 740-362-1429
E-mail: dlanthorn@iwaynet.net

AMERICAN MUSIC CENTER, INC.

MARGARET FAIRBANK JORY COPYING ASSISTANCE
PROGRAM • 180

One-time award to assist composers with the expenses for the copying and reproduction of parts needed for premiere performances. Works must be for four or more instruments. Must be member of AMC. Submit musical score and commitment from performing ensemble. Deadlines: February 1, May 1, and October 1.

Award Grant for use in any year; not renewable. *Number:* 50–150. *Amount:* $250–$5000.
Eligibility Requirements: Applicant must be member of American Music Center. Available to U.S. citizens.
Application Requirements Application.
World Wide Web: http://www.amc.net
Contact: Philip Rothman, Manager of Grantmaking Programs
American Music Center, Inc.
30 West 26th Street, 10th Floor
New York, NY 10010-2011
Phone: 212-366-5260 Ext. 29
E-mail: philip@amc.net

AMERICAN QUARTER HORSE FOUNDATION (AQHF)

AMERICAN QUARTER HORSE FOUNDATION YOUTH
SCHOLARSHIPS • 181

$8,000 scholarships to AQHYA members who have been members for three or more years. The recipient will receive $2,000 per year for four years. Minimum 2.5 GPA required.

Award Scholarship for use in freshman year; renewable. *Number:* 1-25. *Amount:* $2000.

Eligibility Requirements: Applicant must be enrolled full-time at a two-year or four-year or technical institution or university and member of American Quarter Horse Association. Applicant must have 2.5 GPA or higher. Available to U.S. and Canadian citizens.

Application Requirements Application, essay, financial need analysis, photo, references, transcript. *Deadline:* April 1.

World Wide Web: http://www.aqha.org/aqhya

Contact: Laura Owens, Secretary to Director
American Quarter Horse Foundation (AQHF)
2601 I-40 East
Amarillo, TX 79104
Phone: 806-376-5181
Fax: 806-376-1005
E-mail: lowens@aqha.org

ARBY'S FOUNDATION, BIG BROTHERS BIG SISTERS OF AMERICA

ARBY'S-BIG BROTHERS BIG SISTERS SCHOLARSHIP AWARD • 182

Designed to assist exemplary young people from low- and middle-income families. Applicants must be or have been a Little Brother or Little Sister in the Big Brothers or Big Sisters program. Write for more information. Merit considered. Renewable scholarships of up to $5000. Must rank in upper half of class or have a minimum 2.5 GPA.

Award Scholarship for use in freshman or sophomore years; renewable. *Number:* 2–10. *Amount:* $1000–$5000.

Eligibility Requirements: Applicant must be enrolled full-time at a two-year or four-year institution or university; member of Big Brothers/Big Sisters and have employment experience in community service. Applicant must have 2.5 GPA or higher. Available to U.S. citizens.

Application Requirements Application, essay, financial need analysis, photo, references, test scores, transcript. *Deadline:* March 31.

World Wide Web: http://www.bbbsa.org

Contact: Mr. Robert Kearney, Director of Corporate Partnerships
Arby's Foundation, Big Brothers Big Sisters of America
230 North 13th Street
Philadelphia, PA 19107
Phone: 215-665-7762
Fax: 215-567-0394
E-mail: rkearney@bbbsa.org

BOY SCOUTS OF AMERICA, EAGLE SCOUT SERVICE

MABLE AND LAWRENCE S. COOKE SCHOLARSHIP • 183

One scholarship of up to $48,000 (up to $12,000 per year for four years) and four $20,000 scholarships ($5,000 a year for four years) are given annually. The Eagle Scout offered the scholarship must agree to specific conditions before acceptance. Please visit website for information and application. (http://www.bsa.scouting.org)

Award Scholarship for use in freshman, sophomore, junior, or senior years; renewable. *Number:* up to 5. *Amount:* $5000–$12,000.

Eligibility Requirements: Applicant must be enrolled full-time at a four-year institution or university; male and member of Boy Scouts. Applicant must have 3.0 GPA or higher.

Application Requirements Application, essay, financial need analysis, references, test scores, transcript. *Deadline:* February 28.

World Wide Web: http://www.bsa.scouting.org

Contact: Ann Dimond, Manager
Boy Scouts of America, Eagle Scout Service
1325 West Walnut Hill Lane
Box 152079
Irving, TX 75015-2079

BOYS & GIRLS CLUBS OF AMERICA

BOYS & GIRLS CLUBS OF AMERICA NATIONAL YOUTH OF THE YEAR AWARD • 184

This nonrenewable award is available to youths 14-18 who have been active members of their Boys Club or Girls Club for at least one year. Contact local club for nomination form. Minimum 3.0 GPA required. Must be nominated by local club.

Award Scholarship for use in freshman, sophomore, junior, or senior years; not renewable. *Number:* 5. *Amount:* $5000–$10,000.

Eligibility Requirements: Applicant must be high school student; age 14-18; planning to enroll full or part-time at a two-year or four-year or technical institution; single; member of Boys or Girls Club; have employment experience in community service and must have an interest in leadership. Applicant must have 3.0 GPA or higher.

Application Requirements Application, essay, interview, references. *Deadline:* May 15.

Contact: Kelvin Davis, Program Services Director
Boys & Girls Clubs of America
1230 West Peachtree Street, NW
Atlanta, GA 30309

CALIFORNIA TEACHERS ASSOCIATION (CTA)

CALIFORNIA TEACHERS ASSOCIATION SCHOLARSHIP FOR DEPENDENT CHILDREN • 185

Twenty-five $2000 scholarships for study in higher education awarded annually. Twenty-three provided by California Teachers Association; one provided by D. A. Weber Scholarship Fund for student attending continuation high school; and one provided by Ralph J. Flynn Memorial Fund. Must be dependent child of active, retired-life or deceased member of California Teachers Association. Applications available in October.

Award Scholarship for use in any year; not renewable. *Number:* 25. *Amount:* $2000.

Eligibility Requirements: Applicant must be enrolled full-time at a two-year or four-year or technical institution or university and member of California Teachers Association. Applicant must have 3.0 GPA or higher.

Application Requirements Application, essay, references, transcript. *Deadline:* February 15.

World Wide Web: http://www.cta.org

Contact: Human Rights Department
California Teachers Association (CTA)
PO Box 921
Burlingame, CA 94011-0921
Phone: 650-697-1400
E-mail: scholarships@cta.org

DELTA DELTA DELTA FOUNDATION

DELTA DELTA DELTA UNDERGRADUATE SCHOLARSHIP • 186

One-time award based on academic achievement, campus, chapter, and community involvement. Any initiated sophomore or junior member-in-good-standing of Delta Delta Delta may apply. Application and information available on website.

Award Scholarship for use in junior or senior years; not renewable. *Number:* 48–50. *Amount:* $500–$2000.

Eligibility Requirements: Applicant must be enrolled full-time at a four-year institution or university; single female and have employment experience in community service.

Application Requirements Application, references, transcript. *Deadline:* March 1.

World Wide Web: http://www.tridelta.org

Contact: Joyce Allen
Delta Delta Delta Foundation
PO Box 5987
Arlington, TX 76005
Phone: 817-633-8001
Fax: 817-652-0212
E-mail: jallen@trideltaeo.org

ELKS NATIONAL FOUNDATION

ELKS NATIONAL FOUNDATION LEGACY AWARDS • 187

Up to five hundred $1000 one-year scholarships for children and grandchildren of Elks in good standing. Parent or grandparent must have been an Elk for two years. Contact local Elks Lodge for an application or send a SASE to Foundation or see home page (http://www.elks.org, keyword: scholarship). Deadline: November 1.

Award Scholarship for use in freshman year; not renewable. *Number:* up to 500. *Amount:* $1000.

Eligibility Requirements: Applicant must be high school student; planning to enroll full-time at a two-year or four-year institution or university and member of Elks Club. Available to U.S. citizens.

Application Requirements Application, essay, references, self-addressed stamped envelope, test scores, transcript. *Deadline:* November 1.

World Wide Web: http://www.elks.org

Contact: Scholarship Coordinator
Elks National Foundation
2750 Lakeview Avenue
Chicago, IL 60614-1889
Phone: 773-755-4732
Fax: 773-755-4733
E-mail: scholarship@elks.org

GOLDEN KEY INTERNATIONAL HONOUR SOCIETY

UNDERGRADUATE SCHOLARSHIP • 188

Two $500 scholarships are awarded at each chapter every year to members of Golden Key International Honour Society. Minimum 3.5 GPA required. Must be a member of Golden Key International Honour Society to be eligible for awards. Please visit website (http://goldenkey.gsu.edu) for more information. Offered in conjunction with the Ford Motor Company.

Award Scholarship for use in junior or senior years; not renewable. *Number:* 690. *Amount:* $500–$700.

Eligibility Requirements: Applicant must be enrolled full-time at an institution or university and member of Golden Key National Honor Society. Applicant must have 3.5 GPA or higher. Available to U.S. and non-U.S. citizens.

Application Requirements Application, interview, transcript.

World Wide Web: http://goldenkey.gsu.edu

Contact: Michelle Boone, Director of Scholarships and Awards
Golden Key International Honour Society
1189 Ponce de Leon Avenue
Atlanta, GA 30306-4624
Phone: 404-377-2400
E-mail: mboone@goldenkey.gsu.edu

HEBREW IMMIGRANT AID SOCIETY

HEBREW IMMIGRANT AID SOCIETY SCHOLARSHIP AWARDS COMPETITION • 189

Must be Hebrew Immigrant Aid Society-assisted refugee or child thereof who immigrated to the U.S. Must have completed two semesters at a U.S. high school, college, or graduate school. Send self-addressed stamped envelope for application after December 15. Postmark deadline for competition is March 15.

Award Scholarship for use in any year; not renewable. *Number:* 100–134. *Amount:* $1500.

Eligibility Requirements: Applicant must be enrolled full or part-time at a two-year or four-year or technical institution or university and member of Hebrew Immigrant Aid Society. Available to U.S. citizens.

Application Requirements Application, applicant must enter a contest, essay, financial need analysis, self-addressed stamped envelope, test scores, transcript. *Deadline:* March 15.

World Wide Web: http://www.hias.org

Contact: Ms. Irina Reyn, Associate Director of Scholarship
Hebrew Immigrant Aid Society
333 Seventh Avenue
New York, NY 10001-5004
Phone: 212-613-1358
Fax: 212-629-0921
E-mail: info@hias.org

JAPANESE AMERICAN CITIZENS LEAGUE

JAPANESE AMERICAN CITIZENS LEAGUE ENTERING FRESHMAN AWARDS • 190

One-time award for high school seniors planning to attend any institution of higher education. Must be a member of the Japanese-American Citizens League. Send self-addressed stamped envelope for application, specifying application category.

Award Scholarship for use in freshman year; not renewable. *Number:* 10–15. *Amount:* $1000–$5000.

Eligibility Requirements: Applicant must be high school student; planning to enroll full or part-time at a two-year or four-year or technical institution or university and member of Japanese-American Citizens League. Available to U.S. and non-U.S. citizens.

Application Requirements Application, essay, references, self-addressed stamped envelope, test scores, transcript. *Deadline:* March 1.

World Wide Web: http://www.jacl.org

Japanese American Citizens League Entering Freshman Awards (continued)
Contact: National JACL Scholarship & Awards
Japanese American Citizens League
1765 Sutter Street
San Francisco, CA 94115
Phone: 415-921-5225
Fax: 415-931-4671
E-mail: jacl@jacl.org

JAPANESE AMERICAN CITIZENS LEAGUE UNDERGRADUATE AWARDS • 191

One-time award for undergraduates. Must be a member of Japanese-American Citizens League. Send self-addressed stamped envelope for application, specifying application category.

Award Scholarship for use in sophomore, junior, or senior years; not renewable. *Number:* 8–12. *Amount:* $1000–$5000.
Eligibility Requirements: Applicant must be enrolled full or part-time at a two-year or four-year or technical institution or university and member of Japanese-American Citizens League. Available to U.S. and non-U.S. citizens.
Application Requirements Application, essay, references, self-addressed stamped envelope, transcript. *Deadline:* April 1.
World Wide Web: http://www.jacl.org
Contact: National JACL Scholarship & Awards
Japanese American Citizens League
1765 Sutter Street
San Francisco, CA 94115
Phone: 415-921-5225
Fax: 415-931-4671
E-mail: jacl@jacl.org

KAPPA ALPHA THETA FOUNDATION

KAPPA ALPHA THETA FOUNDATION MERIT BASED SCHOLARSHIP PROGRAM • 192

Foundation scholarships are awarded to either graduate or undergraduate members of Kappa Alpha Theta. All scholarships are merit-based. Application postmark date is February 1. Applications may be downloaded from the website or may be obtained by calling 1-888-526-1870 ext. 336.

Award Scholarship for use in sophomore, junior, senior, graduate, or post graduate years; not renewable. *Number:* 120–140. *Amount:* $1000–$12,000.
Eligibility Requirements: Applicant must be enrolled full-time at a four-year institution or university and female. Available to U.S. and non-U.S. citizens.
Application Requirements Application, resume, references, transcript. *Deadline:* February 1.
World Wide Web: http://www.kappaalphatheta.org

Contact: Mrs. Jeni Hilgedag, Director of Programs
Kappa Alpha Theta Foundation
8740 Founders Road
Indianapolis, IN 46268
Phone: 317-876-1870 Ext. 110
Fax: 317-876-1925
E-mail: info@kappaalphatheta.org

KAPPA ALPHA THETA FOUNDATION NAMED TRUST GRANT PROGRAM • 193

The Kappa Alpha Theta Foundation named Trust Grant program was established to provide monies for undergraduate and alumna members of the Fraternity for leadership training and non-degree educational opportunities. Applications may be downloaded from the website. Quarterly deadlines are March 31, June 30, September 30 and December 31.

Award Grant for use in any year; not renewable. *Number:* up to 50. *Amount:* $100–$5000.

Eligibility Requirements: Applicant must be female. Available to U.S. and non-U.S. citizens.

Application Requirements Application, resume, references, budget, proposal, narrative.

World Wide Web: http://www.kappaalphatheta.org

Contact: Mrs. Jeni Hilgedag, Director of Programs
Kappa Alpha Theta Foundation
8740 Founders Road
Indianapolis, IN 46268
Phone: 317-876-1870 Ext. 110
Fax: 317-876-1925
E-mail: info@kappaalphatheta.org

KAPPA SIGMA ENDOWMENT FUND

SCHOLARSHIP-LEADERSHIP AWARDS PROGRAM • 194

Scholarships are given to outstanding undergraduate Kappa Sigma members who excel in the classroom, on campus and within the fraternity. Must have a 2.5 GPA. Applications can be downloaded at http://www.ksefnet.org.

Award Scholarship for use in sophomore, junior, or senior years; not renewable. *Number:* 275–300. *Amount:* $500–$2500.

Eligibility Requirements: Applicant must be enrolled full-time at a four-year institution and male. Applicant must have 2.5 GPA or higher. Available to U.S. and non-U.S. citizens.

Application Requirements Application, transcript. *Deadline:* October 1.

World Wide Web: http://www.ksefnet.org

Scholarship- Leadership Awards Program (continued)
Contact: David Coyne, Chief Development Officer
Kappa Sigma Endowment Fund
PO Box 5643
Charlottesville, VA 22905
Phone: 434-295-3193
Fax: 434-296-5733
E-mail: davidc@imh.kappasigma.org

KNIGHTS OF COLUMBUS

FOURTH DEGREE PRO DEO AND PRO PATRIA SCHOLARSHIPS • 195

Renewable award available to students entering freshman year at a Catholic university or college. Applicant must be a member or child of a member of Knights of Columbus or Columbian Squires. Scholarships are awarded on the basis of academic excellence. Minimum 3.0 GPA required.

Award Scholarship for use in freshman year; renewable. *Number:* 62. *Amount:* $1500.

Eligibility Requirements: Applicant must be Roman Catholic; enrolled full-time at a four-year institution and member of Columbian Squires or Knights of Columbus. Applicant must have 3.0 GPA or higher. Available to U.S. citizens.

Application Requirements Application, autobiography, essay, references, test scores, transcript. *Deadline:* March 1.

Contact: Rev. Donald Barry, Director of Scholarship Aid
Knights of Columbus
PO Box 1670
New Haven, CT 06507-0901
Phone: 203-772-2130 Ext. 332

JOHN W. MC DEVITT (FOURTH DEGREE) SCHOLARSHIPS • 196

Renewable scholarship for students entering freshman year at a Catholic college or university. Applicant must submit Pro Deo and Pro Patria Scholarship application. Must be a member or wife, son, or daughter of a member of the Knights of Columbus. Minimum 3.0 GPA required.

Award Scholarship for use in freshman year; renewable. *Number:* 36. *Amount:* $1500.

Eligibility Requirements: Applicant must be Roman Catholic; enrolled full-time at a four-year institution and member of Knights of Columbus. Applicant must have 3.0 GPA or higher. Available to U.S. citizens.

Application Requirements Application, autobiography, references, test scores, transcript. *Deadline:* March 1.

Contact: Rev. Donald Barry, Director of Scholarship Aid
Knights of Columbus
PO Box 1670
New Haven, CT 06507-0901
Phone: 203-772-2130 Ext. 332
Fax: 203-772-2696

MODERN WOODMEN OF AMERICA

MODERN WOODMEN OF AMERICA FRATERNAL COLLEGE SCHOLARSHIP PROGRAM • 197

Available to high school seniors who have been beneficial members of Modern Woodmen of America for two years by September 30 of senior year. Selection based on scholarship, extracurricular activities, and character. Include photo. Renewable for four years. Must submit biographical questionnaire and a form from official of applicant's high school.

Award Scholarship for use in freshman, sophomore, junior, or senior years; renewable. *Number:* 63. *Amount:* $1000–$4000.

Eligibility Requirements: Applicant must be high school student; planning to enroll full-time at a four-year institution or university and member of Modern Woodmen. Applicant must have 2.5 GPA or higher.

Application Requirements Application, essay, photo, references, test scores, transcript. *Deadline:* January 1.

World Wide Web: http://www.modern-woodmen.org

Contact: Fraternal Scholarship Administrator
Modern Woodmen of America
1701 1st Avenue
Rock Island, IL 61201

NATIONAL ASSOCIATION OF SECONDARY SCHOOL PRINCIPALS

NATIONAL HONOR SOCIETY SCHOLARSHIPS • 198

One-time award available only to high school seniors who are National Honor Society members, for use at an accredited two- or four-year college or university in the U.S. Based on outstanding scholarship, leadership, service, and character. Application fee $6. Contact school counselor or NHS chapter adviser. Minimum 3.0 GPA.

Award Scholarship for use in any year; not renewable. *Number:* 200. *Amount:* $1000.

Eligibility Requirements: Applicant must be high school student; planning to enroll full-time at a two-year or four-year institution or university and member of National Honor Society. Applicant must have 3.0 GPA or higher. Available to U.S. and non-U.S. citizens.

Application Requirements Application, essay, references, test scores, transcript. *Fee:* $6. *Deadline:* January 24.

National Honor Society Scholarships (continued)
World Wide Web: http://www.principals.org
Contact: Local NHS Chapter Advisor

OHIO AMERICAN LEGION

OHIO AMERICAN LEGION SCHOLARSHIPS   • 199

One-time award for full-time students attending accredited institution. Open to students of any postsecondary academic year. Must have minimum 3.0 GPA. Deadline April fifteenth. Must be a member of the American Legion, a direct descendent of a Legionnaire (living or deceased), or surviving spouse or child of a deceased U.S. military person who died on active duty or of injuries received on active duty.

Award Scholarship for use in any year; not renewable. *Number:* 15–18. *Amount:* $2000–$3000.

Eligibility Requirements: Applicant must be enrolled full-time at a two-year or four-year or technical institution or university and member of American Legion or Auxiliary. Applicant must have 3.0 GPA or higher. Available to U.S. and non-U.S. citizens. Applicant or parent must meet one or more of the following requirements: general military experience; retired from active duty; disabled or killed as a result of military service; Prisoner-Of-War; or Missing-In-Action.

Application Requirements Application, transcript. *Deadline:* April 15.

World Wide Web: http://ohioamericanlegion.org

Contact: Donald Lanthorn, Service Director
    Ohio American Legion
    PO Box 8007
    Delaware, OH 43015
    Phone: 740-362-7478
    Fax: 740-362-1429
    E-mail: dlanthorn@iwaynet.net

RECORDING FOR THE BLIND & DYSLEXIC

MARY P. OENSLAGER SCHOLASTIC ACHIEVEMENT AWARDS• 200

Awards for legally blind college seniors, awarded on basis of leadership, scholarship, enterprise, and service to others. Candidates must be registered with Recording for the Blind & Dyslexic for at least one year prior to filing date of February 21 and have an overall GPA of 3.0 or equivalent. Applicants need not plan to continue their education beyond a bachelor's degree.

Award Prize for use in senior year; not renewable. *Number:* 9. *Amount:* $1000–$6000.

Eligibility Requirements: Applicant must be enrolled full-time at a four-year institution; member of Recording for the Blind and Dyslexic; have employment experience in community service and must have an interest in leadership. Applicant must be visually impaired. Applicant must have 3.0 GPA or higher.

Application Requirements Application, essay, references, transcript. *Deadline:* February 21.
World Wide Web: http://www.rfbd.org
Contact: Public Affairs Office
Recording for the Blind & Dyslexic
20 Roszel Road
Princeton, NJ 08540-5443

UNION PLUS SCHOLARSHIP PROGRAM

UNION PLUS SCHOLARSHIP PROGRAM • 201

One-time cash award for AFL-CIO union members, their spouses, or dependent children. Based upon academic achievement, character, leadership, career goals, social awareness, and financial need. Must be from Canada or U.S. including Puerto Rico. Members may download application from website or send a postcard with name, address, phone number and union name to the PO Box. Applications are available from September 1 to January 15.

Award Scholarship for use in freshman, sophomore, junior, or senior years; not renewable. *Number:* 110-130. *Amount:* $500-$4000.
Eligibility Requirements: Applicant must be enrolled full or part-time at a two-year or four-year or technical institution or university and member of AFL-CIO. Available to U.S. and Canadian citizens.
Application Requirements Application, essay, financial need analysis, references, test scores, transcript. *Deadline:* January 31.
World Wide Web: http://www.unionprivilege.org
Contact: Union Plus Scholarship Program
PO Box 34800
Washington, DC 20043-4800
E-mail: info@unionprivilege.org

CORPORATE AFFILIATION_____

ALCOA FOUNDATION

ALCOA FOUNDATION SONS AND DAUGHTERS SCHOLARSHIP PROGRAM • 202

Open to children of Alcoa Inc. employees. Apply in senior year of high school through parent's employment location. Merit is considered.

Award Scholarship for use in freshman year; renewable. *Number:* 100-150. *Amount:* $1500.
Eligibility Requirements: Applicant must be high school student; planning to enroll full-time at a two-year or four-year or technical institution or university and affiliated with Aluminum Company of America. Available to U.S. and non-U.S. citizens.

Alcoa Foundation Sons and Daughters Scholarship Program (continued)

Application Requirements Application, applicant must enter a contest, essay, references, test scores, transcript. *Deadline:* January 22.

Contact: Ms. Carol Greco, Data Analyst
Alcoa Foundation
201 Isabella Street
Pittsburgh, PA 15212-5858
Phone: 412-553-4786
Fax: 412-553-4532
E-mail: carol.greco@alcoa.com

BRIDGESTONE/FIRESTONE TRUST FUND

BRIDGESTONE/FIRESTONE TRUST FUND SCHOLARSHIPS • 203

Award for sons and daughters of Bridgestone/Firestone, Inc. employees and retirees. Must be high school student in junior year. Must be a U.S. citizen. Must also meet all requirements for participation that are published in the PSAT/NMSQT Student Bulletin.

Award Scholarship for use in freshman year; not renewable. *Number:* up to 50. *Amount:* $4000.

Eligibility Requirements: Applicant must be high school student; planning to enroll full-time at a four-year institution or university; affiliated with Bridgestone/Firestone and have employment experience in designated career field. Available to U.S. citizens.

Application Requirements Application. *Deadline:* February 1.

Contact: Bernice Csaszar, Administrator
Bridgestone/Firestone Trust Fund
50 Century Boulevard
Nashville, TN 37214-8900
Phone: 615-872-1415
Fax: 615-872-1414
E-mail: bfstrustfund@bfusa.com

DUKE ENERGY CORPORATION

DUKE ENERGY SCHOLARS PROGRAM • 204

Scholarship is open to graduating high school seniors who are children of eligible employees and retirees of Duke Energy and its subsidiaries. Fifteen four-year scholarships of up to $20,000 and five $1,000 awards given annually. Recipients selected by 5-member outside committee.

Award Scholarship for use in freshman, sophomore, junior, or senior years; renewable. *Number:* 5–15. *Amount:* $1000–$20,000.

Eligibility Requirements: Applicant must be high school student; planning to enroll full-time at a two-year or four-year or technical institution or university; affiliated with Duke Energy Corporation and have employment experience in designated career field. Available to U.S. citizens.

Application Requirements Application, autobiography, essay, financial need analysis, references, test scores, transcript. *Deadline:* December 1.
World Wide Web: http://www.duke-energy.com
Contact: Dianne S. Wilson, Scholarship Administrator
Duke Energy Corporation
PO Box 1642
Houston, TX 77251-1642
Phone: 713-627-4608
Fax: 713-627-4061
E-mail: dswilson@duke-energy.com

HUMANA FOUNDATION

HUMANA FOUNDATION SCHOLARSHIP PROGRAM • 205

Up to 75 scholarships are given to full-time undergraduate students. Eligible applicants must be under 25 and a United States citizen. The deadline is February 1. Must be a dependent of a Humana employee.

Award Scholarship for use in freshman, sophomore, or junior years; renewable. *Number:* up to 75. *Amount:* $1250–$2500.
Eligibility Requirements: Applicant must be age 25 or under; enrolled full-time at a two-year or four-year institution and affiliated with Humana Foundation. Available to U.S. citizens.
Application Requirements Application, transcript. *Deadline:* February 1.
World Wide Web: http://www.humanafoundation.org/scholarship.html
Contact: Charles Jackson, Program Manager
Humana Foundation
Attention: Scholarship Program, 500 West Main Street
Room 208
Louisville, KY 40202
Phone: 502-580-1245
Fax: 502-580-1256
E-mail: cjackson@humana.com

JOHNSON CONTROLS, INC.

JOHNSON CONTROLS FOUNDATION SCHOLARSHIP PROGRAM • 206

Available to high school seniors who are children of Johnson Controls, Inc. employees. Award is distributed over four years of undergraduate study. Renewable scholarships of $8000 each based on merit.

Award Scholarship for use in freshman, sophomore, junior, or senior years; renewable. *Number:* 1–40. *Amount:* $8000.
Eligibility Requirements: Applicant must be high school student; planning to enroll full-time at a four-year institution and affiliated with Johnson Controls, Inc. Applicant must have 3.0 GPA or higher. Available to U.S. citizens.
Application Requirements Application, transcript. *Deadline:* February 15.

Johnson Controls Foundation Scholarship Program (continued)
World Wide Web: http://www.jci.com
Contact: Valerie Adisek, Scholarship Coordinator
Johnson Controls, Inc.
5757 North Green Bay Avenue, X-46
Milwaukee, WI 53209
Phone: 414-524-2296

PROCTER & GAMBLE FUND

PROCTER & GAMBLE FUND SCHOLARSHIP COMPETITION FOR EMPLOYEES' CHILDREN • 207
Award for high school seniors who are dependents of eligible employees, including deceased employees, and retirees of Procter and Gamble Company. All winners receive a one time only award of $2500. Deadline: January 15 of applicant's senior year of high school.

Award Scholarship for use in freshman year; not renewable. *Number:* 250. *Amount:* $2500.
Eligibility Requirements: Applicant must be high school student; planning to enroll full-time at a two-year or four-year or technical institution or university; affiliated with Procter & Gamble Company and have employment experience in designated career field. Available to U.S. citizens.
Application Requirements Application, applicant must enter a contest, essay, references, test scores, transcript. *Deadline:* January 15.
World Wide Web: http://www.pg.com
Contact: Tawnia True, Coordinator, P&G Employee Scholarship Fund
Procter & Gamble Fund
PO Box 599
Cincinnati, OH 45201-0599
Phone: 513-945-8450
Fax: 513-945-8979
E-mail: true.tb@pg.com

TEXACO FOUNDATION

TEXACO FOUNDATION SCHOLARSHIP • 208
Award for children of Texaco Inc. employees. Parent must have worked for Texaco, a subsidiary, or an affiliate for at least one year and must be U.S. citizens or have resident status. Criteria include academic achievement, school recommendation, leadership qualities, involvement in outside activities. Deadline: November 15.

Award Scholarship for use in freshman, sophomore, junior, or senior years; renewable. *Number:* 100. *Amount:* $2500.
Eligibility Requirements: Applicant must be high school student; planning to enroll at a four-year institution or university; affiliated with Texaco, Inc. and must have an interest in leadership. Available to U.S. citizens.

Application Requirements Application, test scores, transcript. *Deadline:* November 15.
World Wide Web: http://www.texaco.com
Contact: Texaco Foundation
2000 Westchester Avenue
White Plains, NY 10650

WAL-MART FOUNDATION

WAL-MART ASSOCIATE SCHOLARSHIPS • 209

Awards for college-bound high school seniors who work for Wal-Mart or whose parents are part-time Wal-Mart associates or have not been with the company for one year. Based on ACT or SAT scores, counselor recommendations, transcripts, class rank, activities, and financial need. One-time award of $1000. For use at an accredited two- or four-year U.S. institution.

Award Scholarship for use in freshman year; not renewable. *Number:* 150–300. *Amount:* $1000.
Eligibility Requirements: Applicant must be high school student; planning to enroll full-time at a two-year or four-year institution or university; affiliated with Wal-Mart Foundation and have employment experience in designated career field. Available to U.S. citizens.
Application Requirements Application, test scores, transcript, federal income tax return. *Deadline:* March 1.
World Wide Web: http://www.walmartfoundation.org
Contact: Jenny Harral
Wal-Mart Foundation
702 Southwest 8th Street
Bentonville, AR 72716-0150
Phone: 800-530-9925
Fax: 501-273-6850

WALTON FAMILY FOUNDATION SCHOLARSHIP • 210

Award for high-school seniors who are children of a Wal-Mart associate who has been employed as a full-time associate for at least one year. $6000 undergraduate scholarship payable over four years. Must submit latest federal income tax return. Contact a member of Wal-Mart management for an application.

Award Scholarship for use in freshman, sophomore, junior, or senior years; renewable. *Number:* 100–120. *Amount:* $6000–$8000.
Eligibility Requirements: Applicant must be high school student; planning to enroll full-time at a two-year or four-year institution or university and affiliated with Wal-Mart Foundation. Available to U.S. citizens.
Application Requirements Application, financial need analysis, test scores, transcript, federal income tax return. *Deadline:* March 1.
World Wide Web: http://www.walmartfoundation.org

Walton Family Foundation Scholarship (continued)
Contact: Jenny Harral
Wal-Mart Foundation
702 Southwest 8th Street
Bentonville, AR 72716-0150
Phone: 800-530-9925
Fax: 501-273-6850

WILLITS FOUNDATION

WILLITS FOUNDATION SCHOLARSHIP PROGRAM   • 211

Renewable awards for children of full-time C. R. Bard, Inc. employees only. Children of Bard officers are not eligible. For domestic Bard branches only. Must be pursuing, or planning to pursue, full-time postsecondary studies in the year in which the application is made.

Award Scholarship for use in any year; renewable. *Number:* 10. *Amount:* $1000–$5000.

Eligibility Requirements: Applicant must be enrolled full-time at a four-year institution or university and affiliated with C.R. Bard, Inc. Available to U.S. and Canadian citizens.

Application Requirements Application, applicant must enter a contest, essay, photo, references, transcript. *Deadline:* March 1.

Contact: Ms. Linda Hrevnack, Secretary
Willits Foundation
730 Central Avenue
Murray Hill, NJ 07974
Phone: 908-277-8182
Fax: 908-277-8098

EMPLOYMENT EXPERIENCE

ALABAMA COMMISSION ON HIGHER EDUCATION

POLICE OFFICERS AND FIREFIGHTERS SURVIVORS EDUCATION ASSISTANCE PROGRAM-ALABAMA   • 212

Provides tuition, fees, books, and supplies to dependents of full-time police officers and firefighters killed in the line of duty. Must attend any Alabama public college as an undergraduate. Must be Alabama resident. Renewable.

Award Grant for use in freshman, sophomore, junior, or senior years; renewable. *Number:* 15–30. *Amount:* $2000–$5000.

Eligibility Requirements: Applicant must be enrolled full or part-time at a two-year or four-year or technical institution or university; single; resident of Alabama; studying in Alabama and have employment experience in police/firefighting. Available to U.S. citizens.

Application Requirements Application, transcript.
World Wide Web: http://www.ache.state.al.us
Contact: Dr. William Wall, Associate Executive Director for Student
Assistance, ACHE
Alabama Commission on Higher Education
PO Box 302000
Montgomery, AL 36130-2000

AMERICAN FOREIGN SERVICE ASSOCIATION

AMERICAN FOREIGN SERVICE ASSOCIATION (AFSA) FINANCIAL AID AWARD PROGRAM
see number 178

ARBY'S FOUNDATION, BIG BROTHERS BIG SISTERS OF AMERICA

ARBY'S-BIG BROTHERS BIG SISTERS SCHOLARSHIP AWARD
see number 182

ARKANSAS DEPARTMENT OF HIGHER EDUCATION

LAW ENFORCEMENT OFFICERS' DEPENDENTS SCHOLARSHIP-ARKANSAS
• 213

For dependents, under 23 years old, of Arkansas law-enforcement officers killed or permanently disabled in the line of duty. Renewable award is a waiver of tuition, fees, and room at two- or four-year Arkansas institution. Submit birth certificate, death certificate, and claims commission report of findings of fact. Proof of disability from State Claims Commission may also be submitted.

Award Scholarship for use in freshman, sophomore, junior, or senior years; renewable. *Number:* 27–32. *Amount:* $2000–$2500.
Eligibility Requirements: Applicant must be age 23 or under; enrolled full or part-time at a two-year or four-year institution or university; resident of Arkansas; studying in Arkansas and have employment experience in police/ firefighting. Available to U.S. citizens.
Application Requirements Application. *Deadline:* Continuous.
World Wide Web: http://www.arscholarships.com
Contact: Lillian Williams, Assistant Coordinator
Arkansas Department of Higher Education
114 East Capitol
Little Rock, AR 72201
Phone: 501-371-2050
Fax: 501-371-2001
E-mail: lillianw@adhe.arknet.edu

TEACHER AND ADMINISTRATOR GRANT
PROGRAM-ARKANSAS   • 214

Reimbursement program for certified teachers and administrators who wish to continue their education and improve their professional skills. Program available for use only during the summer months. For Arkansas resident attending Arkansas institution.

Award Grant for use in any year; not renewable. *Number:* 350–450. *Amount:* $150–$650.

Eligibility Requirements: Applicant must be enrolled at a four-year institution or university; resident of Arkansas; studying in Arkansas and have employment experience in teaching.

Application Requirements Application.

World Wide Web: http://www.arscholarships.com

Contact: Assistant Coordinator
Arkansas Department of Higher Education
114 East Capitol
Little Rock, AR 72201
Phone: 501-371-2050
Fax: 501-371-2001

BOYS & GIRLS CLUBS OF AMERICA

BOYS & GIRLS CLUBS OF AMERICA NATIONAL YOUTH OF THE
YEAR AWARD   see number 184

BRIDGESTONE/FIRESTONE TRUST FUND

BRIDGESTONE/FIRESTONE TRUST FUND SCHOLARSHIPS
see number 203

CALIFORNIA CORRECTIONAL PEACE
OFFICERS ASSOCIATION

CALIFORNIA CORRECTIONAL PEACE OFFICERS ASSOCIATION JOE
HARPER SCHOLARSHIP   • 215

A scholarship program for immediate relatives and/or correctional officers in California.

Award Scholarship for use in any year; not renewable. *Number:* 100. *Amount:* $1000.

Eligibility Requirements: Applicant must be enrolled full or part-time at a two-year or four-year or technical institution or university; resident of California and have employment experience in designated career field. Applicant must have 3.5 GPA or higher. Available to U.S. citizens.

Application Requirements Application, autobiography, essay, financial need analysis, photo, references, test scores, transcript. *Deadline:* April 30.

Contact: Marcia Bartlett, Bookkeeper
California Correctional Peace Officers Association
755 Riverpoint Drive, Suite 200
West Sacremento, CA 95605
Phone: 916-372-6060
Fax: 916-372-6623

CHAIRSCHOLARS FOUNDATION, INC.

CHAIRSCHOLARS FOUNDATION, INC. SCHOLARSHIPS • 216

Award for students who are severely physically challenged. Applicants may be high school seniors or college freshmen. Must be outstanding citizen with history of public service. Minimum 3.5 GPA required. Eight to ten renewable awards of $5000. Deadline: March 1. Must be 17 to 20 years old.

Award Scholarship for use in freshman or sophomore years; renewable. *Number:* 8–10. *Amount:* up to $5000.

Eligibility Requirements: Applicant must be age 17-20; enrolled full-time at a two-year or four-year or technical institution or university and have employment experience in community service. Applicant must be physically disabled. Applicant must have 3.5 GPA or higher. Available to U.S. citizens.

Application Requirements Application, autobiography, essay, financial need analysis, photo, portfolio, references, self-addressed stamped envelope, test scores, transcript, parents' tax return from previous year. *Deadline:* March 1.

World Wide Web: http://www.chairscholars.org

Contact: Hugo and Alicia Keim
Chairscholars Foundation, Inc.
16101 Carencia Lane
Odessa, FL 33556
Phone: 813-920-2737
E-mail: hugokeim@earthlink.net

DELAWARE HIGHER EDUCATION COMMISSION

EDUCATIONAL BENEFITS FOR CHILDREN OF DECEASED MILITARY AND STATE POLICE • 217

Renewable award for Delaware residents who are children of state or military police who were killed in the line of duty. Must attend a Delaware institution unless program of study is not available. Funds cover tuition and fees at Delaware institutions. The amount varies at non-Delaware institutions. Must submit proof of service and related death. Must be ages 16-24 at time of application. Deadline is three weeks before classes begin.

Award Grant for use in freshman, sophomore, junior, or senior years; renewable. *Number:* 1–10. *Amount:* $6255.

Educational Benefits for Children of Deceased Military and State Police (continued)

Eligibility Requirements: Applicant must be age 16-24; enrolled full-time at a two-year or four-year institution or university; resident of Delaware and have employment experience in police/firefighting. Available to U.S. citizens. Applicant or parent must meet one or more of the following requirements: general military experience; retired from active duty; disabled or killed as a result of military service; Prisoner-Of-War; or Missing-In-Action.

Application Requirements Application, verification of service-related death.

Deadline: Continuous.

World Wide Web: http://www.doe.state.de.us/high-ed

Contact: Maureen Laffey, Associate Director
Delaware Higher Education Commission
820 North French Street
Wilmington, DE 19801
Phone: 302-577-3240
Fax: 302-577-6765
E-mail: dhec@state.de.us

DELTA DELTA DELTA FOUNDATION

DELTA DELTA DELTA UNDERGRADUATE SCHOLARSHIP

see number 186

DUKE ENERGY CORPORATION

DUKE ENERGY SCHOLARS PROGRAM

see number 204

FEDERAL EMPLOYEE EDUCATION AND ASSISTANCE FUND

FEEA/NARFE SCHOLARSHIP • 218

Award available to children and grandchildren of National Association of Retired Federal Employees members. Must be full-time students in an accredited two-year or four-year postsecondary school. Minimum 3.0 GPA required.

Award Scholarship for use in freshman, sophomore, junior, or senior years; not renewable. *Number:* 50. *Amount:* $1000.

Eligibility Requirements: Applicant must be enrolled full-time at a two-year or four-year institution or university and have employment experience in federal/postal service. Applicant must have 3.0 GPA or higher. Available to U.S. citizens.

Application Requirements Application, essay, references, test scores, transcript.

World Wide Web: http://www.feea.org

Contact: Stephen Bauer, Director
Federal Employee Education and Assistance Fund
8441 West Bowles Avenue, Suite 200
Littleton, CO 80123-9501
Phone: 303-933-7580
Fax: 303-933-7587

GEORGIA STUDENT FINANCE COMMISSION

GEORGIA PUBLIC SAFETY MEMORIAL GRANT/LAW ENFORCEMENT PERSONNEL DEPARTMENT GRANT • 219

Award for children of Georgia law enforcement officers, prison guards, or fire fighters killed or permanently disabled in the line of duty. Must attend an accredited postsecondary Georgia school. Complete the Law Enforcement Personnel Dependents application.

Award Grant for use in freshman, sophomore, junior, or senior years; renewable. *Number:* 20–40. *Amount:* $2000.

Eligibility Requirements: Applicant must be enrolled full-time at a two-year or four-year or technical institution or university; resident of Georgia; studying in Georgia and have employment experience in police/firefighting. Available to U.S. citizens.

Application Requirements Application. *Deadline:* Continuous.

World Wide Web: http://www.gsfc.org

Contact: William Flook, Director of Scholarships and Grants Division
Georgia Student Finance Commission
2082 East Exchange Place, Suite 100
Tucker, GA 30084

HITACHI FOUNDATION

YOSHIYAMA AWARD • 220

Award for high school seniors based on their community service activities. Must be nominated by someone familiar with their service. Submit nomination form, letter of nomination and two supporting letters by April 1.

Award Prize for use in freshman year; not renewable. *Number:* 10–12. *Amount:* $5000.

Eligibility Requirements: Applicant must be high school student; planning to enroll full-time at an institution or university; single and have employment experience in community service. Available to U.S. citizens.

Application Requirements References, nomination form, letter of nomination. *Deadline:* April 1.

World Wide Web: http://www.hitachi.org

Yoshiyama Award (continued)
Contact: Assistant Coordinator
Hitachi Foundation
1509 22nd Street, NW
Washington, DC 20037-1098
Phone: 202-457-0588
Fax: 202-296-1098

INDEPENDENT OFFICE PRODUCTS AND FURNITURE DEALERS ASSOCIATION

ASSOCIATION SCHOLARSHIP • 221

Funded by contributions from Association members, these awards are given to employees or relatives of employees of Association member companies based on academic achievement and financial need.

Award Scholarship for use in any year; not renewable. *Number:* 65–70. *Amount:* $2000.

Eligibility Requirements: Applicant must be enrolled full-time at a two-year or four-year or technical institution or university and have employment experience in designated career field. Available to U.S. citizens.

Application Requirements Application, references, test scores, transcript. *Deadline:* March 15.

World Wide Web: http://www.iopfda.org

Contact: Faye Peterson, Marketing Projects Coordinator
Independent Office Products and Furniture Dealers Association
301 North Fairfax Street
Suite 200
Alexandria, VA 22314-2696
Phone: 703-549-9040 Ext. 134
Fax: 703-683-7552

J. WOOD PLATT CADDIE SCHOLARSHIP TRUST

J. WOOD PLATT CADDIE SCHOLARSHIP TRUST • 222

Renewable award for high school seniors or college undergraduates who have caddied at least one year at a member club of the Golf Association of Philadelphia. Submit transcript and financial need analysis with application. Interview required.

Award Scholarship for use in freshman, sophomore, junior, senior, or graduate years; renewable. *Number:* 200–300. *Amount:* $200–$15,000.

Eligibility Requirements: Applicant must be enrolled full-time at a two-year or four-year institution or university; have employment experience in private club/caddying and must have an interest in golf. Available to U.S. and non-U.S. citizens.

Application Requirements Application, financial need analysis, interview, references, test scores, transcript. *Deadline:* April 25.
World Wide Web: http://www.gapgolf.org
Contact: Robert Caucci, Program Administrator
J. Wood Platt Caddie Scholarship Trust
Drawer 808
Southeastern, PA 19399-0808
Phone: 610-687-2340 Ext. 21
Fax: 610-687-2082

NATIONAL FASTENER DISTRIBUTORS ASSOCIATION

NATIONAL FASTENER DISTRIBUTORS ASSOCIATION MEMORIAL SCHOLARSHIP FUND • 223

One-time award available to the children and employees of member company firms. Children applying must be incoming full-time freshmen and employees can be at any level of education, but must work for the member company at least 20 hours weekly. Company firm must be a member of the National Fastener Distributors Association.

Award Scholarship for use in any year; not renewable. *Number:* 20–40. *Amount:* $500–$2000.
Eligibility Requirements: Applicant must be enrolled full or part-time at a two-year or four-year or technical institution or university and have employment experience in designated career field. Available to U.S. and non-U.S. citizens.
Application Requirements Application, essay, financial need analysis, references, test scores, transcript. *Deadline:* March 15.
World Wide Web: http://www.nfda-fastener.org
Contact: Tanya Harris-Soeder, Administrative Assistant
National Fastener Distributors Association
1717 East Ninth Street, Suite 1185
Cleveland, OH 44114-2803
Phone: 216-579-1571
Fax: 216-579-1531
E-mail: tsoeder@nfda-fastener.org

NATIONAL FEDERATION OF THE BLIND

NATIONAL FEDERATION OF THE BLIND SCHOLARSHIPS • 224

Award for legally blind students pursuing postsecondary education in the U.S. Must submit recommendation from state officer of the National Federation of the Blind. Award based on academic excellence, service to the community, and financial need. One award given to a person working full-time and is attending or planning to attend a part-time course of study to broaden opportunities in work.

National Federation of the Blind Scholarships (continued)

Award Scholarship for use in any year; not renewable. *Number:* 15. *Amount:* $3000–$5000.

Eligibility Requirements: Applicant must be enrolled full or part-time at an institution or university and have employment experience in community service. Applicant must be visually impaired. Available to U.S. and non-U.S. citizens.

Application Requirements Application, essay, financial need analysis, references, transcript. *Deadline:* March 31.

World Wide Web: http://www.nfb.org

Contact: Peggy Elliot, Chairman, Scholarship Committee
National Federation of the Blind
805 Fifth Avenue
Grinnell, IA 50112
Phone: 641-236-3366

NEW JERSEY STATE GOLF ASSOCIATION

NEW JERSEY STATE GOLF ASSOCIATION CADDIE SCHOLARSHIP • 225

Must caddie for at least one year at a member club of the New Jersey State Golf Association. Based on grades, test scores, references, and financial need. Renewable award for undergraduate use. Minimum 2.5 GPA required. Must be a New Jersey resident.

Award Scholarship for use in freshman, sophomore, junior, or senior years; renewable. *Number:* 200. *Amount:* $1200–$2500.

Eligibility Requirements: Applicant must be enrolled full-time at a two-year or four-year institution or university; resident of New Jersey and have employment experience in private club/caddying. Applicant must have 2.5 GPA or higher.

Application Requirements Application, financial need analysis, references, test scores, transcript. *Deadline:* May 1.

World Wide Web: http://www.njsga.org

Contact: Education Director
New Jersey State Golf Association
PO Box 6947
Freehold, NJ 07728

NORTH CAROLINA STATE EDUCATION ASSISTANCE AUTHORITY

NORTH CAROLINA TEACHING FELLOWS SCHOLARSHIP PROGRAM • 226

Must be high school senior and North Carolina resident. Selection based on high school grades, class standing, SAT scores, writing samples, community service, extracurricular activities and references. Recipients must be accepted at 14 select North Carolina postsecondary institutions. For list see website: http://www.teachingfellows.org. Interviews are required. Financial need is not required.

Award Scholarship for use in freshman, sophomore, junior, or senior years; renewable. *Number:* up to 400. *Amount:* up to $6500.

Eligibility Requirements: Applicant must be high school student; planning to enroll at a four-year institution or university; resident of North Carolina; studying in North Carolina and have employment experience in community service. Available to U.S. citizens.

Application Requirements Application, essay, interview, references, test scores, transcript. *Deadline:* October 27.

World Wide Web: http://www.cfnc.org

Contact: North Carolina Teaching Fellows Program
North Carolina State Education Assistance Authority
3739 National Drive, Suite 210
Raleigh, NC 27612
Phone: 919-781-6833
E-mail: info@teachingfellows.org

PHOENIX SUNS CHARITIES/SUN STUDENTS SCHOLARSHIP

SUN STUDENT COLLEGE SCHOLARSHIP PROGRAM • 227

Applicants must be a senior preparing to graduate from a high school in Arizona. Eligible applicants will have a minimum 2.5 GPA. Applicants must provide evidence of regular involvement in charitable activities or volunteer service in school, church or community organizations. Ten $1,000 scholarships and one $5,000 scholarships will be awarded.

Award Scholarship for use in freshman year; not renewable. *Number:* 1–10. *Amount:* $1000–$5000.

Eligibility Requirements: Applicant must be high school student; planning to enroll full or part-time at a two-year or four-year or technical institution or university; resident of Arizona and have employment experience in community service. Applicant must have 2.5 GPA or higher. Available to U.S. citizens.

Application Requirements Application, essay, transcript. *Deadline:* February 13.

World Wide Web: http://www.suns.com

Contact: Glenna Martinez, Administrative Assistant
Phoenix Suns Charities/Sun Students Scholarship
PO Box 1369
Phoenix, AZ 85001
Phone: 602-379-7767
Fax: 602-379-7596

PROCTER & GAMBLE FUND

PROCTER & GAMBLE FUND SCHOLARSHIP COMPETITION FOR EMPLOYEES' CHILDREN
see number 207

RECORDING FOR THE BLIND & DYSLEXIC

MARY P. OENSLAGER SCHOLASTIC ACHIEVEMENT AWARDS
see number 200

SID RICHARDSON MEMORIAL FUND

SID RICHARDSON MEMORIAL FUND • 228

Eligible applicants are children or grandchildren of persons presently employed (or retired) at a Sid Bass/Richardson company or its subsidiaries. Employee must have a minimum of three years of full-time employment. High seniors may apply for incoming freshman year. Minimum GPA 2.0.

Award Scholarship for use in any year; not renewable. *Number:* 50–60. *Amount:* $500–$7000.

Eligibility Requirements: Applicant must be enrolled full or part-time at a two-year or four-year or technical institution or university and have employment experience in designated career field. Available to U.S. and non-U.S. citizens.

Application Requirements Application, essay, financial need analysis, test scores, transcript. *Deadline:* May 31.

Contact: Jo Helen Rosasker, Administrator
Sid Richardson Memorial Fund
309 Main Street
Fort Worth, TX 76102
Phone: 817-336-0494
Fax: 817-332-2176
E-mail: jhrosacker@sidrichardson.org

SOUTH CAROLINA DEPARTMENT OF EDUCATION

ROBERT C. BYRD HONORS SCHOLARSHIP-SOUTH CAROLINA • 229

Renewable award of $1500 for graduating high school seniors from South Carolina who will be attending a two-year or four-year institution. Applications should be superior students who demonstrate academic achievement and show promise of continued success at a postsecondary institution.

Award Scholarship for use in freshman, sophomore, junior, or senior years; renewable. *Number:* 96. *Amount:* $1500.

Eligibility Requirements: Applicant must be high school student; planning to enroll at a two-year or four-year institution; resident of South Carolina and have employment experience in community service. Applicant must have 3.5 GPA or higher. Available to U.S. citizens.

Application Requirements Application, references, test scores, transcript, extra curricular activities. *Deadline:* February 4.

Contact: Mrs. Beth Cope, Program Administrator
South Carolina Department of Education
1424 Senate Street
Columbia, SC 29201
Phone: 803-734-8116
Fax: 803-734-4387

SUBMARINE OFFICERS' WIVES CLUB

BOWFIN MEMORIAL SCHOLARSHIP • 230

Bowfin Memorial Scholarships are available to Hawaii submariners and their families. Academic scholarships are for children of submariners under 23 years old and Continuing Education Scholarships are for submariners and their spouses.

Award Scholarship for use in any year; not renewable. *Number:* 8–40. *Amount:* $500–$2500.

Eligibility Requirements: Applicant must be enrolled full or part-time at a two-year or four-year or technical institution or university; resident of Hawaii and have employment experience in designated career field. Available to U.S. citizens. Applicant must have served in the Navy.

Application Requirements Application, essay, financial need analysis, interview, references, transcript. *Deadline:* March 1.

Contact: Scholarship Coordinator
Submarine Officers' Wives Club
121 McGrew Loop
Aiea, HI 96701

TEXAS HIGHER EDUCATION COORDINATING BOARD

TRAIN OUR TEACHERS AWARD • 231

Awarded to employed child care workers seeking credentials or an associate degree in child development. Must agree to work 18 consecutive months in a licensed child care facility. Must attend a Texas institution.

Award Scholarship for use in any year; not renewable. *Number:* up to 2000. *Amount:* up to $1000.

Eligibility Requirements: Applicant must be studying in Texas and have employment experience in designated career field.

Application Requirements Application.

Train our Teachers Award (continued)
World Wide Web: http://www.collegefortexans.com
Contact: Financial aid office at college
Texas Higher Education Coordinating Board
PO Box 12788
Austin, TX 78711-2788
Phone: 512-427-6101
Fax: 512-427-6127
E-mail: grantinfo@thecb.state.tx.us

TWO/TEN INTERNATIONAL FOOTWEAR FOUNDATION

TWO/TEN INTERNATIONAL FOOTWEAR FOUNDATION SCHOLARSHIP • 232

Renewable, merit-based award available to students who have 500 hours work experience in footwear, leather, or allied industries during year of application, or have a parent employed in one of these fields for at least one year. Must have proof of employment and maintain 2.0 GPA.

Award Scholarship for use in freshman, sophomore, junior, or senior years; renewable. *Number:* 200–250. *Amount:* $200–$3000.
Eligibility Requirements: Applicant must be enrolled full-time at a two-year or four-year or technical institution or university and have employment experience in leather/footwear. Available to U.S. citizens.
Application Requirements Application, essay, financial need analysis, references, transcript. *Deadline:* December 15.
World Wide Web: http://www.twoten.org
Contact: Catherine Nelson, Scholarship Director
Two/Ten International Footwear Foundation
1466 Main Street
Waltham, MA 02451-1623
Phone: 800-346-3210
Fax: 781-736-1555
E-mail: scholarship@twoten.org

WAL-MART FOUNDATION

WAL-MART ASSOCIATE SCHOLARSHIPS see number 209

WILLIAM G. AND MARIE SELBY FOUNDATION

SELBY SCHOLAR PROGRAM • 233

Scholarships awarded up to $5000 annually, not to exceed 1/3 of individual's financial need. Renewable for four years if student is full-time undergraduate at accredited college or university. Must demonstrate values of leadership and service to the community. Must reside in Sarasota, Manatee, Charlotte, DeSoto, counties in Florida.

Award Scholarship for use in freshman, sophomore, junior, or senior years; renewable. *Number:* 30. *Amount:* up to $5000.

Eligibility Requirements: Applicant must be high school student; planning to enroll full-time at a four-year institution or university; resident of Florida; have employment experience in community service and must have an interest in leadership. Applicant must have 3.0 GPA or higher. Available to U.S. and non-U.S. citizens.

Application Requirements Application, essay, financial need analysis, interview, references, test scores, transcript. *Deadline:* April 1.

World Wide Web: http://www.selbyfdn.org

Contact: Jan Noah, Grants Manager
William G. and Marie Selby Foundation
1800 Second Street, Suite 750
Sarasota, FL 34236
Phone: 941-957-0442
Fax: 941-957-3135
E-mail: jnoah@selbyfdn.org

IMPAIRMENT

AMERICAN COUNCIL OF THE BLIND

AMERICAN COUNCIL OF THE BLIND SCHOLARSHIPS • 234

Merit-based award available to undergraduate, graduate, vocational or technical students who are legally blind in both eyes. Submit certificate of legal blindness and proof of acceptance at an accredited postsecondary institution.

Award Scholarship for use in any year; not renewable. *Number:* 31. *Amount:* $200–$3000.

Eligibility Requirements: Applicant must be enrolled full-time at a two-year or four-year or technical institution or university. Applicant must be visually impaired. Applicant must have 3.5 GPA or higher.

Application Requirements Application, autobiography, essay, references, transcript. *Deadline:* March 1.

World Wide Web: http://www.acb.org

Contact: Terry Pacheco, Affiliate and Membership Services
American Council of the Blind
1155 15th Street, NW, Suite 1004
Washington, DC 20005
Phone: 202-467-5081
Fax: 202-467-5085
E-mail: info@acb.org

CHAIRSCHOLARS FOUNDATION, INC.

CHAIRSCHOLARS FOUNDATION, INC. SCHOLARSHIPS

see number 216

CYSTIC FIBROSIS SCHOLARSHIP FOUNDATION

CYSTIC FIBROSIS FOUNDATION SCHOLARSHIP • 235

Awards for young adults with cystic fibrosis to be used to further their education after high school. Awards may be used for tuition, books and fees. Awards are for one year. Students may reapply in subsequent years.

Award Scholarship for use in any year; not renewable. *Number:* 50. *Amount:* $1000–$2000.

Eligibility Requirements: Applicant must be enrolled full or part-time at a two-year or four-year or technical institution or university. Applicant must be physically disabled. Available to U.S. citizens.

Application Requirements Application, essay, financial need analysis, references, test scores, transcript. *Deadline:* March 15.

Contact: Mary K. Bottorff, President
Cystic Fibrosis Scholarship Foundation
2814 Grant Street
Evanston, IL 60201
Phone: 847-328-0127
Fax: 847-328-0127
E-mail: mkbcfsf@aol.com

IMMUNE DEFICIENCY FOUNDATION

IMMUNE DEFICIENCY FOUNDATION SCHOLARSHIP • 236

One-time award available to individuals diagnosed with a primary immune deficiency disease. Must submit medical verification of diagnosis. Available for study at the undergraduate level at any postsecondary institution. Must be U.S. citizen.

Award Scholarship for use in freshman, sophomore, junior, or senior years; not renewable. *Number:* 25–35. *Amount:* $500–$2000.

Eligibility Requirements: Applicant must be enrolled full or part-time at a two-year or four-year or technical institution or university. Applicant must be physically disabled. Available to U.S. citizens.

Application Requirements Application, autobiography, essay, financial need analysis, references. *Deadline:* March 31.

World Wide Web: http://www.primaryimmune.org

Contact: Tamara Brown, Medical Programs Manager
Immune Deficiency Foundation
40 West Chesapeake Avenue, Suite 308
Towson, MD 21204
Phone: 800-296-4433
Fax: 410-321-9165
E-mail: tb@primaryimmune.org

IOWA DIVISION OF VOCATIONAL REHABILITATION SERVICES

IOWA VOCATIONAL REHABILITATION • 237

Provides vocational rehabilitation services to individuals with disabilities who need these services in order to maintain, retain, or obtain employment compatible with their disabilities. Must be Iowa resident.

Award Grant for use in any year; renewable. *Number:* up to 5000. *Amount:* $500–$4000.

Eligibility Requirements: Applicant must be enrolled full or part-time at a two-year or four-year or technical institution or university and resident of Iowa. Applicant must be hearing impaired, learning disabled, physically disabled, or visually impaired. Available to U.S. and non-U.S. citizens.

Application Requirements Application, financial need analysis, interview. *Deadline:* Continuous.

World Wide Web: http://www.dvrs.state.ia.us

Contact: Ralph Childers, Policy and Workforce Initiatives Coordinator
Iowa Division of Vocational Rehabilitation Services
Division of Vocational Rehabilitation Services
510 East 12th Street
Des Moines, IA 50319
Phone: 515-281-4151
Fax: 515-281-4703
E-mail: rchilders@dvrs.state.ia.us

NATIONAL FEDERATION OF THE BLIND

NATIONAL FEDERATION OF THE BLIND SCHOLARSHIPS

see number 224

NATIONAL PKU NEWS

ROBERT GUTHRIE PKU SCHOLARSHIP AND AWARDS • 238

Award program is open only to persons with phenylketonuria (PKU) who are on a special diet for PKU treatment. PKU is a genetic metabolic disease affecting about 1/12,000 of U.S. births yearly. Award is for full- or part-time study at any accredited U.S. institution.

Robert Guthrie PKU Scholarship and Awards (continued)

Award Scholarship for use in any year; not renewable. *Number:* 6–12. *Amount:* $500–$5000.

Eligibility Requirements: Applicant must be enrolled full or part-time at a two-year or four-year or technical institution or university. Applicant must be physically disabled. Available to U.S. and non-U.S. citizens.

Application Requirements Application, autobiography, essay, references, test scores, transcript. *Deadline:* November 1.

World Wide Web: http://www.pkunews.org

Contact: Virginia Schuett, Director
National PKU News
6869 Woodlawn Avenue NE
Suite 116
Seattle, WA 98115-5469
Phone: 206-525-8140
Fax: 206-525-5023
E-mail: schuett@pkunews.org

RECORDING FOR THE BLIND & DYSLEXIC

MARY P. OENSLAGER SCHOLASTIC ACHIEVEMENT AWARDS

see number 200

MILITARY SERVICE: AIR FORCE_____

AIR FORCE AID SOCIETY

GENERAL HENRY H. ARNOLD EDUCATION GRANT PROGRAM
● 239

$1,500 grant provided to selected sons and daughters of active duty, Title 10 AGR/Reserve, Title 32 AGR performing full-time active duty, retired reserve and deceased Air Force members; spouses (stateside) of active members and Title 10 AGR/Reservist; and surviving spouses of deceased personnel for their undergraduate studies. Dependent children must be unmarried and under the age of 23. High school seniors may apply. Minimum 2.0 GPA required. Applicant must reapply for subsequent years.

Award Grant for use in freshman, sophomore, junior, or senior years; not renewable. *Number:* 4000–5000. *Amount:* $1500.

Eligibility Requirements: Applicant must be enrolled full-time at a two-year or four-year or technical institution or university. Available to U.S. citizens. Applicant or parent must meet one or more of the following requirements: Air Force or Air Force National Guard experience; retired from active duty; disabled or killed as a result of military service; Prisoner-Of-War; or Missing-In-Action.

Application Requirements Application, financial need analysis, self-addressed stamped envelope, transcript, program's own financial forms, USAF military orders (member/parent). *Deadline:* March 15.

World Wide Web: http://www.afas.org

Contact: Education Assistance Department
Air Force Aid Society
1745 Jefferson Davis Highway, Suite 202
Arlington, VA 22202-3410
Phone: 800-429-9475
Fax: 703-607-3022
E-mail: ed@afas-hq.org

MILITARY SERVICE: AIR FORCE NATIONAL GUARD

GENERAL HENRY H. ARNOLD EDUCATION GRANT PROGRAM
see number 239

DEPARTMENT OF MILITARY AFFAIRS

WISCONSIN NATIONAL GUARD TUITION GRANT • 240

Renewable award for active members of the Wisconsin National Guard in good standing, who successfully complete a course of study at a qualifying school. Award covers full tuition, excluding fees, not to exceed undergraduate tuition charged by University of Wisconsin-Madison. Must have a minimum 2.0 GPA.

Award Grant for use in freshman, sophomore, junior, or senior years; renewable. *Number:* up to 4000. *Amount:* $1784.

Eligibility Requirements: Applicant must be enrolled full or part-time at a two-year or four-year or technical institution or university and resident of Wisconsin. Applicant must have 2.5 GPA or higher. Available to U.S. citizens. Applicant must have served in the Air Force National Guard or Army National Guard.

Application Requirements Application. *Deadline:* Continuous.

Contact: Karen Behling, Tuition Grant Administrator
Department of Military Affairs
PO Box 14587
Madison, WI 53714-0587
Phone: 608-242-3159
Fax: 608-242-3154
E-mail: behlik@dma.state.wi.us

ILLINOIS STUDENT ASSISTANCE COMMISSION (ISAC)

ILLINOIS NATIONAL GUARD GRANT PROGRAM • 241

Award for qualified National Guard personnel which pays tuition and fees at Illinois public universities and community colleges. Must provide documentation of service. Deadline: September 15.

Award Grant for use in any year; renewable. *Number:* 2500–3000. *Amount:* $1300–$1700.

Eligibility Requirements: Applicant must be enrolled full or part-time at a two-year or four-year institution or university; resident of Illinois and studying in Illinois. Available to U.S. and non-U.S. citizens. Applicant must have national guard experience.

Application Requirements Application, documentation of service. *Deadline:* September 15.

World Wide Web: http://www.isac-online.org

Contact: David Barinholtz, Client Information
Illinois Student Assistance Commission (ISAC)
1755 Lake Cook Road
Deerfield, IL 60015-5209
Phone: 847-948-8500 Ext. 2385

KANSAS NATIONAL GUARD EDUCATIONAL ASSISTANCE PROGRAM

KANSAS NATIONAL GUARD EDUCATIONAL ASSISTANCE AWARD PROGRAM • 242

Service scholarship for enlisted soldiers in the Kansas National Guard. Pays up to 100% of tuition and fees based on funding. Must attend a state-supported institution. Recipients will be required to serve in the KNG for four years after the last payment of state tuition assistance. Must not have over 15 years of service at time of application. Deadlines are January 15 and August 15. Contact KNG Education Services Specialist for further information. Must be Kansas resident.

Award Scholarship for use in freshman, sophomore, junior, or senior years; not renewable. *Number:* up to 400. *Amount:* up to $617.

Eligibility Requirements: Applicant must be enrolled full or part-time at a two-year or four-year or technical institution or university; resident of Kansas and studying in Kansas. Available to U.S. citizens. Applicant must have served in the Air Force National Guard or Army National Guard.

Application Requirements Application.

Contact: SSG. Anita Istas, Education Services Specialist
Kansas National Guard Educational Assistance Program
Attn: AGKS-DOP-ESO, The Adjutant General of Kansas
2800 South West Topeka Boulevard
Topeka, KS 66611-1287
Phone: 785-274-1060
Fax: 785-274-1617
E-mail: anita.istas@ks.ngb.army.mil

OHIO NATIONAL GUARD

OHIO NATIONAL GUARD SCHOLARSHIP PROGRAM • 243

Scholarships are for undergraduate studies at an approved Ohio postsecondary institution. Applicants must enlist for six years of Selective Service Reserve Duty in the Ohio National Guard. Scholarship pays 100% instructional and general fees for public institutions and an average of cost of public schools is available for private schools. Must be 18 years of age or older. Award is renewable. Deadlines: July 1, November 1, February 1, April 1.

Award Scholarship for use in freshman, sophomore, junior, or senior years; renewable. *Number:* 3500. *Amount:* $3000.

Eligibility Requirements: Applicant must be age 18; enrolled full or part-time at a two-year or four-year institution or university and studying in Ohio. Available to U.S. citizens. Applicant must have served in the Air Force National Guard or Army National Guard.

Application Requirements Application.

Contact: Mrs. Toni Davis, Grants Administrator
Ohio National Guard
2825 West Granville Road
Columbus, OH 43235-2789
Phone: 614-336-7032
Fax: 614-336-7318
E-mail: davist@tagoh.org

STATE OF GEORGIA

GEORGIA NATIONAL GUARD SERVICE CANCELABLE LOAN PROGRAM • 244

Forgivable loans will be awarded to residents of Georgia maintaining good military standing as an eligible member of the Georgia National Guard who are enrolled at least half-time in an undergraduate degree program at an eligible college, university or technical school within the state of Georgia.

Award Forgivable loan for use in freshman, sophomore, junior, or senior years; not renewable. *Number:* 200–250. *Amount:* $438–$1316.

Eligibility Requirements: Applicant must be enrolled full or part-time at a two-year or four-year or technical institution or university; resident of Georgia

Georgia National Guard Service Cancelable Loan Program (continued)
and studying in Georgia. Available to U.S. citizens. Applicant must have served
in the Air Force National Guard or Army National Guard.
Application Requirements Application, financial need analysis. *Deadline:*
Continuous.
World Wide Web: http://www.gsfc.org
Contact: Peggy Matthews, Manager/GSFA Originations
State of Georgia
2082 East Exchange Place, Suite 230
Tucker, GA 30084-5305
Phone: 770-724-9230
Fax: 770-724-9263
E-mail: peggy@mail.gsfc.state.ga.us

STATE STUDENT ASSISTANCE COMMISSION OF INDIANA (SSACI)

INDIANA NATIONAL GUARD SUPPLEMENTAL GRANT • 245

One-time award, which is a supplement to the Indiana Higher Education Grant
program. Applicants must be members of the Indiana National Guard. All
Guard paperwork must be completed prior to the start of each semester. The
FAFSA must be filed by March 1st each year. Award covers tuition and fees at
select public colleges.

Award Grant for use in freshman, sophomore, junior, or senior years; not
renewable. *Number:* 350–735. *Amount:* $200–$4734.
Eligibility Requirements: Applicant must be enrolled full or part-time at a
two-year or four-year institution or university; resident of Indiana and studying
in Indiana. Available to U.S. citizens. Applicant must have served in the Air
Force National Guard or Army National Guard.
Application Requirements Application, financial need analysis. *Deadline:*
March 1.
World Wide Web: http://www.ssaci.in.gov
Contact: Grants Counselor
State Student Assistance Commission of Indiana (SSACI)
150 West Market Street, Suite 500
Indianapolis, IN 46204-2805
Phone: 317-232-2350
Fax: 317-232-2360
E-mail: grants@ssaci.state.in.us

MILITARY SERVICE: ARMY NATIONAL GUARD

DEPARTMENT OF MILITARY AFFAIRS

WISCONSIN NATIONAL GUARD TUITION GRANT   see number 240

ILLINOIS STUDENT ASSISTANCE COMMISSION (ISAC)

ILLINOIS NATIONAL GUARD GRANT PROGRAM   see number 241

KANSAS NATIONAL GUARD EDUCATIONAL ASSISTANCE PROGRAM

KANSAS NATIONAL GUARD EDUCATIONAL ASSISTANCE AWARD PROGRAM   see number 242

OHIO NATIONAL GUARD

OHIO NATIONAL GUARD SCHOLARSHIP PROGRAM   see number 243

STATE OF GEORGIA

GEORGIA NATIONAL GUARD SERVICE CANCELABLE LOAN PROGRAM   see number 244

STATE STUDENT ASSISTANCE COMMISSION OF INDIANA (SSACI)

INDIANA NATIONAL GUARD SUPPLEMENTAL GRANT   see number 245

MILITARY SERVICE: GENERAL_____

DELAWARE HIGHER EDUCATION COMMISSION

EDUCATIONAL BENEFITS FOR CHILDREN OF DECEASED MILITARY AND STATE POLICE   see number 217

ILLINOIS STUDENT ASSISTANCE COMMISSION (ISAC)

ILLINOIS VETERAN GRANT PROGRAM—IVG   **• 246**

Award for qualified veterans for tuition and fees at Illinois public universities and community colleges. Must provide documentation of service (DD214). Deadline is continuous.

Illinois Veteran Grant Program—IVG (continued)
Award Grant for use in any year; renewable. *Number:* 11,000–13,000. *Amount:* $1400–$1600.
Eligibility Requirements: Applicant must be enrolled at a two-year or four-year institution or university; resident of Illinois and studying in Illinois. Available to U.S. and non-U.S. citizens. Applicant must have general military experience.
Application Requirements Application, documentation of service. *Deadline:* Continuous.
World Wide Web: http://www.isac-online.org
Contact: David Barinholtz, Client Information
Illinois Student Assistance Commission (ISAC)
1755 Lake Cook Road
Deerfield, IL 60015-5209
Phone: 847-948-8500 Ext. 2385

MARYLAND STATE HIGHER EDUCATION COMMISSION

EDWARD T. CONROY MEMORIAL SCHOLARSHIP PROGRAM • 247
Scholarship for dependents of deceased or 100% disabled U.S. Armed Forces personnel, Vietnam Missing-In-Action or Prisoner-of-War or sons or daughters of deceased safety personnel, or surviving spouse who has not remarried, deceased state personnel, or deceased safety personnel. Must be a Maryland resident at time of death or disability. Submit applicable VA verification, 100% disability verification and/or chapter 35 letter with application. Must be at least 16 years of age. Must attend Maryland institution.

Award Scholarship for use in freshman, sophomore, junior, senior, or graduate years; renewable. *Number:* up to 80. *Amount:* up to $12,981.
Eligibility Requirements: Applicant must be age 16-24; enrolled full or part-time at a two-year or four-year institution or university; resident of Maryland and studying in Maryland. Available to U.S. citizens. Applicant or parent must meet one or more of the following requirements: general military experience; retired from active duty; disabled or killed as a result of military service; Prisoner-Of-War; or Missing-In-Action.
Application Requirements Application, birth and death certificate, and disability papers. *Deadline:* July 30.
World Wide Web: http://www.mhec.state.md.us
Contact: Margaret Crutchley, Scholarship Administration
Maryland State Higher Education Commission
16 Francis Street
Annapolis, MD 21401-1781
Phone: 410-260-4545
Fax: 410-974-5994
E-mail: ssamail@mhec.state.md.us

OHIO AMERICAN LEGION

OHIO AMERICAN LEGION SCHOLARSHIPS see number 199

RED RIVER VALLEY FIGHTER PILOTS ASSOCIATION

RED RIVER VALLEY ASSOCIATION SCHOLARSHIP GRANT PROGRAM • 248

Annual college tuition grants for legal dependents of U.S. military members listed as Killed-In-Action or Missing-In-Action; or of military aircrew members killed while performing aircrew duties on non-combat missions. Must submit DD Form 1300. Amount of award varies.

Award Grant for use in any year; not renewable. *Number:* 10–40. *Amount:* $500–$4000.

Eligibility Requirements: Applicant must be enrolled full or part-time at a two-year or four-year or technical institution or university. Available to U.S. citizens. Applicant or parent must meet one or more of the following requirements: general military experience; retired from active duty; disabled or killed as a result of military service; Prisoner-Of-War; or Missing-In-Action.

Application Requirements Application, financial need analysis, photo, references, test scores, transcript. *Deadline:* May 15.

World Wide Web: http://www.river-rats.org

Contact: Col. Al Bache, Executive Director
Red River Valley Fighter Pilots Association
PO Box 882
Boothbay Harbor, ME 04538-0882
Phone: 207-633-0333
Fax: 207-633-0330
E-mail: afbridger@aol.com

MILITARY SERVICE: MARINES_____

UNITED STATES MARINE CORPS SCHOLARSHIP FOUNDATION, INC.

MARINE CORPS SCHOLARSHIP FOUNDATION • 249

Available to undergraduate dependent children of current or former Marine Corps members whose family income does not exceed $49,000. Must submit proof of parent's service and should send for applications in the winter.

Award Scholarship for use in freshman, sophomore, junior, or senior years; not renewable. *Number:* 1000. *Amount:* $500–$2500.

Marine Corps Scholarship Foundation (continued)

Eligibility Requirements: Applicant must be enrolled at a two-year or four-year or technical institution or university. Available to U.S. citizens. Applicant or parent must meet one or more of the following requirements: Marine Corp experience; retired from active duty; disabled or killed as a result of military service; Prisoner-Of-War; or Missing-In-Action.

Application Requirements Application, essay, financial need analysis, photo, transcript. *Deadline:* April 1.

World Wide Web: http://www.marine-scholars.org

Contact: United States Marine Corps Scholarship Foundation, Inc.
PO Box 3008
Princeton, NJ 08543-3008

MILITARY SERVICE: NAVY_____

DOLPHIN SCHOLARSHIP FOUNDATION

DOLPHIN SCHOLARSHIPS • 250

Renewable award for undergraduate students under 24 years of age who are children or stepchildren of members or former members of the Submarine Force qualified submariners for a minimum of eight years or of Navy members who served minimum 10 years in submarine support. Based on academic merit, need, and leadership.

Award Scholarship for use in freshman, sophomore, junior, or senior years; renewable. *Number:* 25–30. *Amount:* up to $3000.

Eligibility Requirements: Applicant must be age 23 or under; enrolled full-time at a four-year institution or university and single. Available to U.S. citizens. Applicant or parent must meet one or more of the following requirements: Navy experience; retired from active duty; disabled or killed as a result of military service; Prisoner-Of-War; or Missing-In-Action.

Application Requirements Application, essay, financial need analysis, references, self-addressed stamped envelope, test scores, transcript. *Deadline:* March 15.

World Wide Web: http://www.dolphinscholarship.org

Contact: Tomi Roeske, Scholarship Administrator
Dolphin Scholarship Foundation
5040 Virginia Beach Boulevard, Suite 104A
Virginia Beach, VA 23462
Phone: 757-671-3200
Fax: 757-671-3330

SEABEE MEMORIAL SCHOLARSHIP ASSOCIATION, INC.

SEABEE MEMORIAL ASSOCIATION SCHOLARSHIP • 251

Award available to children or grandchildren of current or former members of the Naval Construction Force (Seabees) or Naval Civil Engineer Corps. High school students may apply. Not available for graduate study or to great-grandchildren of Seabees.

Award Scholarship for use in freshman, sophomore, junior, or senior years; renewable. *Number:* 86. *Amount:* $2200.
Eligibility Requirements: Applicant must be enrolled full-time at a four-year institution. Available to U.S. citizens. Applicant or parent must meet one or more of the following requirements: Navy experience; retired from active duty; disabled or killed as a result of military service; Prisoner-Of-War; or Missing-In-Action.
Application Requirements Application, essay, financial need analysis, test scores, transcript. *Deadline:* May 1.
World Wide Web: http://www.seabee.org
Contact: Sheryl Chiogioji, Administrative Assistant
Seabee Memorial Scholarship Association, Inc.
PO Box 6574
Silver Spring, MD 20916
Phone: 301-570-2850
Fax: 301-570-2873
E-mail: smsa@erols.com

SUBMARINE OFFICERS' WIVES CLUB

BOWFIN MEMORIAL SCHOLARSHIP   see number 230

MILITARY SERVICE: NAVY NATIONAL GUARD

ILLINOIS STUDENT ASSISTANCE COMMISSION (ISAC)

ILLINOIS NATIONAL GUARD GRANT PROGRAM   see number 241

NATIONALITY OR ETHNIC HERITAGE___

ADELANTE! U.S. EDUCATION LEADERSHIP FUND

ADELANTE US EDUCATION LEADERSHIP FUND   • 252

Renewable award for college juniors or seniors of Hispanic descent. Award primarily created to enhance the leadership qualities of the recipients for transition into postgraduate education, business and/or corporate America. Financial need is a factor for this award. Minimum 3.0 GPA required.

Award Scholarship for use in junior or senior years; renewable. *Number:* 20–30. *Amount:* $3000–$6000.

Eligibility Requirements: Applicant must be Hispanic and enrolled full-time at a four-year institution or university. Applicant must have 3.0 GPA or higher. Available to U.S. citizens.

Application Requirements Application, essay, financial need analysis, references, transcript. *Deadline:* Continuous.

Contact: Jan Angelini, Executive Director
Adelante! U.S. Education Leadership Fund
8415 Datapoint Drive
Suite 400
San Antonio, TX 78229
Phone: 210-692-1971
Fax: 210-692-1951
E-mail: jangelini@dcci.com

ALBERTA HERITAGE SCHOLARSHIP FUND

ADULT HIGH SCHOOL EQUIVALENCY SCHOLARSHIPS   • 253

Designed to recognize outstanding achievement in the attainment of high school equivalency. Students are eligible if they have been out of high school for three years, have achieved a minimum average of 80 per cent as a full-time student in courses required for entry into a postsecondary program, and are nominated by their institution. Two hundred awards of Can$500. Must study in and be a resident of Alberta, Canada. Nomination deadline: September 1.

Award Scholarship for use in freshman year; not renewable. *Number:* 200. *Amount:* $500.

Eligibility Requirements: Applicant must be Canadian; enrolled full-time at a two-year or four-year or technical institution or university; resident of Alberta and studying in Alberta. Applicant must have 3.0 GPA or higher.

Application Requirements Application. *Deadline:* September 1.

World Wide Web: http://www.alis.gov.ab.ca/scholarships

Contact: Alberta Heritage Scholarship Fund
9940 106th Street, 9th Floor, Box 28000 Station Main
Edmonton, AB T5J 4R4
Canada
Phone: 780-427-8640
Fax: 780-422-4516
E-mail: heritage@gov.ab.ca

ALEXANDER RUTHERFORD SCHOLARSHIPS FOR HIGH SCHOOL ACHIEVEMENT • 254

The scholarships are awarded to students earning a minimum of 80 percent in five designated subjects in grades 10, 11, and 12. The scholarships are valued at Can$400 for grade 10; Can$800 for grade 11; and Can$1300 for grade 12. Applicants must be Alberta residents who plan to enroll in a full-time post-secondary program. May 1 deadline for September entry; December 1 deadline for January entry.

Award Scholarship for use in freshman year; not renewable. *Number:* 7500. *Amount:* $400–$2500.

Eligibility Requirements: Applicant must be Canadian; high school student; planning to enroll full-time at a two-year or four-year or technical institution or university and resident of Alberta. Applicant must have 3.0 GPA or higher.

Application Requirements Application, transcript.

World Wide Web: http://www.alis.gov.ab.ca/scholarships

Contact: Alberta Heritage Scholarship Fund
9940 106th Street, 9th Floor, Box 28000 Station Main
Edmonton, AB T5J 4R4
Canada
Phone: 780-427-8640
Fax: 780-422-4516
E-mail: heritage@gov.ab.ca

JIMMIE CONDON ATHLETIC SCHOLARSHIPS • 255

One-time award for Canadian citizens who are residents of Alberta and are full-time students in Alberta and members of sports teams. Must be nominated and maintaining at least a 65 percent average.

Award Scholarship for use in any year; not renewable. *Number:* 1700. *Amount:* $1800.

Eligibility Requirements: Applicant must be Canadian; enrolled full-time at a two-year or four-year or technical institution or university; resident of Alberta; studying in Alberta and must have an interest in athletics/sports. Applicant must have 2.5 GPA or higher.

Application Requirements Application. *Deadline:* November 1.

World Wide Web: http://www.alis.gov.ab.ca/scholarships

Jimmie Condon Athletic Scholarships (continued)

Contact: Alberta Heritage Scholarship Fund
9940 106th Street, 9th Floor, Box 28000 Station Main
Edmonton, AB T5J 4R4
Canada
Phone: 780-427-8640
Fax: 780-422-4516
E-mail: heritage@gov.ab.ca

LAURENCE DECORE STUDENT LEADERSHIP AWARDS • 256
A total of 100 awards valued at Can$500 each are available to recognize outstanding leadership in the areas of student government, student societies, clubs or organizations at the postsecondary level. Students are nominated by their Alberta postsecondary institution. Must be a resident of Alberta, Canada.

Award Scholarship for use in freshman, sophomore, junior, or senior years; not renewable. *Number:* 100. *Amount:* $500.

Eligibility Requirements: Applicant must be Canadian; enrolled full-time at a two-year or four-year or technical institution or university; resident of Alberta; studying in Alberta and must have an interest in leadership.

Application Requirements Application. *Deadline:* March 1.

World Wide Web: http://www.alis.gov.ab.ca/scholarships

Contact: Alberta Heritage Scholarship Fund
9940 106th Street, 9th Floor, Box 28000 Station Main
Edmonton, AB T5J 4R4
Canada
Phone: 780-427-8640
Fax: 780-422-4516
E-mail: heritage@gov.ab.ca

LOUISE MCKINNEY POSTSECONDARY SCHOLARSHIPS • 257
Students enrolled in programs within Alberta are nominated by the awards office of their institution. Albertans enrolled in programs outside the province because their program of study is not offered in Alberta should contact the Alberta Heritage Scholarship Fund office. Must be a resident of Alberta. Must be ranked in upper quarter of class or have a minimum 3.5 GPA.

Award Scholarship for use in sophomore, junior, senior, or graduate years; renewable. *Number:* 950. *Amount:* $2500.

Eligibility Requirements: Applicant must be Canadian; enrolled full-time at a two-year or four-year institution or university and resident of Alberta. Applicant must have 3.5 GPA or higher.

Application Requirements Application, transcript. *Deadline:* June 1.

World Wide Web: http://www.alis.gov.ab.ca/scholarships

Contact: Alberta Heritage Scholarship Fund
9940 106th Street, 9th Floor, Box 28000 Station Main
Edmonton, AB T5J 4R4
Canada
Phone: 780-427-8640
Fax: 780-422-4516
E-mail: heritage@gov.ab.ca

NORTHERN ALBERTA DEVELOPMENT COUNCIL BURSARIES • 258

Applicants must have been residents of Alberta for a minimum of three years prior to applying. Students should also be in their latter years of academic study. Recipients are required to live and work for one year within the Northern Alberta Development Council boundary upon graduation.

Award Scholarship for use in junior, senior, or graduate years; not renewable. *Number:* 200–250. *Amount:* up to $3000.

Eligibility Requirements: Applicant must be Canadian; enrolled full-time at a two-year or four-year or technical institution or university and resident of Alberta. Applicant must have 2.5 GPA or higher.

Application Requirements Application, essay, financial need analysis, transcript. *Deadline:* May 31.

World Wide Web: http://www.alis.gov.ab.ca/scholarships

Contact: Alberta Heritage Scholarship Fund
9940 106th Street, 9th Floor, Box 28000 Station Main
Edmonton, AB T5J 4R4
Canada
Phone: 780-427-8640
Fax: 780-422-4516
E-mail: heritage@gov.ab.ca

PERSONS CASE SCHOLARSHIPS • 259

Awards recognize students whose studies will contribute to the advancement of women, or who are studying in fields where members of their sex are traditionally few in number. Selection is based on program of studies, academic achievement and financial need. Awards range from Can$1000 to Can$5000. A maximum of Can$20,000 is available each year. Must study in and be a resident of Alberta, Canada. Must be ranked in upper third of class or have a minimum 3.0 GPA.

Award Scholarship for use in freshman, sophomore, junior, or senior years; not renewable. *Number:* 5–20. *Amount:* $1000–$5000.

Eligibility Requirements: Applicant must be Canadian; enrolled full-time at a two-year or four-year or technical institution or university; resident of Alberta and studying in Alberta. Applicant must have 3.0 GPA or higher.

Application Requirements Application, essay, transcript. *Deadline:* September 30.

World Wide Web: http://www.alis.gov.ab.ca/scholarships

Persons Case Scholarships (continued)

Contact: Alberta Heritage Scholarship Fund
9940 106th Street, 9th Floor, Box 28000 Station Main
Edmonton, AB T5J 4R4
Canada
Phone: 780-427-8640
Fax: 780-422-4516
E-mail: heritage@gov.ab.ca

AMERICAN INSTITUTE FOR FOREIGN STUDY

AMERICAN INSTITUTE FOR FOREIGN STUDY MINORITY SCHOLARSHIPS • 260

Applications will be accepted from African-Americans, Asian-Americans, Native Americans, Hispanic-Americans and Pacific Islanders who are currently enrolled as undergraduates at a U.S. institution applying to an AIFS study abroad program. Applicants must demonstrate financial need, leadership ability, and academic accomplishment and meet program requirements. One full scholarship and three runners-up scholarships are awarded each semester. Submit application by April 15 for fall or October 15 for spring. Application fees are $50.

Award Scholarship for use in sophomore, junior, or senior years; not renewable. *Number:* 8. *Amount:* $2000–$11,500.

Eligibility Requirements: Applicant must be Native American or Eskimo, Asian, African American, or Hispanic; age 17; enrolled full-time at a two-year or four-year institution or university and must have an interest in leadership. Available to U.S. and non-U.S. citizens.

Application Requirements Application, essay, financial need analysis, photo, references, transcript. *Fee:* $50.

World Wide Web: http://www.aifsabroad.com

Contact: David Mauro, Admissions Counselor
American Institute For Foreign Study
River Plaza, 9 West Broad Street
Stamford, CT 06902-3788
Phone: 800-727-2437 Ext. 5163
Fax: 203-399-5598
E-mail: college.info@aifs.com

ARMENIAN STUDENTS ASSOCIATION OF AMERICA, INC.

ARMENIAN STUDENTS ASSOCIATION OF AMERICA, INC. SCHOLARSHIPS • 261

One-time award for students of Armenian descent. Must be undergraduate in sophomore, junior, or senior years, or graduate student, attending accredited

U.S. institution full-time. Award based on need, merit, and character. Show proof of tuition costs and enrollment. Application fee: $15.

Award Scholarship for use in sophomore, junior, senior, or graduate years; not renewable. *Number:* 30. *Amount:* $500–$2500.

Eligibility Requirements: Applicant must be Armenian and enrolled full-time at a four-year institution or university.

Application Requirements Application, essay, financial need analysis, references, transcript. *Fee:* $15. *Deadline:* March 15.

Contact: Nathalie Yaghoobian, Scholarship Administrator
Armenian Students Association of America, Inc.
333 Atlantic Avenue
Warwick, RI 02888
Phone: 401-461-6114
Fax: 401-461-6112
E-mail: headasa.com@aol.com

BLACKFOOT TRIBAL EDUCATION DEPARTMENT

BLACKFOOT TRIBAL EDUCATION GRANTS   • 262

Scholarships available to members of Blackfoot Tribe. Must have a minimum 2.0 GPA. Application deadline is March 1. Write for more information.

Award Grant for use in any year; not renewable. *Number:* 130. *Amount:* $3200–$3800.

Eligibility Requirements: Applicant must be Native American or Eskimo and enrolled full-time at a two-year or four-year institution or university. Available to U.S. citizens.

Application Requirements Application, essay, financial need analysis, transcript. *Deadline:* March 1.

World Wide Web: http://www.blackfeetnation.com

Contact: Mr. Conrad Lafromboise, Director of Higher Education
Blackfoot Tribal Education Department
PO Box 850
Browning, MT 59417

CAP FOUNDATION

RON BROWN SCHOLAR PROGRAM   • 263

Program seeks to identify African-American students who will make significant contributions to society. Applicants must excel academically, show exceptional leadership potential, participate in community service activities and demonstrate financial need. Must be a U.S. citizen or hold permanent resident visa.

Award Scholarship for use in freshman, sophomore, junior, or senior years; renewable. *Number:* 10–20. *Amount:* $10,000–$40,000.

Ron Brown Scholar Program (continued)
Eligibility Requirements: Applicant must be African American; high school student; planning to enroll full-time at a four-year institution or university and must have an interest in leadership. Applicant must have 3.5 GPA or higher. Available to U.S. citizens.
Application Requirements Application, essay, financial need analysis, interview, photo, references, test scores, transcript. *Deadline:* January 9.
World Wide Web: http://www.ronbrown.org
Contact: Fran Hardey, Executive Assistant, Ron Brown Scholar Program
CAP Foundation
1160 Pepsi Place, Suite 206
Charlottesville, VA 22901
Phone: 804-964-1588
Fax: 804-964-1589
E-mail: franh@ronbrown.org

CHEROKEE NATION OF OKLAHOMA

CHEROKEE NATION HIGHER EDUCATION • 264
A supplementary program that provides financial assistance to Cherokee Nation Members only. It is a need based program which provides assistance in seeking a bachelor's degree.

Award Grant for use in freshman, sophomore, junior, or senior years; renewable. *Number:* 1200–1500. *Amount:* $500–$1000.
Eligibility Requirements: Applicant must be Native American or Eskimo and enrolled full-time at a two-year or four-year institution or university. Available to U.S. citizens.
Application Requirements Application, financial need analysis, test scores, transcript, written request for the application. *Deadline:* June 28.
World Wide Web: http://www.cherokee.org
Contact: Bill Miller, Higher Education Specialist
Cherokee Nation of Oklahoma
PO Box 948
Tahlequah, OK 74465
Phone: 918-456-0671
Fax: 918-458-6195

CHICKASAW NATION EDUCATION FOUNDATION

CHICKASAW NATION EDUCATION FOUNDATION PROGRAM • 265
Awards to Chickasaw Nation citizens who might not be eligible for federal grants and aid or other programs for aid. Minimum 3.0 GPA required. Must submit copies of Certificate of Degree of Indian Blood and Chickasaw Nation citizenship card. Deadlines: June 1 for Fall, December 1 for Spring and May 1 for Summer.

Award Scholarship for use in any year; renewable. *Number:* 200–220. *Amount:* $200–$450.

Eligibility Requirements: Applicant must be Native American or Eskimo and enrolled full or part-time at a two-year or four-year or technical institution or university. Applicant must have 3.0 GPA or higher. Available to U.S. citizens.

Application Requirements Application, essay, financial need analysis, test scores, transcript, Certificate of Degree of Indian Blood, Chickasaw Nation citizenship card.

Contact: Chickasaw Nation Education Foundation
224 Rosedale Road
Ada, OK 74820
Phone: 580-421-7711
Fax: 580-436-3733

HIGHER EDUCATION GRANT • 266

The grant is for Chickasaw Citizens who have an unmet need as determined by the Financial Aid office from their college. The maximum award is $750 per semester. Minimum 2.0 GPA required. Application deadlines are June 1 for the fall and December 1 for spring.

Award Grant for use in freshman, sophomore, junior, or senior years; renewable. *Number:* 200–300. *Amount:* up to $750.

Eligibility Requirements: Applicant must be Native American or Eskimo and enrolled full-time at a two-year or four-year institution or university. Available to U.S. citizens.

Application Requirements Application, financial need analysis, test scores, transcript, Certificate of Degree of Indian Blood, Student Aid Report, Chickasaw Citizenship Card, College enrollment verification.

Contact: Andy Kirkpatrick, Director of Education
Chickasaw Nation Education Foundation
224 Rosedale Road
Ada, OK 74820
Phone: 580-421-7711
Fax: 580-436-3733

FIRST CATHOLIC SLOVAK LADIES ASSOCIATION

FIRST CATHOLIC SLOVAK LADIES ASSOCIATION FRATERNAL SCHOLARSHIP AWARD FOR COLLEGE & GRADUATE STUDY • 267

Must be FCSLA member in good standing for at least three years. Must attend accredited college in the U.S. or Canada in undergraduate or graduate degree program. Must submit certified copy of college acceptance. One-time tuition award; win once as undergraduate, up to $1250; once as graduate, up to $1750.

Award Scholarship for use in any year; not renewable. *Number:* 80. *Amount:* up to $1750.

First Catholic Slovak Ladies Association Fraternal Scholarship Award for College &
Graduate Study (continued)

Eligibility Requirements: Applicant must be Roman Catholic; Slavic/Czech and enrolled full-time at a two-year or four-year institution or university. Available to U.S. and non-U.S. citizens.

Application Requirements Application, autobiography, photo, references, test scores, transcript. *Deadline:* March 1.

World Wide Web: http://www.fcsla.com

Contact: Ms. Irene Drotleff, Director of Fraternal Scholarships
First Catholic Slovak Ladies Association
24950 Chagrin Boulevard
Beachwood, OH 44122
Phone: 216-464-8015
Fax: 216-464-8717

FLORIDA STATE DEPARTMENT OF EDUCATION

ROSEWOOD FAMILY SCHOLARSHIP FUND • 268

Renewable award for eligible minority students to attend a Florida public postsecondary institution on a full-time basis. Preference given to direct descendants of African-American Rosewood families affected by the incidents of January 1923. Must be Black, Hispanic, Asian, Pacific Islander, American Indian, or Alaska Native. Free Application for Federal Student Aid (and Student Aid Report for nonresidents of Florida) must be processed by May 15.

Award Scholarship for use in freshman, sophomore, junior, or senior years; renewable. *Number:* up to 25. *Amount:* up to $4000.

Eligibility Requirements: Applicant must be Native American or Eskimo, Asian, African American, or Hispanic; enrolled full-time at a two-year or four-year or technical institution or university and studying in Florida. Available to U.S. citizens.

Application Requirements Application, financial need analysis. *Deadline:* May 15.

World Wide Web: http://www.firn.edu/doe/osfa

Contact: Bureau of Student Financial Assistance
Florida State Department of Education
1940 North Monroe
Suite 70
Tallahassee, FL 32303-4759
Phone: 888-827-2004
E-mail: osfa@mail.doe.state.fl.us

GENERAL BOARD OF GLOBAL MINISTRIES

SPECIAL ADVANCE LEADERSHIP DEVELOPMENT GRANTS • 269

Award for racial and ethnic minority members of the United Methodist Church who are pursuing undergraduate study. Must be U.S. citizen or resident alien. Renewable award of $500 to $2500. Deadline: May 31.

Award Grant for use in freshman, sophomore, junior, or senior years; renewable. *Number:* 75. *Amount:* $500–$2500.

Eligibility Requirements: Applicant must be Methodist; Native American or Eskimo, Asian, African American, or Hispanic and enrolled full-time at a two-year or four-year or technical institution or university. Available to U.S. and non-Canadian citizens.

Application Requirements Application, essay, financial need analysis, photo, references, transcript. *Deadline:* May 31.

World Wide Web: http://www.gbgm-umc.org

Contact: Executive Secretary
General Board of Global Ministries
475 Riverside Drive
New York, NY 10115
Phone: 212-870-3787
E-mail: scholars@gbgm-umc.org

HISPANIC SCHOLARSHIP FUND

HISPANIC SCHOLARSHIP FUND GENERAL PROGRAM • 270

Awards available to full-time undergraduate, or graduate students of Hispanic origin. Applicants must have 15 college units with a minimum 2.7 GPA before applying. Merit-based award for U.S. citizens or permanent residents. Must include financial aid award letter and SAR.

Award Scholarship for use in sophomore, junior, senior, or graduate years; not renewable. *Number:* 3000–4000. *Amount:* $1000–$3000.

Eligibility Requirements: Applicant must be Latin American/Caribbean, Mexican, or Spanish; Hispanic and enrolled full-time at a two-year or four-year institution or university. Available to U.S. citizens.

Application Requirements Application, essay, financial need analysis, references, self-addressed stamped envelope, transcript. *Deadline:* October 15.

World Wide Web: http://www.hsf.net

Contact: General Scholarship Selection Committee
Hispanic Scholarship Fund
One Sansome Street, Suite 1000
San Francisco, CA 94104
Phone: 877-HSF-INFO
E-mail: info@hsf.net

HOPI TRIBE

BIA HIGHER EDUCATION GRANT • 271

Grant provides financial support for eligible Hopi individuals pursuing postsecondary education. Minimum 2.5 GPA required. Deadlines are 4/30 for summer, 7/31 for fall, and 11/30 for spring.

Award Grant for use in any year; not renewable. *Number:* 1–130. *Amount:* $50–$2500.

BIA Higher Education Grant (continued)
Eligibility Requirements: Applicant must be Native American or Eskimo and enrolled full or part-time at a two-year or four-year institution or university. Applicant must have 2.5 GPA or higher. Available to U.S. citizens.
Application Requirements Application, financial need analysis, test scores, transcript, certificate of Indian blood.
Contact: Hopi Tribe
PO Box 123
Kykotsmovi, AZ 86039-0123

HOPI SUPPLEMENTAL GRANT • 272

Grant provides financial support for eligible Hopi individuals pursuing postsecondary education. Minimum 2.5 GPA required. Deadlines are 4/30 for summer, 7/31 for fall, and 11/30 for spring.

Award Grant for use in any year; not renewable. *Number:* 1–400. *Amount:* $50–$1500.
Eligibility Requirements: Applicant must be Native American or Eskimo and enrolled full or part-time at a two-year or four-year institution or university. Applicant must have 2.5 GPA or higher. Available to U.S. citizens.
Application Requirements Application, financial need analysis, test scores, transcript, certificate of Indian blood.
Contact: Hopi Tribe
PO Box 123
Kykotsmovi, AZ 86039-0123

PEABODY SCHOLARSHIP • 273

Scholarship provides financial support for eligible Hopi individuals pursuing postsecondary education. Minimum 3.0 GPA required. Deadlines are 4/30 for summer, 7/31 for fall, and 11/30 for spring.

Award Scholarship for use in any year; not renewable. *Number:* 1–90. *Amount:* $50–$1000.
Eligibility Requirements: Applicant must be Native American or Eskimo and enrolled full or part-time at a two-year or four-year institution or university. Applicant must have 3.0 GPA or higher. Available to U.S. citizens.
Application Requirements Application, financial need analysis, test scores, transcript, certificate of Indian blood.
Contact: Hopi Tribe
PO Box 123
Kykotsmovi, AZ 86039-0123

IDAHO STATE BOARD OF EDUCATION

IDAHO MINORITY AND "AT RISK" STUDENT SCHOLARSHIP • 274

Renewable award for Idaho residents who are disabled or members of a minority group and have financial need. Must attend one of eight postsecondary institutions in the state for undergraduate study. Deadlines vary by institution. Must be a US citizen and be a graduate of an Idaho high school. Contact college financial aid office.

Award Scholarship for use in freshman, sophomore, junior, or senior years; renewable. *Number:* 38–40. *Amount:* $3000.

Eligibility Requirements: Applicant must be Native American or Eskimo, African American, or Hispanic; enrolled full-time at a two-year or four-year institution or university; resident of Idaho and studying in Idaho. Available to U.S. citizens.

Application Requirements Application, financial need analysis.

World Wide Web: http://www.sde.state.id.us/osbe/board.htm

Contact: Financial Aid Office

INTERNATIONAL ORDER OF THE KING'S DAUGHTERS AND SONS

INTERNATIONAL ORDER OF THE KING'S DAUGHTERS AND SONS AMERICAN INDIAN SCHOLARSHIP • 275

For enrolled American Indians. Proof of reservation registration, college acceptance letter, and financial aid office address required. Request application form by March 1 and return by April 15. Merit-based award. Send self-addressed stamped envelope.

Award Scholarship for use in freshman, sophomore, junior, or senior years; renewable. *Number:* 45–60. *Amount:* $500–$1000.

Eligibility Requirements: Applicant must be Native American or Eskimo. Applicant must have 2.5 GPA or higher. Available to U.S. and Canadian citizens.

Application Requirements Application, essay, financial need analysis, references, self-addressed stamped envelope, transcript. *Deadline:* April 15.

Contact: Headquarters Office
International Order of the King's Daughters and Sons
PO Box 1017
Chautauqua, NY 14722-1017
Phone: 716-357-4951

ITALIAN CATHOLIC FEDERATION, INC.

ICF COLLEGE SCHOLARSHIPS TO HIGH SCHOOL SENIORS • 276

Renewable awards for high school students who are residents of California, Illinois, Arizona and Nevada and plan to pursue postsecondary education in same state. Must have minimum 3.2 GPA. Must be a U.S. citizen, Catholic, and of Italian descent or if non-Italian the student's parents or grandparents must be members of the Federation for the student to qualify. Applicants must submit the last two pages of parents' income tax return.

Award Scholarship for use in freshman, sophomore, junior, or senior years; renewable. *Number:* 200. *Amount:* $400–$1000.

ICF College Scholarships to High School Seniors (continued)
Eligibility Requirements: Applicant must be Roman Catholic; Italian; high school student; planning to enroll at a two-year or four-year or technical institution or university; resident of Arizona, California, Illinois, or Nevada and studying in Arizona, California, Illinois, or Nevada. Available to U.S. citizens.
Application Requirements Application, essay, references, transcript. *Deadline:* March 15.
World Wide Web: http://www.icf.org
Contact: Scholarship Director
Italian Catholic Federation, Inc.
675 Hegenberger Road, Suite 230
Oakland, CA 94621
Phone: 510-633-9058
Fax: 510-633-9758

JOSE MARTI SCHOLARSHIP CHALLENGE GRANT FUND

JOSE MARTI SCHOLARSHIP CHALLENGE GRANT • 277

Must apply as a senior in high school or as graduate student. Must be resident of Florida and study in Florida. Need-based, merit scholarship. Must be US citizen or eligible noncitizen. Applicant must certify minimum 3.0 GPA and Hispanic origin.

Award Scholarship for use in freshman, sophomore, junior, senior, or graduate years; renewable. *Number:* 50. *Amount:* $2000.
Eligibility Requirements: Applicant must be Hispanic; enrolled full-time at a two-year or four-year institution or university; resident of Florida and studying in Florida. Applicant must have 3.0 GPA or higher. Available to U.S. citizens.
Application Requirements Application, financial need analysis. *Deadline:* April 1.
World Wide Web: http://www.floridastudentfinancialaid.org
Contact: Jose Marti Scholarship Challenge Grant Fund
1940 North Monroe Street, Suite 70
Tallahassee, FL 32303-4759
Phone: 888-827-2004

KANSAS BOARD OF REGENTS

ETHNIC MINORITY SCHOLARSHIP PROGRAM • 278

This program is designed to assist financially needy, academically competitive students who are identified as members of the following ethnic/racial groups: African-American; American Indian or Alaskan Native; Asian or Pacific Islander; or Hispanic. Must be resident of Kansas and attend college in Kansas. Application fee is $10. Deadline: April 1. Minimum 3.0 GPA required. Must be U.S. citizen.

Award Scholarship for use in freshman, sophomore, junior, or senior years; renewable. *Number:* 200–250. *Amount:* $1850.

Eligibility Requirements: Applicant must be Native American or Eskimo, Asian, African American, or Hispanic; enrolled full-time at a two-year or four-year institution or university; resident of Kansas and studying in Kansas. Applicant must have 3.0 GPA or higher. Available to U.S. citizens.

Application Requirements Application, financial need analysis. *Fee:* $10. *Deadline:* April 1.

World Wide Web: http://www.kansasregents.com

Contact: Diane Lindeman, Director of Student Financial Assistance
Kansas Board of Regents
1000 Southwest Jackson, Suite 520
Topeka, KS 66612-1368
Phone: 785-296-3517
Fax: 785-296-0983
E-mail: dlindeman@ksbor.org

LEAGUE OF UNITED LATIN AMERICAN CITIZENS NATIONAL EDUCATIONAL SERVICE CENTERS, INC.

LULAC NATIONAL SCHOLARSHIP FUND • 279

LULAC Councils will award scholarships to qualified Hispanic students who are enrolled or are planning to enroll in accredited colleges or universities in the United States. Applicants must be U.S. citizens or legal residents. Scholarships may be used for the payment of tuition, academic fees, room, board and the purchase of required educational materials. For additional information applicants should check LULAC website to see a list of participating councils or send a self-addressed stamped envelope.

Award Scholarship for use in any year; not renewable. *Number:* 1500–2000. *Amount:* $250–$1000.

Eligibility Requirements: Applicant must be Hispanic and enrolled full-time at a two-year or four-year institution or university. Available to U.S. citizens.

Application Requirements Application, autobiography, essay, financial need analysis, interview, references, self-addressed stamped envelope, test scores, transcript. *Deadline:* March 31.

World Wide Web: http://www.lnesc.org

Contact: Scholarship Administrator
League of United Latin American Citizens National Educational
Service Centers, Inc.
2000 L Street, NW
Suite 610
Washington, DC 20036

MENOMINEE INDIAN TRIBE OF WISCONSIN

MENOMINEE INDIAN TRIBE ADULT VOCATIONAL TRAINING PROGRAM • 280

Renewable award for enrolled Menominee tribal members to use at vocational or technical schools. Must be at least 1/4 Menominee and show proof of Indian blood. Must complete financial aid form. Deadlines: March 1 and November 1.

Award Grant for use in any year; renewable. *Number:* 50–70. *Amount:* $100–$1100.

Eligibility Requirements: Applicant must be Native American or Eskimo and enrolled full or part-time at a technical institution. Available to U.S. citizens.

Application Requirements Application, financial need analysis. *Deadline:* Continuous.

World Wide Web: http://www.menominee.nsn.us/educationindex/educationhomepage.htm

Contact: Virginia Nuske, Education Director
Menominee Indian Tribe of Wisconsin
PO Box 910
Keshena, WI 54135
Phone: 715-799-5110
Fax: 715-799-1364
E-mail: vnuske@itol.com

MENOMINEE INDIAN TRIBE OF WISCONSIN HIGHER EDUCATION GRANTS • 281

Renewable award for enrolled Menominee tribal member to use at a two- or four-year college or university. Must be at least 1/4 Menominee and show proof of Indian blood. Must complete financial aid form. Contact for deadline information.

Award Grant for use in freshman, sophomore, junior, or senior years; renewable. *Number:* 136. *Amount:* $100–$1100.

Eligibility Requirements: Applicant must be Native American or Eskimo and enrolled full or part-time at a two-year or four-year institution or university. Available to U.S. citizens.

Application Requirements Application, financial need analysis. *Deadline:* Continuous.

World Wide Web: http://www.menominee.nsn.us/educationindex/educationhomepage.htm

Contact: Virginia Nuske, Education Director
Menominee Indian Tribe of Wisconsin
PO Box 910
Keshena, WI 54135
Phone: 715-799-5110
Fax: 715-799-1364
E-mail: vnuske@mitw.org

MONTANA GUARANTEED STUDENT LOAN PROGRAM, OFFICE OF COMMISSIONER OF HIGHER EDUCATION

INDIAN STUDENT FEE WAIVER • 282

This award is a fee waiver awarded by the Montana University System to undergraduate and graduate students meeting the criteria. It waives the registration and tuition fee. The ward amount varies, depending on the tuition and registration fee at each participating college. Students must provide documentation of one-fourth Indian blood or more; must be a resident of Montana for at least one year prior to enrolling in school and must demonstrate financial need. Full-or part-time study qualifies. Complete and submit the FAFSA by March 1 and a Montana Indian Fee Waiver application form. Contact the financial aid office at the college of attendance to determine eligibility.

Award Scholarship for use in freshman, sophomore, junior, senior, or graduate years; renewable. *Number:* 600. *Amount:* $2000.
Eligibility Requirements: Applicant must be Native American or Eskimo; enrolled full or part-time at a two-year or four-year institution or university; resident of Montana and studying in Montana. Available to U.S. citizens.
Application Requirements Application, financial need analysis, FAFSA.
World Wide Web: http://www.mgslp.state.mt.us
Contact: Contact Financial Aid Office
        E-mail: scholars@mgslp.state.mt.us

NATIONAL MERIT SCHOLARSHIP CORPORATION

NATIONAL ACHIEVEMENT SCHOLARSHIP PROGRAM • 283

Competition of African-American students for recognition and undergraduate scholarships. Students enter by taking the Preliminary SAT/National Merit Scholar Qualifying Test and by meeting other participation requirements. Half of the awards are one-time scholarships of $2,500; others are renewable for four years, and valued between $500 and $2,000 or more. Contact high school counselor by fall of junior year. Those qualifying for recognition are notified through their high school. Participation requirements are available in the PSAT/NMSQT Student Bulletin and on the NMSC web site.

Award Scholarship for use in freshman year; renewable. *Number:* 700. *Amount:* $500–$2000.
Eligibility Requirements: Applicant must be African American; high school student and planning to enroll full-time at a four-year institution or university. Available to U.S. citizens.
Application Requirements Application, applicant must enter a contest, autobiography, essay, references, test scores, transcript.
World Wide Web: http://www.nationalmerit.org

National Achievement Scholarship Program (continued)
Contact: High School Counselor
National Merit Scholarship Corporation
1560 Sherman Avenue, Suite 200
Evanston, IL 60201-4897

NORTH CAROLINA COMMISSION OF INDIAN AFFAIRS

INCENTIVE SCHOLARSHIP FOR NATIVE AMERICANS • 284

Merit-based award with a required public service component. Maximum award $3000 per academic year. Must be graduate of a North Carolina high school enrolled at North Carolina institution. Must submit tribal enrollment card. Minimum 2.5 GPA required.

Award Scholarship for use in freshman, sophomore, junior, or senior years; renewable. *Number:* up to 200. *Amount:* up to $3000.

Eligibility Requirements: Applicant must be Native American or Eskimo; enrolled full-time at a four-year institution; resident of North Carolina and studying in North Carolina. Applicant must have 2.5 GPA or higher. Available to U.S. citizens.

Application Requirements Application, financial need analysis, tribal enrollment card. *Deadline:* Continuous.

Contact: Ms. Mickey Locklear, Director, Education Talent Search
North Carolina Commission of Indian Affairs
217 West Jones Street
Raleigh, NC 27603
Phone: 919-733-5998
Fax: 919-733-1207
E-mail: mickey.locklear@ncmail.net

NORTH DAKOTA UNIVERSITY SYSTEM

NORTH DAKOTA INDIAN COLLEGE SCHOLARSHIP PROGRAM • 285

One-time award to Native American residents of North Dakota. Priority given to full-time undergraduate students. Minimum 2.5 GPA required.

Award Scholarship for use in any year; not renewable. *Number:* 147. *Amount:* $700–$2000.

Eligibility Requirements: Applicant must be Native American or Eskimo; enrolled full-time at a two-year or four-year or technical institution or university and resident of North Dakota. Applicant must have 2.5 GPA or higher. Available to U.S. citizens.

Application Requirements Application, financial need analysis, transcript, proof of tribal enrollment. *Deadline:* July 15.

World Wide Web: http://www.ndus.nodak.edu

Contact: Rhonda Schauer, SAA Director
North Dakota University System
600 East Boulevard Avenue
Department 215
Bismarck, ND 58505-0230
Phone: 701-328-9661

NORTHERN CHEYENNE TRIBAL EDUCATION DEPARTMENT

HIGHER EDUCATION SCHOLARSHIP PROGRAM • 286

Scholarships are provided for enrolled Northern Cheyenne Tribal Members only who meet the requirements listed in the guidelines. Must be U.S. citizen enrolled full-time in a postsecondary institution. Minimum 2.5 GPA required. Deadline is March 1.

Award Grant for use in freshman, sophomore, junior, or senior years; renewable. *Number:* 72. *Amount:* $50–$6000.
Eligibility Requirements: Applicant must be Native American or Eskimo and enrolled full-time at a two-year or four-year institution or university. Applicant must have 2.5 GPA or higher. Available to U.S. citizens.
Application Requirements Application, essay, financial need analysis, references, test scores, transcript. *Deadline:* March 1.
Contact: Northern Cheyenne Tribal Education Department
Box 307
Lame Deer, MT 59043

OSAGE TRIBAL EDUCATION COMMITTEE

OSAGE TRIBAL EDUCATION COMMITTEE SCHOLARSHIP • 287

Available for Osage Tribal members only. 150 to 250 renewable scholarship awards. Spring deadline: December 31. Fall deadline: July 1. Summer deadline: May 1.

Award Scholarship for use in any year; renewable. *Number:* 150–250. *Amount:* $200–$400.
Eligibility Requirements: Applicant must be Native American or Eskimo and enrolled full or part-time at a two-year or four-year or technical institution or university.
Application Requirements Photo, references.
Contact: Ms. Cheryl Lewis, Business Manager
Osage Tribal Education Committee
4149 Highline Boulevard, Suite 380
Oklahoma City, OK 73108
Phone: 405-605-6051 Ext. 303
Fax: 405-605-6057

PAGE EDUCATION FOUNDATION

PAGE EDUCATION FOUNDATION GRANT • 288

Grants are available to Minnesota students of color who attend Minnesota postsecondary institutions. Students must be willing to provide a minimum of 50 hours of service each year they accept a grant. This service is focused on K-8th grade children of color and encourages the youngsters to value learning and education. Page scholars are tutors, mentors and role models.

Award Grant for use in any year; renewable. *Number:* 500. *Amount:* $900–$2500.

Eligibility Requirements: Applicant must be Native American or Eskimo, Asian, African American, or Hispanic; enrolled full-time at a two-year or four-year or technical institution or university; resident of Minnesota and studying in Minnesota. Available to U.S. citizens.

Application Requirements Application, essay, financial need analysis, references, transcript. *Deadline:* May 1.

World Wide Web: http://www.page-ed.org

Contact: Ramona Harristhal, Administrative Director
Page Education Foundation
PO Box 581254
Minneapolis, MN 55458-1254
Phone: 612-332-0406
Fax: 612-332-0403
E-mail: pagemail@mtn.org

PRESBYTERIAN CHURCH (USA)

STUDENT OPPORTUNITY SCHOLARSHIP-PRESBYTERIAN CHURCH (U.S.A.) • 289

Available to graduating high school seniors. Applicants must be members of racial minority and be communicant members of the Presbyterian Church (U.S.A.). Renewable award based on academics and financial need. Must be a U.S. citizen. Must rank in upper third of class or have a minimum 3.0 GPA.

Award Scholarship for use in freshman, sophomore, junior, or senior years; renewable. *Number:* up to 200. *Amount:* $100–$1400.

Eligibility Requirements: Applicant must be Presbyterian; Native American or Eskimo, Asian, African American, or Hispanic; high school student and planning to enroll full-time at an institution or university. Applicant must have 3.0 GPA or higher. Available to U.S. citizens.

Application Requirements Application, autobiography, essay, financial need analysis, references, test scores, transcript. *Deadline:* April 1.

World Wide Web: http://www.pcusa.org/highered

Contact: Maria Alvarez, Program Associate
Presbyterian Church (USA)
100 Witherspoon Street
Louisville, KY 40202-1396
Phone: 888-728-7228 Ext. 5760
Fax: 502-569-8766
E-mail: mariaa@ctr.pcusa.org

SACHS FOUNDATION

SACHS FOUNDATION SCHOLARSHIPS • 290

Award for black high school seniors who have been residents of Colorado for at least five years. Based on financial need and GPA of 3.60 or higher. Deadline: March 1.

Award Scholarship for use in freshman year; renewable. *Number:* 250. *Amount:* $4000–$4500.

Eligibility Requirements: Applicant must be African American; high school student; planning to enroll full-time at a two-year or four-year institution or university and resident of Colorado. Available to U.S. citizens.

Application Requirements Application, financial need analysis, interview, photo, references, transcript. *Deadline:* March 1.

World Wide Web: http://www.frii.com/~sachs

Contact: Lisa Harris, Secretary and Treasurer
SACHS Foundation
90 South Cascade Avenue, Suite 1410
Colorado Springs, CO 80903
Phone: 719-633-2353
E-mail: sachs@frii.com

SONS OF ITALY FOUNDATION

SONS OF ITALY FOUNDATION NATIONAL LEADERSHIP GRANTS • 291

Grant for full-time-student of Italian-American descent. Must demonstrate commitment to academic excellence and potential for leadership. Must submit resume. Application fee: $25 (money orders only).

Award Grant for use in any year; not renewable. *Number:* 10–15. *Amount:* $3000–$10,000.

Eligibility Requirements: Applicant must be Italian and enrolled full-time at a four-year institution or university. Available to U.S. citizens.

Application Requirements Application, applicant must enter a contest, essay, resume, references, test scores, transcript. *Fee:* $25. *Deadline:* February 28.

World Wide Web: http://www.osia.org

Sons of Italy Foundation National Leadership Grants (continued)
Contact: Scholarship Information
Sons of Italy Foundation
219 E Street, NE
Washington, DC 20002
E-mail: nationaloffice@osia.org

SWISS BENEVOLENT SOCIETY OF NEW YORK

MEDICUS STUDENT EXCHANGE • 292

One-time award to students of Swiss nationality or parentage. U.S. residents study in Switzerland and Swiss residents study in the U.S. Awards to undergraduates are based on merit and need; those to graduates based only on merit. Open to all U.S. residents. Must be proficient in foreign language of instruction.

Award Grant for use in junior, senior, or graduate years; not renewable. *Number:* 1–5. *Amount:* $2000–$10,000.
Eligibility Requirements: Applicant must be Swiss; enrolled full-time at a four-year institution or university and must have an interest in foreign language. Applicant must have 3.5 GPA or higher. Available to U.S. citizens.
Application Requirements Application, financial need analysis, references, test scores, transcript. *Deadline:* March 31.
World Wide Web: http://www.swissbenevolentny.com
Contact: Anne Marie Gilman, Scholarship Director
Swiss Benevolent Society of New York
608 Fifth Avenue, #309
New York, NY 10020

PELLEGRINI SCHOLARSHIP GRANTS • 293

Award to students who merit an award, have a minimum 3.0 GPA, and show financial need. Must submit proof of Swiss nationality or descent. Must be a resident of Connecticut, Delaware, New Jersey, New York, or Pennsylvania. Fifty grants of up to $2500.

Award Grant for use in any year; not renewable. *Number:* 50. *Amount:* $500–$2500.
Eligibility Requirements: Applicant must be Swiss; enrolled full or part-time at a two-year or four-year or technical institution or university and resident of Connecticut, Delaware, New Jersey, New York, or Pennsylvania. Applicant must have 3.0 GPA or higher.
Application Requirements Application, financial need analysis, references, test scores, transcript. *Deadline:* March 31.
World Wide Web: http://www.swissbenevolentny.com
Contact: Anne Marie Gilman, Scholarship Director
Swiss Benevolent Society of New York
608 Fifth Avenue, #309
New York, NY 10020

TERRY FOX HUMANITARIAN AWARD PROGRAM

TERRY FOX HUMANITARIAN AWARD • 294

Award granted to Canadian students entering postsecondary education. Criteria includes commitment to voluntary humanitarian work, courage in overcoming obstacles and excellence in academics, fitness and amateur sports. Must also show involvement in extra curricular activities. Value of award is $6000 awarded annually for maximum of four years. For those who attend institution that does not charge tuition fees, award is $3500 a year. Must be no older than 25.

Award Scholarship for use in freshman, sophomore, or junior years; renewable. *Number:* 20. *Amount:* $3500–$6000.

Eligibility Requirements: Applicant must be Canadian; age 25 or under and enrolled full-time at a two-year or four-year or technical institution or university.

Application Requirements Application, references, self-addressed stamped envelope, transcript. *Deadline:* February 1.

World Wide Web: http://www.terryfox.org

Contact: Sabrine Barakat, Administrative Assistant
Terry Fox Humanitarian Award Program
AQ 5003, 8888 University Drive
Burnaby, BC V5A-1S6
Phone: 604-291-3057
Fax: 604-291-3311
E-mail: terryfox@sfu.ca

UNITED METHODIST CHURCH

UNITED METHODIST CHURCH ETHNIC SCHOLARSHIP • 295

Awards for minority students pursuing undergraduate degree. Must have been certifiable members of the United Methodist Church for one year. Proof of membership and pastor's statement required. One-time award but is renewable by application each year. Minimum 2.5 GPA required.

Award Scholarship for use in freshman, sophomore, junior, or senior years; not renewable. *Number:* 430–500. *Amount:* $800–$1000.

Eligibility Requirements: Applicant must be Methodist; Native American or Eskimo, Asian, African American, or Hispanic and enrolled full-time at a two-year or four-year institution or university. Applicant must have 2.5 GPA or higher. Available to U.S. and non-Canadian citizens.

Application Requirements Application, essay, references, transcript, membership proof, pastor's statement. *Deadline:* May 1.

World Wide Web: http://www.umc.org/

United Methodist Church Ethnic Scholarship (continued)
Contact: Patti J. Zimmerman, Scholarships Administrator
United Methodist Church
PO Box 340007
Nashville, TN 37203-0007
Phone: 615-340-7344
E-mail: pzimmer@gbhem.org

UNITED METHODIST CHURCH HISPANIC, ASIAN, AND NATIVE AMERICAN SCHOLARSHIP • 296

Award for members of United Methodist Church who are Hispanic, Asian, Native American, or Pacific Islander college juniors, seniors, or graduate students. Need membership proof and pastor's letter. Minimum 2.8 GPA required.

Award Scholarship for use in junior, senior, or graduate years; not renewable. *Number:* 200–250. *Amount:* $1000–$3000.
Eligibility Requirements: Applicant must be Methodist; Native American or Eskimo, Asian, or Hispanic and enrolled full-time at a four-year institution or university. Available to U.S. citizens.
Application Requirements Application, essay, references, transcript, membership proof, pastor's letter. *Deadline:* April 1.
World Wide Web: http://www.umc.org/
Contact: Patti J. Zimmerman, Scholarships Administrator
United Methodist Church
PO Box 340007
Nashville, TN 37203-0007
Phone: 615-340-7344
E-mail: pzimmer@gbhem.org

UNITED NEGRO COLLEGE FUND

MERRILL LYNCH SCHOLARSHIP • 297

Two-year scholarships available to 15 undergraduates at UNCF member colleges and universities. Minimum 3.0 GPA required.

Award Scholarship for use in junior year; not renewable. *Number:* 15. *Amount:* $5000.
Eligibility Requirements: Applicant must be African American and enrolled at a four-year institution or university. Applicant must have 3.0 GPA or higher. Available to U.S. citizens.
Application Requirements Application.
World Wide Web: http://www.uncf.org
Contact: Program Services Department
United Negro College Fund
8260 Willow Oaks Corporate Drive
Fairfax, VA 22031

YAKAMA NATION

YAKAMA NATION SCHOLARSHIP PROGRAM • 298

Scholarship is for enrolled Yakama tribal members studying for a college degree (non-vocational) at an accredited 2-year or 4-year college institution. Applicant must be member of Yakama Nation.

Award Scholarship for use in freshman, sophomore, junior, senior, or graduate years; renewable. *Number:* 150–180. *Amount:* $2000.

Eligibility Requirements: Applicant must be Native American or Eskimo and enrolled full or part-time at a two-year or four-year institution or university. Available to U.S. citizens.

Application Requirements Application, financial need analysis, transcript. *Deadline:* July 1.

Contact: Program Manager
Yakama Nation
PO Box 151
Toppenish, WA 98948

RELIGIOUS AFFILIATION_____

CATHOLIC AID ASSOCIATION

CATHOLIC AID ASSOCIATION COLLEGE TUITION SCHOLARSHIP • 299

Applicants must have been a Catholic Aid Association member for at least two years. $300 scholarships for state and non-Catholic institutions, $500 for Catholic Colleges and Universities. Must be a member of the Catholic Aid Association.

Award Scholarship for use in freshman or sophomore years; not renewable. *Number:* 100–250. *Amount:* $300–$500.

Eligibility Requirements: Applicant must be Roman Catholic and enrolled full-time at a two-year or four-year institution or university. Available to U.S. citizens.

Application Requirements Application, essay, references, transcript. *Deadline:* January 15.

World Wide Web: http://www.catholicaid.com

Contact: Ann Goserud, Fraternal Department Assistant
Catholic Aid Association
3499 North Lexington Avenue
St. Paul, MN 55126-8098
Phone: 651-490-0170

FIRST CATHOLIC SLOVAK LADIES ASSOCIATION

FIRST CATHOLIC SLOVAK LADIES ASSOCIATION FRATERNAL SCHOLARSHIP AWARD FOR COLLEGE & GRADUATE STUDY

see number 267

GENERAL BOARD OF GLOBAL MINISTRIES

SPECIAL ADVANCE LEADERSHIP DEVELOPMENT GRANTS

see number 269

ITALIAN CATHOLIC FEDERATION, INC.

ICF COLLEGE SCHOLARSHIPS TO HIGH SCHOOL SENIORS

see number 276

JEWISH FEDERATION OF METROPOLITAN CHICAGO (JFMC)

JEWISH FEDERATION OF METROPOLITAN CHICAGO ACADEMIC SCHOLARSHIP PROGRAM • 300

Available for Jewish students only in the Chicago metropolitan area. Award available for undergraduates who have entered their junior year in career specific programs which require no postgraduate education for professional level employment or students enrolled in graduate or professional school. Students in a vocational program with a specific educational goal in the helping professions are also eligible.

Award Scholarship for use in junior, senior, graduate, or post graduate years; renewable. *Number:* 75. *Amount:* $5000.

Eligibility Requirements: Applicant must be Jewish; enrolled full-time at an institution or university and resident of Illinois. Available to U.S. and non-U.S. citizens.

Application Requirements Application, essay, financial need analysis, interview, references, transcript. *Deadline:* March 1.

World Wide Web: http://www.jvschicago.org

Contact: Lea Gruhn, Scholarship Secretary
Jewish Federation of Metropolitan Chicago (JFMC)
1 South Franklin Street
Chicago, IL 60606
Phone: 312-357-4521
Fax: 312-553-5544
E-mail: jvs@jvschicago.org

KNIGHTS OF COLUMBUS

FOURTH DEGREE PRO DEO AND PRO PATRIA SCHOLARSHIPS
see number 195

JOHN W. MC DEVITT (FOURTH DEGREE) SCHOLARSHIPS
see number 196

PRESBYTERIAN CHURCH (USA)

APPALACHIAN SCHOLARSHIPS • 301

Renewable scholarship to assist students who are full-time residents of Appalachia. Must be high school graduate or GED recipient and U.S. citizen. Must be member of Presbyterian Church (U.S.A). Must rank in upper third of class or have a minimum 3.0 GPA. Deadline is July 1. Must be a full-time student. High school seniors may apply.

Award Scholarship for use in any year; renewable. *Number:* 100–150. *Amount:* $100–$1500.

Eligibility Requirements: Applicant must be Presbyterian; enrolled full-time at a two-year or four-year or technical institution or university and resident of Alabama, Georgia, Kentucky, Maryland, Mississippi, New York, North Carolina, Ohio, Pennsylvania, South Carolina, Tennessee, Virginia, or West Virginia. Applicant must have 3.0 GPA or higher. Available to U.S. citizens.

Application Requirements Application, autobiography, essay, financial need analysis, references, test scores, transcript. *Deadline:* July 1.

World Wide Web: http://www.pcusa.org/highered

Contact: Kathy Smith, Administrative Assistant
Presbyterian Church (USA)
100 Witherspoon Street
Louisville, KY 40202-1396
Phone: 888-728-7228 Ext. 5745
Fax: 502-569-8766
E-mail: ksmith@ctr.pcusa.org

NATIONAL PRESBYTERIAN COLLEGE SCHOLARSHIP • 302

Available to high school seniors who are members of the Presbyterian Church (U.S.A.) and plan to attend a participating college related to the Presbyterian Church (U.S.A.). Must be a U.S. citizen. Merit-based. Must have 3.0 GPA minimum. Deadline is December 1.

Award Scholarship for use in freshman, sophomore, junior, or senior years; renewable. *Number:* 200. *Amount:* $500–$1400.

Eligibility Requirements: Applicant must be Presbyterian; high school student and planning to enroll full-time at a four-year institution. Applicant must have 3.0 GPA or higher. Available to U.S. citizens.

Application Requirements Application, autobiography, essay, financial need analysis, references, test scores, transcript. *Deadline:* December 1.

National Presbyterian College Scholarship (continued)
World Wide Web: http://www.pcusa.org/highered
Contact: Megan Willman, Program Assistant
  Presbyterian Church (USA)
  100 Witherspoon Street
  Louisville, KY 40202-1396
  Phone: 888-728-7228 Ext. 8235
  Fax: 502-569-8766
  E-mail: megan_willman@yahoo.com

SAMUEL ROBINSON AWARD • 303
One-time award for junior and senior undergraduates attending a college related to the Presbyterian Church (U.S.A.). Must submit a 2,000-word essay and recite answers to the Westminster Shorter Catechism. Contact chaplain for details. Deadline is April 1.

Award Scholarship for use in junior or senior years; not renewable. *Number:* 60. *Amount:* $500–$1400.
Eligibility Requirements: Applicant must be Presbyterian and enrolled full-time at a four-year institution. Available to U.S. citizens.
Application Requirements Essay, references. *Deadline:* April 1.
World Wide Web: http://www.pcusa.org/highered
Contact: Kathy Smith, Administrative Assistant
  Presbyterian Church (USA)
  100 Witherspoon Street
  Louisville, KY 40202-1396
  Phone: 888-728-7228 Ext. 5745
  Fax: 502-569-8766
  E-mail: ksmith@ctr.pcusa.org

STUDENT OPPORTUNITY SCHOLARSHIP-PRESBYTERIAN CHURCH (U.S.A.)
see number 289

UNITED METHODIST CHURCH

GIFT OF HOPE: 21ST CENTURY SCHOLARS PROGRAM • 304
One-time award to reward leadership in the United Methodist Church. Leadership beyond local church given first preference. Minimum undergraduate GPA 3.0. Minimum graduate GPA 3.5.

Award Scholarship for use in any year; not renewable. *Number:* 1000. *Amount:* $1000.
Eligibility Requirements: Applicant must be Methodist and enrolled full-time at a two-year or four-year institution or university. Available to U.S. and non-Canadian citizens.
Application Requirements Application, essay, references, transcript. *Deadline:* May 1.
World Wide Web: http://www.umc.org/

Contact: Patti J. Zimmerman, Scholarships Administrator
United Methodist Church
PO Box 340007
Nashville, TN 37203-0007
Phone: 615-340-7344
E-mail: pzimmer@gbhem.org

UNITED METHODIST CHURCH ETHNIC SCHOLARSHIP see number 295

UNITED METHODIST CHURCH HISPANIC, ASIAN, AND NATIVE AMERICAN SCHOLARSHIP see number 296

STATE OF RESIDENCE_____

ALABAMA COMMISSION ON HIGHER EDUCATION

POLICE OFFICERS AND FIREFIGHTERS SURVIVORS EDUCATION ASSISTANCE PROGRAM-ALABAMA see number 212

ROBERT C. BYRD HONORS SCHOLARSHIP-ALABAMA • 305

Approximately 105 awards. Must be Alabama resident and a high school senior. Contact school guidance counselor for an application.

Award Scholarship for use in freshman, sophomore, junior, or senior years; renewable. *Number:* 105. *Amount:* $1500.
Eligibility Requirements: Applicant must be high school student; planning to enroll full-time at a two-year or four-year institution or university and resident of Alabama. Applicant must have 3.5 GPA or higher. Available to U.S. citizens.
Application Requirements Application, test scores, transcript.
World Wide Web: http://www.ache.state.al.us
Contact: Dr. William Wall, Assoc. Executive Director for Student Assistance
Alabama Commission on Higher Education
PO Box 302000
Montgomery, AL 36130

ALBERTA HERITAGE SCHOLARSHIP FUND

ADULT HIGH SCHOOL EQUIVALENCY SCHOLARSHIPS

see number 253

ALEXANDER RUTHERFORD SCHOLARSHIPS FOR HIGH SCHOOL ACHIEVEMENT see number 254

JIMMIE CONDON ATHLETIC SCHOLARSHIPS   see number 255

LAURENCE DECORE STUDENT LEADERSHIP AWARDS   see number 256

LOUISE MCKINNEY POSTSECONDARY SCHOLARSHIPS
see number 257

NORTHERN ALBERTA DEVELOPMENT COUNCIL BURSARIES
see number 258

PERSONS CASE SCHOLARSHIPS   see number 259

ALBUQUERQUE COMMUNITY FOUNDATION

SUSSMAN-MILLER EDUCATIONAL ASSISTANCE FUND   • 306
Program to provide financial aid to enable students to continue with an undergraduate program. This is a "gap" program based on financial need. Must be resident of New Mexico. Do not write or call for information. Please visit website: http://www.albuquerquefoundation.org for complete information.

Award Grant for use in freshman, sophomore, junior, or senior years; not renewable. *Number:* 40–60. *Amount:* $500–$4000.
Eligibility Requirements: Applicant must be enrolled full-time at a four-year institution or university and resident of New Mexico. Available to U.S. citizens.
Application Requirements Application, autobiography, essay, financial need analysis, resume, references, transcript.
World Wide Web: http://www.albuquerquefoundation.org
Contact: Program Director
        Albuquerque Community Foundation
        PO Box 36960
        Albuquerque, NM 87176-6960

AMERICAN CANCER SOCIETY

AMERICAN CANCER SOCIETY, FLORIDA DIVISION COLLEGE SCHOLARSHIP PROGRAM   • 307
To be eligible for an American Cancer Society Florida Division Scholarship applicants must have had a personal diagnosis of cancer, be under 21, be a Florida resident, and plan to attend college in Florida. Awards will be based on financial need, scholarship, leadership and community service.

Award Grant for use in freshman, sophomore, junior, or senior years; renewable. *Number:* 120–150. *Amount:* $1850–$2300.
Eligibility Requirements: Applicant must be age 21 or under; enrolled full or part-time at a two-year or four-year or technical institution or university; resident of Florida and studying in Florida. Available to U.S. and non-U.S. citizens.
Application Requirements Application, essay, financial need analysis, interview, resume, references, test scores, transcript. *Deadline:* April 10.

World Wide Web: http://www.cancer.org
Contact: Marilyn Westley, Director of Childhood Cancer Programs
American Cancer Society
3709 West Jetton Avenue
Tampa, FL 33629
Phone: 813-253-0541
Fax: 813-254-5857
E-mail: mwestley@cancer.org

AMERICAN CANCER SOCIETY, INC.-GREAT LAKES DIVISION

COLLEGE SCHOLARSHIPS FOR CANCER SURVIVORS • 308

Scholarships for Michigan and Indiana residents who have had a diagnosis of cancer before the age of 21. Applicant must be under 21 at time of application. To be used for undergraduate degrees at any accredited Michigan or Indiana college or university. Deadline: mid-April. Open to U.S. citizens only.

Award Scholarship for use in freshman, sophomore, junior, or senior years; not renewable. *Number:* 1–51. *Amount:* $1000.
Eligibility Requirements: Applicant must be age 17-20; enrolled full-time at a two-year or four-year institution or university; resident of Indiana or Michigan; studying in Indiana or Michigan and must have an interest in leadership. Available to U.S. citizens.
Application Requirements Application, essay, financial need analysis, references, test scores, transcript. *Deadline:* April 2.
World Wide Web: http://www.cancer.org
Contact: Deb Dillingham, Cancer Control Manager
American Cancer Society, Inc.-Great Lakes Division
1755 Abbey Road
East Lansing, MI 48823
Phone: 800-723-0360
Fax: 517-664-1497
E-mail: deb.dillingham@cancer.org

AMERICAN LEGION, DEPARTMENT OF ALABAMA

AMERICAN LEGION DEPARTMENT OF ALABAMA SCHOLARSHIP FOR CHILDREN OF WAR VETERANS • 309

Renewable award available to children of war veterans. Must be resident of Alabama. Application deadline is May 1. Contact for more information.

Award Scholarship for use in any year; renewable. *Number:* 150. *Amount:* $850.
Eligibility Requirements: Applicant must be resident of Alabama. Available to U.S. citizens.

American Legion Department of Alabama Scholarship for Children of War Veterans (continued)

Application Requirements Application, references, test scores, transcript.
Deadline: May 1.
Contact: Braxton Bridgers, Department Adjutant
American Legion, Department of Alabama
PO Box 1069
Montgomery, AL 36101-1069
Phone: 334-262-6638

AMERICAN LEGION, DEPARTMENT OF NEW YORK

AMERICAN LEGION DEPARTMENT OF NEW YORK STATE HIGH SCHOOL ORATORICAL CONTEST • 310

Oratorical contest open to students under the age of twenty in 9th-12th grades of any accredited New York high school. Speech contests begin in November at post levels and continue on to national competition. Contact local American Legion post for deadlines. Must be U.S. citizen or lawful permanent resident. Payments are made directly to college and are awarded over a four-year period.

Award Scholarship for use in any year; not renewable. *Number:* 65. *Amount:* $75–$6000.
Eligibility Requirements: Applicant must be high school student; age 20 or under; resident of New York and must have an interest in public speaking. Available to U.S. citizens.
Application Requirements Application, applicant must enter a contest.
World Wide Web: http://www.ny.legion.org
Contact: Richard Pedro, Department Adjutant
American Legion, Department of New York
112 State Street, Suite 400
Albany, NY 12207
Phone: 518-463-2215
Fax: 518-427-8443
E-mail: newyork@legion.org

AMERICAN LEGION, DEPARTMENT OF NORTH DAKOTA

AMERICAN LEGION DEPARTMENT OF NORTH DAKOTA NATIONAL HIGH SCHOOL ORATORICAL CONTEST • 311

Oratorical contest for high school students in grades 9-12. Contestants must prepare to speak on the topic of the U.S. Constitution. Must graduate from an accredited North Dakota high school. Contest begins at the local level and continues to the national level. Several one-time awards of $100-$1900.

Award Prize for use in any year; not renewable. *Number:* 38. *Amount:* $100–$1900.
Eligibility Requirements: Applicant must be high school student; resident of North Dakota and must have an interest in public speaking. Available to U.S. citizens.
Application Requirements Application, applicant must enter a contest, speech contest. *Deadline:* November 30.
World Wide Web: http://www.ndlegion.org
Contact: David M. Schmidt, Department Adjutant
American Legion, Department of North Dakota
Box 2666
Fargo, ND 58108-2666
Phone: 701-293-3120
Fax: 701-293-9951
E-mail: adjutant@ndlegion.org

ARKANSAS DEPARTMENT OF HIGHER EDUCATION

ARKANSAS STUDENT ASSISTANCE GRANT PROGRAM　● 312
Award for Arkansas residents attending a college within the state. Must be enrolled full-time, have financial need, and maintain satisfactory progress. One-time award for undergraduate use only. Application is the FAFSA.

Award Grant for use in freshman, sophomore, junior, or senior years; not renewable. *Number:* 7000–10,000. *Amount:* $100–$600.
Eligibility Requirements: Applicant must be enrolled full-time at a two-year or four-year or technical institution or university; resident of Arkansas and studying in Arkansas.
Application Requirements Application, financial need analysis, FAFSA. *Deadline:* April 1.
World Wide Web: http://www.arscholarships.com
Contact: Assistant Coordinator
Arkansas Department of Higher Education
114 East Capitol
Little Rock, AR 72201
Phone: 501-371-2050
Fax: 501-371-2001

GOVERNOR'S SCHOLARS—ARKANSAS　● 313
Awards for outstanding Arkansas high school seniors. Must be an Arkansas resident and have a high school GPA of at least 3.5 or have scored at least 27 on the ACT. Award is $4000 per year for four years of full-time undergraduate study. Applicants who attain 32 or above on ACT, 1410 or above on SAT and have an academic 3.50 GPA, or are selected as National Merit or National Achievement finalists may receive an award equal to tuition, mandatory fees, room, and board up to $10K/year at any Arkansas institution.

Governor's Scholars—Arkansas (continued)

Award Scholarship for use in freshman, sophomore, junior, or senior years; renewable. *Number:* 75-250. *Amount:* $4000-$17,690.

Eligibility Requirements: Applicant must be high school student; planning to enroll full-time at a two-year or four-year institution or university; resident of Arkansas and studying in Arkansas. Applicant must have 3.5 GPA or higher. Available to U.S. citizens.

Application Requirements Application, test scores, transcript. *Deadline:* February 1.

World Wide Web: http://www.arscholarships.com

Contact: Melissa Goff, Manager of Student Financial Aid
Arkansas Department of Higher Education
114 East Capitol
Little Rock, AR 72201
Phone: 501-371-2050
Fax: 501-371-2001
E-mail: melissag@adhe.arknet.edu

LAW ENFORCEMENT OFFICERS' DEPENDENTS SCHOLARSHIP-ARKANSAS

see number 213

TEACHER AND ADMINISTRATOR GRANT PROGRAM-ARKANSAS

see number 214

BARBARA ALICE MOWER MEMORIAL SCHOLARSHIP COMMITTEE

BARBARA ALICE MOWER MEMORIAL SCHOLARSHIP • 314

One-time award for women residents of Hawaii who are committed to using their education to help other women, especially women of Hawaii. Must be junior or senior level undergraduate, minimum 2.5 GPA required. Graduate level also eligible.

Award Scholarship for use in junior, senior, graduate, or post graduate years; not renewable. *Number:* 1-25. *Amount:* $1000-$3500.

Eligibility Requirements: Applicant must be enrolled full-time at a four-year institution or university; female and resident of Hawaii. Available to U.S. and non-U.S. citizens.

Application Requirements Application, essay, references, transcript. *Deadline:* May 1.

Contact: Nancy Mower
Barbara Alice Mower Memorial Scholarship Committee
1536 Kamole Street
Honolulu, HI 96821
Phone: 808-373-2901

BIG 33 SCHOLARSHIP FOUNDATION, INC.

BIG 33 SCHOLARSHIP FOUNDATION, INC. SCHOLARSHIPS • 315

Open to all high school seniors in PA and OH. Quantity of scholarships awarded, dollar amount of each and type of scholarships varies each year. They are a one-time award only. Minimum 2.5 GPA required.

Award Scholarship for use in freshman year; not renewable. *Number:* 150–200. *Amount:* $500–$2000.

Eligibility Requirements: Applicant must be high school student; planning to enroll full-time at a two-year or four-year or technical institution or university and resident of Ohio or Pennsylvania. Applicant must have 2.5 GPA or higher. Available to U.S. citizens.

Application Requirements Application, essay, transcript. *Deadline:* February 8.

World Wide Web: http://www.big33.org

Contact: Mickey Minnich, Executive Director
Big 33 Scholarship Foundation, Inc.
511 Bridge Street
PO Box 213
New Cumberland, PA 17070
Phone: 717-774-3303
Fax: 717-774-1749
E-mail: info@big33.org

BIG Y FOODS, INC.

BIG Y SCHOLARSHIPS • 316

Awards are for customers or dependents of customers of Big Y Foods. Big Y Trade area covers western and central Massachusetts and Connecticut. Also awards for Big Y employees and dependents of employees. Awards are based on academic excellence. Grades, board scores and three letters of recommendation required.

Award Scholarship for use in any year; not renewable. *Number:* 200. *Amount:* $500–$2000.

Eligibility Requirements: Applicant must be enrolled full or part-time at a two-year or four-year institution or university and resident of Connecticut or Massachusetts. Available to U.S. citizens.

Application Requirements Application, references, test scores, transcript. *Deadline:* February 1.

World Wide Web: http://www.bigy.com

Contact: Gail Borkosky, Scholarship Administrator
Big Y Foods, Inc.
2145 Roosevelt Avenue
Springfield, MA 01102-7840
Phone: 413-504-4062

BOETTCHER FOUNDATION

BOETTCHER FOUNDATION SCHOLARSHIPS • 317

The Boettcher Scholarship is the most prestigious merit-based scholarship available to graduating seniors in the state of Colorado. Selection based on class rank (top 5%), test scores, leadership, and service. Renewable for four years and can be used at any Colorado university or college. Includes full tuition and fees, living stipend of $2,800 per year and a stipend for books.

Award Scholarship for use in freshman, sophomore, junior, or senior years; renewable. *Number:* 40. *Amount:* $40,000–$120,000.

Eligibility Requirements: Applicant must be high school student; planning to enroll full-time at a four-year institution or university; resident of Colorado and studying in Colorado. Applicant must have 3.5 GPA or higher. Available to U.S. citizens.

Application Requirements Application, essay, interview, references, test scores, transcript. *Deadline:* November 1.

World Wide Web: http://www.boettcherfoundation.org

Contact: Jennie Kenney, Scholarship Administrative Assistant
Boettcher Foundation
500 17th. Street, Suite 2210 S
Denver, CO 80202-5422
Phone: 303-285-6207
E-mail: scholarships@boettcherfoundation.org

BUFFETT FOUNDATION

BUFFETT FOUNDATION SCHOLARSHIP • 318

Scholarship provides assistance for tuition and fees (only) up to $1800 per semester. Must be used at a Nebraska state school or a two-year college or trade school within Nebraska. High school applicant must have maintained a 2.5 GPA, college students a 2.0. Must have already applied for federal financial aid and have printed results. Strict deadlines apply. March 1st for requesting mail applications which must be returned by April 10. Must be Nebraska resident.

Award Scholarship for use in freshman, sophomore, junior, or senior years; renewable. *Number:* 30–50. *Amount:* up to $3600.

Eligibility Requirements: Applicant must be enrolled full-time at a two-year or four-year or technical institution or university; resident of Nebraska and studying in Nebraska. Applicant must have 2.5 GPA or higher. Available to U.S. citizens.

Application Requirements Application, autobiography, essay, financial need analysis, references, transcript, federal tax return. *Deadline:* April 10.

World Wide Web: http://www.buffettscholarships.org

Contact: Devon Buffett, Director of Scholarships
Buffett Foundation
PO Box 4508
Decatur, IL 62525
Phone: 402-451-6011

CALIFORNIA ASSOCIATION OF PRIVATE POSTSECONDARY SCHOOLS

CAPPS SCHOLARSHIP PROGRAM • 319

Schools participating in the CAPPS Scholarship Program offer both full- and $1,000-tuition scholarships to graduating high school students and adults wishing to pursue their education at a private career school. Scholarships are for tuition only. Applications are sent to the school of the applicant's choice; that school selects scholarship recipients using their own criterion. Among other qualifications listed on the application, recipients must meet that school's admissions requirements and be a California resident and a U.S. legal citizen to qualify.

Award Scholarship for use in freshman year; not renewable. *Number:* 250–500. *Amount:* $1000–$10,000.

Eligibility Requirements: Applicant must be enrolled full or part-time at a technical institution and resident of California. Available to U.S. citizens.

Application Requirements Application. *Deadline:* May 17.

World Wide Web: http://www.cappsonline.org

Contact: Lola Woronow, Scholarship Coordinator
California Association of Private Postsecondary Schools
921 11th Street #619
Sacramento, CA 95814-2821
E-mail: info@cappsoline.org

CALIFORNIA CONGRESS OF PARENTS AND TEACHERS, INC.

CALIFORNIA CONGRESS OF PARENTS AND TEACHERS, INC. SCHOLARSHIP • 320

Up to 500 scholarships is awarded to California State PTA members for education and continuing education. Eligible applicants will be California residents. Deadlines are November 30 and March 15.

Award Scholarship for use in any year; not renewable. *Number:* up to 500. *Amount:* $500–$5000.

Eligibility Requirements: Applicant must be enrolled full or part-time at a two-year or four-year or technical institution or university and resident of California. Available to U.S. and non-U.S. citizens.

Application Requirements Application, references, transcript.

Contact: California Congress of Parents and Teachers, Inc.
930 Georgia Street
PO Box 15015
Los Angeles, CA 90015

CALIFORNIA CORRECTIONAL PEACE OFFICERS ASSOCIATION

CALIFORNIA CORRECTIONAL PEACE OFFICERS ASSOCIATION JOE HARPER SCHOLARSHIP
see number 215

CALIFORNIA JUNIOR MISS SCHOLARSHIP PROGRAM

CALIFORNIA JUNIOR MISS SCHOLARSHIP PROGRAM • 321

Scholarship program to recognize and reward outstanding high school junior girls in the areas of academics, leadership, athletics, public speaking and the arts. Must be single, female, a U.S. citizen, and resident of California. Minimum 3.0 GPA required.

Award Scholarship for use in any year; not renewable. *Number:* 10–20. *Amount:* $300–$10,000.

Eligibility Requirements: Applicant must be high school student; planning to enroll full-time at a two-year or four-year institution or university; single female; resident of California and must have an interest in leadership. Applicant must have 3.0 GPA or higher. Available to U.S. citizens.

Application Requirements Application, applicant must enter a contest, interview, test scores, transcript. *Deadline:* January 1.

World Wide Web: http://www.ajm.org/california

Contact: Becky Jo Peterson, California State Chairman
California Junior Miss Scholarship Program
3523 Glenbrook Lane
Napa, CA 94558
Phone: 707-224-5112
E-mail: caljrmiss@aol.com

CAREER COLLEGES AND SCHOOLS OF TEXAS

CAREER COLLEGES AND SCHOOLS OF TEXAS SCHOLARSHIP PROGRAM • 322

One-time award available to graduating high school seniors who plan to attend a Texas trade or technical institution. Must be a Texas resident. Criteria selection, which is determined independently by each school's guidance counselors, may be based on academic excellence, financial need or student leadership. Must be U.S. citizen.

Award Scholarship for use in any year; not renewable. *Number:* up to 6000. *Amount:* up to $1000.

Eligibility Requirements: Applicant must be high school student; planning to enroll full or part-time at a technical institution; resident of Texas and studying in Texas. Available to U.S. citizens.

Application Requirements Determined by high school. *Deadline:* Continuous.
World Wide Web: http://www.colleges-schools.org
Contact: High School counselors
Career Colleges and Schools of Texas
6460 Hiller, Suite D
El Paso, TX 79925

COLORADO COMMISSION ON HIGHER EDUCATION

COLORADO LEVERAGING EDUCATIONAL ASSISTANCE PARTNERSHIP (CLEAP) AND SLEAP • 323

Renewable awards for Colorado residents who are attending Colorado state-supported postsecondary institutions at the undergraduate level. Must document financial need. Contact colleges for complete information and deadlines.

Award Grant for use in freshman, sophomore, junior, or senior years; not renewable. *Number:* 2000–2500. *Amount:* $50–$900.
Eligibility Requirements: Applicant must be enrolled full or part-time at a two-year or four-year or technical institution or university; resident of Colorado and studying in Colorado. Available to U.S. citizens.
Application Requirements Application, financial need analysis.
World Wide Web: http://www.state.co.us/cche
Contact: Financial Aid Office at college/institution
Colorado Commission on Higher Education
1380 Lawrence Street, Suite 1200
Denver, CO 80204-2059

COLORADO MASONS BENEVOLENT FUND ASSOCIATION

COLORADO MASONS BENEVOLENT FUND SCHOLARSHIPS • 324

Applicants must be graduating seniors from a Colorado public high school accepted at a Colorado postsecondary institution. The maximum grant is $5000 renewable over four years. Applicant may not be married. Obtain scholarship materials and specific requirements from high school counselor.

Award Scholarship for use in freshman, sophomore, junior, or senior years; renewable. *Number:* 10–14. *Amount:* up to $5000.
Eligibility Requirements: Applicant must be high school student; planning to enroll full-time at a two-year or four-year or technical institution or university; single; resident of Colorado and studying in Colorado. Available to U.S. and non-U.S. citizens.
Application Requirements Application, essay, financial need analysis, interview, references, transcript. *Deadline:* March 15.

Colorado Masons Benevolent Fund Scholarships (continued)
Contact: Scholarship Administrator
Colorado Masons Benevolent Fund Association
1130 Panorama Drive
Colorado Springs, CO 80904

COMMUNITY FOUNDATION FOR GREATER BUFFALO

COMMUNITY FOUNDATION FOR GREATER BUFFALO SCHOLARSHIPS • 325

Scholarships restricted to current residents of western New York (several only to Erie County), who have been accepted for admission to any nonprofit school in the United States for full-time study at the undergraduate level. Must maintain a "C" average. Must submit estimated family contribution as indicated on Student Aid Report from FAFSA form.

Award Scholarship for use in freshman, sophomore, junior, or senior years; not renewable. *Number:* 125. *Amount:* $200–$4500.
Eligibility Requirements: Applicant must be enrolled full-time at a two-year or four-year institution or university and resident of New York. Available to U.S. and non-U.S. citizens.
Application Requirements Application, essay, financial need analysis, references, self-addressed stamped envelope, transcript. *Deadline:* June 1.
World Wide Web: http://www.cfgb.org
Contact: Program Officer
Community Foundation for Greater Buffalo
712 Main Street
Buffalo, NY 14202

COMMUNITY FOUNDATION OF WESTERN MASSACHUSETTS

JAMES Z. NAURISON SCHOLARSHIP • 326

For undergraduate and graduate students who are residents of Hampden, Kampshire, Franklin, and Berkshire Counties in Massachusetts and Enfield and Suffield, Connecticut. May be awarded up to four years based upon discretion of the scholarship committee. Deadline: April 16. Visit http://www.communityfoundation.org.

Award Scholarship for use in any year; renewable. *Number:* 655. *Amount:* $1000.
Eligibility Requirements: Applicant must be resident of Connecticut or Massachusetts. Available to U.S. citizens.
Application Requirements Application, financial need analysis, references, transcript, personal statement. *Deadline:* April 16.
World Wide Web: http://www.communityfoundation.org

Contact: Community Foundation of Western Massachusetts
1500 Main Street, PO Box 15769
Springfield, MA 01115
Fax: 413-733-8565

DE VRY, INC.

DEVRY BACHELOR'S DEGREE SCHOLARSHIPS • 327

Half-tuition award based on GPA, academic record, letters of recommendation, and essay. Award is renewable if 3.0 GPA is maintained. Award for U.S. and Canadian citizens.

Award Scholarship for use in any year; renewable. *Number:* 4036. *Amount:* up to $16,000.

Eligibility Requirements: Applicant must be enrolled full-time at a four-year institution and studying in Arizona, California, Colorado, Florida, Georgia, Illinois, Missouri, New Jersey, New York, Ohio, Texas, or Virginia. Applicant must have 3.0 GPA or higher. Available to U.S. and Canadian citizens.

Application Requirements Application, essay, interview, references, transcript. *Deadline:* Continuous.

World Wide Web: http://www.devry.edu

Contact: Scholarship Coordinator
De Vry, Inc.
One Tower Lane
Oak Brook Terrace, IL 60181
Phone: 630-571-7700

DEVRY PRESIDENT'S SCHOLARSHIPS • 328

Full-tuition award based on SAT or ACT scores, scholastic achievement, extracurricular activities, essay. Renewable if GPA is maintained.

Award Scholarship for use in any year; renewable. *Number:* 46. *Amount:* $19,075–$35,060.

Eligibility Requirements: Applicant must be high school student; planning to enroll full-time at a four-year institution and studying in Arizona, California, Colorado, Florida, Georgia, Illinois, Missouri, New Jersey, New York, Ohio, Texas, or Virginia. Applicant must have 3.0 GPA or higher. Available to U.S. and Canadian citizens.

Application Requirements Application, essay, interview, references, test scores, transcript. *Deadline:* Continuous.

World Wide Web: http://www.devry.edu

Contact: Scholarship Coordinator
De Vry, Inc.
One Tower Lane
Oak Brook Terrace, IL 60181
Phone: 630-571-7700

DELAWARE HIGHER EDUCATION COMMISSION

DIAMOND STATE SCHOLARSHIP • 329

Renewable award for Delaware high school seniors enrolling full-time at an accredited college or university. Must be ranked in upper quarter of class and score 1200 on SAT or 27 on the ACT.

Award Scholarship for use in freshman year; renewable. *Number:* 50–200. *Amount:* $1250.

Eligibility Requirements: Applicant must be high school student; planning to enroll full-time at a four-year institution or university and resident of Delaware. Applicant must have 3.5 GPA or higher. Available to U.S. citizens.

Application Requirements Application, essay, test scores, transcript. *Deadline:* March 31.

World Wide Web: http://www.doe.state.de.us/high-ed

Contact: Maureen Laffey, Associate Director
Delaware Higher Education Commission
820 North French Street
Wilmington, DE 19801
Phone: 302-577-3240
Fax: 302-577-6765
E-mail: dhec@state.de.us

EDUCATIONAL BENEFITS FOR CHILDREN OF DECEASED MILITARY AND STATE POLICE see number 217

ROBERT C. BYRD HONORS SCHOLARSHIP-DELAWARE • 330

Available to Delaware residents who are graduating high school seniors. Based on outstanding academic merit. Awards are renewable up to four years. Must be ranked in upper quarter of class and have a score of 1200 on SAT or 27 on ACT.

Award Scholarship for use in freshman year; renewable. *Number:* 16–80. *Amount:* $1500.

Eligibility Requirements: Applicant must be high school student; planning to enroll full-time at a two-year or four-year institution or university and resident of Delaware. Applicant must have 3.5 GPA or higher. Available to U.S. citizens.

Application Requirements Application, essay, test scores, transcript. *Deadline:* March 31.

World Wide Web: http://www.doe.state.de.us/high-ed

Contact: Maureen Laffey, Associate Director
Delaware Higher Education Commission
820 North French Street
Wilmington, DE 19801
Phone: 302-577-3240
Fax: 302-577-6765
E-mail: dhec@state.de.us

SCHOLARSHIP INCENTIVE PROGRAM-DELAWARE • 331

One-time award for Delaware residents with financial need. May be used at an institution in Delaware or Pennsylvania, or at another out-of-state institution if a program is not available at a publicly-supported school in Delaware. Must have minimum 2.5 GPA.

Award Grant for use in any year; not renewable. *Number:* 1000–1300. *Amount:* $700–$2200.
Eligibility Requirements: Applicant must be enrolled full-time at a two-year or four-year institution or university; resident of Delaware and studying in Delaware or Pennsylvania. Applicant must have 2.5 GPA or higher. Available to U.S. citizens.
Application Requirements Application, financial need analysis, transcript. *Deadline:* April 15.
World Wide Web: http://www.doe.state.de.us/high-ed
Contact: Maureen Laffey, Associate Director
Delaware Higher Education Commission
820 North French Street
Wilmington, DE 19801
Phone: 302-577-3240
Fax: 302-577-6765
E-mail: dhec@state.de.us

DEPARTMENT OF MILITARY AFFAIRS

WISCONSIN NATIONAL GUARD TUITION GRANT see number 240

DISTRICT OF COLUMBIA STATE EDUCATION OFFICE

DC LEVERAGING EDUCATIONAL ASSISTANCE PARTNERSHIP PROGRAM (LEAP) • 332

Available to Washington, D.C. residents who have financial need. Must also apply for the Federal Pell Grant. Must attend an eligible college at least half-time. Contact financial aid office or local library for more information. Proof of residency may be required. Deadline is June 28.

Award Scholarship for use in freshman, sophomore, junior, or senior years; not renewable. *Number:* 1200–1500. *Amount:* $500–$1000.

DC Leveraging Educational Assistance Partnership Program (LEAP) (continued)
Eligibility Requirements: Applicant must be enrolled full or part-time at a two-year or four-year or technical institution or university and resident of District of Columbia. Available to U.S. citizens.
Application Requirements Application, financial need analysis. *Deadline:* June 28.
Contact: Angela March, Program Manager
District of Columbia State Education Office
441 4th Street NW, Suite 350 North
Washington, DC 20001
Phone: 202-727-6436
Fax: 202-727-2019
E-mail: angela.march@dc.gov

EDMUND F. MAXWELL FOUNDATION

EDMUND F. MAXWELL FOUNDATION SCHOLARSHIP • 333
Scholarships awarded to residents of western Washington to attend accredited independent colleges or universities. Awards of up to $3500 per year based on need, merit, citizenship, and activities. Renewable for up to four years if academic progress is suitable and financial need is unchanged.

Award Scholarship for use in freshman year; renewable. *Number:* 105–135. *Amount:* $1000–$3500.
Eligibility Requirements: Applicant must be enrolled full-time at a four-year institution and resident of Washington. Available to U.S. and non-U.S. citizens.
Application Requirements Application, essay, financial need analysis, test scores, transcript, employment history. *Deadline:* April 30.
World Wide Web: http://www.maxwell.org
Contact: Administrator
Edmund F. Maxwell Foundation
PO Box 22537
Seattle, WA 98122
E-mail: admin@maxwell.com

FINANCE AUTHORITY OF MAINE

MAINE STATE GRANT • 334
Scholarships for residents of Maine attending an eligible school, full-time, in Connecticut, Maine, Massachusetts, New Hampshire, Pennsylvania, Rhode Island, Washington, D.C., or Vermont. Award based on need. Must apply annually. Complete Free Application for Federal Student Aid to apply. One-time award of $500-$1250 for undergraduate study.

Award Grant for use in freshman, sophomore, junior, or senior years; not renewable. *Number:* 8900–12,500. *Amount:* $500–$1250.
Eligibility Requirements: Applicant must be enrolled full-time at a two-year or four-year or technical institution or university; resident of Maine and study-

ing in Connecticut, District of Columbia, Maine, Massachusetts, New Hampshire, Pennsylvania, Rhode Island, or Vermont.
Application Requirements Application, financial need analysis, FAFSA. *Deadline:* May 1.
World Wide Web: http://www.famemaine.com
Contact: Claude Roy, Program Officer
Finance Authority of Maine
5 Community Drive
Augusta, ME 04332-0949
Phone: 800-228-3734
Fax: 207-623-0095
E-mail: claude@famemaine.com

FLORIDA ASSOCIATION OF POSTSECONDARY SCHOOLS AND COLLEGES

FLORIDA ASSOCIATION OF POSTSECONDARY SCHOOLS AND COLLEGES SCHOLARSHIP PROGRAM • 335

Full and partial scholarship to private career schools in Florida are awarded to students either graduating from high school or receiving GED in the current school year. Must be a resident of Florida. Minimum 2.5 GPA required.

Award Scholarship for use in freshman year; not renewable. *Number:* 100–200. *Amount:* $3500.
Eligibility Requirements: Applicant must be high school student; planning to enroll at a technical institution; resident of Florida and studying in Florida. Applicant must have 2.5 GPA or higher. Available to U.S. citizens.
Application Requirements Application, essay, references, transcript. *Deadline:* March 1.
World Wide Web: http://www.fapsc.org
Contact: Heather Fuselier, Membership Director
Florida Association of Postsecondary Schools and Colleges
200 West College Avenue
Tallahassee, FL 32301
Phone: 850-577-3139
Fax: 850-577-3133
E-mail: scholarship@fapsc.org

FLORIDA LEADER MAGAZINE/COLLEGE STUDENT OF THE YEAR, INC.

FLORIDA COLLEGE STUDENT OF THE YEAR AWARD • 336

This award recognizes Florida's finest campus leaders for their service to their campuses and communities. Available to Florida students enrolled at least part-time in a Florida postsecondary school. Must have completed at least eighteen credit hours with minimum GPA of 3.25. Based primarily on leader-

Florida College Student of the Year Award (continued)
ship activities but academic merit and work history are considered. Applicant may be in high school if concurrently enrolled in postsecondary institution. Submit statement of financial self-reliance.

Award Scholarship for use in sophomore, junior, senior, graduate, or post graduate years; not renewable. *Number:* 20. *Amount:* $1500–$4500.

Eligibility Requirements: Applicant must be enrolled full or part-time at a two-year or four-year or technical institution or university; resident of Florida; studying in Florida and must have an interest in leadership. Available to U.S. and non-U.S. citizens.

Application Requirements Application, autobiography, essay, photo, resume, references, self-addressed stamped envelope, transcript. *Deadline:* February 1.

World Wide Web: http://www.floridaleader.com/soty

Contact: W. H. Oxendine, Jr., Publisher/Editor-in-Chief
Florida Leader Magazine/College Student of the Year, Inc.
PO Box 14081
Gainesville, FL 32604-2081
Phone: 352-373-6907
Fax: 352-373-8120
E-mail: info@studentleader.com

FLORIDA STATE DEPARTMENT OF EDUCATION

ROSEWOOD FAMILY SCHOLARSHIP FUND   see number 268

FRANCIS OUIMET SCHOLARSHIP FUND

FRANCIS OUIMET SCHOLARSHIP FUND   • 337

Renewable scholarships are given to students on a need-based schedule who have given two or more years of service to golf in the state of Massachusetts. A knowledge of Francis Ouimet, leadership, community service, and good grades all must be identified. High school golf team members/players are not eligible unless they have met the three year requirement at a course.

Award Scholarship for use in freshman, sophomore, junior, or senior years; renewable. *Number:* 250–360. *Amount:* $1000–$2500.

Eligibility Requirements: Applicant must be enrolled full-time at a two-year or four-year or technical institution or university; resident of Massachusetts and must have an interest in golf. Applicant must have 2.5 GPA or higher. Available to U.S. citizens.

Application Requirements Application, essay, financial need analysis, interview, photo, references, test scores, transcript, proof of service to golf (minimum of three years). *Deadline:* December 1.

World Wide Web: http://www.ouimet.org

Contact: Donna Palen, Scholarship Administrator
Francis Ouimet Scholarship Fund
190 Park Road
Weston, MA 02493
Phone: 781-891-6400 Ext. 112
Fax: 781-891-9471
E-mail: donnap@ouimet.org

GEORGIA STUDENT FINANCE COMMISSION

GEORGIA PUBLIC SAFETY MEMORIAL GRANT/LAW ENFORCEMENT PERSONNEL DEPARTMENT GRANT   see number 219

GEORGIA TUITION EQUALIZATION GRANT (GTEG)   • 338

Award for Georgia residents pursuing undergraduate study at an accredited two- or four-year Georgia private institution. Complete the Georgia Student Grant Application. Award is $1100 per academic year. Deadlines vary.

Award Grant for use in freshman, sophomore, junior, or senior years; renewable. *Number:* 25,000–32,000. *Amount:* $1100.

Eligibility Requirements: Applicant must be enrolled full-time at a two-year or four-year institution or university; resident of Georgia and studying in Georgia. Available to U.S. citizens.

Application Requirements Application.

World Wide Web: http://www.gsfc.org

Contact: William Flook, Director of Scholarships and Grants Division
Georgia Student Finance Commission
2082 East Exchange Place, Suite 100
Tucker, GA 30084

GOVERNOR'S SCHOLARSHIP-GEORGIA   • 339

Award to assist students selected as Georgia scholars, STAR students, valedictorians, and salutatorians. For use at two- and four-year colleges and universities in Georgia. Recipients are selected as entering freshmen. Renewable award of up to $1575. Minimum 3.5 GPA required.

Award Scholarship for use in freshman, sophomore, junior, or senior years; renewable. *Number:* 2000–3000. *Amount:* up to $1575.

Eligibility Requirements: Applicant must be high school student; planning to enroll full-time at a two-year or four-year institution or university; resident of Georgia and studying in Georgia. Applicant must have 3.5 GPA or higher. Available to U.S. citizens.

Application Requirements Application, transcript. *Deadline:* Continuous.

World Wide Web: http://www.gsfc.org

Contact: William Flook, Director of Scholarships and Grants Division
Georgia Student Finance Commission
2082 East Exchange Place, Suite 100
Tucker, GA 30084

HOPE—HELPING OUTSTANDING PUPILS EDUCATIONALLY • 340

Grant program for Georgia residents who are college undergraduates to attend an accredited two- or four-year Georgia institution. Tuition and fees may be covered by the grant. Minimum 3.0 GPA required. Renewable if student maintains grades and reapplies. Write for deadlines.

Award Scholarship for use in freshman, sophomore, junior, or senior years; renewable. *Number:* 140,000–170,000. *Amount:* $300–$3000.

Eligibility Requirements: Applicant must be enrolled full or part-time at a two-year or four-year institution or university; resident of Georgia and studying in Georgia. Applicant must have 3.0 GPA or higher. Available to U.S. citizens.

Application Requirements Application.

World Wide Web: http://www.gsfc.org

Contact: William Flook, Director of Scholarships and Grants Division
Georgia Student Finance Commission
2082 East Exchange Place, Suite 100
Tucker, GA 30084

ROBERT C. BYRD HONORS SCHOLARSHIP-GEORGIA • 341

Complete the application provided by the Georgia Department of Education. Renewable awards for outstanding graduating Georgia high school seniors to be used for full-time undergraduate study at eligible U.S. institution. Minimum 3.5 GPA required.

Award Scholarship for use in freshman, sophomore, junior, or senior years; renewable. *Number:* 600–700. *Amount:* $1500.

Eligibility Requirements: Applicant must be high school student; planning to enroll full-time at a two-year or four-year institution or university and resident of Georgia. Applicant must have 3.5 GPA or higher. Available to U.S. citizens.

Application Requirements Application, transcript. *Deadline:* April 1.

World Wide Web: http://www.gsfc.org

Contact: William Flook, Director of Scholarships and Grants Division
Georgia Student Finance Commission
2082 East Exchange Place, Suite 100
Tucker, GA 30084

GOLDEN STATE MINORITY FOUNDATION

EDUCATIONAL ENRICHMENT SUPPORT PROJECT • 342

The Educational Enrichment Support Project financially enables inner-city schools to enrich the overall educational experience of southern California students.

Award Grant for use in freshman, sophomore, junior, or senior years; not renewable. *Number:* 30–70. *Amount:* $200–$1500.

Eligibility Requirements: Applicant must be resident of California and studying in California. Available to U.S. citizens.
Application Requirements Application, essay, financial need analysis. *Deadline:* Continuous.
World Wide Web: http://www.gsmf.org
Contact: Mr. Jay Johnson, EESP Program Coordinator
Golden State Minority Foundation
419 North Larchmont Boulevard, #98
Los Angeles, CA 90004
Phone: 323-730-5994 Ext. 12
Fax: 323-730-5993
E-mail: education@gsmf.org

GRAND LODGE OF IOWA, AF AND AM

GRAND LODGE OF IOWA MASONIC SCHOLARSHIP • 343

One-time awards for graduating seniors of Iowa public high schools. The scholarship is for the freshman year of college. The application must be submitted by February 1 on an original application provided by the Grand Lodge of Iowa.

Award Scholarship for use in freshman year; not renewable. *Number:* 60–70. *Amount:* $2000.
Eligibility Requirements: Applicant must be high school student; planning to enroll full-time at a four-year institution or university and resident of Iowa. Available to U.S. and non-U.S. citizens.
Application Requirements Application, autobiography, essay, interview, references, transcript. *Deadline:* February 1.
Contact: William Crawford, Grand Secretary
Grand Lodge of Iowa, AF and AM
PO Box 279
Cedar Rapids, IA 52406-0279
Phone: 319-365-1438
Fax: 319-365-1439
E-mail: wrc@netins.net

GREATER BRIDGEPORT AREA FOUNDATION

SCHOLARSHIP AWARD PROGRAM • 344

The Greater Bridgeport Area Foundation Scholarship Award program primarily supports high school seniors entering their freshman year in college. Scholarships average $1000 for one year. Some graduate school scholarships are available. Awards given to students from towns in GBAF service area: Bridgeport, Easton, Fairfield, Milford, Monroe, Shelton, Stratford, Trumbull, and Westport.

Award Scholarship for use in freshman year; not renewable. *Number:* 100–150. *Amount:* $500–$2500.

Scholarship Award Program (continued)

Eligibility Requirements: Applicant must be high school student; planning to enroll full-time at a four-year institution or university and resident of Connecticut. Available to U.S. citizens.

Application Requirements Application, essay, references, transcript. *Deadline:* April 15.

World Wide Web: http://www.gbafoundation.org

Contact: Education Associate
Greater Bridgeport Area Foundation
940 Broad Street
Bridgeport, CT 06604
Phone: 203-334-7511
Fax: 203-333-4652
E-mail: gbaf@snet.net

GREATER KANAWHA VALLEY FOUNDATION

RUTH ANN JOHNSON SCHOLARSHIP • 345

Awarded to students who demonstrate academic excellence and financial need to attend any accredited college or university in any state or county. Scholarships are awarded for one or more years. May apply for two Foundation scholarships but will only be chosen for one. Must be a resident of West Virginia.

Award Scholarship for use in any year; renewable. *Number:* 57. *Amount:* $1000.

Eligibility Requirements: Applicant must be enrolled full-time at a four-year institution or university and resident of West Virginia. Applicant must have 2.5 GPA or higher.

Application Requirements Application, essay, financial need analysis, references, transcript, IRS 1040 form. *Deadline:* February 15.

World Wide Web: http://www.tgkvf.org

Contact: Susan Hoover, Scholarship Coordinator
Greater Kanawha Valley Foundation
PO Box 3041
Charleston, WV 25331
Phone: 304-346-3620
Fax: 304-346-3640

W. P. BLACK SCHOLARSHIP FUND • 346

Renewable award for West Virginia residents who demonstrate academic excellence and financial need and who are enrolled in an undergraduate program in any accredited college or university. May apply for two Foundation scholarships but will only be chosen for one.

Award Scholarship for use in freshman, sophomore, junior, or senior years; renewable. *Number:* 98. *Amount:* $1000.

Eligibility Requirements: Applicant must be enrolled at a two-year or four-year institution or university and resident of West Virginia. Applicant must have 2.5 GPA or higher. Available to U.S. citizens.

Application Requirements Application, essay, financial need analysis, references, self-addressed stamped envelope, test scores, transcript. *Deadline:* February 15.

World Wide Web: http://www.tgkvf.org

Contact: Susan Hoover, Scholarship Coordinator
Greater Kanawha Valley Foundation
PO Box 3041
Charleston, WV 25331
Phone: 304-346-3620
Fax: 304-346-3640

HERSCHEL C. PRICE EDUCATIONAL FOUNDATION

HERSCHEL C. PRICE EDUCATIONAL FOUNDATION SCHOLARSHIPS
• 347

Open to undergraduates, graduates, and high school seniors. Must be a U.S. citizen, resident of West Virginia or attending a West Virginia college. Based on minimum 2.0 GPA and financial need. Deadlines are April 1 for fall and October 1 for spring. Undergraduates are shown preference.

Award Scholarship for use in any year; renewable. *Number:* 200–300. *Amount:* $500–$10,000.

Eligibility Requirements: Applicant must be enrolled full or part-time at a two-year or four-year institution or university; resident of West Virginia and studying in West Virginia. Available to U.S. citizens.

Application Requirements Application, financial need analysis, interview, test scores, transcript.

Contact: Jonna Hughes, Trustee/Director
Herschel C. Price Educational Foundation
PO Box 412
Huntington, WV 25708-0412
Phone: 304-529-3852

IDAHO STATE BOARD OF EDUCATION

IDAHO GOVERNOR'S CHALLENGE SCHOLARSHIP
• 348

Renewable scholarship available to Idaho residents enrolled full-time in an undergraduate academic or vocational-technical program at an eligible Idaho public or private college or university. Minimum GPA: 2.8. Merit-based award. Must be a high school senior and U.S. citizen to apply. Number of awards is conditional on the availability of funds. Must have a demonstrated commitment to public service.

Idaho Governor's Challenge Scholarship (continued)
Award Scholarship for use in freshman, sophomore, junior, or senior years; renewable. *Number:* 15–20. *Amount:* $3000.

Eligibility Requirements: Applicant must be high school student; planning to enroll full-time at a two-year or four-year or technical institution or university; resident of Idaho and studying in Idaho. Available to U.S. citizens.

Application Requirements Application, essay, portfolio, references, test scores, transcript. *Deadline:* December 15.

World Wide Web: http://www.sde.state.id.us/osbe/board.htm

Contact: Caryl Smith, Scholarship Assistant
Idaho State Board of Education
PO Box 83720
Boise, ID 83720-0037
Phone: 208-332-1576
Fax: 208-334-2632
E-mail: csmith@osbe.state.id.us

IDAHO MINORITY AND "AT RISK" STUDENT SCHOLARSHIP

see number 274

IDAHO PROMISE CATEGORY A SCHOLARSHIP PROGRAM • 349

Renewable award available to Idaho residents who are graduating high school seniors. Must attend an approved Idaho college full-time. Based on class rank (must be verified by school official), GPA, and ACT scores. Professional-technical student applicants must take COMPASS.

Award Scholarship for use in freshman, sophomore, junior, or senior years; renewable. *Number:* 25–30. *Amount:* $3000.

Eligibility Requirements: Applicant must be high school student; planning to enroll full-time at a two-year or four-year or technical institution or university; resident of Idaho and studying in Idaho. Applicant must have 3.5 GPA or higher. Available to U.S. citizens.

Application Requirements Application, test scores. *Deadline:* December 15.

World Wide Web: http://www.sde.state.id.us/osbe/board.htm

Contact: Caryl Smith, Scholarship Assistant
Idaho State Board of Education
PO Box 83720
Boise, ID 83720-0037
Phone: 208-332-1576
Fax: 208-334-2632
E-mail: csmith@osbe.state.id.us

ROBERT C. BYRD HONORS SCHOLARSHIP PROGRAM-IDAHO • 350

Renewable scholarships available to Idaho residents based on outstanding academic achievement. Students must apply as high school seniors.

Award Scholarship for use in freshman, sophomore, junior, or senior years; renewable. *Number:* 90. *Amount:* $1500.

Eligibility Requirements: Applicant must be high school student; planning to enroll full-time at a two-year or four-year or technical institution and resident of Idaho. Applicant must have 3.5 GPA or higher. Available to U.S. citizens.

Application Requirements Application, references, test scores, transcript. *Deadline:* March 20.

World Wide Web: http://www.sde.state.id.us/osbe/board.htm

Contact: Sally Tiel, Department of Education, Counseling and Assessment
Idaho State Board of Education
PO Box 83720
Boise, ID 83720-0027
Phone: 208-332-6800
Fax: 208-334-2228

ILLINOIS DEPARTMENT OF CHILDREN AND FAMILY SERVICES

ILLINOIS DEPARTMENT OF CHILDREN AND FAMILY SERVICES SCHOLARSHIPS • 351

Scholarship recipients will receive a medical card, a monthly check of $445 and a tuition waiver for those recipients who chose to attend one of nine Illinois public universities. Scholarship is prorated for a maximum of four years. Applicant must be 16 years of age, possess a diploma or GED accreditation. Must be a ward of the Department of Children and Family Services, or a former ward who has been adopted or placed in private guardianship. ACT or SAT scores and letters of recommendation are required. Contact for application deadline.

Award Scholarship for use in any year; renewable. *Number:* 48. *Amount:* $6000–$8250.

Eligibility Requirements: Applicant must be age 16-21; enrolled full-time at a two-year or four-year institution or university; resident of Illinois and studying in Illinois. Available to U.S. citizens.

Application Requirements Application, autobiography, financial need analysis, references, test scores, transcript.

Contact: Dwight Lambert, Statewide Education Coordinator
Illinois Department of Children and Family Services
406 East Monroe Street, #222
Springfield, IL 62701-1498
Phone: 217-524-2030
Fax: 217-524-2101
E-mail: dlambert@idcfs.state.il.us

ILLINOIS STUDENT ASSISTANCE COMMISSION (ISAC)

ILLINOIS COLLEGE SAVINGS BOND BONUS INCENTIVE GRANT PROGRAM • 352

Program offers holders of Illinois College Savings Bonds a $20 grant for each year of bond maturity payable upon bond redemption if at least 70 percent of proceeds are used to attend college in Illinois. May not be used by students attending religious or divinity schools.

Award Grant for use in any year; not renewable. *Number:* 1200–1400. *Amount:* $40–$220.

Eligibility Requirements: Applicant must be enrolled full or part-time at a two-year or four-year or technical institution or university and studying in Illinois. Available to U.S. and non-U.S. citizens.

Application Requirements Application. *Deadline:* Continuous.

World Wide Web: http://www.isac-online.org

Contact: David Barinholtz, Client Information
Illinois Student Assistance Commission (ISAC)
1755 Lake Cook Road
Deerfield, IL 60015-5209
Phone: 847-948-8500 Ext. 2385

ILLINOIS INCENTIVE FOR ACCESS PROGRAM • 353

Award for eligible first-time freshmen enrolling in approved Illinois institutions. One-time grant of up to $500 may be used for any educational expense. Deadline: October 1.

Award Grant for use in freshman year; not renewable. *Number:* 17,000–19,000. *Amount:* $300–$500.

Eligibility Requirements: Applicant must be enrolled full or part-time at a two-year or four-year or technical institution or university; resident of Illinois and studying in Illinois. Available to U.S. and non-U.S. citizens.

Application Requirements Financial need analysis. *Deadline:* October 1.

World Wide Web: http://www.isac-online.org

Contact: David Barinholtz, Client Information
Illinois Student Assistance Commission (ISAC)
1755 Lake Cook Road
Deerfield, IL 60015-5209
Phone: 847-948-8500 Ext. 2385

ILLINOIS MONETARY AWARD PROGRAM • 354

Award for eligible students attending Illinois public universities, private colleges and universities, community colleges, and some proprietary institutions. Applicable only to tuition and fees. Based on financial need. Deadline: October 1.

Award Grant for use in freshman, sophomore, junior, or senior years; not renewable. *Number:* 135,000–140,000. *Amount:* $300–$4320.

Eligibility Requirements: Applicant must be enrolled full or part-time at a two-year or four-year or technical institution or university; resident of Illinois and studying in Illinois. Available to U.S. and non-U.S. citizens.

Application Requirements Financial need analysis. *Deadline:* October 1.

World Wide Web: http://www.isac-online.org

Contact: David Barinholtz, Client Information
Illinois Student Assistance Commission (ISAC)
1755 Lake Cook Road
Deerfield, IL 60015-5209
Phone: 847-948-8500 Ext. 2385

ILLINOIS NATIONAL GUARD GRANT PROGRAM see number 241

ILLINOIS STUDENT-TO-STUDENT PROGRAM OF MATCHING GRANTS • 355

Award provides matching funds for need-based grants at participating Illinois public universities and community colleges. Deadline: October 1.

Award Grant for use in freshman, sophomore, junior, or senior years; not renewable. *Number:* 2000–4000. *Amount:* $300–$500.

Eligibility Requirements: Applicant must be enrolled full or part-time at a two-year or four-year institution or university; resident of Illinois and studying in Illinois. Available to U.S. and non-U.S. citizens.

Application Requirements Financial need analysis. *Deadline:* October 1.

World Wide Web: http://www.isac-online.org

Contact: David Barinholtz, Client Information
Illinois Student Assistance Commission (ISAC)
1755 Lake Cook Road
Deerfield, IL 60015-5209
Phone: 847-948-8500 Ext. 2385

ILLINOIS VETERAN GRANT PROGRAM—IVG see number 246

MERIT RECOGNITION SCHOLARSHIP (MRS) PROGRAM • 356

Award for Illinois high school seniors graduating in the top 5 percent of their class and attending Illinois postsecondary institution. Deadline: June 15. Contact for application procedures.

Award Scholarship for use in freshman year; not renewable. *Number:* 5000–6000. *Amount:* $900–$1000.

Eligibility Requirements: Applicant must be high school student; planning to enroll full or part-time at a two-year or four-year institution or university; resident of Illinois and studying in Illinois. Applicant must have 3.5 GPA or higher. Available to U.S. and non-U.S. citizens.

Application Requirements Application. *Deadline:* June 15.

World Wide Web: http://www.isac-online.org

Merit Recognition Scholarship (MRS) Program (continued)
Contact: David Barinholtz, Client Information
Illinois Student Assistance Commission (ISAC)
1755 Lake Cook Road
Deerfield, IL 60015-5209
Phone: 847-948-8500 Ext. 2385

ROBERT C. BYRD HONORS SCHOLARSHIP-ILLINOIS • 357

Available to Illinois residents who are graduating high school seniors. Based on outstanding academic merit. Awards are renewable up to four years. Must be accepted on a full-time basis as an undergraduate student.

Award Scholarship for use in freshman, sophomore, junior, or senior years; renewable. *Number:* 1100–1200. *Amount:* $1400–$1500.
Eligibility Requirements: Applicant must be high school student; planning to enroll full-time at a two-year or four-year institution or university and resident of Illinois. Applicant must have 3.5 GPA or higher. Available to U.S. and non-U.S. citizens.
Application Requirements Application, test scores, transcript. *Deadline:* January 15.
World Wide Web: http://www.isac-online.org
Contact: David Barinholtz, Client Information
Illinois Student Assistance Commission (ISAC)
1755 Lake Cook Road
Deerfield, IL 60015-5209
Phone: 847-948-8500 Ext. 2385

IOWA DIVISION OF VOCATIONAL REHABILITATION SERVICES

IOWA VOCATIONAL REHABILITATION   see number 237

ITALIAN CATHOLIC FEDERATION, INC.

ICF COLLEGE SCHOLARSHIPS TO HIGH SCHOOL SENIORS
see number 276

JAMES F. BYRNES FOUNDATION

JAMES F. BYRNES SCHOLARSHIP • 358

Renewable award for residents of South Carolina ages 17-24 with one or both parents deceased. Must show financial need; a satisfactory scholastic record; and qualities of character, ability, and enterprise. Award is for undergraduate study. Results of SAT must be provided.

Award Scholarship for use in freshman, sophomore, junior, or senior years; renewable. *Number:* 70. *Amount:* $2000–$2750.

Eligibility Requirements: Applicant must be age 17-24; enrolled full-time at a four-year institution and resident of South Carolina. Available to U.S. citizens.
Application Requirements Application, autobiography, financial need analysis, interview, photo, references, transcript. *Deadline:* January 31.
World Wide Web: http://www.byrnesscholars.org
Contact: Mrs. Barbara Kirk, Executive Secretary
James F. Byrnes Foundation
PO Box 6781
Columbia, SC 29260-6781
E-mail: jfbfsc@usit.net

JEWISH FEDERATION OF METROPOLITAN CHICAGO (JFMC)

JEWISH FEDERATION OF METROPOLITAN CHICAGO ACADEMIC SCHOLARSHIP PROGRAM
see number 300

JOSE MARTI SCHOLARSHIP CHALLENGE GRANT FUND

JOSE MARTI SCHOLARSHIP CHALLENGE GRANT
see number 277

KANSAS BOARD OF REGENTS

ETHNIC MINORITY SCHOLARSHIP PROGRAM
see number 278

KANSAS COMPREHENSIVE GRANT PROGRAM
• 359

Grants available for Kansas residents attending public or private baccalaureate colleges or universities in Kansas. Based on financial need. Must file Free Application for Federal Student Aid to apply. Renewable award based on continuing eligibility. Up to $3000 for undergraduate use. Deadline: April 1.

Award Grant for use in freshman, sophomore, junior, or senior years; renewable. *Number:* 7000–8200. *Amount:* $1100–$3000.
Eligibility Requirements: Applicant must be enrolled full-time at a two-year or four-year institution or university; resident of Kansas and studying in Kansas. Available to U.S. citizens.
Application Requirements Financial need analysis. *Deadline:* April 1.
World Wide Web: http://www.kansasregents.com
Contact: Diane Lindeman, Director of Student Financial Assistance
Kansas Board of Regents
1000 Southwest Jackson, Suite 520
Topeka, KS 66612-1368
Phone: 785-296-3517
Fax: 785-296-0983
E-mail: dlindeman@ksbor.org

KANSAS STATE SCHOLARSHIP PROGRAM • 360

The Kansas State Scholarship Program provides assistance to financially needy, academically outstanding students who attend Kansas postsecondary institutions. Must be Kansas resident. Minimum 3.0 GPA required for renewal. Application fee is $10. Deadline: May 15.

Award Scholarship for use in freshman, sophomore, junior, or senior years; renewable. *Number:* 1000–1500. *Amount:* $1000.

Eligibility Requirements: Applicant must be enrolled full-time at a two-year or four-year institution or university; resident of Kansas and studying in Kansas. Applicant must have 3.0 GPA or higher. Available to U.S. citizens.

Application Requirements Application, financial need analysis, test scores. *Fee:* $10. *Deadline:* May 15.

World Wide Web: http://www.kansasregents.com

Contact: Diane Lindeman, Director of Student Financial Assistance
Kansas Board of Regents
1000 Southwest Jackson, Suite 520
Topeka, KS 66612-1368
Phone: 785-296-3517
Fax: 785-296-0983
E-mail: dlindeman@ksbor.org

KANSAS NATIONAL GUARD EDUCATIONAL ASSISTANCE PROGRAM

KANSAS NATIONAL GUARD EDUCATIONAL ASSISTANCE AWARD PROGRAM see number 242

KENTUCKY HIGHER EDUCATION ASSISTANCE AUTHORITY (KHEAA)

COLLEGE ACCESS PROGRAM (CAP) GRANT • 361

One-time award for U.S. citizen and Kentucky resident with no previous college degree. Provides $50 per semester hour for a minimum of six hours per semester. Applicants seeking degrees in religion are not eligible. Must demonstrate financial need and submit Free Application for Federal Student Aid. Priority deadline is March 15.

Award Grant for use in freshman, sophomore, junior, or senior years; not renewable. *Number:* 30,000–35,000. *Amount:* up to $1200.

Eligibility Requirements: Applicant must be enrolled full or part-time at a two-year or four-year or technical institution or university; resident of Kentucky and studying in Kentucky. Available to U.S. citizens.

Application Requirements Financial need analysis. *Deadline:* Continuous.

World Wide Web: http://www.kheaa.com

Contact: Mark Wells, Program Coordinator
Kentucky Higher Education Assistance Authority (KHEAA)
1050 U.S. 127 South
Frankfort, KY 40601-4323
Phone: 502-696-7394
Fax: 502-696-7345
E-mail: mwells@kheaa.com

KENTUCKY EDUCATIONAL EXCELLENCE SCHOLARSHIP (KEES) • 362

Annual award based on each Kentucky high school year's GPA of 2.5 or higher and highest ACT or SAT score of 15 or higher received by high school graduation. Awards are renewable if required cumulative GPA maintained at a Kentucky postsecondary school. Must be a Kentucky resident.

Award Scholarship for use in freshman, sophomore, junior, or senior years; renewable. *Number:* 30,000–40,000. *Amount:* $125–$1500.

Eligibility Requirements: Applicant must be high school student; planning to enroll full or part-time at a two-year or four-year or technical institution or university; resident of Kentucky and studying in Kentucky. Applicant must have 2.5 GPA or higher. Available to U.S. citizens.

Application Requirements Test scores, transcript.

World Wide Web: http://www.kheaa.com

Contact: Tim Phelps, KEES Program Coordinator
Kentucky Higher Education Assistance Authority (KHEAA)
1050 U.S. 127 South
Frankfort, KY 40601-4323
Phone: 502-696-7397
Fax: 502-696-7345
E-mail: tphelps@kheaa.com

KENTUCKY TUITION GRANT (KTG) • 363

Available to Kentucky residents who are full-time undergraduates at an independent college within the state. Must not be enrolled in a religion program. Based on financial need. Submit Free Application for Federal Student Aid. Priority deadline is March 15.

Award Grant for use in freshman, sophomore, junior, or senior years; not renewable. *Number:* 9000–10,000. *Amount:* $50–$1600.

Eligibility Requirements: Applicant must be enrolled full-time at a two-year or four-year institution or university; resident of Kentucky and studying in Kentucky. Available to U.S. citizens.

Application Requirements Financial need analysis. *Deadline:* Continuous.

World Wide Web: http://www.kheaa.com

Kentucky Tuition Grant (KTG) (continued)
Contact: Mark Wells, Program Coordinator
Kentucky Higher Education Assistance Authority (KHEAA)
1050 U.S. 127 South
Frankfort, KY 40601-4323
Phone: 502-696-7394
Fax: 502-696-7345
E-mail: mwells@kheaa.com

LONG & FOSTER REAL ESTATE, INC.

LONG & FOSTER SCHOLARSHIP PROGRAM • 364

One-time award for residents of MD, PA, DC , VA and DE. Students may pursue any academic major they desire. The Scholarship Committee will be seeking academically strong high school seniors who are well rounded and demonstrate leadership and involvement in a variety of school activities. Must be U.S. citizen. Minimum 3.0 GPA required.

Award Scholarship for use in freshman year; not renewable. *Number:* 100. *Amount:* $1000.

Eligibility Requirements: Applicant must be high school student; planning to enroll full-time at a four-year institution or university and resident of Delaware, District of Columbia, Maryland, Pennsylvania, or Virginia. Applicant must have 3.0 GPA or higher. Available to U.S. citizens.

Application Requirements Application, essay, financial need analysis, references, transcript. *Deadline:* March 1.

World Wide Web: http://www.longandfoster.com

Contact: Public Relations Coordinator
Long & Foster Real Estate, Inc.
11351 Random Hills Road
Fairfax, VA 22030-6082
Phone: 703-359-1757
Fax: 703-591-5493

LOUISIANA OFFICE OF STUDENT FINANCIAL ASSISTANCE

LEVERAGING EDUCATIONAL ASSISTANCE PROGRAM (LEAP)• 365

LEAP program provides federal and state funds to provide need-based grants to academically qualified students. Individual award determined by Financial Aid Office and governed by number of applicants and availability of funds. File Free Application for Federal Student aid by school deadline to apply each year. For Louisiana students attending Louisiana postsecondary institutions.

Award Grant for use in freshman, sophomore, junior, or senior years; not renewable. *Number:* 3000. *Amount:* $200–$2000.

Eligibility Requirements: Applicant must be enrolled full or part-time at a two-year or four-year or technical institution or university; resident of Louisiana and studying in Louisiana. Available to U.S. citizens.

Application Requirements Application, financial need analysis.
World Wide Web: http://www.osfa.state.la.us
Contact: Public Information
Louisiana Office of Student Financial Assistance
PO Box 91202
Baton Rouge, LA 70821-9202
Phone: 800-259-5626 Ext. 1012
E-mail: custserv@osfa.state.la.us

MAINE COMMUNITY FOUNDATION, INC.

MAINE COMMUNITY FOUNDATION SCHOLARSHIP PROGRAMS • 366

The Maine Community Foundation administers over 150 different scholarship award programs for individuals residing in Maine. For complete information, contact our web site. (http://www.mainecf.org)

Award Scholarship for use in any year; not renewable. *Number:* 150–700. *Amount:* $500–$5000.
Eligibility Requirements: Applicant must be enrolled full or part-time at a two-year or four-year or technical institution or university and resident of Maine. Available to U.S. citizens.
Application Requirements Application.
World Wide Web: http://www.mainecf.org
Contact: Jean Warren, Education Coordinator/ Program Officer
Maine Community Foundation, Inc.
245 Main Street
Ellsworth, ME 04605
Phone: 207-667-9735
Fax: 207-667-0447
E-mail: jwarren@mainecf.org

MARYLAND STATE HIGHER EDUCATION COMMISSION

DELEGATE SCHOLARSHIP PROGRAM-MARYLAND • 367

Delegate scholarships help Maryland residents attending Maryland degree-granting institutions, certain career schools, or nursing diploma schools. May attend out-of-state institution if Maryland Higher Education Commission deems major to be unique and not offered at a Maryland institution. Free Application for Federal Student Aid may be required. Students interested in this program should apply by contacting their legislative district delegate.

Award Scholarship for use in freshman, sophomore, junior, senior, or graduate years; not renewable. *Number:* up to 3500. *Amount:* $200–$12,981.
Eligibility Requirements: Applicant must be enrolled full or part-time at a two-year or four-year or technical institution or university; resident of Maryland and studying in Maryland. Available to U.S. citizens.

Delegate Scholarship Program-Maryland (continued)

Application Requirements Application, financial need analysis. *Deadline:* Continuous.

World Wide Web: http://www.mhec.state.md.us

Contact: Barbara Fantom, Scholarship Administration
Maryland State Higher Education Commission
16 Francis Street
Annapolis, MD 21401-1781
Phone: 410-260-4547
Fax: 410-974-5994
E-mail: ssamail@mhec.state.md.us

DISTINGUISHED SCHOLAR AWARD-MARYLAND • 368

Renewable award for Maryland students enrolled full-time at Maryland institutions. National Merit Scholar Finalists automatically offered award. Others may qualify for the award in satisfying criteria of a minimum 3.7 GPA or in combination with high test scores, or for Talent in Arts competition in categories of music, drama, dance, or visual arts. Must maintain 3.0 GPA in college for award to be renewed. Contact for further details.

Award Scholarship for use in freshman, sophomore, junior, or senior years; renewable. *Number:* up to 2000. *Amount:* up to $3000.

Eligibility Requirements: Applicant must be high school student; planning to enroll full-time at a two-year or four-year institution or university; resident of Maryland and studying in Maryland. Available to U.S. citizens.

Application Requirements Application, test scores, transcript. *Deadline:* February 15.

World Wide Web: http://www.mhec.state.md.us

Contact: Margaret Riley, Scholarship Administration
Maryland State Higher Education Commission
16 Francis Street
Annapolis, MD 21401-1781
Phone: 410-260-4568
Fax: 410-974-5994
E-mail: ssamail@mhec.state.md.us

EDUCATIONAL ASSISTANCE GRANTS-MARYLAND • 369

Award for Maryland residents accepted or enrolled in a full-time undergraduate degree or certificate program at a Maryland institution or hospital nursing school. Must submit financial aid form by March 1. Must earn 2.0 GPA in college to maintain award.

Award Grant for use in freshman, sophomore, junior, or senior years; renewable. *Number:* 11,000–20,000. *Amount:* $400–$2700.

Eligibility Requirements: Applicant must be enrolled full-time at a two-year or four-year institution or university; resident of Maryland and studying in Maryland. Available to U.S. citizens.

Application Requirements Application, financial need analysis. *Deadline:* March 1.

World Wide Web: http://www.mhec.state.md.us

Contact: Barbara Fantom, Scholarship Administration
Maryland State Higher Education Commission
16 Francis Street
Annapolis, MD 21401-1781
Phone: 410-260-4547
Fax: 410-974-5994
E-mail: ssamail@mhec.state.md.us

EDWARD T. CONROY MEMORIAL SCHOLARSHIP PROGRAM

see number 247

GUARANTEED ACCESS GRANT-MARYLAND • 370

Award for Maryland resident enrolling full-time in an undergraduate program at a Maryland institution. Must be under 22 at time of first award and begin college within one year of completing high school in Maryland with a minimum 2.5 GPA. Must have an annual family income less than 130% of the federal poverty level guideline.

Award Grant for use in freshman, sophomore, junior, or senior years; renewable. *Number:* up to 1000. *Amount:* $400–$9200.

Eligibility Requirements: Applicant must be enrolled full-time at a two-year or four-year institution or university; resident of Maryland and studying in Maryland. Applicant must have 2.5 GPA or higher. Available to U.S. citizens.

Application Requirements Application, financial need analysis, transcript. *Deadline:* Continuous.

World Wide Web: http://www.mhec.state.md.us

Contact: Theresa Lowe, Scholarship Administration
Maryland State Higher Education Commission
16 Francis Street
Annapolis, MD 21401-1781
Phone: 410-260-4555
Fax: 410-974-5994
E-mail: ssamail@mhec.state.md.us

J.F. TOLBERT MEMORIAL STUDENT GRANT PROGRAM • 371

Available to Maryland residents attending a private career school in Maryland with at least 18 clock hours per week.

Award Grant for use in any year; not renewable. *Number:* 1500. *Amount:* up to $300.

Eligibility Requirements: Applicant must be enrolled at a technical institution; resident of Maryland and studying in Maryland. Available to U.S. citizens.

Application Requirements Application, financial need analysis. *Deadline:* Continuous.

World Wide Web: http://www.mhec.state.md.us

Contact: Carla Rich, Scholarship Administration
Maryland State Higher Education Commission
16 Francis Street
Annapolis, MD 21401-1781
Phone: 410-260-4513
Fax: 410-974-5994
E-mail: ssamail@mhec.state.md.us

PART-TIME GRANT PROGRAM-MARYLAND • 372

Funds provided to Maryland colleges and universities. Eligible students must be enrolled on a part-time basis (6-11 credits) in an undergraduate degree program. Must demonstrate financial need and also be Maryland resident.

Award Grant for use in freshman, sophomore, junior, or senior years; renewable. *Number:* 2000–2700. *Amount:* $200–$1000.

Eligibility Requirements: Applicant must be enrolled part-time at a two-year or four-year institution or university; resident of Maryland and studying in Maryland. Available to U.S. citizens.

Application Requirements Application, financial need analysis. *Deadline:* March 1.

World Wide Web: http://www.mhec.state.md.us

Contact: Linda Asplin, Scholarship Administration
Maryland State Higher Education Commission
16 Francis Street
Annapolis, MD 21401-1781
Phone: 410-260-4570
Fax: 410-974-5994
E-mail: ssamail@mhec.state.md.us

SENATORIAL SCHOLARSHIPS-MARYLAND • 373

Renewable award for Maryland residents attending a Maryland degree-granting institution, nursing diploma school, or certain private career schools. May be used out-of-state only if Maryland Higher Education Commission deems major to be unique and not offered at Maryland institution.

Award Scholarship for use in freshman, sophomore, junior, senior, or graduate years; renewable. *Number:* up to 7000. *Amount:* $200–$2000.

Eligibility Requirements: Applicant must be enrolled full or part-time at a two-year or four-year or technical institution or university; resident of Maryland and studying in Maryland. Available to U.S. citizens.

Application Requirements Financial need analysis, test scores, application to Legislative District Senator. *Deadline:* March 1.

World Wide Web: http://www.mhec.state.md.us

Contact: Barbara Fantom, Scholarship Administration
Maryland State Higher Education Commission
16 Francis Street
Annapolis, MD 21401-1781
Phone: 410-260-4547
Fax: 410-974-5994
E-mail: ssamail@mhec.state.md.us

MASONIC GRAND LODGE CHARITIES OF RHODE ISLAND

RHODE ISLAND MASONIC GRAND LODGE SCHOLARSHIP • 374

One-time scholarships for Rhode Island residents who have lived in Rhode Island for more than five years and who are enrolled in undergraduate studies. Awards may also be given to students who do not live in Rhode Island but have an association with the Rhode Island Masonic organization. High school students may apply.

Award Scholarship for use in freshman, sophomore, junior, or senior years; not renewable. *Number:* 200–250. *Amount:* $750–$2500.

Eligibility Requirements: Applicant must be enrolled full-time at a two-year or four-year institution or university and resident of Rhode Island. Available to U.S. and non-U.S. citizens.

Application Requirements Application, financial need analysis, transcript. *Deadline:* April 18.

Contact: John Faulhaber, Grand Secretary
Masonic Grand Lodge Charities of Rhode Island
222 Taunton Avenue
East Providence, RI 02914-4556

MASSACHUSETTS OFFICE OF STUDENT FINANCIAL ASSISTANCE

MASSACHUSETTS ASSISTANCE FOR STUDENT SUCCESS PROGRAM • 375

Provides need-based financial assistance to Massachusetts residents to attend undergraduate postsecondary institutions in Connecticut, Maine, Maryland, Massachusetts, New Hampshire, Pennsylvania, Rhode Island, Vermont, and District of Columbia. High school seniors may apply. Timely filing of FAFSA required.

Award Grant for use in freshman, sophomore, junior, or senior years; not renewable. *Number:* 32,000–35,000. *Amount:* $300–$2900.

Eligibility Requirements: Applicant must be enrolled full-time at a two-year or four-year or technical institution or university; resident of Massachusetts and studying in Connecticut, District of Columbia, Maine, Maryland, Massachusetts, New Hampshire, Pennsylvania, Rhode Island, or Vermont. Available to U.S. citizens.

Massachusetts Assistance for Student Success Program (continued)
Application Requirements Financial need analysis, FAFSA. *Deadline:* May 1.
World Wide Web: http://www.osfa.mass.edu
Contact: Scholarship Information
Massachusetts Office of Student Financial Assistance
454 Broadway
Suite 200
Revere, MA 02151

MELLINGER EDUCATIONAL FOUNDATION
MELLINGER SCHOLARSHIPS • 376
Scholarships for undergraduates residing in western Illinois and eastern Iowa.

Award Scholarship for use in freshman, sophomore, junior, or senior years; renewable. *Number:* 300–350. *Amount:* $300–$1200.
Eligibility Requirements: Applicant must be enrolled full or part-time at a two-year or four-year or technical institution or university and resident of Illinois or Iowa. Available to U.S. citizens.
Application Requirements Application, financial need analysis, test scores, transcript. *Deadline:* May 1.
Contact: David Fleming, President
Mellinger Educational Foundation
1025 East Broadway, Box 770
Monmouth, IL 61462
Phone: 309-734-2419
Fax: 309-734-4435

MINNESOTA HIGHER EDUCATION SERVICES OFFICE
MINNESOTA STATE GRANT PROGRAM • 377
Need-based grant program available for Minnesota residents attending Minnesota colleges. Student covers 46% of cost with remainder covered by Pell Grant, parent contribution and state grant. Students apply with FAFSA and college administers the program on campus.

Award Grant for use in freshman, sophomore, junior, or senior years; not renewable. *Number:* 62,000. *Amount:* $100–$7770.
Eligibility Requirements: Applicant must be age 17; enrolled full or part-time at a two-year or four-year or technical institution or university; resident of Minnesota and studying in Minnesota. Available to U.S. citizens.
Application Requirements Application, financial need analysis. *Deadline:* June 30.
World Wide Web: http://www.heso.state.mn.us

Contact: Minnesota Higher Education Services Office
1450 Energy Park Drive, Suite 350
St. Paul, MN 55108
Phone: 651-642-0567 Ext. 1

MISSOURI DEPARTMENT OF ELEMENTARY AND SECONDARY EDUCATION

ROBERT C. BYRD HONORS SCHOLARSHIP • 378

Award for Missouri high school senior who are residents of Missouri. The amount of the award per student each year depends on the amount the state is allotted by the U.S. Department of Education. The highest amount of award per student is $1500. Students must rank in top 10% of high school class and score in top 10% of ACT test.

Award Scholarship for use in freshman year; renewable. *Number:* 150–190. *Amount:* up to $1500.

Eligibility Requirements: Applicant must be high school student; planning to enroll full-time at a two-year or four-year institution or university and resident of Missouri. Applicant must have 3.5 GPA or higher.

Application Requirements Application, test scores, transcript, 7th semester transcripts. *Deadline:* April 15.

World Wide Web: http://www.dese.state.mo.us

Contact: Laura Harrison, Administrative Assistant
Missouri Department of Elementary and Secondary Education
PO Box 480
Jefferson City, MO 65102-0480
Phone: 573-751-1668
Fax: 573-526-3580
E-mail: lharriso@mail.dese.state.mo.us

MITCHELL INSTITUTE

SENATOR GEORGE J. MITCHELL SCHOLARSHIP RESEARCH INSTITUTE SCHOLARSHIPS • 379

The Mitchell Institute awards 160 $4,000 scholarships each year to Maine students entering colleges. One Mitchell Scholar is chosen from every public high school in the state, 15 awarded to private/parochial school students, home-school students, and non-traditional students. Fifteen scholarships are available to Maine seniors going out of state.

Award Grant for use in freshman, sophomore, junior, or senior years; renewable. *Number:* 160. *Amount:* $4000.

Eligibility Requirements: Applicant must be enrolled full-time at a two-year or four-year or technical institution or university and resident of Maine. Available to U.S. and non-U.S. citizens.

Application Requirements Application, essay, financial need analysis, photo, references, transcript. *Deadline:* April 6.

Senator George J. Mitchell Scholarship Research Institute Scholarships (continued)
World Wide Web: http://www.mitchellinstitute.org
Contact: Ms. Patricia Higgins, Director of Scholarship Programs
Mitchell Institute
22 Monument Square, Suite 200
Portland, ME 04106
Phone: 207-773-7700
Fax: 207-773-1133

MONTANA GUARANTEED STUDENT LOAN PROGRAM, OFFICE OF COMMISSIONER OF HIGHER EDUCATION

INDIAN STUDENT FEE WAIVER   see number 282

MONTANA BOARD OF REGENTS HIGH SCHOOL HONOR SCHOLARSHIP   • 380

Scholarship provides a one-year non-renewable fee waiver of tuition and registration and is awarded to graduating high school seniors from accredited high schools in Montana. 500 scholarships are awarded each year averaging $2,000 per recipient. The value of the award varies, depending on the tuition and registration fee at each participating college. Must have a minimum 3.0 GPA, meet all college preparatory requirements and be enrolled in an accredited high school for at least three years prior to graduation. Awarded to highest-ranking student in class attending a participating school. Contact high school counselor to apply. Deadline: April 15.

Award Scholarship for use in freshman year; not renewable. *Number:* 500. *Amount:* $2000.

Eligibility Requirements: Applicant must be high school student; planning to enroll full or part-time at a two-year or four-year institution or university; resident of Montana and studying in Montana. Applicant must have 3.0 GPA or higher. Available to U.S. citizens.

Application Requirements Application, transcript. *Deadline:* April 15.

World Wide Web: http://www.mgslp.state.mt.us

Contact: Contact High School Counselor
E-mail: scholars@mgslp.state.mt.us

MONTANA HIGHER EDUCATION GRANT   • 381

This grant is awarded based on need to undergraduate students attending either part-time or full-time who are residents of Montana and attending participating Montana schools. Awards are limited to the most needy students. A specific major or program of study is not required. This grant does not need to be repaid, and students may apply each year. Apply by filing a Free Application for Federal Student Aid by March 1 and contacting the financial aid office at the admitting college.

Award Grant for use in freshman, sophomore, junior, or senior years; not renewable. *Number:* 500. *Amount:* $400–$600.

Eligibility Requirements: Applicant must be enrolled full or part-time at a two-year or four-year institution or university; resident of Montana and studying in Montana. Available to U.S. citizens.

Application Requirements Financial need analysis, FAFSA.

World Wide Web: http://www.mgslp.state.mt.us

Contact: Contact Financial Aid Office
E-*mail:* scholars@mgslp.state.mt.us

NEBRASKA DEPARTMENT OF EDUCATION

ROBERT C. BYRD HONORS SCHOLARSHIP • 382

Up to $1500 each year for up to four years. Must be U.S. citizen and Nebraska resident. Awards designed to promote student excellence and achievement and to recognize able students who show promise of continued excellence. Applicant must send in a copy of enrollment acceptance.

Award Scholarship for use in freshman, sophomore, junior, or senior years; renewable. *Number:* 40. *Amount:* $1500.

Eligibility Requirements: Applicant must be enrolled full-time at a two-year or four-year or technical institution or university and resident of Nebraska. Available to U.S. citizens.

Application Requirements Application, test scores, transcript, copy of enrollment acceptance. *Deadline:* March 15.

Contact: Robert C. Byrd Scholarship Information
Nebraska Department of Education
301 Centennial Mall South, PO Box 94987
Lincoln, NE 68509-4987
Phone: 402-471-3962

NEVADA DEPARTMENT OF EDUCATION

NEVADA DEPARTMENT OF EDUCATION ROBERT C. BYRD HONORS SCHOLARSHIP PROGRAM • 383

Award for senior graduating from public or private Nevada high school. Must be Nevada resident and Nevada High School Scholars Program recipient. Renewable award of $1500. No application necessary. Nevada scholars are chosen from a database supplied by ACT and SAT. Please request SAT score be mailed to 2707 on your registration form. SAT scores of 1100 and above qualify as initial application. ACT score is automatically submitted for a score of 25 or greater. GPA (unweighted) must be 3.5 or higher.

Award Scholarship for use in freshman, sophomore, junior, or senior years; renewable. *Number:* 50–60. *Amount:* $1500.

Eligibility Requirements: Applicant must be high school student; planning to enroll full-time at a two-year or four-year or technical institution or university and resident of Nevada. Applicant must have 3.5 GPA or higher.

Nevada Department of Education Robert C. Byrd Honors Scholarship Program (continued)

Application Requirements Test scores, transcript. *Deadline:* Continuous.

Contact: Financial aid office at local college
Nevada Department of Education
700 East 5th Street
Carson City, NV 89701

NEVADA STUDENT INCENTIVE GRANT • 384

Award available to Nevada residents for use at an accredited Nevada college or university. Must show financial need. Any field of study eligible. High school students may not apply. One-time award of up to $5000. Contact financial aid office at local college.

Award Grant for use in any year; not renewable. *Number:* 400–800. *Amount:* $100–$5000.

Eligibility Requirements: Applicant must be enrolled full or part-time at a two-year or four-year or technical institution or university; resident of Nevada and studying in Nevada. Available to U.S. citizens.

Application Requirements Application, financial need analysis. *Deadline:* Continuous.

Contact: Financial aid office at local college
Nevada Department of Education
700 East 5th Street
Carson City, NV 89701

NEVADA WOMEN'S FUND

NEVADA WOMEN'S FUND SCHOLARSHIPS • 385

Awards for women for a variety of academic and vocational training scholarships. Must be a resident of Nevada. Preference given to applicants from northern Nevada. Renewable award of $500 to $5000. Application deadline is the last Friday in February. Application can be downloaded from website (http://www.nevadawomensfund.org).

Award Scholarship for use in any year; renewable. *Number:* 50–80. *Amount:* $500–$5000.

Eligibility Requirements: Applicant must be enrolled full or part-time at a two-year or four-year or technical institution or university; female and resident of Nevada.

Application Requirements Application, financial need analysis, references, transcript.

World Wide Web: http://www.nevadawomensfund.org

Contact: Fritsi Ericson, President and CEO
Nevada Women's Fund
770 Smithridge Drive, Suite 300
Reno, NV 89502
Phone: 775-786-2335
Fax: 775-786-8152
E-mail: fritsi@nevadawomensfund.org

NEW HAMPSHIRE CHARITABLE FOUNDATION

ADULT STUDENT AID PROGRAM • 386

One-time award for older students (over age 24) enrolling in undergraduate programs. There are 3 funding cycles during the calendar year: August 15, December 15 and May 15. Applications are available from our website: ⟨http://www.nhcf.org⟩ or at college financial aid offices. Application fee: $15. Must be a resident of New Hampshire.

Award Grant for use in freshman, sophomore, junior, or senior years; not renewable. *Number:* 100–200. *Amount:* $100–$1500.

Eligibility Requirements: Applicant must be age 24; enrolled full or part-time at a two-year or four-year or technical institution or university and resident of New Hampshire. Available to U.S. citizens.

Application Requirements Application, financial need analysis, resume, references. *Fee:* $15. *Deadline:* Continuous.

World Wide Web: http://www.nhcf.org

Contact: Norma Daviault, Program Assistant
New Hampshire Charitable Foundation
37 Pleasant Street
Concord, NH 03301-4005
Phone: 603-225-6641 Ext. 226
E-mail: nd@nhcf.org

NHCF STATEWIDE STUDENT AID PROGRAM • 387

Grants available to students enrolled at accredited institutions. Applicants must be New Hampshire residents. Application fee: $15. Some awards are renewable. Visit website for more information and downloadable application ⟨http://www.nhcf.org⟩.

Award Grant for use in freshman, sophomore, junior, senior, or graduate years; not renewable. *Number:* 300–400. *Amount:* $100–$2500.

Eligibility Requirements: Applicant must be enrolled full-time at a four-year institution or university and resident of New Hampshire. Available to U.S. citizens.

Application Requirements Application, essay, financial need analysis, resume, references, test scores, transcript. *Fee:* $15. *Deadline:* April 26.

World Wide Web: http://www.nhcf.org

Contact: Norma Davaiult, Program Assistant
New Hampshire Charitable Foundation
37 Pleasant Street
Concord, NH 03301-4005
Phone: 603-225-6641 Ext. 226
E-mail: nd@nhcf.org

NEW HAMPSHIRE POSTSECONDARY EDUCATION COMMISSION

NEW HAMPSHIRE INCENTIVE PROGRAM (NHIP) • 388

One-time grants for New Hampshire residents attending school in New Hampshire, Connecticut, Maine, Massachusetts, Rhode Island, or Vermont. Must have financial need. Deadline is May 1. Complete Free Application for Federal Student Aid. Grant is not automatically renewable. Applicant must reapply.

Award Grant for use in freshman, sophomore, junior, or senior years; not renewable. *Number:* 3000–3500. *Amount:* $125–$1000.

Eligibility Requirements: Applicant must be enrolled full or part-time at a two-year or four-year or technical institution or university; resident of New Hampshire and studying in Connecticut, Maine, Massachusetts, New Hampshire, Rhode Island, or Vermont. Available to U.S. citizens.

Application Requirements Application, financial need analysis. *Deadline:* May 1.

World Wide Web: http://www.state.nh.us/postsecondary

Contact: Judith Knapp, Student Financial Assistance Coordinator
New Hampshire Postsecondary Education Commission
Two Industrial Park Drive
Concord, NH 03301-8512
Phone: 603-271-2555
Fax: 603-271-2696
E-mail: jknapp@nhsa.state.nh.us

NEW JERSEY STATE GOLF ASSOCIATION

NEW JERSEY STATE GOLF ASSOCIATION CADDIE SCHOLARSHIP

see number 225

NEW YORK COUNCIL FOR THE HUMANITIES

YOUNG SCHOLARS CONTEST • 389

The Young Scholars Contest is a research essay competition on a predetermined theme in the humanities. New York State high school students who are legal residents of the state are eligible. Deadline is in May.

Award Scholarship for use in any year; not renewable. *Number:* 6–18. *Amount:* $250–$5000.

Eligibility Requirements: Applicant must be high school student; planning to enroll full-time at a two-year or four-year institution or university and resident of New York. Available to U.S. and non-U.S. citizens.

Application Requirements Applicant must enter a contest, essay.

World Wide Web: http://www.nyhumanities.org

Contact: New York Council for the Humanities
150 Broadway, Suite 1700
New York, NY 10038

NEW YORK STATE EDUCATION DEPARTMENT

ROBERT C. BYRD HONORS SCHOLARSHIP-NEW YORK • 390

Award for outstanding high school seniors accepted to U.S. college or university. Based on SAT score and high school average. Minimum 3.5 GPA required; minimum 1250 combined SAT score from one sitting. Must be legal resident of New York and a U.S. citizen. Renewable for up to four years. General Education Degree holders eligible.

Award Scholarship for use in freshman, sophomore, junior, or senior years; renewable. *Number:* 410. *Amount:* $1500.

Eligibility Requirements: Applicant must be high school student; planning to enroll full-time at a two-year or four-year institution or university and resident of New York. Applicant must have 3.5 GPA or higher. Available to U.S. citizens.

Application Requirements Application, test scores, transcript. *Deadline:* March 1.

Contact: Lewis J. Hall, Coordinator
New York State Education Department
Room 1078 EBA
Albany, NY 12234
Phone: 518-486-1319
Fax: 518-486-5346

SCHOLARSHIP FOR ACADEMIC EXCELLENCE • 391

Each requested high school in NY State (public and non-public) will receive at least one $1500 scholarship. Remaining scholarships ($1500) and all $500 scholarships awarded based on size of the preceding year's graduating class. Scholarships can only be used at NY state colleges and universities. Scholarships awarded on academic excellence. Nominees for scholarships selected by high school and will be notified by State Education Department after budget is approved.

Award Scholarship for use in freshman, sophomore, junior, or senior years; renewable. *Number:* 2000–6000. *Amount:* $500–$1500.

Eligibility Requirements: Applicant must be high school student; age 30 or under; planning to enroll full-time at a two-year or four-year institution or university; resident of New York and studying in New York. Applicant must have 3.5 GPA or higher. Available to U.S. citizens.

Application Requirements Application, essay, references, test scores, transcript. *Deadline:* December 20.

Scholarship for Academic Excellence (continued)
Contact: Lewis J. Hall, Coordinator
New York State Education Department
Room 1078 EBA
Albany, NY 12234
Phone: 518-486-1319
Fax: 518-486-5346
E-mail: dmercado@mail.nysed.gov

NEW YORK STATE HIGHER EDUCATION SERVICES CORPORATION

NEW YORK STATE TUITION ASSISTANCE PROGRAM • 392

Award for New York state residents attending New York postsecondary institution. Must be full-time student in approved program with tuition over $200 per year. Must show financial need and not be in default in any other state program. Renewable award of $275-$5000.

Award Grant for use in any year; renewable. *Number:* 300,000–320,000. *Amount:* $275–$5000.
Eligibility Requirements: Applicant must be enrolled full-time at a two-year or four-year institution or university; resident of New York and studying in New York.
Application Requirements Application, financial need analysis. *Deadline:* May 1.
World Wide Web: http://www.hesc.com
Contact: Student Information
New York State Higher Education Services Corporation
99 Washington Avenue, Room 1320
Albany, NY 12255

SCHOLARSHIPS FOR ACADEMIC EXCELLENCE • 393

Renewable awards of up to $1500 for academically outstanding New York State high school graduates planning to attend an approved postsecondary institution in New York State. For full-time study only. Contact high school guidance counselor to apply.

Award Scholarship for use in freshman, sophomore, junior, or senior years; renewable. *Number:* 8000. *Amount:* $500–$1500.
Eligibility Requirements: Applicant must be high school student; planning to enroll full-time at an institution or university; resident of New York and studying in New York.
Application Requirements Application.
World Wide Web: http://www.hesc.com
Contact: Student Information
New York State Higher Education Services Corporation
99 Washington Avenue, Room 1320
Albany, NY 12255

NORTH CAROLINA COMMISSION OF INDIAN AFFAIRS

INCENTIVE SCHOLARSHIP FOR NATIVE AMERICANS   see number 284

NORTH CAROLINA STATE EDUCATION ASSISTANCE AUTHORITY

AUBREY LEE BROOKS SCHOLARSHIPS   • 394

Renewable award for high school seniors who are residents of designated North Carolina counties and are planning to attend North Carolina State University, the University of North Carolina at Chapel Hill or the University of North Carolina at Greensboro. Award provides approximately half of the cost of an undergraduate education. Write for further details and deadlines, or visit website: www.cfnc.org.

Award Scholarship for use in freshman, sophomore, junior, or senior years; renewable. *Number:* 17. *Amount:* up to $6000.

Eligibility Requirements: Applicant must be high school student; planning to enroll full-time at an institution or university; resident of North Carolina and studying in North Carolina. Applicant must have 3.0 GPA or higher. Available to U.S. citizens.

Application Requirements Application, essay, financial need analysis, interview, photo, references, test scores, transcript. *Deadline:* February 1.

World Wide Web: http://www.cfnc.org

Contact: Bill Carswell, Manager of Scholarship and Grant Division
North Carolina State Education Assistance Authority
PO Box 13663
Research Triangle, NC 27709-3663
Phone: 919-549-8614
Fax: 919-549-4687
E-mail: carswellb@ncseaa.edu

NORTH CAROLINA TEACHING FELLOWS SCHOLARSHIP PROGRAM   see number 226

NORTH DAKOTA UNIVERSITY SYSTEM

NORTH DAKOTA INDIAN COLLEGE SCHOLARSHIP PROGRAM
see number 285

OHIO ASSOCIATION OF CAREER COLLEGES AND SCHOOLS

LEGISLATIVE SCHOLARSHIP   • 395

Renewable award to full-time students attending a trade/technical institution in Ohio. Must be U.S. citizen. Minimum 2.5 GPA required. Must be a 2002 Ohio high school graduate.

Legislative Scholarship (continued)

Award Scholarship for use in freshman or sophomore years; renewable. *Number:* 80. *Amount:* $2600–$14,544.

Eligibility Requirements: Applicant must be high school student; planning to enroll full-time at a technical institution; resident of Ohio and studying in Ohio. Applicant must have 2.5 GPA or higher. Available to U.S. citizens.

Application Requirements Application, essay, references, transcript. *Deadline:* January 31.

Contact: Max Lerner, Executive Director
Ohio Association of Career Colleges and Schools
1857 Northwest Boulevard
The Annex
Columbus, OH 43212
Phone: 614-487-8180
Fax: 614-487-8190

OHIO BOARD OF REGENTS

OHIO ACADEMIC SCHOLARSHIP PROGRAM • 396

Award for academically outstanding Ohio residents planning to attend an approved Ohio college. Must be a high school senior intending to enroll full-time. Award is renewable for up to four years. Must rank in upper quarter of class or have a minimum GPA of 3.5.

Award Scholarship for use in freshman, sophomore, junior, or senior years; renewable. *Number:* 1000. *Amount:* $2000.

Eligibility Requirements: Applicant must be high school student; planning to enroll full-time at a two-year or four-year institution; resident of Ohio and studying in Ohio. Applicant must have 3.5 GPA or higher. Available to U.S. citizens.

Application Requirements Application, test scores, transcript. *Deadline:* February 23.

World Wide Web: http://www.regents.state.oh.us

Contact: Sue Minturn, Program Administrator
Ohio Board of Regents
PO Box 182452
Columbus, OH 43218-2452
Phone: 614-752-9536
Fax: 614-752-5903
E-mail: sminturn@regents.state.oh.us

OHIO NATIONAL GUARD

OHIO NATIONAL GUARD SCHOLARSHIP PROGRAM   see number 243

OKLAHOMA STATE REGENTS FOR HIGHER EDUCATION

OKLAHOMA TUITION AID GRANT •397

Award for Oklahoma residents enrolled at an Oklahoma institution at least part-time per semester in a degree program. May be enrolled in two- or four-year or approved vocational-technical institution. Award of up to $1000 per year. Application is made through FAFSA.

Award Grant for use in any year; renewable. *Number:* 23,000. *Amount:* $200–$1000.

Eligibility Requirements: Applicant must be enrolled full or part-time at a two-year or four-year or technical institution or university; resident of Oklahoma and studying in Oklahoma. Available to U.S. citizens.

Application Requirements Application, financial need analysis, FAFSA. *Deadline:* April 30.

World Wide Web: http://www.okhighered.org

Contact: Oklahoma State Regents for Higher Education
PO Box 3020
Oklahoma City, OK 73101-3020
Phone: 405-225-9456
Fax: 405-225-9392
E-mail: otaginfo@otag.org

PAGE EDUCATION FOUNDATION

PAGE EDUCATION FOUNDATION GRANT see number 288

PENNSYLVANIA HIGHER EDUCATION ASSISTANCE AGENCY

PENNSYLVANIA STATE GRANT •398

Award for Pennsylvania residents attending an approved postsecondary institution as undergraduates in a program of at least two years duration. Renewable for up to eight semesters if applicants show continued need and academic progress. Submit Free Application for Federal Student Aid.

Award Grant for use in freshman, sophomore, junior, or senior years; renewable. *Number:* up to 151,000. *Amount:* $300–$3300.

Eligibility Requirements: Applicant must be enrolled full or part-time at a two-year or four-year or technical institution or university and resident of Pennsylvania. Available to U.S. and Canadian citizens.

Application Requirements Application, financial need analysis. *Deadline:* May 1.

World Wide Web: http://www.pheaa.org

Pennsylvania State Grant (continued)
Contact: Keith New, Director of Communications and Press Office
Pennsylvania Higher Education Assistance Agency
1200 North Seventh Street
Harrisburg, PA 17102-1444
Phone: 717-720-2509
Fax: 717-720-3903
E-mail: knew@pheaa.org

PHOENIX SUNS CHARITIES/SUN STUDENTS SCHOLARSHIP

SUN STUDENT COLLEGE SCHOLARSHIP PROGRAM   see number 227

PRESBYTERIAN CHURCH (USA)

APPALACHIAN SCHOLARSHIPS   see number 301

RHODE ISLAND HIGHER EDUCATION ASSISTANCE AUTHORITY

RHODE ISLAND HIGHER EDUCATION GRANT PROGRAM   • 399

Grants for residents of Rhode Island attending an approved school in U.S., Canada, or Mexico. Based on need. Renewable for up to four years if in good academic standing. Applications accepted January 1 through March 1. Several awards of variable amounts. Must be U.S. citizen or registered alien.

Award Grant for use in freshman, sophomore, junior, or senior years; renewable. *Number:* 10,000–12,000. *Amount:* $250–$750.
Eligibility Requirements: Applicant must be enrolled full or part-time at a two-year or four-year or technical institution or university and resident of Rhode Island. Available to U.S. citizens.
Application Requirements Application, financial need analysis. *Deadline:* March 1.
World Wide Web: http://www.riheaa.org
Contact: Mary Ann Welch, Director of Program Administration
Rhode Island Higher Education Assistance Authority
560 Jefferson Boulevard, 222 21st. Avenue South
Warwick, RI 02886
Phone: 401-736-1100
Fax: 401-732-3541

SACHS FOUNDATION

SACHS FOUNDATION SCHOLARSHIPS   see number 290

SOUTH CAROLINA COMMISSION ON HIGHER EDUCATION

PALMETTO FELLOWS SCHOLARSHIP PROGRAM • 400

Renewable award for qualified high school seniors in South Carolina to attend a four-year South Carolina institution. Must rank in top five percent of class at the end of sophomore or junior year, earn a 3.5 GPA on a 4.0 scale, and score at least 1200 on the SAT or 27 on the ACT. Submit official transcript and test scores with application by established deadline (usually January 15th of senior year).

Award Scholarship for use in freshman, sophomore, junior, or senior years; renewable. *Number:* 650–750. *Amount:* up to $5000.

Eligibility Requirements: Applicant must be high school student; planning to enroll full-time at a four-year institution or university; resident of South Carolina and studying in South Carolina. Applicant must have 3.5 GPA or higher. Available to U.S. citizens.

Application Requirements Application, applicant must enter a contest, references, test scores, transcript. *Deadline:* January 15.

World Wide Web: http://www.che400.state.sc.us

Contact: Ms. Sherry Hubbard, Coordinator
South Carolina Commission on Higher Education
1333 Main Street, Suite 200
Columbia, SC 29201
Phone: 803-737-2260
Fax: 803-737-2297
E-mail: shubbard@che400.state.sc.us

SOUTH CAROLINA DEPARTMENT OF EDUCATION

ROBERT C. BYRD HONORS SCHOLARSHIP- SOUTH CAROLINA

see number 229

SOUTH CAROLINA TUITION GRANTS COMMISSION

SOUTH CAROLINA TUITION GRANTS PROGRAM • 401

Assists South Carolina residents attending one of twenty approved South Carolina Independent colleges. Freshmen must be in upper 3/4 of high school class or have SAT score of at least 900. Upper-class students must complete twenty-four semester hours per year to be eligible.

Award Grant for use in freshman, sophomore, junior, or senior years; renewable. *Number:* up to 11,000. *Amount:* $100–$3350.

South Carolina Tuition Grants Program (continued)

Eligibility Requirements: Applicant must be enrolled full-time at a two-year or four-year institution; resident of South Carolina and studying in South Carolina. Available to U.S. citizens.

Application Requirements Application, financial need analysis, test scores, transcript, FAFSA. *Deadline:* June 30.

World Wide Web: http://www.sctuitiongrants.com

Contact: Toni Cave, Financial Aid Counselor
South Carolina Tuition Grants Commission
101 Business Park Boulevard, Suite 2100
Columbia, SC 29203-9498
Phone: 803-896-1120
Fax: 803-896-1126
E-mail: toni@sctuitiongrants.org

SOUTH DAKOTA DEPARTMENT OF EDUCATION AND CULTURAL AFFAIRS

ROBERT C. BYRD HONORS SCHOLARSHIP-SOUTH DAKOTA • 402

For South Dakota residents in their senior year of high school. Must have a minimum 3.5 GPA and a minimum ACT score of 24. Awards are renewable up to four years. Contact high school guidance office for more details.

Award Scholarship for use in freshman, sophomore, junior, or senior years; renewable. *Number:* up to 80. *Amount:* $1500.

Eligibility Requirements: Applicant must be high school student; planning to enroll full-time at a two-year or four-year or technical institution or university and resident of South Dakota. Applicant must have 3.5 GPA or higher. Available to U.S. citizens.

Application Requirements Application, test scores, transcript. *Deadline:* May 1.

World Wide Web: http://www.state.sd.us/deca

Contact: Roxie Thielen, Financial Aid Administrator
South Dakota Department of Education and Cultural Affairs
700 Governors Drive
Pierre, SD 57501-2291
Phone: 605-773-5669
Fax: 605-773-6139
E-mail: roxie.thielen@state.sd.us

SOUTHERN SCHOLARSHIP FOUNDATION, INC.

SOUTHERN SCHOLARSHIP FOUNDATION • 403

The scholarship is for rent-free cooperative living in our houses located at Florida State University, University of Florida, Florida A & M, and (for men only) at Bethune-Cookman College. Students share all household duties while maintaining high academic standards.

Award Scholarship for use in any year; renewable. *Number:* 431. *Amount:* $550–$650.

Eligibility Requirements: Applicant must be enrolled full-time at a four-year institution or university; single and studying in Florida. Applicant must have 3.0 GPA or higher. Available to U.S. and non-U.S. citizens.

Application Requirements Application, autobiography, essay, financial need analysis, photo, references, test scores, transcript, college acceptance letter. *Deadline:* March 1.

World Wide Web: http://www.scholarships.org/ssf

Contact: Thomas Pitcock, President
Southern Scholarship Foundation, Inc.
322 Stadium Drive
Tallahassee, FL 32304
Phone: 850-222-3833
Fax: 850-222-6750
E-mail: tpitcock@scholarships.org

STATE OF GEORGIA

GEORGIA NATIONAL GUARD SERVICE CANCELABLE LOAN PROGRAM
see number 244

STATE OF IOWA

STATE OF IOWA SCHOLARSHIP PROGRAM • 404

Program provides recognition and financial honorarium to Iowa's academically talented high school seniors. Honorary scholarships are presented to all qualified candidates. Approximately 1,700 top-ranking candidates are designated State of Iowa Scholars every March, from an applicant pool of nearly 5,000 high school seniors. Must be used at an Iowa postsecondary institution. Minimum 3.5 GPA required.

Award Scholarship for use in freshman year; not renewable. *Number:* up to 1700. *Amount:* up to $400.

Eligibility Requirements: Applicant must be high school student; planning to enroll full-time at a two-year or four-year or technical institution or university; resident of Iowa and studying in Iowa. Applicant must have 3.5 GPA or higher. Available to U.S. citizens.

Application Requirements Application, test scores. *Deadline:* November 1.

World Wide Web: http://www.iowacollegeaid.org

Contact: Julie Leeper, State Grants Administrator
State of Iowa
200 10th Street, 4th Floor
Des Moines, IA 50309-3609
Phone: 515-242-3370
Fax: 515-242-3388
E-mail: icsac@max.state.ia.us

STATE STUDENT ASSISTANCE COMMISSION OF INDIANA (SSACI)

HOOSIER SCHOLAR AWARD • 405

The Hoosier Scholar Award is a $500 nonrenewable award. Based on the size of the high school, one to three scholars are selected by the guidance counselor(s). The award is based on academic merit and may be used for any educational expense at an eligible Indiana institution of higher education.

Award Scholarship for use in freshman year; not renewable. *Number:* 790–840. *Amount:* $500.

Eligibility Requirements: Applicant must be high school student; planning to enroll full-time at a two-year or four-year institution or university; resident of Indiana and studying in Indiana. Applicant must have 3.5 GPA or higher. Available to U.S. citizens.

Application Requirements *Deadline:* March 1.

World Wide Web: http://www.ssaci.in.gov

Contact: Ms. Ada Sparkman, Program Coordinator
State Student Assistance Commission of Indiana (SSACI)
150 West Market Street, Suite 500
Indianapolis, IN 46204-2805
Phone: 317-232-2350
Fax: 317-232-3260

INDIANA FREEDOM OF CHOICE GRANT • 406

The Freedom of Choice Grant is a need-based, tuition-restricted program for students attending Indiana private institutions seeking a first undergraduate degree. It is awarded in addition to the Higher Education Award. Students (and parents of dependent students) who are U.S. citizens and Indiana residents must file the FAFSA yearly by March 1st for consideration.

Award Grant for use in freshman, sophomore, junior, or senior years; not renewable. *Number:* 10,000–11,830. *Amount:* $200–$5080.

Eligibility Requirements: Applicant must be enrolled full-time at a four-year institution or university; resident of Indiana and studying in Indiana. Available to U.S. citizens.

Application Requirements Application, financial need analysis, FAFSA. *Deadline:* March 1.

World Wide Web: http://www.ssaci.in.gov

Contact: Grant Counselor
State Student Assistance Commission of Indiana (SSACI)
150 West Market Street, Suite 500
Indianapolis, IN 46204-2805
Phone: 317-232-2350
Fax: 317-232-3260
E-mail: grants@ssaci.state.in.us

INDIANA HIGHER EDUCATION AWARD • 407

The Higher Education Award is a need-based, tuition-restricted program for students attending Indiana public, private or proprietary institutions seeking a first undergraduate degree. Students (and parents of dependent students) who are U.S. citizens and Indiana residents must file the FAFSA yearly by March 1st for consideration.

Award Grant for use in freshman, sophomore, junior, or senior years; not renewable. *Number:* 38,000–43,660. *Amount:* $200–$4406.

Eligibility Requirements: Applicant must be enrolled full-time at a two-year or four-year or technical institution or university; resident of Indiana and studying in Indiana. Available to U.S. citizens.

Application Requirements Application, financial need analysis, FAFSA. *Deadline:* March 1.

World Wide Web: http://www.ssaci.in.gov

Contact: Grant Counselors
State Student Assistance Commission of Indiana (SSACI)
150 West Market Street, Suite 500
Indianapolis, IN 46204-2805
Phone: 317-232-2350
Fax: 317-232-3260
E-mail: grants@ssaci.state.in.us

INDIANA NATIONAL GUARD SUPPLEMENTAL GRANT   see number 245

PART-TIME GRANT PROGRAM • 408

Program is designed to encourage part-time undergraduates to start and complete their associate or baccalaureate degrees or certificates by subsidizing part-time tuition costs. It is a term-based award that is based on need. State residency requirements must be met and a FAFSA must be filed. Eligibility is determined at the institutional level subject to approval by SSACI.

Award Grant for use in freshman, sophomore, junior, or senior years; not renewable. *Number:* 4000–5100. *Amount:* $50–$4000.

Eligibility Requirements: Applicant must be enrolled part-time at a two-year or four-year or technical institution or university; resident of Indiana and studying in Indiana. Available to U.S. citizens.

Application Requirements Application, financial need analysis. *Deadline:* Continuous.

World Wide Web: http://www.ssaci.in.gov

Contact: Grant Division
State Student Assistance Commission of Indiana (SSACI)
150 West Market Street, Suite 500
Indianapolis, IN 46204-2805
Phone: 317-232-2350
Fax: 317-232-3260
E-mail: grants@ssaci.state.in.us

ROBERT C. BYRD HONORS SCHOLARSHIP-INDIANA • 409

Scholarship is designed to recognize academic achievement and requires a minimum SAT score of 1300 or ACT score of 31, or recent GED score of 65. The scholarship is awarded equally among Indiana's congressional districts. The amount of the scholarship varies depending upon federal funding and is automatically renewed if the institution's satisfactory academic progress requirements are met.

Award Scholarship for use in freshman, sophomore, junior, or senior years; renewable. *Number:* 550–570. *Amount:* $1500.

Eligibility Requirements: Applicant must be enrolled full-time at a two-year or four-year institution or university and resident of Indiana. Applicant must have 3.0 GPA or higher. Available to U.S. citizens.

Application Requirements Application, test scores, transcript.

World Wide Web: http://www.ssaci.in.gov

Contact: Ms. Yvonne Heflin, Director, Special Programs
State Student Assistance Commission of Indiana (SSACI)
150 West Market Street, Suite 500
Indianapolis, IN 46204-2805
Phone: 317-232-3250
Fax: 317-232-3260

TWENTY-FIRST CENTURY SCHOLARS AWARD • 410

Income-eligible 7th graders who enroll in the program fulfill a pledge of good citizenship and complete the Affirmation Form are guaranteed tuition for four years at any participating public institution. If the student attends a private institution, the state will award an amount comparable to that of a public institution. If the student attends a participating proprietary school, the state will award a tuition scholarship equal to that of Ivy Tech State College. FAFSA must be filed yearly by March 1. Applicant must be a resident of Indiana.

Award Scholarship for use in freshman, sophomore, junior, or senior years; not renewable. *Number:* 2800–8100. *Amount:* $1000–$4734.

Eligibility Requirements: Applicant must be enrolled full-time at a two-year or four-year or technical institution or university; resident of Indiana and studying in Indiana. Applicant must have 2.5 GPA or higher. Available to U.S. citizens.

Application Requirements Application, financial need analysis.

World Wide Web: http://www.ssaci.in.gov

Contact: Twenty-first Century Scholars Program Counselors
State Student Assistance Commission of Indiana (SSACI)
150 West Market Street, Suite 500
Indianapolis, IN 46204-2805
Phone: 317-232-2100
Fax: 317-232-3260

SUBMARINE OFFICERS' WIVES CLUB

BOWFIN MEMORIAL SCHOLARSHIP   see number 230

SWISS BENEVOLENT SOCIETY OF NEW YORK

PELLEGRINI SCHOLARSHIP GRANTS

see number 293

TENNESSEE STUDENT ASSISTANCE CORPORATION

NED MCWHERTER SCHOLARS PROGRAM • 411

Assists Tennessee residents with high academic ability. Must have high school GPA of at least 3.5 and have scored in top five percent of SAT or ACT. Must attend college in Tennessee. Only high school seniors may apply.

Award Scholarship for use in freshman, sophomore, junior, or senior years; renewable. *Number:* 55. *Amount:* $6000.

Eligibility Requirements: Applicant must be high school student; planning to enroll full-time at a two-year or four-year institution or university; resident of Tennessee and studying in Tennessee. Applicant must have 3.5 GPA or higher. Available to U.S. citizens.

Application Requirements Application, test scores, transcript. *Deadline:* February 15.

World Wide Web: http://www.state.tn.us/tsac

Contact: Naomi Derryberry, Grant and Scholarship Administrator
Tennessee Student Assistance Corporation
Suite 1950, Parkway Towers
Nashville, TN 37243-0820
Phone: 615-741-1346
Fax: 615-741-6101

ROBERT C. BYRD HONORS SCHOLARSHIP-TENNESSEE • 412

Available to Tennessee residents graduating from high school. Must have at least a 3.5 GPA. May also qualify with a 24 ACT or 1090 SAT. Renewable up to four years. Those with GED Test score of 57 or above may also apply.

Award Scholarship for use in freshman, sophomore, junior, or senior years; renewable. *Number:* 125. *Amount:* $1100–$1500.

Eligibility Requirements: Applicant must be high school student; planning to enroll full-time at a two-year or four-year institution or university and resident of Tennessee. Applicant must have 3.0 GPA or higher. Available to U.S. citizens.

Application Requirements Application, test scores, transcript. *Deadline:* March 1.

World Wide Web: http://www.state.tn.us/tsac

Robert C. Byrd Honors Scholarship-Tennessee (continued)
Contact: Michael Roberts, Compliance Administrator
Tennessee Student Assistance Corporation
404 James Robertson Parkway, Suite 1950, Parkway Towers
Nashville, TN 37243-0820
Phone: 615-741-1346
Fax: 615-741-6101
E-mail: michael.roberts@state.tn.us

TENNESSEE STUDENT ASSISTANCE AWARD PROGRAM • 413

Assists Tennessee residents attending an approved college or university within the state. Complete a Free Application for Federal Student Aid form. Apply January 1. FAFSA must be processed by May 1 for priority consideration.

Award Grant for use in freshman, sophomore, junior, or senior years; renewable. *Number:* 22,000. *Amount:* $1746.
Eligibility Requirements: Applicant must be enrolled full or part-time at a two-year or four-year or technical institution or university; resident of Tennessee and studying in Tennessee. Available to U.S. citizens.
Application Requirements Application, financial need analysis. *Deadline:* May 1.
World Wide Web: http://www.state.tn.us/tsac
Contact: Naomi Derryberry, Grant and Scholarship Administrator
Tennessee Student Assistance Corporation
Suite 1950, Parkway Towers
Nashville, TN 37243-0820
Phone: 615-741-1346
Fax: 615-741-6101

TEXAS HIGHER EDUCATION COORDINATING BOARD

TRAIN OUR TEACHERS AWARD
see number 231

UNITED FEDERATION OF TEACHERS

ALBERT SHANKER COLLEGE SCHOLARSHIP FUND OF THE UNITED FEDERATION OF TEACHERS • 414

Renewable award for eligible students graduating from New York City public high schools to pursue undergraduate studies. Scholarship is $1250 a year for four years. Submit transcript, autobiography, essay, references, and financial need analysis with application. Deadline is third week of December. There are nine graduate awards including a renewable medical and a renewable law award. Applicants must be current undergraduate award winners.

Award Scholarship for use in freshman, sophomore, junior, senior, or graduate years; renewable. *Number:* 250. *Amount:* $1250.

Eligibility Requirements: Applicant must be enrolled full-time at a two-year or four-year institution or university and resident of New York. Available to U.S. citizens.

Application Requirements Application, autobiography, essay, financial need analysis, references, transcript.

Contact: Jeffrey A. Huart, Director
United Federation of Teachers
260 Park Avenue South
New York, NY 10010

VIRGINIA DEPARTMENT OF EDUCATION

LEE- JACKSON FOUNDATION SCHOLARSHIP   • 415

Essay contest for junior and senior Virginia high school students. Must demonstrate appreciation for the exemplary character and soldierly virtues of Generals Robert E. Lee and Thomas J. "Stonewall" Jackson. Three one-time awards of $1000 in each of Virginia's eight regions. A bonus scholarship of $1000 will be awarded to the author of the best essay in each of the eight regions. An additional award of $8000 will go to the essay judged the best in the state.

Award Scholarship for use in freshman year; not renewable. *Number:* 27. *Amount:* $1000–$8000.

Eligibility Requirements: Applicant must be high school student; planning to enroll at a four-year institution; resident of Virginia and must have an interest in writing. Available to U.S. citizens.

Application Requirements Application, applicant must enter a contest, essay, transcript. *Deadline:* December 21.

World Wide Web: http://www.pen.k12.va.us

Contact: Vernon Wildy, Associate Director for Secondary Instructional
Services
Virginia Department of Education
PO Box 2120
Richmond, VA 23216-2120
Phone: 804-225-2877
Fax: 804-692-3163
E-mail: vwildy@pen.k12.va.us

VIRGINIA STATE COUNCIL OF HIGHER EDUCATION

VIRGINIA TUITION ASSISTANCE GRANT PROGRAM (PRIVATE INSTITUTIONS)   • 416

Renewable awards of approximately $3,000 each for undergraduate, graduate, and first professional degree students attending an approved private, nonprofit college within Virginia. Must be a Virginia resident and be enrolled full-time. Not to be used for religious study. Preferred deadline July 31. Others are

Virginia Tuition Assistance Grant Program (Private Institutions) (continued)
wait-listed. Contact college financial aid office. The application process is
handled by the participating colleges' financial aid office.

Award Grant for use in any year; renewable. *Number:* 15,000. *Amount:*
$3000.
Eligibility Requirements: Applicant must be enrolled full-time at a four-year
institution; resident of Virginia and studying in Virginia.
Application Requirements Application. *Deadline:* July 31.
World Wide Web: http://www.schev.edu
Contact: Financial Aid Office at participating institution
Virginia State Council of Higher Education
James Monroe Building, 10th Floor
101 North 14th Street
Richmond, VA 23219

WATERBURY FOUNDATION

REGIONAL AND RESTRICTED SCHOLARSHIP AWARD
PROGRAM • 417

Supports accredited college or university study for residents of the Waterbury
Foundation's twenty-one town service area. Regional awards are restricted to
Connecticut colleges/universities only. Twenty-four restricted award programs
are based on specific fund criteria (residency, ethnicity or course of study).

Award Scholarship for use in freshman, sophomore, junior, or senior years;
renewable. *Number:* 175–220. *Amount:* $500–$10,000.
Eligibility Requirements: Applicant must be enrolled full or part-time at a
two-year or four-year institution or university and resident of Connecticut.
Applicant must have 2.5 GPA or higher. Available to U.S. citizens.
Application Requirements Application, essay, financial need analysis, refer-
ences, transcript. *Deadline:* April 15.
World Wide Web: http://www.waterburyfoundation.org
Contact: Jill Stone, Program Officer
Waterbury Foundation
81 West Main Street
Waterbury, CT 06702
Phone: 203-753-1315
Fax: 203-756-3054
E-mail: jstone@waterburyfoundation.org

WEST VIRGINIA HIGHER EDUCATION
POLICY COMMISSION-STUDENT SERVICES

ROBERT C. BYRD HONORS SCHOLARSHIP PROGRAM-WEST
VIRGINIA • 418

For West Virginia residents who have demonstrated outstanding academic
achievement. Must be a graduating high school senior. May apply for renewal
consideration for a total of four years of assistance. For full-time study only.

Award Scholarship for use in freshman, sophomore, junior, or senior years; renewable. *Number:* 36. *Amount:* $1500.

Eligibility Requirements: Applicant must be high school student; planning to enroll full-time at a two-year or four-year or technical institution or university and resident of West Virginia. Applicant must have 3.5 GPA or higher. Available to U.S. citizens.

Application Requirements Application, test scores, transcript. *Deadline:* March 15.

World Wide Web: http://www.hepc.wvnet.edu

Contact: Michelle Wicks, Scholarship Coordinator
West Virginia Higher Education Policy Commission-Student Services
1018 Kanawha Boulevard East, Suite 700
Charleston, WV 25301
Phone: 304-558-4618
Fax: 304-558-4622
E-mail: wicks@hepc.wnet.edu

WEST VIRGINIA HIGHER EDUCATION GRANT PROGRAM • 419

For West Virginia residents attending an approved nonprofit degree-granting college or university in West Virginia or Pennsylvania. Must be enrolled full-time. Based on financial need and academic merit. Award covers tuition and fees.

Award Grant for use in freshman, sophomore, junior, or senior years; renewable. *Number:* 10,900–11,200. *Amount:* $350–$2532.

Eligibility Requirements: Applicant must be enrolled full-time at a two-year or four-year institution or university; resident of West Virginia and studying in Pennsylvania or West Virginia. Available to U.S. citizens.

Application Requirements Application, financial need analysis, test scores, transcript. *Deadline:* March 1.

World Wide Web: http://www.hepc.wvnet.edu

Contact: Robert Long, Grant Program Coordinator
West Virginia Higher Education Policy Commission-Student Services
1018 Kanawha Boulevard East, Suite 700
Charleston, WV 25301-2827
Phone: 888-825-5707
Fax: 304-558-4622
E-mail: long@hepc.wvnet.edu

WILLIAM G. AND MARIE SELBY FOUNDATION

SELBY SCHOLAR PROGRAM

see number 233

WISCONSIN FOUNDATION FOR INDEPENDENT COLLEGES, INC.

UPS SCHOLARSHIP • 420

Applicants must attend one of Wisconsin's 21 private colleges and maintain a 3.0 GPA. Each school can award one to three UPS scholarships. Application deadline is May 1.

Award Scholarship for use in freshman, sophomore, junior, or senior years; not renewable. *Number:* 21–63. *Amount:* $1050–$3150.

Eligibility Requirements: Applicant must be enrolled full-time at a four-year institution or university and studying in Wisconsin. Applicant must have 3.0 GPA or higher. Available to U.S. citizens.

Application Requirements Application, autobiography, references. *Deadline:* May 1.

World Wide Web: http://www.wficweb.org

Contact: Christy Miller, Marketing Program Manager
Wisconsin Foundation for Independent Colleges, Inc.
735 North Water Street, Suite 800
Milwaukee, WI 53202
Phone: 414-273-5980
Fax: 414-273-5995
E-mail: wfic@execpc.com

TALENT_____

ALBERTA HERITAGE SCHOLARSHIP FUND

JIMMIE CONDON ATHLETIC SCHOLARSHIPS see number 255

LAURENCE DECORE STUDENT LEADERSHIP AWARDS see number 256

AMERICAN CANCER SOCIETY, INC.-GREAT LAKES DIVISION

COLLEGE SCHOLARSHIPS FOR CANCER SURVIVORS see number 308

AMERICAN INSTITUTE FOR FOREIGN STUDY

AMERICAN INSTITUTE FOR FOREIGN STUDY INTERNATIONAL SCHOLARSHIPS • 421

Awards are available to undergraduates on an AIFS study abroad program. Applicants must demonstrate leadership potential, have a minimum 3.0 cumulative GPA and meet program requirements. Up to 150 $1,000 scholarships are awarded per semester and up to 50 $750 scholarships are awarded each summer. Submit application by March 15 for summer, April 15 for fall or October 15 for spring. The application fee is $50.

Award Scholarship for use in freshman, sophomore, junior, or senior years; not renewable. *Number:* 150. *Amount:* $750–$1000.

Eligibility Requirements: Applicant must be age 17; enrolled full-time at a two-year or four-year institution or university and must have an interest in leadership. Applicant must have 3.0 GPA or higher. Available to U.S. and non-U.S. citizens.

Application Requirements Application, essay, photo, references, transcript. *Fee:* $50.

World Wide Web: http://www.aifsabroad.com

Contact: David Mauro, Admissions Counselor
American Institute For Foreign Study
River Plaza, 9 West Broad Street
Stamford, CT 06902-3788
Phone: 800-727-2437 Ext. 5163
Fax: 203-399-5598
E-mail: college.info@aifs.com

AMERICAN INSTITUTE FOR FOREIGN STUDY MINORITY SCHOLARSHIPS
see number 260

AMERICAN LEGION, DEPARTMENT OF NEW YORK

AMERICAN LEGION DEPARTMENT OF NEW YORK STATE HIGH SCHOOL ORATORICAL CONTEST
see number 310

AMERICAN LEGION, DEPARTMENT OF NORTH DAKOTA

AMERICAN LEGION DEPARTMENT OF NORTH DAKOTA NATIONAL HIGH SCHOOL ORATORICAL CONTEST
see number 311

AMERICAN LEGION, NATIONAL HEADQUARTERS

AMERICAN LEGION NATIONAL HEADQUARTERS NATIONAL HIGH SCHOOL ORATORICAL CONTEST
• **422**

Several prizes awarded to high school students (freshmen through seniors) who give a speech lasting eight to ten minutes on the U.S. Constitution and an

American Legion National Headquarters National High School Oratorical Contest (continued)

assigned topic speech of three to five minutes. Winners advance to higher level. Contact local chapter for entry information. One-time award of $1500–$18,000.

Award Scholarship for use in freshman, sophomore, junior, senior, or graduate years; not renewable. *Number:* 54. *Amount:* $1500–$18,000.

Eligibility Requirements: Applicant must be high school student; planning to enroll full-time at a two-year or four-year institution or university and must have an interest in public speaking. Available to U.S. citizens.

Application Requirements Application. *Deadline:* December 1.

World Wide Web: http://www.legion.org

Contact: Michael Buss, Assistant Director
American Legion, National Headquarters
PO Box 1055
Indianapolis, IN 46206-1055
Phone: 317-630-1249
Fax: 317-630-1369
E-mail: acy@legion.org

AMERICAN STRING TEACHERS ASSOCIATION

NATIONAL SOLO COMPETITION • 423

Twenty-six individual awards totaling $30,000 will be awarded. Instrument categories are violin, viola, cello, double bass, classical guitar and harp. Applicants competing in Junior Division must be under age 19. Senior Division competitors must be ages 19-25. Application fee is $60. Visit website for application forms. Applicant must be a member of ASTA.

Award Prize for use in any year; not renewable. *Number:* 26. *Amount:* $600–$4500.

Eligibility Requirements: Applicant must be enrolled full-time at an institution or university and must have an interest in music. Available to U.S. and Canadian citizens.

Application Requirements Application, applicant must enter a contest, proof of age. *Fee:* $60.

World Wide Web: http://www.astaweb.com

Contact: American String Teachers Association
4153 Chain Bridge Road
Fairfax, VA 22030
Phone: 703-279-2113
Fax: 703-279-2114
E-mail: asta@astaweb.com

ARTIST'S MAGAZINE

THE ARTIST'S MAGAZINE'S ANNUAL ART COMPETITION • 424

One-time award for any artist winning annual art competition. Four separate categories. Send self-addressed stamped envelope for rules and entry form. Deadline is May 1. Must submit slides of work. Application fee: $10 per slide.

Award Prize for use in any year; not renewable. *Number:* 45. *Amount:* $50–$1500.
Eligibility Requirements: Applicant must have an interest in art. Available to U.S. and non-U.S. citizens.
Application Requirements Application, applicant must enter a contest, self-addressed stamped envelope. *Fee:* $10. *Deadline:* May 1.
World Wide Web: http://www.artistsmagazine.com
Contact: Terri Boes, Competition Assistant
Artist's Magazine
1507 Dana Avenue
Cincinnati, OH 45207
Phone: 513-531-2690 Ext. 328
Fax: 513-531-0798
E-mail: competitions@fwpubs.com

AUTHOR SERVICES, INC.

L. RON HUBBARD'S ILLUSTRATORS OF THE FUTURE CONTEST • 425

An ongoing competition for new and amateur artists judged by professional artists. Eligible submissions consist of three science fiction or fantasy illustrations in a black-and-white medium. Quarterly prizes are $500 each for three winners. The Grand Prize, awarded yearly, is $4000. Write for contest rules. Quarterly deadlines are December 31, March 31, June 30 and September 30. Inside California call: 800-624-6504; outside California call: 800-624-7907.

Award Prize for use in any year; not renewable. *Number:* 13. *Amount:* $500–$4000.
Eligibility Requirements: Applicant must have an interest in art. Available to U.S. and non-U.S. citizens.
Application Requirements Applicant must enter a contest, self-addressed stamped envelope, three illustrations.
World Wide Web: http://www.writersofthefuture.com
Contact: Rachel Deuk, Contest Administrator
Author Services, Inc.
PO Box 3190
Los Angeles, CA 90078
Phone: 323-466-3310
Fax: 323-466-6474
E-mail: contests@authorservicesinc.com

L. RON HUBBARD'S WRITERS OF THE FUTURE CONTEST • 426

An ongoing competition for new and amateur writers judged by professional writers. Eligible submissions are short stories and novelettes of science fiction or fantasy. Quarterly prizes are First Place—$1000, Second Place—$750, Third Place—$500. The Grand Prize, awarded yearly, is $4000. Quarterly deadlines

L. Ron Hubbard's Writers of the Future Contest (continued)
are December 31, March 31, June 30 and September 30. Write for contest rules. Inside California call: 800-624-6504; outside California call: 800-624-7907.

Award Prize for use in any year; not renewable. *Number:* 13. *Amount:* $500–$4000.
Eligibility Requirements: Applicant must be enrolled full or part-time at an institution or university and must have an interest in writing. Available to U.S. and non-U.S. citizens.
Application Requirements Applicant must enter a contest, self-addressed stamped envelope, manuscript.
World Wide Web: http://www.writersofthefuture.com
Contact: Rachel Deuk, Contest Administrator
Author Services, Inc.
PO Box 1630
Los Angeles, CA 90078
Phone: 323-466-3310
Fax: 323-466-6474
E-mail: contests@authorservicvesinc.com

AYN RAND INSTITUTE

AYN RAND INSTITUTE COLLEGE SCHOLARSHIP ESSAY CONTEST BASED ON AYN RAND'S NOVELETTE, "ANTHEM" • 427
Entrant must be in the 9th or 10th grade. Essays will be judged on both style and content. Winning essays must demonstrate an outstanding grasp of the philosophical meaning of Ayn Rand's novelette, "Anthem." Contest deadline is March 18. Winners announced June 4. All information necessary to enter the contest is on the website.

Award Prize for use in freshman year; not renewable. *Number:* 251. *Amount:* $30–$2000.
Eligibility Requirements: Applicant must be high school student and must have an interest in writing.
Application Requirements Applicant must enter a contest, essay. *Deadline:* March 18.
World Wide Web: http://www.aynrand.org/contests
Contact: Ayn Rand Institute
4640 Admiralty Way, Suite 406
Marina del Rey, CA 90292
E-mail: marileed@aynrand.org

FOUNTAINHEAD COLLEGE SCHOLARSHIP ESSAY CONTEST • 428
251 prizes totaling $37,500 awarded to 11th and 12th grades for essays on Ayn Rand's "Fountainhead." Essay should be between 800 and 1600 words. Winners announced June 4. Semifinalist and finalist prizes also awarded. All information necessary to enter the contest is on the website.

Award Prize for use in freshman year; not renewable. *Number:* 251. *Amount:* $50–$10,000.

Eligibility Requirements: Applicant must be high school student and must have an interest in writing.

Application Requirements Applicant must enter a contest, essay. *Deadline:* April 15.

World Wide Web: http://www.aynrand.org/contests

Contact: Ayn Rand Institute
4640 Admiralty Way, Suite 406
Marina del Rey, CA 90292
E-mail: marileed@aynrand.org

BMI FOUNDATION, INC.

BMI STUDENT COMPOSER AWARDS • 429

One-time award for original composition in classical genre for young student composers who are under age 26 and citizens of the Western Hemisphere. Must submit original musical score by February 11. Write for further information.

Award Prize for use in any year; not renewable. *Number:* 5–10. *Amount:* $500–$5000.

Eligibility Requirements: Applicant must be age 25 or under; enrolled full or part-time at a two-year or four-year institution or university and must have an interest in music/singing. Available to U.S. and non-U.S. citizens.

Application Requirements Application, applicant must enter a contest. *Deadline:* February 11.

World Wide Web: http://www.bmi.com

Contact: Mr. Ralph Jackson, Director, BMI Student Composer Awards
BMI Foundation, Inc.
320 West 57th Street
New York, NY 10019
Phone: 212-830-2537
Fax: 212-262-2824
E-mail: classical@bmi.com

JOHN LENNON SCHOLARSHIP • 430

Awards for best original song of any genre written by a person between 15 and 24. No applications accepted from individuals. Candidates are chosen by designated schools and other community music organizations. Music tape and lyric sheet required.

Award Grant for use in any year; not renewable. *Number:* 8. *Amount:* $1000–$10,000.

Eligibility Requirements: Applicant must be age 15-24 and must have an interest in music/singing.

Application Requirements Applicant must enter a contest. *Deadline:* March 1.

World Wide Web: http://www.bmi.com

John Lennon Scholarship (continued)
Contact: Ms. Theodora Zavin, President
BMI Foundation, Inc.
320 West 57th Street
New York, NY 10019
Phone: 212-830-2520
Fax: 212-246-2163
E-mail: tzavin@bmi.com

BOYS & GIRLS CLUBS OF AMERICA

BOYS & GIRLS CLUBS OF AMERICA NATIONAL YOUTH OF THE YEAR AWARD
see number 184

CALIFORNIA JUNIOR MISS SCHOLARSHIP PROGRAM

CALIFORNIA JUNIOR MISS SCHOLARSHIP PROGRAM
see number 321

CAP FOUNDATION

RON BROWN SCHOLAR PROGRAM
see number 263

CITIZENS' SCHOLARSHIP FOUNDATION OF AMERICA

VANTAGE POINT PUBLIC EMPLOYEE MEMORIAL SCHOLARSHIP FUND
• 431

Scholarship program available to children and/or spouses of all public sector employees, both emergency and non-emergency personnel, who died in the line of duty. Fund not restricted to September 11th attacks. Five scholarships of up to $10,000 available for children of New York City emergency personnel. Visit website for details http://www.vantagepointscholar.org.

Award Scholarship for use in freshman, sophomore, junior, senior, or graduate years; not renewable. *Number:* 10. *Amount:* up to $10,000.
Eligibility Requirements: Applicant must be enrolled full-time at a two-year or four-year or technical institution or university and must have an interest in leadership. Available to U.S. citizens.
Application Requirements Application, essay, financial need analysis, resume, references, transcript. *Deadline:* March 31.
World Wide Web: http://www.csfa.org

Contact: Scholarship Management Services
Citizens' Scholarship Foundation of America
1505 Riverview Road, PO Box 297
St. Peter, MN 56082
Phone: 507-931-1682

COCA-COLA SCHOLARS FOUNDATION, INC.

COCA-COLA SCHOLARS PROGRAM • 432

Awards based on leadership, academic performance, extracurricular activities, employment, and community involvement. Finalists represent every state in the U.S. 40% of the recipients are minorities. Must apply in senior year of high school. Deadline is October 31. Recipient has six years in which to use award. Two hundred $4000 awards and fifty $20000 awards granted annually. Must apply through website (http://www.coca-colascholars.org). Paper applications not offered.

Award Scholarship for use in freshman, sophomore, junior, or senior years; renewable. *Number:* 250. *Amount:* $4000–$20,000.
Eligibility Requirements: Applicant must be high school student; planning to enroll full or part-time at a two-year or four-year or technical institution or university and must have an interest in leadership. Applicant must have 3.0 GPA or higher. Available to U.S. citizens.
Application Requirements Application, essay, interview, references, transcript. *Deadline:* October 31.
World Wide Web: http://www.coca-colascholars.org
Contact: Mark Davis, President
Coca-Cola Scholars Foundation, Inc.
PO Box 442
Atlanta, GA 30301-0442
Phone: 800-306-2653
Fax: 404-733-5439
E-mail: scholars@na.ko.com

EDUCATIONAL COMMUNICATIONS SCHOLARSHIP FOUNDATION

EDUCATIONAL COMMUNICATIONS SCHOLARSHIP • 433

Award based on scholarship, financial need, leadership, and extracurricular activity. Must be high school student and legal resident of U.S. to apply. Must have a minimum 3.0 GPA and have taken ACT or SAT exam. Semifinalists submit financial need analysis and essay; finalists submit transcript. Application fee is $3.50. Applications are available only at high school guidance offices.

Award Scholarship for use in any year; not renewable. *Number:* 200. *Amount:* $1000.

Educational Communications Scholarship (continued)

Eligibility Requirements: Applicant must be high school student; planning to enroll full or part-time at a two-year or four-year or technical institution or university and must have an interest in leadership. Applicant must have 3.0 GPA or higher. Available to U.S. citizens.

Application Requirements Application, essay, financial need analysis, test scores, transcript. *Fee:* $3.5. *Deadline:* May 15.

Contact: Assistant to the Chairman
Educational Communications Scholarship Foundation
721 North McKinley Road
Lake Forest, IL 60045
Phone: 847-295-6650
Fax: 847-295-3792
E-mail: scholar@ecsf.org

EXECUTIVE WOMEN INTERNATIONAL

EXECUTIVE WOMEN INTERNATIONAL SCHOLARSHIP PROGRAM • 434

Competitive award to high school juniors planning careers in any business or professional field of study which requires a four-year college degree. Award is renewable based on continuing eligibility. Student must have a sponsoring teacher and school to be considered. Awards range from $50-$10,000. Visit website for additional information.

Award Scholarship for use in any year; renewable. *Number:* 130. *Amount:* $50–$10,000.

Eligibility Requirements: Applicant must be high school student; planning to enroll full-time at a four-year institution or university and must have an interest in designated field specified by sponsor.

Application Requirements Application, autobiography, interview, references, transcript. *Deadline:* March 1.

World Wide Web: http://www.executivewomen.org

Contact: Debra Tucker, Scholarship Programs
Executive Women International
515 South 700 East, Suite 2A
Salt Lake City, UT 84102
Phone: 801-355-2800
Fax: 801-362-3212

FLORIDA LEADER MAGAZINE/COLLEGE STUDENT OF THE YEAR, INC.

FLORIDA COLLEGE STUDENT OF THE YEAR AWARD   see number 336

FRANCIS OUIMET SCHOLARSHIP FUND

FRANCIS OUIMET SCHOLARSHIP FUND   see number 337

HOSTESS COMMITTEE SCHOLARSHIPS/MISS AMERICA PAGEANT

MISS AMERICA ORGANIZATION COMPETITION SCHOLARSHIPS • 435

Scholarship competition open to 51 contestants, each serving as state representative. Women will be judged in Private Interview, Swimsuit, Evening Wear and Talent competition. Other awards may be based on points assessed by judges during competitions. Upon reaching the National level, award values range from $5000 to $50,000. Additional awards not affecting the competition can be won with values from $1000 to $10,000. Awards designed to provide contestants with the opportunity to enhance professional and educational goals.

Award Scholarship for use in any year; not renewable. *Amount:* $1000–$50,000.
Eligibility Requirements: Applicant must be female and must have an interest in beauty pageant. Available to U.S. citizens.
Application Requirements Applicant must enter a contest.
World Wide Web: http://www.missamerica.org
Contact: Hostess Committee Scholarships/Miss America Pageant
Two Miss America Way, Suite 1000
Atlantic City, NJ 08401

J. WOOD PLATT CADDIE SCHOLARSHIP TRUST

J. WOOD PLATT CADDIE SCHOLARSHIP TRUST see number 222

LADIES AUXILIARY TO THE VETERANS OF FOREIGN WARS

YOUNG AMERICAN CREATIVE PATRIOTIC ART AWARDS PROGRAM • 436

One-time awards for high school students in grades 9 through12. Must submit an original work of art expressing their patriotism. First-place state-level winners go on to national competition. Five awards of varying amounts. Must reside in same state as sponsoring organization. Award is renewed based on continued eligibility.

Award Prize for use in any year; not renewable. *Number:* 5. *Amount:* $1000–$10,000.
Eligibility Requirements: Applicant must be high school student and must have an interest in designated field specified by sponsor. Available to U.S. citizens.
Application Requirements Application, applicant must enter a contest.
Deadline: December 15.

Young American Creative Patriotic Art Awards Program (continued)
World Wide Web: http://www.ladiesauxvfw.com
Contact: Judy Millick, Administrator of Programs
Ladies Auxiliary to the Veterans of Foreign Wars
406 West 34th Street
Kansas City, MO 64111
Phone: 816-561-8655
Fax: 816-931-4753
E-mail: info@ladiesauxvfw.com

LIEDERKRANZ FOUNDATION

LIEDERKRANZ FOUNDATION SCHOLARSHIP AWARD FOR VOICE • 437

Non-renewable awards for voice for both full- and part-time study. Those studying general voice must be between ages 20 to 35 years old while those studying Wagnerian voice must be between ages 25 to 45 years old. Application fee: $35. Applications not available before August/September. Deadline: November 15.

Award Scholarship for use in any year; not renewable. *Number:* 14–18. *Amount:* $1000–$5000.
Eligibility Requirements: Applicant must be enrolled full or part-time at an institution or university and must have an interest in music/singing. Available to U.S. and non-U.S. citizens.
Application Requirements Application, applicant must enter a contest, driver's license, self-addressed stamped envelope, proof of age. *Fee:* $35. *Deadline:* November 15.
Contact: C. Kessel, Administrative Assistant
Liederkranz Foundation
6 East 87th Street
New York, NY 10128
Phone: 212-534-0880
Fax: 212-828-5372

NATIONAL ALLIANCE FOR EXCELLENCE

NATIONAL ALLIANCE FOR EXCELLENCE HONORED SCHOLARS AND ARTISTS PROGRAM • 438

National competition in four categories: academics, visual arts, performing arts, and technological innovations. Students in arts competitions must send slides or videos of their work. Minimum 1300 SAT and 3.7 GPA for non-arts categories. $5 application fee. All awards are given out in ceremonies with government officials, prominent artists, or business leaders as presenters. Highly competitive. Must send SASE or download application at www.excellence.org.

Award Scholarship for use in any year; not renewable. *Number:* 40–70. *Amount:* $1000–$5000.

Eligibility Requirements: Applicant must be enrolled full-time at a four-year institution or university and must have an interest in art, music/singing, or photography/photogrammetry/filmmaking. Available to U.S. citizens.

Application Requirements Application, applicant must enter a contest, essay, portfolio, resume, references, self-addressed stamped envelope, test scores, transcript. *Fee:* $5. *Deadline:* Continuous.

World Wide Web: http://www.excellence.org

Contact: Linda Paras, President
National Alliance for Excellence
63 Riverside Avenue
Red Bank, NJ 07701
Phone: 732-747-0028
Fax: 732-842-2962
E-mail: info@excellence.org

NATIONAL ASSOCIATION OF SECONDARY SCHOOL PRINCIPALS

PRINCIPAL'S LEADERSHIP AWARD • 439

One-time award available to high school seniors only, for use at an accredited two- or four-year college or university. Based on leadership and school or community involvement. Application fee: $6. Deadline is December 1. Contact school counselor or principal. Citizens of countries other than the U.S. may only apply if they are attending a United States overseas institution. Minimum GPA 3.0.

Award Scholarship for use in any year; not renewable. *Number:* 150. *Amount:* $1000.

Eligibility Requirements: Applicant must be high school student; planning to enroll full-time at a two-year or four-year institution or university and must have an interest in leadership. Applicant must have 3.0 GPA or higher. Available to U.S. and non-Canadian citizens.

Application Requirements Application, essay, references, test scores, transcript. *Fee:* $6. *Deadline:* December 1.

World Wide Web: http://www.principals.org

Contact: Local school principal or guidance counselor

RECORDING FOR THE BLIND & DYSLEXIC

MARY P. OENSLAGER SCHOLASTIC ACHIEVEMENT AWARDS

see number 200

ROOTHBERT FUND, INC.

ROOTHBERT FUND, INC. SCHOLARSHIP • 440

Award for those pursuing undergraduate degree or higher in U.S. institution and satisfying academic standards. Non-U.S. citizens must be living in U.S.

Roothbert Fund, Inc. Scholarship (continued)

Must travel at own expense to interview in Philadelphia, New Haven, or Washington, DC. Deadline: February 1. Provide SASE when requesting an application.

Award Scholarship for use in any year; renewable. *Number:* 50. *Amount:* $2000–$5000.

Eligibility Requirements: Applicant must be enrolled full-time at a two-year or four-year or technical institution or university and must have an interest in designated field specified by sponsor. Available to U.S. and non-U.S. citizens.

Application Requirements Application, autobiography, essay, financial need analysis, interview, photo, references, self-addressed stamped envelope, test scores, transcript. *Deadline:* February 1.

World Wide Web: http://www.roothbertfund.org

Contact: Roothbert Fund, Inc.
475 Riverside Drive, Room 252
New York, NY 10115

ROTARY FOUNDATION OF ROTARY INTERNATIONAL

ROTARY MULTI-YEAR AMBASSADORIAL SCHOLARSHIPS • 441

Awarded for two or three years (depending on availability through sponsoring Rotary district) of degree-oriented study in another country. Applicant must have completed at least two years of university course work and be proficient in language of host country. Application through local Rotary club; appearances before clubs required during award period. Applications are accepted March through July. See website for updated information.

Award Scholarship for use in junior, senior, or graduate years; not renewable. *Number:* 100–150. *Amount:* $12,000.

Eligibility Requirements: Applicant must be enrolled full-time at a four-year institution or university and must have an interest in foreign language.

Application Requirements Application, autobiography, essay, interview, references, transcript.

World Wide Web: http://www.rotary.org

Contact: Scholarship Program
Rotary Foundation of Rotary International
1560 Sherman Avenue
Evanston, IL 60203
Phone: 847-866-4459

SAN ANTONIO INTERNATIONAL PIANO COMPETITION

SAN ANTONIO INTERNATIONAL PIANO COMPETITION • 442

International piano competition for 10 semi-finalists, ages 20-32. Cash awards, ranging from $500 for 5th prize to $10,000 for 1st prize, are determined through a series of daily concerts, with an additional award for the best performance of a commissioned work. Application fee: $50. Deadline: March 31. Additional awards: $350. Competition held every three years.

Award Prize for use in any year; not renewable. *Number:* 7–12. *Amount:* $350–$10,000.

Eligibility Requirements: Applicant must be age 20-32 and must have an interest in music/singing. Available to U.S. and non-U.S. citizens.

Application Requirements Application, applicant must enter a contest, autobiography, driver's license, photo, portfolio, references, self-addressed stamped envelope, tape recording, certified proof of date of birth, clippings and programs from previous performances. *Fee:* $50. *Deadline:* March 31.

World Wide Web: http://www.saipc.org

Contact: Ms. Virginia Lawrence, Registrar
San Antonio International Piano Competition
PO Box 39636
San Antonio, TX 78218
Phone: 210-655-0766
Fax: 210-824-5094
E-mail: info@saipc.org

SCIENCE SERVICE, INC.

DISCOVERY YOUNG SCIENTIST CHALLENGE • 443

Scholarship for students in the fifth through eighth grade to be used for future college enrollment. Must be a U.S. citizen. Must participate in a science fair. Deadline: June 5. For additional information, visit website: http://www.discovery.com/dysc

Award Scholarship for use in any year; renewable. *Number:* up to 40. *Amount:* $500–$15,000.

Eligibility Requirements: Applicant must be enrolled full-time at an institution or university and must have an interest in designated field specified by sponsor. Available to U.S. citizens.

Application Requirements Application, applicant must enter a contest, essay, interview, references. *Deadline:* June 5.

World Wide Web: http://www.sciserv.org

Contact: Michele Glidden, DYSC Program
Science Service, Inc.
1719 N Street, NW
Washington, DC 20036
Phone: 202-785-2255
Fax: 202-785-1243
E-mail: mglidden@sciserv.org

INTEL INTERNATIONAL SCIENCE AND ENGINEERING FAIR • 444

Scholarship for students in the ninth through twelfth grades. Must include research essay and science fair entry. Applicants must compete at local sci-

Intel International Science and Engineering Fair (continued)
ence fair in order to be nominated for national competition. Visit website for additional information: http://www.discovery.com/dysc.

Award Scholarship for use in any year; renewable. *Amount:* $500–$50,000.

Eligibility Requirements: Applicant must be high school student; planning to enroll full-time at an institution or university and must have an interest in designated field specified by sponsor. Available to U.S. and non-U.S. citizens.

Application Requirements Application, applicant must enter a contest, essay, interview.

World Wide Web: http://www.sciserv.org

Contact: Intel ISEF Program Manager
Science Service, Inc.
1719 N Street, NW
Washington, DC 20036
Phone: 202-872-5152
Fax: 205-785-1243

INTEL SCIENCE TALENT SEARCH • 445

Forty scholarships ranging from $5000 to $100,000 will be awarded to the top high school science competition winners. Deadline: December 1. Write for more details. Applicants who are not U.S. citizens must be living in the U.S. and attending a U.S. high school. Visit website for additional information: http://www.discovery.com/dysc.

Award Scholarship for use in freshman, sophomore, junior, or senior years; renewable. *Number:* 40. *Amount:* $5000–$100,000.

Eligibility Requirements: Applicant must be high school student; planning to enroll full-time at a four-year institution or university and must have an interest in designated field specified by sponsor. Available to U.S. citizens.

Application Requirements Application, applicant must enter a contest, autobiography, essay, references, test scores, transcript. *Deadline:* December 1.

World Wide Web: http://www.sciserv.org

Contact: Intel STS Program Manager
Science Service, Inc.
1719 N Street, NW
Washington, DC 20036
Phone: 202-872-5149
Fax: 202-785-1243
E-mail: kstafford@scicerv.org

SWISS BENEVOLENT SOCIETY OF NEW YORK

MEDICUS STUDENT EXCHANGE   see number 292

TEXACO FOUNDATION

TEXACO FOUNDATION SCHOLARSHIP
see number 208

VIRGINIA DEPARTMENT OF EDUCATION

LEE- JACKSON FOUNDATION SCHOLARSHIP
see number 415

W. EUGENE SMITH MEMORIAL FUND, INC.

W. EUGENE SMITH GRANT IN HUMANISTIC PHOTOGRAPHY • 446
Co-sponsored by Nikon Inc. One-time grant available to professional photographers who are unable to complete a major project due to lack of funding. Up to $30,000 awarded for one grant. May be renewed.

Award Grant for use in any year; not renewable. *Number:* 1–3. *Amount:* $30,000.
Eligibility Requirements: Applicant must have an interest in photography/photogrammetry/filmmaking. Available to U.S. and non-U.S. citizens.
Application Requirements Application, portfolio, resume, self-addressed stamped envelope. *Deadline:* July 15.
World Wide Web: http://www.smithfund.org
Contact: Anna Winand
W. Eugene Smith Memorial Fund, Inc.
c/o ICP
1133 Avenue of the Americas
New York, NY 10036
Phone: 212-857-9751

WASHINGTON CROSSING FOUNDATION

WASHINGTON CROSSING FOUNDATION SCHOLARSHIP • 447
Renewable, merit-based awards available to high school seniors who are planning a career in government service. Must write an essay stating reason for deciding on a career in public service. Minimum GPA 3.0 required. Write for details.

Award Scholarship for use in freshman, sophomore, junior, or senior years; renewable. *Number:* 5–10. *Amount:* $1000–$20,000.
Eligibility Requirements: Applicant must be high school student; planning to enroll full-time at a four-year institution and must have an interest in designated field specified by sponsor. Applicant must have 3.0 GPA or higher. Available to U.S. citizens.
Application Requirements Application, essay, references, test scores, transcript. *Deadline:* January 15.
World Wide Web: http://www.gwcf.org

Washington Crossing Foundation Scholarship (continued)
Contact: Eugene Fish, Vice Chairman
Washington Crossing Foundation
PO Box 503
Levittown, PA 19058-0503
Phone: 215-949-8841

WILLIAM G. AND MARIE SELBY FOUNDATION

SELBY SCHOLAR PROGRAM   see number 233

WILLIAM RANDOLPH HEARST FOUNDATION

UNITED STATES SENATE YOUTH PROGRAM   • 448

For high school juniors and seniors holding elected student offices. Must attend high school in state of parents' or guardians' legal residence. Two students selected from each state and the selection process will vary by state. Contact school principal or state department of education for information. Application deadline is in the early fall of each year for most states but the actual date will vary by state. Program is open to citizens and permanent residents of the United States Department of Defense schools overseas and the District of Columbia (not the territories). More information at website, http://www.ussenateyouth.org.

Award Scholarship for use in freshman, sophomore, junior, or senior years; not renewable. *Number:* 104. *Amount:* $2000.
Eligibility Requirements: Applicant must be high school student; planning to enroll full or part-time at a two-year or four-year or technical institution or university and must have an interest in designated field specified by sponsor. Available to U.S. citizens.
Application Requirements Application procedures will vary by state.
World Wide Web: http://www.ussenateyouth.org
Contact: Ms. Rita Almon, Program Director
William Randolph Hearst Foundation
90 New Montgomery Street, Suite 1212
San Francisco, CA 94105-4504
Phone: 800-841-7048
Fax: 415-243-0760
E-mail: ussyp@hearstfdn.org

WOMEN'S SPORTS FOUNDATION

TRAVEL AND TRAINING FUND   • 449

Award to provide financial assistance to aspiring female athletes with successful competitive regional or national records who have the potential to achieve even higher performance levels and rankings. Must be a U.S. citizen or legal resident.

Award Grant for use in any year; not renewable. *Number:* 90–100. *Amount:* $500–$2000.
Eligibility Requirements: Applicant must be female and must have an interest in athletics/sports. Available to U.S. citizens.
Application Requirements Application, references. *Deadline:* July 31.
World Wide Web: http://www.womenssportsfoundation.org
Contact: Women's Sports Foundation
Eisenhower Park
East Meadow, NY 11554
Phone: 800-227-3988
E-mail: wosport@aol.com

WOMEN'S WESTERN GOLF FOUNDATION

WOMEN'S WESTERN GOLF FOUNDATION SCHOLARSHIP • 450

Scholarships for female high school seniors for use at a four-year college or university. Based on academic record, financial need, character, and involvement in golf. (Golf skill not a criterion.) Twenty awards annually for incoming freshmen; approximately 60 scholarships renewed. Must maintain 2.5 GPA as freshman; 3.0 upperclassman GPA. Must continue to have financial need. Award is $2000 per student per year. Applicant must be 17-18 years of age.

Award Scholarship for use in freshman, sophomore, junior, or senior years; renewable. *Number:* up to 80. *Amount:* $2000.
Eligibility Requirements: Applicant must be high school student; age 17-18; planning to enroll full-time at a four-year institution or university; single female and must have an interest in golf. Applicant must have 3.0 GPA or higher. Available to U.S. citizens.
Application Requirements Application, essay, financial need analysis, self-addressed stamped envelope, test scores, transcript. *Deadline:* April 5.
Contact: Mrs. Richard Willis, Scholarship Chairman
Women's Western Golf Foundation
393 Ramsay Road
Deerfield, IL 60015

WRITER'S DIGEST

WRITER'S DIGEST ANNUAL WRITING COMPETITION • 451

Annual writing competition. Only original, unpublished entries in any of the ten categories. Send self-addressed stamped envelope for guidelines and entry form. Deadline is May 31. Application fee: $10.

Award Prize for use in any year; not renewable. *Number:* 1001. *Amount:* $25–$1500.
Eligibility Requirements: Applicant must be enrolled full or part-time at a two-year or four-year or technical institution or university and must have an interest in writing. Available to U.S. and non-U.S. citizens.

Writer's Digest Annual Writing Competition (continued)

Application Requirements Application, applicant must enter a contest, self-addressed stamped envelope. *Fee:* $10. *Deadline:* May 31.

World Wide Web: http://www.writersdigest.com

Contact: Terri Boes, Promotion Assistant
Writer's Digest
1507 Dana Avenue
Cincinnati, OH 45207
Phone: 513-531-2690
Fax: 513-531-0798
E-mail: competitions@fwpubs.com

MISCELLANEOUS CRITERIA

ACADEMY FOUNDATION OF THE ACADEMY OF MOTION PICTURE ARTS AND SCIENCES

ACADEMY OF MOTION PICTURES STUDENT ACADEMY AWARDS • 452

Available to students who have made a narrative, documentary, alternative, or animated film of up to sixty minutes within the curricular structure of an accredited college or university. Initial entry must be on 1/2 inch VHS tape. 16mm or larger format print for further rounds. Prizes awarded in four categories. Each category awards Gold ($5000), Silver ($3000) and Bronze ($2000). Visit website for details and application (http://www.oscars.org/saa).

Award Prize for use in any year; not renewable. *Number:* 3–12. *Amount:* $2000–$5000.

Eligibility Requirements: Applicant must be enrolled full-time at a four-year institution or university. Available to U.S. and non-U.S. citizens.

Application Requirements Application, applicant must enter a contest, VHS tape. *Deadline:* April 1.

World Wide Web: http://www.oscars.org/saa

Contact: Richard Miller, Director of Awards Administration
Academy Foundation of the Academy of Motion Picture Arts and Sciences
8949 Wilshire Boulevard
Beverly Hills, CA 90211-1972
E-mail: rmiller@oscars.org

AFRO-ASIATIC INSTITUTE IN WIEN

ONE WORLD SCHOLARSHIP PROGRAM • 453

Up to eighty-five scholarships and/or grants between $450 and $600 will be given to students who are citizens of a developing country in Africa. Eligible applicants will be between 18 and 35. Deadlines are January 30 and April 2.

Award Scholarship for use in any year; renewable. *Number:* up to 85. *Amount:* $450–$600.

Eligibility Requirements: Applicant must be age 18-35 and enrolled full-time at an institution or university. Available to citizens of countries other than the U.S. or Canada.

Application Requirements Application, autobiography, financial need analysis, interview, references, test scores.

World Wide Web: http://www.aai-wien.at/aai-wien

One World Scholarship Program (continued)
Contact: Pleschko Mankin
Afro-Asiatic Institute in Wien
Turkenstrasse 3
Study Advisory Department
Vienna V-109
Austria
Phone: 43-1-3105145 Ext. 210
Fax: 43-1-3105145 Ext. 312
E-mail: studium@aai-wien.at

ALBERT E. NICHOLL LTD.

NICHOLL SCHOLARSHIPS • 454

This award requires academic excellence, leadership, sport/music achievement, and character. Applicants must be Bermudian.

Award Scholarship for use in any year; not renewable. *Number:* 4. *Amount:* $18,000.
Eligibility Requirements: Applicant must be age 18-24 and enrolled full-time at a four-year institution or university. Available to citizens of countries other than the U.S. or Canada.
Application Requirements Application, essay, photo, resume, references, transcript. *Deadline:* June 14.
World Wide Web: http://www.ask.bm
Contact: Kristina Nusum, Secretary
Albert E. Nicholl Ltd.
PO Box HM 1179
Hamilton HM EX
Bermuda
Phone: 441-295-2244
Fax: 441-298-3307
E-mail: tnusum@ask.bm

AMERICA'S JUNIOR MISS COMPETITION

AMERICA'S JUNIOR MISS SCHOLARSHIP • 455

Awards are given to contestant in local, regional and national levels of competition. Contestants must be female, high school juniors or seniors, U.S. citizens and legal residents of the county and state of competition. Contestants are evaluated on scholastics, interview, talent, fitness and poise. For more information visit http://www.ajm.org.

Award Scholarship for use in freshman, sophomore, junior, or senior years; not renewable. *Number:* up to 36. *Amount:* up to $50,000.
Eligibility Requirements: Applicant must be high school student; planning to enroll at a two-year or four-year institution or university and single female. Available to U.S. citizens.

Application Requirements Application, applicant must enter a contest, test scores, transcript. *Deadline:* Continuous.
World Wide Web: http://www.ajm.org
Contact: Contestant Inquiries
America's Junior Miss Competition
751 Government Street
PO Box 2786
Mobile, AL 36652-2786

AMERICAN ASSOCIATION OF SCHOOL ADMINISTRATORS/DISCOVER CARD TRIBUTE AWARD PROGRAM

DISCOVER CARD TRIBUTE AWARD SCHOLARSHIP PROGRAM
• 456

Applicants should be current high school juniors with minimum 2.75 GPA. Nine scholarships available in each state and Washington, D.C. Nine $25,000 awards at the national level in three categories. Must plan to further education beyond high school in any accredited certification, licensing or training program or institution of higher education. Must demonstrate outstanding accomplishments in three of four areas: special talents, leadership, obstacles overcome, and community service. Visit website for application and more information.

Award Scholarship for use in any year; not renewable. *Number:* up to 478. *Amount:* $2500–$25,000.
Eligibility Requirements: Applicant must be high school student and planning to enroll full or part-time at a two-year or four-year or technical institution or university. Available to U.S. citizens.
Application Requirements Application, essay, references, transcript. *Deadline:* January 11.
World Wide Web: http://www.aasa.org/discover.htm
Contact: Program Director
American Association of School Administrators/Discover Card
Tribute Award Program
PO Box 9338
Arlington, VA 22219
Phone: 703-875-0708
E-mail: tributeaward@aasa.org

AMERICAN ASSOCIATION OF UNIVERSITY WOMEN (AAUW) EDUCATIONAL FOUNDATION

AAUW EDUCATIONAL FOUNDATION COMMUNITY ACTION GRANTS
• 457

Community Action Grants provide seed money for innovative programs or non-degree research projects that promote education and equity for women

AAUW Educational Foundation Community Action Grants (continued)
and girls. Must be U.S. citizen or permanent resident. Projects must have direct public impact, be nonpartisan and take place within the United States or its territories. Preference given to AAUW branch and state projects that seek collaborative partners and to individual AAUW member applicants. Application fee is $25.

Award Grant for use in any year; renewable. *Number:* 20–30. *Amount:* $2000–$10,000.
Eligibility Requirements: Applicant must be female. Available to U.S. citizens.
Application Requirements Application. *Fee:* $25. *Deadline:* February 1.
World Wide Web: http://www.aauw.org
Contact: Program Manager
American Association of University Women (AAUW) Educational
Foundation
2201 North Dodge Street
Iowa City, IA 52243-4030
Phone: 319-337-1716
E-mail: aauw@act.org

ASSOCIATION OF TEACHERS OF JAPANESE BRIDGING CLEARINGHOUSE FOR STUDY ABROAD IN JAPAN

BRIDGING SCHOLARSHIPS • 458

Scholarships for U.S. students studying in Japan on semester or year-long programs. Deadlines are April 3 and October 3.

Award Scholarship for use in sophomore, junior, or senior years; not renewable. *Number:* 40–80. *Amount:* $2500–$4000.
Eligibility Requirements: Applicant must be enrolled full-time at a two-year or four-year institution or university. Available to U.S. citizens.
Application Requirements Application, essay, references, transcript.
World Wide Web: http://www.colorado.edu/ealld/atj/bridging/scholarships.html
Contact: Susan Schmidt, Executive Director
Association of Teachers of Japanese Bridging Clearinghouse for
Study Abroad in Japan
279 UCB
Boulder, CO 80309-0279
Phone: 303-492-5487
Fax: 303-492-5856
E-mail: atj@colorado.edu

CAREER TRAINING FOUNDATION

IMAGINE AMERICA SCHOLARSHIP • 459

One time award available to graduating high school seniors. Must attend an accredited private postsecondary institution. Must be nominated by school counselor or principal. Must enroll by October 31. See website, http://www. petersons.com/cca. Contact the guidance counselor at high school.

Award Scholarship for use in freshman year; not renewable. *Number:* up to 10,000. *Amount:* $1000.

Eligibility Requirements: Applicant must be high school student; age 17-18 and planning to enroll full-time at a two-year or four-year or technical institution. Applicant must have 2.5 GPA or higher. Available to U.S. citizens.

Application Requirements Applicant must enter a contest, financial need analysis, nomination.

World Wide Web: http://www.petersons.com/cca/

Contact: Bob Martin, Executive Director/Vice President
Career Training Foundation
10 G Street, NE, Suite 750
Washington, DC 20002-4213
Phone: 202-336-6800
Fax: 202-408-8102
E-mail: scholarships@career.org

CITIZENS' SCHOLARSHIP FOUNDATION OF AMERICA

DOLLARS FOR SCHOLARS SCHOLARSHIP • 460

Awards totaling $15 million dollars awarded through local community-based Dollars for Scholars chapters. Contact for details and deadlines. Nearly $80 million awarded through sponsored scholarship programs.

Award Scholarship for use in any year; renewable. *Number:* 80,000–90,000. *Amount:* $500.

Eligibility Requirements: Applicant must be enrolled full-time at a two-year or four-year or technical institution. Available to U.S. and Canadian citizens.

Application Requirements Application, essay.

World Wide Web: http://www.csfa.org

Contact: National Headquarters
Citizens' Scholarship Foundation of America
1505 Riverview Road
St. Peter, MN 56082
Phone: 800-248-8080

COCA-COLA SCHOLARS FOUNDATION, INC.

COCA-COLA TWO-YEAR COLLEGES SCHOLARSHIP • 461

Awards based on community involvement, leadership, and academic performance. Finalists represent every state in the U.S. Must pursue a two-year degree. Deadline is May 31. Each institution may nominate up to two applicants. Minimum 2.5 GPA is required. Must apply through website (http://www.coca-colascholars.org). Paper applications not offered.

Coca-Cola Two-Year Colleges Scholarship (continued)

Award Scholarship for use in any year; not renewable. *Number:* 400. *Amount:* $1000.

Eligibility Requirements: Applicant must be enrolled full or part-time at a two-year or technical institution. Applicant must have 2.5 GPA or higher. Available to U.S. citizens.

Application Requirements Application, nomination from institution. *Deadline:* May 31.

World Wide Web: http://www.coca-colascholars.org

Contact: Mark Davis, President
Coca-Cola Scholars Foundation, Inc.
PO Box 442
Atlanta, GA 30301-0442
Phone: 800-306-2653
Fax: 404-733-5439
E-mail: scholars@na.ko.com

COLORADO POLICE CORPS

COLORADO POLICE CORPS SCHOLARSHIP • 462

The Colorado Police Corps is an exciting college scholarship/reimbursement opportunity for individuals interested in law enforcement as a career. Participants can receive up to $30,000 for college expenses. In return participants agree to work as a sworn officer with a participating agency in Colorado for four years after completing the 22 week Colorado Police Corps Academy.

Award Scholarship for use in any year; renewable. *Number:* 20–25. *Amount:* up to $30,000.

Eligibility Requirements: Applicant must be enrolled full-time at a four-year institution or university. Available to U.S. citizens.

Application Requirements Application, driver's license, essay, interview, references, test scores, transcript, background investigation, polygraph and psychological assessment. *Deadline:* Continuous.

World Wide Web: http://cdpsweb.state.co.us/policecorps

Contact: Stephanie Pelster, Training Supervisor
Colorado Police Corps
700 Kipling Street, Suite 1000
Denver, CO 80215
Phone: 303-273-1974
Fax: 303-273-1978
E-mail: stephanie.pelster@cdps.state.co.us

COMMISSION FRANCO-AMERICAINE D'ECHANGES UNIVERSITAIRES ET CULTURELS

FULBRIGHT PROGRAM • 463

Fulbright program offered to senior scholars advanced students, professionals and exchange teachers to carry out research, and/or lecture, study or teach in the United States or France. Program provides grants to approximately 100 nationals from both countries. Applicants must submit proof of their affiliation with their host institution. Grant is only available to American and French citizens. For French citizens, photo must accompany application. Application deadlines: August 1 (for US applicants) and December 15 (for French applicants).

Award Grant for use in senior, graduate, or post graduate years; not renewable. *Number:* 80–100. *Amount:* $1000–$20,000.

Eligibility Requirements: Applicant must be enrolled full or part-time at a four-year or technical institution or university.

Application Requirements Application, essay, interview, photo, references, test scores, transcript.

World Wide Web: http://www.fulbright-france.org

Contact: Dr. Amy Tondu, Program Officer
Commission Franco-Americaine d'Echanges Universitaires et
Culturels
9 Rue Chardin
Paris 75016
France
Phone: 33-1-4414536 Ext. 4
Fax: 33-1-4288047 Ext. 9
E-mail: atondu@fulbright-france.org

CONGRESSIONAL BLACK CAUCUS SPOUSES PROGRAM

CONGRESSIONAL BLACK CAUCUS SPOUSES EDUCATION SCHOLARSHIP FUND • 464

Award made to students who reside or attend school in a Congressional district represented by an African-American member of Congress. Contact the Congressional office in the appropriate district for information and applications (AL, GA, OH, MD, MS, SC, NC, MI, DC, CA, TX, IL, LA, NY, FL, IN, MO, NJ, PA, TN, VA). Any correspondence sent to the CBC Foundation Office on Pennsylvania Avenue will be discarded and may disqualify applicant for the award.

Award Scholarship for use in any year; renewable. *Number:* 200. *Amount:* $500–$4000.

Congressional Black Caucus Spouses Education Scholarship Fund (continued)
Eligibility Requirements: Applicant must be enrolled full-time at a two-year or four-year or technical institution or university. Applicant must have 2.5 GPA or higher. Available to U.S. citizens.
Application Requirements Application, essay, financial need analysis, interview, photo, references, transcript. *Deadline:* Continuous.
Contact: Appropriate Congressional District Office
Congressional Black Caucus Spouses Program
100 Pennsylvania Avenue, SE 80 West Fourth Street
Washington, DC 20003

CORPORATION FOR NATIONAL AND COMMUNITY SERVICE

PRESIDENT'S STUDENT SERVICE SCHOLARSHIPS • 465

The President's Student Service Scholarship program is designed to highlight and promote service and citizenship by students and to recognize students for their leadership in those areas. Each high school in the county may select up to 2 students to receive a $1,000 scholarship. With funds appropriated by Congress, the Corporation for National and Community Service provides $500, which must be matched with $500 secured by the school from the community.

Award Scholarship for use in freshman year; not renewable. *Number:* 10,000. *Amount:* $500.
Eligibility Requirements: Applicant must be high school student and planning to enroll full or part-time at a two-year or four-year or technical institution or university. Available to U.S. citizens.
Application Requirements Application. *Deadline:* June 28.
World Wide Web: http://www.nationalservice.org/scholarships
Contact: President's Student Service Scholarships
Corporation for National and Community Service
1201 New York Avenue, NW
Washington, DC 20525
Phone: 866-291-7700
E-mail: info@studentservicescholarships.org

DATATEL, INC.

RETURNING STUDENT SCHOLARSHIP • 466

For any student returning to higher education within the previous academic year, after a five-year or more absence. Applicant must attend a Datatel client institution. Deadline for requesting applications is January 15. Deadline for submission of applications is February 15. All applications must be submitted to the institution's Financial Aid Office. Applications and eligible institution list available on web.

Award Scholarship for use in any year; not renewable. *Number:* 25–50. *Amount:* $1000.

Eligibility Requirements: Applicant must be enrolled full or part-time at a two-year or four-year or technical institution or university. Available to U.S. and non-U.S. citizens.

Application Requirements Application, essay, references, transcript. *Deadline:* February 15.

World Wide Web: http://www.datatel.com

Contact: Aimee Allenback, Project Leader
Datatel, Inc.
4375 Fair Lakes Court
Fairfax, VA 22033
Phone: 800-486-4332
Fax: 703-968-4573
E-mail: scholars@datatel.com

DAVIS-PUTTER SCHOLARSHIP FUND

DAVIS-PUTTER SCHOLARSHIP FUND • 467

Provides money for students involved in human rights and economic, judicial, and political activism. Eligibility will be based on academic transcripts, recommendations, an essay and a financial need analysis.

Award Scholarship for use in any year; not renewable. *Number:* 25–30. *Amount:* up to $6000.

Eligibility Requirements: Applicant must be enrolled full or part-time at a two-year or four-year institution or university. Available to U.S. and non-U.S. citizens.

Application Requirements Application, essay, financial need analysis, photo, references, transcript. *Deadline:* April 1.

Contact: Jan Phillips, Secretary
Davis-Putter Scholarship Fund
25 Main Street
Belleville, NJ 07109
E-mail: davisputter@hotmail.com

EDDIE G. ROBINSON FOUNDATION

EDDIE ROBINSON FOUNDATION HIGH SCHOOL SENIOR SCHOLARSHIP • 468

Open to all high school seniors. Selection process based on a system using scholastic achievements, athletic accomplishments, leadership skills, and community involvement. Essay also required. Awards overall candidate, not strictly students with high GPA.

Award Scholarship for use in freshman, sophomore, junior, or senior years; renewable. *Number:* 2–4. *Amount:* $20,000.

Eligibility Requirements: Applicant must be high school student and planning to enroll full-time at a four-year institution or university. Applicant must have 2.5 GPA or higher. Available to U.S. citizens.

Eddie Robinson Foundation High School Senior Scholarship (continued)
Application Requirements Application, essay, references, test scores, transcript. *Deadline:* February 16.
World Wide Web: http://www.eddierobinson.com
Contact: Cherie Kirkland, Vice President
Eddie G. Robinson Foundation
5 Concourse Parkway
Suite 3100
Atlanta, GA 30328
Phone: 770-481-1941
Fax: 770-481-1985
E-mail: ckirkland@eddierobinson.com

EDUCAID, A FIRST UNION COMPANY

EDUCAID GIMME FIVE SCHOLARSHIP SWEEPSTAKES • 469
Each year, Educaid will award 12 high school seniors $5000 for their first year at an accredited college or trade school. The scholarships are not based on grades or financial need, so every eligible high school senior who enters has an equal chance of winning. Apply online at: http://www.educaid.com.

Award Prize for use in freshman year; not renewable. *Number:* 12. *Amount:* $5000.
Eligibility Requirements: Applicant must be high school student and planning to enroll full-time at a two-year or four-year or technical institution or university. Available to U.S. citizens.
Application Requirements *Deadline:* Continuous.
World Wide Web: http://www.educaid.com
Contact: applications accepted online only

ELKS NATIONAL FOUNDATION

ELKS MOST VALUABLE STUDENT CONTEST • 470
Five hundred four-year awards are allocated for graduating high school seniors nationally by state quota. Based on scholarship, leadership, and financial need. Renewable awards with first place awards at $60,000, second place awards at $40,000 and third place awards at $20,000. This will be distributed over four years. The remainder of the 494 awards will continue to be worth $4000 over four years. Mid-January deadline. Applications available at local Elks Lodge, at the website (http:// www.elks.org) (keyword: scholarship) or by sending a SASE to the Foundation.

Award Scholarship for use in freshman, sophomore, junior, or senior years; renewable. *Number:* 500. *Amount:* $4000–$60,000.
Eligibility Requirements: Applicant must be high school student and planning to enroll full-time at a two-year or four-year institution or university. Available to U.S. citizens.

Application Requirements Application, applicant must enter a contest, essay, financial need analysis, references, self-addressed stamped envelope, test scores, transcript.

World Wide Web: http://www.elks.org

Contact: Scholarship Coordinator
Elks National Foundation
2750 Lakeview Avenue
Chicago, IL 60614-1889
Phone: 773-755-4732
Fax: 773-755-4733
E-mail: scholarship@elks.org

FINANCIAL SERVICE CENTERS OF AMERICA, INC.

FINANCIAL SERVICE CENTERS OF AMERICA SCHOLARSHIP FUND • 471

The FISCA Scholarship Program awards cash grants of at least $2,500 to two students from each of the 5 geographic regions across the country. Criteria is based on academic achievement, financial need, leadership skills in schools and the community, and an essay written expressly for the competition. Applicant must be single.

Award Grant for use in freshman year; not renewable. *Number:* 10–20. *Amount:* $2500–$5000.

Eligibility Requirements: Applicant must be high school student; planning to enroll full-time at a two-year or four-year institution or university and single. Available to U.S. citizens.

Application Requirements Application, essay, financial need analysis, references, transcript. *Deadline:* June 15.

World Wide Web: http://www.fisca.org

Contact: Henry Shyne, Executive Director
Financial Service Centers of America, Inc.
25 Main Street
PO Box 647
Hackensack, NJ 07602
Phone: 201-487-0412
Fax: 201-487-3954
E-mail: fiscahfs@aol.com

GETCOLLEGE.COM, INC.

THE STRIVERS SCHOLARSHIP • 472

The Strivers Scholarship is for high school students with a GPA of 2.7 to 3.3 and SAT score of 950 to 1100. Renewable if student maintains a 3.0 to 3.3 GPA in a college or university. Must meet all requirements stated in application. Deadline is April 1. Application fee is $35.

The Strivers Scholarship (continued)
Award Scholarship for use in freshman year; renewable. *Number:* 6. *Amount:* $2000–$10,000.

Eligibility Requirements: Applicant must be high school student and planning to enroll full-time at a two-year or four-year institution or university. Applicant must have 3.0 GPA or higher. Available to U.S. citizens.

Application Requirements Application, essay, financial need analysis, references, test scores, transcript, family tax records. *Fee:* $35. *Deadline:* April 1.

World Wide Web: http://www.getcollege.com/scholarship-strivers.html

Contact: Vincent Waterhouse, President
Getcollege.Com, Inc.
1421 14th Lane
Palm Beach Gardens, FL 33418
Phone: 866-624-5591
E-mail: vwaterhouse@getcollege.com

GUIDEPOSTS MAGAZINE

GUIDEPOSTS YOUNG WRITER'S CONTEST • 473

Entrants must be either a high school junior or senior. Submit a first-person story about a memorable or moving experience; story must be the true personal experience of the writer. Authors of top ten manuscripts receive a scholarship. First Prize: $10,000; Second Prize: $8,000; Third Prize: $6,000; Fourth Prize: $4,000; Fifth Prize: $3,000; Sixth through Tenth Prizes: $1,000; Eleventh through Twentieth Prizes receive $250 gift certificate for college supplies.

Award Prize for use in freshman year; not renewable. *Number:* 10. *Amount:* $36,000.

Eligibility Requirements: Applicant must be high school student and planning to enroll at a two-year or four-year or technical institution or university. Available to U.S. and non-U.S. citizens.

Application Requirements Applicant must enter a contest, manuscript (maximum 1200 words). *Deadline:* November 6.

Contact: Surujnie Pooran, Secretary
GUIDEPOSTS Magazine
16 East 34th Street
New York, NY 10016

HELPING HANDS FOUNDATION

HELPING HANDS BOOK SCHOLARSHIP PROGRAM • 474

The HHBSP was created to assist students with the high cost of textbooks and study materials. Awards are open to individuals ages 16 and up who are planning to attend or are currently attending a two- or four-year college or university or a technical/vocational institution. Deadlines are July 15th for the fall and December 15th for the spring. Application fee is $5.

Award Grant for use in any year; not renewable. *Number:* 20–50. *Amount:* $100–$1000.

Eligibility Requirements: Applicant must be age 16 and enrolled full or part-time at a two-year or four-year or technical institution or university. Available to U.S. and non-U.S. citizens.

Application Requirements Application, essay, self-addressed stamped envelope, transcript. *Fee:* $5.

World Wide Web: http://www.helpinghandsbookscholarship.com

Contact: Scholarship Director
Helping Hands Foundation
PO Box 720379
Atlanta, GA 30358
Phone: 877-629-6184
Fax: 770-384-0376
E-mail: director@helpinghandsbookscholarship.com

HORATIO ALGER ASSOCIATION OF DISTINGUISHED AMERICANS

HORATIO ALGER ASSOCIATION SCHOLARSHIP PROGRAM • 475

The Horatio Alger Association provides financial assistance to students in the United States who have exhibited integrity and perseverance in overcoming personal adversity and who aspire to pursue higher education. Renewable award for full-time students seeking undergraduates degree. Minimum 2.0 GPA required.

Award Scholarship for use in freshman, sophomore, junior, or senior years; renewable. *Number:* 800–1000. *Amount:* $1000–$10,000.

Eligibility Requirements: Applicant must be high school student and planning to enroll full-time at a two-year or four-year institution or university. Available to U.S. citizens.

Application Requirements Application, essay, references, transcript. *Deadline:* October 31.

World Wide Web: http://www.horatioalger.com

Contact: Scholarship Coordinator
Horatio Alger Association of Distinguished Americans
99 Canal Center Plaza
Alexandria, VA 22314
E-mail: association@horatioalger.com

INSTITUTE OF INTERNATIONAL EDUCATION

NATIONAL SECURITY EDUCATION PROGRAM DAVID L. BOREN UNDERGRADUATE SCHOLARSHIPS • 476

The National Security Education Program (NSEP) awards scholarships to American undergraduate students for study abroad programs in regions critical to U.S. national interest. Emphasized world areas include Africa, Asia,

National Security Education Program David L. Boren Undergraduate Scholarships (continued)

Eastern and Central Europe, Latin America and the Caribbean, and the Middle East. NSEP scholarship recipients incur a service agreement. Must be a U.S. citizen.

Award Scholarship for use in freshman, sophomore, junior, or senior years; not renewable. *Number:* 130–160. *Amount:* $2500–$20,000.

Eligibility Requirements: Applicant must be enrolled full or part-time at a two-year or four-year institution or university. Available to U.S. citizens.

Application Requirements Application, essay, financial need analysis, references, transcript, campus review. *Deadline:* February 15.

World Wide Web: http://www.iie.org/nsep

Contact: Amy VanDyke, NSEP Program Officer
Institute of International Education
1400 K Street NW, Suite 650
Washington, DC 20005-2403
Phone: 800-618-6737
Fax: 202-326-7698
E-mail: nsep@iie.org

JACKIE ROBINSON FOUNDATION

JACKIE ROBINSON SCHOLARSHIP • 477

Scholarship for graduating minority high school seniors who have been accepted to accredited four-year colleges or universities. Must be U.S. citizen and show financial need, leadership potential and a high level of academic achievement. Application deadline: April 1.

Award Scholarship for use in freshman year; renewable. *Number:* 50–60. *Amount:* up to $6000.

Eligibility Requirements: Applicant must be high school student and planning to enroll full-time at a four-year institution. Available to U.S. citizens.

Application Requirements Application, essay, financial need analysis, references, test scores, transcript, school certification. *Deadline:* April 1.

World Wide Web: http://www.jackierobinson.org

Contact: Scholarship Program
Jackie Robinson Foundation
3 West 35th Street, 11th Floor
New York, NY 10001-2204
Phone: 212-290-8600
Fax: 212-290-8081

JEANNETTE RANKIN FOUNDATION, INC.

JEANNETTE RANKIN FOUNDATION AWARDS • 478

Applicants must be low-income women, age 35 or older, who are pursuing a technical/vocational degree, an associate's degree, or a first-time bachelor's degree. Applications are available November-February. Download materials from the website or send a self-addressed stamped envelope to request an application by mail (http://www.rankinfoundation.org).

Award Grant for use in freshman, sophomore, junior, or senior years; not renewable. *Number:* 25–40. *Amount:* $1500.

Eligibility Requirements: Applicant must be age 35; enrolled full or part-time at a two-year or four-year or technical institution or university and female. Available to U.S. citizens.

Application Requirements Application, essay, financial need analysis, references, self-addressed stamped envelope, transcript. *Deadline:* March 1.

World Wide Web: http://www.rankinfoundation.org

Contact: Andrea Tedrow, Program Coordinator
Jeannette Rankin Foundation, Inc.
PO Box 6653
Athens, GA 30604
Phone: 706-208-1211
Fax: 706-208-1211
E-mail: info@rankinfoundation.org

KAPLAN/NEWSWEEK

"MY TURN" ESSAY COMPETITION • 479

Essay contest open to high school students entering college or university. Can win up to $5,000. Must be U.S. citizen. To enter, student must submit 500-1000 word essay expressing their opinion, experience, or personal feelings on a topic of their own choice. 1st prize, $5,000; 2nd prize, $2,000; 8 finalists awarded $1,000. For more information visit website or call 1-800-KAPTEST.

Award Prize for use in freshman year; not renewable. *Number:* up to 10. *Amount:* $1000–$5000.

Eligibility Requirements: Applicant must be high school student and planning to enroll at a four-year institution or university. Available to U.S. citizens.

Application Requirements Applicant must enter a contest, essay. *Deadline:* March 1.

World Wide Web: http://www.kaptest.com

Contact: Kaplan/Newsweek
888 7th Avenue
New York, NY 10106
Phone: 800-KAP-TEST

MASSACHUSETTS POLICE CORPS

MASSACHUSETTS POLICE CORPS FEDERAL SCHOLARSHIP • 480

The program offers Federal educational assistance to college students who agree to serve 4 years as police officers in MA. In return for this commitment, the Mass Police Corps will award participants scholarships to cover college expenses including tuition, fees, books, supplies, transportation, housing,

Massachusetts Police Corps Federal Scholarship (continued)
meals, and other expenses. Participants can receive up to $7,500 per academic year with a limit of $30,000 per student.

Award Scholarship for use in any year; renewable. *Number:* up to 50. *Amount:* up to $7800.
Eligibility Requirements: Applicant must be enrolled full-time at a four-year institution or university. Available to U.S. citizens.
Application Requirements Application, essay, interview, references, test scores, transcript. *Deadline:* Continuous.
World Wide Web: http://www.masspolicecorps.com
Contact: Lt. Doris Thompson, Training Manager
　　　　　Massachusetts Police Corps
　　　　　South Weymouth Naval Air Station
　　　　　31 Shea Memorial Drive
　　　　　South Weymouth, MA 02190
　　　　　Phone: 781-337-6311
　　　　　Fax: 781-337-6245
　　　　　E-mail: dthoompson@masspolicecorps.com

MINNESOTA GAY/LESBIAN/BISEXUAL/ TRANSGENDER EDUCATIONAL FUND

MINNESOTA GAY/LESBIAN/BISEXUAL/TRANSGENDER SCHOLARSHIP FUND • 481

The Minnesota Gay/Lesbian, Bisexual, Transgender (GLBT) scholarship fund, administered by (GLBT) Philanthrofund Foundation, annually awards students who are gay/lesbian, bisexual, transgender identified, from a GLBT family, and/or pursuing a GLBT course of study. Applicants must either be a Minnesota resident or be planning to study in Minnesota.

Award Scholarship for use in any year; not renewable. *Number:* 20–30. *Amount:* $500–$2500.
Eligibility Requirements: Applicant must be enrolled full or part-time at a two-year or four-year or technical institution or university. Available to U.S. and non-U.S. citizens.
Application Requirements Application, essay, photo, references, transcript, confidentiality statement, press release. *Deadline:* February 1.
World Wide Web: http://www.philanthrofund.org
Contact: Kit Briem, Executive Director
　　　　　Minnesota Gay/Lesbian/Bisexual/Transgender Educational Fund
　　　　　1409 Willow Street
　　　　　Suite 305
　　　　　Minneapolis, MN 55403
　　　　　Phone: 612-870-1806
　　　　　Fax: 612-871-6587
　　　　　E-mail: philanth@scc.net

MISSISSIPPI POLICE CORPS

MISSISSIPPI POLICE CORPS SCHOLARSHIP   • 482

Program designed to motivate highly qualified young people to serve as police officers and sheriffs' deputies in the municipalities and counties that need them the most. Federal scholarships offered on a competitive basis to college students who agree to serve where needed on community patrol for at least 4 years. Participants who seek baccalaureate degrees begin their work as officers shortly after graduation from college. Those who pursue graduate study complete their service in advance. Minimum 2.5 GPA required.

Award Scholarship for use in sophomore, junior, senior, graduate, or post graduate years; not renewable. *Number:* 65. *Amount:* $30,000.
Eligibility Requirements: Applicant must be enrolled full-time at a four-year institution or university. Applicant must have 2.5 GPA or higher. Available to U.S. citizens.
Application Requirements Application, driver's license, essay, interview, resume, references, test scores, transcript. *Deadline:* Continuous.
World Wide Web: http://www.mississippipolicecorps.org
Contact: Rick Weaver, Training Specialist
        Mississippi Police Corps
        c/o University of Southern Mississippi
        Box 5084
        Hattiesburg, MS 39406-5084
        Phone: 601-266-6770
        Fax: 601-266-6786
        E-mail: rick.weaver@usm.edu

NATIONAL ACADEMY OF AMERICAN SCHOLARS

EASLEY NATIONAL SCHOLARSHIPS   • 483

A series of pure, merit-based scholarships available for tuition, room, board, books, and academically-related supplies. Applicants must be high school seniors or equivalent home-school seniors and be U.S. citizen or permanent resident. Application periods are September 15 to May 1. For further information and applications, download applications from website at http://www.naas.org/senior1.htm or visit http://www.naas.org/. Application fee varies, up to $22. Applicants that request an application by mail must enclose a $3 handling fee and a self addressed stamped envelope.

Award Scholarship for use in any year; renewable. *Number:* 10–14. *Amount:* $200–$10,000.
Eligibility Requirements: Applicant must be high school student and planning to enroll full-time at a four-year institution or university. Available to U.S. citizens.
Application Requirements Application, self-addressed stamped envelope, download forms from website. *Fee:* $3.

Easley National Scholarships (continued)
World Wide Web: http://www.naas.org
Contact: Merit Committee, NAAS-I
National Academy of American Scholars
5196 Benito Street, Suite #15, Room A
Montclair, CA 91763-4028
E-mail: team_naas@yahoo.com

NATIONAL BETA CLUB

NATIONAL BETA CLUB SCHOLARSHIP • 484

Applicant must be in 12th grade and a member of the National Beta Club. Must be nominated by school chapter of the National Beta Club, therefore, applications will not be sent to the individual students. Renewable and nonrenewable awards available. Contact school Beta Club sponsor for more information. Application fee: $10.

Award Scholarship for use in freshman year; renewable. *Number:* 209. *Amount:* $1000–$3750.
Eligibility Requirements: Applicant must be high school student and planning to enroll full-time at a two-year or four-year institution or university.
Application Requirements Application, essay, references, test scores, transcript. *Fee:* $10. *Deadline:* December 10.
World Wide Web: http://www.betaclub.org
Contact: Beta Club Sponsor (School Faculty Adviser)
National Beta Club
151 Beta Club Way
Spartanburg, SC 29306-3012

NATIONAL FFA ORGANIZATION

NATIONAL FFA COLLEGE & VOCATIONAL/TECHNICAL SCHOOL SCHOLARSHIP PROGRAM • 485

The National FFA College and Vocational/Technical Scholarship Program currently offers nearly $2 million in money for students who are high school seniors planning to enroll in a full-time course of study at an accredited vocational-technical school, college or university. A smaller number of scholarships are also available to currently enrolled sophomores, juniors and seniors. Most of the awards require that you are an FFA member. However, there are awards offered to non-FFA and former FFA members who are going into the career fields mentioned above. In order to be considered, you will be judged on your academic record, extracurricular activities, volunteer community activities, work experience, a statement of career and educational goals, a counselor or advisor's evaluation and your degree of financial need. Majors may vary from the following career areas: Agriculture, Natural Resources, Communication, Education Specialists, Management, Financial Specialists, Marketing, Engineering, Science, Social Service Professionals and Related Industries.

Award Scholarship for use in any year; not renewable. *Number:* up to 1700. *Amount:* $1000–$10,000.
Eligibility Requirements: Applicant must be enrolled full-time at a two-year or four-year or technical institution or university. Available to U.S. citizens.
Application Requirements Application. *Deadline:* February 15.
World Wide Web: http://www.ffa.org
Contact: Scholarship Coordinator
National FFA Organization
PO Box 68960
Indianapolis, IN 46268-0960
Phone: 317-802-6060
Fax: 317-802-6061

NATIONAL INSTITUTES OF HEALTH

NIH UNDERGRADUATE SCHOLARSHIP PROGRAM FOR STUDENTS FROM DISADVANTAGED BACKGROUNDS • 486
The NIH Undergraduate Scholarship Program offers competitive scholarships to exceptional students from disadvantaged backgrounds who are committed to biomedical, behavioral and social science research careers at the NIH. Citizens of countries outside the U.S. are eligible applicants only if they are permanent residents or nationals. Minimum 3.5 GPA required.

Award Scholarship for use in freshman, sophomore, junior, or senior years; renewable. *Number:* 10–20. *Amount:* up to $20,000.
Eligibility Requirements: Applicant must be enrolled full-time at a four-year institution or university. Applicant must have 3.5 GPA or higher. Available to U.S. citizens.
Application Requirements Application, essay, financial need analysis, references, transcript. *Deadline:* February 28.
World Wide Web: http://ugsp.info.nih.gov
Contact: National Institutes of Health
NIH Office of Loan Repayment and Scholarships
2 Center Drive, MSC 0230
Bethesda, MD 20892-0230
Phone: 800-528-7689
Fax: 301-480-5481
E-mail: ugsp@nih.gov

NATIONAL MERIT SCHOLARSHIP CORPORATION

NATIONAL MERIT SCHOLARSHIP PROGRAM • 487
High school students enter by taking the Preliminary SAT/National Merit Scholar Qualifying Test, and by meeting other participation requirements. Those eligible are contacted through high school. Selection based on test scores, academic abilities, essay, activities, and recommendations. Some awards

are renewable. Contact counselor by fall of junior year for deadline. Participation requirements are available in the PAST/NMSQT Student Bulletin and on NMSE's website.

Award Scholarship for use in freshman year; renewable. *Number:* 9700. *Amount:* $500–$2000.
Eligibility Requirements: Applicant must be high school student and planning to enroll full-time at a four-year institution or university. Available to U.S. citizens.
Application Requirements Application, applicant must enter a contest, autobiography, essay, references, test scores, transcript.
World Wide Web: http://www.nationalmerit.org
Contact: High School Counselor
National Merit Scholarship Corporation
1560 Sherman Avenue, Suite 200
Evanston, IL 60201-4897

NATIONAL SCIENCE TEACHERS ASSOCIATION

TOSHIBA/NSTA EXPLORAVISION AWARDS PROGRAM • 488

Teams of students in grades K-12 consider the impact that science and technology have on society and how innovative thinking can change the future, then use their imaginations and the tools of science to envision new technologies. Students develop written proposals and web pages.

Award Prize for use in any year; not renewable. *Number:* 16–32. *Amount:* $5000–$10,000.
Eligibility Requirements: Applicant must be age 21 or under. Available to U.S. and Canadian citizens.
Application Requirements Application, applicant must enter a contest, essay. *Deadline:* February 3.
World Wide Web: http://www.nsta.org
Contact: Explora vision
National Science Teachers Association
1840 Wilson Boulevard
Arlington, VA 22201
Phone: 800-EXP-LOR9
Fax: 703-243-7177
E-mail: exploravision@nsta.org

NATIONAL TEEN-AGER SCHOLARSHIP FOUNDATION

NATIONAL TEEN-AGER SCHOLARSHIP FOUNDATION • 489

One-time award for young women of leadership and intellect. Award based on school and community leadership, communication skills, academics and personal presentation. 3-5 awards per state. Awards come in the form of savings bonds from $500-1000 and in cash from $5000-10,000. Must be between the ages of 12-18 and be a U.S. citizen. Minimum 3.0 GPA required. $15 application fee.

Award Scholarship for use in freshman year; not renewable. *Number:* 250–1510. *Amount:* $1000–$10,000.

Eligibility Requirements: Applicant must be age 12-18; enrolled full-time at a two-year or four-year institution or university and single female. Applicant must have 3.0 GPA or higher. Available to U.S. citizens.

Application Requirements Application, applicant must enter a contest, interview, photo, self-addressed stamped envelope, transcript. *Fee:* $15. *Deadline:* Continuous.

World Wide Web: http://www.nationalteen.com

Contact: Cheryl Snow, National Director
National Teen-Ager Scholarship Foundation
4708 Mill Crossing West
Colleyville, TX 76034
Phone: 817-577-2220
Fax: 817-428-7232
E-mail: csnow@dallas.net

NINETY-NINES, INC.

AMELIA EARHART MEMORIAL CAREER SCHOLARSHIP FUND
• 490

Scholarships are awarded to members of The Ninety-Nines, Inc. who hold a current medical certificate appropriate for the use of the certificate sought. Applicants must meet the requirements for pilot currency (Flight Review or non-US equivalent) and have financial need. Applicants must agree to complete the course, training and meet the requirements for ratings/certificates specific to the country where training will occur.

Award Scholarship for use in any year; not renewable. *Number:* 15–18. *Amount:* $2000–$10,000.

Eligibility Requirements: Applicant must be enrolled full-time at an institution or university and female. Available to U.S. and non-U.S. citizens.

Application Requirements Application, financial need analysis, photo, resume, references. *Deadline:* December 31.

World Wide Web: http://ninety-nines.org

Contact: Charlene H. Falkenberg, Chairman, Permanent Trustee
Ninety-Nines, Inc.
618 South Washington Street
Hobart, IN 46342-5026
Phone: 219-942-8887
Fax: 219-942-8887
E-mail: charf@prodigy.net

NORTH CAROLINA POLICE CORPS

NORTH CAROLINA POLICE CORPS SCHOLARSHIP   • 491

Selected participants must attend a four-year institution full-time. May receive up to $10,000 per year with a maximum of $30,000. Complete 24-week training course receiving $250 per week while in residence and serve four years in selected law enforcement agency. Must have physical, background investigation, drug test, and psychological evaluation.

Award Scholarship for use in freshman, sophomore, junior, senior, or graduate years; renewable. *Number:* 15–30. *Amount:* $10,000–$30,000.

Eligibility Requirements: Applicant must be enrolled full-time at a four-year institution or university. Available to U.S. citizens.

Application Requirements Application, autobiography, essay, interview, photo, references, test scores, transcript. *Deadline:* November 15.

World Wide Web: http://www.ncpolicecorps.org

Contact: Neil Woodcock, Director, NC Police Corps
North Carolina Police Corps
NC Department of Crime Control and Public Safety, 309
    Chapanoke Rd., Ste. 106
Raleigh, NC 27603-3431
Phone: 919-773-2823
Fax: 919-773-2845
E-mail: nwoodcock@nccrimecontrol.org

ORPHAN FOUNDATION OF AMERICA

OFA 2002 NATIONAL SCHOLARSHIP/CASEY FAMILY SCHOLARS   • 492

Scholarships are given to young people who were in foster care for at least one year at the time of their 18th birthday. Must be under 25 years old. Must have been accepted into an accredited postsecondary school or program. Must not currently be a Casey Family Program CEJT participant.

Award Scholarship for use in freshman, sophomore, junior, or senior years; not renewable. *Number:* 350. *Amount:* $2000–$6000.

Eligibility Requirements: Applicant must be age 24 or under and enrolled full or part-time at a two-year or four-year or technical institution or university. Available to U.S. and non-U.S. citizens.

Application Requirements Application, essay, financial need analysis, photo, references, transcript. *Deadline:* April 15.

World Wide Web: http://www.orphan.org

Contact: Tina Raheem, Office Manager
Orphan Foundation of America
12020—D North Shore Drive
Reston, VA 20190-4507
Phone: 571-203-0270
Fax: 571-203-0273
E-mail: tinar@orphan.org

PHILLIPS FOUNDATION

PHILLIPS FOUNDATION RONALD REAGAN FUTURE LEADERS PROGRAM • 493

The program offers renewable cash grants to college juniors and seniors who demonstrate leadership on behalf of the cause of freedom, American values, and constitutional principles. Winners will receive a grant for their junior year and may apply for renewal before their senior year.

Award Grant for use in junior or senior years; not renewable. *Number:* 10–20. *Amount:* $2500–$10,000.
Eligibility Requirements: Applicant must be enrolled full-time at a four-year institution or university. Available to U.S. citizens.
Application Requirements Application, essay, references. *Deadline:* January 15.
World Wide Web: http://www.thephillipsfoundation.org
Contact: Jeff Hollingsworth, Assistant Secretary
Phillips Foundation
7811 Montrose Road, Suite 100
Potomac, MD 20854
Phone: 301-340-7788 Ext. 6028
E-mail: jhollingsworth@phillips.com

POLISH NATIONAL ALLIANCE

POLISH NATIONAL ALLIANCE SCHOLARSHIP AWARD • 494

This program is awarded to Polish National Alliance members only. Must have a 3.0 GPA. Must currently be enrolled full-time in an accredited college as an undergraduate sophomore, junior or senior.

Award Scholarship for use in sophomore, junior, or senior years; renewable. *Number:* 200. *Amount:* $500.
Eligibility Requirements: Applicant must be enrolled full-time at a four-year institution. Applicant must have 3.0 GPA or higher. Available to U.S. citizens.
Application Requirements Application, photo, test scores, transcript. *Deadline:* April 15.
Contact: Polish National Alliance
Education Department
6100 North Cicero Avenue
Chicago, IL 60646

POLONIA GLOBAL FUND 9-11 SCHOLARSHIP FUND

POLONIA GLOBAL FUND 9-11 SCHOLARSHIP • 495

Funding granted to victims and families of victims of the 9-11 tragedy. 10 one-time awards for both full- or part-time study in any year.

Polonia Global Fund 9-11 Scholarship (continued)

Award Scholarship for use in any year; not renewable. *Number:* up to 10. *Amount:* up to $10,000.

Eligibility Requirements: Applicant must be enrolled full or part-time at an institution or university. Available to U.S. and non-U.S. citizens.

Application Requirements Application, autobiography, financial need analysis, interview, references. *Deadline:* Continuous.

World Wide Web: http://www.pgf.cc

Contact: James Konicki, Co-Chair
Polonia Global Fund 9-11 Scholarship Fund
PO Box 13833
Albany, NY 12212-3833
Phone: 518-765-2657
Fax: 518-765-2657
E-mail: administrator@pgf.cc

RETIRED OFFICERS ASSOCIATION EDUCATIONAL ASSISTANCE PROGRAM (TROA)

RETIRED OFFICERS ASSOCIATION SCHOLARSHIP 200 PROGRAM • 496

Scholarships are awarded to 200 applicants for full-time undergraduate study. Applicant must be 23 years old or child of active duty military member-officer or enlisted. Scholarship is merit-based for $1000. If applicant served in a uniform service before completing college, his or her maximum age or eligibility will increase by the number of years he or she has served up to five years. Must submit online application via TROA website.

Award Scholarship for use in freshman, sophomore, junior, or senior years; not renewable. *Number:* 200. *Amount:* $1000.

Eligibility Requirements: Applicant must be age 23 or under and enrolled full-time at a two-year or four-year institution or university. Available to U.S. citizens.

Application Requirements Application, test scores, transcript, service parent's Leave and Earnings Statement (LES). *Deadline:* March 1.

World Wide Web: http://www.troa.org

Contact: Trey Linnem, Program Development Officer
Retired Officers Association Educational Assistance Program
(TROA)
201 North Washington Street
Alexandria, VA 22314-2529
Phone: 703-838-1654
Fax: 703-838-5819
E-mail: edassist@troa.org

TALBOTS

TALBOTS WOMEN'S SCHOLARSHIP FUND • 497

One-time scholarship for women who earned their high school diploma or GED at least 10 years ago, and who are now seeking an undergraduate college degree.

Award Scholarship for use in freshman, sophomore, junior, or senior years; not renewable. *Number:* 5–50. *Amount:* $1000–$10,000.

Eligibility Requirements: Applicant must be enrolled full or part-time at a two-year or four-year or technical institution or university and female. Available to U.S. citizens.

Application Requirements Application, essay, financial need analysis, references, transcript. *Deadline:* April 2.

World Wide Web: http://www.talbots.com

Contact: Deb Johnson, Citizens Scholarship Foundation
Talbots
1505 Riverview Road, PO Box 297
Saint Peter, MN 56082
Phone: 507-931-1682

TERRY FOX HUMANITARIAN AWARD PROGRAM

TERRY FOX HUMANITARIAN AWARD see number 294

THETA NU EPSILON SOCIETY OF 1870/ NATIONAL ALUMNI ASSOCIATION

THETA NU EPSILON SOCIETY SCHOLARSHIP • 498

Scholarships are awarded to undergraduate or graduate students attending accredited institutions who are related to members of Theta Nu Epsilon. Must have a 2.5 GPA. Must be US citizen.

Award Scholarship for use in freshman, sophomore, junior, senior, or graduate years; renewable. *Number:* 10. *Amount:* $1000–$10,000.

Eligibility Requirements: Applicant must be enrolled full-time at a four-year institution or university. Applicant must have 2.5 GPA or higher. Available to U.S. citizens.

Application Requirements Application, financial need analysis, photo, resume, references, test scores, transcript, verification of member relationship. *Deadline:* Continuous.

World Wide Web: http://www.tne.org

Contact: Theta Nu Epsilon Society of 1870/National Alumni Association
3538 Central Avenue
Suite 2A
Riverside, CA 92506

THIRD WAVE FOUNDATION

SCHOLARSHIP FOR YOUNG WOMEN   • 499

Our scholarship program is available to all full-time or part-time female students age 30 and under who are enrolled in, or have been accepted to, an accredited university, college, or community college in the U.S. The primary criterion for funding is financial need. Students should also be involved as activists, artists, or cultural workers working on issues such as racism, homophobia, sexism, or other forms of inequality. Application deadlines are April 1 and October 1.

Award Grant for use in any year; not renewable. *Number:* 20–30. *Amount:* $500–$5000.

Eligibility Requirements: Applicant must be age 17-30; enrolled full or part-time at a two-year or four-year or technical institution or university and female. Applicant must have 2.5 GPA or higher. Available to U.S. and non-U.S. citizens.

Application Requirements Application, essay, financial need analysis, resume, references, transcript.

World Wide Web: http://www.thirdwavefoundation.org

Contact: Mia Herndon, Network Coordinator
Third Wave Foundation
116 East 16th Street, 7th Floor
New York, NY 10003
Phone: 212-388-1898
Fax: 212-983-3321
E-mail: info@thirdwavefoundation.org

THURGOOD MARSHALL SCHOLARSHIP FUND

THURGOOD MARSHALL SCHOLARSHIP   • 500

Merit scholarships for students attending 1 of 45 member HBPCU's (histori-cally black public colleges, universities) including 5 member law schools. Must maintain an average of 3.0 and have a financial need. Must be a U.S. citizen. 3.0 GPA required to renew. No applications accepted at TMSF. Must apply through the HBPCUs, through a campus scholarship coordinator.

Award Scholarship for use in freshman, sophomore, junior, or senior years; not renewable. *Number:* 50–100. *Amount:* $4400.

Eligibility Requirements: Applicant must be enrolled full-time at a four-year institution or university. Applicant must have 3.0 GPA or higher. Available to U.S. citizens.

Application Requirements Application, essay, interview, photo, references, test scores, transcript. *Deadline:* Continuous.

World Wide Web: http://www.thurgoodmarshallfund.org

Contact: Tawanna L. Whitehead, Manager of Scholarships
Thurgood Marshall Scholarship Fund
100 Park Avenue, 10th Floor
New York, NY 10017
Phone: 917-663-2276
Fax: 917-633-2988
E-mail: twhitehead@tmsf.org

USA TODAY

ALL-USA COLLEGE ACADEMIC TEAM • 501

$2500 prize for four-year college or university sophomores, juniors and seniors who excel in leadership roles both on and off campus. U.S. citizenship is not required but student must be enrolled at a U.S. institution and studying full-time. Students must be nominated by their schools. For more information go to: http://allstars.usatoday.com. Application deadline is November 30.

Award Prize for use in sophomore, junior, or senior years; not renewable. *Number:* 20. *Amount:* $2500.
Eligibility Requirements: Applicant must be enrolled full-time at a four-year institution or university. Available to U.S. and non-U.S. citizens.
Application Requirements Application, applicant must enter a contest, essay, references, transcript. *Deadline:* November 30.
World Wide Web: http://allstars.usatoday.com
Contact: Carol Skalski, Senior Administrator
USA Today
7950 Jones Branch Drive
McLean, VA 22102-3302
Phone: 703-854-5890

ALL-USA COMMUNITY & JR. COLLEGE ACADEMIC TEAM • 502

$2500 prize for community and junior college student. May be full-time or part-time student. Must be nominated by school. Application deadline: December 1. For more information, go to: allstars.usatoday.com or www.ptk.org/schol/aaat/announce.htm. Must be studying in the U.S. or its territories. Must maintain a 3.25 GPA.

Award Prize for use in freshman or sophomore years; not renewable. *Number:* 20. *Amount:* $2500.
Eligibility Requirements: Applicant must be enrolled full or part-time at a two-year institution. Available to U.S. and non-U.S. citizens.
Application Requirements Application, applicant must enter a contest, essay, references, transcript. *Deadline:* December 1.
World Wide Web: http://allstars.usatoday.com
Contact: Carol Skalski, Senior Administrator
USA Today
7950 Jones Branch Drive
McLean, VA 22102-3302
Phone: 703-854-5890

ALL-USA HIGH SCHOOL ACADEMIC TEAM • 503

$2500 prize given to high school students based upon an outstanding original academic, artistic or leadership endeavor. Students must be nominated by their schools. For more information, go to http://allstars.usatoday.com. Deadline is usually the third Friday in February.

Award Prize for use in any year; not renewable. *Number:* 20. *Amount:* $2500.

Eligibility Requirements: Applicant must be high school student and planning to enroll full-time at an institution or university. Available to U.S. and non-U.S. citizens.

Application Requirements Application, applicant must enter a contest, essay, references, test scores, transcript. *Deadline:* February 22.

World Wide Web: http://allstars.usatoday.com

Contact: Carol Skalski, Senior Administrator
USA Today
7950 Jones Branch Drive
McLean, VA 22102-3302
Phone: 703-854-5890

WAL-MART FOUNDATION

SAM WALTON COMMUNITY SCHOLARSHIP • 504

Award for high school seniors not affiliated with Wal-Mart stores. Based on academic merit, financial need, and school or work activities. Each store awards one nonrenewable scholarship. For use at an accredited two- or four-year U.S. institution. Must have 2.5 GPA. Applications available only through local Wal-Mart or Sam's Club stores starting in January. Applications are not available from the corporate office.

Award Scholarship for use in freshman year; not renewable. *Number:* 2900–3400. *Amount:* $1000.

Eligibility Requirements: Applicant must be high school student and planning to enroll full-time at a two-year or four-year institution or university. Applicant must have 2.5 GPA or higher. Available to U.S. citizens.

Application Requirements Application, essay, financial need analysis, test scores, transcript. *Deadline:* March 1.

World Wide Web: http://www.walmartfoundation.org

Contact: Jenny Harral
Wal-Mart Foundation
702 Southwest 8th Street
Bentonville, AR 72716-0150
Phone: 800-530-9925
Fax: 501-273-6850

WASHINGTON STATE PARENT TEACHER ASSOCIATION SCHOLARSHIPS FOUNDATION

WASHINGTON STATE PARENT TEACHER ASSOCIATION SCHOLARSHIPS FOUNDATION • 505

One-time scholarships for students who have graduated from a public high school in state of Washington, and who greatly need financial help to begin full-time postsecondary education. For entering freshmen only.

Award Scholarship for use in freshman year; not renewable. *Number:* 60–80. *Amount:* $1000–$2000.

Eligibility Requirements: Applicant must be enrolled full-time at a two-year or four-year or technical institution or university. Available to U.S. and non-U.S. citizens.

Application Requirements Application, essay, financial need analysis, references, transcript. *Deadline:* March 1.

World Wide Web: http://www.wastatepta.org

Contact: Jean Carpenter, Executive Director
Washington State Parent Teacher Association Scholarships
Foundation
2003 65th Avenue, W
Tacoma, WA 98466-6215

WELLS FARGO EDUCATION FINANCIAL SERVICES

COLLEGE STEPS • 506

CollegeSTEPS offer 250 $1,000 scholarships annually to high school students. Winners are chosen through random drawings, so all students have an equal chance to win. The program also provides timely information preparing for college, taking standardized tests, and applying for financial aid.

Award Scholarship for use in freshman year; not renewable. *Number:* 250. *Amount:* $1000.

Eligibility Requirements: Applicant must be high school student and planning to enroll full or part-time at a two-year or four-year or technical institution or university. Available to U.S. citizens.

Application Requirements Application. *Deadline:* Continuous.

World Wide Web: http://www.wellsfargo.com/student

Contact: Staci Schiller, Product Manager
Wells Fargo Education Financial Services
301 East 58th Street North
Sioux Falls, SD 57104-0422
Phone: 605-575-4649
Fax: 605-575-4550
E-mail: staci.schiller@wellsfargoefs.com

WOODMEN OF THE WORLD

WOODMEN OF THE WORLD SCHOLARSHIP PROGRAM • 507

One-time award for full-time study at a trade/technical school, two-year college, four-year college or university. Applicant must be a member, child of a member or grandchild of a member of Woodman of the World of Denver, Colorado. Applicant must have minimum 2.5 GPA.

Award Scholarship for use in any year; not renewable. *Number:* 65. *Amount:* $500–$2500.

Eligibility Requirements: Applicant must be enrolled full-time at a two-year or four-year or technical institution or university. Applicant must have 2.5 GPA or higher. Available to U.S. citizens.

Application Requirements Application, essay, photo, transcript. *Deadline:* March 15.

World Wide Web: http://www.denverwoodmen.com

Contact: Scholarship Committee
Woodmen of the World
PO Box 266000
Highlands Ranch, CO 80163-6000
Phone: 303-792-9777
Fax: 303-792-9793

Profiles of State-Sponsored Programs

Each state government has established one or more financial aid programs for qualified students. In many instances, these state programs are restricted to legal residents of the state. However, some are available to out-of-state students attending colleges within the state. In addition to residential status, other qualifications frequently exist.

Each of the fifty states' and District of Columbia's gift aid and forgivable loan programs that are open to undergraduate students are described in this section. They are arranged in alphabetical order, first by state name, then by program name. The annotation for each program provides information about the program, eligibility, and the contact addresses for applications or further information.

Students or parents should write to the address given for each program to request that award details for 2002–03 be sent to them as soon as these are available. Descriptive information brochures and application forms for state scholarship programs are usually available in your high school guidance office or from a college financial aid office in your state. Increasingly, state government agencies are putting state scholarship information on their Web sites. Also, the financial aid page of state-administered college or university sites frequently has a list of state-sponsored scholarships and financial aid programs. College and university Web sites can be accessed easily through Peterson's Education Center (www.petersons.com).

Names of scholarship program frequently are used inconsistently or become abbreviated in use. Many programs have variant names by which they are known. The program's sponsor has approved the title of the program that Peterson's uses. However, this name sometimes differs from the program's official name or from the most commonly used name.

States may also offer internship or work-study programs, graduate fellowships and grants, or low-interest loans in addition to the grant aid and forgivable loans programs listed here. If you are interested in learning more about these other kinds of programs, the state higher education office should be able to provide information.

ALABAMA

Alabama National Guard Educational Assistance Program. Renewable award aids Alabama residents who are members of the Alabama National Guard and are enrolled in an accredited college in Alabama. Forms must be signed by a representative of the Alabama Military Department and financial aid officer. Recipient must be in a degree-seeking program. **Award:** Grant for use in freshman, sophomore, junior, senior, or graduate year; renewable. *Award amount:* up to $1000. **Eligibility Requirements:** Applicant must be enrolled full or part-time at a two-year, four-year, or technical institution or university; resident of Alabama and studying in Alabama. Available to U.S. citizens. Applicant must have served in the Air Force National Guard or Army National Guard. **Application Requirements:** Application. **Contact:** Dr. William Wall, Associate Executive Director for Student Assistance, Alabama Commission on Higher Education, PO Box 302000, Montgomery, AL 36130-2000. *Web site:* www.ache. state.al.us.

American Legion Auxiliary Department of Alabama Scholarship Program. Merit-based scholarships for Alabama residents, preferably ages 17-25, who are children or grandchildren of veterans of World War I, World War II, Korea, Vietnam, Operation Desert Storm, Beirut, Grenada, or Panama. Submit proof of relationship and service record. Renewable awards of $850 each. Send self-addressed stamped envelope for application. **Award:** Scholarship for use in any year; renewable. *Award amount:* $850. *Number of awards:* 40. **Eligibility Requirements:** Applicant must be age 17-25; enrolled full or part-time at a four-year institution; resident of Alabama and studying in Alabama. Applicant must have 3.5 GPA or higher. Available to U.S. citizens. Applicant or parent must meet one or more of the following requirements: general military experience; retired from active duty; disabled or killed as a result of military service; Prisoner-Of-War; or Missing-In-Action. **Application Requirements:** Application, financial need analysis, photo, references, self-addressed stamped envelope, test scores, transcript. **Deadline:** April 1. **Contact:** Dola Meckler, Department Secretary, American Legion Auxiliary, Department of Alabama, 120 North Jackson Street, Montgomery, AL 36104-3811. *Phone:* 334-262-1176.

Alabama G.I. Dependents Scholarship Program. Full scholarship for dependents of Alabama disabled, Prisoner-Of-War, or Missing-In-Action veterans. Child or stepchild must initiate training before 26th birthday; age 30 deadline may apply in certain situations. No age deadline for spouses or widows. Contact for application procedures and deadline. **Award:** Scholarship for use in freshman, sophomore, junior, senior, or graduate year; renewable. *Award amount:* up to $7000. **Eligibility Requirements:** Applicant must be enrolled full or part-time at a two-year, four-year, or technical institution or university; resident of Alabama and studying in Alabama. Available to U.S. and non-U.S. citizens. Applicant or parent must meet one or more of the following requirements: general military experience; retired from active duty; disabled or killed as a result of military service; Prisoner-Of-War; or Missing-In-Action. **Application Requirements:** Application. **Contact:** Willy E. Moore, Scholarship Administrator, Alabama Department of Veteran's Affairs, PO Box 1509, Montgomery, AL 36102-1509. *E-mail:* wmoore@va.state.al.us. *Phone:* 334-242-5077. *Fax:* 334-242-5102. *Web site:* www.va.state.al.us/scholarship.htm.

Math and Science Scholarship Program for Alabama Teachers. For full-time students pursuing teaching certificates in mathematics, general science, biology, or physics. Applicants must agree to teach for five years (if a position is offered) in a targeted system with critical needs. Renewable if recipient continues to meet the requirements. Minimum 3.0 GPA required. Must be resident of Alabama and attend school in Alabama. **Academic/Career Areas:** Biology; Earth Science; Meteorology/Atmospheric Science; Natural Sciences; Physical Sciences and Math. **Award:** Forgivable loan for use in junior or senior year; renewable. *Award amount:* $4000. **Eligibility Requirements:** Applicant must be enrolled full-time at an institution or university; resident of Alabama and studying in Alabama. Applicant must have 3.0 GPA or higher. Available to U.S. citizens. **Application Requirements:** Application. **Contact:** Dr. Jayne Meyer, Assistant Superintendent, Alabama State Department of Education, Special Education Services, PO Box 302101, Montgomery, AL 36130-2101. *Phone:* 334-242-9560.

Police Officers and Firefighters Survivors Education Assistance Program-Alabama. Provides tuition, fees, books, and supplies to dependents of full-time police officers and firefighters killed in the line of duty. Must attend any Alabama public college as an undergraduate. Must be Alabama resident. Renewable. **Award:** Grant for use in freshman, sophomore, junior, or senior year; renewable. *Award amount:* $2000–$5000. *Number of awards:* 15–30. **Eligibility Requirements:** Applicant must be enrolled full or part-time at a two-year, four-year, or technical institution or university; single; resident of Alabama; studying in Alabama and have employment experience in police/firefighting. Available to U.S. citizens. **Application Requirements:** Application, transcript. **Contact:** Dr. William Wall, Associate Executive Director for Student Assistance, ACHE, Alabama Commission on Higher Education, PO Box 302000, Montgomery, AL 36130-2000. *Web site:* www.ache.state.al.us.

Alabama Student Grant Program. Renewable awards available to Alabama residents for undergraduate study at certain independent colleges within the state. Both full-time and half-time students are eligible. Deadlines: September 15, January 15, and February 15. **Award:** Grant for use in freshman, sophomore, junior, or senior year; renewable. *Award amount:* up to $1200. **Eligibility Requirements:** Applicant must be enrolled full or part-time at a four-year institution; resident of Alabama and studying in Alabama. Available to U.S. citizens. **Application Requirements:** Application. **Contact:** Dr. William Wall, Associate Executive Director for Student Assistance, ACHE, Alabama Commission on Higher Education, PO Box 302000, Montgomery, AL 36130-2000. *Web site:* www.ache.state.al.us.

ALASKA

Michael Murphy Memorial Scholarship Loan Fund. Assists full-time undergraduate or graduate students enrolled in a program relating to law enforcement. Recipient receives forgiveness of 20 percent of the full loan amount for each year employed in law enforcement. Must be Alaska resident. **Academic/Career Areas:** Criminal Justice/Criminology; Law Enforcement/Police Administration; Social Services. **Award:** Forgivable loan for use in any year; renewable. *Award amount:* up to $1000. *Number of awards:* 3–6. **Eligibility Requirements:** Applicant must be enrolled full-time at a two-year or four-year institution or university and resident of Alaska. Available to U.S. citizens. **Application Requirements:** Application. **Deadline:** April 1. **Contact:** Rodney Dial, Lieutenant, Alaska State Troopers, 5700 East Tudor Road, Anchorage, AK 99507. *E-mail:* rodney_dial@dps.state.ak.us. *Phone:* 907-269-5759. *Fax:* 907-269-5751. *Web site:* www.dps.state.ak.us/ast.

Alaska Commission on Postsecondary Education Teacher Education Scholarship Loan. Renewable loans for Alaska residents who are graduates of an Alaskan high school and pursuing teaching careers in rural elementary and secondary schools in Alaska. Must be nominated by rural school district. Eligible for 100% forgiveness if loan recipient teaches in Alaska upon graduation. Several awards of up to $7500 each. Must maintain good standing at institution. Contact for deadline. **Academic/Career Areas:** Education. **Award:** Forgivable loan for use in freshman, sophomore, junior, or senior year; renewable. *Award amount:* up to $7500. *Number of awards:* 100. **Eligibility Requirements:** Applicant must be enrolled full-time at a four-year institution or university; resident of Alaska and studying in Alaska. **Application Requirements:** Application, transcript. **Contact:** Lori Stedman, Administrative Assistant, Special Programs, Alaska Commission on Postsecondary Education, 3030 Vintage Boulevard, Juneau, AK 99801-7100. *Phone:* 907-465-6741. *Fax:* 907-465-5316. *Web site:* www.state.ak.us/acpe/.

Western Undergraduate Exchange (WUE) Program. Program allowing Alaska residents to enroll at two-or four-year institutions in participating states at a reduced tuition level, which is the in-state tuition plus 50% of that amount. To be used for full-time undergraduate studies. Contact for application procedures, requirements, deadlines, and further information. **Award:** Grant for use in freshman, sophomore, junior, or senior year; renewable. **Eligibility Requirements:** Applicant must be enrolled full-time at a two-year or four-year institution and resident of Alaska. **Contact:** Lori Stedman, Administrative Assistant, Special Programs, Alaska Commission on Postsecondary Education, 3030 Vintage Boulevard, Juneau, AK 99801-7100. *Phone:* 907-465-6741. *Fax:* 907-465-5316. *Web site:* www.state.ak.us/acpe/.

ARKANSAS

Emergency Secondary Education Loan Program. Must be Arkansas resident enrolled full-time in approved Arkansas institution. Renewable award for students majoring in secondary math, chemistry, physics, biology, physical science, general science, special education, or foreign language. Must teach in Arkansas at least five years. Must rank in upper half of class or have a minimum 2.5 GPA. **Academic/Career Areas:** Biology; Education; Foreign Language; Physical Sciences and Math; Special Education. **Award:** Forgivable loan for use in sophomore, junior, senior, or graduate year; renewable. *Award amount:* up to $2500. *Number of awards:* up to 50. **Eligibility Requirements:** Applicant must be enrolled full-time at a two-year or four-year institution or university; resident of Arkansas and studying in Arkansas. Applicant must have 2.5 GPA or higher. Available to U.S. citizens. **Application Requirements:** Application, transcript. **Deadline:** April 1. **Contact:** Assistant Coordinator, Arkansas Department of Higher Education, 114 East Capitol, Little Rock, AR 72201. *Phone:* 501-371-2050. *Fax:* 501-371-2001. *Web site:* www.arscholarships.com.

Arkansas Student Assistance Grant Program. Award for Arkansas residents attending a college within the state. Must be enrolled full-time, have financial need, and maintain satisfactory progress. One-time award for undergraduate use only. Application is the FAFSA. **Award:** Grant for use in freshman, sophomore, junior, or senior year; not renewable. *Award amount:* $100–$600. *Number of awards:* 7000–10,000. **Eligibility Requirements:** Applicant must be enrolled full-time at a two-year, four-year, or technical institution or university; resident of Arkansas and studying in Arkansas. **Application Requirements:** Application, financial need analysis. **Deadline:** April 1. **Contact:** Assistant Coordinator, Arkansas Department of Higher Education, 114 East Capitol, Little Rock, AR 72201. *Phone:* 501-371-2050. *Fax:* 501-371-2001. *Web site:* www.arscholarships. com.

Arkansas Academic Challenge Scholarship Program. Awards for Arkansas residents who are graduating high school seniors to study at an Arkansas institution. Must have at least a 2.75 GPA, meet minimum ACT composite score standards, and have financial need. Renewable up to three additional years. **Award:** Scholarship for use in freshman, sophomore, junior, or senior year; renewable. *Award amount:* up to $2500. **Eligibility Requirements:** Applicant must be high school student; planning to enroll full-time at a two-year or four-year institution or university; resident of Arkansas and studying in Arkansas. **Application Requirements:** Application, financial need analysis, test scores, transcript. **Deadline:** June 1. **Contact:** Assistant Coordinator, Arkansas Department of Higher Education, 114 East Capitol, Little Rock, AR 72201. *Phone:* 501-371-2050. *Fax:* 501-371-2001. *Web site:* www.arscholarships.com.

Second Effort Scholarship. Awarded to those scholars who achieved one of the 10 highest scores on the Arkansas High School Diploma Test (GED). Must be at least age 18 and not have graduated from high school. Students do not apply for this award, they are contacted by the Arkansas Department of Higher Education. **Award:** Scholarship for use in freshman, sophomore, junior, or senior year; renewable. *Award amount:* up to $1000. *Number of awards:* 10. **Eligibility Requirements:** Applicant must be age 18; enrolled full or part-time at an institution or university; resident of Arkansas and studying in Arkansas. Applicant must have 2.5 GPA or higher. **Application Requirements:** Application. **Contact:** Melissa Goff, Manager of Financial Aid, Arkansas Department of Higher Education, 114 East Capitol, Little Rock, AR 72201. *E-mail:* melissag@adhe.arknet.edu. *Phone:* 501-371-2050. *Fax:* 501-371-2001. *Web site:* www.arscholarships.com.

Arkansas Health Education Grant Program (ARHEG). Award provides assistance to Arkansas residents studying dentistry, optometry, veterinary medicine, podiatry, chiropractic medicine, or osteopathic medicine at out-of-state, accredited institutions (programs that are unavailable in Arkansas). **Academic/Career Areas:** Animal/Veterinary Sciences; Dental Health/Services; Health and Medical Sciences. **Award:** Grant for use in any year; not renewable. **Eligibility Requirements:** Applicant must be enrolled full-time at a four-year institution or university and resident of Arkansas. Available to U.S. citizens. **Application Requirements:** Application. **Contact:** Ms. Judy McAinsh, Coordinator, Arkansas Department of Higher Education, 114 East Capitol, Little Rock, AR 72201-3818. *E-mail:* judym@adhe.arknet.edu. *Phone:* 501-371-2013. *Fax:* 501-371-2002. *Web site:* www.arscholarships.com.

Teacher and Administrator Grant Program–Arkansas. Reimbursement program for certified teachers and administrators who wish to continue their education and improve their professional skills. Program available for use only during the summer months. For Arkansas resident attending Arkansas institution. **Award:** Grant for use in any year; not renewable. *Award amount:* $150–$650. *Number of awards:* 350–450. **Eligibility Requirements:** Applicant must be enrolled at a four-year institution or university; resident of Arkansas; studying in Arkansas and have employment experience in teaching. **Application Requirements:** Application. **Contact:** Assistant Coordinator, Arkansas Department of Higher Education, 114 East Capitol, Little Rock, AR 72201. *Phone:* 501-371-2050. *Fax:* 501-371-2001. *Web site:* www.arscholarships.com.

Arkansas Minority Teacher Scholars Program. Renewable award for Native American, African-American, Hispanic and Asian-American students who have completed at least 60 semester hours and are enrolled full-time in a teacher education program in Arkansas. Award may be renewed for one year. Must be Arkansas resident with minimum 2.5 GPA. Must teach for three to five years in Arkansas to repay scholarship funds received. Must pass PPST exam. **Academic/ Career Areas:** Education. **Award:** Forgivable loan for use in junior or senior year; renewable. *Award amount:* up to $5000. *Number of awards:* up to 100. **Eligibility Requirements:** Applicant must be Native American or Eskimo, Asian, African American, or Hispanic; enrolled full-time at a four-year institution or university; resident of Arkansas and studying in Arkansas. Applicant must have 2.5 GPA or higher. Available to U.S. citizens. **Application Requirements:** Application, transcript. **Deadline:** June 1. **Contact:** Lillian Williams, Assistant Coordinator, Arkansas Department of Higher Education, 114 East Capitol, Little Rock, AR 72201. *Phone:* 501-371-2050. *Fax:* 501-371-2001. *Web site:* www. arscholarships.com.

Law Enforcement Officers' Dependents Scholarship–Arkansas. For dependents, under 23 years old, of Arkansas law-enforcement officers killed or permanently disabled in the line of duty. Renewable award is a waiver of tuition, fees, and room at two- or four-year Arkansas institution. Submit birth certificate, death certificate, and claims commission report of findings of fact. Proof of disability from State Claims Commission may also be submitted. **Award:** Scholarship for use in freshman, sophomore, junior, or senior year; renewable. *Award amount:* $2000–$2500. *Number of awards:* 27–32. **Eligibility Requirements:** Applicant must be age 23 or under; enrolled full or part-time at a two-year or four-year institution or university; resident of Arkansas; studying in Arkansas and have employment experience in police/firefighting. Available to U.S. citizens. **Application Requirements:** Application. **Deadline:** continuous. **Contact:** Lillian Williams, Assistant Coordinator, Arkansas Department of Higher Education, 114 East Capitol, Little Rock, AR 72201. *E-mail:* lillianw@adhe.arknet. edu. *Phone:* 501-371-2050. *Fax:* 501-371-2001. *Web site:* www.arscholarships. com.

Missing-in-Action/Killed-in-Action Dependent's Scholarship–Arkansas. Available to Arkansas residents whose parent or spouse was classified either as Missing-In-Action, killed in action or a Prisoner-Of-War. Must attend state-supported institution in Arkansas. Renewable waiver of tuition, fees, room and board. Submit proof of casualty. **Award:** Scholarship for use in any year; renewable. *Award amount:* up to $2500. **Eligibility Requirements:** Applicant must be enrolled full-time at a two-year, four-year, or technical institution or university; resident of Arkansas and studying in Arkansas. Available to U.S. citizens. Applicant or parent must meet one or more of the following requirements: general military experience; retired from active duty; disabled or killed as a result of military service; Prisoner-Of-War; or Missing-In-Action. **Application Requirements:** Application. **Deadline:** continuous. **Contact:** Assistant Coordinator, Arkansas Department of Higher Education, 114 East Capitol, Little Rock, AR 72201. *Phone:* 501-371-2050. *Fax:* 501-371-2001. *Web site:* www. arscholarships.com.

Governor's Scholars–Arkansas. Awards for outstanding Arkansas high school seniors. Must be an Arkansas resident and have a high school GPA of at least 3.5 or have scored at least 27 on the ACT. Award is $4000 per year for four years of full-time undergraduate study. Applicants who attain 32 or above on ACT, 1410 or above on SAT and have an academic 3.50 GPA, or are selected as National Merit or National Achievement finalists may receive an award equal to tuition, mandatory fees, room, and board up to $10K/year at any Arkansas institution. **Award:** Scholarship for use in freshman, sophomore, junior, or senior year; renewable. *Award amount:* $4000–$17,690. *Number of awards:* 75–250. **Eligibility Requirements:** Applicant must be high school student; planning to enroll full-time at a two-year or four-year institution or university; resident of Arkansas and studying in Arkansas. Applicant must have 3.5 GPA or higher. Available to U.S. citizens. **Application Requirements:** Application, test scores, transcript. **Deadline:** February 1. **Contact:** Melissa Goff, Manager of Student Financial Aid, Arkansas Department of Higher Education, 114 East Capitol, Little Rock, AR 72201. *E-mail:* melissag@adhe.arknet.edu. *Phone:* 501-371-2050. *Fax:* 501-371-2001. *Web site:* www.arscholarships.com.

CALIFORNIA

California State University Real Estate Scholarship and Internship Grant Program. Targeted at low income and educationally disadvantaged undergraduate and graduate students at one of twenty-three California State University campuses. Must be enrolled at least half-time in a program related to land use or real estate. Minimum GPA is 2.5 for undergraduate students and 3.0 for graduate students. **Academic/Career Areas:** Architecture; Business/Consumer Services; Civil Engineering; Landscape Architecture; Real Estate. **Award:** Scholarship for use in any year; not renewable. *Award amount:* $500–$2350. *Number of awards:* 22–31. **Eligibility Requirements:** Applicant must be enrolled full or part-time at a four-year institution or university and studying in California. Applicant must have 2.5 GPA or higher. Available to U.S. citizens. **Application Requirements:** Application, essay, financial need analysis, transcript. **Deadline:** continuous. **Contact:** Pam Amundsen, Project Manager, Real Estate and Land Use Institute, 7700 College Town Drive, Suite 200, Sacramento, CA 95826-2304. *E-mail:* amundsenpl@csus.edu. *Phone:* 916-278-6633. *Fax:* 916-278-4500.

Cooperative Agencies Resources for Education Program. Renewable award available to California resident attending a two-year California community college. Must have no more than 70 degree-applicable units, currently receive CALWORKS/TANF, and have at least one child under 14 years of age. Must be in EOPS, single head of household, and 18 or older. Contact local college EOPS-CARE office. **Award:** Grant for use in freshman or sophomore year; renewable.

Number of awards: 11,000. **Eligibility Requirements:** Applicant must be age 18; enrolled full-time at a two-year institution; single; resident of California; studying in California and member of Extended Opportunity Program Service. Available to U.S. citizens. **Application Requirements:** Application, financial need analysis, test scores, transcript. **Deadline:** continuous. **Contact:** Local Community College EOPS/CARE Program, California Community Colleges, 1102 Q Street, Sacramento, CA 95814-6511. *Web site:* www.cccco.edu.

Japanese Studies Scholarship. One-time award open to university-enrolled students ages 18 through 29. (university must be outside Japan). One-year course designed to develop Japanese language aptitude and knowledge of the country's culture, areas which the applicant must currently be studying. Scholarship comprises transportation, accommodations, medical expenses and monthly and arrival allowances. Contact for more information. **Academic/Career Areas:** Area/Ethnic Studies. **Award:** Scholarship for use in freshman, sophomore, junior, or senior year; not renewable. **Eligibility Requirements:** Applicant must be age 18-29; enrolled full-time at an institution or university and must have an interest in Japanese language. Available to U.S. and non-U.S. citizens. **Application Requirements:** Application, autobiography, essay, interview, photo, references, test scores, transcript. **Contact:** Japanese Government/The Monbusho Scholarship Program, 350 South Grand Avenue, Suite 1700, Los Angeles, CA 90071. *Web site:* embjapan.org/la.

COLORADO

Colorado Student Grant. Assists Colorado residents attending eligible public, private, or vocational institutions within the state. Application deadlines vary by institution. Renewable award for undergraduates. Contact the financial aid office at the college/institution for more information and an application. **Award:** Grant for use in freshman, sophomore, junior, or senior year; renewable. **Eligibility Requirements:** Applicant must be enrolled at a two-year, four-year, or technical institution or university; resident of Colorado and studying in Colorado. **Application Requirements:** Application, financial need analysis. **Contact:** Financial Aid Office at college/institution, Colorado Commission on Higher Education, 1380 Lawrence Street, Suite 1200, Denver, CO 80204-2059. *Web site:* www.state.co.us/cche.

Law Enforcement/POW/MIA Dependents Scholarship–Colorado. Aid available for dependents of Colorado law enforcement officers, fire or national guard personnel killed or disabled in the line of duty, and for dependents of Prisoner-Of-War or service personnel listed as Missing-In-Action. Award covers tuition and room and board. **Award:** Scholarship for use in freshman, sophomore, junior, or senior year; renewable. **Eligibility Requirements:** Applicant must be enrolled full or part-time at a two-year, four-year, or technical institution or university. Applicant must have 2.5 GPA or higher. **Application Requirements:** Application. **Deadline:** continuous. **Contact:** Rita Beachem, Colorado Commission on Higher Education, 1380 Lawrence Street, Suite 1200, Denver, CO 80204. *Phone:* 303-866-2723. *Fax:* 303-866-4266. *Web site:* www.state.co.us/cche.

Colorado Nursing Scholarships. Renewable awards for Colorado residents pursuing nursing education programs at Colorado state-supported institutions. Applicant must agree to practice nursing in Colorado upon graduation. Contact colleges for complete information and deadlines. **Academic/Career Areas:** Nursing. **Award:** Scholarship for use in freshman, sophomore, junior, or senior year; not renewable. *Number of awards:* 100. **Eligibility Requirements:** Applicant must be enrolled full or part-time at a two-year, four-year, or technical institution or university; resident of Colorado and studying in Colorado. **Application Requirements:** Application, financial need analysis. **Deadline:** April 1. **Contact:** Financial Aid Office at college/institution, Colorado Commission on Higher Education, 1380 Lawrence Street, Suite 1200, Denver, CO 80204-2059. *Web site:* www.state.co.us/cche.

Colorado Leveraging Educational Assistance Partnership (CLEAP) and SLEAP. Renewable awards for Colorado residents who are attending Colorado state-supported postsecondary institutions at the undergraduate level. Must document financial need. Contact colleges for complete information and deadlines. **Award:** Grant for use in freshman, sophomore, junior, or senior year; not renewable. *Award amount:* $50–$900. *Number of awards:* 2000–2500. **Eligibility Requirements:** Applicant must be enrolled full or part-time at a two-year, four-year, or technical institution or university; resident of Colorado and studying in Colorado. Available to U.S. citizens. **Application Requirements:** Application, financial need analysis. **Contact:** Financial Aid Office at college/institution, Colorado Commission on Higher Education, 1380 Lawrence Street, Suite 1200, Denver, CO 80204-2059. *Web site:* www.state.co.us/cche.

Colorado Undergraduate Merit Scholarships. Renewable awards for students attending Colorado state-supported institutions at the undergraduate level. Must demonstrate superior scholarship or talent. Contact college financial aid office for complete information and deadlines. **Award:** Scholarship for use in freshman, sophomore, junior, or senior year; renewable. **Eligibility Requirements:** Applicant must be enrolled at a two-year, four-year, or technical institution or university and studying in Colorado. Applicant must have 3.0 GPA or higher. **Application Requirements:** Application. **Contact:** Financial Aid Office at college/institution, Colorado Commission on Higher Education, 1380 Lawrence Street, Suite 1200, Denver, CO 80204-2059. *Web site:* www.state.co.us/cche.

Western Undergraduate Exchange Program. Residents of Arkansas, Colorado, Hawaii, Idaho, Montana, Nevada, New Mexico, North Dakota, Oregon, South Dakota, Utah, Washington and Wyoming can enroll in designated two- and four-year undergraduate programs at institutions in participating states at reduced tuition level (resident tuition plus half). Contact Western Interstate Commission for Higher Education for list and deadlines. **Award:** Scholarship for use in freshman, sophomore, junior, or senior year; renewable. **Eligibility Requirements:** Applicant must be enrolled full-time at a two-year or four-year institution; resident of Alaska, Colorado, Hawaii, Idaho, Montana, Nevada, New Mexico, North Dakota, Oregon, South Dakota, Utah, Washington, or Wyoming and studying in Alaska, Colorado, Hawaii, Idaho, Montana, Nevada, New Mexico, North Dakota, Oregon, South Dakota, Utah, or Wyoming. Available to U.S. citizens. **Application Requirements:** Application. **Contact:** Ms. Sandy Jackson, Program Coordinator, Western Interstate Commission for Higher Education, PO Box 9752, Boulder, CO 80301-9752. *E-mail:* info-sep@wiche.edu. *Phone:* 303-541-0210. *Fax:* 303-541-0291. *Web site:* www.wiche.edu.

CONNECTICUT

Connecticut Independent College Student Grants. Award for Connecticut residents attending an independent college or university within the state on at least a half-time basis. Renewable awards based on financial need. Application deadline varies by institution. Apply at college financial aid office. **Award:** Grant for use in any year; renewable. *Award amount:* up to $8600. **Eligibility Requirements:** Applicant must be enrolled full or part-time at a two-year or four-year institution or university; resident of Connecticut and studying in Connecticut. **Application Requirements:** Application, financial need analysis, transcript. **Contact:** John Siegrist, Financial Aid Office, Connecticut Department of Higher Education, 61 Woodland Street, Hartford, CT 06105-2326. *Phone:* 860-947-1855. *Fax:* 860-947-1311. *Web site:* www.ctdhe.org.

Aid for Public College Students Grant Program/Connecticut. Award for students at Connecticut public college or university. Must be state residents and enrolled at least half-time. Renewable award based on financial need and academic progress. Application deadlines vary by institution. Apply at college financial aid office. **Award:** Grant for use in any year; renewable. **Eligibility Requirements:** Applicant must be enrolled full or part-time at a two-year or four-year institution or university; resident of Connecticut and studying in Connecticut. **Application Requirements:** Application, financial need analysis, transcript. **Contact:** John Siegrist, Financial Aid Office, Connecticut Department of Higher Education, 61 Woodland Street, Hartford, CT 06105-2326. *Phone:* 860-947-1855. *Fax:* 860-947-1311. *Web site:* www.ctdhe.org.

Connecticut Tuition Waiver for Senior Citizens. Renewable tuition waiver for a Connecticut senior citizen age 62 or older to use at an accredited two- or four-year public institution in Connecticut. Must show financial need and prove senior citizen status. Award for undergraduate study only. Must be enrolled in credit courses. **Award:** Grant for use in freshman, sophomore, junior, or senior year; renewable. **Eligibility Requirements:** Applicant must be age 62; enrolled at a two-year or four-year institution; resident of Connecticut and studying in Connecticut. **Application Requirements:** Application, financial need analysis. **Deadline:** continuous. **Contact:** John Siegrist, Financial Aid Office, Connecticut Department of Higher Education, 61 Woodland Street, Hartford, CT 06105-2326. *Phone:* 860-947-1855. *Fax:* 860-947-1311. *Web site:* www.ctdhe. org.

Capitol Scholarship Program. Award for Connecticut residents attending eligible institutions in Connecticut or in a state with reciprocity with Connecticut (Delaware, Maine, Massachusetts, New Hampshire, Pennsylvania, Rhode Island, Vermont), or in Washington, D.C. Must be U.S. citizen or permanent resident alien who is a high school senior or graduate with rank in top twenty percent of class or score at least 1200 on SAT and show financial need. **Award:** Scholarship for use in any year; renewable. *Award amount:* up to $2000. **Eligibility Requirements:** Applicant must be enrolled at a two-year or four-year institution or university; resident of Connecticut and studying in Connecticut, Delaware, District of Columbia, Maine, Massachusetts, New Hampshire, Pennsylvania, Rhode Island, or Vermont. Applicant must have 3.5 GPA or higher. Available to U.S. citizens. **Application Requirements:** Application, financial need analysis, test scores. **Deadline:** February 15. **Contact:** John Siegrist,

Financial Aid Office, Connecticut Department of Higher Education, 61 Woodland Street, Hartford, CT 06105-2326. *Phone:* 860-947-1855. *Fax:* 860-947-1311. *Web site:* www.ctdhe.org.

DELAWARE

Critical Need Teacher Scholarship. Teachers in Delaware school districts who are teaching in critical need areas with Temporary or Limited Standard certification may apply for this scholarship to receive reimbursement for successfully completed coursework that enables them to achieve standard certification. Must be nominated. **Academic/Career Areas:** Education. **Award:** Scholarship for use in any year; not renewable. *Award amount:* $1175. **Eligibility Requirements:** Applicant must be enrolled part-time at a four-year institution or university and resident of Delaware. Available to U.S. citizens. **Application Requirements: Deadline:** continuous. **Contact:** Maureen Laffey, Associate Director, Delaware Higher Education Commission, 820 North French Street, Wilmington, DE 19801. *E-mail:* dhec@state.de.us. *Phone:* 302-577-3240. *Fax:* 302-577-6765. *Web site:* www.doe.state.de.us/high-ed.

Diamond State Scholarship. Renewable award for Delaware high school seniors enrolling full-time at an accredited college or university. Must be ranked in upper quarter of class and score 1200 on SAT or 27 on the ACT. **Award:** Scholarship for use in freshman year; renewable. *Award amount:* $1250. *Number of awards:* 50–200. **Eligibility Requirements:** Applicant must be high school student; planning to enroll full-time at a four-year institution or university and resident of Delaware. Applicant must have 3.5 GPA or higher. Available to U.S. citizens. **Application Requirements:** Application, essay, test scores, transcript. **Deadline:** March 31. **Contact:** Maureen Laffey, Associate Director, Delaware Higher Education Commission, 820 North French Street, Wilmington, DE 19801. *E-mail:* dhec@state.de.us. *Phone:* 302-577-3240. *Fax:* 302-577-6765. *Web site:* www.doe.state.de.us/high-ed.

Christa McAuliffe Teacher Scholarship Loan—Delaware. Award for Delaware residents who are pursuing teaching careers. Must agree to teach in Delaware public schools as repayment of loan. Minimum award is $1000 and is renewable for up to four years. Available only at Delaware colleges. Based on academic merit. Must be ranked in upper half of class, and have a score of 1050 on SAT or 25 on the ACT. **Academic/Career Areas:** Education. **Award:** Forgivable loan for use in freshman, sophomore, junior, or senior year; renewable. *Award amount:* $1000–$5000. *Number of awards:* 1–50. **Eligibility Requirements:** Applicant must be enrolled full-time at a four-year institution or university; resident of Delaware and studying in Delaware. Applicant must have 2.5 GPA or higher. Available to U.S. citizens. **Application Requirements:** Application, essay, test scores, transcript. **Deadline:** March 31. **Contact:** Maureen Laffey, Associate Director, Delaware Higher Education Commission, 820 North French Street, Wilmington, DE 19801. *E-mail:* dhec@state.de.us. *Phone:* 302-577-3240. *Fax:* 302-577-6765. *Web site:* www.doe.state.de.us/high-ed.

Delaware Nursing Incentive Scholarship Loan. Award for Delaware residents pursuing a nursing career. Must be repaid with nursing practice at a Delaware state-owned hospital. Based on academic merit. Must have minimum 2.5 GPA. Renewable for up to four years. **Academic/Career Areas:** Nursing. **Award:** Forgivable loan for use in freshman, sophomore, junior, or senior year; renewable.

Award amount: $1000–$5000. *Number of awards:* 1–40. **Eligibility Requirements:** Applicant must be enrolled full-time at a two-year or four-year institution or university and resident of Delaware. Applicant must have 2.5 GPA or higher. Available to U.S. citizens. **Application Requirements:** Application, essay, test scores, transcript. **Deadline:** March 31. **Contact:** Maureen Laffey, Associate Director, Delaware Higher Education Commission, 820 North French Street, Wilmington, DE 19801. *E-mail:* dhec@state.de.us. *Phone:* 302-577-3240. *Fax:* 302-577-6765. *Web site:* www.doe.state.de.us/high-ed.

Educational Benefits for Children of Deceased Military and State Police. Renewable award for Delaware residents who are children of state or military police who were killed in the line of duty. Must attend a Delaware institution unless program of study is not available. Funds cover tuition and fees at Delaware institutions. The amount varies at non-Delaware institutions. Must submit proof of service and related death. Must be ages 16-24 at time of application. Deadline is three weeks before classes begin. **Award:** Grant for use in freshman, sophomore, junior, or senior year; renewable. *Award amount:* $6255. *Number of awards:* 1–10. **Eligibility Requirements:** Applicant must be age 16-24; enrolled full-time at a two-year or four-year institution or university; resident of Delaware and have employment experience in police/firefighting. Available to U.S. citizens. Applicant or parent must meet one or more of the following requirements: general military experience; retired from active duty; disabled or killed as a result of military service; Prisoner-Of-War; or Missing-In-Action. **Application Requirements:** Application. **Deadline:** continuous. **Contact:** Maureen Laffey, Associate Director, Delaware Higher Education Commission, 820 North French Street, Wilmington, DE 19801. *E-mail:* dhec@state.de.us. *Phone:* 302-577-3240. *Fax:* 302-577-6765. *Web site:* www.doe.state.de.us/high-ed.

Scholarship Incentive Program–Delaware. One-time award for Delaware residents with financial need. May be used at an institution in Delaware or Pennsylvania, or at another out-of-state institution if a program is not available at a publicly-supported school in Delaware. Must have minimum 2.5 GPA. **Award:** Grant for use in any year; not renewable. *Award amount:* $700–$2200. *Number of awards:* 1000–1300. **Eligibility Requirements:** Applicant must be enrolled full-time at a two-year or four-year institution or university; resident of Delaware and studying in Delaware or Pennsylvania. Applicant must have 2.5 GPA or higher. Available to U.S. citizens. **Application Requirements:** Application, financial need analysis, transcript. **Deadline:** April 15. **Contact:** Maureen Laffey, Associate Director, Delaware Higher Education Commission, 820 North French Street, Wilmington, DE 19801. *E-mail:* dhec@state.de.us. *Phone:* 302-577-3240. *Fax:* 302-577-6765. *Web site:* www.doe.state.de.us/high-ed.

State Tuition Assistance. Award providing tuition assistance for any member of the Air or Army National Guard attending a Delaware two-year or four-year college. Awards are renewable. Applicant's minimum GPA must be 2.5. For full- or part-time study. Amount of award varies. **Award:** Scholarship for use in freshman, sophomore, junior, or senior year; renewable. **Eligibility Requirements:** Applicant must be enrolled full or part-time at a two-year or four-year institution and studying in Delaware. Applicant must have 2.5 GPA or higher. Available to U.S. citizens. Applicant must have served in the Air Force

National Guard or Army National Guard. **Contact:** Delaware National Guard, First Regiment Road, Wilmington, DE 19808-2191. *Web site:* www.dearng.ngh. army.mil.state.de.us.

Legislative Essay Scholarship. Must be a senior in high school and Delaware resident. Submit an essay of 500 to 2000 words on a designated historical topic (changes annually). Deadline: November 16. For more information visit: http://www.doe.state.de.us/high-ed. **Award:** Scholarship for use in freshman year; not renewable. *Number of awards:* 62. **Eligibility Requirements:** Applicant must be high school student; planning to enroll full or part-time at a two-year, four-year, or technical institution or university and resident of Delaware. Available to U.S. citizens. **Application Requirements:** Application, applicant must enter a contest, essay. **Deadline:** November 16. **Contact:** Maureen Laffey, Associate Director, Delaware Higher Education Commission, 820 North French Street, Wilmington, DE 19801. *E-mail:* dhec@state.de.us. *Phone:* 302-577-3240. *Fax:* 302-577-6765. *Web site:* www.doe.state.de.us/high-ed.

DISTRICT OF COLUMBIA

American Council of the Blind Scholarships. Merit-based award available to undergraduate, graduate, vocational or technical students who are legally blind in both eyes. Submit certificate of legal blindness and proof of acceptance at an accredited postsecondary institution. **Award:** Scholarship for use in any year; not renewable. *Award amount:* $200–$3000. *Number of awards:* 31. **Eligibility Requirements:** Applicant must be enrolled full-time at a two-year, four-year, or technical institution or university. Applicant must be visually impaired. Applicant must have 3.5 GPA or higher. **Application Requirements:** Application, autobiography, essay, references, transcript. **Deadline:** March 1. **Contact:** Terry Pacheco, Affiliate and Membership Services, American Council of the Blind, 1155 15th Street, NW, Suite 1004, Washington, DC 20005. *E-mail:* info@acb.org. *Phone:* 202-467-5081. *Fax:* 202-467-5085. *Web site:* www.acb.org.

DC Leveraging Educational Assistance Partnership Program (LEAP). Available to Washington, D.C. residents who have financial need. Must also apply for the Federal Pell Grant. Must attend an eligible college at least half-time. Contact financial aid office or local library for more information. Proof of residency may be required. Deadline is June 28. **Award:** Scholarship for use in freshman, sophomore, junior, or senior year; not renewable. *Award amount:* $500–$1000. *Number of awards:* 1200–1500. **Eligibility Requirements:** Applicant must be enrolled full or part-time at a two-year, four-year, or technical institution or university and resident of District of Columbia. Available to U.S. citizens. **Application Requirements:** Application, financial need analysis. **Deadline:** June 28. **Contact:** Angela M. March, Program Manager, District of Columbia State Education Office, 441 4th Street NW, Suite 350 North, Washington, DC 20001. *E-mail:* angela.march@dc.gov. *Phone:* 202-727-6436. *Fax:* 202-727-2019.

FLORIDA

Critical Teacher Shortage Tuition Reimbursement–Florida. One-time awards for full-time Florida public school employees who are certified to teach in Florida and are teaching or preparing to teach in critical teacher shortage subject areas. Must earn minimum grade of 3.0 in approved courses. May receive tuition reimbursement up to 9 semester hours or equivalent per academic year, not to exceed $78 per semester hour, for maximum 36 hours. Contact for application and deadline. Must be resident of Florida. **Academic/Career Areas:** Education. **Award:** Scholarship for use in any year; not renewable. *Award amount:* up to $700. *Number of awards:* 1000–1200. **Eligibility Requirements:** Applicant must be enrolled part-time at a two-year or four-year institution or university; resident of Florida; studying in Florida and have employment experience in teaching. Applicant must have 3.0 GPA or higher. Available to U.S. citizens. **Application Requirements:** Application, financial need analysis. **Deadline:** September 15. **Contact:** Bureau of Student Financial Assistance, Florida State Department of Education, 1940 North Monroe, Suite 70, Tallahassee, FL 32303-4759. *E-mail:* osfa@mail.doe.state.fl.us. *Phone:* 888-827-2004. *Web site:* www.firn.edu/doe/osfa.

Florida Postsecondary Student Assistance Grant. Renewable grants for Florida residents who are U.S. citizens or eligible noncitizens attending degree-granting private Florida colleges or universities, but not eligible under the Florida Private Student Assistance Grant. Must enroll full-time and have financial need. Application deadline set by eligible participating institutions. Allow at least 30 days for mailing and processing. **Award:** Grant for use in freshman, sophomore, junior, or senior year; renewable. *Award amount:* $200–$1300. **Eligibility Requirements:** Applicant must be enrolled full-time at a two-year or four-year institution or university; resident of Florida and studying in Florida. Available to U.S. citizens. **Application Requirements:** Application, financial need analysis. **Contact:** Bureau of Student Financial Assistance, Florida State Department of Education, 1940 North Monroe, Suite 70, Tallahassee, FL 32303-4759. *E-mail:* osfa@mail.doe.state.fl.us. *Phone:* 888-827-2004. *Web site:* www.firn.edu/doe/osfa.

Florida Teacher Scholarship and Forgivable Loan Program. Renewable forgivable loan for Florida undergraduates in junior or senior year and graduate students who intend to teach in a critical teacher shortage area in Florida. Undergraduates must have at least 2.5 GPA. Graduate applicants must have B.A. and at least 3.0 GPA or have scored at least 1000 on GRE. Yearly award of up to $4000 awarded for undergraduate and $8000 for graduate. Must be a Florida resident. **Academic/Career Areas:** Education. **Award:** Forgivable loan for use in junior, senior, or graduate year; renewable. *Award amount:* $4000–$8000. **Eligibility Requirements:** Applicant must be enrolled at a four-year institution or university; resident of Florida and studying in Florida. Available to U.S. citizens. **Application Requirements:** Application, financial need analysis, test scores. **Deadline:** March 15. **Contact:** Bureau of Student Financial Assistance, Florida State Department of Education, 1940 North Monroe, Suite 70, Tallahassee, FL 32303-4759. *E-mail:* osfa@mail.doe.state.fl.us. *Phone:* 888-827-2004. *Web site:* www.firn.edu/doe/osfa.

Top Scholars Award. Renewable award for academically top-ranked Florida Bright Futures Scholarship Program recipients from each Florida school district. Must have attended a Florida high school during senior year and be enrolled at an eligible Florida institution. Minimum 3.5 GPA and 1270 SAT or 28 ACT required. **Award:** Scholarship for use in freshman, sophomore, junior, or senior year; renewable. *Award amount:* $1500. **Eligibility Requirements:** Applicant must be high school student; planning to enroll full-time at a two-year, four-year, or technical institution or university; resident of Florida and studying in Florida. Applicant must have 3.5 GPA or higher. Available to U.S. citizens. **Application Requirements:** Application, test scores, transcript. **Contact:** Bureau of Student Financial Assistance, Florida State Department of Education, 1940 North Monroe, Suite 70, Tallahassee, FL 32303-4759. *E-mail:* osfa@mail.doe.state.fl.us. *Phone:* 888-827-2004. *Web site:* www.firn.edu/doe/osfa.

Jose Marti Scholarship Challenge Grant Fund. Award available to Hispanic-American students who were born in or whose parent was born in an Hispanic country. Must have lived in Florida for one year, be enrolled full-time in Florida at an eligible school, and have a GPA of 3.0 or above. Must be U.S. citizen or eligible noncitizen. Renewable award of $2000. Application must be postmarked by April 1. Free Application for Federal Student Aid must be processed by May 15. **Award:** Scholarship for use in any year; renewable. *Award amount:* $2000. **Eligibility Requirements:** Applicant must be Hispanic; enrolled full-time at a two-year or four-year institution or university; resident of Florida and studying in Florida. Applicant must have 3.0 GPA or higher. Available to U.S. citizens. **Application Requirements:** Application, financial need analysis. **Deadline:** May 15. **Contact:** Bureau of Student Financial Assistance, Florida State Department of Education, 1940 North Monroe, Suite 70, Tallahassee, FL 32303-4759. *E-mail:* osfa@mail.doe.state.fl.us. *Phone:* 888-827-2004. *Web site:* www.firn.edu/doe/osfa.

Occupational and Physical Therapist Tuition Reimbursement Program–Florida. Aid to eligible Florida public school occupational or physical therapists or assistants to improve skills and knowledge. Must provide proof of valid license or permit. Must be employed at Florida public school as full-time therapist for minimum of three years. Contact for deadlines. **Academic/Career Areas:** Therapy/Rehabilitation. **Award:** Scholarship for use in any year; not renewable. **Eligibility Requirements:** Applicant must be enrolled part-time at a two-year or four-year institution or university and have employment experience in designated career field. Applicant must have 3.0 GPA or higher. Available to U.S. citizens. **Application Requirements:** Application, financial need analysis. **Deadline:** September 15. **Contact:** Bureau of Student Financial Assistance, Florida State Department of Education, 1940 North Monroe, Suite 70, Tallahassee, FL 32303-4759. *E-mail:* osfa@mail.doe.state.fl.us. *Phone:* 888-827-2004. *Web site:* www.firn.edu/doe/osfa.

Mary McLeod Bethune Scholarship. Available to Florida students with a GPA of 3.0 or above who will attend Florida Agricultural and Mechanical University, Edward Waters College, or Florida Memorial College. Based on need and merit. Apply at the Financial Aid Office at the school. **Award:** Scholarship for use in freshman, sophomore, junior, or senior year; not renewable. *Award amount:* $3000. **Eligibility Requirements:** Applicant must be enrolled full-time at a four-year institution; resident of Florida and studying in Florida. Applicant must have 3.0 GPA or higher. Available to U.S. citizens. **Application Requirements:** Application, financial need analysis. **Contact:** Bureau of Student Financial Assistance, Florida State Department of Education, 1940 North Monroe, Suite 70, Tallahassee, FL 32303-4759. *E-mail:* osfa@mail.doe.state.fl.us. *Phone:* 888-827-2004. *Web site:* www.firn.edu/doe/osfa.

Rosewood Family Scholarship Fund. Renewable award for eligible minority students to attend a Florida public postsecondary institution on a full-time basis. Preference given to direct descendants of African-American Rosewood families affected by the incidents of January 1923. Must be Black, Hispanic, Asian, Pacific Islander, American Indian, or Alaska Native. Free Application for Federal Student Aid (and Student Aid Report for nonresidents of Florida) must be processed by May 15. **Award:** Scholarship for use in freshman, sophomore, junior, or senior year; renewable. *Award amount:* up to $4000. *Number of awards:* up to 25. **Eligibility Requirements:** Applicant must be Native American or Eskimo, Asian, African American, or Hispanic; enrolled full-time at a two-year, four-year, or technical institution or university and studying in Florida. Available to U.S. citizens. **Application Requirements:** Application, financial need analysis. **Deadline:** May 15. **Contact:** Bureau of Student Financial Assistance, Florida State Department of Education, 1940 North Monroe, Suite 70, Tallahassee, FL 32303-4759. *E-mail:* osfa@mail.doe.state.fl.us. *Phone:* 888-827-2004. *Web site:* www.firn.edu/doe/osfa.

Scholarships for Children of Deceased or Disabled Veterans or Children of Servicemen Classified as POW or MIA–Florida. Scholarship provides full tuition assistance for children of deceased or disabled veterans or of servicemen classified as POW or MIA who are in full-time attendance at eligible public or non-public Florida institutions. Service connection must be as specified under Florida statute. Amount of payment to nonpublic institutions is equal to cost at public institutions at the comparable level. Must be between 16 and 22. Qualified veteran and applicant must meet residency requirements. **Award:** Scholarship for use in freshman, sophomore, junior, or senior year; renewable. **Eligibility Requirements:** Applicant must be age 16-22; enrolled full-time at a two-year, four-year, or technical institution or university; resident of Florida and studying in Florida. Available to U.S. citizens. Applicant or parent must meet one or more of the following requirements: general military experience; retired from active duty; disabled or killed as a result of military service; Prisoner-Of-War; or Missing-In-Action. **Application Requirements:** Application, financial need analysis. **Contact:** Executive Director, Florida Department of Veterans Affairs, Florida State Department of Education, P.O. Box 31003, St. Petersburg, FL 33731-8903. *E-mail:* antwort@mail.doe.state.fl.us. *Phone:* 727-319-7400. *Web site:* www.firn. edu/doe/osfa.

Seminole and Miccosukee Indian Scholarship Program. Award is for Florida Seminole and Miccosukee Indians attending eligible Florida institutions as undergraduate or graduate students. Must demonstrate financial need and meet residency requirements. Application may be obtained from and should be submitted to the appropriate tribal higher education committee by the deadline specified by the tribe. **Award:** Scholarship for use in freshman, sophomore, junior, senior, or graduate year; renewable. **Eligibility Requirements:** Applicant must be Native American or Eskimo; enrolled full or part-time at a two-year or four-year institution or university; resident of Florida and studying in Florida. Available to U.S. citizens. **Application Requirements:** Application, financial need analysis. **Contact:** Bureau of Student Financial Assistance, Florida State Department of Education, 1940 North Monroe, Suite 70, Tallahassee, FL 32303-4759. *E-mail:* osfa@mail.doe.state.fl.us. *Phone:* 888-827-2004. *Web site:* www. firn.edu/doe/osfa.

William L. Boyd IV Florida Resident Access Grant. Awards given to Florida residents attending an independent nonprofit college or university in Florida for undergraduate study. Cannot have previously received bachelor's degree. Must enroll minimum 12 credit hours. Deadline set by eligible postsecondary financial aid offices. Contact financial aid administrator for application information. Reapply for renewal. **Award:** Grant for use in freshman, sophomore, junior, or senior year; not renewable. **Eligibility Requirements:** Applicant must be enrolled full-time at a four-year institution or university; resident of Florida and studying in Florida. Available to U.S. citizens. **Application Requirements:** Application. **Contact:** Bureau of Student Financial Assistance, Florida State Department of Education, 1940 North Monroe, Suite 70, Tallahassee, FL 32303-4759. *E-mail:* osfa@mail.doe.state.fl.us. *Phone:* 888-827-2004. *Web site:* www.firn.edu/doe/osfa.

Critical Occupational Therapist or Physical Therapist Shortage Loan Forgiveness Program–Florida. Award is repayment of educational loans to occupational and physical therapists or assistants employed in Florida public schools. Must have Florida license and intend to work minimum three years in position, having already completed one full year. May reapply up to four academic years or a total of $10,000. Assistants may apply for up to 2 years for a maximum of $5,000. **Academic/Career Areas:** Therapy/Rehabilitation. **Award:** Forgivable loan for use in any year; not renewable. *Award amount:* $2500–$5000. **Eligibility Requirements:** Applicant must be enrolled at a two-year or four-year institution or university; resident of Florida and studying in Florida. Available to U.S. citizens. **Application Requirements:** Application, financial need analysis. **Deadline:** July 15. **Contact:** Bureau of Student Financial Assistance, Florida State Department of Education, 1940 North Monroe, Suite 70, Tallahassee, FL 32303-4759. *E-mail:* osfa@mail.doe.state.fl.us. *Phone:* 888-827-2004. *Web site:* www.firn.edu/doe/osfa.

Florida Bright Futures Scholarship Program. Reward for Florida high school graduates who demonstrate high academic achievement, participate in community service projects and enroll in eligible Florida postsecondary institutions. There are three award levels. Each has different academic criteria and awards a different amount. Top ranked scholars from each county will receive additional $1500. Website contains complete information and application which must be completed and submitted to high school guidance counselor prior to graduation. **Award:** Scholarship for use in freshman, sophomore, junior, or senior year; renewable. *Award amount:* up to $1500. **Eligibility Requirements:** Applicant must be high school student; planning to enroll full or part-time at a two-year, four-year, or technical institution or university; resident of Florida and studying in Florida. Available to U.S. citizens. **Application Requirements:** Application, financial need analysis, test scores, transcript. **Contact:** Bureau of Student Financial Assistance, Florida State Department of Education, 1940 North Monroe, Suite 70, Tallahassee, FL 32303-4759. *E-mail:* osfa@mail.doe.state.fl.us. *Phone:* 888-827-2004. *Web site:* www.firn.edu/doe/osfa.

Occupational and Physical Therapist Scholarship Loan Program–Florida. Renewable award for Florida residents enrolled full-time in occupational or physical therapy or assistant program at an eligible Florida institution. Must intend to work as therapist in Florida public schools for minimum of three years or repay loan. **Academic/Career Areas:** Therapy/Rehabilitation. **Award:** Forgivable loan for use in freshman, sophomore, junior, senior, or graduate year; renewable. *Award amount:* up to $4000. **Eligibility Requirements:** Applicant must be enrolled full-time at a two-year, four-year, or technical institution or university; resident of Florida and studying in Florida. Available to U.S. citizens. **Application Requirements:** Application, financial need analysis. **Deadline:** April 15. **Contact:** Bureau of Student Financial Assistance, Florida State Department of Education, 1940 North Monroe, Suite 70, Tallahassee, FL 32303-4759. *E-mail:* osfa@mail.doe.state.fl.us. *Phone:* 888-827-2004. *Web site:* www.firn.edu/doe/osfa.

Florida Public Student Assistance Grant. Grants for Florida residents, U.S. citizens, or eligible noncitizens attending a Florida public college or university full-time. Based on financial need. Renewable up to 9 semesters, 14 quarters, or until receipt of bachelor's degree. Deadline set by eligible participating institutions. **Award:** Grant for use in freshman, sophomore, junior, or senior year; renewable. *Award amount:* $200–$1300. **Eligibility Requirements:** Applicant must be enrolled full-time at a two-year or four-year institution or university; resident of Florida and studying in Florida. Available to U.S. citizens. **Application Requirements:** Application, financial need analysis. **Contact:** Bureau of Student Financial Assistance, Florida State Department of Education, 1940 North Monroe, Suite 70, Tallahassee, FL 32303-4759. *E-mail:* osfa@mail.doe.state.fl.us. *Phone:* 888-827-2004. *Web site:* www.firn.edu/doe/osfa.

Critical Teacher Shortage Student Loan Forgiveness Program–Florida. Eligible Florida teachers may receive up to $5,000 for repayment of undergraduate and graduate educational loans which led to certification in critical teacher shortage subject area. Must teach full-time at a Florida public school in a critical area for a minimum of ninety days to be eligible. Visit Web site for further information. **Award:** Forgivable loan for use in any year; not renewable. *Award amount:* $2500–$5000. **Eligibility Requirements:** Applicant must be enrolled at a two-year or four-year institution or university; resident of Florida; studying in Florida and have employment experience in teaching. Available to U.S. citizens. **Application Requirements:** Application. **Deadline:** July 15. **Contact:** Bureau of Student Financial Assistance, Florida State Department of Education, 1940 North Monroe, Suite 70, Tallahassee, FL 32303-4759. *E-mail:* osfa@mail.doe.state.fl.us. *Phone:* 888-827-2004. *Web site:* www.firn.edu/doe/osfa.

Instructional Aide Scholarship Program. Provides tuition reimbursement for instructional aides to become certified teachers in subject areas of critical state or local need. Areas include math, science, teaching those with specific learning disabilities, etc. Must be employed by a publicly funded Florida school district for at least one year. Must pass classes with a minimum 2.0. See Web site for details. (http://www.firn.edu/doe/ofsa). Must be Florida resident. **Academic/Career Areas:** Education; Special Education. **Award:** Scholarship for use in freshman, sophomore, junior, senior, or graduate year; not renewable. *Award amount:* up to $3000. **Eligibility Requirements:** Applicant must be resident of Florida and have employment experience in teaching. Available to U.S. citizens. **Application Requirements:** Application, financial need analysis. **Contact:** Bureau of Student Financial Assistance, Florida State Department of Education, 1940 North Monroe, Suite 70, Tallahassee, FL 32303-4759. *E-mail:* osfa@mail.doe.state.fl.us. *Phone:* 888-827-2004. *Web site:* www.firn.edu/doe/osfa.

Nursing Scholarship Program. Provides financial assistance for full- or part-time nursing students enrolled in an approved nursing program in Florida. Must be a Florida resident in graduate school or an undergraduate in junior or senior year. **Academic/Career Areas:** Nursing. **Award:** Scholarship for use in junior, senior, or graduate year; renewable. *Award amount:* $4000–$6000. *Number of awards:* 15–30. **Eligibility Requirements:** Applicant must be enrolled full or part-time at a four-year institution or university; resident of Florida and studying in Florida. Available to U.S. and non-U.S. citizens. **Application Requirements:** Application. **Contact:** Florida Department of Health, Division of EMS and Community Health Resources, 4052 Bald Cypress Way, Mail Bin C-15, Tallahassee, FL 32399-1735.

Jose Marti Scholarship Challenge Grant. Must apply as a senior in high school or as graduate student. Must be resident of Florida and study in Florida. Need-based, merit scholarship. Must be US citizen or eligible noncitizen. Applicant must certify minimum 3.0 GPA and Hispanic origin. **Award:** Scholarship for use in freshman, sophomore, junior, senior, or graduate year; renewable. *Award amount:* $2000. *Number of awards:* 50. **Eligibility Requirements:** Applicant must be Hispanic; enrolled full-time at a two-year or four-year institution or university; resident of Florida and studying in Florida. Applicant must have 3.0 GPA or higher. Available to U.S. citizens. **Application Requirements:** Application, financial need analysis. **Deadline:** April 1. **Contact:** Jose Marti Scholarship Challenge Grant Fund, 1940 North Monroe Street, Suite 70, Tallahassee, FL 32303-4759. *Phone:* 888-827-2004. *Web site:* www.floridastudentfinancialaid.org.

Veterans Dependents Scholarships. Scholarships for children and surviving spouses of permanently and totally disabled service-connected veterans or veterans who died of service-connected conditions. Veteran must have entered service from Florida and had qualifying service. Scholar must be attending a Florida state school. Must submit proof of veteran's status. Application forms available at Web site. **Award:** Scholarship for use in any year; renewable. *Award amount:* $2200. **Eligibility Requirements:** Applicant must be enrolled full-time at a two-year, four-year, or technical institution or university; resident of Florida and studying in Florida. Available to U.S. citizens. Applicant or parent must meet one or more of the following requirements: general military experience; retired from active duty; disabled or killed as a result of military service; Prisoner-Of-War; or Missing-In-Action. **Application Requirements:** Application. **Deadline:** continuous. **Contact:** Director, Division of Benefits/Assistance, Florida Department of Veterans Affairs, PO Box 31003, St. Petersburg, FL 33731-8903. *Phone:* 727-319-7400. *Fax:* 727-319-7780. *Web site:* www.floridavets.org.

Ethics in Business Scholarship. Provides assistance to undergraduate college students who enroll at community colleges and eligible Florida colleges or universities. Scholarships are funded by private and state contributions. Awards are dependent on private matching funds. For more information contact the financial aid office at participating institutions, which are listed on the Florida Department of Education Web site. (http://www.firn.edu/doe/ofsa) **Award:** Scholarship for use in freshman, sophomore, junior, or senior year; not renewable. **Eligibility Requirements:** Applicant must be enrolled at a two-year or four-year institution or university and studying in Florida. Available to U.S. citizens. **Application Requirements:** Application. **Contact:** Bureau of Student Financial

Assistance, Florida State Department of Education, 1940 North Monroe, Suite 70, Tallahassee, FL 32303-4759. *E-mail:* osfa@mail.doe.state.fl.us. *Phone:* 888-827-2004. *Web site:* www.firn.edu/doe/osfa.

Chappie James Most Promising Teacher Scholarship. Scholarship to attract capable and promising students to the teaching profession, attract teachers to areas of projected and current critical teaching shortages, and to provide opportunity for persons making mid-career decisions to enter the field. Two year scholarship for freshmen and sophomores. Minimum 3.0 GPA required. Must be Florida resident in attendance at an eligible Florida institution and intend to teach in Florida. Deadline March 1 of senior year in high school. Must be nominated. See Web site (http://www.firn.edu/doe) for details. **Academic/ Career Areas:** Education. **Award:** Scholarship for use in freshman or sophomore year; renewable. *Award amount:* $1500. **Eligibility Requirements:** Applicant must be enrolled full-time at a four-year institution or university; resident of Florida and studying in Florida. Applicant must have 3.0 GPA or higher. Available to U.S. citizens. **Application Requirements:** Application, essay, financial need analysis, references, test scores. **Deadline:** March 1. **Contact:** Bureau of Student Financial Assistance, Florida State Department of Education, 1940 North Monroe, Suite 70, Tallahassee, FL 32303-4759. *E-mail:* osfa@mail.doe.state.fl.us. *Phone:* 888-827-2004. *Web site:* www.firn.edu/doe/osfa.

Florida Minority Participation in Legal Education (MPLE) Scholarship Program. Renewable award to a member of an historically disadvantaged minority group that is underrepresented in the membership of the Florida Bar. Must be a Florida resident and attend a pre-law program at an accredited four-year college or university in the state of Florida. Must be a U.S. citizen. Visit Web site for additional information. **Academic/Career Areas:** Law/Legal Services. **Award:** Scholarship for use in freshman, sophomore, junior, or senior year; renewable. *Award amount:* up to $7500. *Number of awards:* 34. **Eligibility Requirements:** Applicant must be Native American or Eskimo, Asian, African American, or Hispanic; enrolled full-time at a four-year institution or university; resident of Florida and studying in Florida. Available to U.S. citizens. **Application Requirements:** Application, essay, financial need analysis, references, test scores, transcript. **Deadline:** April 30. **Contact:** Lyra Logan, Vice President, Florida Education Fund, 15485 Eagle Nest Lane, Suite 200, Miami Lakes, FL 33014. *E-mail:* mplemail@aol.com. *Phone:* 305-364-3111. *Fax:* 305-364-3128. *Web site:* www.mpleonline.org.

Florida Private Student Assistance Grant. Grants for Florida residents who are U.S. citizens or eligible noncitizens attending eligible independent nonprofit colleges or universities in Florida. Must be full-time student and demonstrate substantial financial need. Renewable for up to nine semesters, fourteen quarters, or until receipt of bachelor's degree. Deadline to be determined by individual eligible institutions. **Award:** Grant for use in freshman, sophomore, junior, or senior year; renewable. *Award amount:* $200–$1300. **Eligibility Requirements:** Applicant must be enrolled full-time at a four-year institution or university; resident of Florida and studying in Florida. Available to U.S. citizens. **Application Requirements:** Application, financial need analysis. **Contact:** Bureau of Student Financial Assistance, Florida State Department of Education, 1940 North Monroe, Suite 70, Tallahassee, FL 32303-4759. *E-mail:* osfa@mail.doe.state.fl.us. *Phone:* 888-827-2004. *Web site:* www.firn.edu/doe/osfa.

GEORGIA

Department of Human Resource Service Cancelable Loan Program. Forgivable loans of $4000 are awarded to current Department of Human Resources employees who will be enrolled in a baccalaureate or advanced nursing degree program at an eligible participating school in Georgia. Loans are cancelled upon two calendar years of service as a registered nurse for the Georgia DHR or any Georgia county board of health. **Academic/Career Areas:** Nursing. **Award:** Forgivable loan for use in freshman, sophomore, junior, senior, or graduate year; not renewable. *Award amount:* $4000. **Eligibility Requirements:** Applicant must be enrolled full or part-time at a four-year institution or university; resident of Georgia and studying in Georgia. Available to U.S. citizens. **Application Requirements:** Application, financial need analysis. **Deadline:** continuous. **Contact:** Peggy Matthews, Manager/GSFA Originations, State of Georgia, 2082 East Exchange Place, Suite 230, Tucker, GA 30084-5305. *E-mail:* peggy@mail. gsfc.state.ga.us. *Phone:* 770-724-9230. *Fax:* 770-724-9263. *Web site:* www.gsfc. org.

Georgia Tuition Equalization Grant (GTEG). Award for Georgia residents pursuing undergraduate study at an accredited two- or four-year Georgia private institution. Complete the Georgia Student Grant Application. Award is $1100 per academic year. Deadlines vary. **Award:** Grant for use in freshman, sophomore, junior, or senior year; renewable. *Award amount:* $1100. *Number of awards:* 25,000–32,000. **Eligibility Requirements:** Applicant must be enrolled full-time at a two-year or four-year institution or university; resident of Georgia and studying in Georgia. Available to U.S. citizens. **Application Requirements:** Application. **Contact:** William Flook, Director of Scholarships and Grants Division, Georgia Student Finance Commission, 2082 East Exchange Place, Suite 100, Tucker, GA 30084. *Web site:* www.gsfc.org.

Georgia National Guard Service Cancelable Loan Program. Forgivable loans will be awarded to residents of Georgia maintaining good military standing as an eligible member of the Georgia National Guard who are enrolled at least half-time in an undergraduate degree program at an eligible college, university or technical school within the state of Georgia. **Award:** Forgivable loan for use in freshman, sophomore, junior, or senior year; not renewable. *Award amount:* $438–$1316. *Number of awards:* 200–250. **Eligibility Requirements:** Applicant must be enrolled full or part-time at a two-year, four-year, or technical institution or university; resident of Georgia and studying in Georgia. Available to U.S. citizens. Applicant must have served in the Air Force National Guard or Army National Guard. **Application Requirements:** Application, financial need analysis. **Deadline:** continuous. **Contact:** Peggy Matthews, Manager/GSFA Originations, State of Georgia, 2082 East Exchange Place, Suite 230, Tucker, GA 30084-5305. *E-mail:* peggy@mail.gsfc.state.ga.us. *Phone:* 770-724-9230. *Fax:* 770-724-9263. *Web site:* www.gsfc.org.

Service-Cancellable Stafford Loan—Georgia. To assist Georgia students enrolled in critical fields of study in allied health (e.g., nursing, physical therapy). For use at GSFA-approved schools. $3500 forgivable loan for dentistry students only. Contact school financial aid officer for more details. **Academic/Career Areas:** Dental Health/Services; Health and Medical Sciences; Nursing. **Award:** Forgivable loan for use in freshman, sophomore, junior, senior, or graduate year; not renewable. *Award amount:* $2000–$4500. *Number of awards:* 500–1200. **Eligibility Requirements:** Applicant must be enrolled full or part-time at a two-year, four-year, or technical institution or university; resident of Georgia and studying in Georgia. Available to U.S. citizens. **Application Requirements:** Application, financial need analysis. **Deadline:** continuous. **Contact:** Peggy Matthews, Manager/GSFA Originations, State of Georgia, 2082 East Exchange Place, Suite 230, Tucker, GA 30084-5305. *E-mail:* peggy@mail.gsfc.state.ga.us. *Phone:* 770-724-9230. *Fax:* 770-724-9263. *Web site:* www.gsfc.org.

Georgia Public Safety Memorial Grant/Law Enforcement Personnel Department Grant. Award for children of Georgia law enforcement officers, prison guards, or fire fighters killed or permanently disabled in the line of duty. Must attend an accredited postsecondary Georgia school. Complete the Law Enforcement Personnel Dependents application. **Award:** Grant for use in freshman, sophomore, junior, or senior year; renewable. *Award amount:* $2000. *Number of awards:* 20–40. **Eligibility Requirements:** Applicant must be enrolled full-time at a two-year, four-year, or technical institution or university; resident of Georgia; studying in Georgia and have employment experience in police/firefighting. Available to U.S. citizens. **Application Requirements:** Application. **Deadline:** continuous. **Contact:** William Flook, Director of Scholarships and Grants Division, Georgia Student Finance Commission, 2082 East Exchange Place, Suite 100, Tucker, GA 30084. *Web site:* www.gsfc.org.

Northeast Georgia Pilot Nurse Service Cancelable Loan. Up to 100 forgivable loans between $2,500 and $4,500 will be awarded to undergraduate students who are residents of Georgia studying nursing at a four-year school in Georgia. Loans can be repaid by working as a nurse in northeast Georgia. **Academic/Career Areas:** Nursing. **Award:** Forgivable loan for use in freshman, sophomore, junior, or senior year; not renewable. *Award amount:* $2500–$4500. *Number of awards:* up to 100. **Eligibility Requirements:** Applicant must be enrolled full or part-time at a four-year institution; resident of Georgia and studying in Georgia. Available to U.S. citizens. **Application Requirements:** Application, financial need analysis. **Deadline:** continuous. **Contact:** Peggy Matthews, Manager/GSFA Originations, State of Georgia, 2082 East Exchange Place, Suite 230, Tucker, GA 30084-5305. *E-mail:* peggy@mail.gsfc.state.ga.us. *Phone:* 770-724-9230. *Fax:* 770-724-9263. *Web site:* www.gsfc.org.

Georgia PROMISE Teacher Scholarship Program. Renewable, forgivable loans for junior undergraduates at Georgia colleges who have been accepted for enrollment into a teacher education program leading to initial certification. Minimum cumulative 3.0 GPA required. Recipient must teach at a Georgia public school for one year for each $1500 awarded. Available to seniors for renewal only. Write for deadlines. **Academic/Career Areas:** Education. **Award:** Forgivable loan for use in junior or senior year; renewable. *Award amount:* $3000–$6000. *Number of awards:* 700–1400. **Eligibility Requirements:** Applicant must be enrolled full or part-time at a four-year institution or university and studying in Georgia. Applicant must have 3.0 GPA or higher. Available to U.S. citizens. **Application Requirements:** Application, transcript. **Deadline:** continuous. **Contact:** William Flook, Director of Scholarships and Grants Division, Georgia Student Finance Commission, 2082 East Exchange Place, Suite 100, Tucker, GA 30084. *Web site:* www.gsfc.org.

Ladders in Nursing Career Service Cancelable Loan Program. Forgivable loans of $2,500 are awarded to students who agree to serve for one calendar year at an approved site within the state of Georgia. Eligible applicants will be residents of Georgia who are studying nursing at a Georgia institution. **Academic/Career Areas:** Nursing. **Award:** Forgivable loan for use in freshman, sophomore, junior, senior, or graduate year; not renewable. *Award amount:* $3000. **Eligibility Requirements:** Applicant must be enrolled full or part-time at a two-year, four-year, or technical institution or university; resident of Georgia and studying in Georgia. Available to U.S. citizens. **Application Requirements:** Application, financial need analysis. **Deadline:** continuous. **Contact:** Peggy Matthews, Manager/GSFA Originations, State of Georgia, 2082 East Exchange Place, Suite 230, Tucker, GA 30084-5305. *E-mail:* peggy@mail.gsfc.state.ga.us. *Phone:* 770-724-9230. *Fax:* 770-724-9263. *Web site:* www.gsfc.org.

Intellectual Capital Partnership Program, ICAPP. Forgivable loans will be awarded to undergraduate students who are residents of Georgia studying high-tech related fields at a Georgia institution. Repayment for every $2500 that is awarded is one-year service in a high-tech field in Georgia. Can be enrolled in a certificate or degree program. **Academic/Career Areas:** Trade/Technical Specialties. **Award:** Forgivable loan for use in freshman, sophomore, junior, or senior year; not renewable. *Award amount:* $7000–$10,000. *Number of awards:* up to 328. **Eligibility Requirements:** Applicant must be enrolled full or part-time at a two-year or four-year institution or university; resident of Georgia and studying in Georgia. Available to U.S. citizens. **Application Requirements:** Application, financial need analysis. **Deadline:** continuous. **Contact:** Peggy Matthews, Manager/GSFA Originations, State of Georgia, 2082 East Exchange Place, Suite 230, Tucker, GA 30084-5305. *E-mail:* peggy@mail.gsfc.state.ga.us. *Phone:* 770-724-9230. *Fax:* 770-724-9263. *Web site:* www.gsfc.org.

Registered Nurse Service Cancelable Loan Program. Forgivable loans will be awarded to undergraduate students who are residents of Georgia studying nursing in a two-year or four-year school in Georgia. Loans can be repaid by working as a Registered Nurse in the state of Georgia. **Academic/Career Areas:** Nursing. **Award:** Forgivable loan for use in freshman, sophomore, junior, or senior year; not renewable. *Award amount:* $200–$4500. **Eligibility Requirements:** Applicant must be enrolled full or part-time at a two-year or four-year institution; resident of Georgia and studying in Georgia. Available to U.S. citizens. **Application Requirements:** Application, financial need analysis. **Deadline:** continuous. **Contact:** Peggy Matthews, Manager/GSFA Originations, State of Georgia, 2082 East Exchange Place, Suite 230, Tucker, GA 30084-5305. *E-mail:* peggy@mail.gsfc.state.ga.us. *Phone:* 770-724-9230. *Fax:* 770-724-9263. *Web site:* www.gsfc.org.

HOPE—Helping Outstanding Pupils Educationally. Grant program for Georgia residents who are college undergraduates to attend an accredited two- or four-year Georgia institution. Tuition and fees may be covered by the grant. Minimum 3.0 GPA required. Renewable if student maintains grades and reapplies. Write for deadlines. **Award:** Scholarship for use in freshman, sophomore, junior, or senior year; renewable. *Award amount:* $300–$3000. *Number of awards:* 140,000–170,000. **Eligibility Requirements:** Applicant must be enrolled full or part-time at a two-year or four-year institution or university; resident of Georgia and studying in Georgia. Applicant must have 3.0 GPA or higher.

Available to U.S. citizens. **Application Requirements:** Application. **Contact:** William Flook, Director of Scholarships and Grants Division, Georgia Student Finance Commission, 2082 East Exchange Place, Suite 100, Tucker, GA 30084. *Web site:* www.gsfc.org.

Governor's Scholarship–Georgia. Award to assist students selected as Georgia scholars, STAR students, valedictorians, and salutatorians. For use at two- and four-year colleges and universities in Georgia. Recipients are selected as entering freshmen. Renewable award of up to $1575. Minimum 3.5 GPA required. **Award:** Scholarship for use in freshman, sophomore, junior, or senior year; renewable. *Award amount:* up to $1575. *Number of awards:* 2000–3000. **Eligibility Requirements:** Applicant must be high school student; planning to enroll full-time at a two-year or four-year institution or university; resident of Georgia and studying in Georgia. Applicant must have 3.5 GPA or higher. Available to U.S. citizens. **Application Requirements:** Application, transcript. **Deadline:** continuous. **Contact:** William Flook, Director of Scholarships and Grants Division, Georgia Student Finance Commission, 2082 East Exchange Place, Suite 100, Tucker, GA 30084. *Web site:* www.gsfc.org.

Robert C. Byrd Honors Scholarship–Georgia. Complete the application provided by the Georgia Department of Education. Renewable awards for outstanding graduating Georgia high school seniors to be used for full-time undergraduate study at eligible U.S. institution. Minimum 3.5 GPA required. **Award:** Scholarship for use in freshman, sophomore, junior, or senior year; renewable. *Award amount:* $1500. *Number of awards:* 600–700. **Eligibility Requirements:** Applicant must be high school student; planning to enroll full-time at a two-year or four-year institution or university and resident of Georgia. Applicant must have 3.5 GPA or higher. Available to U.S. citizens. **Application Requirements:** Application, transcript. **Deadline:** April 1. **Contact:** William Flook, Director of Scholarships and Grants Division, Georgia Student Finance Commission, 2082 East Exchange Place, Suite 100, Tucker, GA 30084. *Web site:* www.gsfc.org.

GAE GFIE Scholarship for Education Support Professionals for Professional Development. At least seven scholarships for up to $10,000 will be awarded to Education Support Professional members who enroll in classes or college programs, which improve their work skills. Scholarships are intended to subsidize applicant's tuition expenses. Must be a member of GAE. **Academic/ Career Areas:** Education. **Award:** Scholarship for use in any year; not renewable. *Award amount:* up to $10,000. *Number of awards:* 7. **Eligibility Requirements:** Applicant must be resident of Georgia and studying in Georgia. Available to U.S. citizens. **Application Requirements:** Application, essay, transcript. **Deadline:** January 18. **Contact:** Sally Bennett, Professional Development Specialist, Georgia Association of Educators, 100 Crescent Centre Parkway, Suite 500, Tucker, GA 30084-7049. *E-mail:* sally.bennett@gae.org. *Phone:* 678-837-1103. *Web site:* www.gae.org.

HAWAII

Hawaii State Student Incentive Grant. Grants are given to residents of Hawaii who are enrolled in a Hawaiian state school. Funds are for undergraduate tuition only. Applicants must submit a financial need analysis. **Award:** Grant for use in freshman, sophomore, junior, or senior year; renewable. **Eligibility**

Requirements: Applicant must be enrolled full or part-time at a two-year or four-year institution or university; resident of Hawaii and studying in Hawaii. Available to U.S. citizens. **Application Requirements:** Financial need analysis. **Contact:** Jo Ann Yoshida, Financial Aid Specialist, Hawaii State Postsecondary Education Commission, University of Hawaii at Manoa, Honolulu, HI 96822. *Phone:* 808-956-6066. *Web site:* www.hern.hawaii.edu.

IDAHO

Education Incentive Loan Forgiveness Contract–Idaho. Renewable award assists Idaho residents enrolling in teacher education or nursing programs within state. Must rank in top fifteen percent of high school graduating class, have a 3.0 GPA or above, and agree to work in Idaho for two years. Deadlines vary. Contact financial aid office at institution of choice. **Academic/Career Areas:** Education; Nursing. **Award:** Forgivable loan for use in freshman, sophomore, junior, or senior year; renewable. *Number of awards:* 29. **Eligibility Requirements:** Applicant must be enrolled full-time at a four-year institution or university; resident of Idaho and studying in Idaho. Applicant must have 3.0 GPA or higher. Available to U.S. citizens. **Application Requirements:** Application, test scores, transcript. **Contact:** Financial Aid Office, Idaho State Board of Education. *Web site:* www.sde.state.id.us/osbe/board.htm.

Leveraging Educational Assistance State Partnership Program (LEAP). One-time award assists students attending participating Idaho colleges and universities majoring in any field except theology or divinity. Idaho residence is not required, but must be U.S. citizen or permanent resident. Must show financial need. Application deadlines vary by institution. **Award:** Grant for use in any year; not renewable. *Award amount:* up to $5000. **Eligibility Requirements:** Applicant must be enrolled full or part-time at a two-year or four-year institution or university and studying in Idaho. Available to U.S. citizens. **Application Requirements:** Application, financial need analysis, self-addressed stamped envelope. **Contact:** Lynn Humphrey, Academic Program Coordinator, Idaho State Board of Education, PO Box 83720, Boise, ID 83720-0037. *Phone:* 208-332-1574. *Fax:* 208-334-2632. *Web site:* www.sde.state.id.us/osbe/board. htm.

Idaho Promise Category B Scholarship Program. Available to Idaho residents entering college for the first time prior to the age of 22. Must have completed high school or its equivalent in Idaho and have a minimum GPA of 3.0 or an ACT score of 20 or higher. Renewable one time only. **Award:** Scholarship for use in freshman or sophomore year; renewable. *Award amount:* $500. **Eligibility Requirements:** Applicant must be age 22 or under; enrolled full-time at a two-year, four-year, or technical institution or university; resident of Idaho and studying in Idaho. Applicant must have 3.0 GPA or higher. Available to U.S. citizens. **Application Requirements:** Application. **Deadline:** continuous. **Contact:** Lynn Humphrey, Academic Program Coordinator, Idaho State Board of Education, PO Box 83720, Boise, ID 83720-0037. *Phone:* 208-332-1574. *Fax:* 208-334-2632. *Web site:* www.sde.state.id.us/osbe/board.htm.

Idaho Promise Category A Scholarship Program. Renewable award available to Idaho residents who are graduating high school seniors. Must attend an approved Idaho college full-time. Based on class rank (must be verified by school official), GPA, and ACT scores. Professional-technical student applicants must take COMPASS. **Award:** Scholarship for use in freshman, sophomore, junior, or senior year; renewable. *Award amount:* $3000. *Number of awards:* 25–30. **Eligibility Requirements:** Applicant must be high school student; planning to enroll full-time at a two-year, four-year, or technical institution or university; resident of Idaho and studying in Idaho. Applicant must have 3.5 GPA or higher. Available to U.S. citizens. **Application Requirements:** Application, test scores. **Deadline:** December 15. **Contact:** Caryl Smith, Scholarship Assistant, Idaho State Board of Education, PO Box 83720, Boise, ID 83720-0037. *E-mail:* csmith@osbe.state.id.us. *Phone:* 208-332-1576. *Fax:* 208-334-2632. *Web site:* www.sde.state.id.us/osbe/board.htm.

Idaho Minority and "At Risk" Student Scholarship. Renewable award for Idaho residents who are disabled or members of a minority group and have financial need. Must attend one of eight postsecondary institutions in the state for undergraduate study. Deadlines vary by institution. Must be a US citizen and be a graduate of an Idaho high school. Contact college financial aid office. **Award:** Scholarship for use in freshman, sophomore, junior, or senior year; renewable. *Award amount:* $3000. *Number of awards:* 38–40. **Eligibility Requirements:** Applicant must be Native American or Eskimo, African American, or Hispanic; enrolled full-time at a two-year or four-year institution or university; resident of Idaho and studying in Idaho. Available to U.S. citizens. **Application Requirements:** Application, financial need analysis. **Contact:** Financial Aid Office, Idaho State Board of Education. *Web site:* www.sde.state.id.us/osbe/board.htm.

ILLINOIS

Illinois Incentive for Access Program. Award for eligible first-time freshmen enrolling in approved Illinois institutions. One-time grant of up to $500 may be used for any educational expense. Deadline: October 1. **Award:** Grant for use in freshman year; not renewable. *Award amount:* $300–$500. *Number of awards:* 17,000–19,000. **Eligibility Requirements:** Applicant must be enrolled full or part-time at a two-year, four-year, or technical institution or university; resident of Illinois and studying in Illinois. Available to U.S. and non-U.S. citizens. **Application Requirements:** Financial need analysis. **Deadline:** October 1. **Contact:** David Barinholtz, Client Information, Illinois Student Assistance Commission (ISAC), 1755 Lake Cook Road, Deerfield, IL 60015-5209. *Phone:* 847-948-8500 Ext. 2385. *Web site:* www.isac-online.org.

Illinois Veteran Grant Program–IVG. Award for qualified veterans for tuition and fees at Illinois public universities and community colleges. Must provide documentation of service (DD214). Deadline is continuous. **Award:** Grant for use in any year; renewable. *Award amount:* $1400–$1600. *Number of awards:* 11,000–13,000. **Eligibility Requirements:** Applicant must be enrolled at a two-year or four-year institution or university; resident of Illinois and studying in Illinois. Available to U.S. and non-U.S. citizens. Applicant must have general military experience. **Application Requirements:** Application. **Deadline:** continuous. **Contact:** David Barinholtz, Client Information, Illinois Student Assistance Commission (ISAC), 1755 Lake Cook Road, Deerfield, IL 60015-5209. *Phone:* 847-948-8500 Ext. 2385. *Web site:* www.isac-online.org.

Illinois College Savings Bond Bonus Incentive Grant Program. Program offers holders of Illinois College Savings Bonds a $20 grant for each year of bond maturity payable upon bond redemption if at least 70 percent of proceeds are used to attend college in Illinois. May not be used by students attending religious or divinity schools. **Award:** Grant for use in any year; not renewable. *Award amount:* $40–$220. *Number of awards:* 1200–1400. **Eligibility Requirements:** Applicant must be enrolled full or part-time at a two-year, four-year, or technical institution or university and studying in Illinois. Available to U.S. and non-U.S. citizens. **Application Requirements:** Application. **Deadline:** continuous. **Contact:** David Barinholtz, Client Information, Illinois Student Assistance Commission (ISAC), 1755 Lake Cook Road, Deerfield, IL 60015-5209. *Phone:* 847-948-8500 Ext. 2385. *Web site:* www.isac-online.org.

Merit Recognition Scholarship (MRS) Program. Award for Illinois high school seniors graduating in the top 5 percent of their class and attending Illinois postsecondary institution. Deadline: June 15. Contact for application procedures. **Award:** Scholarship for use in freshman year; not renewable. *Award amount:* $900–$1000. *Number of awards:* 5000–6000. **Eligibility Requirements:** Applicant must be high school student; planning to enroll full or part-time at a two-year or four-year institution or university; resident of Illinois and studying in Illinois. Applicant must have 3.5 GPA or higher. Available to U.S. and non-U.S. citizens. **Application Requirements:** Application. **Deadline:** June 15. **Contact:** David Barinholtz, Client Information, Illinois Student Assistance Commission (ISAC), 1755 Lake Cook Road, Deerfield, IL 60015-5209. *Phone:* 847-948-8500 Ext. 2385. *Web site:* www.isac-online.org.

Higher Education License Plate Program–HELP. Need-based grants for students at institutions participating in program whose funds are raised by sale of special license plates commemorating the institutions. Deadline: June 30. Must be Illinois resident. **Award:** Grant for use in freshman, sophomore, junior, or senior year; not renewable. *Award amount:* up to $2000. **Eligibility Requirements:** Applicant must be enrolled full or part-time at a two-year or four-year institution or university; resident of Illinois and studying in Illinois. Available to U.S. and non-U.S. citizens. **Application Requirements:** Financial need analysis. **Deadline:** June 30. **Contact:** David Barinholtz, Client Information, Illinois Student Assistance Commission (ISAC), 1755 Lake Cook Road, Deerfield, IL 60015-5209. *Phone:* 847-948-8500 Ext. 2385. *Web site:* www.isac-online.org.

Illinois Monetary Award Program. Award for eligible students attending Illinois public universities, private colleges and universities, community colleges, and some proprietary institutions. Applicable only to tuition and fees. Based on financial need. Deadline: October 1. **Award:** Grant for use in freshman, sophomore, junior, or senior year; not renewable. *Award amount:* $300–$4320. *Number of awards:* 135,000–140,000. **Eligibility Requirements:** Applicant must be enrolled full or part-time at a two-year, four-year, or technical institution or university; resident of Illinois and studying in Illinois. Available to U.S. and non-U.S. citizens. **Application Requirements:** Financial need analysis. **Deadline:** October 1. **Contact:** David Barinholtz, Client Information, Illinois Student Assistance Commission (ISAC), 1755 Lake Cook Road, Deerfield, IL 60015-5209. *Phone:* 847-948-8500 Ext. 2385. *Web site:* www.isac-online.org.

Minority Teachers of Illinois Scholarship Program. Award for minority students planning to teach at an approved Illinois preschool, elementary, or secondary school. Deadline: May 1. Must be Illinois resident. **Academic/Career Areas:** Education; Special Education. **Award:** Forgivable loan for use in sophomore, junior, or senior year; renewable. *Award amount:* $4000–$5000. *Number of awards:* 400–500. **Eligibility Requirements:** Applicant must be Native American or Eskimo, Asian, African American, or Hispanic; enrolled full-time at a four-year institution or university; resident of Illinois and studying in Illinois. Applicant must have 2.5 GPA or higher. Available to U.S. and non-U.S. citizens. **Application Requirements:** Application. **Deadline:** May 1. **Contact:** David Barinholtz, Client Information, Illinois Student Assistance Commission (ISAC), 1755 Lake Cook Road, Deerfield, IL 60015-5209. *Phone:* 847-948-8500 Ext. 2385. *Web site:* www.isac-online.org.

Grant Program for Dependents of Police, Fire, or Correctional Officers. Award for dependents of police, fire, and corrections officers killed or disabled in line of duty. Provides for tuition and fees at approved Illinois institutions. Must be resident of Illinois. Continuous deadline. Provide proof of status. **Award:** Grant for use in any year; renewable. *Award amount:* $3000–$4000. **Eligibility Requirements:** Applicant must be enrolled at a two-year, four-year, or technical institution or university; resident of Illinois; studying in Illinois and have employment experience in police/firefighting. Available to U.S. and non-U.S. citizens. **Application Requirements:** Application. **Deadline:** continuous. **Contact:** David Barinholtz, Client Information, Illinois Student Assistance Commission (ISAC), 1755 Lake Cook Road, Deerfield, IL 60015-5209. *Phone:* 847-948-8500 Ext. 2385. *Web site:* www.isac-online.org.

Illinois Department of Children and Family Services Scholarships. Scholarship recipients will receive a medical card, a monthly check of $445 and a tuition waiver for those recipients who chose to attend one of nine Illinois public universities. Scholarship is prorated for a maximum of four years. Applicant must be 16 years of age, possess a diploma or GED accreditation. Must be a ward of the Department of Children and Family Services, or a former ward who has been adopted or placed in private guardianship. ACT or SAT scores and letters of recommendation are required. Contact for application deadline. **Award:** Scholarship for use in any year; renewable. *Award amount:* $6000–$8250. *Number of awards:* 48. **Eligibility Requirements:** Applicant must be age 16-21; enrolled full-time at a two-year or four-year institution or university; resident of Illinois and studying in Illinois. Available to U.S. citizens. **Application Requirements:** Application, autobiography, financial need analysis, references, test scores, transcript. **Contact:** Dwight Lambert, Statewide Education Coordinator, Illinois Department of Children and Family Services, 406 East Monroe Street, #222, Springfield, IL 62701-1498. *E-mail:* dlambert@idcfs.state.il.us. *Phone:* 217-524-2030. *Fax:* 217-524-2101.

David A. DeBolt Teacher Shortage Scholarship Program. Award to assist Illinois students planning to teach at an Illinois pre-school, elementary school, or high school in a teacher shortage discipline. Must agree to teach one year in teacher shortage area for each year of award assistance received. Deadline: May 1. **Academic/Career Areas:** Education; Special Education. **Award:** Forgivable loan for use in sophomore, junior, senior, or graduate year; not renewable. *Award amount:* $4000–$5000. *Number of awards:* 300–350. **Eligibility Requirements:** Applicant must be enrolled full or part-time at a two-year or four-year institution or university; resident of Illinois and studying in Illinois.

Applicant must have 2.5 GPA or higher. Available to U.S. and non-U.S. citizens. **Application Requirements:** Application, transcript. **Deadline:** May 1. **Contact:** Dave Barinholtz, Client Information, Illinois Student Assistance Commission (ISAC), 1755 Lake Cook Road, Deerfield, IL 60015-5209. *Phone:* 847-948-8500 Ext. 2385. *Web site:* www.isac-online.org.

Illinois Student-to-Student Program of Matching Grants. Award provides matching funds for need-based grants at participating Illinois public universities and community colleges. Deadline: October 1. **Award:** Grant for use in freshman, sophomore, junior, or senior year; not renewable. *Award amount:* $300–$500. *Number of awards:* 2000–4000. **Eligibility Requirements:** Applicant must be enrolled full or part-time at a two-year or four-year institution or university; resident of Illinois and studying in Illinois. Available to U.S. and non-U.S. citizens. **Application Requirements:** Financial need analysis. **Deadline:** October 1. **Contact:** David Barinholtz, Client Information, Illinois Student Assistance Commission (ISAC), 1755 Lake Cook Road, Deerfield, IL 60015-5209. *Phone:* 847-948-8500 Ext. 2385. *Web site:* www.isac-online.org.

Illinois National Guard Grant Program. Award for qualified National Guard personnel which pays tuition and fees at Illinois public universities and community colleges. Must provide documentation of service. Deadline: September 15. **Award:** Grant for use in any year; renewable. *Award amount:* $1300–$1700. *Number of awards:* 2500–3000. **Eligibility Requirements:** Applicant must be enrolled full or part-time at a two-year or four-year institution or university; resident of Illinois and studying in Illinois. Available to U.S. and non-U.S. citizens. Applicant must have national guard experience. **Application Requirements:** Application. **Deadline:** September 15. **Contact:** David Barinholtz, Client Information, Illinois Student Assistance Commission (ISAC), 1755 Lake Cook Road, Deerfield, IL 60015-5209. *Phone:* 847-948-8500 Ext. 2385. *Web site:* www.isac-online.org.

Golden Apple Scholars of Illinois. Between 75 and 100 forgivable loans are given to undergraduate students. Loans are $7,000 a year for 4 years. Applicants must be between 17 and 21 and carry a minimum GPA of 2.5. Eligible applicants will be residents of Illinois who are studying in Illinois. The deadline is December 1. Recipients must agree to teach in high-need Illinois schools. **Academic/Career Areas:** Education. **Award:** Forgivable loan for use in freshman, sophomore, junior, or senior year; renewable. *Award amount:* $7000. *Number of awards:* 75–100. **Eligibility Requirements:** Applicant must be age 17-21; enrolled full-time at a four-year institution or university; resident of Illinois and studying in Illinois. Applicant must have 2.5 GPA or higher. Available to U.S. citizens. **Application Requirements:** Application, autobiography, essay, interview, photo, references, test scores, transcript. **Deadline:** December 1. **Contact:** Pat Kilduff, Director of Recruitment and Placement, Golden Apple Foundation, 8 South Michigan Avenue, Suite 700, Chicago, IL 60603-3318. *E-mail:* patnk@goldenapple.org. *Phone:* 312-407-0006 Ext. 105. *Fax:* 312-407-0344. *Web site:* www.goldenapple.org.

INDIANA

Indiana National Guard Supplemental Grant. One-time award, which is a supplement to the Indiana Higher Education Grant program. Applicants must be members of the Indiana National Guard. All Guard paperwork must be completed prior to the start of each semester. The FAFSA must be filed by March 1st each year. Award covers tuition and fees at select public colleges. **Award:** Grant for use in freshman, sophomore, junior, or senior year; not renewable. *Award amount:* $200–$4734. *Number of awards:* 350–735. **Eligibility Requirements:** Applicant must be enrolled full or part-time at a two-year or four-year institution or university; resident of Indiana and studying in Indiana. Available to U.S. citizens. Applicant must have served in the Air Force National Guard or Army National Guard. **Application Requirements:** Application, financial need analysis. **Deadline:** March 1. **Contact:** Grants Counselor, State Student Assistance Commission of Indiana (SSACI), 150 West Market Street, Suite 500, Indianapolis, IN 46204-2805. *E-mail:* grants@ssaci.state.in.us. *Phone:* 317-232-2350. *Fax:* 317-232-2360. *Web site:* www.ssaci.in.gov.

Indiana Remission of Fees for Child of Disabled Veteran. Renewable award for Indiana residents who are the children of veterans who received the Purple Heart Medal or are rated with a service-connected disability or died from a service-connected disease or injury. Pays partial tuition at Indiana state-supported institutions. Must submit paperwork as proof of decoration, not simply the medal. **Award:** Grant for use in any year; renewable. **Eligibility Requirements:** Applicant must be enrolled full or part-time at a two-year or four-year institution or university; resident of Indiana and studying in Indiana. Available to U.S. citizens. Applicant or parent must meet one or more of the following requirements: general military experience; retired from active duty; disabled or killed as a result of military service; Prisoner-Of-War; or Missing-In-Action. **Application Requirements:** Application. **Deadline:** continuous. **Contact:** Jon Brinkley, State Service Officer, Indiana Department of Veterans' Affairs, 302 West Washington Street, Room E-120, Indianapolis, IN 46204-2738. *E-mail:* jbrinkley@dva.state.in.us. *Phone:* 317-232-3910. *Fax:* 317-232-7721. *Web site:* www.ai.org/veteran/index.html.

Child of Disabled Veteran Grant or Purple Heart Recipient, Grant. Reduction in tuition at Indiana state-supported colleges or universities for children of disabled veterans or Purple Heart recipients. Must submit Form DD214 or service record. **Award:** Grant for use in any year; renewable. **Eligibility Requirements:** Applicant must be enrolled full or part-time at a two-year or four-year institution or university; resident of Indiana and studying in Indiana. Available to U.S. citizens. Applicant or parent must meet one or more of the following requirements: general military experience; retired from active duty; disabled or killed as a result of military service; Prisoner-Of-War; or Missing-In-Action. **Application Requirements:** Application. **Contact:** Jon Brinkley, State Service Officer, Indiana Department of Veterans' Affairs, 302 West Washington Street, Room E-120, Indianapolis, IN 46204-2738. *E-mail:* jbrinkley@dva.state.in.us. *Phone:* 317-232-3910. *Fax:* 317-232-7721. *Web site:* www.ai.org/veteran/index.html.

Department of Veterans Affairs Free Tuition for Children of POW/MIA's in Vietnam. Renewable award for residents of Indiana who are the children of veterans declared Missing-In-Action or Prisoner-Of-War after January 1, 1960. Provides tuition at Indiana state-supported institutions for undergraduate study. **Award:** Grant for use in freshman, sophomore, junior, or senior year; renewable. **Eligibility Requirements:** Applicant must be enrolled at a two-year or four-year institution or university; resident of Indiana and studying in Indiana. Available to U.S. citizens. Applicant or parent must meet one or more of the following requirements: general military experience; retired from active duty; disabled or killed as a result of military service; Prisoner-Of-War; or Missing-In-Action. **Application Requirements:** Application. **Deadline:** continuous. **Contact:** Jon Brinkley, State Service Officer, Indiana Department of Veterans' Affairs, 302 West Washington Street, Roome E-120, Indianapolis, IN 46204-2738. *E-mail:* jbrinkley@dva.state.in.us. *Phone:* 317-232-3910. *Fax:* 317-232-7721. *Web site:* www.ai.org/veteran/index.html.

Part-time Grant Program. Program is designed to encourage part-time undergraduates to start and complete their associate or baccalaureate degrees or certificates by subsidizing part-time tuition costs. It is a term-based award that is based on need. State residency requirements must be met and a FAFSA must be filed. Eligibility is determined at the institutional level subject to approval by SSACI. **Award:** Grant for use in freshman, sophomore, junior, or senior year; not renewable. *Award amount:* $50–$4000. *Number of awards:* 4000–5100. **Eligibility Requirements:** Applicant must be enrolled part-time at a two-year, four-year, or technical institution or university; resident of Indiana and studying in Indiana. Available to U.S. citizens. **Application Requirements:** Application, financial need analysis. **Deadline:** continuous. **Contact:** Grant Division, State Student Assistance Commission of Indiana (SSACI), 150 West Market Street, Suite 500, Indianapolis, IN 46204-2805. *E-mail:* grants@ssaci.state.in.us. *Phone:* 317-232-2350. *Fax:* 317-232-3260. *Web site:* www.ssaci.in.gov.

Indiana Freedom of Choice Grant. The Freedom of Choice Grant is a need-based, tuition-restricted program for students attending Indiana private institutions seeking a first undergraduate degree. It is awarded in addition to the Higher Education Award. Students (and parents of dependent students) who are U.S. citizens and Indiana residents must file the FAFSA yearly by March 1st for consideration. **Award:** Grant for use in freshman, sophomore, junior, or senior year; not renewable. *Award amount:* $200–$5080. *Number of awards:* 10,000–11,830. **Eligibility Requirements:** Applicant must be enrolled full-time at a four-year institution or university; resident of Indiana and studying in Indiana. Available to U.S. citizens. **Application Requirements:** Application, financial need analysis. **Deadline:** March 1. **Contact:** Grant Counselor, State Student Assistance Commission of Indiana (SSACI), 150 West Market Street, Suite 500, Indianapolis, IN 46204-2805. *E-mail:* grants@ssaci.state.in.us. *Phone:* 317-232-2350. *Fax:* 317-232-3260. *Web site:* www.ssaci.in.gov.

Hoosier Scholar Award. The Hoosier Scholar Award is a $500 nonrenewable award. Based on the size of the high school, one to three scholars are selected by the guidance counselor(s). The award is based on academic merit and may be used for any educational expense at an eligible Indiana institution of higher education. **Award:** Scholarship for use in freshman year; not renewable. *Award amount:* $500. *Number of awards:* 790–840. **Eligibility Requirements:** Applicant must be high school student; planning to enroll full-time at a two-year or four-year institution or university; resident of Indiana and studying in Indiana. Applicant must have 3.5 GPA or higher. Available to U.S. citizens. **Application Requirements: Deadline:** March 1. **Contact:** Ms. Ada Sparkman, Program Coordinator, State Student Assistance Commission of Indiana (SSACI), 150 West Market Street, Suite 500, Indianapolis, IN 46204-2805. *Phone:* 317-232-2350. *Fax:* 317-232-3260. *Web site:* www.ssaci.in.gov.

Indiana Higher Education Award. The Higher Education Award is a need-based, tuition-restricted program for students attending Indiana public, private or proprietary institutions seeking a first undergraduate degree. Students (and parents of dependent students) who are U.S. citizens and Indiana residents must file the FAFSA yearly by March 1st for consideration. **Award:** Grant for use in freshman, sophomore, junior, or senior year; not renewable. *Award amount:* $200-$4406. *Number of awards:* 38,000-43,660. **Eligibility Requirements:** Applicant must be enrolled full-time at a two-year, four-year, or technical institution or university; resident of Indiana and studying in Indiana. Available to U.S. citizens. **Application Requirements:** Application, financial need analysis. **Deadline:** March 1. **Contact:** Grant Counselors, State Student Assistance Commission of Indiana (SSACI), 150 West Market Street, Suite 500, Indianapolis, IN 46204-2805. *E-mail:* grants@ssaci.state.in.us. *Phone:* 317-232-2350. *Fax:* 317-232-3260. *Web site:* www.ssaci.in.gov.

Indiana Nursing Scholarship Fund. Need-based tuition funding for nursing students enrolled full- or part-time at an eligible Indiana institution. Must be an Indiana resident and have a minimum 2.0 GPA or meet the minimum requirements for the nursing program. Upon graduation, recipients must practice as a nurse in an Indiana health care setting for two years. **Academic/Career Areas:** Nursing. **Award:** Scholarship for use in any year; not renewable. *Award amount:* $200-$5000. *Number of awards:* 510-595. **Eligibility Requirements:** Applicant must be enrolled full or part-time at a two-year or four-year institution or university; resident of Indiana and studying in Indiana. Available to U.S. citizens. **Application Requirements:** Application, financial need analysis. **Deadline:** continuous. **Contact:** Ms. Yvonne Heflin, Director, Special Programs, State Student Assistance Commission of Indiana (SSACI), 150 West Market Street, Suite 500, Indianapolis, IN 46204-2805. *Phone:* 317-232-2350. *Fax:* 317-232-3260. *Web site:* www.ssaci.in.gov.

Indiana Minority Teacher and Special Education Services Scholarship Program. For Black or Hispanic students seeking teaching certification or for students seeking special education teaching certification or occupational or physical therapy certification. Must be a U.S. citizen and Indiana resident enrolled full-time at an eligible Indiana institution. Must teach in an Indiana-accredited elementary or secondary school after graduation. Contact institution for application and deadline. Minimum 2.0 GPA required. **Academic/Career Areas:** Education; Special Education; Therapy/Rehabilitation. **Award:** Scholarship for use in any year; not renewable. *Award amount:* $1000-$4000. *Number of awards:* 340-370. **Eligibility Requirements:** Applicant must be African American or Hispanic; enrolled full-time at a four-year institution or university; resident of Indiana and studying in Indiana. Available to U.S. citizens. **Application Requirements:** Application, financial need analysis. **Deadline:** continuous. **Contact:** Ms. Yvonne Heflin, Director, Special Programs, State Student Assistance Commission of Indiana (SSACI), 150 West Market Street, Suite 500, Indianapolis, IN 46204-2805. *E-mail:* grants@ssaci.state.un.is. *Phone:* 317-232-2350. *Fax:* 317-232-3260. *Web site:* www.ssaci.in.gov.

Twenty-first Century Scholars Award. Income-eligible 7th graders who enroll in the program fulfill a pledge of good citizenship and complete the Affirmation Form are guaranteed tuition for four years at any participating public institution. If the student attends a private institution, the state will award an amount comparable to that of a public institution. If the student attends a participating proprietary school, the state will award a tuition scholarship equal to that of Ivy Tech State College. FAFSA must be filed yearly by March 1. Applicant must be a resident of Indiana. **Award:** Scholarship for use in freshman, sophomore, junior, or senior year; not renewable. *Award amount:* $1000–$4734. *Number of awards:* 2800–8100. **Eligibility Requirements:** Applicant must be enrolled full-time at a two-year, four-year, or technical institution or university; resident of Indiana and studying in Indiana. Applicant must have 2.5 GPA or higher. Available to U.S. citizens. **Application Requirements:** Application, financial need analysis. **Contact:** Twenty-first Century Scholars Program Counselors, State Student Assistance Commission of Indiana (SSACI), 150 West Market Street, Suite 500, Indianapolis, IN 46204-2805. *Phone:* 317-232-2100. *Fax:* 317-232-3260. *Web site:* www.ssaci.in.gov.

IOWA

Iowa Grants. Statewide need-based program to assist high-need Iowa residents. Recipients must demonstrate a high level of financial need to receive awards ranging from $100 to $1,000. Awards are prorated for students enrolled for less than full-time. Awards must be used at Iowa postsecondary institutions. **Award:** Grant for use in freshman, sophomore, junior, or senior year; not renewable. *Award amount:* $100–$1000. **Eligibility Requirements:** Applicant must be enrolled full or part-time at a two-year, four-year, or technical institution or university; resident of Iowa and studying in Iowa. Available to U.S. citizens. **Application Requirements:** Application, financial need analysis. **Deadline:** continuous. **Contact:** Julie Leeper, State Grants Administrator, Iowa College Student Aid Commission, 200 10th Street, 4th Floor, Des Moines, IA 50309-3609. *E-mail:* icsac@max.state.ia.us. *Phone:* 515-242-3370. *Fax:* 515-242-3388. *Web site:* www.iowacollegeaid.org.

Iowa National Guard Education Assistance Program. Program provides postsecondary tuition assistance to members of Iowa National Guard Units. Must study at a postsecondary institution in Iowa. Contact for additional information. **Award:** Grant for use in freshman, sophomore, junior, or senior year; not renewable. *Award amount:* up to $1200. **Eligibility Requirements:** Applicant must be enrolled full or part-time at a two-year, four-year, or technical institution or university; resident of Iowa and studying in Iowa. Available to U.S. citizens. Applicant must have served in the Air Force National Guard or Army National Guard. **Application Requirements:** Application. **Deadline:** continuous. **Contact:** Julie Leeper, State Grants Administrator, Iowa College Student Aid Commission, 200 10th Street, 4th Floor, Des Moines, IA 50309-3609. *E-mail:* icsac@max.state.ia.us. *Phone:* 515-242-3370. *Fax:* 515-242-3388. *Web site:* www. iowacollegeaid.org.

Iowa Teacher Forgivable Loan Program. Forgivable loan assists students who will teach in Iowa secondary schools. Must be an Iowa resident attending an Iowa postsecondary institution. Contact for additional information. **Academic/Career Areas:** Education. **Award:** Forgivable loan for use in freshman, sophomore, junior, or senior year; not renewable. *Award amount:* $2686. **Eligibility Requirements:** Applicant must be enrolled full or part-time at a four-year institution or university; resident of Iowa; studying in Iowa and have employment experience in teaching. Available to U.S. citizens. **Application**

Requirements: Application, financial need analysis. **Deadline:** continuous. **Contact:** Brenda Easter, Special Programs Administrator, Iowa College Student Aid Commission, 200 10th Street, 4th Floor, Des Moines, IA 50309-3609. *E-mail:* icsac@max.state.ia.us. *Phone:* 515-242-3380. *Fax:* 515-242-3388. *Web site:* www. iowacollegeaid.org.

State of Iowa Scholarship Program. Program provides recognition and financial honorarium to Iowa's academically talented high school seniors. Honorary scholarships are presented to all qualified candidates. Approximately 1,700 top-ranking candidates are designated State of Iowa Scholars every March, from an applicant pool of nearly 5,000 high school seniors. Must be used at an Iowa postsecondary institution. Minimum 3.5 GPA required. **Award:** Scholarship for use in freshman year; not renewable. *Award amount:* up to $400. *Number of awards:* up to 1700. **Eligibility Requirements:** Applicant must be high school student; planning to enroll full-time at a two-year, four-year, or technical institution or university; resident of Iowa and studying in Iowa. Applicant must have 3.5 GPA or higher. Available to U.S. citizens. **Application Requirements:** Application, test scores. **Deadline:** November 1. **Contact:** Julie Leeper, State Grants Administrator, State of Iowa, 200 10th Street, 4th Floor, Des Moines, IA 50309-3609. *E-mail:* icsac@max.state.ia.us. *Phone:* 515-242-3370. *Fax:* 515-242-3388. *Web site:* www.iowacollegeaid.org.

Iowa Tuition Grant Program. Program assists students who attend independent postsecondary institutions in Iowa. Iowa residents currently enrolled, or planning to enroll, for at least three semester hours at one of the eligible Iowa postsecondary institutions may apply. Awards currently range from $100 to $4000. Grants may not exceed the difference between independent college and university tuition and fees and the average tuition and fees at the three public Regent universities. **Award:** Grant for use in freshman, sophomore, junior, or senior year; not renewable. *Award amount:* $100-$4000. **Eligibility Requirements:** Applicant must be enrolled full or part-time at a two-year or four-year institution; resident of Iowa and studying in Iowa. Available to U.S. citizens. **Application Requirements:** Application, financial need analysis. **Deadline:** July 1. **Contact:** Julie Leeper, State Grants Administrator, Iowa College Student Aid Commission, 200 10th Street, 4th Floor, Des Moines, IA 50309-3609. *E-mail:* icsac@max.state.ia.us. *Phone:* 515-242-3370. *Fax:* 515-242-3388. *Web site:* www.iowacollegeaid.org.

Iowa Vocational Rehabilitation. Provides vocational rehabilitation services to individuals with disabilities who need these services in order to maintain, retain, or obtain employment compatible with their disabilities. Must be Iowa resident. **Award:** Grant for use in any year; renewable. *Award amount:* $500-$4000. *Number of awards:* up to 5000. **Eligibility Requirements:** Applicant must be enrolled full or part-time at a two-year, four-year, or technical institution or university and resident of Iowa. Applicant must be hearing impaired, learning disabled, physically disabled, or visually impaired. Available to U.S. and non-U.S. citizens. **Application Requirements:** Application, financial need analysis, interview. **Deadline:** continuous. **Contact:** Ralph Childers, Policy and Workforce Initiatives Coordinator, Iowa Division of Vocational Rehabilitation Services, Division of Vocational Rehabilitation Services, 510 East 12th Street, Des Moines, IA 50319. *E-mail:* rchilders@dvrs.state.ia.us. *Phone:* 515-281-4151. *Fax:* 515-281-4703. *Web site:* www.dvrs.state.ia.us.

Iowa Vocational-Technical Tuition Grant Program. Program provides need-based financial assistance to Iowa residents enrolled in career education (vocational-technical), and career option programs at Iowa area community colleges. Grants range from $150 to $650, depending on the length of program, financial need, and available funds. **Award:** Grant for use in freshman or sophomore year; not renewable. *Award amount:* $150–$650. **Eligibility Requirements:** Applicant must be enrolled full or part-time at a technical institution; resident of Iowa and studying in Iowa. Available to U.S. citizens. **Application Requirements:** Application, financial need analysis. **Deadline:** July 1. **Contact:** Julie Leeper, State Grants Administrator, Iowa College Student Aid Commission, 200 10th Street, 4th Floor, Des Moines, IA 50309-3609. *E-mail:* icsac@max.state.ia.us. *Phone:* 515-242-3370. *Fax:* 515-242-3388. *Web site:* www.iowacollegeaid.org.

KANSAS

Vocational Education Scholarship Program–Kansas. Several scholarships for Kansas residents who graduated from a Kansas accredited high school. Must be enrolled in a vocational education program at an eligible Kansas institution. Based on ability and aptitude. Deadline is July 1. Renewable award of $500. Must be U.S. citizen. **Academic/Career Areas:** Trade/Technical Specialties. **Award:** Scholarship for use in freshman or sophomore year; renewable. *Award amount:* $500. *Number of awards:* 100–200. **Eligibility Requirements:** Applicant must be enrolled full-time at a two-year or technical institution; resident of Kansas and studying in Kansas. Available to U.S. citizens. **Application Requirements:** Application, test scores. **Deadline:** July 1. **Contact:** Diane Lindeman, Director of Student Financial Assistance, Kansas Board of Regents, 1000 Southwest Jackson, Suite 520, Topeka, KS 66612-1368. *E-mail:* dlindeman@ksbor.org. *Phone:* 785-296-3517. *Fax:* 785-296-0983. *Web site:* www.kansasregents.com.

Kansas Teacher Service Scholarship. Several scholarships for Kansas residents pursuing teaching careers. Must teach in a hard-to-fill discipline for underserved area of the state of Kansas for one year for each award received. Renewable award of $5000. Application fee is $10. Deadline: April 1. Must be U.S. citizen. **Academic/Career Areas:** Education. **Award:** Forgivable loan for use in freshman, sophomore, junior, or senior year; renewable. *Award amount:* $5000. *Number of awards:* 60–80. **Eligibility Requirements:** Applicant must be enrolled full-time at a two-year or four-year institution or university; resident of Kansas and studying in Kansas. Applicant must have 3.0 GPA or higher. Available to U.S. citizens. **Application Requirements:** Application, references, test scores, transcript. *Fee:* $10. **Deadline:** April 1. **Contact:** Diane Lindeman, Director of Student Financial Assistance, Kansas Board of Regents, 1000 Southwest Jackson, Suite 520, Topeka, KS 66612-1368. *E-mail:* dlindeman@ksbor.org. *Phone:* 785-296-3517. *Fax:* 785-296-0983. *Web site:* www.kansasregents.com.

Kansas Comprehensive Grant Program. Grants available for Kansas residents attending public or private baccalaureate colleges or universities in Kansas. Based on financial need. Must file Free Application for Federal Student Aid to apply. Renewable award based on continuing eligibility. Up to $3000 for undergraduate use. Deadline: April 1. **Award:** Grant for use in freshman, sophomore, junior, or senior year; renewable. *Award amount:* $1100–$3000.

Number of awards: 7000–8200. **Eligibility Requirements:** Applicant must be enrolled full-time at a two-year or four-year institution or university; resident of Kansas and studying in Kansas. Available to U.S. citizens. **Application Requirements:** Financial need analysis. **Deadline:** April 1. **Contact:** Diane Lindeman, Director of Student Financial Assistance, Kansas Board of Regents, 1000 Southwest Jackson, Suite 520, Topeka, KS 66612-1368. *E-mail:* dlindeman@ ksbor.org. *Phone:* 785-296-3517. *Fax:* 785-296-0983. *Web site:* www.kansasregents. com.

Kansas State Scholarship Program. The Kansas State Scholarship Program provides assistance to financially needy, academically outstanding students who attend Kansas postsecondary institutions. Must be Kansas resident. Minimum 3.0 GPA required for renewal. Application fee is $10. Deadline: May 15. **Award:** Scholarship for use in freshman, sophomore, junior, or senior year; renewable. *Award amount:* $1000. *Number of awards:* 1000–1500. **Eligibility Requirements:** Applicant must be enrolled full-time at a two-year or four-year institution or university; resident of Kansas and studying in Kansas. Applicant must have 3.0 GPA or higher. Available to U.S. citizens. **Application Requirements:** Application, financial need analysis, test scores. *Fee:* $10. **Deadline:** May 15. **Contact:** Diane Lindeman, Director of Student Financial Assistance, Kansas Board of Regents, 1000 Southwest Jackson, Suite 520, Topeka, KS 66612-1368. *E-mail:* dlindeman@ksbor.org. *Phone:* 785-296-3517. *Fax:* 785-296-0983. *Web site:* www.kansasregents.com.

Kansas Nursing Service Scholarship Program. This program is designed to encourage Kansans to enroll in nursing programs and commit to practicing in Kansas. Recipients sign agreements to practice nursing at specific facilities one year for each year of support. Application fee is $10. Deadline: May 15. **Academic/Career Areas:** Nursing. **Award:** Forgivable loan for use in junior or senior year; renewable. *Award amount:* $2500–$3500. *Number of awards:* 100–200. **Eligibility Requirements:** Applicant must be enrolled full-time at a two-year or four-year institution or university; resident of Kansas and studying in Kansas. Available to U.S. citizens. **Application Requirements:** Application, financial need analysis. *Fee:* $10. **Deadline:** May 15. **Contact:** Diane Lindeman, Director of Student Financial Assistance, Kansas Board of Regents, 1000 Southwest Jackson, Suite 520, Topeka, KS 66612-1368. *E-mail:* dlindeman@ksbor.org. *Phone:* 785-296-3517. *Fax:* 785-296-0983. *Web site:* www.kansasregents.com.

Kansas Educational Benefits for Children of MIA, POW, and Deceased Veterans of the Vietnam War. Full-tuition scholarship awarded to students who are children of veterans. Must show proof of parent's status as Missing-In-Action, Prisoner-Of-War, or killed in action in the Vietnam War. Kansas residence required of veteran at time of entry to service. Must attend a state-supported postsecondary school. **Award:** Scholarship for use in any year; not renewable. **Eligibility Requirements:** Applicant must be enrolled at a two-year, four-year, or technical institution or university and studying in Kansas. Available to U.S. citizens. Applicant or parent must meet one or more of the following requirements: general military experience; retired from active duty; disabled or killed as a result of military service; Prisoner-Of-War; or Missing-In-Action. **Application Requirements:** Application. **Deadline:** continuous. **Contact:** Dave DePue, Program Director, Kansas Commission on Veterans Affairs, 700 Southwest

Jackson, Jayhawk Tower, #701, Topeka, KS 66603. *E-mail:* kcva004@ink.org. *Phone:* 785-291-3422. *Fax:* 785-296-1462. *Web site:* www.kcva.org.

Ethnic Minority Scholarship Program. This program is designed to assist financially needy, academically competitive students who are identified as members of the following ethnic/racial groups: African-American; American Indian or Alaskan Native; Asian or Pacific Islander; or Hispanic. Must be resident of Kansas and attend college in Kansas. Application fee is $10. Deadline: April 1. Minimum 3.0 GPA required. Must be U.S. citizen. **Award:** Scholarship for use in freshman, sophomore, junior, or senior year; renewable. *Award amount:* $1850. *Number of awards:* 200–250. **Eligibility Requirements:** Applicant must be Native American or Eskimo, Asian, African American, or Hispanic; enrolled full-time at a two-year or four-year institution or university; resident of Kansas and studying in Kansas. Applicant must have 3.0 GPA or higher. Available to U.S. citizens. **Application Requirements:** Application, financial need analysis. *Fee:* $10. **Deadline:** April 1. **Contact:** Diane Lindeman, Director of Student Financial Assistance, Kansas Board of Regents, 1000 Southwest Jackson, Suite 520, Topeka, KS 66612-1368. *E-mail:* dlindeman@ksbor.org. *Phone:* 785-296-3517. *Fax:* 785-296-0983. *Web site:* www.kansasregents.com.

Kansas National Guard Educational Assistance Award Program. Service scholarship for enlisted soldiers in the Kansas National Guard. Pays up to 100% of tuition and fees based on funding. Must attend a state-supported institution. Recipients will be required to serve in the KNG for four years after the last payment of state tuition assistance. Must not have over 15 years of service at time of application. Deadlines are January 15 and August 15. Contact KNG Education Services Specialist for further information. Must be Kansas resident. **Award:** Scholarship for use in freshman, sophomore, junior, or senior year; not renewable. *Award amount:* up to $617. *Number of awards:* up to 400. **Eligibility Requirements:** Applicant must be enrolled full or part-time at a two-year, four-year, or technical institution or university; resident of Kansas and studying in Kansas. Available to U.S. citizens. Applicant must have served in the Air Force National Guard or Army National Guard. **Application Requirements:** Application. **Contact:** SSG. Anita G. Istas, Education Services Specialist, Kansas National Guard Educational Assistance Program, Attn: AGKS-DOP-ESO, The Adjutant General of Kansas, 2800 South West Topeka Boulevard, Topeka, KS 66611-1287. *E-mail:* anita.istas@ks.ngb.army.mil. *Phone:* 785-274-1060. *Fax:* 785-274-1617.

KENTUCKY

Kentucky Transportation Cabinet Civil Engineering Scholarship Program. Established in 1948, the Kentucky Transportation Cabinet has awarded over 1,400 scholarships to civil engineers, amounting to over $10 million in the 53 years. There are currently 77 scholarships available to eligible applicants at 3 ABET-accredited universities in Kentucky. Our mission is to continually pursue statewide recruitment and retention of bright, motivated civil engineers in the Kentucky Transportation Cabinet. **Academic/Career Areas:** Civil Engineering. **Award:** Scholarship for use in freshman, sophomore, junior, or senior year; renewable. *Award amount:* $3200–$3600. *Number of awards:* 70. **Eligibility Requirements:** Applicant must be enrolled full-time at an institution or university; resident of Kentucky and studying in Kentucky. Available to U.S. citizens.

Application Requirements: Application, essay, interview, references, test scores, transcript. **Deadline:** March 1. **Contact:** Jo Anne Tingle, P.E., Scholarship Program Manager, Kentucky Transportation Cabinet, Attn: Scholarship Coordinator, State Office Building, 501 High Street, Room 913, Frankfort, KY 40622. *E-mail:* jo.tingle@mail.state.ky.us. *Phone:* 877-273-5222. *Fax:* 502-564-6683. *Web site:* www.kytc.state.ky.us/person/ScholarshipProgram.htm.

College Access Program (CAP) Grant. One-time award for U.S. citizen and Kentucky resident with no previous college degree. Provides $50 per semester hour for a minimum of six hours per semester. Applicants seeking degrees in religion are not eligible. Must demonstrate financial need and submit Free Application for Federal Student Aid. Priority deadline is March 15. **Award:** Grant for use in freshman, sophomore, junior, or senior year; not renewable. *Award amount:* up to $1200. *Number of awards:* 30,000–35,000. **Eligibility Requirements:** Applicant must be enrolled full or part-time at a two-year, four-year, or technical institution or university; resident of Kentucky and studying in Kentucky. Available to U.S. citizens. **Application Requirements:** Financial need analysis. **Deadline:** continuous. **Contact:** Mark Wells, Program Coordinator, Kentucky Higher Education Assistance Authority (KHEAA), 1050 U.S. 127 South, Frankfort, KY 40601-4323. *E-mail:* mwells@kheaa.com. *Phone:* 502-696-7394. *Fax:* 502-696-7345. *Web site:* www.kheaa.com.

Kentucky Tuition Grant (KTG). Available to Kentucky residents who are full-time undergraduates at an independent college within the state. Must not be enrolled in a religion program. Based on financial need. Submit Free Application for Federal Student Aid. Priority deadline is March 15. **Award:** Grant for use in freshman, sophomore, junior, or senior year; not renewable. *Award amount:* $50–$1600. *Number of awards:* 9000–10,000. **Eligibility Requirements:** Applicant must be enrolled full-time at a two-year or four-year institution or university; resident of Kentucky and studying in Kentucky. Available to U.S. citizens. **Application Requirements:** Financial need analysis. **Deadline:** continuous. **Contact:** Mark Wells, Program Coordinator, Kentucky Higher Education Assistance Authority (KHEAA), 1050 U.S. 127 South, Frankfort, KY 40601-4323. *E-mail:* mwells@kheaa.com. *Phone:* 502-696-7394. *Fax:* 502-696-7345. *Web site:* www.kheaa.com.

Department of Veterans Affairs Tuition Waiver–KY KRS 164-507. Award provides exemption from matriculation or tuition fee for spouse or child of deceased veteran who served during wartime. Applicant is eligible for 36 months of training, or training until they receive a degree, or training until their 23rd birthday, whichever comes first. There is no age limit for spouse. Must attend a Kentucky state-supported university, junior college or vocational training institution. Must be a Kentucky resident. **Award:** Scholarship for use in freshman, sophomore, junior, or senior year; renewable. **Eligibility Requirements:** Applicant must be enrolled full or part-time at a two-year, four-year, or technical institution or university; resident of Kentucky and studying in Kentucky. Available to U.S. citizens. Applicant or parent must meet one or more of the following requirements: general military experience; retired from active duty; disabled or killed as a result of military service; Prisoner-Of-War; or Missing-In-Action. **Application Requirements:** Application. **Deadline:**

continuous. **Contact:** Lisa Pittman, Coordinator, Kentucky Department of Veterans Affairs, 545 South Third Street, Louisville, KY 40202-9095. *Phone:* 502-595-4447. *Fax:* 502-595-4448.

Department of Veterans Affairs Tuition Waiver-Kentucky KRS 164-505. Award provides exemption from matriculation or tuition fees for dependents, widows or widowers of members of the armed forces or members of the National Guard killed while in service or having died as a result of a service connected disability incurred while serving during a wartime period. Veteran's home of record upon entry into the Armed Forces must have been KY. Applicant is eligible to get undergraduate/graduate degrees. Must attend a state supported post secondary institution. **Award:** Scholarship for use in freshman, sophomore, junior, senior, or graduate year; renewable. **Eligibility Requirements:** Applicant must be enrolled full or part-time at an institution or university; resident of Kentucky and studying in Kentucky. Available to U.S. citizens. Applicant or parent must meet one or more of the following requirements: general military experience; retired from active duty; disabled or killed as a result of military service; Prisoner-Of-War; or Missing-In-Action. **Application Requirements:** Application. **Deadline:** continuous. **Contact:** Lisa Pittman, Coordinator, Kentucky Department of Veterans Affairs, 545 South Third Street, Louisville, KY 40202-9095. *Phone:* 800-928-4012. *Fax:* 502-595-4448.

Kentucky National Guard Tuition Award Program. Tuition award available to all members of the Kentucky National Guard. Award is for study at state institutions. Members must be in good standing to be eligible for awards. Applications deadlines are April 1 and October 1. Completed AGO-18-7 required. Undergraduate study given priority. **Award:** Scholarship for use in any year; not renewable. **Eligibility Requirements:** Applicant must be enrolled full or part-time at a two-year, four-year, or technical institution or university and studying in Kentucky. Available to U.S. citizens. Applicant must have served in the Air Force National Guard or Army National Guard. **Contact:** Linda Hawkins, Education Clerk Chief, Kentucky National Guard, TAG Atten: KG-DOP-ED Boone NG Center, Frankfort, KY 40601. *E-mail:* hawkinslf@bngc.dma.state.ky.us. *Phone:* 502-607-1039. *Fax:* 502-607-1264. *Web site:* www.dma.state.ky.us.

Department of VA Tuition Waiver-KY KRS 164-515. Award provides exemption from tuition for spouse or child of permanently disabled member of the National Guard, war veteran, Prisoner-Of-War, or member of the Armed Services Missing-In-Action. Disability must have been sustained while in service; if not time of service must have been during wartime. Applicant is eligible for 36 months of training or training until they receive a degree; or training until their 23rd birthday whichever comes first. There is no age limit for spouse. Must attend a school funded by the KY Dept. of Ed. **Award:** Scholarship for use in freshman, sophomore, junior, or senior year; renewable. **Eligibility Requirements:** Applicant must be resident of Kentucky and studying in Kentucky. Available to U.S. citizens. Applicant or parent must meet one or more of the following requirements: general military experience; retired from active duty; disabled or killed as a result of military service; Prisoner-Of-War; or Missing-In-Action. **Application Requirements:** Application. **Deadline:** continuous. **Contact:** Lisa Pittman, Coordinator, Kentucky Department of Veterans Affairs, 545 South Third Street, Louisville, KY 40202-9095. *Phone:* 502-595-4447. *Fax:* 502-595-4448.

Kentucky Educational Excellence Scholarship (KEES). Annual award based on each Kentucky high school year's GPA of 2.5 or higher and highest ACT or SAT score of 15 or higher received by high school graduation. Awards are renewable if required cumulative GPA maintained at a Kentucky postsecondary school. Must be a Kentucky resident. **Award:** Scholarship for use in freshman, sophomore, junior, or senior year; renewable. *Award amount:* $125–$1500. *Number of awards:* 30,000–40,000. **Eligibility Requirements:** Applicant must be high school student; planning to enroll full or part-time at a two-year, four-year, or technical institution or university; resident of Kentucky and studying in Kentucky. Applicant must have 2.5 GPA or higher. Available to U.S. citizens. **Application Requirements:** Test scores, transcript. **Contact:** Tim Phelps, KEES Program Coordinator, Kentucky Higher Education Assistance Authority (KHEAA), 1050 U.S. 127 South, Frankfort, KY 40601-4323. *E-mail:* tphelps@kheaa.com. *Phone:* 502-696-7397. *Fax:* 502-696-7345. *Web site:* www.kheaa.com.

Kentucky Teacher Scholarship Program. Award for Kentucky resident attending Kentucky institutions and pursuing initial teacher certification. Must teach one semester for each semester of award received. In critical shortage areas, must teach one semester for every two semesters of award received. Repayment obligation if teaching requirement not met. Submit Free Application for Federal Student Aid and Teacher Scholarship Application by May 1. **Academic/Career Areas:** Education; Special Education. **Award:** Forgivable loan for use in freshman, sophomore, junior, senior, or graduate year; not renewable. *Award amount:* $100–$5000. *Number of awards:* 600–700. **Eligibility Requirements:** Applicant must be enrolled full-time at a two-year or four-year institution or university; resident of Kentucky and studying in Kentucky. Available to U.S. citizens. **Application Requirements:** Application, financial need analysis. **Deadline:** May 1. **Contact:** Pam Polly, Program Coordinator, Kentucky Higher Education Assistance Authority (KHEAA), 1050 U.S. 127 South, Frankfort, KY 40601-4323. *E-mail:* ppolly@kheaa.com. *Phone:* 502-696-7392. *Fax:* 502-696-7345. *Web site:* www.kheaa.com.

Environmental Protection Scholarships. Renewable awards for college juniors, seniors, and graduate students for tuition, fees, and room and board at a Kentucky state university. Awards of $3500 to $4500 per semester for up to four semesters. Minimum 2.5 GPA required. Must agree to work full-time for the Kentucky Natural Resources and Environmental Protection Cabinet upon graduation. Interview is required. **Academic/Career Areas:** Chemical Engineering; Civil Engineering; Materials Science, Engineering and Metallurgy. **Award:** Scholarship for use in junior, senior, or graduate year; renewable. *Award amount:* $3500–$4500. *Number of awards:* 3–5. **Eligibility Requirements:** Applicant must be enrolled full-time at a four-year institution or university and studying in Kentucky. Applicant must have 2.5 GPA or higher. Available to U.S. and non-U.S. citizens. **Application Requirements:** Application, essay, interview, references, transcript. **Deadline:** February 15. **Contact:** Scholarship Program Coordinator, Kentucky Natural Resources and Environmental Protection Cabinet, 233 Mining/Mineral Resources Building, Lexington, KY 40506. *E-mail:* kipp@pop.uky.edu. *Phone:* 859-257-1299. *Fax:* 859-323-1049. *Web site:* www.uky.edu/waterresources.

LOUISIANA

Leveraging Educational Assistance Program (LEAP). LEAP program provides federal and state funds to provide need-based grants to academically qualified students. Individual award determined by Financial Aid Office and governed by number of applicants and availability of funds. File Free Application for Federal Student aid by school deadline to apply each year. For Louisiana students attending Louisiana postsecondary institutions. **Award:** Grant for use in freshman, sophomore, junior, or senior year; not renewable. *Award amount:* $200–$2000. *Number of awards:* 3000. **Eligibility Requirements:** Applicant must be enrolled full or part-time at a two-year, four-year, or technical institution or university; resident of Louisiana and studying in Louisiana. Available to U.S. citizens. **Application Requirements:** Application, financial need analysis. **Contact:** Public Information, Louisiana Office of Student Financial Assistance, PO Box 91202, Baton Rouge, LA 70821-9202. *E-mail:* custserv@osfa.state.la.us. *Phone:* 800-259-5626 Ext. 1012. *Web site:* www.osfa.state.la.us.

Louisiana Department of Veterans Affairs Awards Program. Tuition exemption at any state-supported college, university or technical institute for children of veterans that are rated 90% or above service-connected disabled by the U.S. Department of Veterans Affairs and surviving spouse and children of veterans that died on active duty, in line of duty or where death was the result of a disability incurred in or aggravated by military service. Applicant must be between the ages of 16-25. For residents of Louisiana that are attending a Louisiana institution. **Award:** Scholarship for use in freshman, sophomore, junior, senior, graduate, or post graduate years; renewable. *Award amount:* $12,000–$15,000. **Eligibility Requirements:** Applicant must be age 16-25; enrolled full-time at a two-year, four-year, or technical institution or university; resident of Louisiana and studying in Louisiana. Available to U.S. citizens. Applicant or parent must meet one or more of the following requirements: general military experience; retired from active duty; disabled or killed as a result of military service; Prisoner-Of-War; or Missing-In-Action. **Application Requirements:** Application. **Deadline:** continuous. **Contact:** C. Ray Noland, V.A. Regional Manager, Louisiana Department of Veteran Affairs, PO Box 90495, Capitol Station, Baton Rouge, LA 70804. *E-mail:* rnoland@vetaffairs.com. *Phone:* 225-922-0507. *Fax:* 225-922-0511.

Rockefeller State Wildlife Scholarship. For Louisiana residents attending a public college within the state studying wildlife, forestry, or marine sciences full-time. Renewable up to five years as an undergraduate and two years as a graduate. Must have at least a 2.5 GPA and have taken the ACT or SAT. **Academic/Career Areas:** Animal/Veterinary Sciences; Applied Sciences; Natural Resources. **Award:** Scholarship for use in any year; renewable. *Award amount:* $1000. *Number of awards:* 60. **Eligibility Requirements:** Applicant must be enrolled full-time at a two-year or four-year institution or university; resident of Louisiana and studying in Louisiana. Applicant must have 2.5 GPA or higher. Available to U.S. citizens. **Application Requirements:** Application, test scores, transcript. **Deadline:** July 1. **Contact:** Public Information, Louisiana Office of Student Financial Assistance, PO Box 91202, Baton Rouge, LA 70821-9202. *E-mail:* custserv@osfa.state.la.us. *Phone:* 800-259-5626 Ext. 1012. *Web site:* www. osfa.state.la.us.

Profiles of State-Sponsored Programs

TOPS Opportunity Award. Program awards an amount equal to tuition to students attending a Louisiana public institution, or an amount equal to the weighted average public tuition to students attending a LAICU private institution. Must have a minimum high school GPA of 2.5, the prior year's state average ACT score, and complete a 16.5 unit core curriculum. Must be a Louisiana resident. **Award:** Scholarship for use in freshman, sophomore, junior, or senior year; renewable. *Award amount:* $1240–$3202. **Eligibility Requirements:** Applicant must be high school student; planning to enroll full-time at a two-year, four-year, or technical institution or university; resident of Louisiana and studying in Louisiana. Applicant must have 2.5 GPA or higher. Available to U.S. citizens. **Application Requirements:** Application, test scores. **Deadline:** July 1. **Contact:** Public Information, Louisiana Office of Student Financial Assistance, PO Box 91202, Baton Rouge, LA 70821-9202. *E-mail:* custserv@osfa.state.la.us. *Phone:* 800-259-5626 Ext. 1012. *Fax:* 225-922-0790. *Web site:* www.osfa.state. la.us.

TOPS Performance Award. Program awards an amount equal to tuition plus a $400 annual stipend to students attending a Louisiana public institution, or an amount equal to the weighted average public tuition plus a $400 annual stipend to students attending a LAICU private institution. Must have a minimum high school GPA of 3.5, an ACT score of 23 and completion of a 16.5 unit core curriculum. Must be a Louisiana resident. **Award:** Scholarship for use in freshman, sophomore, junior, or senior year; renewable. **Eligibility Requirements:** Applicant must be high school student; planning to enroll full-time at a two-year, four-year, or technical institution or university; resident of Louisiana and studying in Louisiana. Applicant must have 3.5 GPA or higher. Available to U.S. citizens. **Application Requirements:** Application, test scores. **Deadline:** July 1. **Contact:** Public Information, Louisiana Office of Student Financial Assistance, PO Box 91202, Baton Rouge, LA 70821-9202. *E-mail:* custserv@osfa.state.la.us. *Phone:* 800-259-5626 Ext. 1012. *Fax:* 225-922-0790. *Web site:* www.osfa.state. la.us.

TOPS Honors Award. Program awards an amount equal to tuition plus an $800 per year stipend to students attending a Louisiana public institution, or an amount equal to the weighted average public tuition plus an $800 per year stipend to students attending a LAICU private institution. Must have a minimum high school GPA of 3.5, ACT score of 27, and complete a 16.5 unit core curriculum. Must be resident of Louisiana. **Award:** Scholarship for use in freshman, sophomore, junior, or senior year; renewable. *Award amount:* $2040–$3802. **Eligibility Requirements:** Applicant must be high school student; planning to enroll full-time at a two-year, four-year, or technical institution or university; resident of Louisiana and studying in Louisiana. Applicant must have 3.5 GPA or higher. Available to U.S. citizens. **Application Requirements:** Application, test scores. **Deadline:** July 1. **Contact:** Public Information, Louisiana Office of Student Financial Assistance, PO Box 91202, Baton Rouge, LA 70821-9202. *E-mail:* custserv@osfa.state.la.us. *Phone:* 800-259-5626 Ext. 1012. *Fax:* 225-922-0790. *Web site:* www.osfa.state.la.us.

TOPS Tech Award. Program awards an amount equal to tuition for up to two years of technical training at a Louisiana postsecondary institution that offers a vocational or technical education certificate or diploma program, or a non-academic degree program. Must have a 2.5 high school GPA, an ACT score of 17 and complete the TOPS-Tech core curriculum. Must be a Louisiana resident. **Award:** Scholarship for use in any year; renewable. *Award amount:* $890. **Eligibility Requirements:** Applicant must be high school student; planning to enroll full-time at a technical institution; resident of Louisiana and studying in Louisiana. Applicant must have 2.5 GPA or higher. Available to U.S. citizens. **Application Requirements:** Application, test scores. **Deadline:** July 1. **Contact:** Public Information, Louisiana Office of Student Financial Assistance, PO Box 91202, Baton Rouge, LA 70821-9202. *E-mail:* custserv@osfa.state.la.us. *Phone:* 800-259-5626 Ext. 1012. *Fax:* 225-922-0790. *Web site:* www.osfa.state.la.us.

TOPS Alternate Performance Award. Program awards an amount equal to tuition plus a $400 annual stipend to students attending a Louisiana public institution, or an amount equal to the weighted average public tuition plus a $400 annual stipend to students attending a LAICU private institution. Must have a minimum high school GPA of 3.0 on ACT score of 24, completion of 10 honors courses graded on a 5.0 scale, and completion of a 16.5 unit core curriculum. Must be a resident of Louisiana. **Award:** Scholarship for use in freshman, sophomore, junior, or senior year; renewable. *Award amount:* $1640–$3402. **Eligibility Requirements:** Applicant must be high school student; planning to enroll full-time at a two-year, four-year, or technical institution or university; resident of Louisiana and studying in Louisiana. Applicant must have 3.0 GPA or higher. Available to U.S. citizens. **Application Requirements:** Application, test scores. **Deadline:** July 1. **Contact:** Public Information Officer, Louisiana Office of Student Financial Assistance, PO Box 91202, Baton Rouge, LA 70821-9202. *E-mail:* custserv@osfa.state.la.us. *Phone:* 800-259-5626 Ext. 1012. *Fax:* 225-922-0790. *Web site:* www.osfa.state.la.us.

Louisiana National Guard State Tuition Exemption Program. Renewable award for college undergraduates to receive tuition exemption upon satisfactory performance in the Louisiana National Guard. Must attend a state-funded institution in Louisiana. Must be a resident and registered voter in Louisiana. Must meet the academic and residency requirements of the university attended. Must provide documentation of Louisiana National Guard enlistment. The exemption can be used for up to 15 semesters. Minimum 2.5 GPA required. **Award:** Scholarship for use in freshman, sophomore, junior, or senior year; renewable. **Eligibility Requirements:** Applicant must be enrolled full or part-time at a two-year, four-year, or technical institution or university; resident of Louisiana and studying in Louisiana. Applicant must have 2.5 GPA or higher. Available to U.S. citizens. Applicant must have served in the Air Force National Guard or Army National Guard. **Application Requirements: Deadline:** continuous. **Contact:** Cpt. Jona M. Hughes, Education Services Officers, Louisiana National Guard—State of Louisiana, Military Department, Building 35, Jackson Barracks, DHR-MD, New Orleans, LA 70146-0330. *E-mail:* hughesj@la-arng.ngb.army.mil. *Phone:* 504-278-8531 Ext. 8304. *Fax:* 504-278-8025. *Web site:* www.la.ngb.army. mil.

MAINE

Maine State Grant. Scholarships for residents of Maine attending an eligible school, full-time, in Connecticut, Maine, Massachusetts, New Hampshire, Pennsylvania, Rhode Island, Washington, D.C., or Vermont. Award based on need. Must apply annually. Complete Free Application for Federal Student Aid to apply. One-time award of $500-$1250 for undergraduate study. **Award:** Grant for use in freshman, sophomore, junior, or senior year; not renewable. *Award amount:* $500-$1250. *Number of awards:* 8900-12,500. **Eligibility Requirements:** Applicant must be enrolled full-time at a two-year, four-year, or technical institution or university; resident of Maine and studying in Connecticut, District of Columbia, Maine, Massachusetts, New Hampshire, Pennsylvania, Rhode Island, or Vermont. **Application Requirements:** Application, financial need analysis. **Deadline:** May 1. **Contact:** Claude Roy, Program Officer, Finance Authority of Maine, 5 Community Drive, Augusta, ME 04332-0949. *E-mail:* claude@famemaine.com. *Phone:* 800-228-3734. *Fax:* 207-623-0095. *Web site:* www.famemaine.com.

Veterans Dependents Educational Benefits–Maine. Tuition waiver award for dependents or spouses of veterans who were Prisoner-Of-War, Missing-In-Action, or permanently disabled as a result of service. Veteran must have been Maine resident at service entry for five years preceding application. For use at Maine University system, Technical colleges and Maine Maritime. Must be high school graduate. Must submit birth certificate and proof of VA disability of veteran. Award renewable for eight semesters for those under 22 years of age. **Award:** Scholarship for use in any year; renewable. **Eligibility Requirements:** Applicant must be age 21 or under; enrolled full or part-time at a technical institution or university; resident of Maine and studying in Maine. Applicant or parent must meet one or more of the following requirements: general military experience; retired from active duty; disabled or killed as a result of military service; Prisoner-Of-War; or Missing-In-Action. **Application Requirements:** Application. **Deadline:** continuous. **Contact:** Frank Soares, Administrator, Maine Bureau of Veterans Services, State House Station 117, Augusta, ME 04333-0117. *E-mail:* mvs@me-arng.ngb.army.mil. *Phone:* 207-626-4464. *Fax:* 207-626-4471.

Educators for Maine Program. Loans for residents of Maine who are high school seniors, college students, or college graduates with a minimum 3.0 GPA, studying or preparing to study teacher education. Loan is forgivable if student teaches in Maine upon graduation. Awards are based on merit. **Academic/ Career Areas:** Education. **Award:** Forgivable loan for use in freshman, sophomore, junior, senior, or graduate year; not renewable. *Award amount:* $1500-$3000. **Eligibility Requirements:** Applicant must be enrolled full-time at a four-year institution or university and resident of Maine. Applicant must have 3.0 GPA or higher. Available to U.S. citizens. **Application Requirements:** Application, essay, test scores, transcript. **Deadline:** April 1. **Contact:** Trisha Malloy, Program Officer, Finance Authority of Maine, 5 Community Drive, Augusta, ME 04332-0949. *E-mail:* trisha@famemaine.com. *Phone:* 800-228-3734. *Fax:* 207-623-0095. *Web site:* www.famemaine.com.

MARYLAND

Science and Technology Scholarship. Provides assistance to full-time students in an academic program that will address career shortage areas in the state (computer science, engineering, biological sciences, mathematics, and physical sciences). Must be Maryland resident. Must have cumulative unweighted 3.0 GPA in math, natural or physical science, social science, social studies, English, foreign language, and computer science. **Academic/Career Areas:** Biology; Chemical Engineering; Civil Engineering; Computer Science/Data Processing;

Earth Science; Electrical Engineering/Electronics; Engineering/Technology; Engineering-Related Technologies; Fire Sciences; Physical Sciences and Math. **Award:** Forgivable loan for use in freshman, sophomore, junior, or senior year; renewable. *Award amount:* $1000–$3000. *Number of awards:* up to 2500. **Eligibility Requirements:** Applicant must be enrolled full-time at a two-year or four-year institution or university; resident of Maryland and studying in Maryland. Applicant must have 3.0 GPA or higher. Available to U.S. citizens. **Application Requirements:** Application, transcript. **Deadline:** March 1. **Contact:** Julie Perrotta, Scholarship Administration, Maryland State Higher Education Commission, 16 Francis Street, Annapolis, MD 21401-1781. *E-mail:* ssamail@mhec.state. md.us. *Phone:* 410-260-4564. *Fax:* 410-974-5994. *Web site:* www.mhec.state.md. us.

Distinguished Scholar Award–Maryland. Renewable award for Maryland students enrolled full-time at Maryland institutions. National Merit Scholar Finalists automatically offered award. Others may qualify for the award in satisfying criteria of a minimum 3.7 GPA or in combination with high test scores, or for Talent in Arts competition in categories of music, drama, dance, or visual arts. Must maintain 3.0 GPA in college for award to be renewed. Contact for further details. **Award:** Scholarship for use in freshman, sophomore, junior, or senior year; renewable. *Award amount:* up to $3000. *Number of awards:* up to 2000. **Eligibility Requirements:** Applicant must be high school student; planning to enroll full-time at a two-year or four-year institution or university; resident of Maryland and studying in Maryland. Available to U.S. citizens. **Application Requirements:** Application, test scores, transcript. **Deadline:** February 15. **Contact:** Margaret Riley, Scholarship Administration, Maryland State Higher Education Commission, 16 Francis Street, Annapolis, MD 21401-1781. *E-mail:* ssamail@mhec.state.md.us. *Phone:* 410-260-4568. *Fax:* 410-974-5994. *Web site:* www.mhec.state.md.us.

Distinguished Scholar-Teacher Education Awards. Up to $3,000 scholarship for Maryland high school seniors who have received the Distinguished Scholar Award. Recipient must enroll as a full-time undergraduate in a Maryland institution and pursue a program of study leading to a Maryland teaching certificate. Must maintain 3.0 GPA for renewal. Must teach in a Maryland public school one year for each year scholarship is received. **Academic/Career Areas:** Education. **Award:** Scholarship for use in freshman, sophomore, junior, or senior year; renewable. *Award amount:* up to $3000. *Number of awards:* 20–80. **Eligibility Requirements:** Applicant must be high school student; planning to enroll full-time at a two-year or four-year institution or university; resident of Maryland and studying in Maryland. Applicant must have 3.0 GPA or higher. Available to U.S. citizens. **Application Requirements:** Application, test scores, transcript. **Deadline:** continuous. **Contact:** Margaret Riley, Scholarship Administration, Maryland State Higher Education Commission, 16 Francis Street, Annapolis, MD 21401-1781. *E-mail:* ssamail@mhec.state.md.us. *Phone:* 410-260-4568. *Fax:* 410-974-5994. *Web site:* www.mhec.state.md.us.

Maryland State Nursing Scholarship and Living Expenses Grant. Renewable grant for Maryland residents enrolled in a two-or four-year Maryland institution nursing degree program. Recipients must agree to serve as a full-time nurse in a Maryland shortage area and must maintain a 3.0 GPA in college. Application deadline is June 30. Submit Free Application for Federal Student Aid. **Academic/**

Career Areas: Nursing. **Award:** Forgivable loan for use in freshman, sophomore, junior, senior, or graduate year; renewable. *Award amount:* $200–$4800. *Number of awards:* 186–600. **Eligibility Requirements:** Applicant must be enrolled full or part-time at a two-year or four-year institution or university; resident of Maryland and studying in Maryland. Applicant must have 3.0 GPA or higher. Available to U.S. citizens. **Application Requirements:** Application, financial need analysis, transcript. **Deadline:** June 30. **Contact:** Cis Whittington, Scholarship Administration, Maryland State Higher Education Commission, 16 Francis Street, Annapolis, MD 21401-1781. *E-mail:* ssamail@mhec.state.md.us. *Phone:* 410-260-4546. *Fax:* 410-974-5994. *Web site:* www.mhec.state.md.us.

Physical and Occupational Therapists and Assistants Grant Program. For Maryland residents training as physical, occupational therapists or therapy assistants at Maryland postsecondary institutions. Recipients must provide one year of service for each full, or partial, year of award. Service must be to handicapped children in a Maryland facility that has, or accommodates and provides services to, such children. **Academic/Career Areas:** Therapy/Rehabilitation. **Award:** Forgivable loan for use in freshman, sophomore, junior, senior, or graduate year; renewable. *Award amount:* up to $2000. *Number of awards:* up to 14. **Eligibility Requirements:** Applicant must be enrolled full-time at a two-year or four-year institution or university; resident of Maryland and studying in Maryland. Available to U.S. citizens. **Application Requirements:** Application, transcript. **Deadline:** July 1. **Contact:** Margaret Riley, Scholarship Administration, Maryland State Higher Education Commission, 16 Francis Street, Annapolis, MD 21401-1781. *E-mail:* ssamail@mhec.state.md.us. *Phone:* 410-260-4568. *Fax:* 410-974-5994. *Web site:* www.mhec.state.md.us.

Firefighter, Ambulance, and Rescue Squad Member Tuition Reimbursement Program–Maryland. Award intended to reimburse members of rescue organizations serving Maryland communities for tuition costs of course work towards a degree or certificate in fire service or medical technology. Must attend a two- or four-year school in Maryland. **Academic/Career Areas:** Fire Sciences; Health and Medical Sciences; Trade/Technical Specialties. **Award:** Scholarship for use in any year; not renewable. *Award amount:* $200–$4000. *Number of awards:* 100–300. **Eligibility Requirements:** Applicant must be enrolled full or part-time at a two-year or four-year institution or university; resident of Maryland; studying in Maryland and have employment experience in police/firefighting. Available to U.S. citizens. **Application Requirements:** Application, transcript. **Deadline:** July 1. **Contact:** Margaret Riley, Scholarship Administration, Maryland State Higher Education Commission, 16 Francis Street, Annapolis, MD 21401-1781. *E-mail:* ssamail@mhec.state.md.us. *Phone:* 410-264-4568. *Fax:* 410-974-5994. *Web site:* www.mhec.state.md.us.

Edward T. Conroy Memorial Scholarship Program. Scholarship for dependents of deceased or 100% disabled U.S. Armed Forces personnel, Vietnam Missing-In-Action or Prisoner-Of-War or sons or daughters of deceased safety personnel, or surviving spouse who has not remarried, deceased state personnel, or deceased safety personnel. Must be a Maryland resident at time of death or disability. Submit applicable VA verification, 100% disability verification and/or chapter 35 letter with application. Must be at least 16 years of age. Must attend Maryland institution. **Award:** Scholarship for use in freshman, sophomore, junior, senior, or graduate year; renewable. *Award amount:* up to $12,981.

Number of awards: up to 80. **Eligibility Requirements:** Applicant must be age 16-24; enrolled full or part-time at a two-year or four-year institution or university; resident of Maryland and studying in Maryland. Available to U.S. citizens. Applicant or parent must meet one or more of the following requirements: general military experience; retired from active duty; disabled or killed as a result of military service; Prisoner-Of-War; or Missing-In-Action. **Application Requirements:** Application. **Deadline:** July 30. **Contact:** Margaret Crutchley, Scholarship Administration, Maryland State Higher Education Commission, 16 Francis Street, Annapolis, MD 21401-1781. *E-mail:* ssamail@mhec. state.md.us. *Phone:* 410-260-4545. *Fax:* 410-974-5994. *Web site:* www.mhec. state.md.us.

Guaranteed Access Grant–Maryland. Award for Maryland resident enrolling full-time in an undergraduate program at a Maryland institution. Must be under 22 at time of first award and begin college within one year of completing high school in Maryland with a minimum 2.5 GPA. Must have an annual family income less than 130% of the federal poverty level guideline. **Award:** Grant for use in freshman, sophomore, junior, or senior year; renewable. *Award amount:* $400–$9200. *Number of awards:* up to 1000. **Eligibility Requirements:** Applicant must be enrolled full-time at a two-year or four-year institution or university; resident of Maryland and studying in Maryland. Applicant must have 2.5 GPA or higher. Available to U.S. citizens. **Application Requirements:** Application, financial need analysis, transcript. **Deadline:** continuous. **Contact:** Theresa Lowe, Scholarship Administration, Maryland State Higher Education Commission, 16 Francis Street, Annapolis, MD 21401-1781. *E-mail:* ssamail@ mhec.state.md.us. *Phone:* 410-260-4555. *Fax:* 410-974-5994. *Web site:* www. mhec.state.md.us.

Educational Assistance Grants–Maryland. Award for Maryland residents accepted or enrolled in a full-time undergraduate degree or certificate program at a Maryland institution or hospital nursing school. Must submit financial aid form by March 1. Must earn 2.0 GPA in college to maintain award. **Award:** Grant for use in freshman, sophomore, junior, or senior year; renewable. *Award amount:* $400–$2700. *Number of awards:* 11,000–20,000. **Eligibility Requirements:** Applicant must be enrolled full-time at a two-year or four-year institution or university; resident of Maryland and studying in Maryland. Available to U.S. citizens. **Application Requirements:** Application, financial need analysis. **Deadline:** March 1. **Contact:** Barbara Fantom, Scholarship Administration, Maryland State Higher Education Commission, 16 Francis Street, Annapolis, MD 21401-1781. *E-mail:* ssamail@mhec.state.md.us. *Phone:* 410-260-4547. *Fax:* 410-974-5994. *Web site:* www.mhec.state.md.us.

Developmental Disabilities Tuition Assistance Program. Provides tuition assistance to students who are service employees that provide direct support or care to individuals with mental health disabilities. Must be a Maryland resident attending a Maryland college. **Academic/Career Areas:** Health and Medical Sciences; Nursing; Social Services; Special Education; Therapy/Rehabilitation. **Award:** Forgivable loan for use in freshman, sophomore, junior, senior, or graduate year; renewable. *Award amount:* $500–$3000. *Number of awards:* up to 400. **Eligibility Requirements:** Applicant must be enrolled full or part-time at a two-year or four-year institution or university; resident of Maryland; studying in Maryland and have employment experience in designated career field. Available to U.S. citizens. **Application Requirements:** Application, transcript. **Deadline:** July 1. **Contact:** Deanne Alspach, Scholarship Administration, Maryland State Higher Education Commission, 16 Francis Street, Annapolis, MD 21401-1781. *E-mail:* ssamail@mhec.state.md.us. *Phone:* 410-260-4553. *Fax:* 410-974-5994. *Web site:* www.mhec.state.md.us.

Maryland Teacher Scholarship. Available to Maryland residents attending a college in Maryland with a major in teacher education. Must work as public school teachers within the state of Maryland. **Academic/Career Areas:** Education; Special Education. **Award:** Forgivable loan for use in any year; renewable. *Award amount:* $2000–$5000. *Number of awards:* up to 2300. **Eligibility Requirements:** Applicant must be enrolled full-time at a two-year or four-year institution or university; resident of Maryland and studying in Maryland. Applicant must have 3.0 GPA or higher. Available to U.S. citizens. **Application Requirements:** Application, transcript. **Deadline:** March 1. **Contact:** Julie Perrotta, Scholarship Administration, Maryland State Higher Education Commission, 16 Francis Street, Annapolis, MD 21401-1781. *E-mail:* ssamail@mhec.state.md.us. *Phone:* 410-260-4564. *Fax:* 410-974-5994. *Web site:* www.mhec.state.md.us.

Hope Scholarship. Student must be a high school senior at the time of application and must enroll in an eligible major. Family income may not exceed $95,000 annually. Recipients must agree to work in the state of Maryland for one year for each year they accept the award. **Academic/Career Areas:** Agriculture; Arts; Business/Consumer Services; Communications; Foreign Language; Health and Medical Sciences; Home Economics; Humanities; Literature/English/Writing; Natural Resources; Political Science; Social Sciences. **Award:** Forgivable loan for use in freshman, sophomore, junior, or senior year; renewable. *Award amount:* $1000–$3000. *Number of awards:* up to 300. **Eligibility Requirements:** Applicant must be high school student; planning to enroll full-time at a two-year or four-year institution; resident of Maryland and studying in Maryland. Applicant must have 3.0 GPA or higher. Available to U.S. citizens. **Application Requirements:** Application, financial need analysis, transcript. **Deadline:** March 1. **Contact:** Debbie Smith, Scholarship Administration, Maryland State Higher Education Commission, 16 Francis Street, Annapolis, MD 21401-1781. *E-mail:* ssamail@mhec.state.md.us. *Phone:* 410-260-4594. *Fax:* 410-974-5994. *Web site:* www.mhec.state.md.us.

J.F. Tolbert Memorial Student Grant Program. Available to Maryland residents attending a private career school in Maryland with at least 18 clock hours per week. **Award:** Grant for use in any year; not renewable. *Award amount:* up to $300. *Number of awards:* 1500. **Eligibility Requirements:** Applicant must be enrolled at a technical institution; resident of Maryland and studying in Maryland. Available to U.S. citizens. **Application Requirements:** Application, financial need analysis. **Deadline:** continuous. **Contact:** Carla Rich, Scholarship Administration, Maryland State Higher Education Commission, 16 Francis Street, Annapolis, MD 21401-1781. *E-mail:* ssamail@mhec.state.md.us. *Phone:* 410-260-4513. *Fax:* 410-974-5994. *Web site:* www.mhec.state.md.us.

Janet L. Hoffmann Loan Assistance Repayment Program. Provides assistance for repayment of loan debt to Maryland residents working full-time in nonprofit organizations and state or local governments. Must submit Employment Verification Form and Lender verification form. **Academic/Career Areas:** Education; Law/Legal Services; Nursing; Social Services; Therapy/Rehabilitation. **Award:** Forgivable loan for use in any year; not renewable. *Award amount:* up to $7500. *Number of awards:* up to 400. **Eligibility Requirements:** Applicant must be resident of Maryland and studying in Maryland. Available to U.S. citizens. **Application Requirements:** Application, transcript. **Deadline:** September 30. **Contact:** Cis Whittington, Scholarship Administration, Maryland State Higher Education Commission, 16 Francis Street, Annapolis, MD 21401-1781. *E-mail:* ssamail@mhec.state.md.us. *Phone:* 410-260-4546. *Fax:* 410-974-5994. *Web site:* www.mhec.state.md.us.

Community College Transfer Student Hope Scholarship. Award available to students who transfer with minimum 3.0 GPA and 60 credits from a Maryland two-year college to a Maryland four-year college. Annual family income limit is $95,000. Must agree to work in Maryland for up to three years. **Award:** Forgivable loan for use in junior or senior year; renewable. *Award amount:* up to $3000. **Eligibility Requirements:** Applicant must be enrolled full-time at a four-year institution or university; resident of Maryland and studying in Maryland. Applicant must have 3.0 GPA or higher. Available to U.S. citizens. **Application Requirements:** Application, financial need analysis, transcript. **Deadline:** March 1. **Contact:** Monica Tipton, Scholarship Administration, Maryland State Higher Education Commission, 16 Francis Street, Annapolis, MD 21401-1781. *E-mail:* ssamail@mhec.state.md.us. *Phone:* 410-260-4563. *Fax:* 410-974-5994. *Web site:* www.mhec.state.md.us.

Professional Scholarship Program–Maryland. Professional scholarships provide need-based financial assistance to full-time students attending a Maryland school of medicine, dentistry, law, pharmacy, social work, or nursing. Must be a Maryland resident. **Academic/Career Areas:** Dental Health/Services; Health and Medical Sciences; Law/Legal Services; Nursing; Social Services. **Award:** Scholarship for use in freshman, sophomore, junior, senior, or graduate year; renewable. *Award amount:* $200–$1000. *Number of awards:* 200–500. **Eligibility Requirements:** Applicant must be enrolled full-time at a two-year or four-year institution or university; resident of Maryland and studying in Maryland. Available to U.S. citizens. **Application Requirements:** Application, financial need analysis. **Deadline:** March 1. **Contact:** Cis Whittington, Scholarship Administration, Maryland State Higher Education Commission, 16 Francis Street, Annapolis, MD 21401-1781. *E-mail:* ssamail@mhec.state.md.us. *Phone:* 410-260-4546. *Fax:* 410-974-5994. *Web site:* www.mhec.state.md.us.

Delegate Scholarship Program–Maryland. Delegate scholarships help Maryland residents attending Maryland degree-granting institutions, certain career schools, or nursing diploma schools. May attend out-of-state institution if Maryland Higher Education Commission deems major to be unique and not offered at a Maryland institution. Free Application for Federal Student Aid may be required. Students interested in this program should apply by contacting their legislative district delegate. **Award:** Scholarship for use in freshman, sophomore, junior, senior, or graduate year; not renewable. *Award amount:* $200–$12,981. *Number of awards:* up to 3500. **Eligibility Requirements:** Applicant must be enrolled full or part-time at a two-year, four-year, or technical institution or university; resident of Maryland and studying in Maryland. Available to U.S. citizens. **Application Requirements:** Application, financial need analysis. **Deadline:** continuous.

Contact: Barbara Fantom, Scholarship Administration, Maryland State Higher Education Commission, 16 Francis Street, Annapolis, MD 21401-1781. *E-mail:* ssamail@mhec.state.md.us. *Phone:* 410-260-4547. *Fax:* 410-974-5994. *Web site:* www.mhec.state.md.us.

Child Care Provider Program–Maryland. Scholarship provides assistance for Maryland undergraduates attending a Maryland institution and pursuing studies in a child development program or an early childhood education program. Must serve as a professional day care provider in Maryland for one year for each year award received. Must maintain minimum 2.0 GPA. Contact for further information.**Academic/Career Areas:** Education. **Award:** Scholarship for use in freshman, sophomore, junior, or senior year; renewable. *Award amount:* $500–$2000. *Number of awards:* up to 90. **Eligibility Requirements:** Applicant must be enrolled full or part-time at a two-year or four-year institution or university; resident of Maryland and studying in Maryland. Available to U.S. citizens. **Application Requirements:** Application, transcript. **Deadline:** June 15. **Contact:** Margaret Crutchley, Scholarship Administration, Maryland State Higher Education Commission, 16 Francis Street, Annapolis, MD 21401-1781. *E-mail:* ssamail@mhec.state.md.us. *Phone:* 410-260-4545. *Fax:* 410-974-5994. *Web site:* www.mhec.state.md.us.

Sharon Christa McAuliffe Teacher Education–Critical Shortage Grant Program. Renewable awards for Maryland residents who are college juniors, seniors, or graduate students enrolled in a Maryland teacher education program. Must agree to enter profession in a subject designated as a critical shortage area. Must teach in Maryland for one year for each award year. **Academic/Career Areas:** Education. **Award:** Scholarship for use in junior, senior, or graduate year; renewable. *Award amount:* $200–$12,981. *Number of awards:* up to 100. **Eligibility Requirements:** Applicant must be enrolled full or part-time at a four-year institution or university; resident of Maryland and studying in Maryland. Applicant must have 3.0 GPA or higher. Available to U.S. citizens. **Application Requirements:** Application, essay, resume, transcript. **Deadline:** December 31. **Contact:** Margaret Crutchley, Scholarship Administration, Maryland State Higher Education Commission, 16 Francis Street, Annapolis, MD 21401-1781. *E-mail:* ssamail@mhec.state.md.us. *Phone:* 410-260-4545. *Fax:* 410-974-5994. *Web site:* www.mhec.state.md.us.

Part-time Grant Program–Maryland. Funds provided to Maryland colleges and universities. Eligible students must be enrolled on a part-time basis (6-11 credits) in an undergraduate degree program. Must demonstrate financial need and also be Maryland resident. **Award:** Grant for use in freshman, sophomore, junior, or senior year; renewable. *Award amount:* $200–$1000. *Number of awards:* 2000–2700. **Eligibility Requirements:** Applicant must be enrolled part-time at a two-year or four-year institution or university; resident of Maryland and studying in Maryland. Available to U.S. citizens. **Application Requirements:** Application, financial need analysis. **Deadline:** March 1. **Contact:** Linda Asplin, Scholarship Administration, Maryland State Higher Education Commission, 16 Francis Street, Annapolis, MD 21401-1781. *E-mail:* ssamail@mhec.state.md.us. *Phone:* 410-260-4570. *Fax:* 410-974-5994. *Web site:* www.mhec.state.md.us.

Senatorial Scholarships–Maryland. Renewable award for Maryland residents attending a Maryland degree-granting institution, nursing diploma school, or certain private career schools. May be used out-of-state only if Maryland Higher Education Commission deems major to be unique and not offered at Maryland institution. **Award:** Scholarship for use in freshman, sophomore, junior, senior, or graduate year; renewable. *Award amount:* $200–$2000. *Number of awards:* up to 7000. **Eligibility Requirements:** Applicant must be enrolled full or part-time at a two-year, four-year, or technical institution or university; resident of Maryland and studying in Maryland. Available to U.S. citizens. **Application Requirements:** Financial need analysis, test scores. **Deadline:** March 1. **Contact:** Barbara Fantom, Scholarship Administration, Maryland State Higher Education Commission, 16 Francis Street, Annapolis, MD 21401-1781. *E-mail:* ssamail@mhec.state.md.us. *Phone:* 410-260-4547. *Fax:* 410-974-5994. *Web site:* www.mhec.state.md.us.

MASSACHUSETTS

Massachusetts Assistance for Student Success Program. Provides need-based financial assistance to Massachusetts residents to attend undergraduate postsecondary institutions in Connecticut, Maine, Maryland, Massachusetts, New Hampshire, Pennsylvania, Rhode Island, Vermont, and District of Columbia. High school seniors may apply. Timely filing of FAFSA required. **Award:** Grant for use in freshman, sophomore, junior, or senior year; not renewable. *Award amount:* $300–$2900. *Number of awards:* 32,000–35,000. **Eligibility Requirements:** Applicant must be enrolled full-time at a two-year, four-year, or technical institution or university; resident of Massachusetts and studying in Connecticut, District of Columbia, Maine, Maryland, Massachusetts, New Hampshire, Pennsylvania, Rhode Island, or Vermont. Available to U.S. citizens. **Application Requirements:** Financial need analysis. **Deadline:** May 1. **Contact:** Scholarship Information, Massachusetts Office of Student Financial Assistance, 454 Broadway, Suite 200, Revere, MA 02151. *Web site:* www.osfa.mass.edu.

Tomorrow's Teachers Scholarship Program. Tuition waver for graduating high school senior ranking in Top 25% of class. Must be a resident of Massachusetts and pursue a bachelor's degree at a public college or university in the Commonwealth. Must commit to teach for four years in a Massachusetts public school. **Academic/Career Areas:** Education. **Award:** Scholarship for use in freshman, sophomore, junior, or senior year; renewable. *Number of awards:* up to 700. **Eligibility Requirements:** Applicant must be high school student; planning to enroll full-time at a four-year institution or university; resident of Massachusetts and studying in Massachusetts. Applicant must have 3.5 GPA or higher. Available to U.S. citizens. **Application Requirements:** Application, essay, references, transcript. **Deadline:** February 15. **Contact:** Scholarship Information, Massachusetts Office of Student Financial Assistance, 454 Broadway, Suite 200, Revere, MA 02151. *Web site:* www.osfa.mass.edu.

Higher Education Coordinating Council–Tuition Waiver Program. Renewable award is tuition exemption for up to four years. Available to active members of Air Force, Army, Navy, Marines, or Coast Guard who are residents of Massachusetts. For use at a Massachusetts college or university. Deadlines vary. Contact veterans coordinator at college. **Award:** Scholarship for use in freshman, sophomore, junior, or senior year; renewable. **Eligibility Requirements:** Applicant must be enrolled full or part-time at a two-year or four-year institution or university; resident of Massachusetts and studying in Massachusetts. Available to U.S. citizens. Applicant must have served in the Air Force, Army, Coast Guard, Marine Corp, or Navy. **Application Requirements:** Application, financial need analysis. **Contact:** Scholarship Information, Massachusetts Office of Student Financial Assistance, 454 Broadway, Suite 200, Revere, MA 02151. *Web site:* www.osfa.mass.edu.

Massachusetts Gilbert Matching Student Grant Program. Must be permanent Massachusetts resident for at least one year and attending an independent, regionally accredited Massachusetts school or school of nursing full time. File the Free Application for Federal Student Aid after January 1. Contact college financial aid office for complete details. **Award:** Grant for use in freshman, sophomore, junior, or senior year; not renewable. *Award amount:* $200–$2500. **Eligibility Requirements:** Applicant must be enrolled full-time at a four-year institution or university; resident of Massachusetts and studying in Massachusetts. Available to U.S. citizens. **Application Requirements:** Financial need analysis. **Contact:** Scholarship Information, Massachusetts Office of Student Financial Assistance, 454 Broadway, Suite 200, Revere, MA 02151. *Web site:* www.osfa.mass.edu.

Tuition Waiver (General)–Massachusetts. Need-based tuition waiver for full-time students. Must attend a Massachusetts public institution of higher education and be a permanent Massachusetts resident. File the Free Application for Federal Student Aid after January 1. Award is for undergraduate use. **Award:** Scholarship for use in freshman, sophomore, junior, or senior year; renewable. **Eligibility Requirements:** Applicant must be enrolled full-time at a two-year or four-year institution or university; resident of Massachusetts and studying in Massachusetts. Available to U.S. citizens. **Application Requirements:** Application, financial need analysis. **Deadline:** May 1. **Contact:** School Financial Aid Office, Massachusetts Office of Student Financial Assistance. *Web site:* www. osfa.mass.edu.

Massachusetts Part-time Grant Program. Award for permanent Massachusetts resident for at least one year enrolled part-time in a state-approved post-secondary school. Recipient must not have first bachelor's degree. FAFSA must be filed before May 1. **Award:** Grant for use in freshman, sophomore, junior, or senior year; not renewable. *Award amount:* $200–$1450. **Eligibility Requirements:** Applicant must be enrolled part-time at a two-year, four-year, or technical institution or university; resident of Massachusetts and studying in Massachusetts. Available to U.S. citizens. **Application Requirements:** Financial need analysis. **Contact:** Scholarship Information, Massachusetts Office of Student Financial Assistance, 454 Broadway, Suite 200, Revere, MA 02151. *Web site:* www.osfa.mass.edu.

Performance Bonus Grant Program. One-time award to residents of Massachusetts enrolled in a Massachusetts postsecondary institution. Minimum 3.0 GPA required. Timely filing of FAFSA required. Must be sophomore, junior or senior level undergraduate. **Award:** Grant for use in sophomore, junior, or senior year; not renewable. *Award amount:* $350–$500. **Eligibility Requirements:** Applicant must be enrolled full-time at a two-year or four-year institution or university; resident of Massachusetts and studying in Massachusetts. Applicant must have 3.0 GPA or higher. Available to U.S. citizens. **Application Requirements:** Financial need analysis. **Deadline:** May 1. **Contact:** Scholarship Information, Massachusetts Office of Student Financial Assistance, 454 Broadway, Suite 200, Revere, MA 02151. *Phone:* 617-727-9420. *Fax:* 617-727-0667. *Web site:* www.osfa.mass.edu.

Massachusetts Cash Grant Program. A need based grant to assist with mandatory fees and non-state supported tuition, this supplemental award is available to Massachusetts residents who are undergraduates at two-year colleges, four-year colleges and universities in Massachusetts. Must file FAFSA before May 1. Contact college financial aid office for information. **Award:** Grant for use in freshman, sophomore, junior, or senior year; not renewable. **Eligibility Requirements:** Applicant must be enrolled at a two-year or four-year institution or university; resident of Massachusetts and studying in Massachusetts. Available to U.S. citizens. **Application Requirements:** Financial need analysis. **Contact:** Scholarship Information, Massachusetts Office of Student Financial Assistance, 454 Broadway, Suite 200, Revere, MA 02151. *Web site:* www.osfa.mass.edu.

Christian A. Herter Memorial Scholarship. Renewable award for Massachusetts residents who are in the 10th-11th grades and whose socioeconomic backgrounds and environment may inhibit their ability to attain educational goals. Must exhibit severe personal or family-related difficulties, medical problems, or have overcome a personal obstacle. Provides up to fifty percent of the student's calculated need, as determined by Federal methodology, at the college of their choice within the continental U.S. **Award:** Scholarship for use in freshman, sophomore, junior, or senior year; renewable. *Number of awards:* 25. **Eligibility Requirements:** Applicant must be high school student; planning to enroll full-time at a two-year, four-year, or technical institution or university and resident of Massachusetts. Applicant must have 2.5 GPA or higher. Available to U.S. citizens. **Application Requirements:** Application, autobiography, financial need analysis, interview, references. **Deadline:** March 31. **Contact:** Scholarship Information, Massachusetts Office of Student Financial Assistance, 454 Broadway, Suite 200, Revere, MA 02151. *Web site:* www.osfa.mass.edu.

Massachusetts Public Service Grant Program. Scholarships for children and/or spouses of deceased members of fire, police, and corrections departments who were killed in the line of duty. For Massachusetts residents attending Massachusetts institutions. **Award:** Grant for use in freshman, sophomore, junior, or senior year; not renewable. *Award amount:* $330–$2500. **Eligibility Requirements:** Applicant must be enrolled full-time at a four-year institution or university; resident of Massachusetts; studying in Massachusetts and have employment experience in police/firefighting. Available to U.S. citizens. **Application Requirements: Deadline:** May 1. **Contact:** Scholarship Information, Massachusetts Office of Student Financial Assistance, 454 Broadway, Suite 200, Revere, MA 02151. *Web site:* www.osfa.mass.edu.

MICHIGAN

Michigan Educational Opportunity Grant. Need-based program for Michigan residents who are at least half-time undergraduates attending public Michigan colleges. Must maintain good academic standing. Deadline determined by college. Award of up to $1000. **Award:** Grant for use in freshman, sophomore, junior, or senior year; not renewable. *Award amount:* up to $1000. **Eligibility**

Requirements: Applicant must be enrolled full or part-time at a two-year or four-year institution or university; resident of Michigan and studying in Michigan. Available to U.S. citizens. **Application Requirements:** Application, financial need analysis. **Contact:** Program Director, Michigan Bureau of Student Financial Assistance, PO Box 30466, Lansing, MI 48909-7966. *Web site:* www.michigan. gov/mistudentaid.

Michigan Competitive Scholarship. Awards limited to tuition. Must maintain a C average and meet the college's academic progress requirements. Must file Free Application for Federal Student Aid. Deadlines: February 21 and March 21. Must be Michigan resident. Renewable award of $1300 for undergraduate study at a Michigan institution. **Award:** Scholarship for use in freshman, sophomore, junior, or senior year; renewable. *Award amount:* $100–$1300. **Eligibility Requirements:** Applicant must be enrolled at a two-year or four-year institution or university; resident of Michigan and studying in Michigan. Available to U.S. citizens. **Application Requirements:** Application, financial need analysis, test scores. **Contact:** Scholarship and Grant Director, Michigan Bureau of Student Financial Assistance, PO Box 30466, Lansing, MI 48909. *Web site:* www.michigan. gov/mistudentaid.

Michigan Tuition Grants. Need-based program. Students must attend a Michigan private, nonprofit, degree-granting college. Must file the Free Application for Federal Student Aid and meet the college's academic progress requirements. Deadlines: February 21 and March 21. Must be Michigan resident. Renewable award of $2750. **Award:** Grant for use in any year; renewable. *Award amount:* $100–$2750. **Eligibility Requirements:** Applicant must be enrolled at a two-year or four-year institution or university; resident of Michigan and studying in Michigan. Available to U.S. citizens. **Application Requirements:** Application, financial need analysis. **Contact:** Scholarship and Grant Director, Michigan Bureau of Student Financial Assistance, PO Box 30466, Lansing, MI 48909-7966. *Web site:* www.michigan.gov/mistudentaid.

Michigan Adult Part-time Grant. Grant for part-time, needy, independent undergraduates at an approved, degree-granting Michigan college or university. Eligibility is limited to two years. Must be Michigan resident. Deadlines determined by college. **Award:** Grant for use in freshman, sophomore, junior, or senior year; not renewable. *Award amount:* up to $600. **Eligibility Requirements:** Applicant must be enrolled part-time at a two-year or four-year institution or university; resident of Michigan and studying in Michigan. Available to U.S. citizens. **Application Requirements:** Application, financial need analysis. **Contact:** Program Director, Michigan Bureau of Student Financial Assistance, PO Box 30466, Lansing, MI 48909-7966. *Web site:* www.michigan.gov/ mistudentaid.

Tuition Incentive Program (TIP)–Michigan. Award for Michigan residents who receive or have received Medicaid for required period of time through the Family Independence Agency. Scholarship provides two years tuition towards an associate's degree at a Michigan college or university. Apply before graduating from high school or earning General Education Development diploma. **Award:** Scholarship for use in freshman or sophomore year; renewable. **Eligibility Requirements:** Applicant must be high school student; planning to enroll full or part-time at a two-year or four-year institution or university; resident of

Michigan and studying in Michigan. Available to U.S. citizens. **Application Requirements:** Application, financial need analysis. **Deadline:** continuous. **Contact:** Scholarship and Grant Director, Michigan Bureau of Student Financial Assistance, PO Box 30466, Lansing, MI 48909-7966. *Web site:* www.michigan. gov/mistudentaid.

Michigan Veterans Trust Fund Tuition Grant Program. Tuition grant of $2,800 for children of Michigan veterans who died on active duty or subsequently declared 100 percent disabled as the result of service-connected illness or injury. Must be 17 to 25 years old, be a Michigan resident, and attend a private or public institution in Michigan. **Award:** Grant for use in freshman, sophomore, junior, or senior year; renewable. *Award amount:* up to $2800. **Eligibility Requirements:** Applicant must be age 17-25; enrolled full-time at a two-year, four-year, or technical institution or university; resident of Michigan and study-ing in Michigan. Applicant or parent must meet one or more of the following requirements: general military experience; retired from active duty; disabled or killed as a result of military service; Prisoner-Of-War; or Missing-In-Action. **Application Requirements:** Application. **Deadline:** continuous. **Contact:** Mary Kay Bitten, Michigan Veterans Trust Fund, 611 West Ottawa, 3rd Floor, Lansing, MI 48913. *Phone:* 517-335-1634. *Fax:* 517-335-1631.

MINNESOTA

Minnesota Safety Officers' Survivor Program. Grant for eligible survivors of Minnesota public safety officer killed in the line of duty. Safety officers who have been permanently or totally disabled in the line of duty are also eligible. Must be used at a Minnesota institution participating in State Grant Program. Write for details. Must submit proof of death or disability and Public Safety Officers Benefit Fund Certificate. Must apply each year. Can be awarded for four years. **Award:** Scholarship for use in freshman, sophomore, junior, or senior year; not renewable. *Award amount:* up to $6246. **Eligibility Requirements:** Applicant must be enrolled full or part-time at a two-year, four-year, or technical institution or university; studying in Minnesota and have employment experi-ence in police/firefighting. Available to U.S. citizens. **Application Requirements:** Application. **Deadline:** continuous. **Contact:** Minnesota Higher Education Services Office, 1450 Energy Park Drive, Suite 350, St. Paul, MN 55108-5227. *Phone:* 651-642-0567 Ext. 1. *Web site:* www.heso.state.mn.us.

Minnesota Nurses Loan Forgiveness Program. This program offers loan repayment to registered nurse and licensed practical nurse students who agree to practice in a nursing home or an Intermediate Care Facility for persons with mental retardation for a minimum one-year service obligation after completion of training. Candidates must apply while still in school. Up to 10 selections per year contingent upon state funding. **Academic/Career Areas:** Health and Medical Sciences; Nursing. **Award:** Grant for use in any year; not renewable. *Award amount:* up to $3000. *Number of awards:* up to 10. **Eligibility Requirements:** Applicant must be enrolled full or part-time at an institution or university. Available to U.S. citizens. **Application Requirements:** Application, essay. **Deadline:** December 1. **Contact:** Karen Welter, Minnesota Department of Health, 121 East Seventh Place, Suite 460, PO Box 64975, St. Paul, MN 55164-0975. *E-mail:* karen.welter@health.state.mn.us. *Phone:* 651-282-6302. *Web site:* www.health.state.mn.us.

Postsecondary Child Care Grant Program–Minnesota. Renewable grant available for students not receiving MFIP. Based on financial need. Cannot exceed actual child care costs or maximum award chart (based on income). Must be Minnesota resident. For use at Minnesota two- or four-year school. **Award:** Grant for use in freshman, sophomore, junior, or senior year; renewable. *Award amount:* $300–$2200. **Eligibility Requirements:** Applicant must be enrolled full or part-time at a two-year or four-year institution; resident of Minnesota and studying in Minnesota. Available to U.S. citizens. **Application Requirements:** Application, financial need analysis. **Deadline:** continuous. **Contact:** Minnesota Higher Education Services Office, 1450 Energy Park Drive, Suite 350, St. Paul, MN 55108-5227. *Phone:* 651-642-0567 Ext. 1. *Web site:* www.heso.state.mn.us.

Minnesota State Veterans' Dependents Assistance Program. Tuition assistance to dependents of persons considered to be Prisoner-Of-War or Missing-In-Action after August 1, 1958. Must be Minnesota resident attending Minnesota two- or four-year school. **Award:** Scholarship for use in any year; renewable. **Eligibility Requirements:** Applicant must be enrolled at a two-year or four-year institution; resident of Minnesota and studying in Minnesota. Available to U.S. citizens. Applicant or parent must meet one or more of the following requirements: general military experience; retired from active duty; disabled or killed as a result of military service; Prisoner-Of-War; or Missing-In-Action. **Application Requirements:** Application. **Deadline:** continuous. **Contact:** Minnesota Higher Education Services Office, 1450 Energy Park Drive, Suite 350, St. Paul, MN 55108-5227. *Web site:* www.heso.state.mn.us.

Minnesota Summer Scholarships for Academic Enrichment. Need-based scholarship for students in grades 9-12 who enroll in approved academic enrichment program during the summer. Must be Minnesota resident enrolled in Minnesota school. **Award:** Scholarship for use in any year; not renewable. *Award amount:* $616. **Eligibility Requirements:** Applicant must be high school student; age 19 or under; planning to enroll full or part-time at an institution or university; resident of Minnesota and studying in Minnesota. Applicant must have 3.0 GPA or higher. Available to U.S. citizens. **Application Requirements:** Application, financial need analysis, transcript. **Contact:** Minnesota Higher Education Services Office, 1450 Energy Park Drive, Suite 350, St. Paul, MN 55108-5227. *Phone:* 651-642-0567 Ext. 1. *Web site:* www.heso.state. mn.us.

Minnesota State Grant Program. Need-based grant program available for Minnesota residents attending Minnesota colleges. Student covers 46% of cost with remainder covered by Pell Grant, parent contribution and state grant. Students apply with FAFSA and college administers the program on campus. **Award:** Grant for use in freshman, sophomore, junior, or senior year; not renewable. *Award amount:* $100–$7770. *Number of awards:* 62,000. **Eligibility Requirements:** Applicant must be age 17; enrolled full or part-time at a two-year, four-year, or technical institution or university; resident of Minnesota and studying in Minnesota. Available to U.S. citizens. **Application Requirements:** Application, financial need analysis. **Deadline:** June 30. **Contact:** Minnesota Higher Education Services Office, 1450 Energy Park Drive, Suite 350, St. Paul, MN 55108. *Phone:* 651-642-0567 Ext. 1. *Web site:* www.heso.state.mn.us.

MN VA Educational Assistance for Veterans. One-time $750 stipend given to veterans who have used up all other federal funds, yet have time remaining on their delimiting period. Applicant must be a Minnesota resident and must be attending a Minnesota college or university, but not the University of Minnesota. **Award:** Grant for use in any year; not renewable. *Award amount:* $750. **Eligibility Requirements:** Applicant must be enrolled full or part-time at a two-year, four-year, or technical institution or university; resident of Minnesota and studying in Minnesota. Available to U.S. citizens. Applicant must have general military experience. **Application Requirements:** Application, financial need analysis. **Contact:** Terrence Logan, Director of Veterans Benefits, Minnesota Department of Veterans' Affairs, 20 West 12th Street, Second Floor, St. Paul, MN 55155-2079. *Phone:* 651-296-2652. *Fax:* 651-296-3954. *Web site:* www. state.mn.us/ebranch/mdva.

Minnesota Indian Scholarship Program. One time award for Minnesota Native American Indian. Contact for deadline information. **Award:** Scholarship for use in any year; not renewable. **Eligibility Requirements:** Applicant must be Native American or Eskimo; enrolled full or part-time at a two-year, four-year, or technical institution or university and resident of Minnesota. Available to U.S. citizens. **Application Requirements:** Application. **Contact:** Joe Aitken, Director, Minnesota Indian Scholarship Office, 1819 Bemidji Avenue, Bemidji, MN 56601.

Minnesota Reciprocal Agreement. Renewable tuition waiver for Minnesota residents. Waives all or part of non-resident tuition surcharge at public institutions in Iowa, Kansas, Michigan, Missouri, Nebraska, North Dakota, South Dakota, and Wisconsin. Deadline is last day of academic term. **Award:** Scholarship for use in any year; renewable. **Eligibility Requirements:** Applicant must be enrolled full or part-time at a two-year or four-year institution or university; resident of Minnesota and studying in Iowa, Kansas, Michigan, Missouri, Nebraska, North Dakota, South Dakota, or Wisconsin. Available to U.S. citizens. **Application Requirements:** Application. **Contact:** Minnesota Higher Education Services Office, 1450 Energy Park Drive, Suite 350, St. Paul, MN 55108-5227. *Phone:* 651-642-0567 Ext. 1. *Web site:* www.heso.state.mn.us.

Minnesota Educational Assistance for War Orphans. War orphans may qualify for $750 per year. Must have lost parent through service-related death. Children of deceased veterans may qualify for free tuition at State university, college, or vocational or technical schools, but not at University of Minnesota. Must have been resident of Minnesota for at least two years. **Award:** Grant for use in any year; renewable. *Award amount:* $750. **Eligibility Requirements:** Applicant must be enrolled full or part-time at a two-year, four-year, or technical institution or university; resident of Minnesota and studying in Minnesota. Available to U.S. citizens. Applicant or parent must meet one or more of the following requirements: general military experience; retired from active duty; disabled or killed as a result of military service; Prisoner-Of-War; or Missing-In-Action. **Application Requirements:** Application, financial need analysis. **Contact:** Terrence Logan, Director of Veterans Benefits, Minnesota Department of Veterans' Affairs, 20 West 12th Street, Second Floor, St. Paul, MN 55155-2079. *Phone:* 651-296-2652. *Fax:* 651-296-3954. *Web site:* www.state.mn.us/ebranch/mdva.

Leadership, Excellence and Dedicated Service Scholarship. Awarded to high school seniors who enlist in the Minnesota National Guard. The award recognizes demonstrated leadership, community services and potential for success in the Minnesota National Guard. **Award:** Scholarship for use in freshman year; not renewable. *Award amount:* $1000. *Number of awards:* 25. **Eligibility Requirements:** Applicant must be high school student and planning to enroll full or part-time at a two-year, four-year, or technical institution or university. Applicant must have served in the Air Force National Guard or Army National Guard. **Application Requirements:** Application, essay, references, transcript. **Deadline:** March 15. **Contact:** Barbara O'Reilly, Education Services Officer, Minnesota Department of Military Affairs, Veterans Services Building, 20 West 12th Street, St. Paul, MN 55155-2098. *E-mail:* barbara.oreilly@mn.ngb.army.mil. *Phone:* 651-282-4508. *Web site:* www.dma.state.mn.us.

MISSISSIPPI

Higher Education Legislative Plan (HELP). Eligible applicant must be resident of Mississippi and be freshmen and/or sophomore student who graduated from high school within the immediate past two years. Must demonstrate need as determined by the results of the Free Application for Federal Student Aid, documenting an average family adjusted gross income of $36,500 or less over the prior two years. Must be enrolled full-time at a Mississippi college or university, have a cumulative grade point average of 2.5 and have scored 20 on the ACT. **Award:** Scholarship for use in freshman or sophomore year; renewable. **Eligibility Requirements:** Applicant must be enrolled full-time at a four-year institution or university; resident of Mississippi and studying in Mississippi. Applicant must have 2.5 GPA or higher. Available to U.S. citizens. **Application Requirements:** Application, financial need analysis, test scores, transcript. **Deadline:** March 31. **Contact:** Mississippi State Student Financial Aid, 3825 Ridgewood Road, Jackson, MS 39211-6453. *Phone:* 800-327-2980. *Web site:* www.ihl.state.ms.us.

Mississippi Leveraging Educational Assistance Partnership (LEAP). Award for Mississippi residents enrolled for full-time study at a Mississippi college or university. Based on financial need. Deadline varies with each institution. Contact college financial aid office. **Award:** Grant for use in any year; not renewable. *Award amount:* $100–$1500. **Eligibility Requirements:** Applicant must be enrolled full-time at a two-year or four-year institution or university; resident of Mississippi and studying in Mississippi. Available to U.S. citizens. **Application Requirements:** Application, financial need analysis. **Deadline:** continuous. **Contact:** Student Financial Aid Office, Mississippi State Student Financial Aid. *Web site:* www.ihl.state.ms.us.

Mississippi Health Care Professions Loan/Scholarship Program. Renewable award for junior and senior undergraduates studying psychology, speech pathology or occupational therapy. Must be Mississippi residents attending four-year universities in Mississippi. Must fulfill work obligation in Mississippi or pay back as loan. Renewable award for graduate student enrolled in physical therapy. **Academic/Career Areas:** Health and Medical Sciences; Therapy/Rehabilitation. **Award:** Forgivable loan for use in junior, senior, or graduate year; renewable. *Award amount:* $1500–$3000. **Eligibility Requirements:** Applicant must be enrolled full-time at a four-year institution or·university;

resident of Mississippi and studying in Mississippi. Available to U.S. citizens. **Application Requirements:** Application, driver's license, references, transcript. **Deadline:** March 31. **Contact:** Board of Trustees, Mississippi State Student Financial Aid, 3825 Ridgewood Road, Jackson, MS 39211-6453. *Web site:* www. ihl.state.ms.us.

William F. Winter Teacher Scholar Loan Program. Awarded to Mississippi residents pursuing a teaching career. Must be enrolled full-time in a program leading to a Class A certification and maintain a 2.5 GPA. Must agree to teach one year for each year award is received. **Academic/Career Areas:** Education. **Award:** Forgivable loan for use in freshman, sophomore, junior, or senior year; renewable. *Award amount:* $1000–$3000. **Eligibility Requirements:** Applicant must be enrolled full-time at a two-year or four-year institution or university; resident of Mississippi and studying in Mississippi. Applicant must have 2.5 GPA or higher. Available to U.S. citizens. **Application Requirements:** Application, driver's license, references, transcript. **Deadline:** March 31. **Contact:** Board of Trustees, Mississippi State Student Financial Aid, 3825 Ridgewood Road, Jackson, MS 39211-6453. *Web site:* www.ihl.state.ms.us.

Mississippi Law Enforcement Officers and Firemen Scholarship Program. Award for dependents and spouses of policemen or firemen who were killed or disabled in the line of duty. Must be a Mississippi resident and attend a state-supported college or university. The award is a full tuition waiver. Contact for deadline. **Award:** Scholarship for use in freshman, sophomore, junior, or senior year; renewable. **Eligibility Requirements:** Applicant must be enrolled full-time at a two-year or four-year institution or university; resident of Mississippi; studying in Mississippi and have employment experience in police/firefighting. Available to U.S. citizens. **Application Requirements:** Application, driver's license, references. **Deadline:** continuous. **Contact:** Board of Trustees, Mississippi State Student Financial Aid, 3825 Ridgewood Road, Jackson, MS 39211-6453. *Web site:* www.ihl.state.ms.us.

Mississippi Eminent Scholars Grant. Eligible for high-school seniors who are residents of Mississippi. Applicants must achieve a grade point average of 3.5 after a minimum of seven semesters in high school and must have scored 29 on the ACT. Must enroll full-time at an eligible Mississippi college or university. **Award:** Grant for use in freshman year; renewable. *Award amount:* up to $2500. **Eligibility Requirements:** Applicant must be high school student; planning to enroll full-time at a four-year institution or university; resident of Mississippi and studying in Mississippi. Applicant must have 3.5 GPA or higher. Available to U.S. citizens. **Application Requirements:** Application, test scores, transcript. **Deadline:** September 15. **Contact:** Mississippi State Student Financial Aid, 3825 Ridgewood Road, Jackson, MS 39211-6453. *Phone:* 800-327-2980. *Web site:* www.ihl.state.ms.us.

Critical Needs Teacher Loan/Scholarship. Eligible applicants will agree to employment immediately upon degree completion as a full-time classroom teacher in a public school located in a critical teacher shortage area in the state of Mississippi. Must verify the intention to pursue a first bachelor's degree in teacher education. Award covers tuition and required fees, average cost of room and meals plus a $500 allowance for books. Must be enrolled at a Mississippi college or university. **Academic/Career Areas:** Education. **Award:** Forgivable loan for use in freshman, sophomore, junior, or senior year; not renewable. **Eligibility Requirements:** Applicant must be enrolled full or part-time at a four-year institution or university and studying in Mississippi. Applicant must have 2.5 GPA or higher. Available to U.S. citizens. **Application Requirements:** Application, test scores, transcript. **Deadline:** March 31. **Contact:** Mississippi State Student Financial Aid, 3825 Ridgewood Road, Jackson, MS 39211-6453. *Phone:* 800-327-2980. *Web site:* www.ihl.state.ms.us.

Mississippi Resident Tuition Assistance Grant. Must be a resident of Mississippi enrolled full-time at an eligible Mississippi college or university. Must maintain a minimum 2.5 GPA each semester. MTAG awards may be up to $500 per academic year for freshmen and sophomores and $1,000 per academic year for juniors and seniors. Funds will be made available to eligible participants for eight (8) semesters or the normal time required to complete the degree program, whichever comes first. **Award:** Grant for use in freshman, sophomore, junior, or senior year; renewable. *Award amount:* $500–$1000. **Eligibility Requirements:** Applicant must be enrolled full-time at a two-year or four-year institution or university; resident of Mississippi and studying in Mississippi. Applicant must have 2.5 GPA or higher. Available to U.S. citizens. **Application Requirements:** Application, test scores, transcript. **Deadline:** September 15. **Contact:** Mississippi State Student Financial Aid, 3825 Ridgewood Road, Jackson, MS 39211-6453. *Phone:* 800-327-2980. *Web site:* www.ihl.state.ms.us.

Nursing Education BSN Program–Mississippi. Renewable award for Mississippi undergraduates in junior or senior year pursuing nursing programs in Mississippi in order to earn BSN degree. Include transcript and references with application. Must agree to employment in professional nursing (patient care) in Mississippi. **Academic/Career Areas:** Nursing. **Award:** Forgivable loan for use in junior or senior year; renewable. *Award amount:* up to $2000. **Eligibility Requirements:** Applicant must be enrolled full or part-time at a four-year institution or university; resident of Mississippi and studying in Mississippi. Applicant must have 2.5 GPA or higher. Available to U.S. citizens. **Application Requirements:** Application, driver's license, financial need analysis, references, transcript. **Deadline:** March 31. **Contact:** Board of Trustees, Mississippi State Student Financial Aid, 3825 Ridgewood road, Jackson, MS 39211-6453. *Web site:* www.ihl.state.ms.us.

MISSOURI

Missouri Higher Education Academic Scholarship (Bright Flight). Awards of $2000 for Missouri high school seniors. Must be in top 3% of Missouri SAT or ACT scorers. Must attend Missouri institution as full-time undergraduate. May reapply for up to ten semesters. Must be Missouri resident and U.S. citizen. **Award:** Scholarship for use in freshman, sophomore, junior, or senior year; not renewable. *Award amount:* $2000. **Eligibility Requirements:** Applicant must be high school student; planning to enroll full-time at a two-year, four-year, or technical institution or university; resident of Missouri and studying in Missouri. Available to U.S. citizens. **Application Requirements:** Application, test scores. **Deadline:** July 31. **Contact:** MOSTARS Information Center, Missouri Coordinating Board for Higher Education, 3515 Amazonas Drive, Jefferson City, MO 65109. *E-mail:* icweb@mocbhe.gov. *Phone:* 800-473-6757. *Fax:* 573-751-6635. *Web site:* www.cbhe.state.mo.us.

Missouri Minority Teaching Scholarship. Award may be used any year up to four years at an approved, participating Missouri institution. Scholarship is for minority Missouri residents with a minimum 3.5 GPA in teaching programs. Recipients must commit to teach for five years in a Missouri public elementary or secondary school. Graduate students must teach math or science. Otherwise, award must be repaid. **Academic/Career Areas:** Education. **Award:** Scholarship for use in any year; renewable. *Award amount:* $3000. *Number of awards:* 100. **Eligibility Requirements:** Applicant must be Native American or Eskimo, Asian, African American, or Hispanic; enrolled full-time at a two-year or four-year institution or university; resident of Missouri and studying in Missouri. Applicant must have 3.5 GPA or higher. Available to U.S. citizens. **Application Requirements:** Application, essay, financial need analysis, references, test scores, transcript. **Deadline:** February 15. **Contact:** Laura Harrison, Administrative Assistant II, Missouri Department of Elementary and Secondary Education, PO Box 480, Jefferson City, MO 65102-0480. *E-mail:* lharriso@mail.dese.state.mo.us. *Phone:* 573-751-1668. *Fax:* 573-526-3580. *Web site:* www.dese.state.mo.us.

Missouri Teacher Education Scholarship (General). Nonrenewable award for Missouri high school seniors or Missouri resident college freshmen or sophomores. Must attend approved teacher training program at Missouri four-year institution. Nonrenewable. Must rank in top fifteen percent of high school class or ACT/SAT. Merit-based award. **Academic/Career Areas:** Education. **Award:** Scholarship for use in freshman or sophomore year; not renewable. *Award amount:* $2000. *Number of awards:* 200–240. **Eligibility Requirements:** Applicant must be enrolled full-time at a four-year institution or university; resident of Missouri and studying in Missouri. Applicant must have 3.5 GPA or higher. Available to U.S. citizens. **Application Requirements:** Application, essay, references, test scores, transcript. **Deadline:** February 15. **Contact:** Laura Harrison, Administrative Assistant II, Missouri Department of Elementary and Secondary Education, PO Box 480, Jefferson City, MO 65102-0480. *E-mail:* lharriso@mail.dese.state.mo.us. *Phone:* 573-751-1668. *Fax:* 573-526-3580. *Web site:* www.dese.state.mo.us.

Charles Gallagher Student Assistance Program. Available to Missouri residents attending Missouri colleges or universities full-time. Must be undergraduates with financial need. May reapply for up to a maximum of ten semesters. Free Application for Federal Student Aid (FAFSA) or a renewal must be received by the central processor by April 1 to be considered. **Award:** Grant for use in freshman, sophomore, junior, or senior year; not renewable. *Award amount:* $100–$1500. **Eligibility Requirements:** Applicant must be enrolled full-time at a two-year, four-year, or technical institution or university; resident of Missouri and studying in Missouri. Available to U.S. citizens. **Application Requirements:** Financial need analysis. **Deadline:** April 1. **Contact:** MOSTARS Information Center, Missouri Coordinating Board for Higher Education, 3515 Amazonas Drive, Jefferson City, MO 65109. *E-mail:* icweb@mocbhe.gov. *Phone:* 800-473-6757. *Fax:* 573-751-6635. *Web site:* www.cbhe.state.mo.us.

Advantage Missouri Program. Applicant must be seeking a program of instruction in a designated high demand field. High demand fields are determined each year. Borrower must work in Missouri in the high-demand field for one year for every year the loan is received to be forgiven. For Missouri residents. Must attend a postsecondary institution in Missouri. **Award:** Forgivable loan for use in freshman, sophomore, junior, or senior year; not renewable. *Award amount:* $2500. **Eligibility Requirements:** Applicant must be enrolled full-time at a two-year, four-year, or technical institution or university; resident of Missouri and studying in Missouri. Available to U.S. citizens. **Application Requirements:** Application, financial need analysis. **Deadline:** April 1. **Contact:** MOSTARS Information Center, Missouri Coordinating Board for Higher Education, 3515 Amazonas Drive, Jefferson City, MO 65109. *E-mail:* icweb@mocbhe.gov. *Phone:* 800-473-6757. *Fax:* 573-751-6635. *Web site:* www.cbhe.state.mo.us.

Marguerite Ross Barnett Memorial Scholarship. Applicant must be employed (at least 20 hours per week) and attending school part-time. Must be Missouri resident and enrolled at a participating Missouri postsecondary school. Awards not available during summer term. Minimum age is 18. **Award:** Scholarship for use in freshman, sophomore, junior, or senior year; not renewable. *Award amount:* $849–$1557. **Eligibility Requirements:** Applicant must be age 18; enrolled part-time at a two-year or four-year institution or university; resident of Missouri and studying in Missouri. Available to U.S. citizens. **Application Requirements:** Application, financial need analysis. **Deadline:** April 1. **Contact:** MOSTARS Information Center, Missouri Coordinating Board for Higher Education, 3515 Amazonas Drive, Jefferson City, MO 65109. *E-mail:* icweb@mocbhe.gov. *Phone:* 800-473-6757. *Fax:* 573-751-6635. *Web site:* www.cbhe.state.mo.us.

Missouri College Guarantee Program. Available to Missouri residents attending Missouri colleges full-time. Minimum 2.5 GPA required. Must have participated in high school extracurricular activities. **Award:** Grant for use in freshman, sophomore, junior, or senior year; not renewable. *Award amount:* $100–$4600. **Eligibility Requirements:** Applicant must be enrolled full-time at a two-year or four-year institution or university; resident of Missouri and studying in Missouri. Applicant must have 2.5 GPA or higher. Available to U.S. citizens. **Application Requirements:** Financial need analysis, test scores. **Deadline:** April 1. **Contact:** MOSTARS Information Center, Missouri Coordinating Board for Higher Education, 3515 Amazonas Drive, Jefferson City, MO 65109. *E-mail:* icweb@mocbhe.gov. *Phone:* 800-473-6757. *Fax:* 573-751-6635. *Web site:* www.cbhe.state.mo.us.

Primary Care Resource Initiative for Missouri Loan Program. Forgivable loans for Missouri residents who are attending a Missouri institution doing the following: obtaining a degree as a primary care physician, studying for a bachelor of science degree in a field leading to acceptance into a school of medicine, or studying for a bachelor or master of science degree leading to certification as an Advanced Practice Nurse. This loan is funded privately and by the state. In order to be a forgivable loan, the graduate must work in the health profession in Missouri. **Academic/Career Areas:** Health and Medical Sciences; Nursing. **Award:** Forgivable loan for use in any year; not renewable. *Award amount:* $3000–$20,000. **Eligibility Requirements:** Applicant must be enrolled full or part-time at a four-year institution or university; resident of Missouri and studying in Missouri. Available to U.S. citizens. **Application Requirements:** Application, driver's license. **Deadline:** July 15. **Contact:** Kristie Frank, Health Program Representative, Missouri Department of Health and Senior Services, PO Box 570, Jefferson City, MO 65102-0570. *E-mail:* frank@dhss.state.mo.us. *Phone:* 800-891-7415. *Fax:* 573-522-8146.

MONTANA

Montana Board of Regents High School Honor Scholarship. Scholarship provides a one-year non-renewable fee waiver of tuition and registration and is awarded to graduating high school seniors from accredited high schools in Montana. 500 scholarships are awarded each year averaging $2,000 per recipient. The value of the award varies, depending on the tuition and registration fee at each participating college. Must have a minimum 3.0 GPA, meet all college preparatory requirements and be enrolled in an accredited high school for at least three years prior to graduation. Awarded to highest-ranking student in class attending a participating school. Contact high school counselor to apply. Deadline: April 15. **Award:** Scholarship for use in freshman year; not renewable. *Award amount:* $2000. *Number of awards:* 500. **Eligibility Requirements:** Applicant must be high school student; planning to enroll full or part-time at a two-year or four-year institution or university; resident of Montana and studying in Montana. Applicant must have 3.0 GPA or higher. Available to U.S. citizens. **Application Requirements:** Application, transcript. **Deadline:** April 15. **Contact:** Contact High School Counselor, Montana Guaranteed Student Loan Program, Office of Commissioner of Higher Education. *E-mail:* scholars@mgslp.state.mt.us. *Web site:* www.mgslp.state.mt.us.

Indian Student Fee Waiver. This award is a fee waiver awarded by the Montana University System to undergraduate and graduate students meeting the criteria. It waives the registration and tuition fee. The ward amount varies, depending on the tuition and registration fee at each participating college. Students must provide documentation of one-fourth Indian blood or more; must be a resident of Montana for at least one year prior to enrolling in school and must demonstrate financial need. Full-or part-time study qualifies. Complete and submit the FAFSA by March 1 and a Montana Indian Fee Waiver application form. Contact the financial aid office at the college of attendance to determine eligibility. **Award:** Scholarship for use in freshman, sophomore, junior, senior, or graduate year; renewable. *Award amount:* $2000. *Number of awards:* 600. **Eligibility Requirements:** Applicant must be Native American or Eskimo; enrolled full or part-time at a two-year or four-year institution or university; resident of Montana and studying in Montana. Available to U.S. citizens. **Application Requirements:** Application, financial need analysis. **Contact:** Contact Financial Aid Office, Montana Guaranteed Student Loan Program, Office of Commissioner of Higher Education. *E-mail:* scholars@mgslp.state.mt.us. *Web site:* www.mgslp.state.mt.us.

Montana Higher Education Grant. This grant is awarded based on need to undergraduate students attending either part-time or full-time who are residents of Montana and attending participating Montana schools. Awards are limited to the most needy students. A specific major or program of study is not required. This grant does not need to be repaid, and students may apply each year. Apply by filing a Free Application for Federal Student Aid by March 1 and contacting the financial aid office at the admitting college. **Award:** Grant for use in freshman, sophomore, junior, or senior year; not renewable. *Award amount:* $400–$600. *Number of awards:* 500. **Eligibility Requirements:** Applicant must be enrolled full or part-time at a two-year or four-year institution or university; resident of Montana and studying in Montana. Available to U.S. citizens. **Application Requirements:** Financial need analysis. **Contact:** Contact

Financial Aid Office, Montana Guaranteed Student Loan Program, Office of Commissioner of Higher Education. *E-mail:* scholars@mgslp.state.mt.us. *Web site:* www.mgslp.state.mt.us.

Life Member Montana Federation of Garden Clubs Scholarship. Applicant must be at least a sophomore, majoring in conservation, horticulture, park or forestry, floriculture, greenhouse management, land management, or related subjects. Must be in need of assistance. Must have a potential for a successful future. Must be ranked in upper half of class or have a minimum 2.8 GPA. Must be a Montana resident and all study must be done in Montana. Deadline: May 1. **Academic/Career Areas:** Biology; Earth Science; Horticulture/Floriculture; Landscape Architecture. **Award:** Scholarship for use in sophomore, junior, or senior year; not renewable. *Award amount:* $1000. *Number of awards:* 1. **Eligibility Requirements:** Applicant must be enrolled full-time at a four-year institution or university; resident of Montana and studying in Montana. Available to U.S. citizens. **Application Requirements:** Autobiography, financial need analysis, photo, references, transcript. **Deadline:** May 1. **Contact:** Elizabeth Kehmeier, Life Members Scholarship Chairman, Montana Federation of Garden Clubs, 214 Wyant Lane, Hamilton, MT 59840. *Phone:* 406-363-5693.

Montana Tuition Assistance Program–Baker Grant. This grant is based on need to Montana residents attending participating Montana schools and who have earned at least $2,575 during the previous calendar year. Must be enrolled full time. Grant does not need to be repaid. Award covers the first undergraduate degree or certificate. Apply by filing a Free Application for Federal Student Aid by March 1 and contacting the financial aid office at the admitting college. **Award:** Grant for use in freshman, sophomore, junior, or senior year; not renewable. *Award amount:* $100–$1000. **Eligibility Requirements:** Applicant must be enrolled full-time at a two-year or four-year institution or university; resident of Montana and studying in Montana. Available to U.S. citizens. **Application Requirements:** Financial need analysis. **Contact:** Contact Financial Aid Office, Montana Guaranteed Student Loan Program, Office of Commissioner of Higher Education. *E-mail:* scholars@mgslp.state.mt.us. *Web site:* www.mgslp.state.mt.us.

NEBRASKA

Nebraska National Guard Tuition Credit. Renewable award for members of the Nebraska National Guard. Pays 75% of enlisted soldier's tuition until he or she has received a baccalaureate degree. **Award:** Scholarship for use in freshman, sophomore, junior, or senior year; renewable. *Number of awards:* up to 1200. **Eligibility Requirements:** Applicant must be enrolled full or part-time at a two-year, four-year, or technical institution or university; resident of Nebraska and studying in Nebraska. Applicant must have served in the Air Force National Guard or Army National Guard. **Application Requirements:** Application. **Deadline:** continuous. **Contact:** Cindy York, Staff Assistant, Nebraska National Guard, 1300 Military Road, Lincoln, NE 68508-1090. *Phone:* 402-471-7170. *Fax:* 402-471-7171. *Web site:* www.neguard.com.

American Legion Auxiliary Department of Nebraska President's Scholarships. One-time award for Nebraska high school students who were entered into the national competition and did not win. Contact address below for more information. Must be child of a veteran. Must rank in the upper third of class or have minimum 3.0 GPA. **Award:** Scholarship for use in any year; not renewable. *Award amount:* up to $200. *Number of awards:* 1. **Eligibility Requirements:** Applicant must be high school student; planning to enroll full-time at a two-year, four-year, or technical institution or university and resident of Nebraska. Applicant must have 3.0 GPA or higher. Applicant or parent must meet one or more of the following requirements: general military experience; retired from active duty; disabled or killed as a result of military service; Prisoner-Of-War; or Missing-In-Action. **Application Requirements:** Application, essay, references, test scores, transcript. **Deadline:** April 1. **Contact:** Terry Walker, Department Secretary, American Legion Auxiliary, Department of Nebraska, PO Box 5227, Lincoln, NE 68505. *E-mail:* neaux@alltel.net. *Phone:* 402-466-1808. *Fax:* 402-466-0182.

Postsecondary Education Award Program–Nebraska. Available to undergraduates attending a participating private, nonprofit postsecondary institution in Nebraska. Available to Pell Grant recipients only. Nebraska residency required. Awards determined by each participating institution. Contact financial aid office at respective institution for more information. **Award:** Scholarship for use in freshman, sophomore, junior, or senior year; not renewable. **Eligibility Requirements:** Applicant must be enrolled at a two-year or four-year institution; resident of Nebraska and studying in Nebraska. Available to U.S. citizens. **Application Requirements:** Financial need analysis. **Deadline:** continuous. **Contact:** Contact institution of choice., State of Nebraska, 140 North Eighth Street, Suite 300, PO Box 95005, Lincoln, NE 68509-9500. *Web site:* www.ccpe. state.ne.us.

Nebraska Scholarship Assistance Program. Available to undergraduates attending a participating postsecondary institution in Nebraska. Available to Pell Grant recipients only. Nebraska residency required. Awards determined by each participating institution. Contact financial aid office at respective institution for more information. **Award:** Scholarship for use in freshman, sophomore, junior, or senior year; not renewable. **Eligibility Requirements:** Applicant must be enrolled full or part-time at a two-year, four-year, or technical institution or university; resident of Nebraska and studying in Nebraska. **Application Requirements:** Financial need analysis. **Deadline:** continuous. **Contact:** Contact institution of choice., State of Nebraska, 140 North Eighth Street, Suite 300, PO Box 95005, Lincoln, NE 68509-9500. *Web site:* www.ccpe.state.ne.us.

American Legion Auxiliary Department of Nebraska President's Scholarship for Junior Members. One-time prize for female resident of Nebraska who has been entered into the National President's Scholarship for Junior Members and does not win at the national level. Must be in grades 9-12. Must rank in upper third of class or have a minimum 3.0 GPA. **Award:** Prize for use in freshman year; not renewable. *Award amount:* up to $200. *Number of awards:* 1. **Eligibility Requirements:** Applicant must be high school student; planning to enroll full-time at a two-year, four-year, or technical institution or university; female; resident of Nebraska and member of American Legion or Auxiliary. Applicant must have 3.0 GPA or higher. **Application Requirements:** Application, applicant must enter a contest, financial need analysis, references, transcript. **Deadline:** April 1. **Contact:** Terry Walker, Department Secretary, American Legion Auxiliary, Department of Nebraska, PO Box 5227, Lincoln, NE 68505. *E-mail:* neaux@alltel.net. *Phone:* 402-466-1808. *Fax:* 402-466-0182.

Ruby Paul Campaign Fund Scholarship. One-time award for Nebraska residents who are children, grandchildren or great-grandchildren of an American Legion Auxiliary member or who have been members of the American Legion, American Legion Auxiliary, or Sons of the American Legion or Auxiliary for two years prior to application. Must rank in upper third of class or have minimum 3.0 GPA. **Award:** Scholarship for use in any year; not renewable. *Award amount:* $100–$300. *Number of awards:* 1–3. **Eligibility Requirements:** Applicant must be enrolled full-time at a two-year, four-year, or technical institution or university; resident of Nebraska and member of American Legion or Auxiliary. Applicant must have 3.0 GPA or higher. Applicant or parent must meet one or more of the following requirements: general military experience; retired from active duty; disabled or killed as a result of military service; Prisoner-Of-War; or Missing-In-Action. **Application Requirements:** Application, essay, financial need analysis, references, test scores, transcript. **Deadline:** April 5. **Contact:** Terry Walker, Department Secretary, American Legion Auxiliary, Department of Nebraska, PO Box 5227, Lincoln, NE 68505. *E-mail:* neaux@alltel.net. *Phone:* 402-466-1808. *Fax:* 402-466-0182.

American Legion Auxiliary Department of Nebraska Practical Nurse Scholarship. Nonrenewable scholarship for a veteran or a child of a veteran who served in the Armed Forces during dates of eligibility for American Legion membership. For full-time undergraduate study toward nursing degree at eligible institution. Must be a Nebraska resident. Must rank in upper third of class or have a minimum 3.0 GPA. **Academic/Career Areas:** Nursing. **Award:** Scholarship for use in freshman, sophomore, junior, or senior year; not renewable. *Award amount:* $400–$1000. *Number of awards:* 1–3. **Eligibility Requirements:** Applicant must be enrolled full-time at a two-year or four-year institution or university and resident of Nebraska. Applicant must have 3.0 GPA or higher. Applicant or parent must meet one or more of the following requirements: general military experience; retired from active duty; disabled or killed as a result of military service; Prisoner-Of-War; or Missing-In-Action. **Application Requirements:** Application, essay, financial need analysis, references, test scores, transcript. **Deadline:** April 5. **Contact:** Terry Walker, Department Secretary, American Legion Auxiliary, Department of Nebraska, PO Box 5227, Lincoln, NE 68505. *E-mail:* neaux@alltel.net. *Phone:* 402-466-1808. *Fax:* 402-466-0182.

Nebraska State Scholarship Award Program. Available to undergraduates attending a participating postsecondary institution in Nebraska. Available to Pell Grant recipients only. Nebraska residency not required. Awards determined by each participating institution. Contact financial aid office at respective institution for more details. **Award:** Scholarship for use in freshman, sophomore, junior, or senior year; not renewable. *Award amount:* $516. **Eligibility Requirements:** Applicant must be enrolled full or part-time at an institution or university and studying in Nebraska. **Application Requirements:** Financial need analysis. **Deadline:** continuous. **Contact:** Contact institution of choice., State of Nebraska, 140 North Eighth Street, Suite 300, PO Box 95005, Lincoln, NE 68509-9500. *Web site:* www.ccpe.state.ne.us.

Roberta Marie Stretch Memorial Scholarship. One-time award for Nebraska residents who are children or grandchildren of veterans. Must be enrolled in an undergraduate or graduate program at a four-year institution. Preference given to former Nebraska Girls State Citizens. Must rank in upper third of class or have a minimum 3.0 GPA. **Award:** Scholarship for use in freshman, sophomore, junior, senior, or graduate year; not renewable. *Award amount:* $400. *Number of awards:* 1. **Eligibility Requirements:** Applicant must be enrolled full-time at a four-year institution or university and resident of Nebraska. Applicant must have 3.0 GPA or higher. Applicant or parent must meet one or more of the following requirements: general military experience; retired from active duty; disabled or killed as a result of military service; Prisoner-Of-War; or Missing-In-Action. **Application Requirements:** Application, financial need analysis, test scores, transcript. **Deadline:** April 5. **Contact:** Terry Walker, Department Secretary, American Legion Auxiliary, Department of Nebraska, PO Box 5227, Lincoln, NE 68505. *E-mail:* neaux@alltel.net. *Phone:* 402-466-1808. *Fax:* 402-466-0182.

American Legion Auxiliary Department of Nebraska Nurse's Gift Tuition Scholarship. One-time scholarship for Nebraska resident who is a veteran or a child of a veteran who served in the Armed Forces during dates of eligibility for American Legion membership. Proof of enrollment in nursing program at eligible institution required. Must rank in upper third of class or have a minimum 3.0 GPA. **Academic/Career Areas:** Nursing. **Award:** Scholarship for use in any year; not renewable. *Award amount:* $300–$500. *Number of awards:* 1–20. **Eligibility Requirements:** Applicant must be enrolled full-time at a two-year or four-year institution or university and resident of Nebraska. Applicant must have 3.0 GPA or higher. Available to U.S. citizens. Applicant or parent must meet one or more of the following requirements: general military experience; retired from active duty; disabled or killed as a result of military service; Prisoner-Of-War; or Missing-In-Action. **Application Requirements:** Application, essay, financial need analysis, references, test scores, transcript. **Deadline:** April 5. **Contact:** Terry Walker, Department Secretary, American Legion Auxiliary, Department of Nebraska, PO Box 5227, Lincoln, NE 68505. *E-mail:* neaux@alltel.net. *Phone:* 402-466-1808. *Fax:* 402-466-0182.

American Legion Auxiliary Department of Nebraska Student Aid Grants. One-time award for veteran or veteran's child in financial need. Must be a Nebraska resident of at least five years. Must be accepted or enrolled at an institution of higher learning. If in school, must rank in upper third of class or have a minimum 3.0 GPA. **Award:** Grant for use in any year; not renewable. *Award amount:* $200–$300. *Number of awards:* 1–30. **Eligibility Requirements:** Applicant must be enrolled full-time at a two-year, four-year, or technical institution or university and resident of Nebraska. Applicant must have 3.0 GPA or higher. Applicant or parent must meet one or more of the following requirements: general military experience; retired from active duty; disabled or killed as a result of military service; Prisoner-Of-War; or Missing-In-Action. **Application Requirements:** Application, financial need analysis, test scores, transcript. **Deadline:** April 5. **Contact:** Terry Walker, Department Secretary, American Legion Auxiliary, Department of Nebraska, PO Box 5227, Lincoln, NE 68505. *E-mail:* neaux@alltel.net. *Phone:* 402-466-1808. *Fax:* 402-466-0182.

NEVADA

Nevada Student Incentive Grant. Award available to Nevada residents for use at an accredited Nevada college or university. Must show financial need. Any field of study eligible. High school students may not apply. One-time award of up to $5000. Contact financial aid office at local college. **Award:** Grant for use in any year; not renewable. *Award amount:* $100–$5000. *Number of awards:* 400–800. **Eligibility Requirements:** Applicant must be enrolled full or part-time at a two-year, four-year, or technical institution or university; resident of Nevada and studying in Nevada. Available to U.S. citizens. **Application Requirements:** Application, financial need analysis. **Deadline:** continuous. **Contact:** Financial aid office at local college, Nevada Department of Education, 700 East 5th Street, Carson City, NV 89701.

NEW HAMPSHIRE

New Hampshire Career Incentive Program. Grants available to New Hampshire residents attending New Hampshire institutions in programs leading to certification in special education, foreign language education or licensure as an LPN, RN or an Associate, Baccalaureate or advanced nursing degree. Must work in shortage area following graduation. Deadline: June 1 for fall or December 15 for spring. Foreign language or special education students must be juniors, seniors or graduate students with a 3.0 GPA or higher. Forgivable loan is not automatically renewable. Applicant must reapply. **Academic/Career Areas:** Foreign Language; Nursing; Special Education. **Award:** Forgivable loan for use in freshman, sophomore, junior, senior, or graduate year; not renewable. *Award amount:* $1000–$3000. *Number of awards:* 1–50. **Eligibility Requirements:** Applicant must be enrolled full or part-time at a two-year, four-year, or technical institution or university; resident of New Hampshire and studying in New Hampshire. Available to U.S. citizens. **Application Requirements:** Application, financial need analysis, references. **Contact:** Judith Knapp, Student Financial Assistant Coordinator, New Hampshire Postsecondary Education Commission, Two Industrial Park Drive, Concord, NH 03301-8512. *E-mail:* jknapp@nhsa.state. nh.us. *Phone:* 603-271-2555. *Fax:* 603-271-2696. *Web site:* www.state.nh.us/postsecondary.

New Hampshire Incentive Program (NHIP). One-time grants for New Hampshire residents attending school in New Hampshire, Connecticut, Maine, Massachusetts, Rhode Island, or Vermont. Must have financial need. Deadline is May 1. Complete Free Application for Federal Student Aid. Grant is not automatically renewable. Applicant must reapply. **Award:** Grant for use in freshman, sophomore, junior, or senior year; not renewable. *Award amount:* $125–$1000. *Number of awards:* 3000–3500. **Eligibility Requirements:** Applicant must be enrolled full or part-time at a two-year, four-year, or technical institution or university; resident of New Hampshire and studying in Connecticut, Maine, Massachusetts, New Hampshire, Rhode Island, or Vermont. Available to U.S. citizens. **Application Requirements:** Application, financial need analysis. **Deadline:** May 1. **Contact:** Judith Knapp, Student Financial Assistance Coordinator, New Hampshire Postsecondary Education Commission, Two Industrial Park Drive, Concord, NH 03301-8512. *E-mail:* jknapp@nhsa.state.nh.us. *Phone:* 603-271-2555. *Fax:* 603-271-2696. *Web site:* www.state.nh.us/postsecondary.

Scholarships for Orphans of Veterans–New Hampshire. Awards for New Hampshire residents whose parent died as a result of service in WWI, WWII, the Korean Conflict, or the Southeast Asian Conflict. Parent must have been a New Hampshire resident at time of death. Possible full tuition and $1000 per year with automatic renewal on reapplication. Contact department for application deadlines. Must be under 26. Must include proof of eligibility and proof of parent's death. **Award:** Grant for use in freshman, sophomore, junior, or senior year; renewable. *Award amount:* up to $1000. *Number of awards:* 1–10. **Eligibility Requirements:** Applicant must be age 16-25; enrolled full-time at a two-year or four-year institution or university and resident of New Hampshire. Available to U.S. citizens. Applicant or parent must meet one or more of the following requirements: general military experience; retired from active duty; disabled or killed as a result of military service; Prisoner-Of-War; or Missing-In-Action. **Application Requirements:** Application. **Contact:** Patti Edes, Administrative Assistant, New Hampshire Postsecondary Education Commission, Two Industrial Park Drive, Concord, NH 03301-8512. *E-mail:* pedes@nhsa.state.nh.us. *Phone:* 603-271-2555. *Fax:* 603-271-2696. *Web site:* www.state.nh.us/postsecondary.

Nursing Leveraged Scholarship Loan Program. Forgivable loan available to New Hampshire residents enrolled part- or full-time as a graduate or undergraduate in an approved nursing program at a New Hampshire institute of higher education. Must demonstrate financial need. Loan forgiven through service in New Hampshire as a nurse. **Academic/Career Areas:** Nursing. **Award:** Forgivable loan for use in freshman, sophomore, junior, senior, or graduate year; not renewable. *Award amount:* $100–$2000. **Eligibility Requirements:** Applicant must be enrolled full or part-time at an institution or university; resident of New Hampshire and studying in New Hampshire. Available to U.S. citizens. **Application Requirements:** Application, financial need analysis. **Contact:** Financial Aid Office, New Hampshire Postsecondary Education Commission. *Web site:* www.state.nh.us/postsecondary.

Leveraged Incentive Grant Program. Award open to New Hampshire residents attending school in New Hampshire. Must be in sophomore, junior, or senior year. Award based on financial need and merit. Contact financial aid office for more information. **Award:** Grant for use in sophomore, junior, or senior year; not renewable. *Award amount:* $200–$5000. **Eligibility Requirements:** Applicant must be resident of New Hampshire and studying in New Hampshire. Available to U.S. citizens. **Application Requirements:** Application, financial need analysis. **Contact:** Financial Aid Office, New Hampshire Postsecondary Education Commission. *Web site:* www.state.nh.us/postsecondary.

NEW JERSEY

Tuition Assistance for Children of POW/MIAs. Assists children of military service personnel declared Missing-In-Action or Prisoner-Of-War after January 1, 1960. Must be a resident of New Jersey. Renewable grants provide tuition for undergraduate study in New Jersey. Apply by October 1 for fall, March 1 for spring. Must be high school senior to apply. **Award:** Scholarship for use in freshman, sophomore, junior, or senior year; renewable. **Eligibility Requirements:** Applicant must be high school student; planning to enroll full-time at a two-year or four-year institution; resident of New Jersey and studying in New Jersey. Available to U.S. citizens. Applicant or parent must meet one or more of the following requirements: general military experience; retired from active duty; disabled or killed as a result of military service; Prisoner-Of-War; or Missing-In-Action. **Application Requirements:** Application, transcript.

Contact: Barbara Gilsenan, Veterans Service Officer, New Jersey Department of Military and Veterans Affairs, PO Box 340, Trenton, NJ 08625-0340. *E-mail:* barbara.gilsenan@njdmava.state.nj.us. *Phone:* 609-530-6961. *Fax:* 609-530-6970.

Veterans' Tuition Credit Program–New Jersey. Award for veterans who served in the armed forces between December 31, 1960, and May 7, 1975. Must have been a New Jersey resident at time of induction or discharge or for one year prior to application. Apply by October 1 for fall, March 1 for spring. Renewable award of $200-$400. **Award:** Scholarship for use in any year; renewable. *Award amount:* $200–$400. **Eligibility Requirements:** Applicant must be enrolled full or part-time at a two-year, four-year, or technical institution or university and resident of New Jersey. Available to U.S. citizens. Applicant must have general military experience. **Application Requirements:** Application. **Contact:** Barbara Gilsenan, Veterans Service Officer, New Jersey Department of Military and Veterans Affairs, PO Box 340, Trenton, NJ 08625-0340. *E-mail:* barbara.gilsenan@njdmava.state.nj.us. *Phone:* 609-530-6961. *Fax:* 609-530-6970.

New Jersey War Orphans Tuition Assistance. Renewable award for New Jersey residents who are high school seniors ages 16-21 and who are children of veterans killed or disabled in duty, Missing-In-Action, or Prisoner-Of-War. For use at a two- or four-year college or university. Write for more information. Deadlines: October 1 for fall semester and March 1 for spring semester. **Award:** Scholarship for use in any year; renewable. *Award amount:* $2000–$5000. **Eligibility Requirements:** Applicant must be high school student; age 16-21; planning to enroll full-time at a two-year or four-year institution or university and resident of New Jersey. Applicant or parent must meet one or more of the following requirements: general military experience; retired from active duty; disabled or killed as a result of military service; Prisoner-Of-War; or Missing-In-Action. **Application Requirements:** Application, transcript. **Contact:** Barbara Gilsenan, Veterans Service Officer, New Jersey Department of Military and Veterans Affairs, PO Box 340, Trenton, NJ 08625-0340. *E-mail:* barbara.gilsenan@ njdmava.state.nj.us. *Phone:* 609-530-6961. *Fax:* 609-530-6970.

New Jersey Educational Opportunity Fund Grants. Grants up to $4150 per year. Must be a New Jersey resident for at least twelve consecutive months and attend a New Jersey institution. Must be from a disadvantaged background as defined by EOF guidelines. EOF grant applicants must also apply for financial aid. EOF recipients may qualify for the Martin Luther King Physician/Dentistry Scholarships for graduate study at a professional institution. **Academic/Career Areas:** Dental Health/Services; Health and Medical Sciences. **Award:** Grant for use in freshman, sophomore, junior, senior, or graduate year; renewable. *Award amount:* up to $4150. **Eligibility Requirements:** Applicant must be enrolled full-time at a four-year institution or university; resident of New Jersey and studying in New Jersey. Available to U.S. citizens. **Application Requirements:** Application, financial need analysis. **Contact:** Sandra Rollins, Associate Director of Financial Aid, University of Medicine and Dentistry of NJ School of Osteopathic Medicine, 40 East Laurel Road, Primary Care Center 119, Stratford, NJ 08084. *E-mail:* rollins@umdnj.edu. *Phone:* 856-566-6008. *Fax:* 856-566-6015. *Web site:* www.3.umdnj.edu/faidweb.

NJSA Scholarship Program. One-time award for permanent residents of New Jersey enrolled in an accredited architecture program. Minimum 2.5 GPA required.

Must show evidence of financial need, scholarship, and promise in architecture. Submit portfolio and $5 application fee. **Academic/Career Areas:** Architecture. **Award:** Scholarship for use in sophomore, junior, senior, or graduate year; not renewable. *Award amount:* $1000–$2500. **Eligibility Requirements:** Applicant must be enrolled full-time at a four-year, or technical institution or university and resident of New Jersey. Applicant must have 2.5 GPA or higher. Available to U.S. citizens. **Application Requirements:** Application, essay, financial need analysis, portfolio, references, transcript. *Fee:* $5. **Deadline:** April 29. **Contact:** Robert Zaccone, President, AIA New Jersey Scholarship Foundation, Inc., 212 White Avenue, Old Tappan, NJ 07675-7411. *Fax:* 201-767-5541.

NEW MEXICO

New Mexico Scholars Program. Several scholarships to encourage New Mexico high school graduates to enroll in college at a public or selected private nonprofit postsecondary institution in New Mexico before their 22nd birthday. Selected private colleges are College of Santa Fe, St. John's College in Santa Fe, and College of the Southwest. Must have graduated in top 5% of their class or obtained an ACT score of 25 or SAT score of 1140. One-time scholarship for tuition, books, and fees. Contact financial aid office at college to apply. **Award:** Scholarship for use in freshman, sophomore, junior, or senior year; not renewable. **Eligibility Requirements:** Applicant must be age 22 or under; enrolled full or part-time at a two-year or four-year institution; resident of New Mexico and studying in New Mexico. Available to U.S. citizens. **Application Requirements:** Application, financial need analysis, test scores. **Contact:** Barbara Serna, Clerk Specialist, New Mexico Commission on Higher Education, PO Box 15910, Santa Fe, NM 87506-5910. *Phone:* 505-827-4026. *Fax:* 505-827-7392. *Web site:* www. nmche.org.

Children of Deceased Veterans Scholarship–New Mexico. Award for New Mexico residents who are children of veterans killed or disabled as a result of service, Prisoner-Of-War, or veterans Missing-In-Action. Must be between ages 16 to 26. For use at New Mexico schools for undergraduate study. Submit parent's death certificate and DD form 214. **Award:** Scholarship for use in freshman, sophomore, junior, or senior year; renewable. *Award amount:* $250–$750. **Eligibility Requirements:** Applicant must be age 16-26; enrolled full or part-time at an institution or university; resident of New Mexico and studying in New Mexico. Applicant or parent must meet one or more of the following requirements: general military experience; retired from active duty; disabled or killed as a result of military service; Prisoner-Of-War; or Missing-In-Action. **Application Requirements:** Application, transcript. **Deadline:** continuous. **Contact:** Alan Martinez, Manager of State Benefits, New Mexico Veterans' Service Commission, PO Box 2324, Sante Fe, NM 87504. *Phone:* 505-827-6300. *Fax:* 505-827-6372. *Web site:* www.state.nm.us/veterans.

New Mexico Vietnam Veterans' Scholarship. Renewable award for Vietnam veterans who are New Mexico residents attending state-sponsored schools. Must have been awarded the Vietnam Campaign medal. Submit DD214. Must include discharge papers. **Award:** Scholarship for use in any year; renewable. *Award amount:* up to $1554. **Eligibility Requirements:** Applicant must be resident of New Mexico and studying in New Mexico. Available to U.S. citizens. Applicant must have general military experience. **Application Requirements:**

Application. **Deadline:** continuous. **Contact:** Alan Martinez, Manager State Benefits, New Mexico Veterans' Service Commission, PO Box 2324, Sante Fe, NM 87504. *Phone:* 505-827-6300. *Fax:* 505-827-6372. *Web site:* www.state.nm. us/veterans.

New Mexico Competitive Scholarship. Scholarship available to encourage out-of-state students who have demonstrated high academic achievement to enroll in public institutions of higher education in New Mexico. One-time award for undergraduate students. Deadlines set by each institution. Contact financial aid office of any New Mexico public postsecondary institution to apply. **Award:** Scholarship for use in freshman, sophomore, junior, or senior year; not renewable. *Award amount:* $100. **Eligibility Requirements:** Applicant must be enrolled full or part-time at a two-year or four-year institution or university and studying in New Mexico. Applicant must have 3.0 GPA or higher. Available to U.S. citizens. **Application Requirements:** Application, essay, references, test scores. **Contact:** Barbara Serna, Clerk Specialist, New Mexico Commission on Higher Education, PO Box 15910, Santa Fe, NM 87506-5910. *Phone:* 505-827-4026. *Fax:* 505-827-7392. *Web site:* www.nmche.org.

New Mexico Student Incentive Grant. Several grants available for resident undergraduate students attending public and selected private nonprofit institutions in New Mexico. Must demonstrate financial need. Several one-time awards of varying amounts. To apply contact financial aid office at any public or private nonprofit postsecondary institution in New Mexico. **Award:** Grant for use in freshman, sophomore, junior, or senior year; not renewable. *Award amount:* $200–$2500. **Eligibility Requirements:** Applicant must be enrolled at a two-year or four-year institution or university; resident of New Mexico and studying in New Mexico. Available to U.S. citizens. **Application Requirements:** Application, financial need analysis. **Contact:** Barbara Serna, Clerk Specialist, New Mexico Commission on Higher Education, PO Box 15910, Santa Fe, NM 87506-5910. *Phone:* 505-827-4026. *Fax:* 505-827-7392. *Web site:* www.nmche.org.

Allied Health Student Loan Program–New Mexico. Renewable loans for New Mexico residents enrolled in an undergraduate allied health program. Loans can be forgiven through service in a medically underserved area or can be repaid. Penalties apply for failure to provide service. May borrow up to $12,000 per year for four years. Apply by calling the Commission at the CHE Student Helpline: 1-800-279-9777. **Academic/Career Areas:** Dental Health/Services; Health and Medical Sciences; Nursing; Social Sciences; Therapy/Rehabilitation. **Award:** Forgivable loan for use in freshman, sophomore, junior, or senior year; renewable. *Award amount:* up to $12,000. *Number of awards:* 1–40. **Eligibility Requirements:** Applicant must be enrolled full or part-time at a two-year or four-year institution or university; resident of New Mexico and studying in New Mexico. Available to U.S. citizens. **Application Requirements:** Application, financial need analysis, transcript. **Deadline:** July 1. **Contact:** Barbara Serna, Clerk Specialist, New Mexico Commission on Higher Education, PO Box 15910, Santa Fe, NM 87506-5910. *Phone:* 505-827-4026. *Fax:* 505-827-7392. *Web site:* www.nmche.org.

Nursing Student Loan-For-Service Program. Award for New Mexico residents accepted or enrolled in nursing program at New Mexico public postsecondary institution. Must practice as nurse in designated health professional shortage area in New Mexico. Award dependent upon financial need but may not exceed $12,000. Deadline: July 1. To apply call the Commission at the CHE Student Helpline: 1-800-279-9777. **Academic/Career Areas:** Nursing. **Award:** Forgivable loan for use in freshman, sophomore, junior, or senior year; not renewable. *Award amount:* up to $12,000. **Eligibility Requirements:** Applicant must be enrolled full or part-time at a two-year or four-year institution; resident of New Mexico and studying in New Mexico. Available to U.S. citizens. **Application Requirements:** Application, financial need analysis. **Deadline:** July 1. **Contact:** Barbara Serna, Clerk Specialist, New Mexico Commission on Higher Education, PO Box 15910, Santa Fe, NM 87506-5910. *Phone:* 505-827-4026. *Fax:* 505-827-7392. *Web site:* www.nmche.org.

3% Scholarship Program. Award equal to tuition and required fees for New Mexico residents who are undergraduate students attending public postsecondary institutions in New Mexico. Contact financial aid office of any public postsecondary institution in New Mexico for deadline. **Award:** Scholarship for use in freshman, sophomore, junior, or senior year; not renewable. **Eligibility Requirements:** Applicant must be enrolled full or part-time at a two-year or four-year institution; resident of New Mexico and studying in New Mexico. Available to U.S. citizens. **Application Requirements:** Application. **Contact:** Barbara Serna, Clerk Specialist, New Mexico Commission on Higher Education, PO Box 15910, Santa Fe, NM 87506-5910. *Phone:* 505-827-4026. *Fax:* 505-827-7392. *Web site:* www.nmche.org.

Lottery Success Scholarships. Awards equal to 100 percent of tuition at New Mexico public postsecondary institution. Must have New Mexico high school degree and be enrolled at New Mexico public college or university in first regular semester following high school graduation. Must obtain 2.5 GPA during this semester. May be eligible for up to eight consecutive semesters of support. Deadlines vary by institution. Apply through financial aid office of any New Mexico public postsecondary institution. **Award:** Scholarship for use in freshman, sophomore, junior, or senior year; renewable. **Eligibility Requirements:** Applicant must be enrolled full-time at a two-year or four-year institution; resident of New Mexico and studying in New Mexico. Applicant must have 2.5 GPA or higher. Available to U.S. citizens. **Application Requirements:** Application. **Contact:** Barbara Serna, Clerk Specialist, New Mexico Commission on Higher Education, PO Box 15910, Santa Fe, NM 87506-5910. *Phone:* 505-827-4026. *Fax:* 505-827-7392. *Web site:* www.nmche.org.

Vietnam Veterans Scholarship Program. Award for New Mexico residents who are Vietnam veterans enrolled in undergraduate or master's-level course work at public or selected private New Mexico postsecondary institutions. Award may include tuition, required fees, and book allowance. Contact financial aid office of any public or eligible private New Mexico postsecondary institution for deadline. **Award:** Scholarship for use in freshman, sophomore, junior, senior, or graduate year; not renewable. **Eligibility Requirements:** Applicant must be enrolled full or part-time at a two-year or four-year institution; resident of New Mexico and studying in New Mexico. Available to U.S. citizens. Applicant must have general military experience. **Application Requirements:** Application. **Contact:** Barbara Serna, Clerk Specialist, New Mexico Commission on Higher Education, PO Box 15910, Santa Fe, NM 87506-5910. *Phone:* 505-827-4026. *Fax:* 505-827-7392. *Web site:* www.nmche.org.

Legislative Endowment Scholarships. Awards for undergraduate students with substantial financial need who are attending public postsecondary institutions in New Mexico. Preference given to returning adult students at two-year and four-year institutions and students transferring from two-year to four-year institutions. Deadline set by each institution. Must be resident of New Mexico. Contact financial aid office of any New Mexico public postsecondary institution to apply. **Award:** Scholarship for use in freshman, sophomore, junior, or senior year; not renewable. *Award amount:* $1000–$2500. **Eligibility Requirements:** Applicant must be enrolled full or part-time at a two-year or four-year institution; resident of New Mexico and studying in New Mexico. Available to U.S. citizens. **Application Requirements:** Application, financial need analysis. **Contact:** Barbara Serna, Clerk Specialist, New Mexico Commission on Higher Education, PO Box 15910, Santa Fe, NM 87506-5910. *Phone:* 505-827-7383. *Fax:* 505-827-7392. *Web site:* www.nmche.org.

NEW YORK

New York State Tuition Assistance Program. Award for New York state residents attending New York postsecondary institution. Must be full-time student in approved program with tuition over $200 per year. Must show financial need and not be in default in any other state program. Renewable award of $275–$5000. **Award:** Grant for use in any year; renewable. *Award amount:* $275–$5000. *Number of awards:* 300,000–320,000. **Eligibility Requirements:** Applicant must be enrolled full-time at a two-year or four-year institution or university; resident of New York and studying in New York. **Application Requirements:** Application, financial need analysis. **Deadline:** May 1. **Contact:** Student Information, New York State Higher Education Services Corporation, 99 Washington Avenue, Room 1320, Albany, NY 12255. *Web site:* www.hesc.com.

Native American Postsecondary Grant-in-Aid Program. Must be a New York resident and be on an official tribal roll of a New York state tribe, or be a child of a member. Deadlines are July 15 for fall semester, December 31 for the spring semester, and May 20 for the summer semester. Must maintain a minimum GPA of 2.0. **Award:** Grant for use in freshman, sophomore, junior, or senior year; renewable. *Award amount:* $1750. **Eligibility Requirements:** Applicant must be Native American or Eskimo; enrolled full or part-time at a two-year, four-year, or technical institution or university; resident of New York and studying in New York. Available to U.S. citizens. **Application Requirements:** Application, essay, transcript. **Contact:** Adrian Cooke, Acting Coordinator, New York State Education Department, New York State Education Department, Room 478 EBA, Albany, NY 12234. *Phone:* 518-474-0537. *Fax:* 518-474-3666.

New York Aid for Part-time Study (APTS). Renewable scholarship provides tuition assistance to part-time students who are New York residents attending New York-accredited institutions. Deadlines and award amounts vary. Must be U.S. citizens. **Award:** Grant for use in freshman, sophomore, junior, or senior year; renewable. *Award amount:* up to $2000. **Eligibility Requirements:** Applicant must be enrolled part-time at a two-year or four-year institution; resident of New York and studying in New York. Available to U.S. citizens. **Application Requirements:** Application. **Contact:** Student Information, New

York State Higher Education Services Corporation, 99 Washington Avenue, Room 1320, Albany, NY 12255. *Phone:* 518-473-3887. *Fax:* 518-474-2839. *Web site:* www.hesc.com.

New York Educational Opportunity Program (EOP). Renewable award for New York resident attending New York college/university for undergraduate study. For educationally and economically disadvantaged students; includes educational assistance such as tutoring. Contact prospective college for information. **Award:** Scholarship for use in freshman, sophomore, junior, or senior year; renewable. **Eligibility Requirements:** Applicant must be enrolled full-time at a two-year or four-year institution or university; resident of New York and studying in New York. Available to U.S. citizens. **Application Requirements:** Application, financial need analysis, transcript. **Contact:** Student Information, New York State Higher Education Services Corporation, 99 Washington Avenue, Room 1320, Albany, NY 12255. *Web site:* www.hesc.com.

New York Memorial Scholarships for Families of Deceased Police Officers, Firefighters and Peace Officers. Renewable scholarship for families of New York police officers, peace officers or firefighters who died in the line of duty. Must be a New York resident pursuing undergraduate study at a SUNY college or university. **Award:** Scholarship for use in freshman, sophomore, junior, or senior year; renewable. **Eligibility Requirements:** Applicant must be enrolled full-time at a four-year institution or university; resident of New York; studying in New York and have employment experience in police/ firefighting. Available to U.S. citizens. **Application Requirements:** Application, financial need analysis. **Deadline:** May 1. **Contact:** Student Information, New York State Higher Education Services Corporation, 99 Washington Avenue, Room 1320, Albany, NY 12255. *Web site:* www.hesc.com.

New York Vietnam Veterans Tuition Awards. Scholarship for veterans who served in Vietnam. Must be a New York resident attending a New York institution. Renewable award of $500-$1000. Deadline: May 1. Must establish eligibility by September 1. **Award:** Scholarship for use in any year; renewable. *Award amount:* $500–$1000. **Eligibility Requirements:** Applicant must be enrolled full or part-time at a two-year, four-year, or technical institution or university; resident of New York and studying in New York. Applicant must have served in the Air Force, Army, Marine Corp, or Navy. **Application Requirements:** Application, financial need analysis. **Deadline:** May 1. **Contact:** Student Information, New York State Higher Education Services Corporation, 99 Washington Avenue, Room 1320, Albany, NY 12255. *Web site:* www.hesc.com.

New York State Aid to Native Americans. Award for enrolled members of a New York State tribe and their children who are attending or planning to attend a New York State college and who are New York State residents. Award for full-time-students up to $1550 annually; part-time awards approximately $65 per credit hour. **Award:** Scholarship for use in freshman, sophomore, junior, or senior year; not renewable. *Award amount:* up to $1550. **Eligibility Requirements:** Applicant must be Native American or Eskimo; enrolled full or part-time at a two-year, four-year, or technical institution or university; resident of New York and studying in New York. **Application Requirements:** Application. **Deadline:** July 15. **Contact:** Native American Education Unit, New

York State Education Department, New York State Higher Education Services Corporation, EBA Room 374, Albany, NY 12234. *Phone:* 518-474-0537. *Web site:* www.hesc.com.

Regents Award for Child of Veteran. Award for students whose parent, as a result of service in U.S. Armed Forces during war or national emergency, died; suffered a 40 percent or more disability; or is classified as Missing-In-Action or a Prisoner-Of-War. Veteran must be current New York State resident or have been so at time of death. Must be New York resident attending, or planning to attend, college in New York State. Must establish eligibility before applying for payment. **Award:** Scholarship for use in freshman, sophomore, junior, or senior year; not renewable. *Award amount:* $450. **Eligibility Requirements:** Applicant must be enrolled full-time at a two-year or four-year institution or university; resident of New York and studying in New York. Available to U.S. citizens. Applicant or parent must meet one or more of the following requirements: general military experience; retired from active duty; disabled or killed as a result of military service; Prisoner-Of-War; or Missing-In-Action. **Application Requirements:** Application. **Deadline:** May 1. **Contact:** Student Information, New York State Higher Education Services Corporation, 99 Washington Avenue, Room 1320, Albany, NY 12255. *Web site:* www.hesc.com.

Regents Professional Opportunity Scholarships. Award for New York State residents pursuing career in certain licensed professions. Must attend New York State college. Priority given to economically disadvantaged members of minority group underrepresented in chosen profession and graduates of SEEK, College Discovery, EOP, and HEOP. Must work in New York State in chosen profession one year for each annual payment. **Award:** Forgivable loan for use in freshman, sophomore, junior, senior, or graduate year; not renewable. *Award amount:* $1000–$5000. **Eligibility Requirements:** Applicant must be enrolled full-time at a two-year or four-year institution or university; resident of New York and studying in New York. Available to U.S. citizens. **Application Requirements:** Application. **Deadline:** May 1. **Contact:** Scholarship Processing Unit-New York State Education Department, New York State Higher Education Services Corporation, EBA Room 1078, Albany, NY 12234. *Phone:* 518-486-1319. *Web site:* www.hesc.com.

Scholarship for Academic Excellence. Each requested high school in NY State (public and non-public) will receive at least one $1500 scholarship. Remaining scholarships ($1500) and all $500 scholarships awarded based on size of the preceding year's graduating class. Scholarships can only be used at NY state colleges and universities. Scholarships awarded on academic excellence. Nominees for scholarships selected by high school and will be notified by State Education Department after budget is approved. **Award:** Scholarship for use in freshman, sophomore, junior, or senior year; renewable. *Award amount:* $500–$1500. *Number of awards:* 2000–6000. **Eligibility Requirements:** Applicant must be high school student; age 30 or under; planning to enroll full-time at a two-year or four-year institution or university; resident of New York and studying in New York. Applicant must have 3.5 GPA or higher. Available to U.S. citizens. **Application Requirements:** Application, essay, references, test scores, transcript. **Deadline:** December 20. **Contact:** Lewis J. Hall, Coordinator, New York State Education Department, Room 1078 EBA, Albany, NY 12234. *E-mail:* dmercado@mail.nysed.gov. *Phone:* 518-486-1319. *Fax:* 518-486-5346.

Scholarships for Academic Excellence. Renewable awards of up to $1500 for academically outstanding New York State high school graduates planning to attend an approved postsecondary institution in New York State. For full-time study only. Contact high school guidance counselor to apply. **Award:** Scholarship for use in freshman, sophomore, junior, or senior year; renewable. *Award amount:* $500–$1500. *Number of awards:* 8000. **Eligibility Requirements:** Applicant must be high school student; planning to enroll full-time at an institution or university; resident of New York and studying in New York. **Application Requirements:** Application. **Contact:** Student Information, New York State Higher Education Services Corporation, 99 Washington Avenue, Room 1320, Albany, NY 12255. *Web site:* www.hesc.com.

Regents Professional Opportunity Scholarship Program–New York. Renewable award for New York residents in programs leading to a degree in a profession licensed by the Board of Regents. Priority given to minority or disadvantaged students. Must practice full time, professionally in New York for one year for each award received. **Academic/Career Areas:** Architecture; Business/Consumer Services; Civil Engineering; Dental Health/Services; Electrical Engineering/Electronics; Food Science/Nutrition; Interior Design; Landscape Architecture; Law/Legal Services; Nursing; Social Sciences; Therapy/Rehabilitation. **Award:** Forgivable loan for use in freshman, sophomore, junior, senior, or graduate year; renewable. *Award amount:* $1000–$5000. *Number of awards:* 220. **Eligibility Requirements:** Applicant must be Native American or Eskimo, African American, or Hispanic; enrolled full-time at a two-year or four-year institution or university; resident of New York and studying in New York. Available to U.S. citizens. **Application Requirements:** Application. **Deadline:** May 1. **Contact:** Lewis J. Hall, Coordinator, New York State Education Department, Room 1078 EBA, Albany, NY 12234. *Phone:* 518-486-1319. *Fax:* 518-486-5346.

Young Scholars Contest. The Young Scholars Contest is a research essay competition on a pre-determined theme in the humanities. New York State high school students who are legal residents of the state are eligible. Deadline is in May. **Award:** Scholarship for use in any year; not renewable. *Award amount:* $250–$5000. *Number of awards:* 6–18. **Eligibility Requirements:** Applicant must be high school student; planning to enroll full-time at a two-year or four-year institution or university and resident of New York. Available to U.S. and non-U.S. citizens. **Application Requirements:** Applicant must enter a contest, essay. **Contact:** New York Council for the Humanities, 150 Broadway, Suite 1700, New York, NY 10038. *Web site:* www.nyhumanities.org.

NORTH CAROLINA

State Contractual Scholarship Fund Program–North Carolina. Renewable award for North Carolina residents already attending an approved private college or university in the state in pursuit of an undergraduate degree. Must have financial need. Contact college financial aid office for deadline and information. May not be enrolled in a program leading to a religious vocation. **Award:** Scholarship for use in freshman, sophomore, junior, or senior year; renewable. *Award amount:* up to $1100. **Eligibility Requirements:** Applicant must be enrolled full or part-time at a two-year or four-year institution or university; resident of North Carolina and studying in North Carolina. Available to U.S.

citizens. **Application Requirements:** Financial need analysis. **Contact:** Bill Carswell, Manager of Scholarship and Grant Division, North Carolina State Education Assistance Authority, PO Box 13663, Research Triangle, NC 27709-3663. *Web site:* www.cfnc.org.

Incentive Scholarship for Native Americans. Merit-based award with a required public service component. Maximum award $3000 per academic year. Must be graduate of a North Carolina high school enrolled at North Carolina institution. Must submit tribal enrollment card. Minimum 2.5 GPA required. **Award:** Scholarship for use in freshman, sophomore, junior, or senior year; renewable. *Award amount:* up to $3000. *Number of awards:* up to 200. **Eligibility Requirements:** Applicant must be Native American or Eskimo; enrolled full-time at a four-year institution; resident of North Carolina and studying in North Carolina. Applicant must have 2.5 GPA or higher. Available to U.S. citizens. **Application Requirements:** Application, financial need analysis. **Deadline:** continuous. **Contact:** Ms. Mickey Locklear, Director, Education Talent Search, North Carolina Commission of Indian Affairs, 217 West Jones Street, Raleigh, NC 27603. *E-mail:* mickey.locklear@ncmail.net. *Phone:* 919-733-5998. *Fax:* 919-733-1207.

North Carolina Sheriffs' Association Undergraduate Criminal Justice Scholarships. One-time award for full-time North Carolina resident undergraduate students majoring in criminal justice at a University of North Carolina school. Priority given to child of any North Carolina law enforcement officer. Letter of recommendation from county sheriff required. **Academic/Career Areas:** Criminal Justice/Criminology; Law Enforcement/Police Administration. **Award:** Scholarship for use in freshman, sophomore, junior, or senior year; not renewable. *Award amount:* up to $2000. *Number of awards:* up to 10. **Eligibility Requirements:** Applicant must be enrolled full-time at a four-year institution; resident of North Carolina; studying in North Carolina and have employment experience in police/firefighting. Available to U.S. citizens. **Application Requirements:** Essay, financial need analysis, references, transcript. **Deadline:** continuous. **Contact:** Sharon Scott, Assistant, Scholarship and Grant Division, North Carolina State Education Assistance Authority, PO Box 13663, Research Triangle, NC 27709-3663. *Web site:* www.cfnc.org.

North Carolina Student Loan Program for Health, Science, and Mathematics. Renewable award for North Carolina residents studying health-related fields, or science or math education. Based on merit, need, and promise of service as a health professional or educator in an underserved area of North Carolina. Need two co-signers. Submit surety statement. **Academic/Career Areas:** Dental Health/Services; Health Administration; Health and Medical Sciences; Nursing; Physical Sciences and Math; Therapy/Rehabilitation. **Award:** Forgivable loan for use in any year; renewable. *Award amount:* $3000–$8500. **Eligibility Requirements:** Applicant must be enrolled full-time at a two-year or four-year institution or university; resident of North Carolina and studying in North Carolina. Available to U.S. citizens. **Application Requirements:** Application, financial need analysis, transcript. **Deadline:** June 1. **Contact:** Edna Williams, Manager, Selection and Origination, HSM Loan Program, North Carolina State Education Assistance Authority, PO Box 14223, Research Triangle, NC 27709-4223. *Phone:* 919-549-8614. *Web site:* www.cfnc.org.

North Carolina Legislative Tuition Grant Program. Renewable aid for North Carolina residents attending approved private colleges or universities within the state. Must be enrolled full-time in an undergraduate program not leading to a religious vocation. Contact college financial aid office for deadlines. **Award:** Grant for use in freshman, sophomore, junior, or senior year; renewable. *Award amount:* up to $1800. **Eligibility Requirements:** Applicant must be enrolled full-time at a two-year or four-year institution or university; resident of North Carolina and studying in North Carolina. Available to U.S. citizens. **Application Requirements:** Application. **Contact:** Bill Carswell, Manager of Scholarship and Grant Division, North Carolina State Education Assistance Authority, PO Box 13663, Research Triangle, NC 27709-3663. *Web site:* www.cfnc.org.

North Carolina Veterans Scholarships. Renewable awards for children of deceased or disabled veterans or veterans who were listed as Prisoner-Of-War or Missing-In-Action who were residents of North Carolina at time of entry into service. Award covers up to four years of tuition, room and board, and fees at a North Carolina institution. Children do not have to be residents of North Carolina to qualify. **Award:** Scholarship for use in any year; renewable. *Award amount:* $1500–$4500. **Eligibility Requirements:** Applicant must be enrolled full-time at a two-year, four-year, or technical institution or university and studying in North Carolina. Available to U.S. citizens. Applicant or parent must meet one or more of the following requirements: general military experience; retired from active duty; disabled or killed as a result of military service; Prisoner-Of-War; or Missing-In-Action. **Application Requirements:** Application, financial need analysis, interview, transcript. **Deadline:** May 30. **Contact:** Charles Smith, Director, North Carolina Division of Veterans' Affairs, 325 North Salisbury Street, Raleigh, NC 27603. *Phone:* 919-733-3851. *Fax:* 919-733-2834.

North Carolina Student Incentive Grant. Renewable award for North Carolina residents who are enrolled full-time in an undergraduate program not leading to a religious vocation at a North Carolina postsecondary institution. Must demonstrate substantial financial need. Must complete Free Application for Student Aid. Must be U.S. citizen and must maintain satisfactory academic progress. **Award:** Grant for use in freshman, sophomore, junior, or senior year; renewable. *Award amount:* $200–$1500. **Eligibility Requirements:** Applicant must be enrolled full-time at a two-year or four-year institution or university; resident of North Carolina and studying in North Carolina. Available to U.S. citizens. **Application Requirements:** Financial need analysis. **Deadline:** March 15. **Contact:** Bill Carswell, Manager of Scholarship and Grant Division, North Carolina State Education Assistance Authority, PO Box 13663, Research Triangle, NC 27709-3663. *Web site:* www.cfnc.org.

North Carolina National Guard Tuition Assistance Program. For members of the North Carolina Air and Army National Guard who will remain in the service for two years following the period for which assistance is provided. Applicants must reapply for each academic period. For use at approved North Carolina institutions. Deadline: 30 days before start of semester. Applicant must currently be serving in the Air National Guard or Army National Guard. Career maximum of $8,000. Annual maximum (1 Jul through 30 Jun) of $2,000. **Award:** Grant for use in any year; not renewable. *Award amount:* up to $2000. **Eligibility Requirements:** Applicant must be enrolled full or part-time at a two-year, four-year, or technical institution or university and studying in North

Carolina. Available to U.S. citizens. Applicant must have served in the Air Force National Guard or Army National Guard. **Application Requirements:** Application. **Deadline:** continuous. **Contact:** Cpt. Miriam Gray, Education Services Officer, North Carolina National Guard, 4105 Reedy Creek Road, Raleigh, NC 27607-6410. *E-mail:* miriam.gray@nc.ngb.army.mil. *Phone:* 800-621-4136 Ext. 6272. *Fax:* 919-664-6439. *Web site:* www.ncguard.com/.

North Carolina Teaching Fellows Scholarship Program. Renewable award for North Carolina high school seniors pursuing teaching careers. Must agree to teach in a North Carolina public or government school for four years or repay award. Must attend one of the fourteen approved schools in North Carolina. Merit-based. Must interview at the local level and at the regional level as a finalist. **Academic/Career Areas:** Education. **Award:** Forgivable loan for use in freshman, sophomore, junior, or senior year; renewable. *Award amount:* $6500. *Number of awards:* up to 400. **Eligibility Requirements:** Applicant must be high school student; planning to enroll full-time at a four-year institution; resident of North Carolina and studying in North Carolina. Applicant must have 3.5 GPA or higher. Available to U.S. citizens. **Application Requirements:** Application, essay, interview, references, test scores, transcript. **Deadline:** October 31. **Contact:** Ms. Sherry Woodruff, Program Officer, North Carolina Teaching Fellows Commission, 3739 National Drive, Suite 210, Raleigh, NC 27612. *E-mail:* tfellows@ncforum.org. *Phone:* 919-781-6833. *Fax:* 919-781-6527. *Web site:* www. teachingfellows.org.

NORTH DAKOTA

North Dakota Department of Transportation Engineering Grant. Educational grants for civil or construction engineering, or civil engineering technology, are awarded to students who have completed one-year of course study at an institution of higher learning in North Dakota. Recipients must agree to work for the Department for a period of time at least equal to the grant period or repay the grant at 6 percent interest. Minimum 2.5 GPA required. **Academic/Career Areas:** Civil Engineering; Engineering/Technology. **Award:** Grant for use in sophomore, junior, or senior year; renewable. *Award amount:* $2000. *Number of awards:* 1–10. **Eligibility Requirements:** Applicant must be enrolled full-time at a four-year, or technical institution and studying in North Dakota. Applicant must have 2.5 GPA or higher. Available to U.S. citizens. **Application Requirements:** Application, financial need analysis, interview, transcript. **Deadline:** continuous. **Contact:** Lorrie Pavlicek, Human Resources Manager, North Dakota Department of Transportation, 503 38th Street S, Fargo, ND 58103. *E-mail:* lpavlice@state.nd.us. *Phone:* 701-239-8934. *Fax:* 701-239-8939. *Web site:* www.state.nd.us/dot/.

North Dakota Indian College Scholarship Program. One-time award to Native American residents of North Dakota. Priority given to full-time undergraduate students. Minimum 2.5 GPA required. **Award:** Scholarship for use in any year; not renewable. *Award amount:* $700–$2000. *Number of awards:* 147. **Eligibility Requirements:** Applicant must be Native American or Eskimo; enrolled full-time at a two-year, four-year, or technical institution or university and resident of North Dakota. Applicant must have 2.5 GPA or higher. Available to U.S. citizens. **Application Requirements:** Application, financial need analysis, transcript. **Deadline:** July 15. **Contact:** Rhonda Schauer, SAA Director, North

Dakota University System, 600 East Boulevard Avenue, Department 215, Bismarck, ND 58505-0230. *Phone:* 701-328-9661. *Web site:* www.ndus.nodak.edu.

OHIO

Robert C. Byrd Honors Scholarship. Renewable award for graduating high school seniors who demonstrate outstanding academic achievement. Each Ohio high school receives applications by January of each year. School can submit one application for each 200 students in the senior class. **Award:** Scholarship for use in freshman, sophomore, junior, or senior year; renewable. *Award amount:* $1500. **Eligibility Requirements:** Applicant must be high school student; planning to enroll at a two-year or four-year institution or university and resident of Ohio. Applicant must have 3.5 GPA or higher. Available to U.S. citizens. **Application Requirements:** Application, test scores. **Deadline:** March 10. **Contact:** Charles Shahid, Program Coordinator, Ohio Board of Regents, PO Box 182452, Columbus, OH 43218-2452. *E-mail:* cshahid@regents.state.oh.us. *Phone:* 614-644-5959. *Fax:* 614-752-5903. *Web site:* www.regents.state.oh.us.

Ohio Instructional Grant. Award for low- and middle-income Ohio residents attending an approved college or school in Ohio or Pennsylvania. Must be enrolled full-time and have financial need. Average award is $630. May be used for any course of study except theology. **Award:** Grant for use in freshman, sophomore, junior, or senior year; renewable. *Award amount:* $210–$3750. **Eligibility Requirements:** Applicant must be enrolled full-time at a two-year or four-year institution or university; resident of Ohio and studying in Ohio or Pennsylvania. Available to U.S. citizens. **Application Requirements:** Application, financial need analysis. **Deadline:** October 1. **Contact:** David Bastian, Program Supervisor, Ohio Board of Regents, PO Box 182452, Columbus, OH 43218-2452. *E-mail:* dbastian@regents.state.oh.us. *Phone:* 614-752-9489. *Fax:* 614-752-5903. *Web site:* www.regents.state.oh.us.

Ohio Missing in Action and Prisoners-of-War Orphans Scholarship. Renewable award aids children of Vietnam conflict servicemen who have been classified as Missing-In-Action or Prisoner-Of-War. Must be an Ohio resident, be 16-21, and be enrolled full-time at an Ohio college. Full tuition awards. **Award:** Scholarship for use in freshman, sophomore, junior, or senior year; renewable. *Number of awards:* 1-5. **Eligibility Requirements:** Applicant must be age 16-21; enrolled full-time at a two-year or four-year institution; resident of Ohio and studying in Ohio. Available to U.S. citizens. Applicant or parent must meet one or more of the following requirements: general military experience; retired from active duty; disabled or killed as a result of military service; Prisoner-Of-War; or Missing-In-Action. **Application Requirements:** Application. **Deadline:** July 1. **Contact:** Sue Minturn, Program Administrator, Ohio Board of Regents, PO Box 182452, Columbus, OH 43218-2452. *E-mail:* sminturn@regents.state.oh.us. *Phone:* 614-752-9536. *Fax:* 614-752-5903. *Web site:* www.regents.state.oh.us.

Ohio War Orphans Scholarship. Aids Ohio residents attending an eligible college in Ohio. Must be between the ages of 16-21, the child of a disabled or deceased veteran, and enrolled full-time. Renewable up to five years. Amount of award varies. Must include Form DD214. **Award:** Scholarship for use in freshman, sophomore, junior, or senior year; renewable. *Number of awards:* 300–450. **Eligibility Requirements:** Applicant must be age 16-21; enrolled full-time at a two-year or four-year institution; resident of Ohio and studying in Ohio. Available to U.S. citizens. Applicant or parent must meet one or more of the following requirements: general military experience; retired from active duty; disabled or killed as a result of military service; Prisoner-Of-War; or Missing-In-Action. **Application Requirements:** Application. **Deadline:** July 1. **Contact:** Sue Minturn, Program Administrator, Ohio Board of Regents, PO Box 182452, Columbus, OH 43218-2452. *E-mail:* sminturn@regents.state.oh.us. *Phone:* 614-752-9536. *Fax:* 614-752-5903. *Web site:* www.regents.state.oh.us.

Ohio Safety Officers College Memorial Fund. Renewable award available to children and surviving spouses of peace officers and fire fighters killed in the line of duty in any state. Children must be under 26 years of age. Must be an Ohio resident and enroll full-time or part-time at an Ohio college or university. **Award:** Scholarship for use in freshman, sophomore, junior, or senior year; renewable. *Number of awards:* 50–65. **Eligibility Requirements:** Applicant must be age 25 or under; enrolled full or part-time at a two-year or four-year institution or university; resident of Ohio; studying in Ohio and have employment experience in police/firefighting. Available to U.S. citizens. **Application Requirements: Deadline:** continuous. **Contact:** Barbara Metheney, Program Administrator, Ohio Board of Regents, PO Box 182452, Columbus, OH 43218-2452. *E-mail:* bmethene@regents.state.oh.us. *Phone:* 614-752-9535. *Fax:* 614-752-5903. *Web site:* www.regents.state.oh.us.

Ohio National Guard Scholarship Program. Scholarships are for undergraduate studies at an approved Ohio postsecondary institution. Applicants must enlist for six years of Selective Service Reserve Duty in the Ohio National Guard. Scholarship pays 100% instructional and general fees for public institutions and an average of cost of public schools is available for private schools. Must be 18 years of age or older. Award is renewable. Deadlines: July 1, November 1, February 1, April 1. **Award:** Scholarship for use in freshman, sophomore, junior, or senior year; renewable. *Award amount:* $3000. *Number of awards:* 3500. **Eligibility Requirements:** Applicant must be age 18; enrolled full or part-time at a two-year or four-year institution or university and studying in Ohio. Available to U.S. citizens. Applicant must have served in the Air Force National Guard or Army National Guard. **Application Requirements:** Application. **Contact:** Mrs. Toni Davis, Grants Administrator, Ohio National Guard, 2825 West Granville Road, Columbus, OH 43235-2789. *E-mail:* davist@tagoh.org. *Phone:* 614-336-7032. *Fax:* 614-336-7318.

Ohio Academic Scholarship Program. Award for academically outstanding Ohio residents planning to attend an approved Ohio college. Must be a high school senior intending to enroll full-time. Award is renewable for up to four years. Must rank in upper quarter of class or have a minimum GPA of 3.5. **Award:** Scholarship for use in freshman, sophomore, junior, or senior year; renewable. *Award amount:* $2000. *Number of awards:* 1000. **Eligibility Requirements:** Applicant must be high school student; planning to enroll full-time at a two-year or four-year institution; resident of Ohio and studying in Ohio. Applicant must have 3.5 GPA or higher. Available to U.S. citizens. **Application Requirements:** Application, test scores, transcript. **Deadline:** February 23. **Contact:** Sue Minturn, Program Administrator, Ohio Board of Regents, PO Box 182452, Columbus, OH 43218-2452. *E-mail:* sminturn@regents.state.oh.us. *Phone:* 614-752-9536. *Fax:* 614-752-5903. *Web site:* www.regents.state.oh.us.

Part-time Student Instructional Grant. Renewable grants for part-time undergraduates who are Ohio residents. Award amounts vary. Must attend an Ohio institution. **Award:** Grant for use in freshman, sophomore, or junior year; renewable. *Number of awards:* up to 40,000. **Eligibility Requirements:** Applicant must be enrolled part-time at a two-year or four-year institution or university; resident of Ohio and studying in Ohio. Available to U.S. citizens. **Application Requirements:** Application, financial need analysis. **Deadline:** continuous. **Contact:** Barbara Metheney, Program Administrator, Ohio Board of Regents, PO Box 182452, Columbus, OH 43218-2452. *E-mail:* bmethene@regents. state.oh.us. *Phone:* 614-752-9535. *Fax:* 614-752-5903. *Web site:* www.regents. state.oh.us.

Ohio Student Choice Grant Program. Renewable award available to Ohio residents attending private colleges within the state. Must be enrolled full-time in a bachelor's degree program. Do not apply to state. Check with financial aid office of college. **Award:** Grant for use in freshman, sophomore, junior, or senior year; renewable. *Award amount:* up to $1062. **Eligibility Requirements:** Applicant must be enrolled full-time at a four-year institution; resident of Ohio and studying in Ohio. Available to U.S. citizens. **Application Requirements: Deadline:** continuous. **Contact:** Barbara Metheney, Program Administrator, Ohio Board of Regents, PO Box 182452, Columbus, OH 43218-2452. *E-mail:* bmethene@regents.state.oh.us. *Phone:* 614-752-9535. *Fax:* 614-752-5903. *Web site:* www.regents.state.oh.us.

OKLAHOMA

Future Teacher Scholarship–Oklahoma. Open to outstanding Oklahoma high school graduates who agree to teach in shortage areas. Must rank in top fifteen percent of graduating class or score above 85th percentile on ACT or similar test, or be accepted in an educational program. Students nominated by institution. Reapply to renew. Must attend college/university in Oklahoma. **Academic/Career Areas:** Education. **Award:** Scholarship for use in any year; not renewable. *Award amount:* up to $1500. **Eligibility Requirements:** Applicant must be high school student; planning to enroll full or part-time at a two-year or four-year institution or university; resident of Oklahoma and studying in Oklahoma. Available to U.S. and non-U.S. citizens. **Application Requirements:** Application, essay, test scores, transcript. **Contact:** Oklahoma State Regents for Higher Education, PO Box 108850, Oklahoma City, OK 73101-8850. *Phone:* 800-858-1840. *Fax:* 405-225-9230. *Web site:* www.okhighered.org.

Oklahoma Tuition Aid Grant. Award for Oklahoma residents enrolled at an Oklahoma institution at least part-time per semester in a degree program. May be enrolled in two- or four-year or approved vocational-technical institution. Award of up to $1000 per year. Application is made through FAFSA. **Award:** Grant for use in any year; renewable. *Award amount:* $200–$1000. *Number of awards:* 23,000. **Eligibility Requirements:** Applicant must be enrolled full or part-time at a two-year, four-year, or technical institution or university; resident of Oklahoma and studying in Oklahoma. Available to U.S. citizens. **Application Requirements:** Application, financial need analysis. **Deadline:** April 30. **Contact:** Oklahoma State Regents for Higher Education, PO Box 3020, Oklahoma City, OK 73101-3020. *E-mail:* otaginfo@otag.org. *Phone:* 405-225-9456. *Fax:* 405-225-9392. *Web site:* www.okhighered.org.

Academic Scholars Program. Encourages students of high academic ability to attend institutions in Oklahoma. Renewable up to four years. ACT or SAT scores must fall between 99.5 and 100th percentiles, or be designated as a National Merit Scholar or finalist. **Award:** Scholarship for use in any year; renewable. *Award amount:* $3500–$5500. **Eligibility Requirements:** Applicant must be enrolled full-time at a two-year or four-year institution or university and studying in Oklahoma. Available to U.S. and non-U.S. citizens. **Application Requirements:** Application, test scores, transcript. **Deadline:** continuous. **Contact:** Oklahoma State Regents for Higher Education, PO Box 108850, Oklahoma City, OK 73101-8850. *E-mail:* studentinfo@osrhe.edu. *Phone:* 800-858-1840. *Fax:* 405-225-9230. *Web site:* www.okhighered.org.

OREGON

Woodard Family Scholarship. Scholarships are available to employees and children of employees of Kimwood Corporation or Middlefield Estates. Applicants must have graduated from a U.S. high school. Awards may be used at Oregon colleges only, and may be received for a maximum of twelve quarters of undergraduate study. **Award:** Scholarship for use in freshman, sophomore, junior, or senior year; renewable. **Eligibility Requirements:** Applicant must be enrolled at a two-year or four-year institution; resident of Oregon; studying in Oregon; affiliated with Kimwood Corporation or Middlefield Village and have employment experience in designated career field. Available to U.S. citizens. **Application Requirements:** Application, essay, financial need analysis, references, transcript. **Deadline:** March 1. **Contact:** Director of Grant Programs, Oregon Student Assistance Commission, 1500 Valley River Drive, Suite 100, Eugene, OR 97401-7020. *E-mail:* awardinfo@mercury.osac.state.or.us. *Phone:* 800-452-8807 Ext. 7395. *Web site:* www.osac.state.or.us.

Ford Scholars. Award for Oregon graduating seniors, Oregon high school graduates not yet full-time undergraduates, or those who have completed two years of undergraduate study at an Oregon community college and will enter junior year at a four-year Oregon college. Minimum cumulative 3.0 GPA or 260 GED score. If minimum requirements not met, Special Recommendation Form (see high school counselor or contact OSAC) must be submitted. May apply for this program OR Ford Opportunity OR Ford Restart. **Award:** Scholarship for use in freshman, sophomore, or junior year; renewable. **Eligibility Requirements:** Applicant must be enrolled at a four-year institution; resident of Oregon and studying in Oregon. Applicant must have 3.0 GPA or higher. Available to U.S. citizens. **Application Requirements:** Application, essay, financial need analysis, test scores, transcript. **Deadline:** March 1. **Contact:** Director of Grant Programs, Oregon Student Assistance Commission, 1500 Valley River Drive, Suite 100, Eugene, OR 97401-7020. *E-mail:* awardinfo@mercury.osac.state.or.us. *Phone:* 800-452-8807 Ext. 7395. *Web site:* www.osac.state.or.us.

Ford Opportunity Program. Award for Oregon residents who are single heads of household with custody of a dependent child or children. Only for use at Oregon colleges. Minimum 3.0 GPA or 260 GED score required. If minimum requirements not met, Special Recommendation Form (see high school counselor or contact OSAC) must be submitted. May apply for this program or Ford Scholars or Ford Restart. **Award:** Scholarship for use in freshman, sophomore, junior, or senior year; renewable. **Eligibility Requirements:** Applicant must be enrolled at a two-year or four-year institution; single; resident of Oregon and studying in Oregon. Applicant must have 3.0 GPA or higher. **Application Requirements:** Application, essay, financial need analysis, test scores, transcript. **Deadline:** March 1. **Contact:** Director of Grant Programs, Oregon Student Assistance Commission, 1500 Valley River Drive, Suite 100, Eugene, OR 97401-7020. *E-mail:* awardinfo@mercury.osac.state.or.us. *Phone:* 800-452-8807 Ext. 7395. *Web site:* www.osac.state.or.us.

Oregon Dungeness Crab Commission Scholarship. One scholarship available to graduating high school senior who is a dependent of licensed Oregon Dungeness Crab fisherman or crew member. One-time award. Identify name of vessel in place of work site. **Award:** Scholarship for use in freshman year; not renewable. *Number of awards:* 1. **Eligibility Requirements:** Applicant must be high school student; resident of Oregon; affiliated with Oregon Dungeness Crab Commission and have employment experience in designated career field. Available to U.S. citizens. **Application Requirements:** Application, essay, financial need analysis, transcript. **Deadline:** March 1. **Contact:** Director of Grant Programs, Oregon Student Assistance Commission, 1500 Valley River Drive, Suite 100, Eugene, OR 97401-7020. *E-mail:* awardinfo@mercury.osac.state.or.us. *Phone:* 800-452-8807 Ext. 7395. *Web site:* www.osac.state.or.us.

Lawrence R. Foster Memorial Scholarship. One-time award to students enrolled or planning to enroll in a public health degree program. First preference given to those working in the public health field and those pursuing a graduate degree in public health. Undergraduates entering junior or senior year health programs may apply if seeking a public health career, and not private practice. Must provide 3 references. Additional essay required. Must be resident of Oregon. **Academic/Career Areas:** Health and Medical Sciences. **Award:** Scholarship for use in junior, senior, graduate, or post graduate years; not renewable. **Eligibility Requirements:** Applicant must be enrolled at a four-year institution and resident of Oregon. Available to U.S. citizens. **Application Requirements:** Application, essay, financial need analysis, references, transcript. **Deadline:** March 1. **Contact:** Director of Grant Programs, Oregon Student Assistance Commission, 1500 Valley River Drive, Suite 100, Eugene, OR 97401-7020. *E-mail:* awardinfo@mercury.osac.state.or.us. *Phone:* 800-452-8807 Ext. 7395. *Web site:* www.osac.state.or.us.

Alpha Delta Kappa/Harriet Simmons Scholarship. One-time award for elementary and secondary education majors entering their senior year, or graduate students enrolled in a fifth-year program leading to a teaching certificate. Visit Web site http://www.osac.state.or.us for more information. **Academic/ Career Areas:** Education. **Award:** Scholarship for use in senior or graduate year; not renewable. **Eligibility Requirements:** Applicant must be enrolled at a four-year institution or university and resident of Oregon. Available to U.S. citizens. **Application Requirements:** Application, essay, financial need analysis, transcript. **Deadline:** March 1. **Contact:** Director of Grant Programs, Oregon Student Assistance Commission, 1500 Valley River Drive, Suite 100, Eugene, OR 97401-7020. *E-mail:* awardinfo@mercury.osac.state.or.us. *Phone:* 800-452-8807 Ext. 7395. *Web site:* www.osac.state.or.us.

Troutman's Emporium Scholarship. One scholarship available to Troutman's Emporium full-time or part-time employees and dependents. Employee must have been employed for at least one year. Applicants must be planning to enroll at least half-time in an undergraduate course of study. Preference given to those planning to attend college in California, Idaho, Oregon, or Washington. One-time award. **Award:** Scholarship for use in freshman, sophomore, junior, or senior year; not renewable. **Eligibility Requirements:** Applicant must be enrolled full or part-time at a two-year or four-year institution; resident of Oregon; studying in California, Idaho, Oregon, or Washington; affiliated with Troutman's Emporium and have employment experience in designated career field. Available to U.S. citizens. **Application Requirements:** Application, essay, financial need analysis, references, transcript. **Deadline:** March 1. **Contact:** Director of Grant Programs, Oregon Student Assistance Commission, 1500 Valley River Drive, Suite 100, Eugene, OR 97401-7020. *E-mail:* awardinfo@ mercury.osac.state.or.us. *Phone:* 800-452-8807 Ext. 7395. *Web site:* www.osac. state.or.us.

Oregon Metro Federal Credit Union Scholarship. One scholarship available to an Oregon high school graduate who is a Oregon Metro Federal Credit Union member. Preference given to graduating high school senior and applicant who plans to attend an Oregon college. One-time award. **Award:** Scholarship for use in freshman, sophomore, junior, or senior year; not renewable. *Number of awards:* 1. **Eligibility Requirements:** Applicant must be enrolled at a four-year institution; resident of Oregon; studying in Oregon and affiliated with Oregon Metro Federal Credit Union. Available to U.S. citizens. **Application Requirements:** Application, essay, financial need analysis, references, transcript. **Deadline:** March 1. **Contact:** Director of Grant Programs, Oregon Student Assistance Commission, 1500 Valley River Drive, Suite 100, Eugene, OR 97401-7020. *E-mail:* awardinfo@mercury.osac.state.or.us. *Phone:* 800-452-8807 Ext. 7395. *Web site:* www.osac.state.or.us.

Teamsters Clyde C. Crosby/Joseph M. Edgar Memorial Scholarship. One scholarship available for a graduating high school senior with a minimum 3.0 cumulative GPA who is a child, or dependent stepchild of an active, retired, disabled, or deceased member of local union affiliated with Teamsters #37. Member must have been active for at least one year. Award may be received for a maximum of twelve quarters. **Award:** Scholarship for use in freshman, sophomore, junior, or senior year; renewable. *Number of awards:* 1. **Eligibility Requirements:** Applicant must be high school student; planning to enroll full or part-time at an institution or university; resident of Oregon; member of Teamsters and have employment experience in designated career field. Applicant must have 3.0 GPA or higher. Available to U.S. citizens. **Application Requirements:** Application, essay, financial need analysis, transcript. **Deadline:** March 1. **Contact:** Director of Grant Programs, Oregon Student Assistance Commission, 1500 Valley River Drive, Suite 100, Eugene, OR 97401-7020. *E-mail:* awardinfo@mercury.osac.state.or.us. *Phone:* 800-452-8807 Ext. 7395. *Web site:* www.osac.state.or.us.

Oregon Trucking Association Scholarship. One scholarship available to a child of an Oregon Trucking Association member, or child of employee of member. Applicants must be Oregon residents who are graduating high school seniors from an Oregon high school. One-time award. **Award:** Scholarship for use in freshman year; not renewable. *Number of awards:* 1. **Eligibility Requirements:** Applicant must be high school student; planning to enroll at a four-year institution; resident of Oregon; affiliated with Oregon Trucking Association and have employment experience in designated career field. Available to U.S. citizens. **Application Requirements:** Application, essay, financial need analysis, references, transcript. **Deadline:** March 1. **Contact:** Director of Grant Programs, Oregon Student Assistance Commission, 1500 Valley River Drive, Suite 100, Eugene, OR 97401-7020. *E-mail:* awardinfo@mercury.osac.state.or. us. *Phone:* 800-452-8807 Ext. 7395. *Web site:* www.osac.state.or.us.

Albina Fuel Company Scholarship. One scholarship available to a dependent child of a current Albina Fuel Company employee. The employee must have been employed for at least one full year as of October 1 prior to the scholarship deadline. One-time award. **Award:** Scholarship for use in freshman, sophomore, junior, or senior year; not renewable. **Eligibility Requirements:** Applicant must be resident of Oregon; affiliated with Albina Fuel Company and have employment experience in designated career field. Available to U.S. citizens. **Application Requirements:** Application, essay, financial need analysis, transcript. **Deadline:** March 1. **Contact:** Director of Grant Programs, Oregon Student Assistance Commission, 1500 Valley River Drive, Suite 100, Eugene, OR 97401-7020. *E-mail:* awardinfo@mercury.osac.state.or.us. *Phone:* 800-452-8807 Ext. 7395. *Web site:* www.osac.state.or.us.

Roger W. Emmons Memorial Scholarship. One scholarship available to a graduating Oregon high school senior who is a child or grandchild of an employee (for at least three years) of member of the Oregon Refuse and Recycling Association. One-time award for use at an Oregon college. **Award:** Scholarship for use in freshman year; renewable. *Number of awards:* 1. **Eligibility Requirements:** Applicant must be high school student; planning to enroll at a four-year institution; resident of Oregon; studying in Oregon; affiliated with Oregon Refuse and Recycling Association and have employment experience in designated career field. Available to U.S. citizens. **Application Requirements:** Application, essay, financial need analysis, references, transcript. **Deadline:** March 1. **Contact:** Director of Grant Programs, Oregon Student Assistance Commission, 1500 Valley River Drive, Suite 100, Eugene, OR 97401-7020. *E-mail:* awardinfo@mercury.osac.state.or.us. *Phone:* 800-452-8807 Ext. 7395. *Web site:* www.osac.state.or.us.

Glenn Jackson Scholars Scholarships (OCF). Award for graduating high school seniors who are dependents of employees or retirees of Oregon Department of Transportation or Parks and Recreation Department. Employees must have worked in their department at least three years. Award for maximum twelve undergraduate quarters or 6 quarters at a two-year institution. Must be U.S. citizen or permanent resident. Visit Web site (http://www.osac.state.or.us) for more details. **Award:** Scholarship for use in freshman, sophomore, junior, or senior year; renewable. **Eligibility Requirements:** Applicant must be high school student; planning to enroll at a four-year institution; resident of Oregon; affiliated with Oregon Department of Transportation Parks and Recreation and have employment experience in designated career field. Available to U.S. citizens. **Application Requirements:** Application, essay, financial need analysis, references, transcript. **Deadline:** March 1. **Contact:** Director of Grant Programs, Oregon Student Assistance Commission, 1500 Valley River Drive, Suite 100, Eugene, OR 97401-7020. *E-mail:* awardinfo@mercury.osac.state.or.us. *Phone:* 800-452-8807 Ext. 7395. *Web site:* www.osac.state.or.us.

Profiles of State-Sponsored Programs

Robert D. Forster Scholarship. One scholarship available to a dependent child of a Walsh Construction Co. employee who has completed 1,000 hours or more in each of three consecutive fiscal years. Award may be received for a maximum of twelve quarters of undergraduate study and may only be used at four-year colleges. **Award:** Scholarship for use in freshman, sophomore, junior, or senior year; renewable. *Number of awards:* 1. **Eligibility Requirements:** Applicant must be enrolled at a four-year institution; resident of Oregon; affiliated with Walsh Construction Company and have employment experience in designated career field. Available to U.S. citizens. **Application Requirements:** Application, essay, financial need analysis, references, transcript. **Deadline:** March 1. **Contact:** Director of Grant Programs, Oregon Student Assistance Commission, 1500 Valley River Drive, Suite 100, Eugene, OR 97401-7020. *E-mail:* awardinfo@mercury.osac.state.or.us. *Phone:* 800-452-8807 Ext. 7395. *Web site:* www.osac.state.or.us.

Ben Selling Scholarship. Award for Oregon residents enrolling as sophomores or higher in college. College GPA 3.50 or higher required. Apply/compete annually. Must be U.S. citizen or permanent resident. Wells Fargo employees, their children or near relatives must provide complete disclosure of employment status to receive this award. **Award:** Scholarship for use in sophomore, junior, or senior year; not renewable. **Eligibility Requirements:** Applicant must be resident of Oregon. Applicant must have 3.5 GPA or higher. Available to U.S. citizens. **Application Requirements:** Application, essay, financial need analysis, references, transcript. **Deadline:** March 1. **Contact:** Director of Grant Programs, Oregon Student Assistance Commission, 1500 Valley River Drive, Suite 100, Eugene, OR 97401-7020. *E-mail:* awardinfo@mercury.osac.state.or. us. *Phone:* 800-452-8807 Ext. 7395. *Web site:* www.osac.state.or.us.

Walter and Marie Schmidt Scholarship. One scholarship available to a student who is enrolled or planning to enroll in a program of training to become a registered nurse. Applicants must submit an additional essay describing their desire to pursue a nursing career in geriatrics. U.S. Bancorp employees and their relatives are not eligible. One-time award. **Academic/Career Areas:** Nursing. **Award:** Scholarship for use in freshman or sophomore year; not renewable. *Number of awards:* 1. **Eligibility Requirements:** Applicant must be enrolled full or part-time at a two-year or four-year institution and resident of Oregon. Available to U.S. citizens. **Application Requirements:** Application, essay, financial need analysis, references, transcript. **Deadline:** March 1. **Contact:** Director of Grant Programs, Oregon Student Assistance Commission, 1500 Valley River Drive, Suite 100, Eugene, OR 97401-7020. *E-mail:* awardinfo@ mercury.osac.state.or.us. *Phone:* 800-452-8807 Ext. 7395. *Web site:* www.osac. state.or.us.

David Family Scholarship. Award for residents of Clackamas, Lane, Linn, Marion, Multnomah, Washington, and Yamill counties. First preference to applicants enrolling at least half-time in upper-division or graduate programs at four-year colleges. Second preference to graduating high school seniors from West Linn-Wilsonville, Lake Oswego, Portland, Tigard-Tualatin, or Beaverton school districts. **Award:** Scholarship for use in any year; not renewable. **Eligibility Requirements:** Applicant must be enrolled full or part-time at a four-year institution and resident of Oregon. Applicant must have 2.5 GPA or higher. Available to U.S. citizens. **Application Requirements:** Application, essay, financial need analysis, test scores, transcript. **Deadline:** March 1. **Contact:** Director of Grant Programs, Oregon Student Assistance Commission, 1500 Valley River Drive, Suite 100, Eugene, OR 97401-7020. *E-mail:* awardinfo@ mercury.osac.state.or.us. *Phone:* 800-452-8807 Ext. 7395. *Web site:* www.osac. state.or.us.

Oregon Collectors Association Bob Hasson Memorial Scholarship. One-time award for graduating Oregon high school seniors and recent Oregon high school graduates, enrolling in college within one year of graduation. Children and grandchildren of owners and officers of collection agencies registered in Oregon are not eligible. Award is based on a 3-4 page essay titled "The Proper Use of Credit." See Web site (http://www.osac.state.or.us) for important application information. **Award:** Scholarship for use in freshman year; not renewable. *Award amount:* $1500-$3000. **Eligibility Requirements:** Applicant must be enrolled at a two-year, four-year, or technical institution; resident of Oregon and studying in Oregon. Available to U.S. citizens. **Application Requirements:** Application, applicant must enter a contest, essay, financial need analysis, test scores, transcript. **Deadline:** March 1. **Contact:** Director of Grant Programs, Oregon Student Assistance Commission, 1500 Valley River Drive, Suite 100, Eugene, OR 97401-7020. *E-mail:* awardinfo@mercury.osac.state.or.us. *Phone:* 800-452-8807 Ext. 7395. *Web site:* www.osac.state.or.us.

Dorothy Campbell Memorial Scholarship. Renewable award for female Oregon high school senior with a minimum 2.75 GPA. Must submit essay describing strong, continuing interest in golf and the contribution that sport has made to applicant's development. See Web site for more information. **Award:** Scholarship for use in freshman, sophomore, junior, or senior year; renewable. **Eligibility Requirements:** Applicant must be high school student; planning to enroll at a four-year institution; female; resident of Oregon; studying in Oregon and must have an interest in golf. Available to U.S. citizens. **Application Requirements:** Application, essay, financial need analysis, test scores, transcript. **Deadline:** March 1. **Contact:** Director of Grant Programs, Oregon Student Assistance Commission, 1500 Valley River Drive, Suite 100, Eugene, OR 97401-7020. *E-mail:* awardinfo@mercury.osac.state.or.us. *Phone:* 800-452-8807 Ext. 7395. *Web site:* www.osac.state.or.us.

Ida M. Crawford Scholarship. One-time scholarship awarded to Oregon high school seniors with a cumulative GPA of 3.5. Not available to applicants majoring in law, medicine, theology, teaching, or music. U.S. Bancorp employees, their children or near relatives, are not eligible. Must supply proof of birth in the continental U.S. **Award:** Scholarship for use in freshman year; not renewable. **Eligibility Requirements:** Applicant must be high school student and resident of Oregon. Applicant must have 3.5 GPA or higher. Available to U.S. citizens. **Application Requirements:** Application, essay, financial need analysis, test scores, transcript. **Deadline:** March 1. **Contact:** Director of Grant Programs, Oregon Student Assistance Commission, 1500 Valley River Drive, Suite 100, Eugene, OR 97401-7020. *E-mail:* awardinfo@mercury.osac.state.or.us. *Phone:* 800-452-8807 Ext. 7395. *Web site:* www.osac.state.or.us.

American Ex-Prisoner-of-War Scholarships: Peter Connacher Memorial Scholarship. Renewable award for American Prisoners-Of-War and their descendants. Written proof of Prisoner-Of-War status and discharge papers from the U.S. Armed Forces must accompany application. Statement of relationship between applicant and former Prisoner-Of-War is required. See Web site for details. **Award:** Scholarship for use in any year; renewable. **Eligibility Requirements:** Applicant must be enrolled at a two-year or four-year institution and resident of Oregon. Available to U.S. citizens. Applicant or parent must meet one or more of the following requirements: general military experience; retired from active duty; disabled or killed as a result of military service; Prisoner-Of-War; or Missing-In-Action. **Application Requirements:** Application, essay, financial need analysis, transcript. **Deadline:** March 1. **Contact:** Director of Grant Programs, Oregon Student Assistance Commission, 1500 Valley River Drive, Suite 100, Eugene, OR 97401-7020. *E-mail:* awardinfo@mercury.osac.state. or.us. *Phone:* 800-452-8807 Ext. 7395. *Web site:* www.osac.state.or.us.

Pacific NW Federal Credit Union Scholarship. One scholarship available to graduating high school senior who is a member of Pacific North West Federal Credit Union. A special essay is required employing the theme, "Why is My Credit Union an Important Consumer Choice?" Employers and officials of the Credit Union and their dependents are not eligible. One-time award. **Award:** Scholarship for use in freshman year; not renewable. *Number of awards:* 1. **Eligibility Requirements:** Applicant must be high school student; planning to enroll at a four-year institution; resident of Oregon and affiliated with Pacific Northwest Federal Credit Union. Available to U.S. citizens. **Application Requirements:** Application, essay, financial need analysis, references, transcript. **Deadline:** March 1. **Contact:** Director of Grant Programs, Oregon Student Assistance Commission, 1500 Valley River Drive, Suite 100, Eugene, OR 97401-7020. *E-mail:* awardinfo@mercury.osac.state.or.us. *Phone:* 800-452-8807 Ext. 7395. *Web site:* www.osac.state.or.us.

Mentor Graphics Scholarship. One-time award for computer science, computer engineering, or electrical engineering majors entering junior or senior year at a four-year institution. Preference for one award to female, African-American, Native American, or Hispanic applicant. **Academic/Career Areas:** Computer Science/Data Processing; Electrical Engineering/Electronics. **Award:** Scholarship for use in junior or senior year; not renewable. **Eligibility Requirements:** Applicant must be Native American or Eskimo, African American, or Hispanic; enrolled at a four-year institution; female and resident of Oregon. Available to U.S. citizens. **Application Requirements:** Application, essay, financial need analysis, references, transcript. **Deadline:** March 1. **Contact:** Director of Grant Programs, Oregon Student Assistance Commission, 1500 Valley River Drive, Suite 100, Eugene, OR 97401-7020. *E-mail:* awardinfo@ mercury.osac.state.or.us. *Phone:* 800-452-8807 Ext. 7395. *Web site:* www.osac. state.or.us.

Ford Restart Program Scholarship. Award for Oregon residents 26 years of age or older who have a high school degree or GED and wish to pursue technical, community college, or 4-year degrees. Preference given to those with limited college experience. Must complete ReStart Reference Form Contact OSAC. Apply for this program OR Ford Opportunity OR Ford Scholars. **Award:** Scholarship for use in freshman, sophomore, junior, or senior year; renewable. **Eligibility Requirements:** Applicant must be age 26; enrolled at a two-year, four-year, or technical institution; resident of Oregon and studying in Oregon. Available to U.S. citizens. **Application Requirements:** Application, essay, financial need analysis, transcript. **Deadline:** March 1. **Contact:** Director of Grant Programs, Oregon Student Assistance Commission, 1500 Valley River Drive, Suite 100, Eugene, OR 97401-7020. *E-mail:* awardinfo@mercury.osac.state. or.us. *Phone:* 800-452-8807 Ext. 7395. *Web site:* www.osac.state.or.us.

PENNSYLVANIA

Pennsylvania State Grant. Award for Pennsylvania residents attending an approved postsecondary institution as undergraduates in a program of at least two years duration. Renewable for up to eight semesters if applicants show continued need and academic progress. Submit Free Application for Federal Student Aid. **Award:** Grant for use in freshman, sophomore, junior, or senior year; renewable. *Award amount:* $300–$3300. *Number of awards:* up to 151,000. **Eligibility Requirements:** Applicant must be enrolled full or part-time at a two-year, four-year, or technical institution or university and resident of Pennsylvania. Available to U.S. and Canadian citizens. **Application Requirements:** Application, financial need analysis. **Deadline:** May 1. **Contact:** Keith New, Director of Communications and Press Office, Pennsylvania Higher Education Assistance Agency, 1200 North Seventh Street, Harrisburg, PA 17102-1444. *E-mail:* knew@pheaa.org. *Phone:* 717-720-2509. *Fax:* 717-720-3903. *Web site:* www.pheaa.org.

Veterans Grant–Pennsylvania. Renewable awards for Pennsylvania residents who are qualified veterans attending an approved undergraduate program full-time. Up to $3300 for in-state study or $800 for out-of-state study. Deadlines: May 1 for all renewal applicants, new applicants who plan to enroll in an undergraduate baccalaureate degree program, and those in college transfer programs at two-year public or junior colleges; August 1 for all first-time applicants who plan to enroll in a business, trade, or technical school; a hospital school of nursing; or a two-year terminal program at a community, junior, or four-year college. **Award:** Grant for use in freshman, sophomore, junior, or senior year; renewable. *Award amount:* $800–$3300. **Eligibility Requirements:** Applicant must be enrolled full or part-time at a two-year, four-year, or technical institution or university and resident of Pennsylvania. Available to U.S. citizens. Applicant must have general military experience. **Application Requirements:** Application. **Contact:** Keith New, Director of Communications and Press Office, Pennsylvania Higher Education Assistance Agency, 1200 North Seventh Street, Harrisburg, PA 17102-1444. *E-mail:* knew@pheaa.org. *Phone:* 717-720-2509. *Fax:* 717-720-3903. *Web site:* www.pheaa.org.

Agriculture Education Loan Forgiveness Program. Loan forgiveness to help agriculture and veterinary medicine graduates repay student loans when they return to operate a family farm, a family farm corporation, or practice veterinary medicine on agricultural animals in Pennsylvania. Must hold a degree in agriculture or veterinary medicine from a Pennsylvania institution. Limited to a lifetime maximum of $10,000 in loan forgiveness payments. The program will forgive up to $2,000 per year of PHEAA guaranteed student loans for each year the borrower is employed or works full-time. **Academic/Career Areas:** Agriculture; Animal/Veterinary Sciences. **Award:** Forgivable loan for use in any year; renewable. *Award amount:* up to $2000. **Eligibility Requirements:** Applicant must be studying in Pennsylvania. Available to U.S. citizens. **Application Requirements:** Application. **Deadline:** November 15. **Contact:** Keith

New, Director of Communications and Press Office, Pennsylvania Higher Education Assistance Agency, 1200 North Seventh Street, Harrisburg, PA 17102-1444. *E-mail:* knew@pheaa.org. *Phone:* 717-720-2509. *Fax:* 717-720-3903. *Web site:* www.pheaa.org.

RHODE ISLAND

Rhode Island Higher Education Grant Program. Grants for residents of Rhode Island attending an approved school in U.S., Canada, or Mexico. Based on need. Renewable for up to four years if in good academic standing. Applications accepted January 1 through March 1. Several awards of variable amounts. Must be U.S. citizen or registered alien. **Award:** Grant for use in freshman, sophomore, junior, or senior year; renewable. *Award amount:* $250–$750. *Number of awards:* 10,000–12,000. **Eligibility Requirements:** Applicant must be enrolled full or part-time at a two-year, four-year, or technical institution or university and resident of Rhode Island. Available to U.S. citizens. **Application Requirements:** Application, financial need analysis. **Deadline:** March 1. **Contact:** Mary Ann Welch, Director of Program Administration, Rhode Island Higher Education Assistance Authority, 560 Jefferson Boulevard, 222 21st. Avenue South, Warwick, RI 02886. *Phone:* 401-736-1100. *Fax:* 401-732-3541. *Web site:* www.riheaa.org.

SOUTH CAROLINA

South Carolina Tuition Grants Program. Assists South Carolina residents attending one of twenty approved South Carolina Independent colleges. Freshmen must be in upper 3/4 of high school class or have SAT score of at least 900. Upper-class students must complete twenty-four semester hours per year to be eligible. **Award:** Grant for use in freshman, sophomore, junior, or senior year; renewable. *Award amount:* $100–$3350. *Number of awards:* up to 11,000. **Eligibility Requirements:** Applicant must be enrolled full-time at a two-year or four-year institution; resident of South Carolina and studying in South Carolina. Available to U.S. citizens. **Application Requirements:** Application, financial need analysis, test scores, transcript. **Deadline:** June 30. **Contact:** Toni Cave, Financial Aid Counselor, South Carolina Tuition Grants Commission, 101 Business Park Boulevard, Suite 2100, Columbia, SC 29203-9498. *E-mail:* toni@sctuitiongrants.org. *Phone:* 803-896-1120. *Fax:* 803-896-1126. *Web site:* www.sctuitiongrants.com.

South Carolina Need-Based Grants Program. Need-based grant awarded based on results of Free Application for Federal Student Aid. A student may receive up to $2500 annually for full-time and up to $1250 annually for part-time. The grant must be applied toward the cost of attendance at a South Carolina college for up to eight full-time equivalent terms. Student must be degree-seeking. **Award:** Grant for use in freshman, sophomore, junior, or senior year; renewable. **Eligibility Requirements:** Applicant must be enrolled full or part-time at a two-year, four-year, or technical institution or university; resident of South Carolina and studying in South Carolina. Available to U.S. citizens. **Application Requirements:** Financial need analysis. **Deadline:** continuous. **Contact:** Ms. Sherry Hubbard, Coordinator, South Carolina Commission on

Higher Education, 1333 Main Street, Suite 200, Columbia, SC 29201. *E-mail:* shubbard@che400.state.sc.us. *Phone:* 803-737-2260. *Fax:* 803-737-2297. *Web site:* www.che400.state.sc.us.

Palmetto Fellows Scholarship Program. Renewable award for qualified high school seniors in South Carolina to attend a four-year South Carolina institution. Must rank in top five percent of class at the end of sophomore or junior year, earn a 3.5 GPA on a 4.0 scale, and score at least 1200 on the SAT or 27 on the ACT. Submit official transcript and test scores with application by established deadline (usually January 15th of senior year). **Award:** Scholarship for use in freshman, sophomore, junior, or senior year; renewable. *Award amount:* up to $5000. *Number of awards:* 650–750. **Eligibility Requirements:** Applicant must be high school student; planning to enroll full-time at a four-year institution or university; resident of South Carolina and studying in South Carolina. Applicant must have 3.5 GPA or higher. Available to U.S. citizens. **Application Requirements:** Application, applicant must enter a contest, references, test scores, transcript. **Deadline:** January 15. **Contact:** Ms. Sherry Hubbard, Coordinator, South Carolina Commission on Higher Education, 1333 Main Street, Suite 200, Columbia, SC 29201. *E-mail:* shubbard@che400.state.sc.us. *Phone:* 803-737-2260. *Fax:* 803-737-2297. *Web site:* www.che400.state.sc.us.

Legislative Incentives for Future Excellence Program. The goals of the LIFE Scholarship Program are to increase access to higher education, improve the employability of South Carolina's students so as to attract business to the State, provide incentives for students to be better prepared for college, to improve SAT scores, and to graduate from college on time. Must meet two of the following three criteria for students graduating from high school in 2002: 1) minimum 3.0 GPA, 2) 1100 SAT or 24 ACT, or 3) Graduate in top 30% of graduating class. **Award:** Scholarship for use in freshman, sophomore, junior, or senior year; renewable. *Award amount:* $3700–$5090. **Eligibility Requirements:** Applicant must be enrolled full-time at a four-year institution or university; resident of South Carolina and studying in South Carolina. Applicant must have 3.0 GPA or higher. Available to U.S. citizens. **Application Requirements:** Test scores, transcript. **Deadline:** continuous. **Contact:** Bichevia Green, LIFE Scholarship Coordinator, South Carolina Commission on Higher Education, 1333 Main Street, Suite 200, Columbia, SC 29201. *E-mail:* bgreen@che400.state.sc.us. *Phone:* 803-737-2280. *Fax:* 803-737-2297. *Web site:* www.che400.state.sc.us.

South Carolina Teacher Loan Program. One-time awards for South Carolina residents attending four-year postsecondary institutions in South Carolina. Recipients must teach in the South Carolina public school system in a critical-need area after graduation. 20% of loan forgiven for each year of service. Write for additional requirements. **Academic/Career Areas:** Education; Special Education. **Award:** Forgivable loan for use in any year; not renewable. *Award amount:* $2500–$5000. *Number of awards:* up to 1121. **Eligibility Requirements:** Applicant must be enrolled full or part-time at a four-year institution or university; resident of South Carolina and studying in South Carolina. Applicant must have 3.0 GPA or higher. **Application Requirements:** Application, test scores. **Deadline:** June 1. **Contact:** Jennifer Jones-Gaddy, Vice President,

South Carolina Student Loan Corporation, PO Box 21487, Columbia, SC 29221. *E-mail:* jgaddy@slc.sc.edu. *Phone:* 803-798-0916. *Fax:* 803-772-9410. *Web site:* www.slc.sc.edu.

Educational Assistance for Certain War Veteran's Dependents–South Carolina. Renewable aid to South Carolina Disabled Veterans' dependents under age 26. Veterans must have had wartime service in World War II, the Vietnam War, Persian Gulf or the Korean War. Must have received the Purple Heart or Medal of Honor. Applicant must show DD214 (birth certificate and VA rating). For undergraduate study at any South Carolina state supported college. Must be South Carolina resident. **Award:** Scholarship for use in freshman, sophomore, junior, or senior year; renewable. **Eligibility Requirements:** Applicant must be age 18-26; enrolled full or part-time at a two-year, four-year, or technical institution or university; resident of South Carolina and studying in South Carolina. Available to U.S. citizens. Applicant or parent must meet one or more of the following requirements: general military experience; retired from active duty; disabled or killed as a result of military service; Prisoner-Of-War; or Missing-In-Action. **Application Requirements:** Application. **Contact:** Ms. Lauren Hugg, Free Tuition Assistant, South Carolina Division of Veterans Affairs, 1801 Assembly Street, Room 141, Columbia, SC 29201. *Phone:* 803-255-4317. *Fax:* 803-255-4257.

SOUTH DAKOTA

Haines Memorial Scholarship. One-time scholarship for South Dakota public university students who are sophomores, juniors, or seniors having at least a 2.5 GPA and majoring in a teacher education program. Include resume with application. Must be South Dakota resident. **Academic/Career Areas:** Education. **Award:** Scholarship for use in sophomore, junior, or senior year; not renewable. *Award amount:* $2150. *Number of awards:* 1. **Eligibility Requirements:** Applicant must be resident of South Dakota and studying in South Dakota. Applicant must have 2.5 GPA or higher. **Application Requirements:** Application, autobiography, essay, resume. **Deadline:** February 25. **Contact:** South Dakota Board of Regents, 306 East Capitol Avenue, Suite 200, Pierre, SD 57501-3159. *Web site:* www.ris.sdbor.edu.

South Dakota Aid to Dependents of Deceased Veterans. Program provides free tuition for children of deceased veterans who are under the age of 25, are residents of South Dakota, and whose mother or father was killed in action or died of other causes while on active duty. ("Veteran" for this purpose is as defined by South Dakota Codified Laws.) Parent must have been a bona fide resident of SD for at least six months immediately preceding entry into active service. Eligibility is for state supported schools only. Must use SDDVA form E-12 available at financial aid offices. **Award:** Scholarship for use in freshman, sophomore, junior, or senior year; not renewable. **Eligibility Requirements:** Applicant must be age 25 or under; enrolled at a two-year or four-year institution; resident of South Dakota and studying in South Dakota. Available to U.S. citizens. Applicant or parent must meet one or more of the following requirements: general military experience; retired from active duty; disabled or killed as a result of military service; Prisoner-Of-War; or Missing-In-Action. **Application Requirements:** Application. **Contact:** Dr. Lesta V. Turchen, Senior

Administrator, South Dakota Board of Regents, 306 East Capitol Avenue, Suite 200, Pierre, SD 57501-3159. *Phone:* 605-773-3455. *Fax:* 605-773-2422. *Web site:* www.ris.sdbor.edu.

Education Benefits for Dependents of POWs and MIAs. Children and spouses of Prisoners-Of-War, or of persons listed as Missing-In-Action, are entitled to attend a state-supported school without the payment of tuition or mandatory fees provided they are not eligible for equal or greater federal benefits. File SDDVA for E-12 available at financial aids offices. Must be a South Dakota resident intending to study in South Dakota. **Award:** Scholarship for use in any year; not renewable. **Eligibility Requirements:** Applicant must be resident of South Dakota and studying in South Dakota. Available to U.S. citizens. Applicant or parent must meet one or more of the following requirements: general military experience; retired from active duty; disabled or killed as a result of military service; Prisoner-Of-War; or Missing-In-Action. **Application Requirements:** Application. **Contact:** Dr. Lesta V. Turchen, Senior Administrator, South Dakota Board of Regents, 306 East Capitol Avenue, Suite 200, Pierre, SD 57501-3159. *Phone:* 605-773-3455. *Fax:* 605-773-2422. *Web site:* www.ris.sdbor.edu.

South Dakota Education Benefits for National Guard Members. Guard members who meet the requirements for admission are eligible for a fifty percent reduction in undergraduate tuition charges at any state-supported school for up to a maximum of four academic years. Provision also covers one program of study, approved by the State Board of Education, at any state vocational school. Must be state resident and member of the SD Army or Air Guard throughout period for which benefits are sought. Must contact financial aid office for full details and forms at time of registration. **Award:** Scholarship for use in freshman, sophomore, junior, or senior year; not renewable. **Eligibility Requirements:** Applicant must be enrolled at a two-year, four-year, or technical institution or university; resident of South Dakota and studying in South Dakota. Available to U.S. citizens. Applicant must have served in the Air Force National Guard, Army National Guard, or Navy National Guard. **Application Requirements:** Application. **Contact:** Dr. Lesta V. Turchen, Senior Administrator, South Dakota Board of Regents, 306 East Capitol Avenue, Suite 200, Pierre, SD 57501-3159. *Phone:* 605-773-3455. *Fax:* 605-773-2422. *Web site:* www.ris.sdbor.edu.

SD Education Benefits for Veterans. Certain veterans are eligible for free undergraduate tuition assistance at state-supported schools provided they are not eligible for educational payments under the GI Bill or any other federal educational program. Contact financial aid office for full details and forms. May receive one month of free tuition for each month of qualifying service (minimum one year, maximum four years). Must be resident of South Dakota. **Award:** Scholarship for use in freshman, sophomore, junior, or senior year; not renewable. **Eligibility Requirements:** Applicant must be resident of South Dakota and studying in South Dakota. Available to U.S. citizens. Applicant must have general military experience. **Application Requirements:** Application. **Contact:** Dr. Lesta V. Turchen, Senior Administrator, South Dakota Board of Regents, 306 East Capitol Avenue, Suite 200, Pierre, SD 57501-3159. *Phone:* 605-773-3455. *Fax:* 605-773-2422. *Web site:* www.ris.sdbor.edu.

TENNESSEE

Tennessee Student Assistance Award Program. Assists Tennessee residents attending an approved college or university within the state. Complete a Free Application for Federal Student Aid form. Apply January 1. FAFSA must be processed by May 1 for priority consideration. **Award:** Grant for use in freshman, sophomore, junior, or senior year; renewable. *Award amount:* $1746. *Number of awards:* 22,000. **Eligibility Requirements:** Applicant must be enrolled full or part-time at a two-year, four-year, or technical institution or university; resident of Tennessee and studying in Tennessee. Available to U.S. citizens. **Application Requirements:** Application, financial need analysis. **Deadline:** May 1. **Contact:** Naomi Derryberry, Grant and Scholarship Administrator, Tennessee Student Assistance Corporation, Suite 1950, Parkway Towers, Nashville, TN 37243-0820. *Phone:* 615-741-1346. *Fax:* 615-741-6101. *Web site:* www.state.tn.us/tsac.

Tennessee Teaching Scholars Program. Forgivable loan for college juniors, seniors, and college graduates admitted to an education program in Tennessee with a minimum GPA of 2.5. Students must commit to teach in a Tennessee public school one year for each year of the award. **Academic/Career Areas:** Education. **Award:** Forgivable loan for use in junior, senior, or graduate year; not renewable. *Award amount:* $1000–$3900. *Number of awards:* 30–250. **Eligibility Requirements:** Applicant must be enrolled full-time at a four-year institution or university; resident of Tennessee and studying in Tennessee. Applicant must have 2.5 GPA or higher. Available to U.S. citizens. **Application Requirements:** Application, references, test scores, transcript. **Deadline:** April 15. **Contact:** Mike McCormack, Scholarship Administrator, Tennessee Student Assistance Corporation, Suite 1950, Parkway Towers, Nashville, TN 37243-0820. *Phone:* 615-741-1346. *Fax:* 615-741-6101. *Web site:* www.state.tn.us/tsac.

Minority Teaching Fellows Program/Tennessee. Forgivable loan for minority Tennessee residents pursuing teaching careers. High school applicant minimum 2.75 GPA. Must be in the top quarter of the class or score an 18 on ACT. College applicant minimum 2.50 GPA. Submit statement of intent, test scores, and transcripts with application and two letters of recommendation. Must teach one year per year of award or repay as a loan. **Academic/Career Areas:** Education; Special Education. **Award:** Forgivable loan for use in freshman, sophomore, junior, or senior year; renewable. *Award amount:* $5000. *Number of awards:* 19–29. **Eligibility Requirements:** Applicant must be Native American or Eskimo, Asian, African American, or Hispanic; enrolled full-time at a two-year or four-year institution or university; resident of Tennessee and studying in Tennessee. Available to U.S. citizens. **Application Requirements:** Application, essay, references, test scores, transcript. **Deadline:** April 15. **Contact:** Michael Roberts, Compliance Administrator, Tennessee Student Assistance Corporation, 404 James Robertson Parkway, Suite 1950, Parkway Towers, Nashville, TN 37243-0820. *E-mail:* michael.roberts@state.tn.us. *Phone:* 615-741-1346. *Fax:* 615-741-6101. *Web site:* www.state.tn.us/tsac.

Ned McWherter Scholars Program. Assists Tennessee residents with high academic ability. Must have high school GPA of at least 3.5 and have scored in top five percent of SAT or ACT. Must attend college in Tennessee. Only high school seniors may apply. **Award:** Scholarship for use in freshman, sophomore, junior, or senior year; renewable. *Award amount:* $6000. *Number of awards:* 55. **Eligibility Requirements:** Applicant must be high school student; planning to enroll full-time at a two-year or four-year institution or university; resident of Tennessee and studying in Tennessee. Applicant must have 3.5 GPA or higher. Available to U.S. citizens. **Application Requirements:** Application, test scores, transcript. **Deadline:** February 15. **Contact:** Naomi Derryberry, Grant and Scholarship Administrator, Tennessee Student Assistance Corporation, Suite 1950, Parkway Towers, Nashville, TN 37243-0820. *Phone:* 615-741-1346. *Fax:* 615-741-6101. *Web site:* www.state.tn.us/tsac.

TEXAS

Texas Yes! Scholarships. Texas YES! Scholarships are awarded to women and minorities, or to applicants who have participated in the educational programs sponsored by the Texas Society of Professional Engineers: MATHCOUNTS, NEDC, TEC, TEAMS, TESC. Applicants must have a 3.0 GPA. Must major in a field of engineering, be a resident of Texas and attend a postsecondary institution in Texas. Must be a high school senior. **Academic/Career Areas:** Chemical Engineering; Civil Engineering; Electrical Engineering/Electronics; Engineering/Technology; Mechanical Engineering. **Award:** Scholarship for use in freshman year; not renewable. *Award amount:* $500–$1000. *Number of awards:* 3–5. **Eligibility Requirements:** Applicant must be high school student; planning to enroll full-time at an institution or university; resident of Texas and studying in Texas. Applicant must have 3.0 GPA or higher. Available to U.S. citizens. **Application Requirements:** Application, essay, references, transcript. **Deadline:** January 15. **Contact:** Kelly Melnyk, Assistant Director of Education Programs, Texas Engineering Foundation, Attn: Programs Director, 3501 Manor Road, PO Box 2145, Austin, TX 78768. *E-mail:* kellym@tspe.org. *Phone:* 512-472-9286. *Fax:* 512-472-2934. *Web site:* www.tspe.org.

Texas Tuition Exemption for Students in Foster Care or other Residential Care. Exemption from tuition and fees at Texas institution. Must have been in foster care under the conservatorship of the Department of Protection and Regulatory Services on or after 18th birthday; or on the day of the student's 14th birthday, if the student was also eligible for adoption on or after that day; or the day the student graduated from high school or completed the equivalent of a high school diploma. Must enroll as undergraduate student within three years of discharge. Must be Texas resident. Contact the admissions/registrar's office for application information. **Award:** Scholarship for use in freshman, sophomore, junior, or senior year; renewable. **Eligibility Requirements:** Applicant must be enrolled full or part-time at a two-year, four-year, or technical institution or university; resident of Texas and studying in Texas. Available to U.S. citizens. **Application Requirements:** Application. **Deadline:** continuous. **Contact:** Financial aid office at college, Texas Higher Education Coordinating Board, PO Box 12788, Austin, TX 78711-2788. *E-mail:* grantinfo@thecb.state.tx. us. *Phone:* 512-427-6101. *Fax:* 512-427-6127. *Web site:* www.collegefortexans. com.

License Plate Insignia Scholarship. One-time award to Texas residents enrolled at least half-time at public or private nonprofit senior colleges and universities in Texas. Must demonstrate financial need. Contact financial aid office at college for application. **Award:** Scholarship for use in freshman, sophomore, junior, or senior year; not renewable. **Eligibility Requirements:** Applicant must be enrolled full or part-time at a four-year institution or university; resident of Texas and studying in Texas. **Application Requirements:** Application, financial need analysis. **Contact:** Financial aid office at college, Texas Higher Education Coordinating Board, PO Box 12788, Austin, TX 78711-2788. *E-mail:* grantinfo@ thecb.state.tx.us. *Phone:* 512-427-6101. *Fax:* 512-427-6127. *Web site:* www. collegefortexans.com.

Leveraging Educational Assistance Partnership Program (LEAP) (formerly SSIG). Renewable award available to residents of Texas attending public colleges or universities in Texas. Must be enrolled at least half-time and show financial need. Deadlines vary by institution. Contact the college/university financial aid office for application information. **Award:** Grant for use in any year; renewable. *Award amount:* up to $1250. **Eligibility Requirements:** Applicant must be enrolled full or part-time at a two-year, four-year, or technical institution or university; resident of Texas and studying in Texas. Available to U.S. citizens. **Application Requirements:** Financial need analysis. **Deadline:** continuous. **Contact:** Financial aid office at college, Texas Higher Education Coordinating Board, PO Box 12788, Austin, TX 78711-2788. *E-mail:* grantinfo@ thecb.state.tx.us. *Phone:* 512-427-6101. *Fax:* 512-427-6127. *Web site:* www. collegefortexans.com.

Train our Teachers Award. Awarded to employed child care workers seeking credentials or an associate degree in child development. Must agree to work 18 consecutive months in a licensed child care facility. Must attend a Texas institution. **Award:** Scholarship for use in any year; not renewable. *Award amount:* up to $1000. *Number of awards:* up to 2000. **Eligibility Requirements:** Applicant must be studying in Texas and have employment experience in designated career field. **Application Requirements:** Application. **Contact:** Financial aid office at college, Texas Higher Education Coordinating Board, PO Box 12788, Austin, TX 78711-2788. *E-mail:* grantinfo@thecb.state.tx. us. *Phone:* 512-427-6101. *Fax:* 512-427-6127. *Web site:* www.collegefortexans. com.

Teach for Texas Conditional Grant Program. This is a student loan with cancellation provisions for teaching. Prospective teachers must be enrolled in degree programs leading to certification in a teaching field designated as having a critical shortage of teachers, or agree to teach in a Texas community certified as experiencing a critical shortage of teachers. For upper division college students only. **Academic/Career Areas:** Education. **Award:** Forgivable loan for use in junior or senior year; not renewable. *Award amount:* $3584–$10,752. **Eligibility Requirements:** Applicant must be enrolled full or part-time at a four-year institution or university; resident of Texas and studying in Texas. Applicant must have 2.5 GPA or higher. Available to U.S. citizens. **Application Requirements:** Application, financial need analysis, references. **Deadline:** continuous. **Contact:** Special Accounts Servicing, Texas Higher Education Coordinating Board, PO Box 12788, Austin, TX 78711-2788. *E-mail:* grantinfo@thecb.state.tx.us. *Phone:* 800-242-3062. *Web site:* www.collegefortexans. com.

Educational Aides Exemption. Assist certain educational aides by exempting them from payment of tuition and fees at public colleges or universities in

Texas. Applicants must have worked as an educational aide in a Texas public school for at least one year and must be enrolled in courses required for teacher certification. Contact your college or university financial aid office for information on applying for this scholarship. **Academic/Career Areas:** Education. **Award:** Scholarship for use in any year; not renewable. *Award amount:* up to $605. **Eligibility Requirements:** Applicant must be enrolled at a four-year institution or university; resident of Texas and studying in Texas. **Application Requirements:** Application, financial need analysis. **Contact:** Financial aid office at college, Texas Higher Education Coordinating Board, PO Box 12788, Austin, TX 78711-2788. *E-mail:* grantinfo@thecb.state.tx.us. *Phone:* 512-427-6101. *Fax:* 512-427-6127. *Web site:* www.collegefortexans.com.

Toward Excellence, Access, and Success (TEXAS) Grant II Program. Provides grant aid to financially needy students enrolled in Texas public two-year colleges. Complete FAFSA. Contact college financial aid office for additional assistance. **Award:** Grant for use in freshman or sophomore year; renewable. *Award amount:* $582–$1344. **Eligibility Requirements:** Applicant must be enrolled full or part-time at a two-year or technical institution; resident of Texas and studying in Texas. Applicant must have 2.5 GPA or higher. Available to U.S. citizens. **Application Requirements:** Financial need analysis, transcript. **Deadline:** continuous. **Contact:** Financial aid office at college, Texas Higher Education Coordinating Board, PO Box 12788, Austin, TX 78711-2788. *E-mail:* grantinfo@thecb.state.tx.us. *Phone:* 512-427-6101. *Fax:* 512-427-6127. *Web site:* www.collegefortexans.com.

Texas Tuition Exemption for TANF Students. Tuition and fee exemption for Texas residents who during last year of high school received financial assistance for not less than 6 months. Must enroll at Texas institution within 24 TANF months of high school graduation. Award is good for one year. Contact the admissions/registrar's office for application information. **Award:** Scholarship for use in freshman year; not renewable. **Eligibility Requirements:** Applicant must be age 21 or under; enrolled full or part-time at a two-year, four-year, or technical institution or university; single; resident of Texas and studying in Texas. **Application Requirements:** Application, financial need analysis. **Deadline:** continuous. **Contact:** Financial aid office at college, Texas Higher Education Coordinating Board, PO Box 12788, Austin, TX 78711-2788. *E-mail:* grantinfo@thecb.state.tx.us. *Phone:* 512-427-6101. *Fax:* 512-427-6127. *Web site:* www.collegefortexans.com.

Early High School Graduation Scholarships. Award of $1000 for Texas residents who have completed the requirements for graduation from a Texas high school in no more than 36 consecutive months. Eligibility continues until full $1000 tuition award is received. Must submit high school certificate of eligibility to Coordinating Board. For more information, contact your high school counselor. **Award:** Scholarship for use in any year; not renewable. *Award amount:* $1000. **Eligibility Requirements:** Applicant must be high school student; planning to enroll full or part-time at a two-year, four-year, or technical institution or university; resident of Texas and studying in Texas. Available to U.S. citizens. **Application Requirements:** Application. **Deadline:** continuous. **Contact:** Texas Higher Education Coordinating Board, PO Box 12788, Austin, TX 78711-2788. *E-mail:* grantinfo@thecb.state.tx.us. *Phone:* 800-242-3062 Ext. 6387. *Web site:* www.collegefortexans.com.

Fifth-Year Accounting Student Scholarship Program. One-time award for students enrolled as fifth-year accounting students at a Texas institution. Must sign statement confirming intent to take the written exam for the purpose of being granted a certificate of CPA to practice in Texas. Contact college/ university financial aid office for application information. **Academic/Career Areas:** Business/Consumer Services. **Award:** Scholarship for use in senior or graduate year; not renewable. *Award amount:* up to $3000. **Eligibility Requirements:** Applicant must be enrolled full or part-time at a four-year institution or university and studying in Texas. Available to U.S. and non-U.S. citizens. **Application Requirements:** Application, financial need analysis, transcript. **Deadline:** continuous. **Contact:** Financial aid office at college, Texas Higher Education Coordinating Board, PO Box 12788, Austin, TX 78711-2788. *E-mail:* grantinfo@thecb.state.tx.us. *Phone:* 512-427-6101. *Fax:* 512-427-6127. *Web site:* www.collegefortexans.com.

Conditional Grant Program. A grant that provides female minorities financial education assistance up to $3,000 per semester for approved degree plans. At present, it is for civil engineering degrees. Must be a Texas resident and study in Texas. **Academic/Career Areas:** Civil Engineering. **Award:** Grant for use in freshman, sophomore, junior, or senior year; renewable. *Award amount:* up to $3000. *Number of awards:* 50. **Eligibility Requirements:** Applicant must be Native American or Eskimo, Asian, African American, or Hispanic; enrolled full-time at a four-year institution; female; resident of Texas and studying in Texas. Applicant must have 2.5 GPA or higher. Available to U.S. citizens. **Application Requirements:** Application, essay, interview, references, test scores, transcript. **Deadline:** March 1. **Contact:** Minnie Brown, Program Coordinator, Texas Department of Transportation, 125 East 11th Street, Austin, TX 78701-2483. *E-mail:* www.mbrown2@dot.state.tx.us. *Phone:* 512-416-4979. *Fax:* 512-416-4980. *Web site:* www.dot.state.tx.us.

Dental Education Loan Repayment Program. Award will repay student loans for licensed dentists. Must agree to work in underserved area of Texas for one year. Repayment applied to undergraduate or graduate loans for studies in Texas. May reapply up to five years. **Award:** Scholarship for use in any year; not renewable. *Award amount:* up to $10,000. **Eligibility Requirements:** Applicant must have employment experience in designated career field. **Application Requirements:** Application. **Contact:** Special Accounts, Texas Higher Education Coordinating Board, PO Box 12788, Austin, TX 78711. *E-mail:* grantinfo@ thecb.state.tx.us. *Web site:* www.collegefortexans.com.

Exemption for Disabled in the Line of Duty Peace Officers. Renewable award for persons who were injured in the line of duty while serving as Peace Officers. Must be Texas resident and attend a public college or university in Texas. Submit documentation of disability from employer. **Award:** Scholarship for use in freshman, sophomore, junior, or senior year; renewable. **Eligibility Requirements:** Applicant must be enrolled at a four-year institution or university; resident of Texas; studying in Texas and have employment experience in police/firefighting. **Application Requirements:** Application. **Contact:** Texas Higher Education Coordinating Board, PO Box 12788, Austin, TX 78711. *E-mail:* grantinfo@thecb.state.tx.us. *Web site:* www.collegefortexans.com.

Early Childhood Care Provider Student Loan Repayment. Award will repay student loans for child-care workers with a degree in Early Child Development. Must be employed at a licensed facility and work a minimum of 31 hours per week. Must agree to provide service for two years. **Award:** Scholarship for use in any year; not renewable. *Award amount:* up to $3830. **Eligibility Requirements:** Applicant must have employment experience in designated career field. Available to U.S. citizens. **Application Requirements:** Application. **Contact:** Special Accounts, Texas Higher Education Coordinating Board, PO Box 12788, Austin, TX 78711. *E-mail:* grantinfo@thecb.state.tx.us. *Web site:* www.collegefortexans.com.

Outstanding Rural Scholar Recognition Program. Forgivable loan for Texas residents to pursue a health-related career in rural Texas. Must be sponsored by a rural community. A student repays the loan by returning to the sponsoring rural community and fulfilling a service obligation equal to the number of years sponsored through school. Deadlines are the third Fridays in September, January, and May. College applicants must have a minimum 3.0 GPA. High school applicants must be in the upper quarter of their class. **Academic/Career Areas:** Biology; Dental Health/Services; Food Science/Nutrition; Health Administration; Health and Medical Sciences; Health Information Management/Technology; Nursing; Social Services; Therapy/Rehabilitation. **Award:** Forgivable loan for use in any year; renewable. *Award amount:* $4536–$43,217. **Eligibility Requirements:** Applicant must be enrolled full-time at a two-year, four-year, or technical institution or university; resident of Texas and must have an interest in designated field specified by sponsor. Applicant must have 3.0 GPA or higher. Available to U.S. citizens. **Application Requirements:** Application, essay, interview, references, test scores, transcript. **Contact:** Susan Kolliopoulos, Program Administrator, Center for Rural Health Initiatives- Texas, PO Drawer 1708, Austin, TX 78767-1708. *E-mail:* crhi@crhi.state.tx.us. *Phone:* 512-479-8891. *Fax:* 512-479-8898. *Web site:* www.crhi.state.tx.us.

Texas Physician Assistant Loan Reimbursement Program. Educational loan reimbursement program for physician assistants who have worked twelve consecutive months in a qualified rural Texas county. Submit a copy of diploma from accredited physician assistant school. **Academic/Career Areas:** Health and Medical Sciences. **Award:** Grant for use in any year; not renewable. *Award amount:* $2500–$5000. *Number of awards:* 18–36. **Eligibility Requirements:** Applicant must be resident of Texas. **Application Requirements:** Application. **Deadline:** June 30. **Contact:** Susan Kolliopoulos, Program Administrator, Center for Rural Health Initiatives- Texas, PO Drawer 1708, Austin, TX 78767-1708. *E-mail:* crhi@crhi.state.tx.us. *Phone:* 512-479-8891. *Fax:* 512-479-8898. *Web site:* www.crhi.state.tx.us.

Border County Waiver. Award provides waiver of nonresident tuition for students of neighboring states (Louisiana, Oklahoma, Arkansas and New Mexico). Must attend a Texas public institution. Contact the registrar's office for details. **Award:** Scholarship for use in freshman, sophomore, junior, or senior year; not renewable. **Eligibility Requirements:** Applicant must be enrolled at a four-year institution or university; resident of Arkansas, Louisiana, New Mexico, or Oklahoma and studying in Texas. **Application Requirements:** Application. **Contact:** Financial aid office at college, Texas Higher Education Coordinating

Board, PO Box 12788, Austin, TX 78711-2788. *E-mail:* grantinfo@thecb.state.tx. us. *Phone:* 512-427-6101. *Fax:* 512-427-6127. *Web site:* www.collegefortexans. com.

Professional Nursing Scholarships. Several awards for Texas residents enrolled at least half-time in a nursing program leading to a professional degree at a Texas institution. **Academic/Career Areas:** Nursing. **Award:** Scholarship for use in any year; not renewable. *Award amount:* up to $3000. **Eligibility Requirements:** Applicant must be enrolled full or part-time at a four-year institution or university; resident of Texas and studying in Texas. Available to U.S. citizens. **Application Requirements:** Application, financial need analysis, test scores, transcript. **Contact:** Student Services Division, Texas Higher Education Coordinating Board, PO Box 12788, Austin, TX 78711-2788. *E-mail:* grantinfo@thecb.state.tx.us. *Phone:* 800-242-3062. *Web site:* www.collegefortexans. com.

Physician Assistant Loan Reimbursement Program. Award will repay loans for physician assistants working in rural Texas counties. Must have worked at least 12 consecutive months in a rural Texas county designated medically underserved. **Award:** Grant for use in any year; renewable. *Award amount:* up to $5000. **Eligibility Requirements:** Applicant must have employment experience in designated career field. Available to U.S. citizens. **Application Requirements:** Application. **Contact:** Financial aid office at college, Texas Higher Education Coordinating Board, PO Box 12788, Austin, TX 78711-2788. *E-mail:* grantinfo@thecb.state.tx.us. *Phone:* 512-427-6101. *Fax:* 512-427-6127. *Web site:* www.collegefortexans.com.

Firefighter Exemption Program–Texas. One-time award assists firemen enrolled in fire science courses as part of a fire science curriculum. Award is exemption from tuition and laboratory fees at publicly supported Texas colleges. Contact the admissions/registrar's office for information on how to apply. **Academic/Career Areas:** Applied Sciences; Physical Sciences and Math; Trade/ Technical Specialties. **Award:** Scholarship for use in freshman, sophomore, junior, or senior year; not renewable. *Award amount:* up to $217. **Eligibility Requirements:** Applicant must be enrolled full or part-time at a two-year, four-year, or technical institution; resident of Texas; studying in Texas and have employment experience in fire service or police/firefighting. Available to U.S. citizens. **Application Requirements:** Application. **Deadline:** continuous. **Contact:** Financial aid office at college, Texas Higher Education Coordinating Board, PO Box 12788, Austin, TX 78711-2788. *E-mail:* grantinfo@thecb.state.tx. us. *Phone:* 512-427-6101. *Fax:* 512-427-6127. *Web site:* www.collegefortexans. com.

Good Neighbor Scholarship Waiver. Renewable aid for students residing in Texas who are citizens of another country of the Americas and intend to return to their country upon completion of the course of study. Must attend public college in Texas. Student will be exempt from tuition. **Award:** Scholarship for use in any year; renewable. **Eligibility Requirements:** Applicant must be Canadian or Latin American/Caribbean; enrolled full or part-time at a two-year, four-year, or technical institution or university and studying in Texas. Available to Canadian and non-U.S. citizens. **Application Requirements:** Application, test scores, transcript. **Deadline:** March 15. **Contact:** Texas Higher Education

Coordinating Board, PO Box 12788, Austin, TX 78711-2788. *E-mail:* grantinfo@thecb.state.tx.us. *Phone:* 800-242-3062. *Web site:* www.collegefortexans.com.

Texas Tuition Exemption for Senior Citizens–65+. Tuition exemption for Texas residents over the age of 65 at eligible Texas institutions. Pays tuition for up to six semester credit hours per semester or summer term. Nonrenewable. Awards made on a space-available basis. Contact the admissions/registrar's office for application information. **Award:** Scholarship for use in any year; not renewable. *Award amount:* up to $146. **Eligibility Requirements:** Applicant must be age 65; enrolled part-time at a two-year, four-year, or technical institution or university; resident of Texas and studying in Texas. Available to U.S. citizens. **Application Requirements:** Application. **Deadline:** continuous. **Contact:** Financial aid office at college, Texas Higher Education Coordinating Board, PO Box 12788, Austin, TX 78711-2788. *E-mail:* grantinfo@thecb.state.tx.us. *Phone:* 512-427-6101. *Fax:* 512-427-6127. *Web site:* www.collegefortexans.com.

Professional Nurses' Student Loan Repayment. Award for licensed nurses practicing in Texas to pay off student loans. Must demonstrate financial need. **Award:** Scholarship for use in any year; not renewable. *Award amount:* up to $2000. **Eligibility Requirements:** Applicant must have employment experience in designated career field. **Application Requirements:** Application, financial need analysis. **Deadline:** January 15. **Contact:** Grants and Special Programs Office, Texas Higher Education Coordinating Board, PO Box 12788, Austin, TX 78711. *E-mail:* grantinfo@thecb.state.tx.us. *Phone:* 800-242-3062. *Web site:* www.collegefortexans.com.

Tuition Exemptions for Texas Veterans (Hazelwood Act). Renewable tuition and partial fee exemptions for Texas veterans who have been honorably discharged after at least 180 days of active duty. Must be a Texas resident at time of entry into service. Must have exhausted federal education benefits. Contact the admissions/registrar's office for information on how to apply. Must be used at a Texas public institution. **Award:** Scholarship for use in any year; renewable. *Award amount:* $855. **Eligibility Requirements:** Applicant must be enrolled full or part-time at a two-year, four-year, or technical institution or university; resident of Texas and studying in Texas. Available to U.S. citizens. Applicant or parent must meet one or more of the following requirements: general military experience; retired from active duty; disabled or killed as a result of military service; Prisoner-Of-War; or Missing-In-Action. **Application Requirements:** Application. **Deadline:** continuous. **Contact:** Financial aid office at college, Texas Higher Education Coordinating Board, PO Box 12788, Austin, TX 78711-2788. *E-mail:* grantinfo@thecb.state.tx.us. *Phone:* 512-427-6101. *Fax:* 512-427-6127. *Web site:* www.collegefortexans.com.

Texas National Guard Tuition Assistance Program. Provides exemption from the payment of tuition to certain members of the Texas National Guard, Texas Air Guard or the State Guard. Must be Texas resident and attend school in Texas. Visit the TNG Web site at: http://www.agd.state.tx.us/education_office/state_tuition.htm. **Award:** Scholarship for use in freshman, sophomore, junior, or senior year; renewable. *Award amount:* up to $551. **Eligibility Requirements:** Applicant must be resident of Texas and studying in Texas. Applicant must have served in the Air Force National Guard, Army National

Guard, or Navy National Guard. **Application Requirements:** Application. **Contact:** State Adjutant General's Office, Texas Higher Education Coordinating Board, PO Box 5218/AGTX-PAE, Austin, TX 78763-5218. *Phone:* 512-465-5001. *Web site:* www.collegefortexans.com.

Texas Tuition Exemption for Blind/Deaf Students. Renewable award aids certain blind or deaf students by exempting them from payment of tuition and fees at public colleges or universities in Texas. Must be a resident of Texas. Deadlines vary. Must submit certificate of deafness or blindness. Contact the admissions/registrar's office for application information. **Award:** Scholarship for use in any year; renewable. **Eligibility Requirements:** Applicant must be enrolled full or part-time at a two-year, four-year, or technical institution or university; resident of Texas and studying in Texas. Applicant must be hearing impaired or visually impaired. Available to U.S. citizens. **Application Requirements:** Application. **Contact:** Financial aid office at college, Texas Higher Education Coordinating Board, PO Box 12788, Austin, TX 78711-2788. *E-mail:* grantinfo@ thecb.state.tx.us. *Phone:* 512-427-6101. *Fax:* 512-427-6127. *Web site:* www. collegefortexans.com.

Texas–Tuition Fee Exemption for Children of Disabled/Deceased Firemen, Peace Officers, Game Wardens, Employees of Correctional Institutions. Renewable award for children of paid or volunteer firemen, game wardens, peace officers, or custodial employees of the Department of Corrections disabled or deceased while serving in Texas. Must attend a Texas institution. Must apply before 21st birthday. Must provide certification of parent's disability or death. Contact institution's admissions or registrar's office for application information. **Award:** Scholarship for use in any year; renewable. **Eligibility Requirements:** Applicant must be age 20 or under; enrolled full or part-time at a two-year, four-year, or technical institution or university; resident of Texas; studying in Texas and have employment experience in designated career field, fire service, or police/firefighting. Available to U.S. citizens. **Application Requirements:** Application. **Deadline:** continuous. **Contact:** Financial aid office at college, Texas Higher Education Coordinating Board, PO Box 12788, Austin, TX 78711-2788. *E-mail:* grantinfo@thecb.state.tx.us. *Phone:* 512-427-6101. *Fax:* 512-427-6127. *Web site:* www.collegefortexans.com.

Tuition and Fee Exemption for Children of Prisoners-of-War or Persons Missing-in-Action–Texas. Renewable awards assists children of Prisoner-Of-War or veterans classified as Missing-In-Action. Must be a Texas resident and attend a public college or university within Texas. Submit proof of service and proof of MIA/POW status. Award is exemption from tuition and fees. Must be under 21 years of age. Contact the admissions/registrar's office for application information. **Award:** Scholarship for use in any year; renewable. **Eligibility Requirements:** Applicant must be age 20 or under; enrolled at a two-year, four-year, or technical institution or university; resident of Texas and studying in Texas. Applicant or parent must meet one or more of the following requirements: general military experience; retired from active duty; disabled or killed as a result of military service; Prisoner-Of-War; or Missing-In-Action. **Application Requirements:** Application. **Deadline:** continuous. **Contact:** Financial aid office at college, Texas Higher Education Coordinating Board, PO Box 12788, Austin, TX 78711-2788. *E-mail:* grantinfo@thecb.state.tx.us. *Phone:* 512-427-6101. *Fax:* 512-427-6127. *Web site:* www.collegefortexans.com.

Vocational Nursing Scholarships. Scholarships for Texas residents must be enrolled in a vocational nursing program at an institution in Texas. Deadline varies. **Academic/Career Areas:** Nursing. **Award:** Scholarship for use in any year; not renewable. *Award amount:* up to $1500. **Eligibility Requirements:** Applicant must be enrolled full or part-time at a four-year institution or university; resident of Texas and studying in Texas. Available to U.S. citizens. **Application Requirements:** Application, financial need analysis, test scores, transcript. **Contact:** Texas Higher Education Coordinating Board, PO Box 12788, Austin, TX 78711-2788. *E-mail:* grantinfo@thecb.state.tx.us. *Web site:* www.collegefortexans. com.

Tuition Equalization Grant (TEG) Program. Renewable award for Texas residents enrolled at least half-time at an independent college or university within the state. Based on financial need. Deadlines vary by institution. Must not be receiving athletic scholarship. Contact college/university financial aid office for application information. **Award:** Grant for use in any year; renewable. *Award amount:* up to $3572. **Eligibility Requirements:** Applicant must be enrolled full or part-time at a two-year or four-year institution or university; resident of Texas and studying in Texas. Available to U.S. citizens. **Application Requirements:** Financial need analysis. **Contact:** Financial aid office at college, Texas Higher Education Coordinating Board, PO Box 12788, Austin, TX 78711- 2788. *E-mail:* grantinfo@thecb.state.tx.us. *Phone:* 512-427-6101. *Fax:* 512-427- 6127. *Web site:* www.collegefortexans.com.

Military Stationed in Texas Waiver. Award provides tuition waiver for nonresident military personnel stationed in Texas. Limited to public institutions only. Contact financial aid office at college for application. **Award:** Scholarship for use in freshman, sophomore, junior, or senior year; not renewable. **Eligibility Requirements:** Applicant must be studying in Texas. Applicant must have general military experience. **Application Requirements:** Application. **Contact:** Financial aid office at college, Texas Higher Education Coordinating Board, PO Box 12788, Austin, TX 78711-2788. *E-mail:* grantinfo@thecb.state.tx.us. *Phone:* 512-427-6101. *Fax:* 512-427-6127. *Web site:* www.collegefortexans.com.

Toward Excellence, Access and Success (TEXAS Grant). Renewable aid for students enrolled in a public or private nonprofit, college or university in Texas. Based on need. Amount of award is determined by the financial aid office of each school. Deadlines vary. Contact the college/university financial aid office for application information. **Award:** Grant for use in freshman, sophomore, junior, or senior year; renewable. *Award amount:* up to $1976. **Eligibility Requirements:** Applicant must be enrolled full or part-time at a two-year, four-year, or technical institution or university; resident of Texas and studying in Texas. Applicant must have 2.5 GPA or higher. Available to U.S. citizens. **Application Requirements:** Application, financial need analysis, transcript. **Deadline:** continuous. **Contact:** Financial aid office at college, Texas Higher Education Coordinating Board, PO Box 12788, Austin, TX 78711-2788. *E-mail:* grantinfo@thecb.state.tx.us. *Phone:* 512-427-6101. *Fax:* 512-427-6127. *Web site:* www.collegefortexans.com.

Academic Common Market Waiver. For Texas residents who are students pursuing a degree in a field of study not offered in Texas. May qualify for special tuition rates. Deadlines vary by institution. Must be studying in the South.

Award: Scholarship for use in freshman, sophomore, junior, senior, or graduate year; renewable. **Eligibility Requirements:** Applicant must be enrolled full or part-time at an institution or university; resident of Texas and studying in Alabama, Arkansas, Florida, Georgia, Kentucky, Louisiana, Mississippi, Missouri, Oklahoma, South Carolina, Tennessee, or Virginia. Available to U.S. citizens. **Application Requirements:** Application. **Contact:** Linda McDonough, Associate Program Director, Texas Higher Education Coordinating Board, PO Box 12788, Austin, TX 78711-2788. *E-mail:* grantinfo@thecb.state.tx.us. *Phone:* 512-427-6525. *Web site:* www.collegefortexans.com.

Texas Tuition Exemption Program: Highest Ranking High School Graduate. Award available to Texas residents who are the top ranked seniors of their high school. Must attend a public college or university within Texas. Recipient is exempt from certain charges for first two semesters. Deadlines vary. Contact admissions/registrar's office for application information. Must provide proof of valedictorian ranking to the registrar. **Award:** Scholarship for use in freshman year; not renewable. **Eligibility Requirements:** Applicant must be enrolled full or part-time at a two-year, four-year, or technical institution or university; resident of Texas and studying in Texas. Applicant must have 3.5 GPA or higher. Available to U.S. citizens. **Application Requirements:** Transcript. **Contact:** Financial aid office at college, Texas Higher Education Coordinating Board, PO Box 12788, Austin, TX 78711-2788. *E-mail:* grantinfo@thecb.state.tx.us. *Phone:* 512-427-6101. *Fax:* 512-427-6127. *Web site:* www.collegefortexans.com.

Outstanding Rural Scholar Program. Award enables rural communities to sponsor a student going into health professions. The students must agree to work in that community once they receive their degree. Must be Texas resident entering a Texas institution on a full-time basis. Must demonstrate financial need. **Academic/Career Areas:** Health and Medical Sciences. **Award:** Scholarship for use in any year; renewable. **Eligibility Requirements:** Applicant must be enrolled full-time at a four-year institution or university; resident of Texas and studying in Texas. **Application Requirements:** Application, financial need analysis, transcript. **Contact:** Center for Rural Health Initiatives, Texas Higher Education Coordinating Board, PO Drawer 1708, Austin, TX 78767. *E-mail:* grantinfo@thecb.state.tx.us. *Phone:* 512-479-8891. *Web site:* www.collegefortexans.com.

UTAH

Utah Society of Professional Engineers Scholarship. One-time award for entering freshman pursuing studies in the field of engineering (civil, chemical, electrical, or engineering related technologies.) Minimum 3.0 GPA required. Must be a U.S. citizen and Utah resident attending school in Utah. Application deadline is April 29. **Academic/Career Areas:** Chemical Engineering; Civil Engineering; Economics; Electrical Engineering/Electronics; Engineering/Technology; Engineering-Related Technologies; Mechanical Engineering. **Award:** Scholarship for use in freshman year; not renewable. *Award amount:* $1000. *Number of awards:* 2. **Eligibility Requirements:** Applicant must be high school student; planning to enroll full or part-time at a four-year institution or university; resident of Utah and studying in Utah. Applicant must have 3.0 GPA or higher. Available to U.S. citizens. **Application Requirements:** Application, essay, resume, references, test scores, transcript. **Deadline:** March 29. **Contact:** Owen Mills, Scholarship Coordinator, Utah Society of Professional Engineers, 488 East Winchester Street, Suite 400, Murray, UT 84107. *E-mail:* omills@uta. cog.ut.us. *Phone:* 801-262-3735. *Fax:* 801-262-4303. *Web site:* www.uspeonline. com.

T.H. Bell Teaching Incentive Loan–Utah. Renewable awards for Utah residents who are high school seniors and wish to pursue teaching careers. Award pays for tuition and fees at a Utah institution. Must agree to teach in a Utah public school or pay back loan through monthly installments. Must be a U.S. citizen. **Academic/Career Areas:** Education; Special Education. **Award:** Forgivable loan for use in freshman, sophomore, junior, or senior year; renewable. *Number of awards:* 50. **Eligibility Requirements:** Applicant must be high school student; planning to enroll full-time at a two-year or four-year institution or university; resident of Utah and studying in Utah. Available to U.S. citizens. **Application Requirements:** Application, essay, test scores, transcript. **Deadline:** March 29. **Contact:** Diane DeMan, Executive Secretary, Utah State Office of Education, 250 East 500 South, Salt Lake City, UT 84111. *Phone:* 801-538-7741. *Fax:* 801-538-7973. *Web site:* www.usoe.k12.ut.us/cert/scholarships/scholars. htm.

New Century Scholarship. Scholarship for qualified high school graduates of Utah. Must attend Utah operated state college. Award depends on number of hours student enrolled. Please contact for further eligibility requirements. Students must complete an associate degree at a Utah-state operated institution by September 1 of the year they graduate from a UT accredited high school. Eligible recipients receive an award equal to 75% of tuition for 60 credit hours toward the completion of a bachelors degree. **Award:** Scholarship for use in junior or senior year; renewable. *Award amount:* $500–$1000. **Eligibility Requirements:** Applicant must be high school student; planning to enroll full or part-time at a four-year institution or university; resident of Utah and studying in Utah. Available to U.S. citizens. **Application Requirements:** Application, test scores, transcript. **Deadline:** continuous. **Contact:** Angie Loving, Manager for Programs/Administration, State of Utah, 3 Triad Center, Suite 500, Salt Lake City, UT 84180-1205. *E-mail:* aloving@utahsbr.edu. *Phone:* 801-321-7124. *Fax:* 801-321-7199. *Web site:* www.utahsbr.edu.

Terrel H. Bell Teaching Incentive Loan. Designed to provide financial assistance to outstanding Utah students pursuing a degree in education. The incentive loan funds full-time tuition and general fees for eight semesters. After graduation/certification the loan may be forgiven if the recipient teaches in a Utah public school or accredited private school (K-12). Loan forgiveness is done on a year for year basis. Application deadline depends on institution. **Academic/ Career Areas:** Education. **Award:** Forgivable loan for use in freshman, sophomore, junior, or senior year; renewable. *Award amount:* $600–$1500. *Number of awards:* 365. **Eligibility Requirements:** Applicant must be enrolled full-time at a two-year or four-year institution or university; resident of Utah and studying in Utah. Available to U.S. citizens. **Application Requirements:** Application, essay, test scores, transcript. **Contact:** Angie Loving, Manager for Programs and Administration, State of Utah, 3 Triad Center, Suite 550, Salt Lake City, UT 84180. *E-mail:* aloving@utahsbr.edu. *Phone:* 801-321-7124. *Fax:* 801-321-7199. *Web site:* www.utahsbr.edu.

VERMONT

Vermont Incentive Grants. Renewable grants for Vermont residents based on financial need. Must meet needs test. Must be college undergraduate or graduate student enrolled full-time at an approved postsecondary institution. Only available to U.S. citizens or permanent residents. **Award:** Grant for use in freshman, sophomore, junior, senior, or graduate year; renewable. *Award amount:* $500–$8650. **Eligibility Requirements:** Applicant must be enrolled full-time at an institution or university and resident of Vermont. Available to U.S. citizens. **Application Requirements:** Application, financial need analysis. **Deadline:** continuous. **Contact:** Grant Program, Vermont Student Assistance Corporation, PO Box 2000, Winooski, VT 05404-2000. *Phone:* 802-655-9602. *Fax:* 802-654-3765. *Web site:* www.vsac.org.

Barbara Jean Barker Memorial Scholarship for a Displaced Homemaker. A nontraditional scholarship designed for a woman who has been primarily a homemaker for 14-20 years and has lost her main means of support through divorce, separation or death of a spouse, and needs retraining for re-entry to the world of work. Must be a Vermont resident. **Award:** Grant for use in any year; not renewable. *Award amount:* $500–$1500. *Number of awards:* 1–3. **Eligibility Requirements:** Applicant must be age 35; enrolled full or part-time at a two-year, four-year, or technical institution or university; female and resident of Vermont. Available to U.S. citizens. **Application Requirements:** Application, autobiography, financial need analysis, interview, references. **Deadline:** March 15. **Contact:** Marie A. Hall, Scholarship Chairman, General Federation of Women's Clubs of Vermont, PO Box 787, Milton, VT 05468. *Phone:* 802-893-2378.

Vermont Non-Degree Student Grant Program. Renewable grants for Vermont residents enrolled in non-degree programs at colleges, vocational centers, and high school adult courses. May receive funds for two enrollment periods per year, up to $650 per course, per semester. Award based upon financial need. **Award:** Grant for use in any year; renewable. *Award amount:* up to $650. **Eligibility Requirements:** Applicant must be resident of Vermont. **Application Requirements:** Application, financial need analysis. **Deadline:** continuous. **Contact:** Grant Program, Vermont Student Assistance Corporation, PO Box 2000, Winooski, VT 05404-2000. *Phone:* 802-655-9602. *Fax:* 802-654-3765. *Web site:* www.vsac.org.

Vermont Part-time Student Grants. For undergraduates carrying less than twelve credits per semester who have not received a bachelor's degree. Must be Vermont resident. Based on financial need. Complete Vermont Financial Aid Packet to apply. May be used at any approved postsecondary institution. **Award:** Grant for use in freshman, sophomore, junior, or senior year; renewable. *Award amount:* $250–$6490. **Eligibility Requirements:** Applicant must be enrolled part-time at an institution or university and resident of Vermont. **Application Requirements:** Application, financial need analysis. **Deadline:** continuous. **Contact:** Grant Program, Vermont Student Assistance Corporation, PO Box 2000, Winooski, VT 05404-2000. *Phone:* 802-655-9602. *Fax:* 802-654-3765. *Web site:* www.vsac.org.

VIRGINIA

Mary Marshall Practical Nursing Scholarships. One-time award for practical nursing students who are Virginia residents. Must attend a full-time nursing program in Virginia. Recipient must agree to work in Virginia after graduation. Minimum 3.0 GPA required. **Academic/Career Areas:** Nursing. **Award:** Scholarship for use in any year; not renewable. *Award amount:* $150–$500. **Eligibility Requirements:** Applicant must be enrolled full-time at a two-year or technical institution; resident of Virginia and studying in Virginia. Applicant must have 3.0 GPA or higher. Available to U.S. citizens. **Application Requirements:** Application, financial need analysis, references, transcript. **Deadline:** June 30. **Contact:** Norma Marrin, Business Manager, Virginia Department of Health, Office of Health Policy and Planning, PO Box 2448, Richmond, VA 23218. *E-mail:* nmarrin@ vdh.state.va.us. *Phone:* 804-371-4090. *Fax:* 804-371-0116. *Web site:* www.vdh. state.va.us/primcare/index.html.

Walter Reed Smith Scholarship. Award for full-time female undergraduate student who is a descendant of a Confederate soldier, studying nutrition, home economics or nursing. Must carry a minimum of 12 credit hours each semester and have a minimum 3.0 GPA. Submit letter of endorsement from sponsoring chapter of the United Daughters of the Confederacy. **Academic/Career Areas:** Food Science/Nutrition; Home Economics; Nursing. **Award:** Scholarship for use in freshman, sophomore, junior, or senior year; renewable. *Award amount:* $800–$1000. *Number of awards:* 1–2. **Eligibility Requirements:** Applicant must be enrolled full-time at a four-year institution or university; female and member of United Daughters of the Confederacy. Applicant must have 3.0 GPA or higher. Available to U.S. citizens. **Application Requirements:** Application, essay, financial need analysis, photo, references, self-addressed stamped envelope, transcript. **Deadline:** February 15. **Contact:** Second Vice President General, United Daughters of the Confederacy, 328 North Boulevard, Richmond, VA 23220-4057. *Phone:* 804-355-1636. *Web site:* www.hqudc.org.

Mary Marshall Registered Nursing Program Scholarships. One-time award for registered nursing students who are Virginia residents. Must attend a full-time nursing program in Virginia. Recipient must agree to work in Virginia after graduation. Minimum 3.0 GPA required. **Academic/Career Areas:** Nursing. **Award:** Scholarship for use in freshman, sophomore, junior, or senior year; not renewable. *Award amount:* $1000–$2000. **Eligibility Requirements:** Applicant must be enrolled full-time at a two-year or four-year institution or university; resident of Virginia and studying in Virginia. Applicant must have 3.0 GPA or higher. Available to U.S. citizens. **Application Requirements:** Application, financial need analysis, references, transcript. **Deadline:** June 30. **Contact:** Norma Marrin, Business Manager, Virginia Department of Health, Office of Health Policy and Planning, PO Box 2448, Richmond, VA 23218. *E-mail:* nmarrin@ udh.state.va.us. *Phone:* 804-371-4090. *Fax:* 804-371-0116. *Web site:* www.vdh. state.va.us/primcare/index.html.

General Mills Scholars Program/Internship. Scholarships awarded to college sophomores and juniors majoring in business, accounting, information systems, or liberal arts at a UNCF member college or university. Minimum 2.5 GPA required. **Academic/Career Areas:** Business/Consumer Services; Computer Science/Data Processing. **Award:** Scholarship for use in sophomore or junior year; not renewable. *Award amount:* up to $11,000. **Eligibility Requirements:** Applicant must be African American and enrolled at a four-year institution or university. Applicant must have 2.5 GPA or higher. Available to U.S. citizens. **Application Requirements:** Application. **Contact:** Program Services Department, United Negro College Fund, 8260 Willow Oaks Corporate Drive, Fairfax, VA 22031. *Web site:* www.uncf.org.

Virginia Tuition Assistance Grant Program (Private Institutions). Renewable awards of approximately $3,000 each for undergraduate, graduate, and first professional degree students attending an approved private, nonprofit college within Virginia. Must be a Virginia resident and be enrolled full-time. Not to be used for religious study. Preferred deadline July 31. Others are wait-listed. Contact college financial aid office. The application process is handled by the participating colleges' financial aid office. **Award:** Grant for use in any year; renewable. *Award amount:* $3000. *Number of awards:* 15,000. **Eligibility Requirements:** Applicant must be enrolled full-time at a four-year institution; resident of Virginia and studying in Virginia. **Application Requirements:** Application. **Deadline:** July 31. **Contact:** Financial Aid Office at participating institution, Virginia State Council of Higher Education, James Monroe Building, 10th Floor, 101 North 14th Street, Richmond, VA 23219. *Web site:* www.schev.edu.

WASHINGTON

Washington National Guard Scholarship Program. A state funded retention incentive/loan program for both Washington Army and Air Guard members meeting all eligibility requirements. The loans are forgiven if the soldier/airman completes their service requirements. Failure to meet/complete service obligations incurrs the requirement to repay the loan plus eight percent interest. Minimum 2.5 GPA required. Deadline is April 30. **Award:** Forgivable loan for use in any year; not renewable. *Number of awards:* 25–30. **Eligibility Requirements:** Applicant must be enrolled full or part-time at a two-year, four-year, or technical institution or university and resident of Washington. Applicant must have 2.5 GPA or higher. Available to U.S. and non-U.S. citizens. Applicant must have served in the Air Force National Guard or Army National Guard. **Application Requirements:** Application, transcript. **Deadline:** April 30. **Contact:** Mark M. Rhoden, Educational Officer, Washington National Guard, Building 1, Camp Murray, Tacoma, WA 98430-5073. *E-mail:* mark.rhoden@wa. ngb.army.mil. *Phone:* 253-512-8899. *Fax:* 253-512-8936. *Web site:* www. washingtonguard.com/education/education.htm.

WEST VIRGINIA

Underwood-Smith Teacher Scholarship Program. For West Virginia residents at West Virginia institutions pursuing teaching careers. Must have a 3.25 GPA after completion of two years of course work. Must teach two years in West Virginia public schools for each year the award is received. Recipients will be required to sign an agreement acknowledging an understanding of the program's requirements and their willingness to repay the award if appropriate teaching service is not rendered. **Academic/Career Areas:** Education. **Award:** Scholarship for use in junior, senior, or graduate year; renewable. *Award amount:* up to $5000. *Number of awards:* 53. **Eligibility Requirements:** Applicant must be enrolled full-time at a four-year institution or university; resident of West Virginia and studying in West Virginia. Available to U.S. citizens. **Application Requirements:** Application, essay, references. **Deadline:** April 15. **Contact:** Michelle Wicks, Scholarship Coordinator, West Virginia Higher Education Policy Commission-Student Services, 1018 Kanawha Boulevard East, Suite 700, Charleston, WV 25301. *E-mail:* wicks@hepc.wvnet.edu. *Phone:* 304-558-4618. *Fax:* 304-558-4622. *Web site:* www.hepc.wvnet.edu.

West Virginia Higher Education Grant Program. For West Virginia residents attending an approved nonprofit degree-granting college or university in West Virginia or Pennsylvania. Must be enrolled full-time. Based on financial need and academic merit. Award covers tuition and fees. **Award:** Grant for use in freshman, sophomore, junior, or senior year; renewable. *Award amount:* $350–$2532. *Number of awards:* 10,900–11,200. **Eligibility Requirements:** Applicant must be enrolled full-time at a two-year or four-year institution or university; resident of West Virginia and studying in Pennsylvania or West Virginia. Available to U.S. citizens. **Application Requirements:** Application, financial need analysis, test scores, transcript. **Deadline:** March 1. **Contact:** Robert Long, Grant Program Coordinator, West Virginia Higher Education Policy Commission-Student Services, 1018 Kanawha Boulevard East, Suite 700, Charleston, WV 25301-2827. *E-mail:* long@hepc.wvnet.edu. *Phone:* 888-825-5707. *Fax:* 304-558-4622. *Web site:* www.hepc.wvnet.edu.

West Virginia Division of Veterans' Affairs War Orphans Education Program. Renewable waiver of tuition award for West Virginia residents who are children of deceased veterans. Parent must have died of war-related service-connected disability. Must be ages 16-23. Minimum 2.6 GPA required. Must attend a state-supported West Virginia postsecondary institution. Deadline: July 1 and December 1. **Award:** Scholarship for use in any year; renewable. **Eligibility Requirements:** Applicant must be age 16-23; enrolled full or part-time at a two-year, four-year, or technical institution or university; resident of West Virginia and studying in West Virginia. Applicant must have 2.5 GPA or higher. Available to U.S. citizens. Applicant or parent must meet one or more of the following requirements: general military experience; retired from active duty; disabled or killed as a result of military service; Prisoner-Of-War; or Missing-In-Action. **Application Requirements:** Application, references. **Contact:** Ms. Susan Kerns, Secretary, West Virginia Division of Veterans' Affairs, 1321 Plaza East, Suite 101, Charleston, WV 25301-1400. *E-mail:* wvvetaff@aol.com. *Phone:* 304-668-3661. *Fax:* 304-668-3662.

West Virginia Engineering, Science & Technology Scholarship Program. For students attending WV institutions full-time pursuing a career in engineering, science or technology. Must have a 3.0 GPA on a 4.0 scale. Must work in the fields of engineering, science or technology in West Virginia one year for each year the award is received. **Academic/Career Areas:** Electrical Engineering/Electronics; Engineering/Technology; Engineering-Related Technologies; Science, Technology and Society. **Award:** Scholarship for use in freshman, sophomore, junior, or senior year; renewable. *Award amount:* up to $3000. *Number of awards:* 300. **Eligibility Requirements:** Applicant must be enrolled full-time at a two-year, four-year, or technical institution or university and studying in West Virginia. Applicant must have 3.0 GPA or higher. Available to U.S. citizens. **Application Requirements:** Application, essay, test scores, transcript.

Deadline: April 1. **Contact:** Michelle Wicks, Scholarship Coordinator, West Virginia Higher Education Policy Commission-Student Services, 1018 Kanawha Boulevard East, Suite 700, Charleston, WV 25301. *E-mail:* wicks@hepc.wvnet. edu. *Phone:* 304-558-4618. *Fax:* 304-558-4622. *Web site:* www.hepc.wvnet.edu.

WISCONSIN

Teacher of the Visually Impaired Loan Program. Provides forgivable loans to students who enroll in programs that lead to be certified as a teacher of the visually impaired or an orientation and mobility instructor. Must be a Wisconsin resident. **Award:** Forgivable loan for use in freshman, sophomore, junior, senior, or post graduate years; not renewable. *Award amount:* $250–$10,000. **Eligibility Requirements:** Applicant must be enrolled full or part-time at a two-year, four-year, or technical institution or university and resident of Wisconsin. Available to U.S. and non-U.S. citizens. **Application Requirements:** Application, financial need analysis. **Deadline:** continuous. **Contact:** Jim Buske, Manager-Programs and Policy, Wisconsin Higher Educational Aid Board, 131 West Wilson Street, Madison, WI 53707-7885. *E-mail:* james.buske@heab.state.wi.us. *Phone:* 608-266-0888. *Fax:* 608-267-2808. *Web site:* www.heab.state.wi.us.

Minnesota-Wisconsin Reciprocity Program. Wisconsin residents may attend a Minnesota public institution and pay the reciprocity tuition charged by Minnesota institution. All programs are eligible except doctoral programs in medicine, dentistry, and veterinary medicine. **Award:** Scholarship for use in any year; renewable. **Eligibility Requirements:** Applicant must be enrolled full or part-time at a two-year, four-year, or technical institution or university; resident of Wisconsin and studying in Minnesota. Available to U.S. citizens. **Application Requirements:** Application. **Deadline:** continuous. **Contact:** Cindy Lehrman, Wisconsin Higher Educational Aid Board, 131 West Wilson Street #902, Madison, WI 53707-7885. *E-mail:* cindy.lehrman@heab.state.wi.us. *Phone:* 608-267-2209. *Fax:* 608-267-2808. *Web site:* www.heab.state.wi.us.

Wisconsin Higher Education Grants (WHEG). Grants for residents of Wisconsin attending a campus of the University of Wisconsin or Wisconsin Technical College. Must be enrolled at least half-time and show financial need. Renewable for up to five years. **Award:** Grant for use in freshman, sophomore, junior, or senior year; not renewable. *Award amount:* $250–$1800. **Eligibility Requirements:** Applicant must be enrolled full or part-time at a two-year, four-year, or technical institution or university; resident of Wisconsin and studying in Wisconsin. Available to U.S. and non-U.S. citizens. **Application Requirements:** Financial need analysis. **Deadline:** continuous. **Contact:** Sandra Thomas, Program Coordinator, Wisconsin Higher Educational Aid Board, 131 West Wilson Street, Madison, WI 53707-7885. *E-mail:* sandy.thomas@heab.state. wi.us. *Phone:* 608-266-0888. *Fax:* 608-267-2808. *Web site:* www.heab.state.wi. us.

Wisconsin Academic Excellence Scholarship. Renewable award for high school seniors with the highest GPA in graduating class. Must be a Wisconsin resident. Award covers tuition for up to four years. Must maintain 3.5 GPA for renewal. Scholarships of up to $2250 each. Must attend a nonprofit Wisconsin institution full-time. **Award:** Scholarship for use in freshman, sophomore, junior, or senior year; renewable. *Award amount:* $250–$2250. **Eligibility Requirements:** Applicant must be high school student; planning to enroll full-time at a two-year, four-year, or technical institution or university; resident of Wisconsin and studying in Wisconsin. Applicant must have 3.5 GPA or higher. Available to U.S. and non-U.S. citizens. **Application Requirements:** Transcript. **Deadline:** continuous. **Contact:** Alice Winters, Program Coordinator, Wisconsin Higher Educational Aid Board, 131 West Wilson Street, Madison, WI 53707-7885. *E-mail:* alice.winters@heab.state.wi.us. *Phone:* 608-267-2213. *Fax:* 608-267-2808. *Web site:* www.heab.state.wi.us.

Handicapped Student Grant–Wisconsin. One-time awards available to residents of Wisconsin who have severe or profound hearing or visual impairment. Must be enrolled at least half-time at a nonprofit institution. If the handicap prevents the student from attending a Wisconsin school, the award may be used out-of-state in a specialized college. **Award:** Grant for use in freshman, sophomore, junior, or senior year; not renewable. *Award amount:* $250–$1800. **Eligibility Requirements:** Applicant must be enrolled full or part-time at a two-year, four-year, or technical institution or university and resident of Wisconsin. Applicant must be hearing impaired or visually impaired. Available to U.S. and non-U.S. citizens. **Application Requirements:** Application, financial need analysis. **Deadline:** continuous. **Contact:** Sandra Thomas, Wisconsin Higher Educational Aid Board, 131 West Wilson Street, Madison, WI 53707-7885. *E-mail:* sandy.thomas@heab.state.wi.us. *Phone:* 608-266-0888. *Fax:* 608-267-2808. *Web site:* www.heab.state.wi.us.

Wisconsin Tuition Grant Program. Available to Wisconsin residents who are enrolled at least half-time in degree or certificate programs at independent, nonprofit colleges or universities in Wisconsin. Must show financial need. **Award:** Grant for use in freshman, sophomore, junior, or senior year; not renewable. *Award amount:* $250–$2172. **Eligibility Requirements:** Applicant must be enrolled full or part-time at a four-year institution or university; resident of Wisconsin and studying in Wisconsin. Available to U.S. and non-U.S. citizens. **Application Requirements:** Application, financial need analysis. **Contact:** Mary Lou Kuzdas, Program Coordinator, Wisconsin Higher Educational Aid Board, 131 West Wilson Street, Madison, WI 53707-7885. *E-mail:* mary.kuzdas@ heab.state.wi.us. *Phone:* 608-267-2212. *Fax:* 608-267-2808. *Web site:* www.heab. state.wi.us.

Minority Retention Grant–Wisconsin. Provides financial assistance to African-American, Native American, Hispanic, and former citizens of Laos, Vietnam, and Cambodia, for study in Wisconsin. Must be Wisconsin resident, enrolled at least half-time in a two-year or four-year nonprofit college, and must show financial need. **Award:** Grant for use in sophomore, junior, senior, or graduate year; not renewable. *Award amount:* $250–$2500. **Eligibility Requirements:** Applicant must be Native American or Eskimo, Asian, African American, or Hispanic; enrolled full or part-time at a two-year, four-year, or technical institution; resident of Wisconsin and studying in Wisconsin. Available to U.S. and non-U.S. citizens. **Application Requirements:** Application, financial need analysis. **Deadline:** continuous. **Contact:** Mary Lou Kuzdas, Program Coordinator, Wisconsin Higher Educational Aid Board, 131 West Wilson Street, Madison, WI 53707-7885. *E-mail:* mary.kuzdas@heab.state.wi.us. *Phone:* 608-267-2212. *Fax:* 608-267-2808. *Web site:* www.heab.state.wi.us.

Wisconsin Native American Student Grant. Grants for Wisconsin residents who are at least one-quarter American Indian. Must be attending a college or university within the state. Renewable for up to five years. Several grants of up to $1100. **Award:** Grant for use in any year; not renewable. *Award amount:* $250–$1100. **Eligibility Requirements:** Applicant must be Native American or Eskimo; enrolled full or part-time at a two-year, four-year, or technical institution or university; resident of Wisconsin and studying in Wisconsin. Available to U.S. and non-U.S. citizens. **Application Requirements:** Application, financial need analysis. **Deadline:** continuous. **Contact:** Sandra Thomas, Program Coordinator, Wisconsin Higher Educational Aid Board, 131 West Wilson Street, Madison, WI 53707-7885. *E-mail:* sandy.thomas@heab.state.wi.us. *Phone:* 608-266-0888. *Fax:* 608-267-2808. *Web site:* www.heab.state.wi.us.

Wisconsin Department of Veterans Affairs Retraining Grants. Renewable award for veterans, unmarried spouses of deceased veterans, or dependents of deceased veterans. Must be resident of Wisconsin and attend an institution in Wisconsin. Veteran must be recently unemployed and show financial need. Must enroll in a vocational or technical program that can reasonably be expected to lead to employment. Course work at four-year colleges or universities does not qualify as retraining. **Award:** Grant for use in any year; renewable. *Award amount:* up to $3000. **Eligibility Requirements:** Applicant must be enrolled at a technical institution; resident of Wisconsin and studying in Wisconsin. Applicant or parent must meet one or more of the following requirements: general military experience; retired from active duty; disabled or killed as a result of military service; Prisoner-Of-War; or Missing-In-Action. **Application Requirements:** Application, financial need analysis. **Contact:** Mr. Steve Olson, Public Relations Officer, Wisconsin Department of Veterans Affairs, PO Box 7843, Madison, WI 53707-7843. *Phone:* 608-266-1311. *Web site:* www.dva.state. wi.us.

Wisconsin Veterans Part-time Study Reimbursement Grant. Open only to Wisconsin veterans and dependents of deceased Wisconsin veterans. Renewable for continuing study. Contact office for more details. Application deadline is sixty days prior to course completion. Veterans may be reimbursed up to 85% of tuition and fees. **Award:** Grant for use in any year; renewable. *Award amount:* $300–$1100. **Eligibility Requirements:** Applicant must be enrolled part-time at an institution or university; resident of Wisconsin and studying in Wisconsin. Available to U.S. citizens. Applicant or parent must meet one or more of the following requirements: general military experience; retired from active duty; disabled or killed as a result of military service; Prisoner-Of-War; or Missing-In-Action. **Application Requirements:** Application. **Contact:** Mr. Steve Olson, Public Relations Officer, Wisconsin Department of Veterans Affairs, PO Box 7843, Madison, WI 53707-7843. *Phone:* 608-266-1311. *Web site:* www.dva. state.wi.us.

Tuition and Fee Reimbursement Grants. Up to 85% tuition and fee reimbursement for Wisconsin veterans who were discharged from active duty within the last 10 years. Undergraduate courses must be completed at accredited Wisconsin schools. Those attending Minnesota public colleges, universities, and technical schools that have a tuition reciprocity agreement with Wisconsin may also qualify. Must meet military service requirements. **Award:** Grant for use in freshman, sophomore, junior, or senior year; renewable. **Eligibility**

Requirements: Applicant must be enrolled full-time at an institution or university; resident of Wisconsin and studying in Minnesota or Wisconsin. Available to U.S. citizens. Applicant must have general military experience. **Application Requirements:** Application. **Contact:** Mr. Steve Olson, Public Relations Officer, Wisconsin Department of Veterans Affairs, PO Box 7843, Madison, WI 53707-7843. *Phone:* 608-266-1311. *Web site:* www.dva.state.wi.us.

Wisconsin National Guard Tuition Grant. Renewable award for active members of the Wisconsin National Guard in good standing, who successfully complete a course of study at a qualifying school. Award covers full tuition, excluding fees, not to exceed undergraduate tuition charged by University of Wisconsin-Madison. Must have a minimum 2.0 GPA. **Award:** Grant for use in freshman, sophomore, junior, or senior year; renewable. *Award amount:* $1784. *Number of awards:* up to 4000. **Eligibility Requirements:** Applicant must be enrolled full or part-time at a two-year, four-year, or technical institution or university and resident of Wisconsin. Applicant must have 2.5 GPA or higher. Available to U.S. citizens. Applicant must have served in the Air Force National Guard or Army National Guard. **Application Requirements:** Application. **Deadline:** continuous. **Contact:** Karen Behling, Tuition Grant Administrator, Department of Military Affairs, PO Box 14587, Madison, WI 53714-0587. *E-mail:* behlik@dma.state.wi.us. *Phone:* 608-242-3159. *Fax:* 608-242-3154.

Talent Incentive Program–Wisconsin. Assists residents of Wisconsin who are attending a nonprofit institution in Wisconsin and have substantial financial need. Must meet income criteria, be considered economically and educationally disadvantaged and be enrolled at least half-time. **Award:** Grant for use in freshman, sophomore, junior, or senior year; renewable. *Award amount:* $600–$1800. **Eligibility Requirements:** Applicant must be enrolled full or part-time at a two-year, four-year, or technical institution or university; resident of Wisconsin and studying in Wisconsin. Available to U.S. and non-U.S. citizens. **Application Requirements:** Application, financial need analysis. **Deadline:** continuous. **Contact:** John Whitt, Wisconsin Higher Educational Aid Board, 131 West Wilson Street, Madison, WI 53707-7885. *E-mail:* john.whitt@heab.state.wi.us. *Phone:* 608-266-1665. *Fax:* 608-267-2808. *Web site:* www.heab.state.wi.us.

WYOMING

Superior Student in Education Scholarship–Wyoming. Available to Wyoming high school graduates who have demonstrated high academic achievement and plan to teach in Wyoming public schools. Award is for tuition at Wyoming institutions. Must maintain 3.0 GPA. **Academic/Career Areas:** Education. **Award:** Scholarship for use in freshman, sophomore, junior, or senior year; renewable. *Number of awards:* 16–80. **Eligibility Requirements:** Applicant must be enrolled full-time at a two-year or four-year institution or university; resident of Wyoming; studying in Wyoming and must have an interest in leadership. Applicant must have 3.0 GPA or higher. Available to U.S. citizens. **Application Requirements:** Application, references, test scores, transcript. **Deadline:** October 31. **Contact:** Joel Anne Berrigan, Assistant Director, Scholarships, State of Wyoming, PO Box 3335, Laramie, WY 82071-3335. *Phone:* 307-766-2117. *Fax:* 307-766-3800.

Vietnam Veterans Award/Wyoming. Available to Wyoming residents who served in the armed forces between August 5, 1964, and May 7, 1975, and received a Vietnam service medal. Award is free tuition at the University of Wyoming or a state (WY) community college. **Award:** Scholarship for use in any year; renewable. **Eligibility Requirements:** Applicant must be enrolled full or part-time at a two-year or four-year institution or university; resident of Wyoming and studying in Wyoming. Available to U.S. citizens. Applicant must have general military experience. **Application Requirements:** Application. **Deadline:** continuous. **Contact:** JoelAnne Berrigan, Assistant Director, Scholarships, State of Wyoming, PO Box 3335, Laramie, WY 82071-3335. *E-mail:* finaid@uwyo.edu. *Phone:* 307-766-2117. *Fax:* 307-766-3800.

Appendix: Special Terminology Related to College Financing

T he terms in this glossary are used in this book with some special meaning to scholarships. The glossary is not an exhaustive list, so be sure to contact the sponsor for clarification of any words or terms whose meanings are unclear to you.

accredited program; accredited college—a program of study or an academic institution that has been evaluated and recognized by an accrediting agency as one that provides a sufficient education. There are general regional accrediting agencies and accrediting agencies for specific academic areas. Regional accreditation guarantees a minimum of adequacy in terms of academic facilities and programs. Many scholarships are for use only in colleges or universities that have regional accreditation or in programs that have been accredited by a federally recognized professional education accrediting body or association.

ACT—a standardized test offered by American College Testing required for admission to some colleges. (See also SAT.)

Advanced Placement tests (AP)—tests used to earn credit for college subjects while in high school.

African American—a U.S. citizen who has a Negroid racial identity. U.S. citizens with a Negroid racial identity who have ancestry from countries outside of Africa usually are considered by sponsors to be African American, although there may be ambiguity about individuals with ancestry in Latin America and the Caribbean countries. U.S. citizens with ancestry from countries in Africa, but who have a racial identity other than Negroid, are usually not considered to be African American. If you are uncertain about a sponsor's definition with regard to your eligibility for a scholarship, contact the sponsor for a more specific explanation.

American—a native, inhabitant, or citizen of the United States. Sponsors usually mean "U.S. citizen" when American is a criterion descriptor. People from other countries of the Western Hemisphere usually are referred to by the name of their specific country (e.g., Canadian, Mexican, Colombian, Brazilian, Argentine, etc.). If this is an important factor to you, and there is any question about the definition, contact the sponsor for further explanation.

appeal—a formal request to have a college's financial aid administrator review one's aid eligibility and possibly adjust the amounts offered. An appeal should be requested especially when circumstances (e.g., unemployment, a death) have caused the information on a financial aid application to misrepresent a family's current ability to pay.

Asian American—a U.S. citizen or resident immigrant who is identified by ancestry from East Asia or the countries of the Indian subcontinent. In typical usage, people with ancestry from the countries west of Pakistan, in central Asia, and Siberia, are not considered to be Asian American. This term sometimes is restricted to citizens with Mongoloid racial identity. If national distinctions are important to you in relation to award eligibility, contact the sponsor to ascertain their definition.

assistantships—graduate-level awards, usually waiving all or some tuition expenses, plus an allowance for living expenses. In return, the recipient works at teaching or research duties. Teaching Assistants teach in their field of study. Research Assistants work on projects often, but not necessarily, related to their dissertation or thesis research.

associate degree—the degree granted by two-year colleges. A typical course of study to earn an associate degree is two years. See *community college* below.

award—a general term for gift aid that encompasses scholarships, grants, fellowships, and prizes. Awards do not have to be repaid.

baccalaureate, bachelor's degree—the degree awarded upon successful completion of three to five years of study in the liberal arts and sciences, in professional, or in preprofessional areas.

campus-based aid—student financial aid programs administered by the college or university. Most campus-based aid comes from federal funds.

class rank—a student's standing in the secondary school class relative to her or his peers. This is reported either as a number (such as third out of a class of 30) or as a percentile (top third, top 10 percent, etc.).

community college—a postsecondary institution governed by a local governmental agency (usually county or city) at which the associate degree is the highest credential awarded. A typical course of study is two years. Community college curricula are often characterized by career and vocational training programs and nondegree continuing education programs. Community colleges usually lack residential facilities, and their students commute to classes. Many students begin their higher education at community colleges with plans to eventually transfer to a four-year college or university program to obtain their bachelor's degree.

contest—a procedure for giving awards that typically entails the submission of material (an essay, documentation of research, a creative work, a portfolio, autobiographical information) that is judged. The candidate whose material is deemed by the judges to be superior is awarded the gift aid. Contests in the performing arts may require actual competitive performances.

cooperative education—a program organized by a school or department in which work, either on a part-time basis or full-time for a limited period, in a job related to a student's major is combined with regular classroom study.

cost of attendance (COA)—the total amount it should cost the student to go to school. This includes tuition and mandatory fees, room and board, books and supplies, transportation, and personal expenses. Schools apply different COA standards for students who are living on-campus or off-campus, married or unmarried, and in-state or out-of-state.

credit, credit hours, credits—the unit of measurement of academic work successfully completed. There are several different credit systems. Under one system, a course might be worth 1 credit, while in another system the same course would be worth 3 "credit hours" or "hours," indicating the amount of time spent each week in class. Sometimes courses that are more advanced or that meet for more hours offer greater credit.

curriculum vitae (*c.v.*)—a summary account of one's life, familiarly called a *c.v.* In academe, this is a relatively lengthy document. In addition to basic biographical data, it typically covers an individual's education, employment, teaching or research positions, administrative responsibilities, ongoing research, delivered and published papers, lengthier publications, awards and honors, professional memberships and posts, and other relevant accomplishments.

demonstrated financial need—proof that one's income and assets are insufficient to cover college expenses. This is usually a formal document in which an applicant will provide required information and backup documentation concerning income and assets. This form may be supplied by the sponsor or the sponsor may rely upon a standard methodology—Federal Methodology (FM) or Institutional Methodology (IM).

dependent, dependent child—an immediate family member or spouse who lives with and receives over half of his or her support from another family member. The actual definitions of which family members may qualify and how old they can be may differ from sponsor to sponsor. Be sure to check with the sponsor to find out their particular definition of dependent status if this is a factor in your eligibility.

disability, disabilities, disabled—a limitation in one or more life functions, including sight, hearing, thinking, walking, breathing, performing manual tasks, or speaking. Some disabilities are obvious physical impediments. There is also widespread recognition of disabilities, such as learning disabilities and attention deficit disorders, that can greatly affect a student's ability to perform well academically.

entering students, entering freshmen—students who have been recently enrolled by a postsecondary institution but who may or may not have begun to attend classes.

expected family contribution (EFC)—the amount of money that a family is expected to be able to contribute to their student's education as determined by the Federal Methodology (FM). The EFC includes parent and student contributions. The EFC deducted from the Cost of Attendance (COA) is the student's financial need, which is the basis for determining any need-based financial aid.

Federal Methodology (FM)—the need analysis formula established by the federal government for analyzing the FAFSA to determine the expected family contribution (EFC).

Federal Work-Study (FWS)—a federally supported program that provides students with part-time employment during the school year. Part of the student's salary is paid by the government. Employers frequently are college or university departments or facilities. However, local businesses can and frequently do participate in the program. Eligibility for FWS is based on need. Work-Study is often one component in the financial aid package that a college offers prospective students.

fellowship—graduate and postgraduate-level awards to individuals to cover their living expenses while they take advanced courses, carry out research, or work on a project. Some fellowships include a tuition waiver.

financial aid office—college or university office that is responsible for the determination of financial need and the awarding of financial aid.

financial aid package—the complete collection of gift aid, loans, and work-study employment from all sources offered by the college or university to a student.

financial need analysis—the formula for calculating a student's financial need. This may be individual to a scholarship sponsor or be one of numerous standardized formulas, such as the Federal Methodology (FM) or the Institutional Methodology (IM). See *demonstrated financial need*, above.

forgivable loan—a form of student financial aid under which the student borrower commits to apply their training for a finite period of time in a way dictated by the lender and thereby win cancellation of the loan. Commitments may be to practicing health care in a rural or underserved area, teaching in a rural or inner-city district, or serving in a branch of the armed services. Failure to graduate or follow through on the service commitment entails repayment of the loan amount with interest.

four-year institution—a postsecondary institution or college offering one or more four-year programs of study leading to a bachelor's degree. A four-year institution may be a unit within a university or an independent college.

Free Application for Federal Student Aid (FAFSA)—the financial aid application form used to apply for all other need-based aid from the federal government, as well as the majority of aid from state governments and college-based sources. Many noninstitutional award programs that take need into account will use data that are reported on the FAFSA. In addition to the standard print version, which is available at any college financial aid office and most high school guidance offices, there are two versions available in electronic media—FAFSA Express on diskette and FAFSA on the Web that can be completed and submitted via the Internet.

freshman, freshmen—a student in the first year or with first-year standing at a college or secondary school. The term applies to both men and women.

full-time, full-time course load, full-time study—denotes a student who meets a specific minimal criterion regarding the number of credits being taken in a particular period. Colleges differ in the standards that they use to determine full-time status, and they apply different standards to different levels of study. A typical undergraduate program requires 12 credit hours or four courses each term to qualify as full-time. This standard is reduced, usually progressively, for each graduate level. You will have to check with the specific institution to find out how they define a "full-time" course load.

gift aid—financial aid which does not need to be repaid. Scholarships, grants, prizes, and fellowships are some types of gift aid.

GPA (grade point average)—a system of scoring student achievement used by many colleges and universities. A student's GPA is computed by multiplying the numerical grade received in each course by the number of credits offered for each course, then dividing by the total number of credit hours studied. Most institutions use the following grade conversion scale: A = 4, B = 3, C = 2, D = 1, and E and F = 0.

graduate student, graduate study—refers to the level of higher education that will lead to a master's degree or doctoral degree. Graduate degrees are required to enter professional careers in medicine, business, college or university teaching, and many other fields. Among other requirements, admission to a graduate program will require a bachelor's degree or its equivalent.

grant—gift aid usually awarded to support research or specific projects. Grants provide funds directly related to carrying out proposed research, but can include funds for travel and living expenses while conducting research away from a home institution. Many grant programs support doctoral dissertation research, and some can be applied to research related to a master's thesis. The term "grant" very frequently is used to refer to any form of gift aid, including scholarships and fellowships.

Hispanic—an adjective for people, regardless of race, who identify with ancestry in Mexico, Puerto Rico, Cuba, Central or South America, and other countries with Spanish cultural roots. There is ambiguity as to whether Europeans of the Iberian Peninsula, Brazilians, and American Indians with a mixed heritage of Mexican or Central or South American tribes are included in this category. If these distinctions are important to you, check with the specific award's sponsor to find out their definition.

independent student—a student who does not have over half of his or her support provided by an immediate family member.

Institutional Methodology (IM)—the need analysis formula established by CSS for analyzing the Financial Aid PROFILE used to determine the expected family contribution. Unlike the Federal Methodology (FM), the net value of the family residence is part of the consideration.

internship—a program for students to gain practical experience in their field of interest by working with and under the supervision of the professional staff of an organization. Paid internships offer a wage or fixed allowance to the student during the period of internship. Often an intern works on projects of interest to the host organization or learns specific techniques. Internships can range in length up to an entire academic year.

interview—a conversation between the candidate for an award and the individual or group that will decide who receives the award. Usually this is an actual meeting of the parties that is conducted at the sponsor's offices. The purpose is to allow the judges the opportunity to better evaluate the suitability of the candidate in accordance with the program's goals.

junior—a student in the third year or with third-year standing at a college or secondary school.

letter of recommendation—a document written and signed by an individual of professional authority or credence, typically a teacher, school administrator, or professional in a subject field, that attests to the quality of an applicant's qualifications, work, character, or abilities. The letter may be specifically addressed or written to any recipient who may be interested. Sponsors may request that the signer send the letter directly.

loan—a type of financial aid which must be repaid, with interest.

major—the academic area in which a student chooses to concentrate. Generally, major course requirements take up one quarter to one half of the student's undergraduate studies and are combined with other general education requirements.

merit-based—describes awards that are given on the basis of criteria other than financial need, including the academic field chosen, career goals, grades, test scores, athletic ability, hobbies, talents, place of residence or birth, ethnic identity, religious affiliation, one's or one's parents' military or public safety service, disability, union memberships, employment history, community service, or club affiliations.

minority—a group of people with a coherent identity that historically has been frustrated in achieving parity with an antithetical group that comprises the "majority." In the U.S., the traditional and most common usage of the term is in reference to racial or ethnic populations, specifically African Americans, Hispanics, and Native Americans. In higher education, the "minority" label has been claimed by or attached to other kinds of groups, such as women, homosexuals, and people with disabilities, that have experienced bias or relative lack of economic opportunity or progress.

Native American—denotes identity with one of the aboriginal tribal populations of the Americas, excluding Inuit or Eskimo people. American Indian is a widely used alternative term. If this is used as a criterion for a scholarship award, proof of tribal membership usually will be required.

need, needy, needy student—in the jargon of student financial aid, the difference between the cost of attendance (COA) and the expected family contribution (EFC). The financial aid package is based on the amount of financial need. Needy describes student need in this context and does not connote that the student or family is in poverty.

nominated, nomination—describes the action of having one's eligibility for an award brought to the consideration of a sponsor by a third party or organization. Usually the nominator must be in a position of professional authority or high reputation, be unrelated to the candidate, and be familiar with the candidate's academic achievements, community service record, talents, or character.

nonrenewable—description of awards that will not be awarded more than once to the same recipient.

one-time award—description of awards that have a term limit of coverage. Check with the sponsor to find out if reapplication for a new award is allowed when the current award period ceases.

postsecondary—description of any organized education above grade 12 of the secondary (high school or preparatory school) level.

prize—gift aid given for outstanding achievement or winning a competition.

professional degree—a degree in a field such as law, education, medicine, pharmacy, or dentistry. Many fields that require advanced or specialized educational degrees are also referred to as professions, and a sponsor may be referring to a profession other than one of these specifically cited. It is advisable to check with a scholarship's sponsor if this distinction may be important to you.

PROFILE—the financial aid application form distributed through the College Scholarship Service (CSS) that is used by about 300 private colleges and universities as the basis for awarding college-based aid. The FAFSA also must be filed to receive aid from these colleges. There is an application fee with the PROFILE form.

quarter—a division of a college or university's academic year if the institution divides its year into four terms (quarters).

reapplication, reapply—indicates that a new application is required to secure renewal of an award. Frequently in a reapplication you have no intrinsic advantage over other applicants for the award.

recommendation—see *letter of recommendation*, above.

registration fee—a fee charged by certain sponsors to consider your application.

renewable—describes awards that may be for a length of study beyond a single year. Some renewable scholarships will require the student to reapply for the scholarship each year; others will just require a report on the student's progress to a degree.

resident—a reference to having one's primary residence within a place for a specified length of time. Many awards require that recipients be residents of a particular state. Each state of the United States sets its own criteria for what conditions must be met to be considered a "legal" resident. A "permanent resident" of the U.S. is a non-U.S. citizen who has been granted this official status by the U.S. Immigration and Naturalization Service. A "permanent resident" can be considered to be a legal resident of one of the United States if he or she otherwise can meet that specific state's residence criteria.

résumé—a summary account of one's life, education, and experience. Typically this is shorter than a *curriculum vitae,* usually between one and two pages in length. In addition to basic biographical data, it typically covers an individual's education, employment, teaching or research positions, responsibilities, and other relevant information.

SASE—a stamped, self-addressed envelope to be included with inquiry or application material to ensure a response.

SAT—a standardized test, offered by the College Board through the Educational Testing Service, required for admission to many colleges.

scholarship—precisely defined, gift aid to cover tuition and fees for undergraduate study. Usually a scholarship can be applied to tuition and fees, but rarely to room and board. Scholarship programs occasionally cover room and board, but this is rare. However, scholarship is frequently used generically to describe all forms of gift aid, including fellowships and grants. You will need to read the full description of a scholarship award program in order to ascertain to what level of study it may apply.

school—a general term used to refer to any institution of secondary or higher education. This includes high schools, colleges, universities, and graduate or professional institutions.

self-help aid—financial aid in the form of loans and student employment. Many college and university financial aid packages automatically include a minimum amount of self-help aid before any gift aid is granted.

semester—a division of a college or university's academic year if the institution divides its year into two terms (semesters).

seminar—an advanced or graduate-level class or course of study on a particular subject in which each student does original research under the guidance of a faculty member.

seminary—a professional school or other institution of higher education for training in religion, usually as preparation for priesthood, ministry, or rabbinate.

senior—a student in the fourth year or with fourth-year standing at a college or secondary school.

sophomore—a student in the second year or with second-year standing at a college or secondary school.

Student Aid Report (SAR)—an official document based on the FAFSA that goes to the Financial Aid Office and describes the amount of any possible Pell Grant funds, and the expected family contribution (EFC). The SAR usually arrives one to two months after the FAFSA is filed. This is the basis for the individual college's student financial aid decisions. It should be reviewed carefully to ensure that there are no errors.

Test of English as a Foreign Language (TOEFL)—test of a student's ability to communicate in and understand English that most colleges and universities require international students to take as part of their application.

transcript—the record of one's academic work. Many award programs will require the submission of an official copy, translated into English, of your secondary school transcript.

trimester—a division of a college or university's academic year if the institution divides its year into three terms (trimesters).

tuition—fees that pay for instruction in an academic institution. Other expenses, such as those for room and board (lodging and meals), health insurance, activities, and transportation, are not included in tuition figures.

two-year institution—a postsecondary institution at which the associate degree is the highest credential awarded. A typical course of study is two years. Credits earned at an accredited two-year institution generally will be transferable for study at a four-year college or university.

undergraduate—an associate or bachelor's degree candidate or a description of such candidate's courses. Once students have earned a bachelor's degree, they are eligible for entry to graduate programs at the master's and doctoral levels.

university—a large educational institution comprising a number of divisions, including graduate and professional schools. Academic offerings are usually more comprehensive than at colleges. A few universities have no professional schools or offer no doctoral programs.

veteran—a former member of the U.S. armed forces. Awards to veterans usually require active service duty in one of the U.S. armed service branches (Army, Air Force, Coast Guard, Navy, Marines) and an honorable discharge.

vocational-technical schools—institutions of postsecondary education that offer certificates or diplomas requiring fewer than two years of study. Programs of study usually are directly related to preparation for specific careers.

INDEXES

(Please note: The number reference found in these indexes is the sequence number of the award, not the number of the page on which it is found.)

AWARD NAME INDEX

AACE International Competitive Scholarship • 15
AACN Educational Advancement Scholarships-BSN Completion • 145
AAUW Educational Foundation Community Action Grants • 457
Academy of Motion Pictures Student Academy Awards • 452
Actuarial Scholarships for Minority Students • 43
Adelante US Education Leadership Fund • 252
Adult High School Equivalency Scholarships • 253
Adult Student Aid Program • 386
AGC Education and Research Foundation Undergraduate Scholarships • 62
AIAA Undergraduate Scholarship • 9
Alaska Commission on Postsecondary Education Teacher Education Scholarship Loan • 75
Albert and Florence Newton Nurse Scholarship Newton Fund • 159
Albert Shanker College Scholarship Fund of the United Federation of Teachers • 414
Alberta Heritage Scholarship Fund Aboriginal Health Careers Bursary • 33
Alberta Heritage Scholarship Fund Fellowships for full-time Studies in French—College/Technical Schools • 118
Alcoa Foundation Sons and Daughters Scholarship Program • 202
Alexander Rutherford Scholarships for High School Achievement • 254
Alice M. and Samuel Yarnold Scholarship • 125
All-USA College Academic Team • 501
All-USA Community & Jr. College Academic Team • 502
All-USA High School Academic Team • 503
Allied Health Student Loan Program-New Mexico • 72
AMBUCS Scholars-Scholarships for Therapists • 131
Amelia Earhart Memorial Career Scholarship Fund • 490
America's Junior Miss Scholarship • 455
American Cancer Society, Florida Division College Scholarship Program • 307
American Chemical Society Scholars Program • 59
American Council of the Blind Scholarships • 234
American Foreign Service Association (AFSA) Financial Aid Award Program • 178
American Institute For Foreign Study International Scholarships • 421
American Institute For Foreign Study Minority Scholarships • 260
American Institute of Architects Minority/Disadvantaged Scholarship • 16
American Institute of Architects/American Architectural Foundation Scholarship for Professional Degree Candidates • 17
American Legion Department of Alabama Scholarship for Children of War Veterans • 309
American Legion Department of New York State High School Oratorical Contest • 310
American Legion Department of North Dakota National High School Oratorical Contest • 311
American Legion National Headquarters National High School Oratorical Contest • 422
American Legion Scholarship—Ohio • 179
American Ornithologists' Union Research Awards • 7
American Quarter Horse Foundation Youth Scholarships • 181
American Society of Composers, Authors, and Publishers Foundation Morton Gould Young Composer Awards • 162

Colorado Leveraging Educational Assistance Partnership (CLEAP) and SLEAP • 323
Colorado Masons Benevolent Fund Scholarships • 324
Colorado Police Corps Scholarship • 462
Community Foundation for Greater Buffalo Scholarships • 325
Conditional Grant Program • 64
Congressional Black Caucus Spouses Education Scholarship Fund • 464
Consulting Engineers and Land Surveyors of California Scholarship Award • 60
Critical Teacher Shortage Tuition Reimbursement-Florida • 79
Cystic Fibrosis Foundation Scholarship • 235
David A. DeBolt Teacher Shortage Scholarship Program • 83
Davis-Putter Scholarship Fund • 467
DC Leveraging Educational Assistance Partnership Program (LEAP) • 332
Delaware Nursing Incentive Scholarship Loan • 147
Delegate Scholarship Program-Maryland • 367
Delta Delta Delta Undergraduate Scholarship • 186
Developmental Disabilities Tuition Assistance Program • 130
DeVry Bachelor's Degree Scholarships • 327
DeVry President's Scholarships • 328
Diamond State Scholarship • 329
Discover Card Tribute Award Scholarship Program • 456
Discovery Young Scientist Challenge • 443
Distinguished Scholar Award-Maryland • 368
Distinguished Scholar-Teacher Education Awards • 88
Dollars for Scholars Scholarship • 460
Dolphin Scholarships • 250
Donald W. Fogarty International Student Paper Competition • 42
Donna Reed Performing Arts Scholarships • 166
Duke Energy Scholars Program • 204
Easley National Scholarships • 483
Econo-Clad Literature Program Award • 140
Ed E. and Gladys Hurley Foundation Scholarship • 171
Eddie Robinson Foundation High School Senior Scholarship • 468
Edmund F. Maxwell Foundation Scholarship • 333
EDS Corporate Scholars Program • 68
Educaid Gimme Five Scholarship Sweepstakes • 469
Educational Assistance Grants-Maryland • 369
Educational Benefits for Children of Deceased Military and State Police • 217
Educational Communications Scholarship • 433
Educational Enrichment Support Project • 342
Educational Foundation Scholarships • 46
Edward T. Conroy Memorial Scholarship Program • 247
Eight & Forty Lung and Respiratory Disease Nursing Scholarship Fund • 146
Elizabeth Greenshields Award/Grant • 27
Elks Most Valuable Student Contest • 470
Elks National Foundation Legacy Awards • 187
Emergency Secondary Education Loan Program • 35
Ernest and Eurice Miller Bass Scholarship Fund • 172
Ethnic Minority Scholarship Program • 278
Executive Women International Scholarship Program • 434
FAMSI 2002 Annual Grant Competition • 14
FCCLA Houston Livestock Show and Rodeo Scholarship • 135
FEEA/NARFE Scholarship • 218
Fellowships for Full-time Studies in French—University • 119
FICPA Chapter Scholarship Program • 47
Financial Service Centers of America Scholarship Fund • 471

SPONSOR INDEX

Sponsor Index

Massachusetts Office of Student Financial Assistance • 375
Massachusetts Police Corps • 480
Mellinger Educational Foundation • 376
Menominee Indian Tribe of Wisconsin • 280, 281
Minnesota Gay/Lesbian/Bisexual/Transgender Educational Fund • 481
Minnesota Higher Education Services Office • 377
Mississippi Police Corps • 482
Missouri Department of Elementary and Secondary Education • 92, 93, 378
Missouri Department of Health and Senior Services • 156
Mitchell Institute • 379
Modern Woodmen of America • 197
Montana Guaranteed Student Loan Program, Office of Commissioner of Higher
  Education • 282, 380, 381
Namepa National Scholarship Foundation • 29
NASA Minnesota Space Grant Consortium • 30
NASA Nevada Space Grant Consortium • 31
National Academy for Nuclear Training • 144
National Academy of American Scholars • 483
National Alliance for Excellence • 438
National AMBUCS, Inc. • 131
National Association of Black Accountants, Inc. • 50
National Association of Secondary School Principals • 198, 439
National Association of Women in Construction • 20
National Athletic Trainers' Association • 173
National Beta Club • 484
National Dental Association Foundation • 71
National Fastener Distributors Association • 223
National Federation of the Blind • 224
National FFA Organization • 485
National Fish and Wildlife Foundation • 142
National Institutes of Health • 486
National Merit Scholarship Corporation • 283, 487
National PKU News • 238
National Restaurant Association Educational Foundation • 115, 116
National Science Teachers Association • 488
National Teen-Ager Scholarship Foundation • 489
Nebraska Department of Education • 382
Nevada Department of Education • 383, 384
Nevada Women's Fund • 385
New Hampshire Charitable Foundation • 386, 387
New Hampshire Postsecondary Education Commission • 120, 388
New Jersey Society of Certified Public Accountants • 51, 52
New Jersey State Golf Association • 225
New Mexico Commission on Higher Education • 72
New York Council for the Humanities • 389
New York State Education Department • 21, 390, 391
New York State Higher Education Services Corporation • 392, 393
Ninety-Nines, Inc. • 490
North Carolina Commission of Indian Affairs • 284
North Carolina CPA Foundation, Inc. • 53
North Carolina Police Corps • 491
North Carolina State Education Assistance Authority • 157, 226, 394
North Carolina Teaching Fellows Commission • 94
North Dakota Board of Nursing • 158
North Dakota University System • 285
Northern Cheyenne Tribal Education Department • 286

ACADEMIC FIELDS/CAREER GOALS INDEX

Agribusiness
California Farm Bureau Scholarship • 1
Cenex Harvest States Foundation Cooperative Studies Scholarships • 2
Hispanic College Fund Scholarship Program • 3
The Hispanic College Fund/INROADS/Sprint Scholarship Program • 4
United Agribusiness League Scholarship Program • 5

Agriculture
California Farm Bureau Scholarship • 1
Cenex Harvest States Foundation Cooperative Studies Scholarships • 2
Hope Scholarship • 6
United Agribusiness League Scholarship Program • 5

Animal/Veterinary Sciences
American Ornithologists' Union Research Awards • 7
Rockefeller State Wildlife Scholarship • 8
United Agribusiness League Scholarship Program • 5

Applied Sciences
AIAA Undergraduate Scholarship • 9
American Society of Naval Engineers Scholarship • 10
Astronaut Scholarship Foundation • 11
Barry M. Goldwater Scholarship and Excellence in Education Program • 12
Rockefeller State Wildlife Scholarship • 8
SPIE Educational Scholarships in Optical Science and Engineering • 13

Archaeology
FAMSI 2002 Annual Grant Competition • 14

Architecture
AACE International Competitive Scholarship • 15
American Institute of Architects Minority/Disadvantaged Scholarship • 16
American Institute of Architects/American Architectural Foundation Scholarship
 for Professional Degree Candidates • 17
California State University Real Estate Scholarship and Internship Grant Program
 • 22
FAMSI 2002 Annual Grant Competition • 14
IFMA Foundation Scholarships • 18
Kennedy Research Grants • 19
NAWIC Undergraduate Scholarships • 20
Regents Professional Opportunity Scholarship Program—New York • 21
Worldstudio Foundation Scholarship Program • 23

Area/Ethnic Studies
FAMSI 2002 Annual Grant Competition • 14
Irish Research Funds • 24

Art History
FAMSI 2002 Annual Grant Competition • 14

Arts
Elizabeth Greenshields Award/Grant • 27
FAMSI 2002 Annual Grant Competition • 14

Emergency Secondary Education Loan Program • 35
GAE GFIE Scholarship for Education Support Professionals for Professional Development • 80
Georgia PROMISE Teacher Scholarship Program • 81
Golden Apple Scholars of Illinois • 82
Harry A. Applegate Scholarship • 45
Indiana Minority Teacher and Special Education Services Scholarship Program • 99
International Teacher Education Scholarship • 76
Janet L. Hoffmann Loan Assistance Repayment Program • 89
Kansas Teacher Service Scholarship • 85
Kennedy Research Grants • 19
Kentucky Teacher Scholarship Program • 86
Maryland Teacher Scholarship • 90
Minority Teachers of Illinois Scholarship Program • 84
Minority Teaching Fellows Program/Tennessee • 100
Missouri Minority Teaching Scholarship • 92
Missouri Teacher Education Scholarship (General) • 93
North Carolina Teaching Fellows Scholarship Program • 94
Ordean Loan Program • 95
Scholarship Grants for Prospective Educators • 96
Sharon Christa McAuliffe Teacher Education-Critical Shortage Grant Program • 91
South Carolina Teacher Loan Program • 97
Tennessee Teaching Scholars Program • 101
Terrel H. Bell Teaching Incentive Loan • 98
Underwood-Smith Teacher Scholarship Program • 102

Electrical Engineering/Electronics

AACE International Competitive Scholarship • 15
AIAA Undergraduate Scholarship • 9
American Society of Naval Engineers Scholarship • 10
Astronaut Scholarship Foundation • 11
Consulting Engineers and Land Surveyors of California Scholarship Award • 60
Hispanic College Fund Scholarship Program • 3
Instrumentation, Systems, and Automation Society (ISA) Scholarship Program • 28
Mas Family Scholarships • 44
National Association of Minority Engineering Program Administrators National Scholarship Fund • 29
NAWIC Undergraduate Scholarships • 20
Regents Professional Opportunity Scholarship Program—New York • 21
SAE Engineering Scholarships • 32
Science and Technology Scholarship • 38
SPIE Educational Scholarships in Optical Science and Engineering • 13
The Hispanic College Fund/INROADS/Sprint Scholarship Program • 4
University and Community College System of Nevada NASA Space Grant and Fellowship Program • 31
USENIX Student Programs • 61
West Virginia Engineering, Science & Technology Scholarship Program • 103

Engineering-Related Technologies

AACE International Competitive Scholarship • 15
American Welding Society District Scholarship Program • 104
Astronaut Scholarship Foundation • 11
BPW Career Advancement Scholarship Program for Women • 37
Consulting Engineers and Land Surveyors of California Scholarship Award • 60

Mas Family Scholarships • 44

Landscape Architecture
California State University Real Estate Scholarship and Internship Grant Program
• 22
NAWIC Undergraduate Scholarships • 20
Regents Professional Opportunity Scholarship Program—New York • 21
United Agribusiness League Scholarship Program • 5

Law Enforcement/Police Administration
Arkansas Police Corps Scholarship • 138

Law/Legal Services
BPW Career Advancement Scholarship Program for Women • 37
Florida Minority Participation in Legal Education (MPLE) Scholarship Program
• 139
Janet L. Hoffmann Loan Assistance Repayment Program • 89
Professional Scholarship Program-Maryland • 70
Regents Professional Opportunity Scholarship Program—New York • 21

Library Sciences
Econo-Clad Literature Program Award • 140
Kennedy Research Grants • 19

Literature/English/Writing
Hope Scholarship • 6
International Reading Association Elva Knight Research Grant • 141
Kennedy Research Grants • 19
Scholastic Art and Writing Awards-Art Section • 25
Scholastic Art and Writing Awards-Writing Section Scholarship • 26

Materials Science, Engineering and Metallurgy
AIAA Undergraduate Scholarship • 9
American Chemical Society Scholars Program • 59
American Society of Naval Engineers Scholarship • 10
Astronaut Scholarship Foundation • 11
Barry M. Goldwater Scholarship and Excellence in Education Program • 12
National Association of Minority Engineering Program Administrators National
Scholarship Fund • 29
Plastics Pioneers Scholarships • 105
SAE Engineering Scholarships • 32
Society of Plastics Engineers Scholarship Program • 56
SPIE Educational Scholarships in Optical Science and Engineering • 13
USENIX Student Programs • 61

Mechanical Engineering
AACE International Competitive Scholarship • 15
AIAA Undergraduate Scholarship • 9
American Society of Naval Engineers Scholarship • 10
Astronaut Scholarship Foundation • 11
Barry M. Goldwater Scholarship and Excellence in Education Program • 12
Consulting Engineers and Land Surveyors of California Scholarship Award • 60
Hispanic College Fund Scholarship Program • 3
Mas Family Scholarships • 44
National Association of Minority Engineering Program Administrators National
Scholarship Fund • 29
NAWIC Undergraduate Scholarships • 20
SAE Engineering Scholarships • 32
Society of Plastics Engineers Scholarship Program • 56

Registered Nurse Education Loan Repayment Program • 152
RN Education Scholarship Program • 153
Service-Cancellable Stafford Loan-Georgia • 73
Youth for Adolescent Pregnancy Prevention Leadership Recognition Program
• 128

Peace and Conflict Studies
Hugh Fulton Byas Memorial Grant • 134

Performing Arts
American Society of Composers, Authors, and Publishers Foundation Morton
Gould Young Composer Awards • 162
Donna Reed Performing Arts Scholarships • 166
Gina Bachauer International Artists Piano Competition Award • 167
Princess Grace Scholarships in Dance, Theater, and Film • 108
The Raissa Tselentis Memorial, Johann Sebastian Bach International
Competitions • 168
University of Maryland International Leonard Rose Cello Competition • 163
University of Maryland International Marian Anderson Vocal Arts Competition
and Festival • 164
University of Maryland International William Kapell Piano Competition • 165
YMF Scholarship Program • 170
Young Artist Competition • 169

Photojournalism
Joel Garcia Memorial Scholarship • 65
Los Angeles Times Scholarship Program • 67

Physical Sciences and Math
AIAA Undergraduate Scholarship • 9
American Society of Naval Engineers Scholarship • 10
Barry M. Goldwater Scholarship and Excellence in Education Program • 12
BPW Career Advancement Scholarship Program for Women • 37
Emergency Secondary Education Loan Program • 35
Minnesota Space Grant Consortium Minnesota Space Grant Consortium • 30
NIH Undergraduate Scholarship for Individuals from Disadvantaged Backgrounds
• 40
Science and Technology Scholarship • 38
Society of Exploration Geophysicists Foundation Scholarship • 74
Student Research Fellowships-American Liver Foundation • 34
University and Community College System of Nevada NASA Space Grant and
Fellowship Program • 31

Political Science
FAMSI 2002 Annual Grant Competition • 14
Hope Scholarship • 6
Kennedy Research Grants • 19
Mas Family Scholarships • 44

Real Estate
California State University Real Estate Scholarship and Internship Grant Program
• 22

Religion/Theology
Ed E. and Gladys Hurley Foundation Scholarship • 171
Ernest and Eurice Miller Bass Scholarship Fund • 172
FAMSI 2002 Annual Grant Competition • 14

Science, Technology and Society
AIAA Undergraduate Scholarship • 9
West Virginia Engineering, Science & Technology Scholarship Program • 103

ASSOCIATION AFFILIATION
INDEX

CORPORATE AFFILIATION INDEX

EMPLOYMENT EXPERIENCE INDEX

Community service
Arby's-Big Brothers Big Sisters Scholarship Award • 182
Boys & Girls Clubs of America National Youth of the Year Award • 184
Chairscholars Foundation, Inc. Scholarships • 216
Delta Delta Delta Undergraduate Scholarship • 186
Mary P. Oenslager Scholastic Achievement Awards • 200
National Federation of the Blind Scholarships • 224
North Carolina Teaching Fellows Scholarship Program • 226
Robert C. Byrd Honors Scholarship- South Carolina • 229
Selby Scholar Program • 233
Sun Student College Scholarship Program • 227
Yoshiyama Award • 220

Designated career field
AACN Educational Advancement Scholarships-BSN Completion • 145
Association Scholarship • 221
Bowfin Memorial Scholarship • 230
Bridgestone/Firestone Trust Fund Scholarships • 203
California Correctional Peace Officers Association Joe Harper Scholarship • 215
Developmental Disabilities Tuition Assistance Program • 130
Duke Energy Scholars Program • 204
Econo-Clad Literature Program Award • 140
Eight & Forty Lung and Respiratory Disease Nursing Scholarship Fund • 146
National Fastener Distributors Association Memorial Scholarship Fund • 223
Procter & Gamble Fund Scholarship Competition for Employees' Children • 207
Sid Richardson Memorial Fund • 228
Train our Teachers Award • 231
Wal-Mart Associate Scholarships • 209

Federal/postal service
FEEA/NARFE Scholarship • 218

Food service
IACP Foundation Culinary Scholarships • 112
National Restaurant Association Educational Foundation Undergraduate
    Scholarships for College Students • 115
National Restaurant Association Educational Foundation Undergraduate
    Scholarships for High School Seniors • 116
Schwan's Food Service Scholarship • 110

Leather/footwear
Two/Ten International Footwear Foundation Scholarship • 232

Police/firefighting
Educational Benefits for Children of Deceased Military and State Police • 217
Firefighter, Ambulance, and Rescue Squad Member Tuition Reimbursement
    Program-Maryland • 109
Georgia Public Safety Memorial Grant/Law Enforcement Personnel Department
    Grant • 219
Law Enforcement Officers' Dependents Scholarship-Arkansas • 213
Police Officers and Firefighters Survivors Education Assistance Program-Alabama
    • 212

Employment Experience Index

Private club/caddying
J. Wood Platt Caddie Scholarship Trust • 222
New Jersey State Golf Association Caddie Scholarship • 225

Teaching
Critical Teacher Shortage Tuition Reimbursement-Florida • 79
Teacher and Administrator Grant Program-Arkansas • 214

U.S. Foreign Service
American Foreign Service Association (AFSA) Financial Aid Award Program
• 178

IMPAIRMENT INDEX

Hearing Impaired
Iowa Vocational Rehabilitation • 237

Learning Disabled
Iowa Vocational Rehabilitation • 237

Physically Disabled
Chairscholars Foundation, Inc. Scholarships • 216
Cystic Fibrosis Foundation Scholarship • 235
Immune Deficiency Foundation Scholarship • 236
Iowa Vocational Rehabilitation • 237
Robert Guthrie PKU Scholarship and Awards • 238

Visually Impaired
American Council of the Blind Scholarships • 234
Iowa Vocational Rehabilitation • 237
Mary P. Oenslager Scholastic Achievement Awards • 200
National Federation of the Blind Scholarships • 224

MILITARY SERVICE INDEX

NATIONALITY OR ETHNIC HERITAGE INDEX

African-American
Actuarial Scholarships for Minority Students • 43
American Chemical Society Scholars Program • 59
American Institute For Foreign Study Minority Scholarships • 260
American Institute of Architects Minority/Disadvantaged Scholarship • 16
Arkansas Minority Teacher Scholars Program • 77
Citigroup Fellows Program • 57
Coca-Cola Corporate Scholarship/Intern Program • 58
Conditional Grant Program • 64
EDS Corporate Scholars Program • 68
Ethnic Minority Scholarship Program • 278
Florida Minority Participation in Legal Education (MPLE) Scholarship Program
    • 139
Idaho Minority and "At Risk" Student Scholarship • 274
Indiana Minority Teacher and Special Education Services Scholarship Program
    • 99
Knight Ridder Minority Scholarship Program • 48
Merrill Lynch Scholarship • 297
Minority Teachers of Illinois Scholarship Program • 84
Minority Teaching Fellows Program/Tennessee • 100
Minority Undergraduate Student Awards • 39
Missouri Minority Teaching Scholarship • 92
National Achievement Scholarship Program • 283
National Association of Black Accountants National Scholarship • 50
National Association of Minority Engineering Program Administrators National
    Scholarship Fund • 29
NDAF/Colgate Palmolive Scholarship Program • 71
Page Education Foundation Grant • 288
Regents Professional Opportunity Scholarship Program—New York • 21
Ron Brown Scholar Program • 263
Rosewood Family Scholarship Fund • 268
SACHS Foundation Scholarships • 290
Special Advance Leadership Development Grants • 269
Student Opportunity Scholarship-Presbyterian Church (U.S.A.) • 289
United Methodist Church Ethnic Scholarship • 295

Armenian
Armenian Students Association of America, Inc. Scholarships • 261

Asian
American Institute For Foreign Study Minority Scholarships • 260
American Institute of Architects Minority/Disadvantaged Scholarship • 16
Arkansas Minority Teacher Scholars Program • 77
Coca-Cola Corporate Scholarship/Intern Program • 58
Conditional Grant Program • 64
Ethnic Minority Scholarship Program • 278
Florida Minority Participation in Legal Education (MPLE) Scholarship Program
    • 139
Knight Ridder Minority Scholarship Program • 48
Minority Teachers of Illinois Scholarship Program • 84

Special Advance Leadership Development Grants • 269
Student Opportunity Scholarship-Presbyterian Church (U.S.A.) • 289
The Hispanic College Fund/INROADS/Sprint Scholarship Program • 4
United Methodist Church Ethnic Scholarship • 295
United Methodist Church Hispanic, Asian, and Native American Scholarship
    • 296

Italian
ICF College Scholarships to High School Seniors • 276
Sons of Italy Foundation National Leadership Grants • 291

Latin American/Caribbean
Hispanic College Fund Scholarship Program • 3
Hispanic Scholarship Fund General Program • 270
Joel Garcia Memorial Scholarship • 65
Mas Family Scholarships • 44
The Hispanic College Fund/INROADS/Sprint Scholarship Program • 4

Mexican
Hispanic College Fund Scholarship Program • 3
Hispanic Scholarship Fund General Program • 270
The Hispanic College Fund/INROADS/Sprint Scholarship Program • 4

Native American
Actuarial Scholarships for Minority Students • 43
Alberta Heritage Scholarship Fund Aboriginal Health Careers Bursary • 33
American Chemical Society Scholars Program • 59
American Institute For Foreign Study Minority Scholarships • 260
American Institute of Architects Minority/Disadvantaged Scholarship • 16
Arkansas Minority Teacher Scholars Program • 77
BIA Higher Education Grant • 271
Blackfoot Tribal Education Grants • 262
Cherokee Nation Higher Education • 264
Chickasaw Nation Education Foundation Program • 265
Coca-Cola Corporate Scholarship/Intern Program • 58
Conditional Grant Program • 64
Ethnic Minority Scholarship Program • 278
Florida Minority Participation in Legal Education (MPLE) Scholarship Program
    • 139
Higher Education Grant • 266
Higher Education Scholarship Program • 286
Hopi Supplemental Grant • 272
Idaho Minority and "At Risk" Student Scholarship • 274
Incentive Scholarship for Native Americans • 284
Indian Student Fee Waiver • 282
International Order of the King's Daughters and Sons American Indian
    Scholarship • 275
Knight Ridder Minority Scholarship Program • 48
Menominee Indian Tribe Adult Vocational Training Program • 280
Menominee Indian Tribe of Wisconsin Higher Education Grants • 281
Minority Teachers of Illinois Scholarship Program • 84
Minority Teaching Fellows Program/Tennessee • 100
Minority Undergraduate Student Awards • 39
Missouri Minority Teaching Scholarship • 92
National Association of Black Accountants National Scholarship • 50
National Association of Minority Engineering Program Administrators National
    Scholarship Fund • 29
North Dakota Indian College Scholarship Program • 285

RELIGIOUS AFFILIATION INDEX

Jewish
Jewish Federation of Metropolitan Chicago Academic Scholarship Program
  • 300

Methodist
Ernest and Eurice Miller Bass Scholarship Fund • 172
Gift of Hope: 21st Century Scholars Program • 304
Special Advance Leadership Development Grants • 269
United Methodist Church Ethnic Scholarship • 295
United Methodist Church Hispanic, Asian, and Native American Scholarship
  • 296

Presbyterian
Appalachian Scholarships • 301
National Presbyterian College Scholarship • 302
Samuel Robinson Award • 303
Student Opportunity Scholarship-Presbyterian Church (U.S.A.) • 289

Protestant
Ed E. and Gladys Hurley Foundation Scholarship • 171

Roman Catholic
Catholic Aid Association College Tuition Scholarship • 299
First Catholic Slovak Ladies Association Fraternal Scholarship Award for College
  & Graduate Study • 267
Fourth Degree Pro Deo and Pro Patria Scholarships • 195
ICF College Scholarships to High School Seniors • 276
John W. Mc Devitt (Fourth Degree) Scholarships • 196

STATE OF RESIDENCE INDEX

Rhode Island
Albert and Florence Newton Nurse Scholarship Newton Fund • 159
Rhode Island Higher Education Grant Program • 399
Rhode Island Masonic Grand Lodge Scholarship • 374

South Carolina
Appalachian Scholarships • 301
James F. Byrnes Scholarship • 358
Palmetto Fellows Scholarship Program • 400
Robert C. Byrd Honors Scholarship-South Carolina • 229
South Carolina Teacher Loan Program • 97
South Carolina Tuition Grants Program • 401

South Dakota
Cenex Harvest States Foundation Cooperative Studies Scholarships • 2
Robert C. Byrd Honors Scholarship-South Dakota • 402
Young Artist Competition • 169

Tennessee
Appalachian Scholarships • 301
Minority Teaching Fellows Program/Tennessee • 100
Ned McWherter Scholars Program • 411
Robert C. Byrd Honors Scholarship-Tennessee • 412
Tennessee Student Assistance Award Program • 413
Tennessee Teaching Scholars Program • 101

Texas
Career Colleges and Schools of Texas Scholarship Program • 322
Conditional Grant Program • 64
FCCLA Houston Livestock Show and Rodeo Scholarship • 135
Texas Physician Assistant Loan Reimbursement Program • 126

Utah
Cenex Harvest States Foundation Cooperative Studies Scholarships • 2
Terrel H. Bell Teaching Incentive Loan • 98

Virginia
Appalachian Scholarships • 301
Lee-Jackson Foundation Scholarship • 415
Long & Foster Scholarship Program • 364
Virginia Tuition Assistance Grant Program (Private Institutions) • 416

Washington
Cenex Harvest States Foundation Cooperative Studies Scholarships • 2
Edmund F. Maxwell Foundation Scholarship • 333

West Virginia
Appalachian Scholarships • 301
Herschel C. Price Educational Foundation Scholarships • 347
Robert C. Byrd Honors Scholarship Program-West Virginia • 418
Ruth Ann Johnson Scholarship • 345
Underwood-Smith Teacher Scholarship Program • 102
W. P. Black Scholarship Fund • 346
West Virginia Higher Education Grant Program • 419

TALENT INDEX

TALENT INDEX

Art
Elizabeth Greenshields Award/Grant • 27
L. Ron Hubbard's Illustrators of the Future Contest • 425
National Alliance for Excellence Honored Scholars and Artists Program • 438
Scholastic Art and Writing Awards-Art Section • 25
The Artist's Magazine's Annual Art Competition • 424

Athletics/sports
Jimmie Condon Athletic Scholarships • 255
Travel and Training Fund • 449

Beauty pageant
Miss America Organization Competition Scholarships • 435

Designated field specified by sponsor
Discovery Young Scientist Challenge • 443
Executive Women International Scholarship Program • 434
Intel International Science and Engineering Fair • 444
Intel Science Talent Search • 445
Knight Ridder Minority Scholarship Program • 48
Print and Graphics Scholarships • 124
Roothbert Fund, Inc. Scholarship • 440
United States Senate Youth Program • 448
Washington Crossing Foundation Scholarship • 447
Women's Jewelry Association Scholarship Program • 176
Young American Creative Patriotic Art Awards Program • 436

Foreign language
Medicus Student Exchange • 292
Rotary Foundation Academic-Year Ambassadorial Scholarships • 121
Rotary Multi-Year Ambassadorial Scholarships • 441

Golf
Francis Ouimet Scholarship Fund • 337
J. Wood Platt Caddie Scholarship Trust • 222
Women's Western Golf Foundation Scholarship • 450

Leadership
American Institute For Foreign Study International Scholarships • 421
American Institute For Foreign Study Minority Scholarships • 260
Boys & Girls Clubs of America National Youth of the Year Award • 184
California Junior Miss Scholarship Program • 321
Coca-Cola Scholars Program • 432
College Scholarships for Cancer Survivors • 308
Educational Communications Scholarship • 433
Eight & Forty Lung and Respiratory Disease Nursing Scholarship Fund • 146
Florida College Student of the Year Award • 336
Harry A. Applegate Scholarship • 45
Laurence Decore Student Leadership Awards • 256
Mary P. Oenslager Scholastic Achievement Awards • 200
Mas Family Scholarships • 44
Principal's Leadership Award • 439
Ron Brown Scholar Program • 263
Rotary Foundation Cultural Ambassadorial Scholarship • 122

NOTES

NOTES

NOTES

NOTES

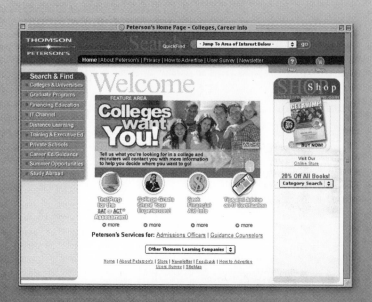